Moral Issues
of the Marketplace
in Jewish Law

Aaron Levine

YASHAR ETHICS SERIES: VOLUME III
MORAL ISSUES OF THE MARKETPLACE IN JEWISH LAW
by Aaron Levine

Library of Congress Cataloging-in-Publication Data

Levine, Aaron.
    Moral issues of the marketplace in Jewish law / by Aaron Levine
        p. cm.
    Includes bibliographical references and index.
    1. Busines ethics. 2. Ethics, Jewish. 3. Business—Religious
    aspects—Judaism. I. Title. II. Levine, Aaron.
ISBN 1-933143-08-8 (hardcover)
ISBN 1-933143-09-6 (softcover)

For information and catalog write to Yashar Books Inc., 1548 E. 33rd Street, Brooklyn, NY 11234, or visit our website: www.YasharBooks.com

For Sarah
My beloved wife and life companion,
My wisest and best friend.

Contents

Preface

Moral Issues of the Marketplace in Jewish Law is the fifth volume of my research into the interface between economics and Jewish law. My primary goal in these works has always been to show that economic analysis is vital for elucidating a Torah perspective on commercial issues and economic public policy.

My present offering together with my previous volume, _Case Studies in Jewish Business Ethics_, fit best into the area of study called Jewish Business Ethics. In his recent review article on Jewish Business Ethics, Rabbi Dr. Asher Meir identified many strands of contributions in this field. In some of the works, the major objective is the inculcation of Jewish values; in others the thrust is hortatory preachment. In still others the aim is prescriptive conduct. While these categories undoubtedly overlap, Rabbi Meir categorized my own work as falling into the category of prescriptive conduct.[1] The diversity of perspectives in the field of Jewish Business Ethics reflects the maturity that the scholarship in this field has achieved. In his review article, Rabbi Meir makes mention of the expanding literature of this field. I would be remiss if I did not mention that the reviewer himself, Rabbi Dr. Asher Meir, is very much a part of this expanding literature. His recent publication, _The Jewish Ethicist: Everyday Ethics in Business and Life_ (Ktav Publishing Company Inc. 2005), is an important contribution to the discipline. It is my pleasant collegial duty to also take note of the work of Professor Moses Pava of the Sy Syms School of Business of Yeshiva University.

His scholarship on Jewish Business Ethics has made a significant impact on the secular business ethics literature.

When I began my research thirty years ago into the interface between economics and Jewish law, I felt that my work found its home in the field of scholarship called *Mishpat ha-Ivri* (lit. The Hebrew Law). This field of study extracts principles from the Talmudic and Responsa literature to provide guideposts for commercial, social and political interactions for the State of Israel. My early writings drew upon the scholarship of the well known works in this field of Menachem Elon, Nahum Rakover, Shmuel Shilo and Shillem Wahrhaftig.

While excellent works on economic topics in the Hebrew language have appeared in various journals and publications over the years, a break-through of sorts occurred when Yehoshua Liebermann, Manfred Ohrenstein and Aharon Shapiro penetrated the economic journals with the publication of their works. Hence, in the early years of my writing on economics and Jewish law, I felt that my work was a contribution to a developing branch of an established field in economics called Economics and Law. The importance of the specialty of Economics and Law for the discipline of Economics was no more evident than when Ronald Coase, the editor of the *Journal of Economics and Law*, won the Nobel Prize in economics in 1991.

Over the years, research into economics and Jewish law has become, on occasion, connected with mainstream economic research. From the perspective of my own experiences, let me note a few highlights.

In 1982, the Fraser Institute sponsored an international symposium on the "Morality of the Market." The conference took place in Vancouver, British Columbia. In one of the sessions, I was the respondent to the Nobel laureate Milton Friedman's paper "Capitalism and the Jews."[2]

In June, 2000 the Hebrew University sponsored a conference on biblical economics. The conference was held in Jerusalem. Chaired by the Nobel laureate, Kenneth Arrow, the conference attracted an international array of scholars. Among the many papers delivered, I presented a paper: *"Ona'ah* and The Modern Marketplace."[3]

One final highlight: Professor Morris Altman of the University of Saskatchewan has recently written a pioneering work that revises the neo-classical theory of the firm. His model shows that ethical and altruistic conduct on the part of the firm is consistent with the profit maximizing conduct theorized by neoclassical theory. Altman's work will be published in a forth-coming issue of the *Journal of Economic Psychology*. My critique of his work from the perspective of Jewish law will appear in the same issue.

NOTES

1. Asher Meir, [on] Aaron Levine, "Case Studies in Jewish Business Ethics (2000), *Bekhol Derakhekha Daehu* 11 (2000), pp. 47–57.
2. The papers of this conference, including my comments on Milton Friedman's paper, were later published in the form of a book: Walter Block, Geoffrey Brennan and Kenneth Elzinga, Eds., *"Morality of the Market: Religious and Economic Perspectives."* (Canada: The Fraser Institute, 1985)
3. Subsequently, my paper was published: *"Ona'ah* and The Operation of The Modern Marketplace," *Jewish Law Annual*, Hebrew University, vol. XIV, 2003, pp. 225–258.

Acknowledgments

The first four books of my research into economics and Jewish law were published by Ktav Publishing House Inc. and Yeshiva University Press as part of Rabbi Dr. Norman Lamm's Library of Jewish Law and Ethics. When I presented the manuscript of my first volume *Free Enterprise and Jewish Law* to Rabbi Lamm, then president of Yeshiva University, for consideration for publication in his series, he responded in a most enthusiastic manner. My appreciation for this warm acceptance only grows with the passage of time. Consider that I presented my work not as the fruits of labor of one his faculty at the Rabbi Isaac Elchanan Theological Seminary (RIETS), but rather as the research protocol of an aspiring Assistant Professor of Economics at Yeshiva University. Despite being president of the University, Rabbi Lamm never questioned how my work fit into mainstream economic research. Instead, his entire focus was then, and has always been, on my contribution to the halakhic literature.

My heartfelt appreciation is extended to Rabbi Dr. Norman Lamm, long-time president of Yeshiva University, who now serves as its chancellor and continues as *Rosh ha-Yeshiva* of RIETS, for the friendship, the kindnesses and the support he has extended me over the years.

Yeshiva University has been my professional home for the past 34 years. My heartfelt gratitude to its head, president Richard M. Joel. Mr. Joel brings to the position charisma, warmth and purpose. May our esteemed president's leadership propel Yeshiva to ever greater heights in Jewish accomplishment and service to humanity.

My profound gratitude to Dr. Morton Lowengrub, Academic Vice President, Yeshiva University. Dr. Lowengrub has done much in many concrete ways to foster and encourage research by the faculty of the undergraduate colleges. I gratefully acknowledge the warm encouragement he has given my work. I express appreciation for the summer faculty fellowship I received in 2003, as well as the grant to finance the final stages in the technical preparation of this volume.

The preparation and publication of my previous volume, *Case Studies in Jewish Business Ethics*, was made possible in part by a grant from the Memorial Foundation for Jewish Culture. In my grant application, I submitted a preliminary outline for a second volume, which comprises my present work. I therefore gratefully acknowledge again the financial assistance of The Memorial Foundation for Jewish Culture.

For the past twenty-four years, I have offered courses in Jewish business ethics and economics and Jewish law at both Stern College for Women and Yeshiva College. I offer my heartfelt appreciation to Dr. Norman Rosenfeld, former Dean of Yeshiva College, and Dr. Karen Bacon, Monique C. Katz, Dean, Stern College for Women, for the strong support and encouragement they gave for inaugurating and continuing my courses in the curriculum of the economics department.

Dr. Bacon has for many years been one of the visionary personalities in the Yeshiva University community. My profound thanks is given to Dr. Bacon for her unstinting support and enthusiastic encouragement of my scholarship.

My gratitude is extended to Rabbi Dr. Ephraim Kanarfogel, Director of the Rebecca Ivry Department of Jewish Studies at Stern College, for his excellent scholarly and administrative leadership.

My thanks is offered to Dean Dr. Norman Adler for the academic and intellectual leadership he has given Yeshiva College and for the enthusiasm he has always shown for my work.

In recent years, Rabbi Zevulun Charlop, Max and Marion Grill Dean of RIETS, has invited me to teach a course in Jewish business ethics for the Bella and Harry Wexner Kollel Elyon and Semikhah Honors Program. I express my profound appreciation to Rabbi Charlop for the enthusiastic interest he has taken in my work and for encouraging the students to maintain a dialogue with me on a long term basis on Jewish business ethics issues.

The courses I give at Yeshiva College in economics and Jewish law have served as an impetus to get students involved in a serious way with my research. For my present work, *Moral Issues of the Marketplace in Jewish Law*, I benefited from the research and technical assistance of a number of students. In the early stages of the work, Nathaniel Weider-Blank helped me in the literature search for several topics. His critiques helped me develop the twists and turns of a number of issues. Shalom Morris meticulously verified the accuracy of all the sources I quoted in the chapter entitled "Truth Telling in Labor and Crisis Negotiation." His insightful comments were also helpful. Jonathan Grossman provided a critique, verified sources and made some fine editorial suggestions for the chapters entitled "Leverage is the Thing" and "Whistleblowing." Jonathan's enthusiasm for the project was always evident and gave me quite a lift. David Sidney's work on the chapters entitled "Regulation of Advertising," "Employee Agreements Not to Compete," and "Girard's Law of 250" provided me with significant challenges. In addition, David meticulously verified sources. His editorial suggestions were superb. Chaim Sultan did a yeoman's job in preparing the name index and giving me very substantial help in preparing the glossaries and the subject index. In a pinch, he was always available to locate missing sources. The single-minded devotion and alacrity Chaim applied to the work has made an indelible impression on me.

I gave out earlier drafts of much of the material of this book for critical comment. My foremost acknowledgment goes to my dear friend, Leon M. Metzger. Mr. Metzger, MBA, vice-chairman Paloma Partners Management Company, is sophisticated and adept in both the worlds of halakhic and abstract economic reasoning as well as in the real marketplaces that I discuss in my book. This combination makes for provocative challenges, probing questions and insightful comments.

David Schwartz, Esq., of Wachtell, Lipton, Rosen & Katz provided a critique for the chapter called "Goldfarb's 15 Year Turf War." Particularly valuable to me was his input on the comparison I made between Halakhah and secular law on the issue of fair competition.

My appreciation to Professor Elias Grivoyannis, my friend and colleague in the department of economics at Yeshiva University, for the education he gave me on forensic economics. His expertise in expanding the present value formula for a wrongful death suit was vital in making the comparison between Halakhah and American law on this issue.

Throughout the period I researched my book, I benefited from conversations I had with various people on the topics I covered. My thanks to the following for their insights and comments: Rabbi Shalom Carmy, Rabbi Dr. Joshua Krausz, Rabbi Dr. Shnayer Leiman, Rabbi Dr. Dov Levine, Rabbi Efraim Yaakov Levine, Rabbi Nosson Levine, Rabbi Yosef Chaim Levine, Rabbi Dr. Asher Meir, Rabbi Dr. David Shatz, Mr. Judah Rosensweig, Esq., and Rabbi Hershel Schachter.

Throughout the project, my research was aided by the professionalism and the many amenities extended to me by the library staff of Yeshiva University. In particular, I would like to thank Zalman Alpert, Zvi Ehrenyi, Chaya Gordon, Rabbi Moshe Schapiro and Jeffrey Shulevitz of the Mendel Gottesman Library; John Moryl and Mary Ann Linahan of the Pollack Library; and Professor Edith Lubetski (head) and Vivian Moskowitz of the Hedi Steinberg Library.

My profound gratitude is given to the publisher of Yashar Books, Rabbi Gil Student. In our working relationship, Gil proved to be author friendly beyond reasonable expectation. In his capacity as publisher of this work, Rabbi Student thoroughly reviewed the entire manuscript and offered some valuable and substantive suggestions. I offer my heartfelt best wishes that the passion and sense of mission he brings to his calling to disseminate Torah scholarship will be crowned with great success.

My thanks is given to Dana Salzman of Yashar Books for her expertise and technical assistance in preparing my book for publication.

CREDITS

Several of the chapters of this study draw upon earlier published works: "Ethical Dilemmas in the Telemarketer Industry" is reprinted from *Tradition* 38:3, Fall 2004, pp. 1–30. The chapter "Regulation of Advertising" is an expansion and elaboration of my paper "Regulation of Advertising in Jewish Law: A Prototype Model—The Kraft Singles Case," delivered at the Thirtieth Biennial Conference of the Jewish Law Association, Boston University, August, 2004. "The Mean Boss" is adapted from my article by that title in *Tradition*. 35:1, Spring 2001, pp. 3–43. "Employee Agreements Not to Compete" is adapted from my article "Employee Agreements Not to Compete in American Law, Economic Theory and Halakhah," *Torah U-Madda Journal*, vol. 10, 2001, pp. 95–141; "False Goodwill" is adapted from my article by that title in *Tradition* 34:1, Spring 2000, pp. 1–43.

Translations of Talmudic passages were taken from the Schottenstein Edition of *Talmud Bavli*, Mesorah Publications, Ltd.

Introduction

This book uses the case study method to present and analyze moral dilemmas of the marketplace from the perspective of Jewish and American law, and secular business ethics. The types of moral dilemmas that I will deal with are those that one may encounter in everyday life in the roles of market participant and citizen. Economic analysis and public policy considerations are a feature of this work.

I hope to show with my interdisciplinary approach that issues arising from modern-day technology, secular scholarship, and economic analysis open up vistas, nuances, and subtleties for cases discussed in ancient and modern Jewish law sources.

Moral Issues of the Marketplace in Jewish Law builds on the philosophical underpinnings of my previous work *Case Studies in Jewish Business Ethics*.[1] In that book, my main objective was to lay out the case for moral education as well as to investigate by means of the case study method specific issues revolving around advertising, marketing, salesmanship, pricing policies, labor relations, consumer, and social ethics. Occasional reference will be made here to the material on moral education. The specific issues covered here, as described below, are different from the issues covered in *Case Studies in Jewish Business Ethics*. Nonetheless, there is an inevitable, but slight, intersection between the two works. With the aim of making the present study as user friendly as possible, the references to *Case Studies* will be in the form of either summaries or quotes, as the occasion warrants.

The moral dilemmas in this work are organized topically. The topics include: professional ethics, fair competition, marketing ethics, labor relations, privacy issues, public policy, and ethical issues in the protection of property.

The first two chapters deal with professional ethics.

In Chapter 1, I discuss the issue of false goodwill. The concern here will be to identify the parameters wherein the capture of goodwill is the legitimate entitlement of the person who generated it. Another issue for investigation is the identification of the circumstances where the opportunity to capture legitimately earned goodwill must be foregone.

By means of the case study method, I set out to explore these issues in the setting of a number of moral dilemmas a rabbi faces in the course of going about his professional duties.

Chapter 2 deals with the issue of truth telling in the context of labor and crisis negotiations. Specific issues discussed include the ethics of the use of tactics like false demands, false promises, false threats, diversions, and insincerity of both the transparent and nontransparent variety. The acceptability of these various tactics will form the basis of the judgment on whether the standard of truth telling in the setting of negotiation is any different from the standard of truth telling in other settings.

Chapters 3, 4, and 5 deal with the ethics of various competitive tactics in the marketplace.

Chapter 3 focuses on the extent to which Halakhah (Jewish law) protects a firm from the competitive pressures of the marketplace. For purposes of analytical simplicity, I use as my model the protection Halakhah affords an existing firm from the competitive pressures of a new entrant. Through a case study, I show that Halakhah espouses rules of "fair competition" for the marketplace. For Halakhah, maximizing consumer welfare by adopting rules to ensure that the product or service involved is produced at the lowest possible social cost is not the only criterion for governance of the marketplace. Last, I contrast the protection Jewish and American law afford a firm from the competitive pressures of the marketplace.

Chapter 4 deals with the "post-employment restrictive covenant." In this agreement an employee agrees, upon being employed, to conform to certain conditions following termination of employment with his or her present employer. From the perspective of Halakhah, one must overcome many technicalities to create valid non-compete employee agreements. Within the context of Halakhah's concept of "fair play" in the marketplace, there is a balance between the economic interests of an established firm and the legitimate rights of a former employee of that firm to compete in the same business.

Parties to a mutually advantageous transaction rarely meet on equal terms. Instead, one party has an advantage over the other. If the leverage consists of market power, it will come as no surprise that the stronger party usually walks away from the transaction with the lion's share of the gains. This is the way of the marketplace.

The case studies in chapter 5 focus on the ethics of exploiting an existing leveraged situation for further gains. Indeed, the distinction between negotiating a lopsided deal and unilaterally changing the terms of that deal once it has been negotiated may become blurred or even lost entirely in the mind of the advantaged party.

In what one could call reverse leverage, the seemingly weaker party can maneuver to escape an obligation because it is so insignificant from the perspective of the advantaged party that the weaker party hopes the obligation will go unnoticed. Alternatively, the weaker party can maneuver to escape payment because on a cost-benefit basis it is not worthwhile for the advantaged party to pursue its claim through legal channels.

Exercising leverage may turn into violation of *oshek* (extortion) and the prohibition of *lo tahmod* (coveting). In inter-Jewish loan transactions, the exercise of leverage may run afoul of the rabbinical extensions of the biblical prohibition of *ribbit* (the charging and the payment of interest on loans).

Chapters 6 and 7 deal with ethical issues in marketing and salesmanship.

Chapter 6 examines the philosophy and salesmanship techniques Joe Girard employed in becoming the world's best salesperson. Joe dubs the philosophy behind his phenomenal success Girard's Law of 250. This philosophy begins with the observation that the average attendance at a funeral and a wedding is 250 and 500 people, respectively. What this told Joe was that an average person interacts in a socially meaningful way with approximately 250 people. A satisfied customer could therefore potentially spread goodwill about him to 250 people and a dissatisfied customer could potentially "badmouth" him to as many as 250 people. The customer at hand was therefore really 250 people wrapped up together in one.

Joe's philosophy is examined not in terms of how it promoted success, but rather, in terms of whether it resulted in virtuous and ethically acceptable behavior in the marketplace.

Chapter 7 explores the ethics of marketing techniques that relate to the telemarketing industry. Both the business practices of this industry and the way consumers have reacted to these practices present a number of serious moral dilemmas. These include the use of pressure tactics, pricing policies, conduct consumers engage in to thwart the telemarketer, and using the information the telemarketer offers without compensating him or her for the provision of that information.

Chapter 8 deals with the ethics of an employer who springs work rules on an employee when the employee did not agree to these rules before he or she signed the contract.

Chapter 9 takes up the issue of privacy in the workplace. Does Halakhah validate prehiring screening for drug, tobacco, and alcohol abuse? Moreover, does Halakhah treat the issue of screening job applicants with pencil-and-paper integrity testing and handwriting analysis in the same way? What is Halakhah's attitude toward the use of the polygraph in the workplace? If prehiring screening for some purpose is halakhically valid, perhaps once a candidate is hired, the employer has no right to retest. Instead, the employer may only periodically elicit the employee's self-declaration that he or she is not violating the policy the employer seeks to enforce. Is privacy in the workplace all a matter of contract between the employee and employer? Finally, I discuss the issue of the extent and manner in which an employer may monitor the electronic communications coming into and out of the office.

Chapters 10 and 11 deal with ethical issues in the marketplace that require government involvement in the form of public policy.

Chapter 10 concentrates on the issue of government regulation of advertising. For secular society, this issue essentially revolves around deception. Halakhah's concept of deception is far stricter, however. Beyond rules against deception, Halakhah promotes truth telling as a positive value in society. Finally, Halakhah prescribes strict rules against negative commercial speech.

Chapter 11 deals with the issue of whistleblowing. In this chapter I draw a comparison between the secular and halakhic approaches. A major difference arises. The secular approach is distinctly utilitarian. If whistle-blowing is justified, it is only because the good it produces outweighs the harm it causes to those responsible for the harm. In sharp contrast, Halakhah focuses entirely on the victim or would-be victims. To be sure, satisfaction of a number of conditions must be met before one can justify the disclosure. Nonetheless, these conditions are constraints and nothing more. Accordingly, if the disclosure will produce a benefit in the form of restitution for a victim or deterrence against future harm, the disclosure should be made.

In dealing with whisleblowing I am also interested in creating both an organizational structure and a corporate culture that precludes the problem of whistleblowing in the first place. I then turn to a consideration of the protection the whistleblower enjoys under law today. I will analyze these laws from the perspective of Halakhah.

The final two chapters of this work deal with identifying the permissible bounds for protecting and defending one's property and other rights against infringement. Does this right extend even to causing possible harm, loss, and even death to potential infringers and intruders?

By means of the case study method, Chapter 12 deals with the right to protect and defend one's property in the following two settings: the right of a homeowner to protect his or her property against theft, and the right and duty of a student to protect him- or herself against cheaters. Finally, does a teacher's responsibility to discipline his or her students extend even to the prerogative of confiscating their property?

Last, the task of Chapter 13 is to explore the duty a property owner has to ensure that his or her premises will not cause injury to someone who enters them. Moreover, if an entrant injures himself/herself on the property, to what extent is the owner of the property liable? In the comparison I draw between the secular and halakhic approaches, I will use the cases of *Lee v. Chicago Transit Authority* and *Smith v. Wal-Mart Stores* to illustrate the differences in law.

ETHICAL NORMS FOR WHOM?

The focus of this work is the duties of a Jew vis-à-vis, a fellow Jew in the context of the marketplace. In this regard, the phrase *Torah society* appears occasionally in this volume. What I mean to convey with this phrase is a community where *all* its members are committed to Halakhah. Indeed, only in such a society would everything discussed in this volume be given consideration for adoption.

Basic to our belief system is the notion that the mission and the destiny of the Jewish people is to be the "light for the nations."[2] Accordingly, the public and business policies for the Torah society can often serve as models for secular society.

In the marketplace of the real world, we interact with non-Jews, both in the settings of being members of the same team and members of opposing teams. To what extent do the marketplace ethics described in this book apply to our interactions with non-Jews? Preliminarily, let us note that the overriding objective behind the Torah's prescriptions is the creation of rules for honest dealing and against hurtful conduct. These same objectives stand behind the various enactments of American civil law. Consider, however, that we, as Jews, are forbidden to put our disputes in these matters before a non-Jewish court. Instead, we must submit these disputes to a Jewish court (*Bet Din*) that will decide the matter based on Jewish law.[3] In these *Bet Din* proceedings, American civil law has, however, some applicability based on the principle of *dina d'malkhuta dina*, i.e. the law of the kingdom is law.[4] Elsewhere in this volume, I make note of four different views on the parameters of this matter. Some of these views reject *dina d'malkhuta* when it is in conflict with the law of the Torah.[5] *Dina d'malkhuta* is, however, always the operative principle in a dispute between a Jew and non-Jew, even when the rule contradicts the law of the Torah.[6] Once it is recognized that *dina d'malkhuta* is the operative principle in resolving disputes between Jews and non-Jews, Halakhah is already protecting the non-Jew at the *very beginning stages* of his or her dealings with a Jew. This is so because the ethical person will be sure to educate himself or herself as to what *dina d'malkhuta* requires and not first discover these requirements in a court proceeding. Moreover, the ethical person will not exploit the legal system by refusing to satisfy a just and rightful claim until a court, whether Jewish or secular, orders him or her to do so.

The aforementioned brings us to the following conundrum. Consider that the code of ethics that Halakhah prescribes for the marketplace, as we shall see in this volume, often goes considerably beyond the strictures of

American legislation. The issue before us is therefore whether the rules of the Torah for interpersonal conduct pertain only to our interactions with fellow Jews. However, as far as our duties to non-Jews, the whole matter is *dina d'malkhuta* and nothing more. Put in stark terms, the issue is whether Halakhah countenances a dual morality for us in interpersonal conduct: one standard for our interactions with fellow Jews and a lower standard in respect to our interaction with non-Jews.

Repudiation of the notion that Halakhah countenances a dual morality system begins with the diatribe R. Tzevi Hirsch Ashkenazi (*Hakham Tzevi*, Germany, 1660–1718) issued *against* the notion that Halakhah's rules for honest dealing apply with less stringency in transactions with non-Jews. Quite to the contrary, R. Ashkenazi tells us, Halakhah's rules for honest conduct apply with even greater stringency regarding transactions with gentiles.

In rejecting the dual morality thesis, R. Ashkenazi, at the outset, points out that by dint of *Torah* law, theft (*geneivah*) is prohibited even when the motive of the perpetrator is salutary. This would be the case, for instance, if the thief *T* intends to return his or her pilferage to the rightful owner and carries out the caper only to teach the intended victim *V* a lesson to guard his or her property more carefully. Another qualifying case occurs when *T* desires to give *V* a gift, but *V* demurs. As a means of accomplishing his objective, *T* steals an item from *V* and makes sure that two witnesses catch him red- handed in the act. Predictably, the two witnesses will come forward and implicate *T* in the crime. *T* will now finally get his wish to give *V* a gift, as the Jewish court will order *T* to pay *V* the "double indemnity" (*kefel*) payment imposed on a thief. Notwithstanding the salutary motives in both of the above-described cases, the action of the thief in both cases is prohibited conduct. What this tells us, avers R. Ashkenazi, is that theft is *inherently* an abhorrent act. Dishonest conduct debilitates the character of the perpetrator and sullies his soul. Hence dishonest conduct directed at any human being is equally prohibited.[7] R. Joseph b. Moses Babad (Poland, 1800–1872) makes this same point.[8]

The stricter standard we have vis-à-vis a non-Jew comes into play in the instance where the non-Jewish victim gets wind that the perpetrator was Jewish. Here, the offender compounds the sin of theft with the additional sin of disgracing God's name (*hillul ha-Shem*)[9] For the same case involving a Jewish victim, the perpetrator does not violate *hillul ha-Shem*. Why it makes a difference whether the victim is a co-religionist or not is explained by R. Bahya b. Asher (Saragossa, 13th cent.): In the instance where the victim is a gentile, the discovery that the perpetrator is a Jew could incite the non-Jewish victim to disgrace the Jewish religion and call it a false-belief system. When the victim is, however, a Jew, discovery that the per-petrator is a fellow Jew *presumably does not move the offended party to rail out against his* own religion and call it a false belief.[10]

Hakham Tzevi's diatribe has much import for the modern marketplace. Most fundamentally, it must be appreciated that the types of misconduct falling under the rubric of robbery and theft go considerably beyond the readily recognizable violations of these transgressions. A case in point is the use of leverage to unilaterally change the terms of a done deal. Notwith-standing that the disadvantaged party raises no protest, the change is effected by means of intimidation, and hence is extortion.[11] Another case in point is the use of unlawful sales pressure to effect a deal. This conduct vio-lates the prohibitions of *lo tit'avveh*[12] (do not desire) and *lo tahmod*[13] (do not covet).[14] In Jewish law, misrepresentation (*geneivat da'at*) falls under the rubric of either the prohibition against falsehood or the prohibition against theft.[15] Examples of this type of prohibited conduct are found throughout this work.

Hakham Tzevi's notion that dishonest conduct debilitates character should have ramifications for the prohibitions of the Torah that relate to hurtful conduct as well. Representative of the prohibitions of the Torah of this genre that will be encountered in this work are the prohibition to cause someone needless mental anguish (*ona'at devarim*)[16] and the prohibition to deliver a true, but damaging report about someone (*lashon ha-ra*).[17] In for-mulating these duties of character, the Torah refers to the target of the hurt-ful conduct as *ahiv* (brother) and *amekhah* (your people), respectively. These expressions seem to indicate that the duties apply only in interactions with fellow Jews.

However, we must recognize that hurtful conduct done for a bad motive surely debilitates character, and this conduct should therefore be prohib-ited, at least on a hortatory level, irrespective of who the target of the mis-treatment is.

Explication of what constitutes dishonest and hurtful conduct is not the whole story of this book. Many of the ethical norms presented in this volume relate not to dishonest or hurtful conduct, but rather to a duty to manifest a refined and elevated character in one's interactions with one's fellow man. Examples of such conduct are the duty to conduct one's self "beyond the letter of the law" (*lifnim mi-shurat ha-din*)[18] and the duty to judge someone favorably.[19] During a lull in the work flow, an employee is entitled to communicate minimally with the outside world. The employee need not secure advanced permission for this privilege. Diminished expectations of privacy at the work scene do not empower an employer to claim a business interest in reading the private communications of his workers.[20] Perhaps these types of refined duties apply only to interactions with fellow Jews. This conclusion is unwarranted. First, let us take note that despite important differences in faith between Judaism and the other major religions of the world. Jewish law does not put the great preponderance of civilized society today in the category of idolaters.[21] Consider, however, that even in respect to non-Jews who the rabbis of the Talmud (ca. 500 C.E.) regarded as idolaters, positive duties were prescribed. These duties consisted of specific welfare ordinances the sages instituted in the name of *darkhei shalom* (literally, ways of peace) and changes in the law aimed at preventing resentment and enmity (*eivah*).[22] I will briefly describe these principles as they pertain to interpersonal relations and draw out the implications for interactions in the modern marketplace:

Under the *darkhei shalom* legislation Jews affirmed the dignity of the gentile, expressed sympathy for him, and rendered material assistance to the poor. This material assistance took the form of allowing the non-Jewish poor to collect along with the Jewish poor the mandated agricultural gifts from the fields.[23] These gifts included the gleanings, the forgotten sheaves, and the corner of the field.[24] At the same time, in Jewish towns, a welfare duty devolved upon the Jewish community to respond to calls for assistance from the non-Jewish poor.[25] For example, if there was no one to attend to the burial of a non-Jewish person, this responsibility fell to the Jewish community of the town.[26]

Finally, under the *darkhei shalom* ordinance Jews expressed their humanity towards non-Jews by showing solidarity with them in time of suffering. Specifically, Jews visited the sick, made eulogies for their dead, and made condolence calls to the bereaved.[27]

The *eivah* principle is illustrated by the duty to respond to a call from an individual to help him load his animal. The *Torah* formulates this duty in terms of responding to the call for help coming from a fellow Jew: "You shall not see your brother's (*ahikha*) donkey or his ox fallen in the road and hide from them; raise up, you shall raise up with him [the owner]" (Deuteronomy 22:4). Nonetheless, if the one who calls for assistance is a non-Jew, the rabbis instituted that the passerby is also duty bound to respond. The obligation is rooted in a concern to prevent *eivah* on the part of the non-Jew.[28] (The passerby may precondition his or her agreement to render assistance upon the promise that the gentile will compensate him or her with the relevant competitive wage, just as he or she would be entitled to do if the request came from a Jew).[29]

Many of the ethical norms appearing in this volume come in the form of policy recommendations for the firm and legislative suggestions for government. If a committed Jew is in a strategic position to push or implement a halakhic policy, practical considerations will ordinarily demand that the idea be implemeted on a nondiscriminatory basis, for Jew and non-Jew alike.

Beyond practicalities, consider that having one policy for Jewish workers and another policy for non-Jewish ones easily can lead to resentment from the non-Jewish workers. The *eivah* principle, therefore, tells us that one must implement the policy on a uniform, non-discriminatory basis, for Jew and non-Jew alike.

To illustrate, suppose a company institutes a policy of repeat testing for drug abuse for non-Jewish hires, but only prehiring drug testing for Jewish hires. This policy will undoubtedly foster resentment among the non-Jewish workers.

Another example of a policy that undoubtedly would generate resentment is for an employer to set up an interest-free loan fringe benefit for Jewish workers, but to charge interest, albeit even a below-market interest rate, on loans to non-Jewish workers. Consider that in inter-Jewish loan transactions, the payment and receipt of interest is prohibited. But, if one of the parties is non-Jewish, the prohibition against interest does not apply. Although one can defend the fringe-benefit policy based on technical Halakhah, it will deservedly generate resentment among the non-Jewish workers.

There can be no doubt that the *eivah* doctrine issues a strong condemnation against engaging in hurtful conduct against gentiles. Let there be no illusions, however, about the mileage we can get out of the *eivah* principle. It is a doctrine of fear. It will hence do no more than produce policies for the workplace based on pragmatism, rather than humanism and idealism.

In evaluating the motivational potential of the *darkhei shalom* principle to bring about a uniform nondiscriminatory policy in the marketplace, we must recognize the historical context of this legislation. At the same time the rabbis were busy legislating *darkhei shalom* ordinances, other legislation was already on the books to create social barriers between Jews and idolaters.[30] The two strains of legislation hence are designed to achieve a balance between the desire to have harmonious relations with non-Jews and not exposing us too closely to their idolatrous practices. It is in this vein that R. Samuel b. David ha-Levi (*Turei Zahav*, Poland, 1586–1667) understood all the *darkhei shalom* legislation mentioned. In the opinion of *Turei Zahav*, what the rabbis meant to say with the specific items of the *darkhei shalom* legislation was that these forms of conduct do not infringe upon the social barriers the rabbis created between Jews and idolaters. Darkhei shalom conduct, according to *Turei Zahav*, is permissible, but not obligatory conduct.[31]

We must, however, recognize that *darkhei shalom* legislation is inexorably intertwined with the principle of *eivah*. Accordingly, if a gentile mendicant comes to a Jewish home and makes a request for assistance, the request may not be refused. This is so because denying or deflecting the legitimate request for aid will generate resentment and ill feeling.

In his treatment of *darkhei shalom* duties, Maimonides explicitly says that a request for assistance by the non-Jewish poor may not be refused.[32] Presumably, the same principle should apply to other prescribed *darkhei shalom* duties when the request for the particular assistance comes at the initiative of the gentile. Moreover, let us take note that Maimonides informs us that *darkhei shalom* conduct in relation to non-Jews is rooted in the verses "The Lord is good to all; and His tender mercies are over all His works" (Psalms 145:9) and "Its ways are the ways of pleasantness, and all its paths are peace" (Proverbs 3:17).[33] What this tells us is that *darkhei shalom* duties regarding non-Jews are not just permissible actions, but *required ethical duties*.

Like the *eivah* dictum, the *darkhei shalom* dictum issues a strong condemnation against engaging in hurtful conduct against non-Jews. In terms of affirmative duties, however, *darkhei shalom* mandates no specific conduct for the marketplace. Rather, it offers nothing more than general guideposts consistent with sensible business practices.

The specificity we are looking for proceeds from the teachings of the medieval exegete, R. Menahem b. Solomon *Meiri* (*Meiri*, France, ca. 1249–1306).

Meiri puts all non-Jews who observe the seven Noahide laws[34] in the category of people that are "disciplined in the ways of religion and civilization." As such, these people have a certain fraternity with the Jewish faith community. This judgment led *Meiri* to squarely place these people as qualifying beneficiaries of deeds of mandated kindness seemingly meant only for fellow Jews. A case in point is the duty of a passerby to restore a lost article (*hashavat aveidah*) to its rightful owner. Notwithstanding that the Torah formulates this obligation as a duty owed "your brother" (*ahikha*),[35] *Meiri* includes a non-Jew that is "disciplined in the ways of religion and civilization" as also being the beneficiary of this mandate.

Meiri makes the same point in connection with the treatment of an income transfer P_1 realizes from P_2 that was not called for by the terms of their commercial transaction. In realizing this "windfall," P_1 was not guilty of affirmative deception. Instead, P_1's "windfall" was entirely due to P_2's error (*ta'ut*). Suppose further that P_1 adjured P_2 to "carefully look into this transaction because I'm relying on you." For the above case, if P_2 is an idolater, P_1, may, as a strict matter of law, keep the "windfall." In the opinion of *Meiri*, keeping the "windfall" is not an option when P_2 is a gentile but not an idolater. Here, the rule is that P_1 must always rectify the mistake.[36]

The 19th century halakhic authority R. Tzevi Chajes (Poland, 1805–1855) quotes *Meiri*'s attitude toward non-Jews approvingly. Both the Christian and Muslim governments of his time, R. Chajes tells us, strenuously enforced the Noahide laws.[37]

Meiri's formulation has direct implications for the prohibitions of the Torah that relate to hurtful conduct. If the non-Jew that is "disciplined in the ways of religion and civilization" qualifies as a beneficiary for supererogatory ethical conduct, afflicting this person with hurtful conduct is certainly morally repugnant.

Within *Meiri*'s formulation, *hashavat aveidah* and the case of *ta'ut* serve as models for the infusion of positive energy into the proposition that all policies in the workforce must apply uniformly to Jew and non-Jew alike.

Meiri's embracing attitude toward the gentile should not be taken as advocacy for equality of treatment between Jew and non-Jew. Consider that *Meiri* understands the verses in the Torah dealing with the prohibition against interest payments in a loan to differentiate between a Jewish and non-Jewish debtor: "You may not pay interest to your brother, interest on money, interest on food; interest on any matter where it is paid. You may *tashikh* (take)[38] from a stranger, but from your brother do not take interest" (Deuteronomy 23:20-21). Given the fraternity *Meiri* saw between Jews and the gentiles of his time, we would expect *Meiri* to say that interest should not be charged to gentiles. However, *Meiri* does move in this direction by saying that the phrase "you may *take* from a stranger" conveys that the livelihood of the non-Jew should be of our concern. If the non-Jew comes for a loan, we should not turn him away. Though we are not obliged to extend ourselves to him with an interest free loan, we should at least lend him money on interest. In addition, as far as making loans is concerned, priority must be given to a Jew over a non-Jew.[39] What *Meiri* is saying is that within the refined character trait of engaging in acts of kindness to our fellow man, we certainly owe a duty to the gentile, but a higher level of kindness is due our own brethren.

INTERACTION WITH NON-JEWS AND *KIDDUSH-HA-SHEM*

This book is being published against the backdrop of the relatively recent revelations of major scandals in corporate America. High-ranking executives in Enron, WorldCom, Tyco, and Computer Associates were implicated for such crimes as fraudulent accounting at their companies. Regulators have accused some executives at mutual funds of treating some investors more favorably than others notwithstanding assurances to the contrary. Furthermore, regulators have charged leaders of insurance-related companies of defrauding policyholders. The brazenness with which these alleged crimes were committed has had the effect of severely damaging the moral climate of society. If brazenness of the evil variety is what is damaging the moral climate, it takes brazenness of the virtuous variety to get us back on track. What comes to mind is the following episode in the life of Talmudic sage R. Shimon b. Shetah (first century B.C.E.):

> It is related of R. Shimon b. Shetah that he once bought a donkey from an Ishmaelite. His disciples came and found a precious stone suspended from its neck. They said to him: "Master, 'The blessing of the Lord will bring riches . . .' (Proverbs 10:22)." R. Shimon b. Shetah replied: "I purchased a donkey, but I have not purchased a precious stone." He then went and returned it to the Ishmaelite, and the latter exclaimed of him, "Blessed be the lord God of Shimon b. Shetah."[40]

Because the Ishmaelite despaired of ever getting back his lost precious stone, we can well understand the gratitude he felt toward R. Shimon b. Shetah. But, the sentiment of gratitude should have caused the Ishmaelite to bless R. Shimon b. Shetah; instead, the Ishmaelite blesses the God of R. Shimon b. Shetah. Addressing himself to this issue, R. Jeroham Leibovitz (Poland, 1874–1936) posits that the Ishmaelite was not only filled with a sense of gratitude, but was *nonplussed* by R. Shimon b. Shetah's conduct. What the Ishmaelite witnessed was no ordinary act of kindness, but the type of deed that made the *tzalem Elokim* (image of God) evident in the person of R. Shimon b. Shetah. The reaction of the Ishmaelite was in every way akin to the making of a blessing over a fruit before partaking of it. In the blessing over the fruit, we thank God for creating the "fruit of the tree." What we are saying is that we see the *greatness* of the Creator in the fruit that we are about to consume. So, too, the Ishmaelite saw the greatness of the Creator in the grand act of kindness of R. Shimon b. Shetah.[41]

The words of R. Shimon b. Shetah, "I purchased a donkey, but I have not purchased a precious stone," ring out against veiled misconduct in the marketplace. Because man is no more vulnerable to the wiles of the evil inclination than in a setting for veiled misconduct, overcoming this temptation represents for man his greatest triumph. This triumph is that much more magnified when our opposite number is a non-Jew and overcoming the temptation is *Kiddush ha-Shem*. Accordingly, overcoming veiled misconduct in interactions with non-Jews represents the greatest possibilities for sanctification of God's name.

RELATIONS WITH NON-JEWS IN THE MARKETPLACE—A SUMMARY

At this juncture, a summary of what has been said concerning the relations between Jews and non-Jews in the marketplace is in order. First, *dina d'malkhuta dina* makes American civil law fully operative vis-à-vis the non-Jew.

In respect to the Torah's rules against dishonesty, deception, falsehood, and hurtful conduct, the code is a uniform one and applies equally, to whomever we interact with. One of the purposes of this work is to show that the limits of these prohibitions go considerably beyond the readily recognizable manifestations of these transgressions.

Expanding the realm of the uniformity of Halakhah's code of interpersonal ethics to the treatment of non-Jews are the *eivah* and *darkhei shalom* principles. At the very least, these principles tell us that any policy for the workforce or marketplace must be implemented on a nondiscriminatory basis, treating Jew and non-Jew equally. Pragmatic considerations, in any case, recommend a nondiscriminatory policy, so Halakhah reinforces what good business practice would, in any case, recommend.

Meiri's doctrine provides, at the very least, a hortatory ring as well as positive energy to the notion that all policies in the workforce must apply uniformly, to Jew and non-Jew alike.

Finally, we must be cognizant that interactions with non-Jews in the marketplace present the extreme possibilities of *hillul ha-Shem* if we fail, and the glorious prospect of sanctifying God's name if we succeed.

POSTPRANDIUM

Upon completing work on this volume, I went over it again very carefully, chapter by chapter. I would like to say a bit more! The additions are a potpourri of items that defy categorization into a homogenous grouping. One category consists of problems at the end of some of the chapters. For other additions, my aim is either to extend the material of the chapter a bit further or take the topic in a new direction. Because the pattern of these addenda form no recognizable mosaic, I call this section of my book *POSTPRANDIUM* (from Latin *post*, after, and *prandium*, dinner). In the manner of an after-dinner conversation with a friend, these additions are intended to be provocative and to stimulate interest in the subject matter. More importantly, this section is to tell the reader something about myself: "It is not upon you to complete the work, yet you are not free to withdraw from it."[42]

NOTES

1. Aaron Levine, *Case Studies in Jewish Business Ethics* (Hoboken, NJ: Ktav Publishing, Yeshiva University Press, 2000).
2. For an excellent exposition of various nuances of this concept, see David Shatz, Chaim I. Waxman, & Nathan J. Diament, *Tikun Olam: Social Responsibility in Jewish Thought and Law* (Northvale, NJ: Jason Aronson, 1997).

3. *Baraita, Gittin* 88a. For sources and treatment of the many nuances of this topic, Cf. R. Simcha Krauss, "Litigation in Secular Courts," *Journal of Halacha and Contemporary Society*, vol. 2, no.1, pp. 35–53; R. Dr. Dov Bressler, "Arbitration and the Courts in Jewish Law," *Journal of Halacha and Contemporary Society*, no. 9, Spring 1985, pp. 105–117.

4. Samuel, *Gittin* 10a. The preponderant opinion among halakhic authorities is that *dina d'malkhuta dina* has the force of biblical law. Cf. R. Avraham Duber Kahana Shapira (Poland, 1870–1943), *Devar Avraham* 1:1. A minority position here is taken by R. Shemu'el b. Uri Shraga Phoebus (Poland, 1650–1705). In his view, *dina d'malkhuta* operates on the force of rabbinical law (*Beit Shemu'el, Even ha-Ezer* 28 note 3).

5. Please turn to pp. 144–145 of this volume.

6. R. Mosheh Isserles (Poland, 1525 or 1530–1572), *Rema, Shulhan Arukh, Hoshen Mishpat* 369:11; R. Abraham Isaiah Karelitz (Israel, 1878–1953), *Hazon Ish, Bava Kamma* 10:9, *Likkutim* 16:1.

7. R. Tzvi Hirsch Ashkenazi, *Hakham Tzevi* 26.

8. R. Joseph b. Moses Babad (Poland, 1800-1872), *Minhat Hinnukh, Mitzvah* 224. The notion that the *Torah* prohibits bad conduct not just on account of the hurtful effect it has on the victim, but also because it sullies the character of the perpetrator, finds expression in the work of Maimonides (*Sefer ha-Mitzvot* 317). Maimonides espouses this principle in connection with the prohibition "You shall not curse a deaf person. . . ." (Leviticus 19:14). Although the deaf person will not hear the curses, this conduct fosters for the perpetrator the character traits of revenge and anger.

9. *Hakham Tzevi*, op. cit.

10. R. Bahya b. Asher, *Rabbenu Bahya al-ha-Torah*, Leviticus 25:50.

11. For explication of the various violations that may be involved in exercising leverage in commercial and other settings, please turn to pp. 175–200 of this volume.

12. Deuteronomy 5:18.

13. Exodus 20:14.

14. For explication of these prohibitions, please turn to pp. 189–191, 234–244 of this volume.

15. For sources on the prohibition of *geneivat da'at*, please turn to pp. 8–9, 266 n.26 of this volume.

16. Leviticus 25:17.

17. Leviticus 19:16.

18. Deuteronomy 6:18.

19. Leviticus 19:15.

20. For detailed treatment of these points, please turn to pp. of this volume.

21. R. Tzevi Chajes (Poland, 1805–1855, *Kol Sifrei Maharats Hayyot, Tiferet L'Yisrael*, pp. 489–491); R. Yosef Eliyahu Henkin, "Ketz ha-Yamim," *Hadorom, Elul*, 1958, 5–9. For review articles on this issue, see R. Elisha Aviner, "Maamad ha-Ishmaellim bi-Medinat Israel lefi ha-Halakhah," *Tehumim* 8, 337–362; R. Hayyim David ha-Levi (Israel, 1924–1998), "Darkhei Shalom ba-Yahasin she-bein Yehudim le-She-enan Yehudim," *Tehumim* 9, 71–81. Maimonides regarded the Christians of his time as idolaters (Cf. *Yad, Avodah Zarah* 9:4, 10:1; *Ma'akholot Asurot* 11:7). For the thesis that Maimonides may not have regarded the Christians of our time in the same category, see Dror Fixler and Gil Nadle, "Ha'im ha-Notsrim be-Yamenu Ovdei Avodah Zarah Hem?" *Tehumim*, 22, 2001, 68–78.

22. In a wide variety of settings, the rabbis instituted ordinances to prevent *eivah*. For an overview of these ordinances, see *Encyclopedia Talmudit*, vol.1, pp. 488–493.

23. *Mishnah, Gittin* 5:8; R. Isaac b. Jacob Alfasi (Algeria, 1012–1103), *Rif,* ad locum;. Maimonides, *Yad, Mattenot Aniyyim* 7:7; R. Asher b. Jehiel (Germany, 1250–1327), *Rosh, Gittin* 5:20; R. Jacob b. Asher (Spain, 1250–1327), *Tur, Yoreh De'ah* 251; R. Joseph Caro (Israel, 1488–1575), *Shulhan Arukh, Yoreh De'ah* 251:12.

24. Leviticus 19:9–10.

25. *Gittin* 61a; *Rif* ad locum; *Yad, Avodah Zorah* 10:5; *Rosh,* op. cit. 3:23; *Tur,* op. cit. 251; *Sh. Ar.,* op. cit. 251:12. Rabbi Dr. Alter Hilvitz, "Lebiur he-Sugiya 'Mipnei Darkhei Shalom' be-Yahas le-Goyim," *Sinai,* 100, 1986, 325–358.

26. *Gittin* 61a; *Rif* ad locum; *Yad, Melakhim* 10:12; *Rosh,* op. cit.; *Tur,* op. cit.; *Sh. Ar.,* op. cit.; Hilvitz, op. cit.

27. *Tosefta, Gittin* 3:14; *Rosh,* op. cit.; *Tur,* op. cit.; *Sh. Ar.,* op. cit.; *Hilvitz,* op. cit.

28. *Tosafot, Bava Metzia* 32b.

29. *Bava Metzia* 32b; R. Isaac b. Jacob Alfasi, *Rif,* ad locum; Maimonides, *Yad, Rotseah,* 13:7; R. Asher b. Jehiel, *Rosh, Bava Metzia* 2:28; R. Jacob b. Asher, *Tur, Hoshen Mishpat* 272; R. Joseph Caro, *Shulhan Arukh, Hoshen Mishpat* 272:6; R. Jehiel Michel Epstein, *Arukh ha-Shulhan, Hoshen Mishpat* 272:4. The sources cited speak of the right of a Jew to demand compensation for the loading operation when the one seeking this help is a fellow Jew. I assume that the right to demand compensation remains intact when the one who requests assistance is a non-Jew.

30 *Shabbat* 17b.

31. R. Samuel b. David ha-Levi, *Turei Zahav, Yoreh De'ah* 152 note 9.

32. *Yad, Avodah Zorah* 10:5.

33. *Yad,* Melakhim 10:12.

34. The seven Noahide laws consist of six prohibitions and one positive command. The six prohibitions are: 1) murder, 2) incest, 3) robbery, 4) eating the flesh of animals taken from the animal while it was still alive, 5) idolatry, and 6) blasphemy (Maimonides, *Yad, Melakhim* 9:1). The seventh law is a matter of dispute. In the opinion of Maimonides the seventh commandment consists of a duty to set up an administration of justice to enforce the other six (*Yad,* op. cit. 9:14). Nahmanides (Spain, 1194–1270, *Ramban,* Genesis 34:13), however, expands the ambit of the seventh commandment to include the setting up of civil law and a penal code modeled after the laws of the *Torah* in these matters.

35. "You may not observe your *brother's* ox or his sheep lost and conceal yourself from them; you must surely return them to your *brother*" (Deuteronomy 22:1).

36. R. Menahem b. Solomon *Meiri, Beit ha-Behirah, Bava Kamma* 113b. For the type of social barrier the rabbis continued to maintain between the Jew and the non-Jew who is "disciplined in the ways of religion and civilization," see *Beit Behirah, Hullin* 13b, *Avodah Zarah* 6a.

37. R. Tzevi Chajes, *Kol Sifrei Maharats Hayyot, Tiferet L'Yisrael,* op. cit., 489–491. *Meiri's* view has been subject to much discussion and analysis in the scholarly literature. Cf. Mosheh Halbertal, *"Bein Torah Le-Hohkhmah,"* (Jerusalem: Hebrew University Magnes Press, 2000), 80–109; Y. Blidstein, *"Meiri's* Attitude to Gentiles-Between Apologetics and Internalization" (Heb.), *Zion* 51 (1986): 153–166; J. Katz, "More on the Religious Tolerance of *Meiri"*(Heb.), *Zion* 46 (1961): 243–246; E.E. Urbach, "The Origins and Limitations of Tolerance in *Meiri"* (Heb.), in *Jacob Katz Jubilee Volume* (Jerusalem,1960), 34–44; J. Katz, "Exclusiveness and Tolerance (Oxford: Oxford University Press, 1986), 185–202.

38. *Meiri*'s interpretation of Deuteronomy 23:21 follows *Sifrei* which interprets *tashikh* to be the active form (*kal*) of the verb and therefore to mean *take*. Although understanding verse 21 differently than *Meiri*, *Maimonides* (*Yad*, Malveh 5:1) also understands the word *tashikh* in that verse to mean take. *Bava Metzia* 70b, however, interprets *tashikh* as the causative form (*hiphil*), i.e. to cause to take and therefore *to pay*. In this interpretation, the entire intent of the verse is just to make us draw an inference: that it is only permissible to cause a non-Jew to pay interest on a loan; however, it is forbidden to cause a Jew to pay interest on a loan. What the verse does, therefore, is heap another transgression on the one already spelled out in verse 20.

39. R. Menahem b. Solomon *Meiri, Beit ha-Behirah, Bava Metzia* 71a. See, however, Maimonides' interpretation of this verse (*Yad, Malveh* 5:1).

40. Deuteronomy *Rabbah* 3:3.

41. R. Jeroham Leibovitz, *Da'at Torah Parshat Bo*, 123–127; *Parshat Metzora*, 130–133.

42. R. Tarfon, *Avot* 2:21.

I. Professional Ethics

1

False Goodwill

Goodwill is the lubricant of harmonious human relations. In some professions, success or failure is heavily predicated upon the ability of the practitioner to inspire an abundance of goodwill in everyone with whom he or she professionally interacts. The goodwill an individual's actions produce is, however, sometimes unwarranted because it is produced by a false impression. My purpose here will be to identify the parameters wherein the capture of goodwill is the legitimate entitlement of the person who generated it. Another issue I will investigate is the identification of the circumstances where the opportunity to capture legitimately earned goodwill must be passed up.

By means of the case study method, I will set out to explore these issues in the context of a number of moral dilemmas a rabbi faces in the course of going about his professional duties. After presenting these dilemmas I will proceed to develop, in general terms, the halakhic principles I will draw upon to analyze these cases. I will then proceed to apply these principles to the specific cases presented.

Although the scenarios I present in this chapter relate to false goodwill issues encountered in the rabbinate, the principles developed can be generalized for the treatment of false goodwill in other professions as well.

GOODWILL CAPTURED: ALL IN A DAY'S WORK

Rabbi Ari Samson paced up and down the third floor of the Gabriel Pavilion of Bet Miriam Hospital, nervously awaiting the results of the diagnostic tests on his son, Tzvi. Three hours had passed since the rabbi and his wife, Matilda, had arrived at the hospital. The couple had received a call from the Refuah Volunteer Ambulance Society that Tzvi had been found in a dazed condition after he had apparently rammed into a tree while riding his bicycle. When the medical tests showed that Tzvi had sustained no serious injuries, the Samsons breathed a sigh of relief and offered thanksgiving to God for His kindness. At this moment Matilda spoke up: "Ari, you've had a pretty rough time for the last three hours, why don't you go to the cafeteria for a bite and then visit Joshua Farbstein. On Shabbat, I heard that Mr. Farbstein is in Bet Miriam as a patient."

When Rabbi Samson came calling on Mr. Farbstein, he found Mrs. Farbstein at her husband's bedside. Some of the Farbstein children and grandchildren were there, too. The couple was very glad to see him. While extending his hand to the rabbi, Farbstein exclaimed, "The doctors just gave me a clean bill of health. Please God I will be going home soon. I sure appreciate that you made a *special visit* to the hospital to see me." Doing his best to hide his uneasiness, Samson blurted out, "Uh, uh, I'm very flattered that you value my presence so much." Samson continued socializing with the Farbsteins for a while and left the couple in good cheer with his blessing that Mr. Farbstein should have a speedy recovery.

As Rabbi Samson returned to his son Tzvi's room, he was overcome with a sense of guilt for having failed to disabuse Farbstein of the notion that he made a *special* trip to the hospital to visit him. Samson's sense of guilt was reinforced when he realized that similar incidents had occurred to him over the course of the previous year and in each episode he had lacked the *fortitude* to disabuse the congregant of the false impression he or she had harbored.

In one incident, Samson had made a special trip to the hospital to visit Paul Dubchek. Dubchek was the president of Rabbi Samson's shul, the Bet Kodesh of Eden Commons, and a good friend as well. Samson, while still in the hospital, decided to pay a call on Dave Plotkin. Plotkin, suffering from cellulitis, was being treated with intravenous antibiotics. If not for the urgency he felt in visiting Dubchek, he would not have visited Plotkin on that particular day, and perhaps not even make a special trip to see him in the hospital. When Samson visited Plotkin, Plotkin was surprised to see him and exclaimed, "Rabbi, you surely did not make a special trip to the hospital to see me. Who else is here from the shul?" "I am disappointed to hear you speak this way," snapped back the rabbi. "You certainly deserve a special visit; I *came* to Bet Miriam to see you."

In another incident, Beryl Lemnick fell on a banana peel on a Manhattan street. The EMS rushed him to the emergency room of Royal Blue Hospital. The doctors decided to keep him overnight for observation. Coincidentally, Samson was at this time visiting his uncle at Royal Blue. As the rabbi made his way to the cafeteria for a snack, he noticed Beryl being wheeled to his room. As soon as Beryl made eye contact with Rabbi Samson, Beryl exclaimed, "I'm overwhelmed that you rushed over to be at my side so soon after my unfortunate accident. What a relief! All the tests were negative. I'm so appreciative that you are *here* for me." In response to this outpouring of emotion, Samson just smiled in a supportive way and wished his congregant a speedy recovery.

In contexts other than hospital visits, Rabbi Samson also apparently reaped undeserved goodwill. Let us look, for instance, at what happened at the annual Rodef Hesed breakfast in Eden Commons. Because the Rabbinical Board of Eden Park sponsored this event, Samson looked forward to the affair as an opportunity to socialize with his colleagues and exchange insights with them on the weekly portion. He often told Matilda that these exchanges provided unexpected fodder for his sermons. Samson's practice was only to selectively open mail. When the Rodef Hesed invitation arrived, Samson saw no need to open it, as he could pick up the relevant information incidentally in conversation with colleagues. When Samson arrived at the breakfast, he quickly picked up for the first time that Solomon Drake was this year's honoree. Rabbi Samson knew Drake and occasionally used him as a sounding board for his homiletic ideas. Drake was not a member of Bet Kodesh. Samson's relationship with him was only cordial. A moment's reflection told Samson that the circumstance that a charitable institution was honoring Drake would not in and of itself oblige his personal appearance at the event. Just as Rabbi Samson began to formulate what he should say by way of congratulations to Drake, Drake appeared from nowhere and effusively thanked the rabbi for coming to the affair in his honor. Before

Rabbi Samson could get a word in edgewise, Drake went on to say, "My rabbi, Rav Irving Beck, will be presenting me with the plaque. As a speaker, he always delivers a 'nugget.' I'm sure you'll agree." Not wanting to deflate or disappoint Drake, Samson responded warmly: "I'm so glad to be here. It's people like you, Sol, that keep Rodef Hesed's wheels spinning."

A misunderstanding of this sort also occurred at the Hyde Park Torah Academy annual banquet. The affair was held at the plush Jefferson Meadowlands Hotel in North Adams, New Jersey. One of the honorees at this affair was a former member of Bet Kodesh of Eden Commons, Walter Belzag. Belzag had moved out of Eden Commons several years before. At the smorgasbord, Belzag warmly greeted Rabbi Samson and his wife and thanked them lavishly for coming to the affair in his honor. In actuality, the Samsons were guests of another honoree of the evening, Eytan Kramer. Bear in mind, the cost per person was $250. Without the benefit of Kramer's largesse, the Samsons would not have attended the affair altogether. Instead of disabusing Belzag of his false notion, Samson responded to Belzag's exuberance by saying, "May the Almighty give you health and inspiration to continue your great work."

Let's examine one final setting where Rabbi Samson apparently captured unwarranted goodwill: his Friday night lectures at Bet Kodesh. In these lectures Rabbi Samson deals with Halakhah and contemporary society. This past year Samson chose to lecture on *ribbit* (the prohibition to pay and accept interest in an inter-Jewish loan transaction) problems in everyday life. He showed that such everyday transactions as investment in Israeli government bonds, using a friend's credit card, customer return policies at department stores, and magazine subscriptions, all involve possible *ribbit* issues. Samson's lecture was very well received. Many of the congregants complimented him for the fascinating insights he provided them with. Samson was delighted to overhear the shul president, Paul Dubchek, beam to Matilda in earshot of Dave Plotkin that "the rabbi has an incredible command over the entire range of rabbinical literature."

The impression the congregants gathered of Samson's erudition was, however, overly favorable. In preparing his lecture Samson made use of Rabbi Yaakov Yeshayahu Bloi's excellent work *Berit Yehudah*. For every case Samson presented, *Berit Yehudah* cited Talmudic sources and the modern halakhic authorities that dealt with the issues. *Berit Yehudah* opened Samson's eyes to issues he was never aware of before. In preparing his lecture, Samson did not look up any of the sources quoted in *Berit Yehudah* but instead relied totally on the summaries the author made of these works. Despite the vital role *Berit Yehudah* played for Samson in the preparation of his lecture, Samson made no mention of either the work or the author during the course of his lecture.

CAUSING AGGRAVATION TO A SERIOUSLY ILL PATIENT

Several of the scenarios discussed in this chapter involve interactions with patients in a hospital setting. The sages of the Talmud were particularly sensitive to the delicate mental state of a seriously ill patient. Out of concern that receiving aggravating news could cause the condition of a seriously ill patient to deteriorate (*shema tittaref da'ato*), the sages decreed that such a patient should not be given the news that a close relative of his had died. News of the death should be withheld even if the patient would not be obligated to sit in mourning upon hearing the report.[1] What the above law points to, according to R. Jehiel Michel Epstein (Belorussia, 1829-1908), is a prohibition against causing aggravation of any kind to a seriously ill patient.[2]

What emerges from the above law is that the standard Halakhah sets for the treatment of a seriously ill person stands on a higher level than that prescribed for an ordinary, healthy person. With respect to an ordinary, healthy person, the standard consists of a prohibition not to cause someone *needless mental anguish (ona'at devarim)*.[3] Illustrating the *ona'at devarim* interdict is the prohibition for *B* to price an article with no intention of buying it.[4] Because *B* makes his inquiry to *A* *with a closed mind*, the subsequent disappointment A experiences when *B's* inquiry does not culminate in a sale is regarded as needless mental anguish and is hence the responsibility of *B*.[5] But, if *B's* inquiry is sincere, *B* is not liable for the disappointment *A* experiences if *B's* inquiry does not culminate in a sale.[6] Similarly, if *A* insults *B*, *B* has every right to respond, without concern that his response may cause pain to *A*.[7] In the latter two instances, the pain *B* inflicts on *A* is not regarded as needless mental anguish.

A clear-cut application of the *ona'at devarim* interdict as it relates to interaction with the seriously ill is the duty to withhold from the patient aggravating news of any sort that can wait. Imparting aggravating information to someone who is suffering mentally and physically only exacerbates the pain of receiving the bad news. Since the information can wait, the *extra* pain the patient experiences by being presented with it on his sickbed is the responsibility of the reporter and violates the *ona'at devarim* interdict.

The standard the sages set for the treatment of a seriously ill patient, however, goes beyond the *ona'at devarim* interdict. Causing a seriously ill patient mental anguish is prohibited, even if the pain involved cannot be said to amount to *needless* mental anguish.

Let us suppose for the moment that the patients Samson visits are all seriously ill. Disabusing them of their false belief that he made a special trip to the hospital to visit them causes their expectations to be dashed. In this regard, a patient will be disappointed even if his expectation was produced by an unreasonable assumption. The prohibition not to cause aggravation to a seriously ill patient therefore suggests the proposition that Rabbi Samson should not disabuse a patient of his erroneous belief that he made a special trip to the hospital to visit him. Note, however, that the special protection from mental anguish Halakhah affords the seriously ill does not give Samson a license to tell the patient a lie or engage in *affirmative* deception for the purpose of enhancing his relationship with that person.

In order to determine when the requirement of extra sensitivity applies, the criterion for defining a seriously ill patient must be clarified. Not all hospital patients should be classified as seriously ill and thus protected beyond the law of *ona'at devarim*.[8] In the opinion of this writer, if the patient knows that his condition has been *definitively diagnosed and his doctors tell him that he is clearly not in any life-threatening danger and will recover*, the usual strictures of *ona'at devarim* should apply, with no extra delicate sensitivity required.[9]

With the aim of simplifying the analysis of the above scenarios, we will assume that the patients Rabbi Samson visits do not fall into the category of the seriously ill.

FALSE GOODWILL AND HALAKHAH

Rabbi Samson's failure to correct his congregants' overestimate of the goodwill he displayed toward them may violate various halakhic principles. Let us begin with the prohibition against creating a false impression (*geneivat da'at*).[10]

The biblical source of the *geneivat da'at* interdict is disputed by Talmudic decisors. R. Jonah b. Abraham Gerondi (Spain, ca. 1200–1264) places such conduct under the rubric of falsehood (*sheker*).[11] R. Yom Tov Ishbili (Seville, ca. 1250–1330), however, subsumes it under the *Torah*'s admonition against theft (*lo tignovu*, Leviticus 19:11). What *lo tignovu* enjoins is both theft of property and the acquisition of something by means of deception.[12]

Illustrating the *geneivat da'at* prohibition is R. Meir's dictum at *Hullin* 94a:

> A person should not urge his fellow to dine with him, when he knows that he will not dine; nor should he make numerous offerings of gifts, when he knows that he does not accept [gifts]; nor should he open for him barrels that have been sold to a shopkeeper unless he notifies him [that they were sold]; nor should he say to him, "Anoint [yourself with] oil," [when he is actually offering] from an empty flask. However, if [he does so] for his honor, it is permitted.

The underlying rationale for prohibiting the above behavior, according to R. Solomon b. Isaac (*Rashi*, France, 1040-1105), is that such conduct generates an unwarranted sense of indebtedness on the part of the friend (*mahazik tovah be-hinnam*).[13]

In assessing whether Rabbi Samson violated the *geneivat da'at* prohibition, let us consider that the rabbi, in all but one of the scenarios described above, did not *affirmatively* create false impressions, but instead was guilty of only a failure to correct the overly favorable impressions he knew that various people had formed of him. Perhaps *geneivat da'at* is violated only when one actively creates a false impression by either word or deed. But, failure to correct a false impression does not violate the *geneivat da'at* interdict.

Bearing directly on this issue in Halakhah is the disclosure formula the rabbis of the Talmud devised to inform townspeople that the day's supply of meat was not kosher. A public announcement to this effect served a double purpose. It communicated to the Gentile patrons that the meat they were buying was not kosher. The proprietors of kosher butcher shops would hence not violate *geneivat da'at* vis-á-vis their Gentile patrons. It also alerted the Jews of the town not to purchase meat from a Gentile supplier on that day.

In respect to the exact formulation of the announcement, the following discussion takes place at *Hullin* 94b:

What is the [text of the] announcement that we make [to notify the public about the occurrence of a *terefah*]? Rav Yitzhak bar Yosef said: [We announce:] "Meat for the general populace has fallen [into our hands, henceforth *nafla bisra*]."

But let us say [explicitly], "*Terefah* [meat] for the general populace has fallen [into our hands, *nafla trefta*]."

Then [the idolaters] will not buy [the meat].

But [the meat sellers] are misleading them, [for they are under the impression that they are purchasing kosher meat]!

It is they who are misleading themselves!

Like that [incident involving] Mar Zutra the son of Rav Nahman [who] was going from Sikhra to Bei Mehoza, and Rava and Rav Safra were coming to Sikhra. They met each other [on the road]. [Mar Zutra] thought that they were coming to greet him. He said to them, "Why was it necessary for the rabbis to trouble themselves and come so far?" Rav Safra said to him, "We did not know that the master was coming; [but] had we known, we would have troubled ourselves even more." Rava said to [Rav Safra], "What is the reason that you said so to him [and] disheartened him [so]?" [Rav Safra] said to [Rava], "But [had I not said so], we would be misleading him [into thinking that we came to honor him]!" [Rava replied,] "It is he who misled himself, [and we are under no obligation to correct his mistake]."

The support the Talmud draws for the *nafla bisra* proclamation from the Mar Zutra incident requires explanation. First, given that an explicit announcement of the presence of nonkosher meat in the butcher shops repels Gentile customers, formulating the announcement in ambiguous terms should amount to a deliberate attempt at deception. Why, then, do we regard the purchase of nonkosher meat by Gentiles based on the ambiguous announcement as constituting only self-deception on their part? Second, how can the Mar Zutra episode serve as support for the permissibility of making a calculated ambiguous announcement when the encounter between the rabbis and Mar Zutra was entirely coincidental and the rabbis did nothing to create the false impression that they constituted a welcoming party for him?

The previous difficulties are removed with the proposition that *passivity* on the part of the offender is not an extenuating factor in deciding whether one violates *geneivat da'at*. Instead, what makes for a *geneivat da'at* violation is that (1) the offender *knows* that the victim has a false impression of him, and (2) the deception is the result of the victim's *reasonable* interpretation of the circumstances confronting him. Let us proceed now to demonstrate how the above criteria explains the connection between *nafla bisra* and the Mar Zutra incident:

Given that no announcement whatsoever is made on days when the meat supply is kosher, the *nafla bisra* announcement should be understood by the ordinary shopper as conveying the message that the meat supply that day is not kosher, notwithstanding that the word *trefta* was not used in the announcement. Both the *nafla bisra* and the *nafla trefta* proclamation communicate the same message, but with different promotional slants. *Nafla trefta* is decidedly negative, openly proclaiming that the meat is unfit for Jewish consumption, but available for sale to Gentiles. *Nafla bisra*, on the other hand, openly conveys only that Gentiles are the desired customer base of the product; the unfitness of the product for Jewish consumption is indicated only by means of reasonable implication.

The proposition that the difference between the two proclamations is merely a matter of promotional slant is supported by the comment *ad locum* of R. Solomon b. Isaac (*Rashi*; Troyes, 1040–1105) as to why Gentiles are repulsed by the *nafla trefta* proclamation: "It is a disgrace for them, since we do not want to eat it." What makes nonkosher meat repulsive to the Gentile is not the essentially valueless datum that Jews do not eat it, but rather the formal declaration that they do not *desire* to eat it. The following observation will clarify the point. There are two categories of nonkosher meat. One is meat derived from an animal that was not slaughtered in accordance with Jewish ritual law (*nevelah*). The second is meat derived from an organically defective animal (*terefah*). Since there is no qualitative difference between *nevelah* and kosher meat, the Gentile should rationally be indifferent between the two. Similarly, at fair market value, a Gentile should find no reason to reject *terefah*. If the Gentile finds nonkosher meat repulsive, it is therefore not the product itself that repulses him, but rather the manner in which it is marketed. Expressly representing to him that the meat is *terefah* makes it a disgrace for him to purchase it, as the declaration openly proclaims that it is unfit for Jewish consumption, but suitable for Gentiles.

Thus, *nafla bisra* is not deceptive disclosure, but a creative way of marketing a product so that it becomes acceptable to Gentiles, whose sole reason for rejecting it would be the word *trefta* used in its promotion. Because no announcement whatsoever is made when the butcher shops are selling only kosher meat, *nafla bisra* should convey to a reasonable person that the meat is not kosher.

Recall that the Talmud characterizes those misled by *nafla bisra* as being guilty of self-deception. The result of the analysis in the preceding paragraphs shows that this applies only to the few who mistakenly think that the meat being offered for sale is kosher in the absence of an explicit declaration to the contrary. But for the vast majority of patrons, no misunderstanding whatsoever takes place, for they correctly read into *nafla bisra* an implicit notification that nonkosher meat is being offered for sale.

Given the role the "reasonable man" principle plays in extricating *nafla bisra* from a deceptive characterization, the similarity of this case to the Mar Zutra incident is readily apparent. In the latter case, too, it is the "reasonable man" standard that frees the rabbis' conduct from the *geneivat da'at* interdict. Consider that Mar Zutra gave no advance notice of his plan to travel to Bei Mahoza. In addition, Rava and Rav Safra, who were traveling in the opposite direction from Bei Mahoza to Sikhra, met Mar Zutra, not in the outskirts of Bei Mahoza, but rather, in the Bei Mahoza roadway toward Sikhra. Any reasonable person would, therefore, regard the rabbis' encounter with Mar Zutra as clearly coincidental. Because Mar Zutra's assessment that the rabbis constituted a greeting party for him was unreasonable, the rabbis bore no responsibility to disabuse him of his misimpression.[14] The case is thus comparable to the *nafla bisra* case in that in both instances the "reasonable man" would not have erred in his perception of what was transpiring.

Further support for this thesis can be derived by comparing the text at hand with a point in *geneivat da'at* law expounded in the Jerusalem Talmud at *Makkot* 2:6. The case entails the following elements: *A* is well versed in one tractate of the Talmud, but the townspeople mistakenly think he is proficient in two tractates and accord him the honor due someone who is proficient in two tractates. The Jerusalem Talmud rules that *A* is obligated to disabuse the townspeople of their mistaken impression of him. This ruling apparently contradicts the rule, elucidated at *Hullin* 94b, that an individual is exempt from correcting a mistaken impression that is rooted in self-deception. Ready reconciliation of the two texts follows, however, from the "reasonable man" hypothesis. An individual need only be concerned about a "reasonable misimpression." Because the various tractates of the Talmud, especially those in the same order,[15] are interconnected, complement each other, and overlap somewhat, proficiency in one tractate can easily be mistaken for proficiency in two tractates. Accordingly, a Talmudic scholar must disabuse the townspeople of their inaccurate assessment of him. In sharp contrast, since a reasonable person would interpret Mar Zutra's encounter with Rava and Rav Safra as nothing more than coincidental, no corrective obligation devolved upon the rabbis to disabuse Mar Zutra of his error. In a similar vein, a reasonable person will take *nafla bisra* as constituting an implicit declaration that the meat at hand is not kosher. Accordingly, use of this formulation does not constitute deception.[16]

The notion that *geneivat da'at* can be violated passively comports well with the biblical sources of the interdict. Recall that R. Yom Tov Ishbili regards *geneivat da'at* as a form of theft. Now, if *A* knows that he has *B*'s property in his possession he is obligated to return it to *B*, notwithstanding that he played no role whatsoever in removing the property from *B*'s domain.[17] Similarly, if *A* knows that *B* holds an unwarranted feeling of indebtedness towards him, he should be obligated to set *B* straight, provided, of course, that the objective facts make *B*'s judgment reasonable. The circumstance that *A* did not actively create the unwarranted sense of indebtedness should not alter this obligation. This selfsame conclusion is indicated if we conceptualize *geneivat da'at*, along with R. Gerondi, as a form of falsehood. Consider that one biblical source for the prohibition against falsehood is "Distance yourself from falsehood" (Exodus 23:7). The *Torah*'s choice of phrase, *distance yourself*, indicates that affirmative misconduct is not essential for the prohibition against falsehood to be violated.

THE RELIABILITY OF SELF-ASSESSMENT

Since the existence of a false impression is, in the final analysis, a matter of judgment, perhaps the person who the false impression is about has a role in deciding whether a disabusing duty devolves upon her- or himself.

Bearing directly on this issue is the wine-barrel hospitality case, discussed at *Hullin* 94a. Here we are told that a host (*H*) should not delude his guest (*G*) into believing that he has acted toward him with magnanimous hospitality when in fact he has not done so. Opening a barrel of wine in honor of someone usually constitutes a gesture of magnanimous hospitality, as the wine remaining in the barrel may deteriorate as a result of its exposure to the air. The magnanimity of the gesture is considerably reduced, however, when *H* happens to have sold the barrel of wine to a retailer just before the arrival of *G*. (A price adjustment, of course, will be made with the retailer). Accordingly, if *H* sold the barrel of wine prior to the arrival of *G*, *H* must inform *G* that he sold the barrel prior to his arrival.[18]

In relation to the above disclosure requirement, the Talmud relates a hospitality incident involving R. Judah and Ulla. R. Judah opened a barrel of wine in honor of Ulla. The barrel had been sold before Ulla arrived. Two versions of the incident are recorded. In one, R. Judah told his guest about the sale. In the other, no such disclosure took place. The Talmud defends the second version on the grounds that Ulla was very dear to R. Judah, and, consequently, he would have extended him the hospitality gesture even if it entailed considerable expense.

Curiously, the point of leniency in *geneivat da'at* law that emerges from the R. Judah-Ulla incident is conspicuously omitted by Maimonides and R. Jacob b. Asher (Germany, 1270–1343) in their treatments of the wine-barrel hospitality case. Noting the omission, R. Aryeh Judah b. Akiba (Poland, 1759–1819) posits that the aforementioned codifiers regard the Talmudic incident as lacking general applicability. Only a host like R. Judah, that is, someone of exceptional moral character, is free of the obligation to correct his guest's false impression that he treated him with magnanimous hospitality. In the instance of someone like R. Judah, the host's self-assessment that he would confer generous hospitality on his guest even if it entailed a considerable expense is completely reliable. Such a self-assessment would not, however, free an individual of ordinary moral character from his obligation to make the disclosure. For an ordinary person, such a self-assessment amounts to self-delusion. Confronted with an actual opportunity to confer generous hospitality on a friend only at a considerable expense, the average person would find many convenient excuses not to do so. Since the point of leniency in *geneivat da'at* law that emerges from the R. Judah-Ulla incident does not have general applicability, Maimonides and R. Jacob b. Asher omit it.[19]

R. Aryeh Judah b. Akiba's conclusion regarding the unreliability of self-assessment apparently places him at odds with the responsa literature with respect to an issue dealing with the counteracting of unwarranted bias in the labor market. The specific issue involves the question of whether an individual is permitted to achieve a more youthful appearance by dyeing his beard to enhance his chances of securing employment. Addressing this question, R. Mosheh Mordecai Epstein (Hebron, 1866–1922) permits the conduct provided the employer's expectations with respect to performance will be met. Realizing that productivity could decline sharply with advancing age, R. Epstein points out that, in the final analysis, the conduct's legitimacy rests on the honesty of the job seeker's self-assessment.[20] Advancing a similar analysis, R. Elazar Meir Preil (Luthuania, 1881–1934) arrives at the same conclusion.[21] R. Mosheh Feinstein (New York, 1895–1986) concurs with these rulings.[22]

If we distinguish between self-assessment cases relating to routine circumstances and those relating to extraordinary hypothetical situations, we approach a reconciliation of the opinions. Self-assessment may very well be reliable when it relates to ordinary, predictable life situations. Although productivity may decline with advancing age, honest self-appraisal can indicate to the senior job seeker whether he can meet the employer's performance standards. The reliability of self-assessment in the realm of the hypothetical is another matter. Individuals of ordinary moral character cannot extrapolate with any degree of accuracy how they would react to a hypothetical situation requiring extraordinary effort on their part.

In the final analysis, the job seeker's self-assessment of his ability is reliable because he knows that it will be subject to objective verification. This is supported by the Talmudic text at *Hullin* 94a, referred to earlier. Recall that Mar Zutra jumped to the conclusion that Rava and Rav Safra, whom he met on his way to Bei Mahoza, were a welcoming party in his honor. Rava felt that Mar Zutra was guilty of self-deception and thus that there was no need to disabuse him of his error. Rava's confidence that his judgment was correct was rooted, as it appears to this writer, in the knowledge that Mar Zutra himself would soon come to the same conclusion. After all, Rava and Rav Safra were traveling in the opposite direction of Mar Zutra. As soon as the three men parted company and went their separate ways, Mar Zutra would realize that Rava and Rav Safra had not come as a welcoming party for him. The certainty that Mar Zutra's hindsight judgment would confirm his own *a priori* judgment gave Rava the confidence that his assessment was correct.

The selfsame feature of objective verifiability is what gave the rabbis, in the same reference text at *Hullin* 94a, the confidence that the marketplace would understand *nafla bisra* as an implicit declaration of *terefah*. If the rabbis were wrong, then the *nafla bisra* proclamation would unsettle the marketplace greatly. Sellers would think that they were representing their meat as nonkosher, but the Gentile clientele would take the representation to mean that the meat was kosher. This misunderstanding would manifest itself in a significant number of complaints of deception against the Jewish butchers. Any unsettling of the marketplace as a result of the proclamation of *nafla bisra* informs the rabbis that they erred in expecting the marketplace to read the meaning they intended into *nafla bisra*. This, in turn, will necessitate its replacement with a *nafla terefah* announcement.[23]

HEVER IR

Another consideration in assessing whether Rabbi Samson violated *geneivat da'at* law is the following dictum at *Hullin* 94a:

> A person may not go to the house of mourning and [hold] in his hand a flask [of wine] that splashes [i.e., that is partially empty], nor should he fill it with water, for he deceives him. However, if there is an assembly of townsfolk *hever ir* there, [and he does so to enhance the mourner's prestige in their eyes,] it is permitted.

What proceeds from the above dictum is that in the presence of *hever ir* an individual may affirmatively create the impression that the honor he is bestowing upon the mourner is greater than it actually is.[24] The backdrop against which *hever ir* operates, according to R. Samuel Edels (Poland, 1555–1631), is the custom, prevalent in the time of the Talmud, for visitors to bring jugs of wine for the mourner to drink. The mourner will, of course, not drink from all the jugs of wine brought by the visitors. Under these conditions, a visitor may bring a largely empty jug and maneuver so that the mourner takes someone else's jug from which to drink. Later, when the mourner notices the mostly empty jug, he will imagine that it was one of the jugs from which he drank. Hence, the mourner will not discover the ruse that one of the visitors brought a mostly empty jug. Since the visitor with the largely empty jug clearly desires to honor the mourner in the presence of *hever ir*, his action is permissible, notwithstanding the overly favorable impression of honor he makes on the mourner.[25] What proceeds from R. Edels' analysis is that *hever ir* is not an extenuating factor unless we are reasonably certain that the individual who is the target of the honor will not catch on later that the impression of honor he got from his caller was overly favorable.

Is *hever ir* relevant for the scenarios of our case study? Yes. To show how, we need only mention that if *affirmative action* to create an overly favorable impression of honor is permissible in the presence of *hever ir*, then a duty to correct an overly favorable impression of honor in the presence of *hever ir* should also not exist.

SHEKER (FALSEHOOD)

Another relevant ethical principle in analyzing the various scenarios is the prohibition against falsehood: "Distance yourself from a false word . . ." (Exodus 23:7). One aspect of *sheker* that is relevant here is the prohibition for *A* to conceal from *B* the primary motive behind his action and reveal to him only the secondary motive behind the action. This prohibition is derived from an analysis of R. Natan's dictum at *Yevamot* 65b. Here, R. Natan expounds that it is not only permissible to alter the truth for the sake of peace, but a positive duty (*mitzvah*) to do so. This is called the *darkhei shalom* (promotion of peace) principle. R. Natan derives this from an episode in the life of Samuel the prophet: God charged Samuel to go to Bethlehem and anoint one of Jesse's sons as King of Israel, whereupon Samuel inquired: "How shall I go? For, if Saul hears, he will kill me" (I Samuel 16:2). In response to Samuel's concern, God created a pretext for him: "You shall take a heifer with you, and you shall say, "I have come to slaughter [a sacrifice] to the Lord" (ibid. 16:2).

R. Natan's dictum requires further elaboration. In what manner did Samuel alter the truth? True to his word, Samuel offered the sacrifice and invited the elders of Bethlehem to join him in the sacrificial feast (ibid.). Addressing himself to this issue, R. Yom Tov Ishbili points out that Samuel's *primary* mission was to anoint one of Jesse's sons King of Israel. Concealing this from the inquisitive elders of Bethlehem and revealing to them only his secondary purpose in coming constituted a form of *sheker*. What allowed Samuel to conduct himself in this fashion was his motive to preserve peace. Since God Himself provided Samuel with the pretext, R. Natan was justified in deriving that it is a *mitzvah* to alter the truth to preserve peace. Absent the *darkhei shalom* motive, concealing the primary motive behind one's actions while revealing only the secondary motive behind the action is a form of *sheker*.[26]

Another nuance of the prohibition against *sheker* that is relevant for our case studies is the biblical interdict: *lo tisa shema shav* (Do not accept a false report, Exodus 23:1). Quoting *Targum Onkelos*, *Rashi* understands the verse as a general prohibition against accepting false reports.[27] Following this line of thought, R. Pinhas ha-Levi (Barcelona, 1235–1300) understands the prohibition to accept false reports to be an aspect of the *Torah*'s concern that we should *distance* ourselves from falsehood (Exodus 23:7).[28] In his analysis of the prohibition to accept a false report, R. Nahum Yavruv (Israel, contemp.) posits that the prohibition does not apply to all forms of falsehood. In his view, the prohibition applies only to a lie that causes an injustice or perversion in interpersonal relations.[29]

DARKHEI SHALOM PRINCIPLE

Another ethical norm that should inform R. Samson's conduct, referred to earlier, is the *darkhei shalom* principle. However, *darkhei shalom* is not a blanket license to lie for the sake of peace. Many caveats are attached to this principle.[30] The caveats that are applicable to our case study are the following:

1. Lying for the purpose of promoting peace, according to R. Menahem b. Solomon Meiri (*Meiri*, Perpignan, 1249–1316), is permissible only if the objective is to end discord or prevent an actual rift. If the objective of the lie, however, is merely to mollify or prevent the occurrence of a ruffled feeling, the lie is not permitted.[31]

2. *A* may not lie to *B* to promote peace if the consequence is to make *B* feel an unwarranted debt to *A*.[32]

3. *Darkhei shalom* considers the long-term impact of a lie. Accordingly, if it is assessed that in the long-run, when the lie is discovered, the discord will return in exasperated form, the lie is not permitted, notwithstanding that the lie does end the discord temporarily.[33]

PROMOTING PEACE (BAKESH SHALOM)

In assessing Rabbi Samson's duty to disabuse in the scenarios described in the opening vignettes, consideration of the prohibitions against *geneivat da'at* and *sheker* is not the whole story. Rabbi Samson has the positive duty to conduct himself in a manner that will not cause strained relations with his congregants. This duty derives from the Divine mandate: *bakesh shalom ve-rodefehu* ("Seek peace and pursue it," Psalms 34:15). In the opinion of R. Isaac of Corbeil (France, d. 1280) *bakesh shalom* is an aspect of the *mitzvah* of "You must love your neighbor as [you love] yourself" (Leviticus 19:18).[34]

In Judaism, the guidepost for interpersonal conduct is the duty to emulate God's Attributes[35] of Mercy. This behavioral norm is called *imitatio Dei* ("imitation of God").[36] One Attribute of God's Mercy is *Shalom* (peace).[37] The duty to conduct oneself with the aim of producing harmonious relations hence also follows from the *imitatio Dei* principle.

Once it is recognized that *bakesh shalom* is an aspect of *imitatio Dei* conduct, *bakesh shalom* translates into a duty to promote harmonious relations not just in the short run, but for the long term as well. This is because God's mercy is designed for man's ultimate good.[38] Accordingly, conduct that "buys temporary peace," but will surely unravel and result in bad relations in the long-term, violates *bakesh shalom* and *imitatio Dei*.

Recall that the Talmud records two instances where a misimpression is deemed to be the product of self-deception. The one who inspired the misimpression is hence under no duty to correct it. If our proposition is correct that *bakesh shalom* and *imitatio Dei* must also be considered, it becomes necessary to demonstrate that the conduct will also not cause a strain in relations.

Let us begin with the *nafla bisra* announcement. *Geneivat da'at* law tells us that the "reasonable man" will not be misled by the wording of this announcement and hence will not read into the message that the day's supply of meat is kosher. But, an insignificant minority will assuredly be misled by the message and understand it to convey that the day's supply of meat *is* kosher. When the "duped" customers later discover the truth, will they not feel outrage against the Jewish butchers for deceiving them? Taking measures to prevent Gentiles from harboring *eivah* (enmity) toward us is a legitimate concern of Halakhah. It is an aspect of the *darkhei shalom* principle. The general rule here, according to R. Mosheh Sofer (Hungary,

1762–1839), is that if a prohibition that is only rabbinical in nature must be transgressed in order to prevent *eivah* from erupting against Jews, violation of the prohibition is sanctioned.[39] Now, if a rabbinical decree is suspended in order to prevent enmity from erupting, how could the sages sanction *nafla bisra*, which entails the possible *creation* of enmity? The above difficulty disappears under the assumption that the predictable reaction of those who were deceived when they are set straight is not enmity, but rather self-blame. This is so because deception here is the result of a failure on the part of the victim to inform him- or herself minimally of the workings of the marketplace. Consider also that after the *nafla bisra* announcement is made Jewish customers are conspicuously absent in the butchery and the price of meat is lower than it ordinarily is. Reflection on these anomalies should make self-blame rather than outrage the predictable reaction when the duped customers discover the truth. The contention that the *nafla bisra* announcement causes *eivah* in the long run is hence misplaced.

Further support for the above proposition can also be derived from an analysis of the Mar Zutra incident. Recall that Rava objected to Rav Safra's approach of setting Mar Zutra straight on the spot on the grounds that the disclosure caused Mar Zutra aggravation. Objecting on this ground is surprising. Consider that in the give and take between Rava and Rav Safra, Rava's bottom line was that the rabbis bore no disabusing obligation because Mar Zutra was guilty of self-deception. Now, if the release from the disabusing duty is fundamentally rooted in the assessment that Mar Zutra was guilty of self-deception, then the judgment of whether the disclosure would hurt Mar Zutra's feelings is irrelevant. Moreover, Rava's approach also entailed inevitable aggravation for Mar Zutra. We can see this by extrapolating how Rava would have preferred to handle the situation. To be sure, Rav Safra's conduct preempted Rava and precluded him from implementing the reaction to Mar Zutra that he thought appropriate. But, if setting Mar Zutra straight was not appropriate, then what Rava preferred, as it appears to this writer, was for the rabbis to *graciously sidetrack* Mar Zutra's misimpression and continue along with their original travel plans to Sikhra.[40] Conducting themselves in this manner would make Mar Zutra discover on his own in short shrift that his meeting with the rabbis just moments ago was on their part entirely unintended. A rude awakening of this sort would certainly deflate Mar Zutra from the sense of self-importance that made him feel that the rabbis should have known of his itinerary, even though he gave no advance notice of it. Accordingly, Rava's approach would have apparently also entailed aggravation for Mar Zutra.

The previous difficulties are readily resolved under the thesis that Rava held that if a misimpression is the result of an "unreasonable" assumption, self-discovery of the truth at a later time is not something that will hurt the feelings of the one who carried the false impression until now.

The give and take between Rava and Rav Safra is now understandable. For Rava, the behavioral guidepost for the situation he and Rav Safra faced was clear-cut. Because Mar Zutra's false impression was rooted in an unreasonable assumption, Mar Zutra was guilty of self-deception and the rabbis bore no responsibility to disabuse Mar Zutra. In objecting to Rav Safra's reaction of setting Mar Zutra straight, Rava initially thought that Rav Safra also agreed that what the rabbis faced was essentially a case of self-deception, and there was thus no disabusing responsibility. But, Rav Safra, who is cited in the Talmud as the paragon of truth telling,[41] felt that it would be right to go *lifnim mi-shurat ha-din* (beyond the letter of the law)[42] and set Mar Zutra straight. To this, Rava reacted by saying that there is no room for stringency here because disclosure of the truth will surely hurt Mar Zutra's feelings. To be sure, when Mar Zutra discovers on his own that the rabbis' meeting with him was unintended, he might become momentarily deflated. But, compared to being explicitly set straight, Mar Zutra will experience but a momentary twinge when he discovers the truth on his own. Here is an example of the Talmudic adage *millah be-sela mashtuka be-trein* ("a word is worth a *sela*, silence two *selas*").[43] Moreover, once Mar Zutra realizes the truth, he should take the rabbis' *original* silence as a kindness rather than as a reason to bear ill feeling toward them. Silence is a very fungible commodity. It allows Mar Zutra to read into it that the rabbis *wished* that circumstances were different and *regretted* that they were not in fact a greeting party.

What proceeds from the above analysis is that the rabbis of the Talmud assessed that under certain conditions a duped individual will not harbor ill feeling toward the individual who originally failed to correct his misconception. This results when the duped feeling is essentially the victim's own doing. In such a case, when the victim discovers his error, he will either blame himself for it or even be happy that he discovered the error himself, instead of having someone correct him.

THE REASONABLENESS CRITERION AND THE HOSPITAL VISIT CASES

Central to analyzing the various scenarios presented is the reasonableness criterion with its various nuances. Before applying this criterion to the specific scenarios presented, let's relate this principle in general terms to the hospital visit cases. One salient feature to consider in applying the "reasonableness" criterion is a consideration of Rabbi Samson's job description and the demographics of his shul. With the aim of facilitating the analysis, let us assume that visiting the sick was part of the job description that Rabbi Samson received when he accepted his position as the rabbi of Bet Kodesh. Let us further assume that Bet Kodesh is a small synagogue and thus that two members of the synagogue being in the same hospital at the same time is rare. For a patient to assume that Rabbi Samson made a special trip to the hospital to see him or her is therefore reasonable.

Farbstein

The Farbstein scenario breaks down into two considerations. One is whether Samson is entitled to the goodwill his visit generated. The second is whether Samson should forego the opportunity to capture this goodwill if he feels that his silence might have an unfavorable impact on his long-term relationship with Farbstein.

With respect to the first issue, one cannot make a strong case for relieving Rabbi Samson of a responsibility to disabuse Mr. Farbstein. The most basic point to make here is that Farbstein's assumption that Samson made a special trip to the hospital to see him is reasonable.

Perhaps Samson should be relieved of a responsibility to disabuse Farbstein on the basis of his assessment that had Tzvi not been in the hospital that day he would have made a special trip to Bet Miriam to visit Farbstein. Is Rabbi Samson's assessment in this regard reliable? No. Consider that Samson has no consistent practice regarding hospital visits for congregants. In practice, he responds to the demands of *bikkur holim* (visiting the sick) sometimes with a telephone call, sometimes with a hospital visit and sometimes with a post hospital stay call or home visit. Given the variety of these responses, Samson's assessment that he would have made a special trip to visit Farbstein had circumstances not made this unnecessary relates to the realm of the hypothetical. Unless Farbstein had a previous hospital stay and Samson had visited him, Samson's assessment should be regarded as unreliable.

The fact that Farbstein was surrounded by his family when Rabbi Samson made his visit creates a *hever ir* situation. Nevertheless, *hever ir* is not an extenuating factor unless we are reasonably certain that the individual who is the target of the honor will not catch on later to the misimpression. This is certainly not the case here. Consider that a sizable crowd of curious onlookers watched as Refuah brought Tzvi to the Hospital. The likelihood is that the entire community, Farbstein included, will soon know of Tzvi's accident in all its minutiae. Because Farbstein will soon learn of the primary reason Samson came to Bet Miriam that day, the *hever ir* leniency does not apply.

Reinforcing the judgment that Rabbi Samson should disabuse Mr. Farbstein of his erroneous impression is that the *bakesh shalom* principle requires him to consider the impact his silence will have on his long-term relations with Farbstein. To be sure, playing along with the notion that he made a special trip to visit Farbstein will buy that man's goodwill in the short run. But as soon as Farbstein gets wind of what brought Samson to the hospital that day, the goodwill he originally felt toward Rabbi Samson might dissipate into resentment for being misled. Moreover, when the Farbsteins learn of Tzvi's accident they might even feel slighted that the rabbi did not share the event with them, especially in view of the fact that the entire episode would soon become a matter of public knowledge.

The upshot of the above analysis is that Samson bears a disabusing responsibility to Farbstein. Because the goodwill Samson reaps is undeserved, listening to Farbstein's *false* statement without protest makes Samson guilty also of accepting a *false* report.

Let us change the scenario a bit. Suppose Rabbi Samson, in addition to being the rabbi of Bet Kodesh, is also the chaplain of the hospital. Because it is part of rabbi Samson's almost daily routine to see the Jewish patients in the hospital, Mr. Farbstein's effusive thank you for making a "special visit" to see him is a product of Mr. Farbstein ignorance that the rabbi is in the hospital *anyway* on almost a daily basis. Because it is generally well-known among rabbi Samson's congregants that the rabbi is the chaplain at Bet Miriam, the "generous gesture" Farbstein imagined the rabbi bestowed him must be characterized as "self-deception" à la the Mar Zutra incident discussed on the previous page. *Geneivat da'at* law, hence, would not require Rabbi Samson to disabuse Mr. Farbstein of his erroneous impression.

While *geneivat da'at* law does not require Rabbi Samson to disabuse Mr. Farbstein in the above scenario, the *bakesh shalom* imperative should require this disclosure. Consider that sooner or later Farbstein will surely pick up on the fact that Samson made no special gesture when he visited him. When Farbstein comes to this realization he will wonder why the rabbi did not reveal his chaplaincy position when he came visiting. Was the rabbi perhaps hoping that Farbstein might just not pick up on the chaplaincy matter and earn underserved "goodwill"? With the aim of avoiding possible strained feelings with Farbstein later, *bakesh shalom* tells the rabbi to disclose now what Farbstein will surely pick up on later.

Although the scenario just described bears a resemblance to the Mar Zutra incident, the two cases differ fundamentally in respect to the *bakesh shalom* duty. We take it as a given that Rava's and Rav Safra's encounter with Mar Zutra did not cause them to change their travel plans. Accordingly, after exchanging pleasantries with Mar Zutra, the rabbis were planning to continue with their journey in the opposite direction to Sikhra. If so, the rabbis in short shrift would be implicitly communicating to Mar Zutra that *all along* they were not a greeting party to welcome him into Bei Mehoza. Since the rabbis would in any case be disabusing Mar Zutra, the issue becomes whether *bakesh shalom* demands an upfront disclosure to Mar Zutra as soon they made contact with him. No. Given the awkward situation the rabbis found themselves in, the dictum of *millah be-sela mashtuka be-trein* tells them that *bakesh shalom* is best served by not verbally discussing the matter at all. In sharp contrast, the choice Rabbi Samson confronts is either to disabuse Mr. Farbstein himself or face the consequences of having someone else do the job later. Far better that Samson take on the task himself. Passing up the opportunity runs the risk that Farbstein will suspect the rabbi of capturing underserved goodwill by taking the chance that his grateful congregant will never catch on that his rabbi's visit, in fact, entailed no special effort.

Plotkin

The salient feature of the Plotkin scenario is that Rabbi Samson *affirmatively* misleads Plotkin into thinking that he made a special trip to the hospital to visit him. Samson does this by saying to Plotkin, "I came to Bet Miriam to see you." On the face of it, this statement is not false. Specifically, Samson did leave his home with the intention to visit Plotkin. Consider, however, that Samson's main purpose in coming to Bet Miriam was to visit Dubchek. His statement hence violates the interdict against *sheker*. Moreover, by conveniently omitting mention of his main reason for coming to Bet Miriam, Samson, at least temporarily, reaps from Plotkin more goodwill from his visit than he deserves. Consequently, Samson violates *geneivat da'at* law as well as *sheker*.

The *darkhei shalom* principle provides only limited defense here. Halakhah gives legitimacy to *sheker* and *geneivat da'at* to promote peace only when the objective is to end discord or prevent a rift. Telling Plotkin "you certainly deserve a special visit" prevents a strain with him and hence should be said even if Samson does not himself *believe* the statement. Samson, nonetheless, should have stopped right there! The use of *sheker* and *geneivat da'at* is, however, not legitimate when the objective at hand is only to mollify or prevent the occurrence of a momentary ruffled feeling. Telling Plotkin that he "came to Bet Miriam to see him" hence violates for Samson the prohibition against *sheker*. Moreover, if the consequence of promoting peace by the use of a lie is to secure a benefit for oneself, the tactic is prohibited. This is the case here, as Samson buys with his lie not only peace with Plotkin, but also an unwarranted feeling of indebtedness from him to boot. Last, Samson's lie surely will explode in his face in the end, when Plotkin learns that Dubchek was in Bet Miriam the same time he was there. When Plotkin gets wind of this, the original cynicism he expressed to the rabbi might very well turn into smoldering hatred. Moreover, consider the distinct possibility that as soon as Plotkin hears that Dubchek was in Bet Miriam at the same time that he was there, he will begin to tell his friends that the rabbi was a "liar" for saying he came to Bet Miriam to visit him. Hence, the risk Samson runs by not telling Plotkin the truth is that his conduct may very well *provoke* Plotkin to "badmouth" him. If, in fact, Plotkin does snarl about Rabbi Samson, Plotkin violates the Biblical prohibition against *lashon ha-ra* (tale bearing).[44] In fact, it will be Rabbi Samson's conduct that provokes Plotkin to carp about him. If *A* provokes *B* to speak *lashon ha-ra*, A violates the prohibition of *lashon ha-ra* on a rabbinical level, called *avak lashon ha-ra*.[45]

Given these nasty long-term consequences for Samson's relationship with Plotkin, *bakesh shalom* and *imitatio Dei* reinforce the above judgment that Samson should not withhold from Plotkin his primary reason for coming to Bet Miriam.

Lemnick

The Lemnick scenario bears a striking similarity to the Mar Zutra incident discussed earlier. Recall that Beryl Lemnick bumped into Rabbi Samson as he was being wheeled into his room at Royal Blue Hospital and imagined that the rabbi had rushed to his side to be there for him. Consider that Samson lives and works in Eden Commons, and in no more than twenty minutes after Lemnick was brought to Royal Blue, a forty-minute drive from Eden Commons, the rabbi was already at his side. What an amazing feat! Given that Lemnick's sizing up of the situation was unrealistic, *geneivat da'at* law does not require the rabbi to set Lemnick straight and inform him that he just happened at the time to be in the hospital to visit his uncle and was not even aware of the accident.

Because Rabbi Samson is entitled to any goodwill he reaps from the incident, the false assessment Lemnick makes of the nature of Samson's visit will not result in any injustice or perversion of interpersonal relations. Accordingly, listening to Lemnick's misimpression of his hospital visit without protest does not make Samson guilty of accepting a false report.

Suppose we inject a *hever ir* element into the Lemnick scenario. Specifically, let us assume that when Rabbi Samson encountered Lemnick, his family was surrounding the patient. Does *hever ir* provide additional grounds for relieving Samson of a disabusing responsibility in the Lemnick scenario? No. Recall that Samson's encounter with Lemnick was *unintended*. Hence, injecting a *hever ir* element into the case does not introduce an extenuating element for the rabbi not to disabuse Beryl of his misperception. *Hever ir* can be invoked only when G sets out to honor H and devises a scheme to make H imagine that he has honored him more than is actually the case. But, in the case at hand, the fact remains that the encounter between Samson and Lemnick was coincidental, notwithstanding that Lemnick was surrounded by a *hever ir* at the time of their encounter.

Let us now turn to Rabbi Samson's duty to Lemnick in regard to the *bakesh shalom* imperative. We take it as a given that if Rabbi Samson does not disabuse Lemnick, Lemnick's friends will assuredly set him straight when he relates the story to them. Rabbi Samson's mandate is therefore to choose the path that will maximize harmonious relations with Lemnick. Is *bakesh shalom* optimally promoted by requiring the rabbi to disabuse Lemnick on the spot? Or, perhaps, *bakesh shalom* is better served if the Rabbi relies on Lemnick's friends to do this task later. In resolving this dilemma, the salient feature to focus on is that Lemnick's mistake is not that he thinks the rabbi honored him more than was the case. Rather, Lemick's mistake was thinking that the Rabbi bestowed upon him a magnanimous gesture, when, in fact, *there was no gesture at all because the encounter was entirely fortuitous.* Because Lemick's error is not just one of degree, but, is rather a fundamental one, it will make a difference to Lemnick both who and when he is disabused of his error. From Lemnick's perspective, what could be worse than to learn the error of his thinking while on an emotional high and directly from the rabbi? The rabbi's disclosure will assuredly set the record straight, but will also *deflate* Lemnick and make him feel *very foolish.* Far better for Lemnick would be to learn the truth later in a calm state and from a friend that uses the reasonable assumption method to arrive at his conclusions. Getting to the truth this way straightens out Lemnick without the accompanying negative emotional fallout. *Bakesh shalom* hence reinforces *geneivat da'at* law and tells Rabbi Samson to keep to his own counsel the real reason he was at the Royal Blue at the same time Lemnick was brought there.

Drake

The basic issue the Drake scenario presents is the "reasonableness" of Drake's assumption that Rabbi Samson came to the breakfast to honor him. Arguing in the negative is the consideration that the sponsor of the breakfast was the Rabbinical Board of Eden Commons. Should Drake not consider that some of the rabbis of the Board would attend no matter what? A loyalist will *plan* to attend the event even if it turns out that he has no or little connection with this year's honoree. And, in fact, Samson fell into this category. Counterbalancing this argument is that only an insider or someone who attended the breakfast on a regular basis would notice this. Another factor supporting the reasonableness of Drake's assumption is that the

Rodef Hesed affair took place in the Hidekel section of Eden Commons, which was within walking distance of Samson's home. Consider also that Rodef Hesed did not charge for attending the breakfast. Instead, all contributions at the breakfast were voluntary. Hence, coming to the affair involved no extraordinary expenditure of time or money for Samson. The balance of the above considerations argues that Drake's assumption that Rabbi Samson came to the breakfast in his honor was reasonable. Based on the reasonableness criterion, Samson should have disabused Drake of his misimpression. *Geneivat da'at* law, therefore, apparently calls for Samson to say something like: "Sol, congratulations on your well deserved honor. You need not, however, thank me for coming. I come every year to this affair."

Consider that Drake's effusive thank-you to Samson is based on a false premise. If Samson fails to disabuse Drake, Samson will be guilty of accepting a false report. Since Samson's silence reaps for him undeserved goodwill, accepting the false report violates for Samson the prohibition against *sheker*.

While Samson has a duty to disabuse Drake, he should surely not reveal the naked truth to Drake. Telling Drake that the reason he came to the breakfast was to socialize with his rabbinical colleagues and trade *bon mots* with them on the weekly portion will surely hurt Drake's feelings, and perhaps even cause enmity. *Darkhei shalom*, in fact, demands that Samson not speak to Drake in this fashion. But, playing along with Drake's misimpression goes beyond preventing enmity and results in the rabbi capturing unwarranted goodwill from Drake.

A saving factor can, however, be identified that points to a scenario where Samson will be under no duty to disabuse Drake of his misimpression. Recall that Drake strongly hinted to Samson that he would like him to remain for the presentation of his award. This points to the judgment that attendees at the Rodef Hesed affair confer on Drake honor on different levels. Some guests make only a brief appearance. These people come only to personally congratulate Drake and leave a check for the organization in his honor. If all the attendees comported themselves in this very rushed manner, Drake would probably feel insulted as he would get the impression that "no one has any time for me." Accordingly, those attendees that mill about the hall for a substantial amount of time contribute to making the affair confer greater honor to Drake. Finally, those who remain for the presentation, other things being equal, contribute the most in honoring Drake at the affair. Given that attendees fall into different categories as far as the amount of honor they confer on Drake, Samson has the ability to spontaneously create a *hever ir* situation by remaining for the presentation. To be sure, Drake imagines that Rabbi Samson planned all along *to do this* while, in fact, the rabbi decided on doing this only *after* he came to the affair. But the *hever ir* leniency allows an attendee to maneuver the honoree into thinking that he conferred on him more honor than was actually the case. Recall that for the *hever ir* leniency to be operative, a crowd must be present and it must be reasonably certain that the honoree will never get wind of the illusion. These two conditions are met here.

One caveat should, however, be noted. To spontaneously create a *hever ir* situation, Rabbi Samson must have the ability to increase his participation in the Rodef Hesed affair beyond his ordinary participation. Because Rabbi Samson's motive in participating in this event is social and professional, he certainly does not fit into the category of those who honor Drake via only minimal participation. If Samson's ordinary practice is to slip away from the affair just before the program begins, the rabbi can avoid being saddled with a duty to disabuse Drake by committing himself to stay through the program. Samson's spontaneous decision to stay for the program, something he never does,[46] makes his presence at that part of the affair *specifically* in honor of Drake. Staying the course hence triggers the *hever ir* leniency and allows Samson to maneuver Drake into thinking that he had planned all along to come for the entire affair in his honor. But, suppose Samson always stays for the program with the hope of gleaning a nugget from one of the speakers; then, Samson has no maneuverability to spontaneously transform his presence at the affair for social and professional reasons to being there for the purpose of honoring Drake. Accordingly, in the latter scenario the disabusing duty for Samson remains intact.

Belzag

The Belzag scenario bears a striking resemblance to the Mar Zutra incident. Consider that the cost per person was $250. Coming to the banquet would have entailed a $500 expense for the Samsons. This sum represents a sizable chunk of Rabbi Samson's weekly salary at Bet Kodesh. Given that Torah Academy is not an Eden Commons institution and Samson is not an alumnus of the yeshiva, is it reasonable to assume that the Samsons would incur such a large expense to be at the banquet? Because of the considerable expense involved, almost all of Belzag's close friends came to the affair without their spouses. If nothing else, Matilda's presence at the affair should have been a "giveaway" to the "reasonable man" that the Samsons were the guests of one of the other honorees. Perhaps Belzag erroneously assumed that rabbis attend the affair either on a complimentary or cost basis. Consider, however, that anyone who operates under this assumption would concede readily that this would apply only to either a rabbi whom the honoree told the yeshiva to invite in his or her honor or to a rabbi who is connected to the yeshiva. In any case, the privileged rabbi theory would not explain the presence of Matilda. Moreover, as a former member of Bet Kodesh, Belzag should have known that the usual practice is for the honoree to treat Rabbi Samson with a complimentary ticket. Belzag knew full well that he had neither asked Rabbi Samson to be his guest at the affair nor requested that the yeshiva send an invitation. Did Belzag assume that Rabbi Samson got wind of the affair through a newspaper ad, called the yeshiva, and requested an invitation? Highly unlikely! Should Belzag not have considered the reasonable possibility that his inaction sent a clear signal to Samson that he was not interested in the rabbi attending the affair? Given this backdrop, it was unreasonable for Belzag to imagine that Rabbi and Mrs. Samson had come to the banquet in his honor. Because Belzag's assumption is unreasonable, Samson bears no responsibility to correct his misperception.

Does the *hever ir* leniency apply to the Belzag scenario? No. Two essential conditions are missing here. For one, the Samsons are Eytan Kramer's guests. To be sure, the Samsons' presence at the affair contributes to the public recognition of Belzag. But, the Samsons did not come to the affair to give recognition to Belzag, and Belzag's indebtedness to the Samsons is unwarranted.

Another reason that *hever ir* does not apply is that before the evening is over Belzag will surely realize that the Samsons were Kramer's guests. Because he, himself, is an honoree, Belzag will surely peruse the banquet journal the yeshiva gives to each attendee. If he bothers to read Kramer's message, he will see that Kramer gives honorable mention to the rabbi. What Belzag may not know is that many years before Kramer's meteoric rise in the financial world, Rabbi Samson was his youth leader at Torah for Teens, an outreach program for youth in public schools. Samson knew all this when Belzag thanked him and his wife for coming to the affair in his honor. Moreover, Samson knew that Kramer would be one of the speakers that evening. Is it out of the realm of reasonable possibility that Kramer would give him honorable mention in his speech? Finally, precisely because Belzag's assumption that the Samsons came *primarily* to honor him is unreasonable, many of Belzag's friends will be wondering what in the world the Samsons are doing at this banquet. The drive to solve this puzzle will undoubtedly sprinkle the chitchat of the cocktail hour. Someone will hit upon the idea of taking a peek at the banquet journal to solve this mystery. Soon the secret will be out and everyone will know, including Belzag. Since Samson should realize in advance that before the evening is out Belzag will discover that Eytan Kramer is the reason for his coming to the banquet, *hever ir* does not supply an extenuating factor for excusing him from disabusing Belzag of his error at the beginning of the affair.

We now move to Rabbi Samson's duty to Belzag in regard to the *bakesh shalom* imperative. The analysis here parallels the reasoning we offered for the same issue in the Lemnick case. Consider that the error Belzag makes here is not whether Rabbi Samson came to the dinner primarily or only secondarily to honor him. No. Had Kramer not made the Samsons his guests at the dinner, the rabbi would never consider showing up at the affair. Given the magnitude of Belzag's error, it surely makes a difference to him how and when he discovers his error. If the rabbi disabuses him on the spot, the disclosure will assuredly set him straight, but will also deflate him and make him feel foolish. Far better for Belzag that he pick up his error himself by means of discovering the revealing information from the yeshiva journal or by listening to Eytan Kramer's speech. Promotion of *bakesh shalom* hence requires Samson not to disabuse Belzag on the spot of his error.

THE FRIDAY NIGHT LECTURE

The reasonableness criterion provides the starting point for analyzing the ethics of Samson not disclosing to his audience that he made use of *Berit Yehudah* to prepare his lecture. Consider that thorough preparation combined with the knowledge of which sources to consult will assuredly generate goodwill for Samson for the lecture he delivers. There can be no doubt that this goodwill is his legitimate entitlement. Accordingly, if the audience generally presumes that Samson makes use of secondary sources and eclectic works to prepare his lecture, his failure to give attribution to *Berit Yehudah* does not project him as more scholarly and learned than he actually is. Does *Halakhah* give Samson a license to rely on his own intuition that this is in fact the case? Recall that the sages devised the formulation *nafla bisra* to inform the townspeople that the day's supply of meat was not kosher. The rabbis relied here on their *intuition* that this formulation would not deceive Gentiles into thinking that the meat was actually kosher. The difference between the two cases is, however, clear-cut. Intuition is reliable only when the decision maker faces the certainty of adverse consequences should circumstances prove he was in error. The prospect that an erroneous judgment will inflict punishment on the decision maker works to thrust that person into the realm of unbiased thinking. This was the case in the *nafla bisra* scenario. If circumstances were to prove that the rabbis erred in their judgment and that *nafla bisra* had misled non-Jews into believing that the meat they were buying was kosher, then, the marketplace would become unsettled and the number of complaints against Jewish butchers would have proliferated. In addition, the rabbis themselves would be accused of profaning God's name (*hillul ha-Shem*). The knowledge that these frightening consequences follow on the heels of error objectified the sages' thinking and enhanced the reliability of their original assessment.

A different judgment must, however, be made for the case at hand. What adverse consequences does Samson face in the event his assessment is wrong? Because punishing consequences do not follow on the heels of error, Samson's intuition in the matter must be regarded as self-serving and hence unreliable.

Why is it wrong for Samson to rely on his intuition in this matter? The operative principle here is the *mi'ut ha-matzui* (small, but significant percentage) rule. This rule states that Halakhah concerns itself with a condition as prevailing even though it is not based on observed fact but, rather, only on a small, yet significant statistical probability.[47] To illustrate: the rule is that the majority of those who engage in ritual slaughter are presumed to be competent and certified. Nonetheless, a small, but significant minority of ritual slaughterers are not competent and are not certified. Because the number of those not certified constitutes *mi'ut ha-matzui*, we may not rely on the majority rule when the would-be ritual slaughterer stands in front of us.

Here, we may not allow him to proceed without first investigating his credentials.[48]

The *mi'ut ha-matzui* rule tells us that there will certainly be some people in the audience who will gather an overly favorable impression of Samson's scholarship on account of the rabbi's failure to disclose that he used *Berit Yehudah* to prepare his lecture. Failure to make the disclosure hence puts Samson at risk of violating the *geneivat da'at* interdict. But, what of the principle, discussed earlier, that an individual is not responsible for disabusing others of a false impression when that impression is the product of self-deception? There must be a quantitive measure for *mi'ut ha-matzui*. If the percentage of people in the audience left with the misimpression falls below this threshold number, then, the judgment will be that these people were guilty of self-deception. If, on the other hand, the percentage of people left with the misimpression is higher than this benchmark, then Samson's nondisclosure of his sources is not acceptable.

How is *mi'ut ha-matzui* translated into quantitative terms? Addressing himself to this issue, R. Jacob b. Aaron (Karlin, d. 1844) regards *mi'ut ha-matzui* as generally translating into a 10 percent benchmark.[49] Disputing R. Jacob b. Aaron, R. Yosef Shalom Elyashiv (Israel, contemp.) feels that *mi'ut ha-matzui* translates into a 15–20 percent range. The specific issue R. Elyashiv dealt with is the prohibition to eat fruits and vegetables without first being sure that the produce is free of worms. If 15–20 percent of a particular species is known to contain worms, it is prohibited to eat the species without first ascertaining that the fruit or vegetable at hand is worm-free.[50]

Let us adopt R. Elyashiv's benchmark of *mi'ut ha-matzui* for the case at hand. Accordingly, if Samson does not want to disclose to his audience that he used *Berit Yehudah* to prepare his lecture, he must first conduct a scientifically valid survey to confirm that less than 15–20 percent of his audience assumes he uses primary sources directly in preparing his lecture.

Suppose that Samson conducts the necessary survey and the data confirm his intuition. What the outcome of the survey does is only to make Samson's nondisclosure of *Berit Yehudah* free of a *geneivat da'at* violation. Not telling the audience of his debt to *Berit Yehudah* may, however, violate other ethical duties.

One problem Samson's nondisclosure entails is that his conduct falls short of the demands of the law of attribution. Repeating a saying in the name of the person who said it is counted by the *Tanna* in *Avot* as one of the 48 qualities necessary to acquire the *Torah*. The Tanna goes on to say: "Whoever repeats a thing in the name of the one who said it brings redemption to the world, as it is said: 'And Esther said to the king in the name of Mordecai' "(*Avot* 6:6).[51] To be sure, Samson gives proper attribution to the originators of all of the concepts and rulings he mentions. But, he does not look up these sources in their original works, but instead relies on R. Bloi's summaries of these works. R. Bloi hence assumes the role of the *first teacher* in a chain of teachers. In this regard, the Talmud at *Nazir* 56b informs us that for a teaching reported in a chain of three or more teachers, we mention, in the attribution, the first and last conveyors of the law, but we need not mention the intermediate conveyors. Thus, R. Yehudah ha-Nassi presents in his *Mishna* a teaching of R. Elazar in the name of R. Yehoshua b. Hananya; even though R. Elazar did not learn the dictum directly from R. Yehoshua b. Hananya, but instead only from R. Yehoshua b. Mamal, who, in turn, learned it from R. Yehoshua b. Hananya. Since R. Bloi is for Rabbi Samson the *first teacher* in a chain of teachers, the law of attribution requires Samson to mention R. Bloi.

A variation of this case occurs when Samson looks up all the sources R. Bloi quotes and studies them in the original. Because Samson is now in a position to directly report on what these authorities have to say, these authorities now become Samson's *first teachers in a chain of teachers* and the role R. Bloi plays here is reduced to someone who made Samson aware of their teachings. In the latter scenario, the law of attribution does not require Samson to make mention of R. Bloi.

Samson's failure to acknowledge R. Bloi not only violates the law of attribution, but also bespeaks of ingratitude and disrespect for someone who has effectively become his teacher of *Torah*. We need only take note of the dictum of the *Tanna* in *Avot* (6:3): "He who learns from his fellow a single chapter, a single Halakhah, a single verse, a single *Torah* statement, or even a single letter, must *treat him with honor . . .* "

The upshot of the above analysis is that without a validating survey to confirm his intuition that the audience is well aware without being explicitly told that he uses secondary sources to prepare the lecture, Samson's silence on the role *Berit Yehudah* played in preparing his lecture violates *geneivat da'at* law. Moreover, even if Samson has this validating survey in hand, not to acknowledge R. Bloi does injustice to the law of attribution and bespeaks of ingratitude and disrespect to someone who has effectively become his teacher of *Torah*. The extent to which Samson should acknowledge R. Bloi will depend on the degree to which Samson relied on *Berit Yehudah* in preparing his lecture. Greatest acknowledgment will be owed if *Berit Yehudah* both laid out his lecture for him and made him aware for the first time of the issues he spoke about.

THE REASONABLENESS CRITERION AND LETTING SOMEONE DO HIMSELF IN

For the various scenarios we have taken up in this chapter, the reasonableness criterion is the starting point in making the judgment whether the one who captures false goodwill has a disabusing duty or not. As important as this principle is for *genevat da'at* law, its limitation for settings other than allowing someone to reap false goodwill must be recognized. Suppose, for instance, that *A* is poised to engage in self-hurtful conduct. *B's* knowledge that *A's* planned action is rooted in an unreasonable assumptions does not relieve him of a duty to warn *A* against the harm or the detriment. The moral principle here is "Do not stand idly by the blood of your neighbor" (*lo ta'amod al dam rei'akha*, Leviticus 19:16). While the verse speaks of the prohibition of a bystander's remaining idle in a life threatening situation, *Sifra* extends the interdict to the prohibition of withholding testimony in a monetary matter. [52] Basing himself on *Sifra*, R. Israel Meir ha-Kohen Kagan (Radin, 1838–1933) understands the monetary application of the *lo ta'amod* interdict in broad terms: *A's* failure to supply *B* with timely information that would avert a financial loss for *B* is a violation of the *lo ta'amod* interdict.[53] This self-same duty for A not to allow B to do himself in is affirmatively demanded of A on the basis of the imperative "You must love your neighbor as [you love] yourself" (Leviticus 19:18).

SUMMARY AND CONCLUSION

Building a successful professional career requires the practitioner to work hard at creating goodwill with both colleagues and clients. Because goodwill is the stock of trade of the professional, it becomes inevitable that the professional will, at times, find himself, reaping goodwill that is not deserved. The starting point in deciding whether a disabusing duty is operative is whether the false impression was arrived at by means of reasonable assumption. Because self-assessment is usually not reliable, it is not legitimate to rely on one's own judgment without falling back on a previously demonstrated track record. Assessing what one would do in a hypothetical situation is certainly not reliable. Nonetheless, even when the assumption behind the false impression is reasonable, a disabusing duty may not apply. Such factors as *darkhei shalom* and *hever ir* may be operative and consequently obviate the duty to set the misinformed party straight.

For cases where the disabusing duty does not apply, no *carte blanche* license for exploiting all the goodwill possible in the situation exists. What disallows this is the various nuances of the prohibition against *sheker*. In addition, the affirmative duty of *bakesh shalom* requires one to insure that capturing undeserved goodwill does not in any way compromise long term harmonious relations with the person who harbors the misimpression.

In the area of scholarship, the parameters for guidance in the ethics of capturing goodwill expands to include the norms the *Torah* sets for giving proper attribution to the source and authority of a teaching.

POSTPRANDIUM

PROBLEM 1

Heather sends Fraydel an invitation to her wedding. Heather's intention is to invite Fraydel only to the *Huppah*. Accordingly, Heather does not include a response card in the invitation she sends Fraydel. When Fraydel receives the invitation she assumes that she is invited to the entire wedding and the omission of the response card was just a mistake. Fraydel calls Heather to tell her that she is coming to the meal at the wedding and lets her know that the invitation had no response card.

1. When Fraydel calls, is it O.K. for Heather to lie and tell Fraydel that she was, of course, all along invited to the entire wedding and apologize that the return card was inadvertently missing in Fraydel's invitation.

2. Another scenario: Fraydel does not call Heather. Fraydel meets Pam, who is Heather's best friend. The conversation turns to Heather's wedding. Pam tells Fraydel that she plans to go to Heather's wedding with her husband. Fraydel blurts out "I'm going too. Can I get a ride with you? You know, the weirdest thing happened; I got no return card with my invitation. It must have been a mistake. I'm coming to the whole affair. When you speak to Heather tell her I'm coming and ask her to seat me with you."

When Pam filters through Fraydel's message, Heather decides that she does not want to call up Fraydel and tell her that she is invited only to the Huppah, but she also does not want to incur the expense of another plate either. To get out of the dilemma, Heather calls up ten friends and asks each of them a hypothetical question: "Suppose you got an invitation to a wedding with no return card, would you take that to mean that you were just invited to the Huppah?" All ten friends responded the same way: "An invitation without a return card means that you are invited only to the Huppah."

Relieved that Fraydel was guilty of self-deception, Heather decides that she will not put up a place card for Fraydel. If Fraydel ends up suffering any embarrassment as a result, it would be all her own doing. Is Heather right?[54]

PROBLEM 2

Berish Langer is employed as a driver and delivery person for The George Goodside Beverage Company. His job is to deliver cases of soda to restaurants and hotels along a 15 mile route. One day when Berish returned to his truck from the delivery of a large order, he was shocked to find that a motorcyclist had crashed into his pick up truck and hundreds of bottles of soda were spilled out all over the road. No sooner than Berish discovered the fiasco than the motorist escaped the crime scene with his motorcycle. It was a case of hit and run. A large crowd of curiosity seekers gathered at the scene. When the enormity of the loss sank in, Berish broke out in a sob: "Mr. Goodside will surely fire me for this." Sighs of sympathy could be heard from the crowd. Whereon, there suddenly appeared from the crowd a distinguished figure, wearing a homburg. The man in a very dignified tone said, "why are we all just standing around and watching this spectacle, we can do something to save this man's job;" whereupon, the distinguishing looking man, removed his homburg and deposited $20 in the hat and began to move about the crowd, hat in hand, with an invitation that everyone should join. After much money was thrown in the hat, the distinguished man removed the collection from the hat and brought it over to Berish, "take this money, young man, it's a tidy sum. It will be enough to make your boss happy." The noble initiative and quick thinking of the distinguished stranger filled the crowd with warm compliments for his heroics. Amidst the animated conversations of the people in the crowd, the distinguished stranger slipped away unnoticed. As the crowd dispersed, Berish muttered to himself, again and again, "generosity, nobility, my eye! The man with the homburg was my boss, George Goodside."[55]

Evaluate the conduct of Mr. Goodside.

Notes

1. *Mo'ed Katan* 26b; Nahmanides (Spain, 1194–1270), *Torat ha-Adam, Sha'ar ha-Sof*; R. Jacob b. Asher (Spain, 1270–1343), *Tur, Yoreh De'ah* 337 on understanding of R. Joel Sirkes (Poland, 1561–1650), *Bah, ad locum*; R. Joseph Caro (Israel, 1488–1575), *Shulhan Arukh, Yoreh De'ah* 337; R. Jehiel Michel Epstein (Belorussia, 1829–1908), *Yoreh De'ah* 337:1–2.
2. R. Jehiel Michel Epstein, *Ar. ha-Sh., op. cit.* 337:2.
3. Leviticus 25:17.
4. *Mishnah, Bava Metzia* 4:10.
5. R. Menahem b. Solomon Meiri (Perpignan, 1249–1316), *Beit ha-Behirah, Bava Metzia* 59a. Pricing an article with no intention to buy it is prohibited, according to R. Samuel b. Meir (France, ca. 1080–1174, *Rashbam, Pesahim* 112b) on account of the possible loss this behavior might cause the vendor. While the vendor is preoccupied with the insincere inquiry, serious customers may turn elsewhere.
6. R. Solomon b. Isaac, *Rashi*, Leviticus 25:17.
7. R. Pinhas ha-Levi (Barcelona, 1235–1300), *Sefer ha-Hinnukh* 338.
8. R. Aaron Levine (Toronto, 1942–, *Zikhron Meir*, p. 83, notes 83–84) makes this point in general terms without drawing a distinction between the standard Halakhah prescribes for interaction with the seriously ill and the ordinary standard prescribed by the *ona'at devarim* interdict.
9. Supportive of the notion that the extra sensitivity Halakhah prescribes regarding the seriously ill does not apply across the board to all hospital patients is the definition Halakhah adopts for the seriously ill in connection with a related issue, that is, the transfer of property. Ordinarily, the transfer of property is effected only by means of the execution of an appropriate symbolic act (*kinyan*). The sages, however, simplified the

process for the seriously ill. The simplification becomes operative in the instance where the seriously ill person communicates a desire to transfer his entire property, without specifically expressing that he is doing so in anticipation of his death. This case is referred to in the Talmudic literature as *mattenot shekhiv me'ra's* (lit. the death bed gift). Out of concern that the *shekhiv me'ra's* condition will deteriorate if he feels that his instructions will have no legal effect, the sages ruled that the instructions of the *shekhiv me'ra* are retroactively binding should he die, without the need for any symbolic act. *Shekhiv me'ra* is defined by Maimonides (Egypt, 1135-1204, *Zekhiyyah u-Mattanah* 8: 1–2) as follows:

> A blind, lame or handless person, and similarly, one who feels pain in his head, his eye, his hand, his foot or the like, is considered to be a healthy person with regard to all matters that concern his purchases, his sales or gifts that he gives.
>
> However, when a person becomes ill to the extent that he feels weak throughout his entire body. Indeed, because of his illness, his strength has dwindled to the extent he cannot walk on his feet in the market place, and he is confined to his bed—he is referred to as a *shekhiv me'ra.*'The laws applying to his gifts differ from those applying to the gifts given by a healthy person.

Maimonides' text, according to R. Joshua b. Alexander ha-Kohen Falk (Poland, 1555–1614), *Derishah, Tur, Hoshen Mishpat* 250:8) lends itself to the interpretation that qualifying as *shekhiv me'ra* is a patient whose general weakness in strength does not allow him to venture outside his home, even if that person is not actually bedridden. If this person gives an instruction regarding the distribution of his entire property, his instructions become retroactively legally binding if he dies, with no need for a *kinyan*. If, however, the patient is so weak that he is actually bedridden, any instruction he gives regarding the disposition of his property, whether it relates to his entire wealth or not, becomes legally binding without need for a *kinyan* because we assume that the instruction was made in anticipation of imminent death.

Another view is expressed here by R. Yom Tov Vidal (Toloso, 14th cent., *Maggid Mishneh*, Yad, loc. cit.). In his understanding, Maimonides' definition of *shekhiv me'ra* is more narrow. In the latter's thinking, *shekhiv me'ra* status obtains only if the patient (P) is actually bed ridden. A special variant of *shekhiv me'ra* obtains when an illness suddenly befell P and the condition worsened. Here, any instruction P gives regarding the disposition of his assets, whether in full or in part, is presumed to have been made in anticipation of death, and therefore becomes effective without the usual legal requirements. (See *Yad, ad loc.* 8: 24).

Let us take note that the rationale behind both the extra sensitivity prescribed for the seriously ill and the easing of the usual procedures required for the transfer of property for the *shekhiv me'ra* is the same, namely, the concern that the condition of the patient may deteriorate (*shema tittaref da'ato*). Given that the rationale behind the two laws is the same, the medical condition the two laws refer to should also be the same. What all definitions describing the *shekhiv me'ra* portray is an illness that has so generally debilitated the strength of the patient that he anticipates death. The definition we have adopted in the text for a seriously ill person in respect to when the extra sensitivity requirement kicks in is therefore consistent with both R. Vidal and R. Falk's views' on Maimonides.

10. The treatment of the *geneivat da'at* in this chapter draws upon my previous work *Case Studies in Jewish Business Ethics* (Hoboken, N.J.: Ktav Publishing House, Yeshiva University Press, 2000), pp. 33–48.

11. R. Jonah b. Abraham Gerondi (Spain, ca. 1200-1264), *Sha'arei Teshuvah, sha'ar 3, ot* 184.

12. R. Yom Tov Ishbili (Seville, ca. 1250-1330), *Ritva, Hullin* 94a.

13. *Rashi, Hullin* 94a.

14. Aaron Levine, *Economic Public Policy And Jewish Law* (Hoboken, N.J.: Ktav Publishing House, Yeshiva University Press, 1987), 69-72.

15. The Mishnah is divided into six orders (sedarim). These are (1) *Zera'im* ("seeds"), (2) *Mo'ed* ("festivals"), (3) *Nashim* ("women"), (4) *Nezikin* ("damages"), (5) *Kodashim* ("holy things"), and (6) Toharot ("purities"). The various tractates of the Babylonian Talmud fit into these orders. For the Jerusalem Talmud, the *Kodashim* and *Toharot* orders are missing.

16. *Economic Public Policy and Jewish Law, op. cit.*, 72–7.

17. R. Solomon b. Abraham Adret (Barcelona, 1235-1314, *Rashba, Ketubbot* 34a) explicitly espouses this position. The specific case he deals with is the following: *A* becomes aware that *B*'s animal is lying in his courtyard. *B* decides not to return the animal to *A* and instead to acquire it unlawfully by virtue of the fact that the animal is lying in his property *(kinyan hatzer)*. Notwithstanding that *A* committed no affirmative act of misappropriation *(ma'aseh geneivah)*, his acquisition of *B*'s animal by means of *kinyan hatzer* makes him a thief. In the opinion of R. Aryeh Loeb b. Joseph ha-kohen Heller (Poland, 1745–1813, *Ketzot ha-Hoshen, Shulhan Arukh, Hoshen Mishpat,* 348:2), a person does not legally become a thief unless he commits an affirmative act of misappropriation *(ma'aseh geneivah)*. If we follow *Ketzot*'s line we should formulate the *geneivat da'at* interdict in terms of the prohibition against *sheker*.

18. *Tosafot, Hullin* 94a. R. Solomon b. Isaac *(Rashi,* France, 1040–1105), however, takes the view that *H* is merely prohibited from telling *G* that he is opening the barrel especially for him. For an explanation of the dispute between *Rashi* and *Tosafot*, see *Case Studies in Jewish Business Ethics, op. cit.* 118-121.

19. R. Aryeh Judah b. Akiba, *Lev Aryeh, Hullin* 94a.

20. R. Mosheh Mordecai Epstein, *Resp. Levush Mordecai* 24.

21. R Elazar Meir Preil, *Ha-Ma'or* 1:26-27.

22. R. Mosheh Feinstein, *Iggerot Mosheh, Yoreh De'ah* 2:61.

23. *Economic Public Policy and Jewish Law, op. cit.* 69–73.

24. See R. Isaac b. Jacob Alfasi (Algeria, 1012–1103), *Rif, ad loc.*; R. Asher b. Jehiel, *Rosh, Hullin* 7:18; *Tur, Hoshen Mishpat* 228; *Sh. Ar., Hoshen Mishpat* 228:8; *Arukh ha-Shulhan, Hoshen Mishpat* 228:3.

    R. Hayyim David ha-Levi (Israel, 1924–1998, *Ase Lekha Rav* 4:61) contends that a *baraita* cited in *Jerusalem Talmud, Demai* 4:3 stands in opposition to the *hever ir* leniency. Maimonides' omission of the *hever ir* leniency is therefore taken by him to amount to a rejection of this dictum, in accordance with the *Jerusalem Talmud*.

25. R. Samuel Eliezer b. Judah ha-Levi Edels, *Maharsha, Hullin* 94a.

26. R. Yom Tov Ishbili, *Ritva, Yevamot* 65b.

27. *Rashi* at Exodus 23:1.

28. R. Pinhas ha-Levi, *Sefer ha-Hinnukh* 74.

29. R. Nahum Yavruv, *Niv Sifatayyim*, p. 70.

30. For further discussion of caveats for the *darkhei shalom* principle, turn to pp. 49–52, 393 of this volume.

31. R. Menahem b. Solomon Meiri, *Beit ha-Behirah*, *Yevamot* 63a; R. Joseph Epstein (New York, contemp.), *Mitzvat ha-Shalom*, 547.

32. R. Jonah b. Abraham Gerondi (Spain, ca.1200–1264) on interpretation of R. Nahum Yavruv, *Niv Sifatayyim*, 3rd edition, *helek alef*, pp. 39–40.

33. *Niv Sefatayyim*, op. cit. *helek alef*, p. 40.

34. R. Isaac of Corbeil quoted by R. Aaron ha-Kohen of Lunel in *Orhot Hayyim*, vol. 1 *siman* 5 *ot* 5.

35. In the opinion of R. Naftali Zevi Yehudah Berlin, *imitatio Dei* extends beyond a duty to emulate those Attributes of God's mercies explicitly enumerated at Exodus 34:67. By the exegesis of Joel 3:5, a duty to emulate God in every manifestation of His mercy is established (*Emek Netziv*, *Sifrei* at Deuteronomy 10:2, *piska* 13).

36. *Sotah* 14a; *Sifrei* at Deuteronomy 10:12.

37. Cf. Psalms 29:11; *Sanhedrin* 37a; *Ukzin* 3:11; *Leviticus Rabbah* 9:9; *Deuteronomy Rabbah* 5:12.

38. Deuteronomy 8:16.

39. R. Mosheh Sofer, Resp. *Hatam Sofer*, *Yoreh De'ah* 131.

40. In his treatment of the Mar Zutra incident, R. Joseph Hayyim b. Elijah al-Hakham (Baghdad, 1834–1909, *Ben Yehoyada*, *Hullin* 94b) understands that the rabbis, at the initiative of Rav Safra, actually escorted Mar Zutra back to Bei Mahoza. Rav Safra's initiative preempted Rava. What would Rava have done? He, too, according to R. Joseph Hayyim, would have taken the initiative to spontaneously change his and Rav Safra's travel plans and escort Mar Zutra to Bei Mahoza. What Rava objected to was that Rav Safra revealed to Mar Zutra that he and Rava did not come to greet him. In Rava's opinion, the rabbis should have *silently* escorted Mar Zutra to Bei Mahoza. For an analysis of R. Joseph Hayyim's view, see Aaron Levine, "False Goodwill and Halakhah," *Tradition*, 34:1, Spring, 2000, pp. 24–28.

41. *Makkot* 24a and *Rashi* ad locum.

42. For an explication of this principle please turn to pp. 371–372 of this volume.

43. *Megillah* 18a.

44. Leviticus 19: 16. Depending upon the circumstance, tale bearing, according to R. Israel Meir ha-Kohen (Radin, 1838–1933, *Hafetz Hayyim*, *Lavin* 1–7, *Essin* 1–14), may involve the violation of a total of 31 Pentateuchal positive commands.

45. *Arakhin* 16a; R. Isaac b. Jacob Alfasi (Algeria, 1013–1103), *Rif*, *Shabbat* 14a; *Yad*, *De'ot*; *Hafetz Hayyim Hilkhot Issurei lashon ha-Ra* 9:1.

46. In my opinion, Samson makes a mistake by slipping away before the official program begins. His main reason for coming to the breakfast, as mentioned in the text, is to get material for his sermons by trading *bon mots* with colleagues. Samson should know better! The best *Torah* insights will come from the prepared remarks of the official program.

47. For a comprehensive treatment of *mi'ut ha-matzui*, see R. Shmuel ha-Levi Wosner (Israel, contemp.), Resp. *Shevat ha-Levi*, 4 *Yoreh De'ah* 81.

48. *Hullin* 12a and R. Nissim b. Reuben Gerondi (Barcelona, ca. 1290–ca. 1375), on R. Isaac b. Jacob Alfasi (Algeria, 1013–1104), *Rif*, *Hullin* 12a.

49. R. Jacob b. Aaron, *Mishkenot Ya'akov*, *Yoreh De'ah* 17.

50. Ruling of R. Yosef Shalom Elyashiv as reported by R. Joseph I. Efrati in a letter to Rabbi A. Panet, dated 1995. I am indebted to R. Yosef Eisen of the Orthodox Union for making available to me this letter.
51. The duty to repeat a *Torah* teaching in the name of the originator proceeds from ethical principles other than *Avot* 6:6. For these sources see R. Ahron Maged, *Bet Ahron*, vol. 3, pp. 376–94.
52. *Sifre* at Leviticus 19:16 ot 41.
53. R. Israel Meir ha-Kohen Kagan, *Hafez Hayyim, Be'er Mayim Hayyim, Hilkhot Issurei Rekhilut* 9:1
54. Adapted from a question submitted by Judith Kaplan, member of class, Topics in Jewish Ethics, JUD1501, SCW, Yeshiva University, Fall, 2002.
55. Adapted from a story told by Aryeh Warshavchik

2

Truth Telling in Labor and Crisis Negotiation

The purpose of this chapter is to investigate the standard for truth telling that Halakhah (Jewish law) prescribes for labor and crisis negotiation. By means of the case study method we will investigate the ethics of the use of such tactics as false demands, false promises, false threats, diversionary tactics, and insincerity of both the transparent and nontransparent variety. The acceptability of these various tactics will form the basis of the judgment on whether the standard of truth telling in the setting of negotiation is any different from the standard of truth telling in other settings.

CONTRACT NEGOTIATIONS BETWEEN BRICKMIRE UNIVERSITY AND ITS TEACHERS UNION

As contract negotiations between Brickmire University and its Teachers Union got under way, the tension in the air was so thick that it could be cut only with a chain saw. Much of the responsibility for building up the tension could be blamed on the student publications of the university. Based on both interviews with some of the feisty and militant professors and leaks from reliable, anonymous sources in the administration, the student newspapers built up expectations of large gaps between union demands and the financial ability and/or willingness of the university to meet these demands at the upcoming contract talks.

43

Professor Lance Wineman, an economics professor, headed the negotiating team for the faculty. No novice at the task, Wineman often spiced his
incisive comments with references to economic theory, especially integra-
tive bargaining theory. Wineman was accustomed to working with models
and abstractions. In a previous negotiation with the university administration, Wineman purportedly reacted to a proposal by quipping, "Sure, that
works well in practice, *but will it work well in theory*." His counterpart for
the administration was Gary Pelt. Pelt, who sported Ivy League credentials
in both his law and business administration degrees, had a reputation as a
hard nosed negotiator that would not "give away ice in the winter."

Pelt and Wineman were no strangers. They had locked horns in the past
on a number of lengthy contract negotiations. Mutual dislike and distrust
best described the relationship between the two men. Nonetheless, before
the nitty gritty of the negotiations actually began, Pelt and Wineman
exchanged pleasantries and inquired about the welfare of their opposite
member's family. In addition, they feigned laughter at each other's jokes.

In the opening round, Wineman laid out the Union's demands. Wineman's demands included a 15 percent raise across the board for all professorial ranks, an increase in the university's pension fund contribution from
7 percent to 10 percent, and a vastly improved health plan, which would
feature lower deductibles and a lower co-insurance rate. All these demands
were more or less expected. But, Pelt and his team were in for a few surprises. Wineman put on the table a demand that the sabbatical leave benefit should expand from half pay for a full year or full pay for a semester to
full pay for a full year. Another surprise was the demand of a course reduction for all ranks, with the largest reduction demanded for full professors
from eight courses to six courses for the school year. Lesser amounts of
course reduction were demanded for the other ranks. Finally, the union
demanded that the university provide teaching assistants for all full professors. The main function of these personnel would be to conduct review sessions and to grade papers.

Pelt responded to the initial recital of union demands with conciliatory
words:

> Professor Wineman, it's in the self-interest of the university to improve
> faculty welfare. We believe, as you do, that increased salaries will
> improve faculty productivity. The other side of the coin is that higher

faculty salaries produce better students, who go on to have more suc-cessful careers. When alumni gifts begin to pile up and these same sat-isfied and successful alumni eagerly send their children to their alma mater, the ingredients of a self-feeding virtuous cycle are in place. Your proposals are therefore theoretically sound. But, please recognize our financial exigencies. At this juncture, the University is prepared to offer a 3 percent across the board raise and a 1 percent increase in our con-tribution to the pension fund.

Reacting to the university's counterproposal with obvious anguish and disappointment, Wineman portrayed the faculty at Brickmire as being embittered over historical wrongs and smarting badly over a pay scale and fringe benefit package that was clearly inferior to universities that it could legitimately compare itself to.

"Unless the 'pay gap' is considerably narrowed, I predict significant attrition, a significant increase in faculty moonlighting and, a very sub-stantial deterioration in both the quality of teaching here and in time faculty spends on campus. The pay gap will also take a significant toll on faculty productivity in the area of research. So much for the long run. In the short run, we're open to "creative flexibility," but if our demands are not met, I predict a strike."

On this ominous note the talks ended for the day. When the talks resumed the next day, Pelt set a hard line tone:

"Understand that our goal for achieving excellence is a partnership with our faculty. We won't tolerate dead wood. All raises will have to be linked to merit. The criteria here will be publications and teaching per-formance evaluation. In addition, I'm afraid we'll have to insist that the pay of a professor be docked if he or she misses a class, a faculty assem-bly, or even an important committee meeting. The latter would be at the discretion of the dean. Moreover, suitable penalties must be imposed if grades are handed in late."

"We also need to look for ways to be more efficient. Greater effi-ciency in anything we do frees up money for faculty salary increases and other amenities. In this regard what I have in mind is to put a block on faculty office long-distance calling. If faculty need to receive or make work-related long-distance calls, it can be done in the dean's office with the prior approval of the dean."

Not wanting to end his response to the union's demands on a sour note, Pelt ended his presentation with a quip. Looking at Wineman with a mischievous twinkle in his eye, Pelt said, "Professor Wineman, you're trying to extend your famous law of household consumption to new frontiers." Very flattered that Pelt was familiar with his law and visibly moved to have it invoked in the collective bargaining session, Wineman waited with baited breath to hear if Pelt really understood his law and how he was applying it to the situation at hand. Pelt continued,

"Your law, Professor Wineman, as I recall, theorizes that consumption for the household is directly proportional to its accessibility. The importance of the law is that a household cannot expect to beat inflation by stockpiling nonperishables. This is so because the more food a family has around over a given time period, the faster it will be consumed over that given period of time. Extending your law to the world of university endowments apparently leads to the proposition that when philanthropists move from promise to actual donation, the accessibility of university resources for faculty consumption increases. But, the flaw here is that the endowments are typically earmarked for particular projects. These include capital projects and renovations and the funding of academic programs that we ordinarily don't get involved in. So you see, more money does not always mean greater accessibility of university resources for faculty consumption."

On the basis of the position opposing sides took, observers held out little hope that a strike could be averted. But, when all the rhetoric settled down, both parties moved in the direction of settlement.

The turning point, at least according to the student publication *Asymmetric Information Fixer*, came when Pelt broke the icy silence and quipped, "Well, perhaps Wineman's law of food accessibility applies in a modified manner to university finances. By the way, I'm fascinated with your law. When this is over we really should do lunch and discuss your law in all its minutiae [polite laughter]. The university is prepared to up our last offer, provided you recognize the merit principle."

From this critical juncture it was smooth sailing, and a compromise set-tlement was in the works. It took no more than four bargaining sessions, the last one an all nighter, for a final settlement to be hammered out. The break-through came when the university dropped its insistence that it would block long-distance calling in faculty offices. Once this draconian measure got off the table, the *quid pro quo* process began in earnest. By dropping its insis-tence on punitive measures for teacher absences from classes, no shows in meetings, and handing in grades late, the university got the union to agree on the principal that raises beyond a cost of living increase would be based on merit. Joint faculty-administration committees were set up to determine the formula for merit and who would have authority in this matter. Subject to qualification on the basis of merit, the agreement called for a graduated increase in salary and other benefits over a three-year period. In the first year the increase would be 4 percent. In the second year 5 percent, and in the third year 7 percent In addition, the university agreed to immediately lower the deductible on the health plan from $1000 to $300. In regard to teaching assistants and the policy for sabbatical leaves, the university agreed to commission a cost-benefit study and report to the faculty on its findings. No deadline for the report was set and no follow-up commitments were made.

BILATERAL MONOPOLY AND ETHICS IN NEGOTIATION

The negotiation between Brickmire University and the Teachers Union raises a number of ethical issues in the area of truth telling and integrity. Before turning to these issues, let us take note of the mutual dependence the parties of the negotiation must face up to. To be sure, a strike is a possibil-ity. But even in that eventuality, the parties will presumably want to come back together and reach a settlement, rather than face the financial costs and emotional scars of protracted labor-management strife. The upshot is therefore that, for all intents and purposes, Brickmire has no alternative but to deal with the faculty union as its *only* source for teaching personnel and the union has no alternative but to regard Brickmire as the *only* source of employment for its members. Economists refer to the above setting as a *bilateral monopoly model*.

In Halakhah the price terms of a commercial transaction are usually subject to a fairness test when a competitive market price exists for the article at hand. This is called the law of *ona'ah*. Depending on how widely the price of the subject transaction departs from the competitive norm, the injured party may have recourse to void or adjust the transaction.[1] The biblical source of *ona'ah* deals with a commodity.[2] Biblical exegesis extends the law of *ona'ah* to the labor market.[3] The scope of this application is, however, limited.[4] In any case, the law of *ona'ah* generally does not apply when the commodity at hand is sold under monopoly conditions.[5] By extension, the law of *ona'ah* should not apply to the bilateral monopoly case. The settlement terms of Brickmire's labor contract would hence not be subject by Halakhah to a comparison reference price.

The upshot of the above analysis is that the outcome of the bilateral monopoly negotiation between Brickmire and the Teachers Union is up for grabs. Because the agreement that is hammered out is not subject to revision based on comparing it to any reference teacher's contract, what the final outcome will be is a matter of both the leverage and the relative bargaining skills of the parties to the negotiations.

DARKHEI SHALOM AND LYING TO AVERT A STRIKE

Let us now consider the implication of the mutual dependency factor for the issue of lying and engaging in deceptive conduct in the collective bargaining process. We begin with the concept of reservation price. Reservation price is the minimum offer a party to a negotiation would accept. Typically, the initial position a party to a negotiation adopts is above his reservation price. But, there is no guarantee that the initial position one adopts will fall above the reservation price of one's opposite number. This was the case in the opening vignette. If Pelt and Wineman had held onto their initial positions, a strike would surely have taken place. But, both modified their original positions. As the bargaining proceeded, their positions narrowed sufficiently to make the prospect of a strike nil. Because both Pelt and Wineman were seasoned and shrewd bargainers, neither gave away when the offer on the table fell into the boundaries of their respective reservation prices.

The concept of reservation price identifies the crisis point in a labor negotiation. Suppose, for instance, Wineman is convinced that the deal before him is the final offer of the university and it will be rejected by the Teachers Union. With the aim of breaking the impasse and *averting a strike*, is it permissible for Wineman to lie with the aim of making the university offer a better deal? Given the bilateral monopoly nature of the negotiation at hand, any additional advantage Wineman secures for the union by means of this ploy should in no way be regarded as an ill-gotten gain. Within this context, perhaps lying is permissible. Consider the Talmudic dictum that lying for the purpose of preserving peace is permissible.[6] This teaching is referred to as the *darkhei shalom* (ways of peace) principle. In fact, one opinion in the Talmud makes *darkhei shalom* not just permissible, but a positive duty.[7]

Darkhei shalom is not, however, a blanket dispensation for lying. Consideration of the many caveats attached to *darkhei shalom* will show that the application of this principle to collective bargaining is limited.

1. One caveat, enunciated by R. Israel Meir ha-Kohen Kagan (Radin, 1838–1933) is that lying for the purpose of preserving peace is permissible only when the objective cannot be achieved without lying.[8] R. Nahum Yavruv (Israel, contemp.), basing himself on R. Hayyim Kanievsky (Israel, contemp.), avers that even if considerable toil and effort must be exerted to achieve peace without lying, it is preferable to go this route rather than engage in lying.[9]

2. The *darkhei shalom* motive, in the opinion of R. Nahum Yavruv, legitimizes the telling of a lie, even if the one who tells the lie realizes that with time the lie will be exposed and the peace it achieved will dissipate. This is so because telling a lie with the aim of achieving a *temporary* peace is also legitimate. Nonetheless, if the peacemaker assesses that when his lie is exposed the discord it ended will reemerge in exasperated form, *darkhei shalom* does not permit the telling of the lie.[10]

3. *Darkhei shalom*, according to R. Judah b. Samuel he-Hasid (Regensburg, c. 1150–1217) et al, is permitted only in respect to making false statements about an event that already happened. Uttering falsehood in respect to matters of the present or future is, however, prohibited.[11] The rationale behind this distinction is that compared to lying about the past, lying about the present and future exerts a greater influence to habituate a person to continue the trait of lying in the future.[12]

Another school of thought, led by Maimonides (Egypt, 1135–1204), makes no distinction between a lie that relates to an event in the past and a lie that relates to the present or future. If the motive is *darkhei shalom*, a lie—whether relating to the past, present, or future is permitted.[13]

Noting this dispute among the authorities, R. Nahum Yavruv posits that the stringent view is a very substantial view to the extent that we should conduct ourselves in the first instance according to this view. In difficult circumstances, we can follow the lenient view. Even under difficult circumstances the use of double entendres or vague language is preferred over outright lies.[14]

4. Lying for the purpose of ending discord, according to R. Solomon b. Jehiel Luria (Poland, 1510–1573) is acceptable only when the *darkhei shalom* setting requires a one-shot lie. If, on the other hand, peace is only possible if the lie is repeated again and again, the lie is not permitted.[15] The basis for this stringency is that repeated lies will accustom the peacemaker to lie.[16]

5. In his treatment of the prohibitions of lying and deception, R. Jonah b. Abraham Gerondi (Spain, ca. 1200–1264) places liars in order of severity into nine categories. In the fourth category, R. Jonah places a person who lies because he "loves falsehood."[17] If someone "loves falsehood" telling a lie, even for the purpose of achieving peace, is prohibited.[18]

Before relating these caveats to the specifics of the Pelt-Wineman negotiations, it should be clear that they point to an ethical norm for the schooling of labor-management negotiators and for the mock sessions that precede an actual negotiation. The point here is that the training and the mock sessions should not include honing skills in making up non detectable lies. Such training surely *habituates* the trainees in falsehood and therefore cannot be justified on the basis that the prepared lies will be used only for a *darkhei shalom* purpose. Moreover, if honing skills in nondetectable lies becomes part of the repertoire of the professional negotiator, the negotiator will easily develop an "acquired taste for lying" and descend into R. Jonah's category of a "lover of falsehood."

Precautions to prevent negotiators from becoming habituated in falsehood are clearly needed. What is minimally necessary here is a game plan that does not feature advance preparation for lying and deception. Within the framework of this attitude and approach, if negotiations threaten to break down, and one of the parties *spontaneously* comes up with some nondetectable lie to save the day, his success will not habituate him to lie. Does this say that Halakhah's standard for collective bargaining entails a level of forthrightness that is tantamount to requiring the opposing parties to reveal to each other their respective reservation prices? No. Within the context of collective bargaining the use of diversionary tactics, as will be discussed below, is permitted. Devising these strategies in advance should be permissible, as the non acceptable form of deception is not involved here. Preparing diversionary tactics in advance bespeaks of shrewdness, not duplicity.

Let us now relate these caveats to the specifics of the Pelt-Wineman negotiations. The most fundamental point to be made is that a *darkhei shalom* setting comes into play only when either Pelt or Wineman faces an offer from his opposite number that fails to meet his reservation price. It is here that the party that faces the unacceptable offer might be permitted to lie as a means of averting a strike. If, on the other hand, the purpose of injecting a lie into the negotiation is to accrue additional gains, the *darkhei shalom* principle will not legitimize the telling of a lie. Moreover, lying is permitted only if all other legitimate means of effecting movement on the other side are unavailable.

Within the framework of a *darkhei shalom* setting, let us show how the Pelt-Wineman negotiation could violate one or more of the various caveats discussed above. Pelt faces an unacceptable demand from Wineman. As an alternative to walking away from the talks, Pelt decides to lie about the value of the university's endowment fund. The figure Pelt gives can easily be confirmed on the basis of publicly available documents. But, consider that Wineman relies on Pelt to quote him a figure that includes a "good faith" estimate of what the fund will amount to by the end of the current fiscal year. Pelt knows that by the end of the year there will be several announcements regarding newly endowed professorial chairs, but the figure he gives does not include these chairs. The figure Pelt quotes for the endowment fund is for the moment an "undetectable lie." Pelt's game plan is to disavow knowledge that these chairs were in the works when the announcements will finally come. Because the estimate Pelt offers is a lie in respect to the present and future as opposed to what already transpired, Pelt's *darkhei shalom* motive does not license him to make this lie. Relatedly, Pelt's lie at the negotiating table will inevitably force him to lie again when the announcement of the chairs is made. Moreover, Pelt's claim of ignorance that the chairs were in the works strains credulity and will only work to increase the level of distrust the faculty community will harbor against the university.

To be sure, when Pelt's lie comes to light the faculty won't react with a wildcat strike, and for that matter, with any job action whatsoever. Nonetheless, the faculty will at that time be filled with a smoldering resentment because they will suspect that they were lied to. To say the least, much ill feeling will be directed toward the university. All this is quite predictable in advance. Pelt's desperate lie seals the contract agreement for the next three years, but predictably destroys any goodwill that may have existed between the faculty and the administration. Because Pelt's ploy exasperates long-term relations between administration and faculty, the ploy cannot be legitimized on the basis of the *darkhei shalom* principal.

At this juncture let us change the scenario. Instead of lying about the size of the university's endowments, Pelt lies about the maximum size of the tuition hike the university is willing to implement. Here, all of the caveats for *darkhei shalom* are not violated. First, the lie relates to a decision that was already made. In addition, because that decision is for now the secret of a few people, there is little chance that the lie will explode in Pelt's face later. Finally, there is no inevitability that there will be a need to repeat the lie again and again.

TRANSPARENT INSINCERITY

Before getting down to brass tacks, we find Pelt and Wineman engaged in pleasantries. In reality, they dislike each other intensely. Yet, for the sake of show, each expresses interest in the well-being of both his opposite number and his family, and even feigns laughter at the other's jokes. Given that Pelt and Wineman's words don't reflect their true feelings, the pleasantries they exchange should be regarded as hypocritical conduct. In the Talmudic literature such conduct is called "one thing with the heart (*ahat ba-lev*) and another thing with the mouth (*ve-ahat ba-peh*). Henceforth, we will refer to such conduct by the shorthand notation of *ahat ba-lev*.

Relevant here is the comparison Genesis Rabbah draws between the conduct of Absalom (son of King David) and Joseph's brothers:

"His [Joseph's] brothers saw that it was he whom their father loved most of all his brothers so they hated him; and they were not able to speak to him peaceably" (Genesis 37:4). Out of this remark of disparagement of them we may learn their praise, that they did not speak one thing with their mouth and another with their heart. Elsewhere it says, "And Absalom spoke unto Amnon neither good nor bad" (2 Samuel 13:22), keeping in his heart what he felt in his heart. Whereas here, what was in their hearts was on their tongues.[19]

Two moral lessons proceed from the above comparison. One lesson is the deadly consequence that ensues when an individual harbors a complaint against someone and never confronts that person with the complaint. The second lesson is the *integrity* that is required of one who does speak out and articulate to his friend a complaint he has against him. Amnon raped Absalom's sister, Tamar. Absalom was enraged at this offense, but never confronted Amnon about it. Because Absalom never excoriated Amnon for raping his sister, Amnon was never made to realize the depth of Absalom's rage against him. Quite to the contrary, Absalom's silence inveigled Amnon into treating the sin much more lightly than he should have. Absalom's silent treatment of Amnon produced nothing less than tragedy for both of them. Specifically, had Absalom only confronted Amnon, the latter might have been moved to repent and feel a need to placate Absalom and reconcile himself with him. Similarly, because Absalom did not express his anger against Amnon openly, Amnon never guarded himself against Absalom and hence became easy prey for Absalom to murder. In sharp contrast, Joseph's brothers openly expressed complaints and anger to him for his conduct. Because they openly contended with him, they felt it would be hypocritical on their part to return Joseph's friendly greetings. Reciprocating to Joseph his friendly gestures would send a false signal to him that they were, in fact, not so terribly angry with him for his conduct.

Proceeding from the above is a rationale of why *ahat ba-lev* conduct is prohibited. It is prohibited because such conduct sends out a false signal. In the case at hand, no false signal is sent out by the pleasantries Pelt and Wineman exchange before the bargaining session begins. This is so because each party does not mistakenly take his opposite number's inquires about family as a gesture of friendship. Instead, these inquires are taken as conversation for the sake of signaling to each other that they desire to be on speaking terms. Consider that in the understanding of the sages of the Talmud, deliberate non communication with a fellow for three days is taken as a sign of enmity.[20] Now, Pelt and Wineman could have just as easily dispensed with the pleasantries and gone straight into their negotiations. Instead, they chose to engage in civil discourse. What each party signaled with this is that despite their mutual dislike, they desired to be on speaking terms. The feigned laughter reinforces the mutual signal that they desire to suppress their hostility to the level of civil discourse. Let us recognize that ideas put on the table in collective bargaining sessions can sometimes be transformed into mutual gains, if the parties would only be attuned to such a possibility. By putting their relationship on the level of civil discourse, both Pelt and Wineman signal they will not automatically shoot down and reject out of hand what comes out from the other side. Thus, by suppressing personal hostility, both Pelt and Wineman will more effectively represent the interests of their principals. Naked self-interest hence dictates that they conduct their negotiations against the backdrop of being on speaking terms.

The pleasantries Pelt and Wineman exchange before their negotiation begins therefore amounts to nothing more than transparent insincerities that serve a mutually beneficial purpose and should therefore be permitted.

Moreover, let us consider the possibility that Pelt and Wineman's pre-negotiation session conduct was even laudatory. This judgment can be reached by considering the duty in Halakhah not to perpetuate a quarrel. This duty is derived from the manner in which Moses conducted himself vis-à-vis Datan and Abiram when they joined forces with Korah to rebel against his authority: "Moses sent forth to summon Datan and Abiram, the sons of Eliab, but they said, 'We shall not go up! Is it not enough that you have brought us up from a land flowing with milk and honey to cause us to die in the wilderness, yet you seek to dominate us, even to dominate further?'" (Numbers 16:13). Notwithstanding this calumny, Moses reached out to them to desist from their rebellion before he called for the destruction of Korah and his cohorts: "So Moses stood up and went to Datan and Abiram." (Numbers 16:25). The lesson the Talmud derives from this episode is that one should not perpetuate a quarrel even if he is in the right.[21]

Given the sour note on which Pelt and Wineman parted ways in their last encounter, it would be a matter of religious duty for either of them to initiate conversation and pleasantries in their next encounter. Doing so fulfills the duty not to perpetuate a quarrel. Exchanging pleasantries in no way communicates a mutual desire to have a relationship of friendship. Instead, it communicates that neither party wants their relationship to deteriorate to the level where the only conversation possible is the discussion of collective bargaining issues in the context of official meetings.

FALSE PRAISE AND INSINCERITY OF THE NONTRANSPARENT VARIETY

Recall that by injecting Wineman's law of household consumption into the negotiation talks, Pelt got the stalled talks back on track. In reality, Pelt regards Wineman's law as a piece of "pretentious flummery." Pelt's false praise of Wineman amounts therefore to *ahat ba-lev* conduct.

Another consideration here is the prohibition against *hanuppah* (forbidden flattery). The biblical source of this prohibition is, "You shall not corrupt (*tahanippu*) the land" (Numbers 35:33).[22] To be sure, the basic conduct the verse prohibits is to flatter the wicked;[23] but, in the thinking of R. Ephraim Solomon b. Aaron of Lenczycza (d. 1619) the ambit of *hanuppah* extends further. In his view, *hanuppah* is defined as "giving a fellow something that he is not worthy of out of expectation to receive something in return."[24] Another authority that extends the ambit of *hanuppah* beyond the prohibition to flatter the wicked is R. Hayyim Hezekiah Medini (Russia, 1832–1904). This is evident by the criticism he levies against the prevailing practice of his time for rabbis to address their colleagues with excessively lavish titles and praises.[25] Because Pelt feels that Wineman's theory of accessible consumption is nothing but a piece of pretentious flummery, heaping public praise on it in Wineman's presence should place him in violation of *hanuppah*.

Pelt's gesture to Wineman to join him as his guest over lunch to discuss the household consumption theory should also be objectionable. In reality, Pelt has no plans whatsoever to follow up on his invitation. In the unlikely event that Wineman takes the gesture as a firm invitation and goes ahead and presses Pelt for a time and place, Pelt will give Wineman the runaround and slip away. Pelt's gesture is therefore insincere and is designed to create an unwarranted sense of indebtedness (*mahazik tova be-hinnam*) on the part of Wineman. Such conduct, specifically mentioned in the Talmud, is an aspect of the prohibition against *geneivat da'at* (literally, stealing of the mind).[26] Given the insincerity of Pelt's invitation, his gesture also should be categorized as *ahat ba-lev* conduct.

The objections against both Pelt's false praise of Wineman and his insincere invitation to him can, however, be removed. Consider that Pelt's motive in engaging in this conduct is to lighten the mood with the aim of restarting the stalled talks. Because Pelt's motive is clearly *darkhei shalom*, his conduct should be permissible. However, engaging in various forms of lies for the purpose of promoting peace is permitted *only* when these lies are absolutely essential in achieving the desired result. Accordingly, if Pelt can lighten the mood by falsely praising Wineman's law of household consumption, his *darkhei shalom* license ends there and he has no right to heap on top of this an insincere invitation to discuss this law with Wineman over lunch. Moreover, if Pelt decides to go ahead with the insincere invitation, it will be his duty to minimize the false goodwill proceeding from it. At a minimum, this requires Pelt not to give Wineman the runaround if Wineman calls him to fix a time and place for their lunch. Consider also that Pelt tendered his invitation in the heat of a negotiating session. Wineman will therefore probably expect a follow-up call from Pelt to both extend him a formal invitation and finalize arrangements with him. By following through in this manner when the negotiations are over, Pelt will minimize the false goodwill his gesture generated. Instead of being guilty of expressing both false interest in Wineman's theory and failure to follow up on the lunch invitation, Pelt will be guilty only of expressing false interest in Wineman's theory.

COLLECTIVE BARGAINING AND DIVERSIONARY TACTICS

In the opening vignette we find Pelt deflecting Wineman's claim that the university is able to pay by pointing out that endowment funds don't conform to Wineman's law of household consumption. The unexpected mention of his law in the collective bargaining session throws Wineman off and he neglects to probe deeper into the minutiae of the endowment funds. Wineman should have pressed on that surely *some* of the endowment funds do relieve the university of the need to finance a portion of its regular budget from other sources. What percentage of the endowment funds falls into this category? What was the increase in endowments over last year? Because

Wineman's ego became a bit inflated by the surprise mention of his law, he neglected to pursue these matters. The ploy of mentioning Wineman's law was a carefully calculated one by Pelt. Among professional economists, Wineman himself is probably the only one that is acquainted with his law. But, Wineman gives his law prominent mention in the courses he teaches at Brickmire. Pelt knew of the law because his son, Tzvi, had Wineman for a course and Tzvi entertained the family with the law over dinner one night.

Pelt's surprise mention of Wineman's law at the collective bargaining session provides an example of the use of a *diversionary tactic*. The tactic is designed to throw off one's opposite number from pursuing a particular line of questioning. Note that giving honorable mention to Wineman's law was not the first instance of Pelt's use of the diversionary tactic at the collective bargaining session. Recall that Wineman obsessively focused on theory over practical considerations to the point of quipping in a previous negotiation: "Sure, that works well in practice, *but will it work well in theory*." By warmly acknowledging, "Wineman's proposals are *theoretically* sound," Pelt was hoping to send Wineman off into the abstract world of theory and models. Perhaps Wineman would get caught up in the ivory tower world and forget to make demands for the mundane real world that the union members lived in. Pelt's first attempt at a diversionary tactic was a total disaster. It failed to deflect Wineman from the beaten path even momentarily. But, Pelt's second attempt at the diversionary tactic was a resounding success. The prominence Pelt gave Wineman's law so flustered Wineman that Wineman became diverted from pursuing an obvious and compelling line of inquiry.

In evaluating the ethics of using diversionary tactics in a collective bargaining session, one fundamental concern is that the tactic might violate the prohibition against creating a false impression (*geneivat da'at*). The prototype of the *geneivat da'at* personality, in the teaching of the Talmudic sages, was the biblical figure Absalom, son of King David.[27] In the insurrection he engineered to usurp the crown from his father, Absalom used a number of ploys that entailed *geneivat da'at* conduct. Let us review the story of his insurrection and relate his *geneivat da'at* conduct to the ethics of making use of diversionary tactics in a collective bargaining session.

Absalom's plot to usurp the crown from his father, King David, entailed the "deceiving of three hearts."[28] His elaborate scheme began by "deceiving the heart of the men of Israel."[29] With the aim of both undermining King David's system of justice and ingratiating himself with the masses, Absalom mingled with those who sought adjudication of their disputes in King David's court and proclaimed: ". . . see your words are good and right; but there is none of the King's [judges] to hear you . . . Oh, who will appoint me judge in the land, and every man who has a quarrel or suit, will come to me, then I will [surely] do him justice" (2 Samuel 15:3, 4). In the first phase of his plan, Absalom succeeds in generating for himself a massive amount of unwarranted goodwill. His objective was to draw upon this goodwill to support his quest for the crown.

In the next phase of his plot, Absalom deceived the heart of his father, King David, as well as the heart of the Sanhedrin (the Jewish high court).

Absalom approached his father, King David, to receive permission to go to Hebron to fulfill a sacrificial vow he made. King David consented (2 Samuel 15:7, 9), whereupon Absalom maneuvered the king into issuing a royal order for two people of Absalom's choice to accompany him to Hebron. Absalom showed the royal order to separate groups of two, again and again, and thereby amassed an entourage consisting of 200 associates of the Sanhedrin.[30]

In the last phase of his plot, Absalom dispersed spies throughout the tribes of Israel and instructed them: "As soon as you hear the sound of the *shofar* [ram's horn], then you shall say: 'Absalom is King in Hebron'"(2 Samuel 15:10).

Absalom's religious journey to Hebron was the event that launched his public quest to usurp his father's crown. Because Absalom hid his true motive in seeking permission to go to Hebron, he was guilty of lying. Absalom's misconduct violated *geneivat da'at* law as well because his pretext was a duping mechanism to secure what he never would otherwise be given. Had King David known Absalom's primary designs, he would not have granted Absalom permission to go to Hebron. Absalom's plot would have been stillborn.

In a similar vein, Absalom's misuse of the royal order for an entourage violated *geneivat da'at*. Had the individuals who were approached known Absalom's primary motive, they presumably would not have joined him. By making repeated use of the royal order, Absalom created the false impression that the Sanhedrin as an institution supported his quest for the crown. Absalom was therefore guilty of deceiving the heart of the Jewish court.

What emerges from this story is that Absalom employed two variants of *geneivat da'at* conduct to advance his insurrection. In the first stage, he engineered false goodwill among the populace, which he later drew upon to support his insurrection. In the second variety, Absalom induced both his father and the Sanhedrin to take action they certainly would not have taken had they only known the motive behind Absalom's request to them.

It is the second variant of Absalom's *geneivat da'at* conduct that bears directly on the ethics of making use of diversionary tactics in a collective bargaining negotiation. One can, however, discern a fundamental difference between the two modes of conduct. Absalom's conduct is deceitful because he *requests* people to take action they would not otherwise take had they only known the *motive* behind his request. In sharp contrast, Pelt requests no action, instead, he merely *introduces* into the negotiations a *distraction*. It is entirely up to Wineman to react or not react to this distraction. Pelt, on his part, does nothing to keep Wineman from pursuing any line of questioning or agenda. Nothing, therefore, is stopping Wineman from getting back on course.

Within the confines of the bilateral monopoly model, the ability of the players to make use of diversionary tactics should be broad. Consider that the outcome of this negotiation in terms of the distribution of relative gains is up for grabs. The law of *ona'ah*, as discussed earlier, does not apply here. Because neither player has an ethical duty to reveal his reservation price to his opposite number, each player should have latitude to block his opposite number from easy access to telltale signs of what that figure is. As a means of illustrating this point, let us consider the ethics of the following real estate transaction:

Eitan Kramer, the head of a multi-billion dollar real estate development conglomerate, wants to build a Disneyland-like project in Seattle. Realizing that open entry into the real estate market would give away his entrepreneurial intent and enormously bid up the value of the desired parcels of land, Kramer uses several of his less-known subsidiaries to negotiate the real estate deals. Alternatively, Kramer creates a dummy corporation for the purpose of acquiring the desired parcels. With obscurity thereby achieved, Kramer acquires the parcels at relatively low prices.

In evaluating the ethics of Kramer's ploy, consider that Kramer has no ethical duty to make the owners of the real estate parcels as partners in his venture. Accordingly, Kramer bears no duty to volunteer to the owners of the parcels what he intends to do with their land or how important a particular parcel is for his overall plan. Although Kramer bears no duty to *volunteer* this information, if he is directly asked this question he has two options. One option is to respond to the query. If Kramer chooses this option, he must respond in an open and forthright manner. But, Kramer has a right *to refuse to answer* as well. If he chooses to stonewall, the seller will probably conclude that Kramer has in mind a very valuable project and will increase his asking price. What Kramer accomplishes with his ploy of masquerading his true identity is to capture a larger share of the value of his entrepreneurial effort than would have been otherwise possible.

Let us look at the same transaction from the standpoint of the sellers. Given that the landowners have no right to demand to become partners in Kramer's venture, the onus is upon them to probe him as best they can about his entrepreneurial intent. Accordingly, when these landowners are approached by an obscure corporation to buy up their parcels, the onus is upon them to grill the buyer with queries such as: Do you know of any investments made in my land to determine its mineralization? Are you aware of any entrepreneurial project that plans to use my land? Are you a principal or an agent? Are you an independent company or a subsidiary of some other company? Kramer's agent may, of course, refuse to answer these questions. Doing so will signal the landowner to increase his or her asking price. The landowner neglects pursuing these inquiries at his or her own risk. Masquerading his true identity hence does not make Kramer guilty of either deceiving or misleading the landowner. Rather, his ploy only makes it more difficult for them to pick up on information that they are, in any case, not entitled to.

The upshot of this analysis is that within the framework of a collective bargaining setting, each party is entitled to protect his reservation price from discovery by his opposite number. Toward this end, legitimacy would be given to the use of diversionary tactics. The permissible objective for the use of this tactic is to take measures by word or deed that will either deflect one's opposite number from pursuing a particular line of inquiry or make it more difficult for that person to pick up on information that he, in any case, is not entitled to have.

THE BILATERAL MONOPOLY IN THE TORAH

Precedent for the permissibility of using diversionary tactics within the framework of the bilateral monopoly can be found by an analysis of the biblical account of how Jacob acquired the birthright from his brother Esau:

> Once when Jacob was making a stew, Esau came in from the fields famished. Whereupon Esau said to Jacob: "Let me swallow some of that red pottage, for I am famished!" Said Jacob: "First sell me your birthright." Said Esau: "I am about to die; of what use is a birthright to me?" "Said Jacob: "First give me your oath." So he gave him his oath, and sold his birthright to Jacob. Jacob then gave Esau bread and stewed lentils. He ate and drank, then rose and went away. Thus did Esau disdain the birthright. (Genesis 25:29, 34).

A superficial reading of the biblical account of the sale of the birthright leaves the impression that Jacob secured the birthright for a nominal sum by means of exploiting Esau's famished condition. Far from finding fault with Jacob's conduct, the sages defend him. The key to the defense, in the opinion of this writer, is scripture's characterization of Esau's attitude toward the birthright as one of disdain (*ve-yivez et ha-bekhorah*), even after he had relieved his hunger with stewed lentils and bread. What this tells us is that absent his feelings of desperation, Esau would still have regarded the pot of lentils as a fair price for transferring the birthright to his brother Jacob.[31]

In modern economic terminology, *ve-yivez et ha-bekhorah* translates into the thesis that Esau's reservation price for giving up the birthright was very low. The following commentators supply various reasons why Esau's *reservation price* for giving up the birthright was very low:

1. Esau's contempt for the birthright, according to R. Abraham Ibn Ezra (Spain, 1108 ca. 1164), stemmed from his assessment that it entailed no material benefit for him. Since his father, Isaac, was destitute, the double-portion inheritance right of the firstborn offered no prospect of material advantage.[32]

2. Before Sinai, the sole advantage of the firstborn, according to Nahmanides, (Spain, 1194–1270), consisted of inheriting the authority of the father. This conferred the firstborn with honor and distinction

in relation to the younger brothers. Since the birthright carried with it no distinction until after the passing of the father, it had no value to a man like Esau, who was in constant mortal danger from the animals he hunted. His brutal lifestyle convinced him that in all likelihood he would not outlive his father.[33]

3. The value of the birthright, according to R. Solomon b. Isaac (*Rashi*, France, 1040–1105), consisted of the privilege of being the family priest in offering sacrifices to the Almighty. The negotiation between Jacob and Esau focused, according to *Rashi*, around this aspect of the birthright. When Jacob informed Esau of the various stringencies in law surrounding this privilege, Esau regarded it as a burden, exclaiming,

"I am about to die; of what use is a birthright to me?" (Genesis 25:32) "I will surely deserve death on account of it."[34]

Regarding Esau as a wicked man, unworthy of representing the family in offering sacrifices, Jacob eagerly sought to acquire the birthright, thereby preventing Esau from performing the priestly service. Esau's contempt for the birthright made it of little value in his own eyes, but Jacob's keen interest in it created a lucrative commercial opportunity for Esau. Seizing the moment of Esau's famished condition to initiate negotiations for the birthright represented an opportune time for Jacob to secure it. Since Esau intrinsically valued the right as worth no more than a pot of lentils, the tactic amounted to nothing more than a diversionary maneuver. In his weakened state Esau would be quite amenable to thinking of the birthright in terms of his own reservation price for giving it up, rather than in terms of his brother Jacob's reservation price for acquiring it.

Since the birthright could not theoretically be transferred to anyone other than Jacob, the latter's tactic did not deprive Esau of the opportunity to secure a higher price for the right from another party.

Supporting this assertion is R. Ephraim Solomon b. Aaron of Lenczycza's (d. 1619) interpretation of the birthright sale. It was no mere coincidence that upon his return from a hunting expedition, Esau encountered Jacob while the latter was preparing a lentil stew. Rather, Jacob carefully planned this encounter. Noting that lentils are the food of mourners, R. Ephraim suggests that Jacob's intent was to reproach Esau immediately upon his return from his dangerous adventure, in effect saying, "Esau, your brutal style of living will result in imminent death for you. Soon, I will be sitting in mourning for you."[35] Jacob hence used the lentil dish as a device to dramatize for Esau his reckless lifestyle. Jacob's hope was therefore that the lentil dish would drive Esau into an amenable state of mind for the purpose of conducting the sale of the birthright. Instead of fixating on Jacob's *reservation price* for acquiring the birthright, Esau would be satisfied to accept his own *reservation price*, which amounted to nothing more than a pittance.

FALSE DEMANDS

In the opening vignette we find both Pelt and Wineman putting forth a plethora of demands on the bargaining table. Some of these demands are false demands. They were put on the table only for the purpose of increasing the supply of negotiating currency. Wineman, for instance, was prepared all along to pull back the union's demand for expanding the Sabbatical leave privilege as well as the demand for teacher assistants. The same could be said of Pelt's demand for punitive measures against faculty who were delinquent in various ways. Insofar as false demands are not a forthright and sincere statement of what a party to collective bargaining really wants, are these demands a violation of *ahat ba-lev*?

In evaluating the ethics of making false demands at a collective bargaining session, it will be useful to distinguish between two variants of false demands. One variant consists of the false demand that can be described as wishful thinking. The other category is the false demand that serves the purpose of a decoy in respect to what the party really wants. Let us discuss each of these variants in turn.

In the wishful thinking case, the false demand represents something the negotiating party really wants but is prepared to pull back on because there is something else on the table he or she wants even more. Wineman's demand for teaching assistants illustrates this variety of false demand. There can be no doubt that every member of the faculty puts value on this amenity. But, there is no free lunch! A price tag must be put on this benefit and pushing for this benefit is possibly at the expense of getting a smaller raise and a smaller increase in health benefits. It is for this reason that when

push comes to shove, Wineman is prepared to either drop this demand altogether or trade it in for additional concessions in salary and health benefits.
In a similar vein, some portion of the initial 15 percent raise the union
sought is a false demand in the sense that it would be willing to drop it or
trade it away for securing concessions on other items in play. Does the
union's foreknowledge that it can't possibly get everything it puts initially
on the table have the effect of characterizing the package it initially
demands as an *ahat ba-lev* demand? No, because the union really wants
each and every item in the package *at least on the level of wishful thinking*;
therefore, the union's demand cannot be said to be insincere. If the administration can't figure out what the union will bend on and what it will go on
strike for, this does not make the union demands insincere; rather, it signals
the success of the union in hiding its reservation price from the administration. False demands in the form of wishful thinking items hence are a permissible diversionary tactic.

Another variety of false demand entails a demand a negotiating party is
set to pull back even if the other side agrees to it. Here, the false demand
serves as a decoy. The hope is that the opposite party will not pick up on the
decoy nature of the false demand and will make concessions to have the
false demand removed. Pelt's demand to put a block on long-distance calling in the faculty offices provides a case in point. First, Wineman and his
team had no idea what the savings to the university would be to remove this
amenity from the faculty. Pelt, who was privy to the volume of long-distance
calls made by faculty and what the block feature would cost to install, knew
what the savings would be. Pelt thought this out carefully and decided to nip
the idea in the bud on the basis of a cost-benefit analysis. Implementing the
policy would be counterproductive. The cost saving would not outweigh the
annoyance and resentment the faculty would harbor regarding this policy, to
say nothing of the intolerable increase in traffic at the dean's office for legitimate business-related long-distance calls. Pelt decided against the deal,
but threw it in anyway as a false demand for the purpose of increasing the
supply of negotiating currency. Because the university had no plans to
implement the long-distance telephone block even if the union agreed to it,
the demand amounts to *ahat ba-lev* conduct.

The union's demand for expanded Sabbatical leave privileges also
amounted to an *ahat ba-lev* demand. Few faculty members really wanted

this amenity; those that wanted it were the new faculty who were very research oriented. The bulk of the faculty was, however, not into heavy research. Many feared that if the sabbatical leave would be for a full year at full pay, the university would insist on a much higher standard to qualify. Gone would be the days when a faculty member could look forward to a "semester spent in leisure, with some dabbling in scholarship for show." Some feared that the change in policy in regard to sabbatical leave would signal that raises would mainly be based on research rather than on teaching excellence and involvement with students. Because the sabbatical demand was a false demand the faculty was quite content to drop this demand in the eleventh hour and have the university set up a committee to effectively "study the matter to death."

FALSE THREATS

In the opening vignette we find Wineman flatly predicting significant attrition and even possibly a strike if the union demands are not met. In reality, Wineman does not believe that failure to meet the union's demands will result in the dire consequences he claims. Reacting to Pelt's proposal with a threat of a strike amounts, therefore, to no more than a bluff on the part of Wineman.

Bluffing conduct violates the imperative in Halakhah that requires an individual who makes a commitment to do so in good faith.[36]

A mitigating factor here is that in the context of collective bargaining negotiation, the threat of a strike by the union is commonplace. Because the threat of a strike is so commonly used, management often does not take the threat at face value. Instead, the threat conveys to them that a temporary impasse has been reached, and what happens next will be a "test of wills" situation. Who will blink first?

If the above-described mitigating factor is valid, two varieties of bluff can be identified. One variety is the bluff that deceives. Illustrating this variant is the instance where Pelt takes Wineman's false threat to strike at face value. Wineman's bluff here violates the imperative to deal in good faith. The second variety of bluff is the transparent bluff. This bluff entails no deception and is understood as no more than a notice to one's opposite number that talks have reached an impasse and a "test of wills" has commenced. In this variant, *the imperative to deal in good faith* is not violated. The crucial question then becomes when does a false threat become transparent and hence permissible on account of the implicit message that it transmits? Given the propensity of man to solve moral dilemmas in his own favor, the self-assessment of the one who wants to make use of the false threat is certainly not reliable.

In searching for a criterion on what constitutes a permissible bluff, an appropriate model is the law of vows (*nedarim*). The imperative to deal in good faith and the law of vows share a crucial feature: Both require that the commitment of the heart must conform to what the mouth articulates. When this conformity is not in place, the speaker is not conducting himself in good faith. In the realm of vows, if this condition, which is called *piv ve-lebo shavim* (literally, his mouth and heart are the same), is not in place, the vow does not take effect.[37]

Vows come in two varieties. In one variety the vow impacts only on the speaker and no one else. In a second variety, the vow impacts on others.

In the first category of vow, the mere declaration on the part of the speaker that he did not intend to say what he actually articulated is sufficient to prevent the vow from ever getting off the ground. To illustrate, suppose *A* prohibits himself, by means of a vow, from eating wheat bread. Subsequent to making the vow, *A* tells us that he meant to prohibit on himself barley bread, but accidentally blurted out wheat bread. Because *piv ve-lebo* is lacking here, the vow takes effect in respect to neither wheat nor barley bread.[38]

When the vow impacts on others, the speaker cannot knock out the vow by simply declaring, "What I meant I didn't say" or "What I said I didn't mean." When the vow impacts on others, the meaning of the words one utters takes on an objective meaning. Investigation of the *piv ve-lebo* condition as it relates to vows of motivation (*nidrei zeiriezin*) will clarify this matter. *Nidrei zeiriezin* will provide us with a criterion as to when a bluff should be regarded as transparent and hence permissible.

Suppose a seller (*S*) and a buyer (*B*) are locked in a price negotiation. *S* asks a *sela* (4 *dinars*) for his article. *B* counters with an offer of a *shekel* (2 *dinars*). Upon hearing *B*'s bid, *S* proclaims "If I accept anything less than a *sela* for this item, the money you pay me for it shall be forbidden to me as a *konem* (consecrated animal)." *B* then counters "If I pay you anything more than a *shekel* for this item the item should become forbidden to me as a *konem.*" The sages see in this dialogue no more than business parlance. Accordingly, though each party fortified his negotiating position by means of a vow, the vows are not regarded as a result of firm resolution. Because the vows lack legal force, the deal may be concluded at three *dinars* and the money *S* acquires and the item *B* receives is not forbidden to them. The permissibility of the item and the money to the respective parties does not require the parties to resort to *hatarat nedarim* (the absolution process).[39] *Tosafot* and others point out that common business practice makes the intention of the parties clear-cut. Far from communicating intransigence, as his formulation appears to indicate, *S* merely wants to put *B* on notice that they are now locked in "a contest of wills." *B's* intentions are similarly interpreted. Though non-verbalized thoughts are usually of no account in Halakhah, *S's* and *B's* non-verbalized thoughts regarding their intentions are universally understood. Anyone hearing the vows would interpret each party's intentions to consist merely of forewarning his opposite number to adopt a more flexible position.[40]

Though *nidrei zeiriezin* are not legally binding, an individual is prohibited to utter such a vow. This lesson is exegetically derived from the verse "He shall not break (*yahel*) his word" (Numbers: 30:3), i.e., he shall not make profane (*hullin*) his own words.[41]

What proceeds from this discussion is that, other than in the language of *nidrei zeiriezin*, the face value of language does not automatically convey a commitment on the part of the speaker. If the context in which the words were uttered objectively indicates that no commitment was meant, the verbal utterance generates no consequences for the speaker.

Before drawing implications from *nidrei zeiriezin* when false threats can be regarded as transparent and hence permissible, let's demonstrate that the ambit of this case is extremely narrow.

Most crucial is that what makes the words of the vow void is not just *S's* and *B's* stating that they meant no vow, but rather, the circumstance that everyone else also picks up on this and understands that *B* and *S* meant no vow with their declarations. Remove this universality element, and we must take *B's* and *S's* declarations at face value, despite their protestations to the contrary.

The delicate underpinning of vows of motivation can be seen by taking note of a variant case put forward by Ravina in the Talmud. Suppose S declares to B: "If I accept anything less than a *sela* and a *perutah* [the smallest denomination coin] the money I receive from you for this item will be prohibited to me as a *konem*." Upon hearing this, B declares: "If I offer anything more than a *shekel* less a *perutah*, the item I acquire from you will be prohibited to me as a *konem*." Whether the ambit of vows of motivation expands to include Ravina's case is a question that remains unresolved in the Talmud.[42] R. Nissim b. Reuben Gerondi (Barcelona, ca. 1290–ca. 1375) offers two explanations of what is at issue in Ravina's variant. One possibility is that vows of motivation don't apply when the parties go to the trouble to formulate their declarations in specific and precise terms. This is the case when S goes to the trouble of saying a *sela* and a *perutah* and B goes the trouble of saying more than a *shekel* less a *perutah*. Another possibility is that when the differences between the parties expand to *more* than four[43] *dinars*, the vows made must be taken seriously.[44] Commenting on Ravina's query, R. Joshua b. Alexander ha-Kohen Falk (Poland, 1555–1614) picks up on R. Nissim's second explanation and puts the matter in percentage terms: Consider, he tells us, that the usual commercial practice is for both B and S to put forward opening positions that are as much as 25 percent off what their final positions would be. Because the vows B and S make diverge more than 25 percent from a three-dinar settlement, we must presume B and S were serious on the level of making a vow not to settle at 3 *dinars*.[45]

Let us take note of another caveat for the *nidrei zeiriezin* case offered by R. Moshe Sofer (Hungary, 1762–1839). In his view, the liberty of B and S to conclude their negotiation at a price other than the original positions they vowed not to depart from exists only if they fortified their original position by means of a vow. But, if they fortified their original positions by means of an *oath*, the oath they made binds them to their original positions. If they want to relent, they can do so only by having their oaths absolved. Fortifying one's initial position by invoking the name of God communicates seriousness beyond the usual commercial talk. Consequently, the claim that the intent of nonabsolute intransigence was universally understood is rejected. Here, what each party thought in their heart is handled in the usual manner as "the nonverbalized thoughts of the heart," which have no halakhic or moral significance.[46]

Let us now draw the implications of the *piv ve-lebo shavim* rule for a criterion as to when a false threat becomes transparent and therefore permissible. If a false threat is legitimate it is only because it is *universally* understood not as a promise to take specific action, but rather as an urgent admonishment to one's opposite number to show flexibility and accommodation. Preliminarily, let us take note that the current legal environment that governs collective bargaining negotiations creates an expectation for "good faith" bargaining on the part of the negotiating partners. Within the current legal environment for collective bargaining, a number of scenarios can be identified where the universality assumption stands on shaky grounds. These are situations where one of the parties makes use of a stratagem that calls in to question whether he is bargaining in "good faith."

In the United States, the Wagner Act, as amended by the Taft Hartley Act, governs the standards of conduct for labor and management at the bargaining table. Over the years the National Labor Relations Board (NLRB) interpretation of these standards has created strict guidelines to ensure that both sides are engaged in a good faith effort to secure agreement. Let us consider two specific modes of conduct that the NLRB has ruled as breaching its good faith imperative and relate them to the ethics of making false threats.

Providing an example of a "bad faith" tactic is the Supreme Court's ruling against the collective bargaining stratagem the General Electric Corporation utilized in the 1950s and 1960s.[47] Referred to as Boulwarism,[48] G.E's strategy was twofold. First, the company thoroughly researched the market conditions and its ability to pay, and on this basis formulated its opening bargaining position to the union. In a break with tradition, this position was also the company's final position. The company would make no concessions unless the union would present new information not available to General Electric when they formulated their proposal.

The second aspect of the strategy was to apply G.E,'s considerable experience in marketing its products to selling the agreement directly to the rank and file union members.

The Union filed a series of unfair labor practice charges against General Electric, and eventually succeeded in convincing the NLRB and the courts that General Electric was not bargaining in good faith.[49]

In its ruling, the court did not outlaw the "take it or leave it" approach per se. What the court held was that an employer may not combine "take it or leave it" bargaining methods with a widely publicized stance of unbending firmness.[50]

Let us now relate the court ruling against Boulwarism to our case study. Pelt and Wineman are locked in a negotiation. Pelt tenaciously refuses to budge from his initial position. Notwithstanding the significant gap, Wineman feels that Pelt's initial offer is livable, and if he had to he could squeak it through the membership. But, why accept it so easily? It's only the first offer. In the hope of getting a slightly better deal, is it permissible for Wineman to bluff and predict that the union will go out on strike rather than accept the offer? No. Wineman's bluff here is in no way transparent. Given that Pelt may be moving dangerously down the road of the prohibited conduct of Boulwarism, the objective onlooker expects labor to react in a combative manner, and not in a manner that signals that the agreement is in hand and the only issue is who will get a slightly better deal. Because the response to what appears to be Boulwarism should be either to threaten the filing of a "bad faith" bargaining complaint or to threaten a strike, the universality condition is clearly missing. Wineman's threat of a strike will therefore not be understood as a bluff that conveys no more than that a test of wills will follow. Wineman's false threat here is hence not transparent and therefore violates the good faith imperative.

Another scenario where the universality condition fails entails the following elements: Pelt rejects Wineman's proposal on the grounds of inability to pay, but steadfastly refuses to substantiate his "plea of poverty" by producing financial data. Wineman finds Pelt's approach very distasteful, but believes the offer on the table would, in any case, pass muster with the union. In Wineman's mind, however, the show of some toughness at this juncture in the negotiations might work to nudge out a slightly better deal. To this end, Wineman, in a voice that expresses outrage, bluffs Pelt with a threat of a strike if the university doesn't come through with a better offer. Because Pelt's stratagem of stonewalling Wineman's request for financial data characterizes his tactic as bargaining in bad faith,[51] an objective observer might very well understand Wineman's strike threat to mean nothing less than a work stoppage. Given that the universality condition fails here, the threat of a strike as a bluffing tactic cannot be countenanced here. The use of a bluff in this context will hence find no legitimacy from the model of *nidrei zeiriezin*.

EXAGGERATION

In the opening vignette we find Wineman making dire predictions regarding the consequences the university could expect if the "pay gap" is not narrowed. Wineman makes his predictions without factual basis. Instead, his predictions are based on how the "economic man" generally reacts to differentials in the reward system. In Wineman's mind, the faculty at Brickmire *should* react to the pay gap in the manner he describes. In short, Wineman takes general economic theory to describe *reality* at Brickmire. Wineman's statements raise the issue of the legitimate use of hyperbole.

One fundamental point in formulating Halakhah's attitude toward the ethics of exaggeration is that a distinction must be drawn between pernicious and innocent exaggeration.

R. Israel Meir ha-Kohen Kagan (Radin, 1838–1933) addresses the issue of pernicious exaggeration in the context of his classical exposition on the prohibition to make an evil but true report (*lashon ha-ra*) about a fellow. In R. Kagan's teaching, it is generally permissible for A to make an evil report to B about C if A's intention is to save B from harm. R. Kagan attaches many caveats before the prohibition of *lashon ha-ra* is suspended. One caveat is that A may not exaggerate the evil conduct that is the subject of his report. Exaggeration, R. Kagan tells us, is an aspect of falsehood and it falls under the prohibition against slander (*motzi shem ra*). This can be seen by the Talmud's understanding of the case of the husband who falsely accuses his wife of adultery (Deuteronomy (22:13–18): The husband (H) produces two witnesses, W_1 and W_2, who state that his spouse (S) committed adultery. The testimony of the witnesses, if it stands, will put S to death. Two other witnesses, W_3 and W_4, come forward and testify that at the time W_1 and W_2 claim that the adultery took place they were with them at a different location. In this scenario the Torah gives credibility to W_3 and W_4 over W_1 and W_2. S is hence exonerated. In consequence, it is now evident that H slandered S. His punishments consist of lashes, a fine of 100 *sela*, and the removal of a right to divorce his wife against her will.[52] Suppose W_3 and W_4 add in their testimony that S had indeed had relations with a man but it happened when she was single. Notwithstanding that the sexual crime she committed before she was married to H was of the severity that she was liable to *karet* (divine punishment through premature death), the prescribed punishments for H remain intact. Consider that in the final analysis, the court has evidence before it that *S* was guilty of serious sexual misconduct. Instead of being guilty of a capital crime, she was guilty of *karet*. What this shows, points out R. Kagan, is that *motzi shem ra* is slander even when it amounts to not a total falsehood but only an *exaggeration* of prohibited conduct. R. Kagan applies this lesson to the laws of *lashon ha-ra*: The prohibition against *lashon ha-ra* is not suspended when the report exaggerates the evil the perpetrator intends, notwithstanding that the motive of the speaker is to prevent harm.[53]

R. Kagan's thesis regarding the prohibition against exaggeration stands in sharp contrast to R. Ammi's dictum at *Hullin* 90b. Here, R. Ammi observes that *divrei havaee* (inaccurate speech) is utilized by the Torah, the prophets, and the sages. The use of *divrei havaee* in the holy sphere puts the stamp of legitimacy on this type of speech.

R. Kagan's thesis is readily reconcilable with R. Ammi's dictum. What is prohibited is *pernicious* exaggeration. R. Ammi, however, speaks of exaggeration that generates harm to no one. The matter is not closed. Consider R. Kagan's statement that exaggeration is a form of falsehood. Ordinarily, in the absence of special warrant, falsehood is prohibited speech even when it is innocent and generates harm to no one. If *divrei havaee* is *absolutely permissible speech*, there must be something about it that separates it from the vanilla variety of innocent falsehood. *Rashi's* definition of *divrei havaee* identifies the distinctive factor we are looking for. In Rashi's view, *divrei havaee* is the speech employed by ordinary people. It entails a misstatement, but the misstatement is not the result of a deliberate attempt to lie, but rather the result of imprecision.[54]

Examination of the specific examples of *divrei havaee* that R. Ammi cites add further refinement to both the parameters of and limits to inaccurate speech. With the aim of discovering a common denominator in the instances of *divrei havaee* that R. Ammi identifies, let us take a look at the specific examples R. Ammi cites.

Let us begin with the use of *divrei havaee* by the sages. In connection with the Temple service, R. Ammi cites a number of inaccurate statements. One such instance is the statement in the *Mishnah* that the ash-heap on top of the altar at times reached 300 *Kor*. Commenting on this dictum, Raba avers that it is an exaggeration, as this weight exceeded the capacity of the altar.

Divrei havaee by the prophets is illustrated by one of the descriptions Jeremiah[55] makes of the coronation of King Solomon. He tells us: "And all the people came up after him and the people played the flutes and rejoiced with great joy, and the earth was split by their sound" (1 Kings1:44). Now, the description that "the earth was split by their sound" must be an exaggeration, as the sounds of the rejoicing, although loud, certainly did not actually split the earth.

Finally, the use of *divrei havaee* in the Torah is illustrated by the difference in the report the scouts made to Moses regarding the Land of *Cana'an* and the review of that report Moses made to the Jewish people 39 years later. In the original report, the scouts reported to Moses: "However, the nation is mighty, those who inhabit the land and the *cities are greatly fortified*, and we saw the offspring of the giant over there (Numbers 13:28). In his address of reproof to the Jewish people 39 years later, Moses refers to that report and says: "Where are we going up to? Our brothers have shattered our hopes by saying, 'A people greater and more powerful than we, cities *great and fortified to the heaven*, and also descendants of the Anakim-did we see there'" (Deuteronomy1: 28). By ascribing to the scouts the description of the cities of the *Cana'an* as *"fortified to the heaven,"* when they actually said only *"greatly fortified,"* Moses was apparently exaggerating the evil report the scouts issued thirty-nine years before.

The common denominator of the aforementioned expressions of *divrei havaee* is that the basic reality that each expression is rooted in is preserved and is still fully recognized. What each expression does is no more than embellish or heighten the reality that it is rooted in.

Let us begin with the statement that the weight of the ash-heap on the altar reached, at times, as much as 300 *Kor*. Although the actual weight never reached 300 *Kor*, the accumulation was in any case, at times, massive. Accordingly, the exaggeration does not distort reality, but only embellishes it. Likewise, Jeremiah's use of the expression that the "earth was split by the sound" does not pervert what actually happened at King Solomon's coronation. To be sure, the sounds of the people's joy did not "split the earth," but the jubilation did generate a tremendous sound. Jeremiah's description hence does not distort what actually happened, it only embellishes it.

Our criterion for *divrei havaee* apparently does not work in rationalizing the alteration Moses made in reviewing the report of the scouts. Consider that there is a qualitative difference between *"greatly fortified"* and *"forti-fied up to the heaven."* The latter conveys impregnability, whereas the former does not. R. Ephraim Solomon b. Aaron of Lenczycza, however, brings these phrases together. To be sure, Numbers 13:28, *out of context*, does not convey the same thing as does the phrase at Deuteronomy 1:28. But to understand what the scouts meant to convey with their phrase *"greatly fortified"* we need to consider this phrase within the context of their entire report. Taken as a whole, the scouts report was that the conquest of the land of *Cana'an* is impossible. The key phrase in their report is: "But the men who went up with him (Caleiv) said 'we are not able to go up against the nation, for they are more powerful than *(mimenu)*.'" (Numbers 13:28). The word *mimenu* can mean either *him or we*. The sages tell us "do not read it as meaning 'than we,'[56] but rather as meaning 'than Him.'—They were saying, as it were,—that even the Householder (i.e. the Master of the World) cannot remove his utensils from there." The scouts hence blasphemed against God. Given the blasphemous intentions of the scouts, Moses took license to report that the scouts described the cities of the land of *Cana'an* as *fortified up to the heaven*, even though the actual phrase they used was *"fortified greatly."*[57]

Recall that Rashi defined *divrei havaee* as a misstatement that is rooted in inattention to precision rather than in a deliberate attempt to mischaracterize. R. Ephraim's exposition is at odds with Rashi's definition of *divrei havaee*, at least as it relates to Moses's alteration of the report of the scouts.

Let us now put R. Ephraim's understanding of the meaning of *"fortified up to the heaven"* in the context of the license one has to engage in *divrei havaee*. What the license consists of is the right to summarize a report. To be sure some degree of accuracy is always lost in a summary. But, provided a good faith effort is made to avoid distortion, making a summary does not violate Halakhah's standards for truth telling.

Let us now relate these parameters for *divrei havaee* to the dire consequences Wineman predicted would ensue if the "pay gap" was not significantly narrowed. Now, if Wineman knows as a fact that some of the faculty at Brickmire are actively on the job market or are making tentative plans for moonlighting pending the outcome of the talks, then the predictions he makes about attrition and productivity are firmly rooted in a *reality* at Brickmire. In this scenario, Wineman's predictions merely embellish or heighten a reality. What he does is merely formulate a *reality* into *an extrap-olation for the future*. Wineman's conduct is hence a permissible exercise of his license to engage in *divrei havaee*. But, the fact is that none of the predictions Wineman makes are rooted in any reality other than in a model of how the economic man *should generally* react to differences in the reward system of the marketplace. The model may have no relevancy or predictive value for the particular situation at Brickmire. Predicting from the top of one's head dire consequences of increased attrition and productivity setbacks amounts to the mouthing of possible lies. Uttering comments with full knowledge that the statement may not be true violates Halakhah's standards for truth telling.[58]

TRUTH TELLING IN CRISIS NEGOTIATION

Let us now turn to a consideration of the standard for truth telling in a crisis situation involving negotiation with a hostage taker. Consider the James Harvey case:

> In February 1988, James Harvey held a classroom of children hostage in Tuscaloosa, Alabama. As conditions for his surrender, Harvey demanded and got a videotaped pardon by Governor Guy Hunt and the promise that he would be permitted a news conference to air publicly his grievances concerning social ills. Law enforcement officials deceived Harvey in respect to the news conference. The pardon was also later rescinded.
>
> Harvey was subsequently convicted and was given a life sentence. Interviewed while in prison, Harvey's deep resentment was evident by his statement, "you cannot trust the government because they lie."
>
> In addition, the broken promises perpetrated upon James Harvey were aired publicly during news coverage of the incident and a subsequent television documentary.[59]

The basic ethical issue the Harvey scenario raises is whether it is ethical to secure the release of the hostages by means of lies.

One possible approach here is to take the position that by committing the immoral act of taking hostages, Harvey *forfeits* any right to expect truthful information. In his treatment of the issue of truth telling in a hostage situation, Martin Golding points out that the Roman philosopher Cicero took this approach more than 2000 years ago:

> Suppose that one does not deliver the amount agreed upon with pirates as the price of one's life, that would be counted no deception—not even if one should fail to deliver the amount after having sworn to do so; for a pirate is not included in the number of lawful enemies, but is the common foe of all the world; and with him there ought not to be any pledged word or oath mutually binding.[60]

The *forfeiture* approach can apparently find support in Halakhah in the treatment of a worker who threatens to walk out of his or her job. Workers are classified into two categories. If a worker hires himself out for fixed hours he or she is called a *po'el* (P). If the worker is paid for the completed job he or she is called a *kabbelan*.[61] Ordinarily, by dint of Torah law P has a right to withdraw without penalty from his contract to work.[62] Let us illustrate the nature of this right by means of an arithmetic example:

Employer E hires P_1 to work for him for eight hours at $10 an hour. At the end of four hours P_1 tells E that he is quitting. At this juncture the wage rate has gone up to $15 an hour. Hiring a replacement worker, P_2, requires E to expend an additional $60 to complete the job. Because P has a right to withdraw from work without penalty, P is entitled to the entire $40 prorated wages he earned up to the point of his withdrawal, and is not docked $20 to compensate E for the *extra cost* resulting from his withdrawal.[63]

P's retraction right is not recognized when leaving the work scene will generate a material loss to E. This circumstance is referred to as the *davar ha-avud* case.

An example of *davar ha-avud*, cited in the Talmud, is the hiring of a worker to remove flax from its steeping. If the task is not performed immediately, E will suffer material loss. Another example is the hiring of a worker to bring litter-carriers and pipers to a wedding ceremony. Since the litter-carriers and pipers are sent with the purpose of enhancing the ceremony, delay in their dispatch will defeat the purpose of the sender because they will arrive after the ceremony is already over.[64]

In the *davar ha-avud* case, E has the right to cajole the reneging P to stay on the job by offering him a raise. If the tactic succeeds, the employer bears no responsibility to make good on his promise for a raise. Moreover, if *P* demands the extra fee up front, the differential pay is recoverable in a *Bet Din* (Jewish court). This tactic is referred to as *mat'an* (literally, he deceives them).[65]

Standing behind the *mat'an* principle is apparently the notion that because *P* acted unethically he loses his right to expect truthful information. Apparently understanding the *mat'an* principle in this manner, R. Nahum Yavruv offers the following Talmudic passage at *Megillah* 13b as the underpinning of this principle:

And what was the modesty exhibited by Rachel? i.e., where do we see that she displayed modesty? For it is written: "And Jacob told Rachel that he was the brother of her father (Genesis 29:12)." Now, was [Jacob] really the brother of her father? Was he not rather the son of Rebecca, her father's sister? Rather, this is what transpired: He said to [Rachel], "Will you marry me?" She answered him, "Yes, However, I must warn you that father is a deceiver—and you will not be able to outwit him." He said to her; "I am his brother in deceit," i.e., I am a match for him. This was what Jacob meant when he told Rachel "that he was the brother of her father." [Rachel] then asked him "Are the righteous permitted to act deceitfully?" He answered her: "Yes, they are, when others are trying to deceive them, as it is written: 'With a pure person you act purely and with a crooked person you act crookedly (11 Samuel 22:27).'" [Jacob] asked her, "What deceit would he use against me?" She answered him: "I have a sister, Leah, who is older than I, and [my father] will not marry me off before he marries her off. He will therefore try to trick you into marrying her instead of me." To prevent this from occurring, [Jacob] gave [Rachel] signs, i.e., passwords, through which he would be able to identify her as Rachel, thereby preventing Laban from substituting Leah for Rachel. When the wedding night arrived, and Rachel saw that her father was indeed planning on secretly substituting Leah for her, she said to herself, "Now my sister will be put to shame, for Jacob will ask her for the passwords and she will not know them." She therefore conveyed [the prearranged signs] to her [Leah] And thus it is written: "And it came to pass in the morning, and behold, it was Leah" (Genesis 29:25). Is this to imply that until now [in the morning] it was not Leah? Certainly not! Rather, through the pre-arranged signs that Rachel conveyed to Leah, [Jacob] did not know until now [in the morning] that it was Leah and not Rachel. Therefore, because Rachel acted modestly, she merited that the modest Saul descended from her.

R. Yavruv's proposition that *mat'an* is rooted in II Samuel 22:27 can be put to question. Consider that on the basis of Rachel warning to Jacob that her father, Laban, was a deceiver, Jacob did no more than adopt *defensive measures* against expected duplicity on the part of Laban to subvert their marriage plans. One aspect of these measures, as the above Talmudic passage records, was the secret codes he devised with Rachel to foil any attempt on the part of Laban to substitute Leah for Rachel. But, perhaps, the most fundamental defensive measure Jacob took was the manner in which he formulated his marriage proposal to Laban: "I will work for you seven years, for Rachel your younger daughter" (Genesis 29:18). Jacob's proposal appears somewhat verbose. Since Jacob was speaking directly to Laban, it would have been sufficient for him to say, "I will work for you seven years for *Rachel*." Why, then, did Jacob formulate his proposal . . . *"for Rachel your younger daughter."* Addressing this difficulty Genesis Rabbah 70:17 makes the following comment:

Said he [Jacob] to him [Laban]: "Knowing that the people of your town are deceivers, I make my demands absolutely clear." Thus: And He said: 'I will serve you seven years for Rachel your younger daughter. *For Rachel*, not for Leah; *your daughter*–you are not to bring some other woman from the market place named Rachel; *younger*—you are not to exchange their names.'" But even if you fix a wicked man in a carpenter's vice, it will avail you naught.

Given that Jacob took only defensive measures against Laban, the inference to be drawn is that "with a crooked person you act crookedly" is no more than *pragmatic advice* to conduct oneself in a guarded fashion when dealing with the wicked. The verse does not, however, confer a general license to relax any ethical standards in dealing with the wicked. If the situation at hand permits the relaxation of a particular ethical norm, it will find its basis in a source other than 2 Samuel 22:27.

Bolstering this understanding of "with a crooked person you act crookedly" is Jacob's dealings with Laban in the economic sphere: Laban offers to pay Jacob a wage for tending his sheep: "Specify your wage to me and I will give it" (Genesis 30:28). In response, Jacob proposes that Laban should remove from the herd he tended for him all the spotted and mottled lambs, leaving in Jacob's care only the single-colored lambs. Jacob proposes that his wage should consist of the mottled and spotted sheep that will be born from the single-colored herd. Notwithstanding that Jacob formulated his wage in precise terms, Laban unilaterally changed the definition of "speckled and spotted" no less than ten times in five years (Genesis 31:7). Now, if "with a crooked person you act crookedly" is a license to use deceit to retrieve from the wicked person what is lawfully ours, why did Jacob allow Laban to unilaterally change his wage five times in ten years? Jacob should have stopped the unethical conduct by showing Laban that he (Jacob) is Laban's brother in the craft of deceit. If 2 Samuel 22:27 teaches that the wicked are subject to the forfeiture principle, it surely is nowhere evident in Jacob's dealings with Laban.

Two options present themselves in explaining why Jacob did not act more assertively and aggressively against Laban. One possibility is that Jacob chose not to make use of all his rights inherent in "with a crooked person you act crookedly." Alternatively, this verse teaches no *general license* to relax our ethical standards in dealings with the wicked. Instead, the verse imparts only pragmatic advice to put up our guard in dealing with the wicked. In his dealings with Laban, Jacob, on a selective basis, availed himself of this advice. What follows is that there is no solid basis for claiming that *mat'an* is rooted in 2 Samuel 22:27.

Another reason for rejecting the forfeiture principle as the basis of *mat'an* is that falsehood is prohibited even when it causes no harm.[66] This stringency, as R. Dov Berish Gottlieb (Poland, mid eighteenth century) points out, proceeds from an analysis of the wording employed in the biblical source of the prohibition: " Distance yourself from a false word" (Exodus 23:7). Instead of prohibiting the *speaking* of false *speech*, the Torah bids us to *distance* ourselves from a false *word*. The phraseology *distance* and *word* imparts that a lie is prohibited even if it does not deceive and it causes no harm.[67]

The aforementioned points to the need to find an alternate ethical basis for *mat'an*. We suggest that the basis for *mat'an* is the dictum of *avid inish dina l'nafshai* (a man may take the law into his own hands for the protection of his interests; henceforth, *avid inish*).

The ambit of this legal principle is a matter of dispute between Rav Nahman and Rav Yehudah.[68] Resorting to self-help instead of suing a defendant in court is, of course, legitimate only if plaintiff has solid objective proof to substantiate his claim. The plaintiff's subjective certainty alone does not give him an *avid inish* license. Following Rav Nahman's line, decisors extend *avid inish* to even the instance where the plaintiff would suffer no loss if he or she would sue the defendant in court instead of resorting to self-help.[69] In the instance where thief T tries to steal some object from owner O by wresting it away from him, *avid inish* allows O, according to all disputants, to thwart T's designs. If all persuasion and pleading fail, O's *avid inish* license allows him, according to R. Asher b. Jehiel (Germany, 1250–1327), to even assault T to prevent him from taking his property.[70] R. Jehiel Michel Epstein (Belarus, 1829–1908), however, would not empower O to assault T even as a last recourse unless O assesses that he would incur an irretrievable loss if he would sue T in *Bet Din* instead of resorting to self-help.[71]

The *mat'an* case is very much analogous to the case where T tries to steal something from O by wresting the object from him. Consider that in the *davar ha-avud* job, it is unethical for P to quit before completing the job. Though no one can be forced to work against his will,[72] P will be responsible for E's losses.[73] Suppose E's pleadings with P to stay on the job or to make good on his loss fail. Suppose further that E assesses that suing P in *Bet Din* instead of resorting to self-help will subject him to the risk that the debt owed him will be uncollectible.[74] What it boils down to for E is either *mat'an* or resorting to violence against P. What should E do? *Mat'an* is surely preferable. To be sure, *avid inish* does not give one a license to *fabricate* evidence to support his claim. This amounts to the use of an outright lie.[75] But, *mat'an* is not an outright lie. This is so because under the *avid inish* rule, E, if summoned by P, must submit to a judicial review of what he did.[76] What this implies is that under *avid inish* E has no right to make a false promise to P unless he all along commits himself, if summoned by P, to have his action reviewed by a *Bet Din* and abide by whatever decision they make. Because *E* fully intends to actually give *P* the raise he promised him if *Bet Din* subsequently orders it, the promise he makes to *P* stands on higher moral ground compared to the ordinary bluff.

If the forfeiture principle does not proceed from II Samuel 22:27, then the *preferred* way to induce Harvey to release his hostages is to use only instruments of truth, such as persuasion. What countenances the use of lies, if necessary, is the judgment that our duty to save the hostages overrides our ethical duty not to be guilty of lies. Let us make this case. By holding the children hostage at gunpoint, Harvey puts himself in the category of a *rodef* (one who pursues another with the intent to kill). To extricate the children from danger, any bystander is obligated to intervene, even at the cost of taking Harvey's life.[77] But, becoming a *rodef* does not put Harvey's life in absolute forfeit, as the rescue must be made by means of inflicting the least possible harm to Harvey. If it is evident that a bystander could have neutralized the threat Harvey presented with minimal force, but instead killed him, the bystander is guilty of a capital offense.[78] The logical extension of the least harm principle is that securing the release of the hostages by means of a lie is preferable to securing their release by means of violence.

Consider also that the use of lies prevents the outbreak of violence between society and Harvey. The *darkhei shalom* principle should therefore provide another basis for the permissible use of lies as a means of securing the release of the hostages.

CONSIDERING THE LONG-TERM IMPACT

The issue of truth telling in crisis negotiation is complicated by consideration of the long-term impact the use of lies has on the credibility of law enforcement officials. Psychologist Harvey Schlossberg warns: "Remember, tomorrow's hostage-taker is watching today's news report."[79]

In formulating public policy, Halakhah takes into account the long-term impact of alternative courses of action. A case in point is the monetary limits the sages set for redeeming captives. In this regard the *Mishna* states: Captives should not be redeemed for more than their value.[80] The basis for this restriction is discussed in the Talmud. Two alternative rationales are offered. One possibility is that the concern is that the burden on the community should not become excessively onerous. Another possibility is that the restriction was set so as not to encourage the bandits to increase their efforts on this front.[81] Maimonides and others take the second rationale as controlling and generally prohibit a victim's family from acceding to excessive demands, even though no funds are solicited from the community or taken from the public purse.[82] Analogously, if *carte blanche* were given to crisis negotiators to employ lies, if necessary, the prospects for successful negotiation in future crises would be undermined.

What this dilemma points to is a need to train crisis negotiators to minimize the use of lies in their work. Francis V. Burke, Jr., a hostage-crisis negotiator with the Gloucester County New Jersey Critical Incident Team, advocates this position. Burke notes that ignoring the statements and bizarre demands of a hostage taker is sometimes an effective response.[83]

The aforementioned points to a difference in the training program and preparation of a labor negotiator versus a crisis negotiator.

The essential feature of a collective bargaining negotiation is that both sides are involved in a perfectly legitimate enterprise. Relating this point to the opening vignette, we can say that Pelt and Wineman each have the right to seek an outcome that will be maximally satisfying to the groups they represent. Neither Pelt nor Wineman has a right to enter the bargaining session with the attitude that his opposite number is holding onto some property right that was *stolen from him* and the use of any means to wrest it away is fair game. Because each side is involved in a legitimate enterprise, each must operate under the assumption that the outcome will be arrived at by means of the production of facts and figures and the artful use of leverage and persuasion. Coming into the session with prepared lies and deception with the aim of springing them loose when and if circumstances warrant is illegitimate. Such a stratagem amounts to a deliberate plan to use deception to achieve monetary gain. Irrespective of whether the plan is actually implemented or if its use is halakhically valid, the fact remains that the training, readiness, and preparation to use lies and deceptions *acclimates* one to lie and therefore debilitates the character. This stratagem should be prohibited on the basis of "They have taught their tongue to speak lies. . . ." (Jeremiah 9:4). If lies and deception have any legitimacy in a collective bargaining session it would only be as a *spontaneous* reaction to the situation at hand, with the motive being to avert a strike.

The situation is entirely different in the setting of a crisis negotiation.

Consider that by virtue of committing the crime of holding people against their will at gunpoint, the hostage taker has lost his *hezkat kashrut* (presumption of righteousness). Given that they are negotiating with a miscreant, law enforcement officials must understand that the crisis will not always be diffused exclusively by peaceful means and instruments of truth. It is for this reason that the team at hand is trained in rescue operations. But, a rescue operation is fraught with extreme danger to life. Because lying is always preferable to the loss of life, part of the training for crisis negotiators must be the artful use of deception and lying.

Once it is recognized that training in the artful use of lies is an integral part of the training and preparation for crisis negotiators, steps must be taken to ensure that these professionals don't subconsciously become habituated to engaging in deception outside of discharging their professional duties. The concern that the character of crisis negotiators should not become tainted is intensified when one considers that these individuals are heroic figures and will be regarded as role models. What is therefore indicated is that a program of moral education should also be an integral part of the professional training of crisis negotiators.

SUMMARY AND CONCLUSION

In searching for the standard for truth telling in a commercial transaction, perhaps the key element to focus on is the disclosure obligations of the parties conducting the transaction. Collective bargaining is essentially a bilateral monopoly model. The distribution of the relative gains will depend upon the leverage and skill the negotiating parties bring with them to the bargaining table. Neither side is obligated to divulge his reservation price. Because neither party is entitled to know each other's reservation price, legitimacy would be given for either to make use of diversionary tactics as a means of preventing discovery of their reservation prices. To be legitimate, the diversionary tactic must not mislead, but only introduce a distraction or detour. Because the choice of either refusing to go on the detour or traveling along it but returning on point is within the reasonable capacity of the opposite number at the negotiating table, the tactic is not a form of deception.

Illustrating the permissible use of the diversionary tactic is a false demand that can be characterized as wishful thinking. The essential feature of this type of demand is that the item is something the negotiating party *really wants* but is prepared to use as *trading currency* to get something that it wants even more. The wishful thinking false demand can take the form of either an inflated demand or a demand the negotiating party is prepared to drop entirely in exchange for some other concession or because it decides that it has already bargained for the best possible deal.

Another variety of false demand entails a demand a negotiating party is set to pull back even if the other side agrees to it. Here, the false demand serves as a decoy. The hope is that the opposite side will not pick up on the decoy nature of the false demand and will make concessions to have the false demand removed by the other side. This type of false demand amounts to a violation of *ahat ba-lev* conduct.

Exaggerations and hyperbole fall into two categories. When the exaggeration distorts, it is prohibited speech and falls into the rubric of falsehood. When the exaggeration is, however, firmly rooted in a reality but merely embellishes that reality, it is permitted speech.

Our investigation has shown that the use of a false threat is legitimate only if it is objectively evident that the threat is false and hence the opposite number is not misled as he also does not take it at face value.

The most crucial aspect of this chapter dealt with the application of the *darhei shalom* dictum to the setting of collective bargaining. Consider that if negotiations reach an impasse, a lie on the part of one side may avert a strike and bring on a settlement. Because the lie promotes peace, it should be permissible on the basis of *darkhei shalom*. Many caveats were, however, noted. The import of these caveats is to both bar the use of certain tactics in collective bargaining negotiations and set guideposts for the preparation of these talks.

Darkhei shalom has much to say on the preparations for the collective bargaining session. The notion that a negotiator should come into the bargaining session with *prepared lies*, of the nondetectable variety, and be in a state of readiness to spring these lies on the opposition when the situation is ripe is an attitude Halakhah would find very distasteful. Making the art of deception part of the preparation one brings into the bargaining table works only to *habituate* one in lying. Another reason to be concerned with the training and preparation the negotiator goes through is that there is no *darkhei shalom* license for someone who is infatuated with lying. Accordingly, if success as a negotiator is to some degree predicated on the *honing* of the skill of artful lying, the practitioner faces the long-term danger that his profession will develop for him "an acquired taste" for lying.

What is minimally necessary to meet Halakhah's standard is that the schooling and training of negotiators should not include advance preparation for lying and deception. Within the framework of this attitude and approach, if negotiations threaten to break down and one of the protagonists *spontaneously* comes up with a nondetectable lie to save the day, his success will not habituate him to lie.

Our investigation has found that the widest discretion to engage in deception as a means of promoting an end occurs in a crisis negotiation seeking the release of hostages. Consider that by virtue of committing the crime of holding people against their will at gunpoint, the hostage taker, from the standpoint of Halakhah, loses his *hezkat kashrut*. Does the hostage taker forfeit thereby his right to have people speak to him truthfully? No. Irrespective of the fact that the hostage taker has no spiritual worthiness, those seeking to diffuse the crisis enjoy no *carte blanche* right to lie to the hostage taker. Accordingly, the *preferred* way out of the crisis is persuasion and the use of instruments of truth.

Notwithstanding that the immoral act of taking hostages does not forfeit for the hostage taker the right to expect truthful information, there can be no doubt that our duty to save the hostages overrides our ethical duty not to be guilty of lies. The act of taking hostages puts the hostage taker in the category of *rodef*. To extricate the would-be victims from danger, any bystander is obligated to intervene, even at the cost of taking the hostage taker's life. But, becoming a *rodef* does not put the perpetrator's life in absolute forfeit, as the rescue must be made by means of inflicting the least possible harm to him. If it is evident that a bystander could have neutralized the threat the perpetrator presented with minimal force, but instead killed him, the bystander is guilty of a capital offense. The logical extension of the least harm principle is that securing the release of the hostages by means of a lie is preferable to securing their release by means of violence.

Consider also that the use of lies prevents the outbreak of violence between society and the perpetrator. The *darkhei shalom* principle should therefore provide another basis for the permissible use of lies as a means of securing the release of the hostages.

The issue of truth telling in crisis negotiation is complicated by consideration of the long-term impact the use of lies has on the credibility of law enforcement officials. If *carte blanche* were given to crises negotiators to employ lies, if necessary, the prospects for successful negotiation in future crisis would be undermined. What this consideration points to is that hostage negotiators should be trained to minimize the use of lies in their work.

Recognition that the hostage negotiator is dealing with a man that has lost his *hezkat kashrut* points to the proposition that the artful use of deception must be an integral part of the training and preparation for crisis negotiators. Because training in deception and its not infrequent use in crisis intervention *habituate* the practitioner to engage in deception outside the permitted circumstances, measures to counteract the debilitating impact on character are necessary. What this points to is that moral education must be an integral part of both the training and the professional enrichment of the crisis negotiator.

POSTPRANDIUM

PROBLEM

Massachusetts law prohibits an employer from asking an applicant questions concerning any admission to a facility for the care and treatment of mentally ill persons. In connection with his application for an appointment as a Boston police officer, Martin Kraft falsely failed to disclose, as the form required, that on five occasions between April 1976 and March 1978 he had voluntarily been a patient receiving psychological treatment in Veteran's Administration Hospital.

In March of 1983, Kraft was appointed a police officer. He completed his one-year probationary term and served the next several years with an unblemished record, including various commendations. In June of 1988, the Boston police department terminated Kraft "for the stated reason that Kraft had failed to disclose his hospital admissions in his sworn answers to the department's application questions."

In its review of the case, the Supreme Court of Massachusetts ruled that the police commissioner had no authority to discharge Kraft for giving false answers to questions that the commissioner had no right to ask under law. Accordingly, the Court stated that Martin Kraft should be reinstated with back pay and damages for emotional distress.[84]

The case was no fluke. In many other cases, lawyers succeeded in advancing the notion that if a question is improper, a job applicant needn't answer it truthfully. As one commentator, Walter Olson, put it: "If the question is improper, the job applicant has a right to lie about it.[85]

NOTES

1. Rava, *Bava Metzia* 50b; R. Isaac b. Jacob Alfasi (Algeria, 1012–1103, *Rif* ad locum; Maimonides (Egypt, 1135–1204), *Yad, Mekhirah* 12:1–4; R. Asher b. Jehiel (Germany, 1250–1327), *Rosh, Bava Metzia* 4:15; R. Jacob b. Asher (Spain, 1270–1343), *Tur, Hoshen Mishpat* 227; R. Joseph Caro (Israel, 1488–1575), *Shulhan Arukh, Hoshen Mishpat* 227:1–6; R. Jehiel Michel Epstein (Belarus, 1829–1908), *Arukh ha-Shulhan, Hoshen Mishpat* 227:1–6.
2. Leviticus 25:14.
3. See *Yad*, op. cit., 13:15–19.
4. For the development of this thesis, see Aaron Levine, *Economic Public Policy and Jewish Law* (Hoboken, NJ: Ktav Publishing, Yeshiva University Press, 1993), pp. 40–48.
5. *Mishnah, Ketubbot* 13:7; *Bava Metzia* 58b. For the development of this thesis, see Aaron Levine, "Ona'ah and the Operation of the Modern Marketplace," *Jewish Law Annual*, Hebrew University, vol. XIV, 2003, pp. 225–258.
6. *Yevamot* 65b.
7. R. Nathan, *Yevamot* ad loc.
8. R. Israel Meir ha-Kohen Kagan (Radin, 1838–1933), *Hafetz Hayyim, Hilkhot Rekhilot* 1:8.
9. R. Nahum Yavruv, *Niv Sefatayyim*, 3rd edition, *helek alef*, pp. 27–29.
10. *Niv Sefatayyim*, op. cit., *helek alef*, p. 40, *ot* 25.
11. R. Judah b. Samuel he-Hasid, *Sefer Hassidim* 426. R. Abraham Abele b. Hayyim ha-Levi Gombiner (Poland, ca. 1637–1683, *Magan Avraham, Sh Ar. Orah Hayyim* 156) and R. Mosheh Sofer (Hungary, 1762–1839, *Hatam Sofer* 6:59) follow R. Judah b. Samuel he-Hasid's line.
12. *Niv Sefatayyim*, op. cit., *helek alef*, p. 41.
13. Maimonides, *Yad, Gezeilah ve-Aveidah* 14:13.
14. *Niv Sefatayyim*, op. cit., *helek alef*, p. 28.
15. R. Solomon b. Jehiel Luria, *Yam Shel Shelomoh, Yevamot* 6:46.
16. *Niv Sifatayyim*, op. cit., *helek alef*, p. 34.
17. R. Jonah b. Abraham Gerondi, *Sha'arei Teshuvah* 3: 178–186.
18. *Niv Sefatayyim*, op. cit., *helek alef*, p. 38, *helek bet*, Chapter 12, p. 30.
19. Genesis Rabbah 37:4.
20. *Sanhedrin* 27b.
21. *Sanhedrin* 110a; *Tanhuma* 10.

22 *Sifre*i, Numbers *piska* 161.

23. *Sota* 41b and R Menahem b. Solomon Meiri (France, 1249–1316) *Beit ha-Behirah* ad locum; R. Eliezer b. Samuel (Metz, 1115–1198), *Yere'im ha-Shalem* 248; R. Jonah b. Abraham Gerondi, *Shar'arei Teshuvah* 3:187.

24. R. Ephraim Solomon b. Aaron of Lenczycza, *Keli Yakar* at Numbers 35:33.

25. R. Hayyim Hezekiah Medini, *Sedei Hemed* vol. 2 , p. 447, *k'lal* 140.

26. *Hullin* 94a. For a discussion of various nuances of the law of *geneivat da'at* see pp. 8–17, 389–391 of this volume.

27. *Mishnah Sotah* 1:8.

28. Loc. cit.

29. II Samuel 15:6.

30. Jerusalem Talmud *Sotah* 1:8.

31. Support for this thesis can be found in the introductory words of Nahmanides in his commentary at Genesis 25:34.

32. R. Abraham Ibn Ezra, *Ibn Ezra*, Genesis 25:34. Nahmanies, ad locum, strenuously objects to R. Abraham Ibn Ezra's pauperization of Isaac. Nahmanides avers that Isaac, along with the other Patriarchs, was an individual of prodigious wealth. The double-portion right of the firstborn was, however, not instituted until the Sinaitic Covenant.

33. Nahmanides, *Ramban*, Genesis 25:34.

34. R. Solomon b. Isaac, *Rashi*, Genesis 25:32.

35. R. Ephraim Solomon b. Aaron Lenczycza, *Keli Yakar*, Genesis 25:34.

36. For the derivation of the imperative to deal in "good faith" please turn to pp. 152–154, 395–396 of this volume.

37. *Shavuot* 26b; *Rif*, ad loc; *Yad, Nedarim* 2:2; *Rosh, Shavuot* 3:14; *Tur, Yoreh De'ah* 210; *Sh. Ar., Yoreh De'ah* 210:1.

38. Ibid.

39. *Nedarim* 21a; *Rif*, ad locum; *Yad, Nedarim* 4:3; *Rosh, Nedarim* 3:1; *Tur*, op. cit. 232; *Sh. Ar.*, op. cit. 232:1–2. Given the negotiating intent of both buyer and seller, some authorities take the view that the respective vows are not legally binding even in regard to the original positions that prompted the vows. Hence, the buyer would not be prohibited by force of his vow from settling and concluding the deal at the initial four *dinar* asking price of the seller. Similarly, the seller's vow would not prohibit him from concluding the transaction at the initial two *dinar* bid of the buyer. Other authorities regard the vows as legally not binding only in respect to some compromise sum. By force of these vows, each party, however, would be prohibited from concluding the transaction at the opening price of his opposite number. (See R. Nissim b. Reuben Gerondi (Spain, 1310–1375), *Ran, Nedarim* 21a and R. Mosheh Isserles (Poland, 1525 or 1530–1572), *Rema, Sh. Ar. Yoreh De'ah* 232:2.) R. Joel Sirkes (Poland, 1561–1650, *Bah, Tur*, loc. cit.) point out that common practice is in accordance with the lenient view.

40. *Tosafot, Nedarim* 20b; R. Yom Tov Ishbili (Spain, 1270–1342), *Ritba, Nedarim* 20b.

41. *Tosefta, Nedarim* 4:4; *Yad*, op. cit., 4:4; *Tur*, op. cit., 232; *Sh. Ar.*, op. cit., 232:13.

42. *Nedarim* 21a.

43. In *Ran's* version of the text, *S* declares to *B* "I will not give it to you for less than a *sela* and a *dinar*, i.e. five *dinars*)." At the same time *B* declares to *S*: "I will pay no more than less a *shekel* (i.e., one *dinar*)." The difference between *S* and *B*, in R. Nissim's understanding, is hence four *dinars*. See, however, R. Solomon b. Isaac, *Rashi, Nedarim* 21a.

44. R. Nissim b. Reuben Gerondi, *Ran, Nedarim* 21a.
45. R. Joshua b. Alexander ha-Kohen Falk, *Perishah, Tur, Yoreh De'ah* 232, note 6.
46. R. Mosheh Sofer, *Hiddushei Hatam Sofer, Nedarim* 21b.
47. *NLRB v. General Electric Company*, 418F. 2nd 736 (1969).
48. Boulwarism takes its name from Lemuel Boulware, who was a GE vice-president and chief architect of the strategy.
49. *National Labor Relations Board v. General Electric Company* 418F 2d 736 (1969).
50. E. Edward Herman, Joshua L. Schwartz & Alfred Kuhn, *Collective Bargaining and Labor Relations, 3rd Ed.*, (Englewood Cliffs, NJ: Prentice Hall, 1992), pp. 207–209; *National Labor Relations Board v. General Electric Company* 418 F2d 736 (1969).
51. The Supreme Court has stated that when an employer claims financial inability to pay as the reason for not accepting a union proposal a duty arises to provide financial data to substantiate that claim. See *NLRB v. Truitt Mfg.*, 351 U.S. 149 (1956), at 152–153.
52. These penalties apply only when the husband initiated his slander case against his wife when she was between twelve and twelve and a half and the accusation of adultery is claimed by the husband to have occurred in the same time frame. See *Yad, Na'arah Betullah* 3:1–12. It should be noted that since the ordinance by R. Gershom b. Judah Me'Or ha-Golah (France, ca. 960–1040) no woman can be divorced against her will.
53. R. Israel Meir ha-Kohen Kagan, *Hilkhot Lashon ha-Ra, Mekor Hayyim K'lal* 10, 2 and *Be'ar Mayyim Hayyim* ad locum, *ot* 9.
54. R. Solomon b. Isaac, *Rashi, Hullin* 90b.
55. The Talmud (*Bava Batra* 14b) notes that Jeremiah the prophet authored the Book of Kings. It was incorporated into the Holy Scriptures by the men of the Great Assembly.
56. The key to understanding why the sages reject reading into *mimenu* the meaning "than we," according to R. Judah Loew Bezalel (Bohemia, ca. 1525–1609, *Gur Aryeh*, Numbers 13:31), is the spies' declaration: ". . . [W]e were like grasshoppers in our eyes, and so we were in their eyes!" This assessment tells us that the spies regarded the inhabitants of *Cana'an* as not just stronger than them in a comparative sense, but superior in a qualitative sense. Given that the phrase *mimenu* speaks no more than of comparative strength and says nothing about qualitative superiority, the comparison inherent in *mimenu* cannot be between the inhabitants of *Cana'an* and the nation of Israel. Instead, *mimenu* must be taken to mean "than He" and therefore is a statement of apostasy.
57. R. Ephraim Solomon b. Aaron of Lenczycza, *Keli Yakar*, Numbers 13:27.
58. R. Nahum Yavruv (Israel, contemp.), *Niv Sefatayyim*, 3rd ed., *helek alef*, p. 14.
59. Francis V. Burke, Jr. "Lying During Crisis Negotiations: A Costly Means To Expedient Resolution," *Criminal Justice Ethics*, Winter–Spring 1995 vol. 14, no. 1, pp. 49–62.
60. Martin Golding, "Agreements with Hostage-Takers," in *Hobbes: War Among Nations*, (Timo Airaksinen & Martin A. Bertman, eds., (Brookfield, VT; Avebury Publishers, 1989), p. 154.
61. R. Meir b. Barukh (Rothenburg, 1215–1293), Responsa *Maharam* 477; R. Isaac b. Moses (Vienna, ca. 1180–1250), *Or Zaru'a* 3, *Bava Metzia, piska* 242; R. Meir ha-Kohen (end of 13th cent.), *Haggahot Maimuniyyot, Sekhirut* 9:4; R. Jekuthiel Asher Zalman Zausmir (d. 1858), Responsa *Mahariaz, siman* 15, *amud* 14, *tur* 1.
62. *Bava Metzia* 10a; *Rif, Bava Metzia* 77b; *Yad, Sekhirut* 9:4; *Rosh*, op. cit., 6:6; *Tur*, op. cit., 332:2; *Sh. Ar.*, op. cit., 333:3; *Ar. ha-Sh.*, op. cit., 333:6.
63. *Yad*, op. cit.; *Tur*, op. cit., 333:4 *Sh. Ar.*, op. cit. 333:4; *Ar. ha-Sh.*, op. cit. 333:16. How

P_1's right to withdraw works itself out if the wage rate went down is a matter of dispute. In this scenario, P_1, according to R. Jacob b. Asher (*ad loc.*), is entitled to collect more than his prorated wage for the time he actually put in. Let us use the example in the text to illustrate this: Suppose the wage rate went down to $5 an hour. The cost to hire P_2 to complete the job is hence only $20. Since E agreed to pay P_1 $80 for an eight-hour work day and P_2 is paid only $20, P_1 is entitled to wages of $60. Disputing R. Jacob, R. Shabbetai b. Meir ha-Kohen (Poland, 1621–1662, *Siftei Kohen, Sh. Ar.*, loc. cit., n. 19) finds no basis to allow P_1 to parlay his withdrawal right into a profit. In his view, P_1's entitlement here is no more than what he would get if the wage rate went up, and hence P_1 is due only $40. R. Aryeh Loeb Joseph ha-Kohen (Poland, 1745–1813) rules in accordance with R. Jacob b. Asher's view (*Ketzot ha-Hoshen, Sh. Ar.*, op. cit., n. 8).

The right to withdraw without penalty was not given to a worker who is paid for the finished product and is not required to work at fixed hours. This type of worker is called a *kabbelan*. Accordingly, in the illustration of the text, if the wage rate went up to $20 an hour, the *kabbelan* faces a penalty of $20 and has his earnings reduced to $20. (See sources cited in the beginning of this footnote.)

64. *Bava Metzia* 77b; *Rif*, ad locum; *Yad*, op. cit., *Rosh*, op. cit., *Tur*, op. cit., 333; *Sh. Ar.*, op. cit., 333:18; *Ar. ha-Sh.*, op. cit., 333:18–24.

65. *Mishna, Bava Metzia* 6:1; *Rosh*, op. cit.; *Yad*, op cit.; *Tur*, op. cit., *Sh. Ar.*, op. cit; *Ar. ha-Sh.*, op. cit., 333:19.

66. R. Jonah b. Abraham Gerondi, *Sha'arei Teshuvah* 3:4,9; R. Israel Meir ha-Kohen Kagan, *Sefat Tamim*, chapter 6; R. Abraham Isaiah Karelitz (Israel, 1878–1953), 4:13.

67. R. Dov Berish Gottlieb, *Yad ha-Ketanah, De'ot* 10 *ot alef.*

68. *Bava Kamma* 27b.

69. *Bava Kamma* 27b; R. Isaac b. Jacob Alfasi, *Rif, Bava Kamma* 27b; Maimonides, *Yad, Sanhedrin* 2:12; R. Asher b. Jehiel, *Rosh, Bava Kamma* 3:3; R. Jacob b. Asher, *Tur, Hoshen Mishpat* 4; R. Joseph Caro, *Sh. Ar., Hoshen Mishpat* 4:1; R. Jehiel Michel Epstein, *Ar. ha-Sh., Hoshen Mishpat* 4:1.

70. *Rosh*, loc. cit. See Shimshon Etinger, *Self Help in Jewish Law (Hebrew)*, Thesis submitted for the degree Doctor of Law, Hebrew University of Jerusalem, June, 1982, p. 68, n. 14.

71. *Ar. ha-Sh.*, loc. cit., 4:1.

72. See sources cited by Shillem Warhaftig, *Dinei Avodah ba-Mishpat ha-Ivri*, vol. 1 (Jerusalem: Moreshet, 1968), pp. 123–131.

73. R. Mosheh Isserles, *Rema, Sh. Ar. Hoshen Mishpat* 333:6.

74. The Talmud (*Bava Metzia* 83a) relates that Rabbah b. Bar Hanna hired porters to transport wine barrels for him. Due to their negligence the workers broke the wine barrels, causing a loss for Rabbah b. Bar Hannan. Rabbah b. Bar Hannan felt he had a legitimate damage claim against the porters, but Rav told him that, as a matter of pious conduct, he should forego the damage claim and even pay the porters for the time they spent on the job.

In rationalizing Rav's ruling, R. Mosheh Feinstein assumes that the workers would not have the ability to pay the debt they owed Rabbah b. Bar Hannan. Because the debt they owed him was an abstract debt with no prospects of eventual payment, it would be a matter of pious conduct on the part of Rabbah b. Bar Hannan to relieve the porters of the psychological burden of the debt they owed him and waive his rights in the matter

(*Iggerot Mosheh Hoshen Mishpat* 1:60). Implicit in R. Feinstein's analysis is that in Talmudic times, it would not be an easy matter to collect on a damage claim against a worker. The difficulty arises out of the presumed impoverished state the worker would be in. What follows is that in the *davar ha-avud* case, E has the right to presume that collecting on his damage claim will be unlikely. Suing P in *Bet Din* instead of resorting to self-help will result in an irretrievable loss for E. Resorting to self-help as a means of preventing the harm in the first place is hence for E a legitimate application of *avid inish*.

75. R. Solomon b. Abraham Adret (Spain, c. 1235–1310), Responsa *Rashba* 3:81.
76. *Yad*, loc. cit.; *Tur*, loc. cit.
77. *Mishnah, Sanhedrin* 8:7; *Rif*, ad locum; *Yad, Rotzeah* 1:7; *Rosh, Sanhedrin* 8:1; *Tur*, op. cit., 425; *Sh. Ar.*, op. cit., 425:1; *Ar. ha-Sh.*, op. cit., 425:5.
78. *Baraita, Sanhedrin* 74a; *Yad*, op. cit.; *Rosh*, op. cit., 8:2; *Tur*, op. cit.; *Sh. Ar.*, op. cit.; *Ar. ha-Sh.*, op. cit., 425:6.
79. Francis V. Burke Jr., "Lying During Crisis Negotiations: A Costly Means to Expedient Resolution," *Criminal Justice Ethics*, Winter-Spring 1995, p. 53.
80. *Mishnah, Gittin* 4:6.
81. *Gittin* 45a.
82. *Yad, Mattenot Aniyyim* 8:12; *Tur, Yoreh De'ah*, op. cit.; *Sh. Ar., Yoreh De'ah*, op. cit.; *Ar. ha-Sh.* 252:4.
83. Burke, op. cit., p. 54.
84. 410 Mass. 155, 571 N.E.; 1991.
85. Walter Olson, *The Excuse Factory* (New York: Martin Kessler Books, 1997), p. 17.

II. Fair Competition

3

Goldfarb's 15-Year Turf War

In this chapter our focus is on the extent to which Halakhah protects a firm from the competitive pressures of the marketplace. For purposes of analytical simplicity, we use as our model the protection Halakhah affords an incumbent firm from the competitive pressures of a new entrant. Through a case study, we will show that Halakhah espouses rules of "fair competition" for the marketplace. For Halakhah, maximizing consumer welfare by adopting rules to ensure that the product or service involved is produced at the lowest possible social cost is not the only criterion for governance of the marketplace. We will then contrast the approaches of Halakhah and American law protecting an established firm from the competitive pressures of new entrants.

INTRODUCTION

In 1985 Donald Goldfarb established a kosher grocery store in Plainville, a small town in the Northeast. In the early years of its business, Goldfarb's store was the only one in town that carried various lines of kosher food. Over a 15-year period, Goldfarb tenaciously sought to block new entrants from opening competing stores in the local area. As soon as he became aware of a potential competitor, Goldfarb swiftly solicited the local *Bet Din* (Jewish court) to enjoin the new entrant. In some of the skirmishes Goldfarb proved victorious. In others, *Bet Din* ruled against him. But, in 2000, Goldfarb

95

suffered a very painful defeat. The court decision was so devastating that it practically sounded the death knell for his business.

In dealing with these disputes, *Bet Din*, as you shall see, articulated various halakhic norms for "fair competition" in the marketplace. Beyond specific prescriptions for conduct, *Bet Din* articulated the philosophy that a firm is entitled, at least for a limited time, to protection against ruination of the kind that it is powerless to counteract. The following Talmudic discussions provide the background for the philosophical position the *Bet Din* adopted:

> R. Huna [d. 296] said: If a resident of an alley sets up a hand mill and another resident of the alley wants to set up one next to him, the first has the right to stop him, because he can say to him "You are interfering with my livelihood."
>
> R. Huna b. Joshua said: It is quite clear to me that the resident of one town can prevent the resident of another town [from establishing a competing outlet in his town]—not, however if he pays the poll tax to that town—and that the resident of an alley cannot prevent another resident of the same alley [from establishing a competing outlet in his alley]. R. Huna b. Joshua then raised the question: Can the resident of one alley prevent the resident of another [from competing with him]?— This question remains unresolved.[1]

Talmudic decisors rule in accordance with R. Huna b. Joshua's view.[2] What follows from this advocacy of freedom of entry is that an established firm is entitled to protection against intrusion into its territory only when the potential entrant is an out-of-town tradesman who does not pay taxes in the complainant's town. Given the unresolved entry status of a resident of a different alley, the Jewish court would not enjoin him from entering the complainant's alley.[3] (Rabbinical courts in Israel today have understood the modern "neighborhood" to correspond to the Talmudic "alley").[4]

THE DEPRIVATION-GENERATING CRITERION

Although R. Huna's protectionist philosophy is apparently rejected, several rishonic[5] rulings indicate that his view is not entirely discarded. R. Eliezer

b. Joel ha-Levi of Bonn (1140–1225) confers monopoly status to a store located at the extreme end of a closed alley. Allowing another firm to locate immediately in front of the established firm would effectively ruin the livelihood of the original competitor because passersby would be blocked from seeing it and would take all their business to the new entrant.[6]

Commenting on R. Eliezer b. Joel ha-Levi's ruling, R. Mosheh Isserles (*Rema*, Poland, 1525 or 1530–1572) suggests that whenever the expected impact of a competitive tactic is to financially ruin an established rival, the tactic must be disallowed in accordance with the protectionist philosophy of R. Huna. Price cutting that an established firm cannot match without undergoing financial ruin is, according to R. Isserles, analogous to R. Eliezer b. Joel ha-Levi's closed-alley case.[7]

Another Rishon following a protectionist philosophy is R. Joseph Ibn MiGash (1077–1141). His protectionist advocacy is clearly seen by his comments on the following Talmudic passage at *Bava Batra* 21b:

> May we say that this view [R. Huna's] is supported by the following: Fishing nets must be kept away from [the hiding place of] a fish [which has been spotted by another fisherman] the full length of the fish's swim! And how much is this? Rabbah son of R. Huna [d. 322] says: A parasang?—Fish are different because they look about [for food].

Why a fisherman is conferred a territorial preserve while a tradesman is not similarly treated is explained by R. Joseph Ibn MiGash as follows: A fisherman's design to capture a large fish he sights is effectively frustrated when another fisherman places his net between this fish's hiding place and the bait. The second fisherman's action has the effect of intercepting the swarm of little fish that surround the large fish. Insofar as the large fish will change direction as soon as he notices that the small fish have been caught, the action of the intruder effectively deprives the first fisherman of his catch.[8]

R. Joseph Ibn MiGash's understanding of the fisherman case leads to the proposition that Halakhah would protect an established firm from a new entrant when the effect of the new entrant would be to ruin the established firm. R. Joseph Ibn MiGash appears, therefore, to follow the same line as R. Isserles and R. Eliezer b. Joel ha-Levi.

The aforementioned leads R. Mosheh Sofer (Hungary, 1762–1839) to reconcile the dispute between R. Huna and R. Huna b. Joshua: R. Huna's protectionist philosophy is restricted to instances where the effect of the new entry would ruin, not merely reduce, the livelihood of the established firm. The free-entry advocacy of R. Huna b. Joshua, on the other hand, is confined to instances where the effect of the new entry would be merely to reduce the profit margin of the entrenched competitor and not deprive him of his livelihood entirely.[9]

The complainant's wealth level and the number of sources of his livelihood are, according to R. Mosheh Sofer, irrelevant in considering the merits of a ruinous-competition case. To qualify for judicial intervention, a complainant need only demonstrate that a particular source of his livelihood is cut off as a result of his competitor's action.[10]

Concurring with R. Sofer's deprivation-generating criterion, R. Mosheh Feinstein (New York, 1895–1986) would enjoin a new entrant whenever the expected result is to reduce the earnings of the owner of the incumbent firm below the mean earnings of his socioeconomic peer group.[11] Deprivation, in R. Feinstein's formulation, is hence not associated with below-subsistence earnings. A complainant, depending upon his socioeconomic status, may aspire for protection of an earnings floor above the margin of subsistence.

R. Feinstein's approach to ruinous competition is akin to an opportunity-cost formulation. This is so because what drives an individual to abandon his current livelihood pursuits in favor of something else is not the fall of his earnings below subsistence, but rather the conviction that he will do better by pursuing a new enterprise. Since maintaining the earnings of one's socioeconomic peer group is what it takes to retain one's status in society, a fall in earnings below this level drives an individual to seek alternative employment as a means of keeping his place in society. Accordingly, let us formulate the distinction between deprivation of livelihood and reduction of earnings in opportunity-cost terms: Provided the competitive tactic does not entirely ruin a rival's particular source of income, the court will not enjoin a business initiative unless the complainant's livelihood, as a result, is driven below his opportunity-cost earnings. Here, the direct impact of the rival's initiative is to force the complainant to withdraw from his present enterprise. The complainant's protectionist plea would, however, be rejected when it is assessed that he can maintain his opportunity-cost earnings within the framework of the new competitive environment.

SUSPENSION OF PROTECTION WHEN THE COMPLAINANT CAN BECOME MORE EFFICIENT

Protecting a competitor's opportunity-cost earnings in no way guarantees that the subject product or service will be produced at its lowest possible social cost. The Torah's notion of the rules of fair competition hence clashes with the criterion of efficiency. This conflict is, however, somewhat lessened by the consideration that the complainant's protectionist plea is rejected when the means are objectively available to him to counter his rival's initiative and thereby maintain his opportunity-cost earnings. This point emerges from the following Talmudic passage:

> Said Ravina [d. 422] to Rava [d. 352]: May we say that R. Huna adopts the same principle as R. Judah? For we have learnt: R. Judah says that a shopkeeper should not give presents of parched corn and nuts to children, because he thus entices them to come back to him. The sages, however, allow this!—You may even say that he is in agreement with the sages also. For the ground on which the sages allowed the shopkeeper to do this was because he can say to his rival: "Just as I make presents of nuts so you can make presents of prunes;" but in this case they would agree that the first man can say to the other: "You are interfering with my livelihood."[12]

Given the permissibility of business promotional activities in Jewish law, in accordance with the sages' view,[13] the import of the Talmud's question, "May we say that R. Huna adopts the same principle as R. Judah?" is that R. Huna's protectionist philosophy is rooted in R. Judah's minority view and should therefore be rejected. What follows is that the distinction the Talmud draws in its rejoinder between ability to counter a rival's initiative and inability to do so is critical in rationalizing R. Huna's protectionist philosophy. To qualify for protection against a competitive tactic, a complainant must demonstrate to the court's satisfaction that it is not within his means to counter the tactic without falling below his opportunity-cost earnings.

Within this framework, the court would deny a complainant protection whenever it assessed that it was within his means to reduce cost by improving the efficiency of his operation. To illustrate, suppose M_1 and M_2 are rival leather-bag manufacturers. M_1 sells at a profit but his price falls below M_2's per unit cost. Examination of their respective enterprises reveals, however, that M_1's operation is much more efficient than M_2's. Whereas M_2 tolerates sloth on the production line, M_1 does not. Similarly, M_2's cutting technique wastes relatively more leather than the technique M_1 employs. Since it is within M_2's means to modify his operation and reduce costs, he is not entitled to price protection.

THE FREEDOM OF ENTRY SCHOOL

Another school of thought in Jewish law conceptualizes fair competition in terms that call for much less insulation from unpleasantness of competition than proceeds from the deprivation-generating rule. The Anti-protectionist School views the dispute between R. Huna and R. Huna b. Joshua as irreconcilable and rules in accordance with the free-entry advocacy of R. Huna b. Joshua.

What follows is a sampling of the anti-protectionist school. We begin with the restraint of trade case dealt with by R. Hayyim Halberstam (Sanz, 1793–1876).

In that case two wool farmers, W_1 and W_2, secured a written agreement with the garment manufacturers of the area that they would buy their wool only from them. All the garment manufacturers were non-Jewish. After fifteen of the garment manufacturers broke loose from the restraint of trade agreement by petitioning the secular courts, the remaining wool producers were emboldened to petition R. Halberstam to void W_1's and W_2's restraint of trade agreement on the grounds that the contract financially ruined the business of the remaining wool farmers.

R. Halberstam refused to void the restraint of trade agreement. In issuing his ruling, R. Halberstam insisted that the circumstance that a competitive tactic exerts a ruinous impact on rival firms is not a basis to restrain that tactic. Protection against ruinous competition proceeds only from the protectionist position R. Eliezer b. Joel ha-Levi took in the closed alley case. But the majority opinion, avers R. Halberstam, rejects R. Eliezer b. Joel's approach.

Another mitigating factor in the previous case, avers R. Halberstam, is that W_1 and W_2 did not take action to void an existing contract the other wool farmers had with the garment manufacturers. Quite to the contrary, no contracts existed at the time W_1 and W_2 secured their restraint of trade agreement. Consider that W_1 and W_2 have every right to sell their entire output and are under no obligation to hold back on the quantity of wool they sell so that other wool farmers could also earn a livelihood. Now, suppose the quantity of wool W_1 and W_2 have available to sell meets the entire market demand for wool; no restraint on their sales would be ordered in order to ensure that the other wool farmers not be ruined. Accordingly, there should be no objection for W_1 and W_2 to take the initiative and negotiate a restraint of trade agreement with the garment manufacturers, even though the effect of this agreement is to exert a ruinous impact on the other wool farmers. Just as the ingenuity of W_1 and W_2 secured an advantage for themselves, the other wool farmers could have come up with some other contrivance to secure the same kind of advantage.[14]

Representative of the anti-protectionist school in the modern era is R. Mordecai Yaakov Breisch (Israel, 1895–1977). R. Breisch's anti-protectionist stance emerges from his handling of the following complaint by the owners of a luncheonette: On the basis of the promises of patronage from the students and staff of a Yeshiva, S_1 opened a luncheonette outside the institution. For a period of three years, two partners earned a livelihood from this business. At this juncture, S_2, who sold tea and sweets inside the study hall of the yeshiva during this period, decided to expand his business to include many of the food items available in the luncheonette. S_1 complained that the availability of the same food items in the study hall makes it inevitable that the Yeshiva students would switch their patronage to the in-house vendor because eating lunch without leaving the walls of the study hall minimizes idleness from Torah study. S_1 hence complained that the impact of S_2 on their business would be ruinous.

In his analysis of the opposing views, R. Breisch notes *inter alia* that the plaintiff's claim of ruinous competition need not be accepted as fact. Given that the students have permission to leave the study hall at lunch hour, it may well turn out that the competition of the inside vendor will not be so severe as to drive the luncheonette out of business. With its customer base no longer taken for granted, the luncheonette will be forced to differentiate its product offering from that of the in-house vendors to enable it to survive commercially. In any case, competition will, in all likelihood, benefit consumers by forcing each firm to do what it can to attract customers.

More fundamentally, even if we accept S_1's claim at face value, S_2 cannot be prevented from competing with S_1. R. Breisch's approach is to collect the opinions that appear to espouse the position that a firm is entitled to protection against ruinous competition and show that each of those views is a minority view.

R. Breisch begins with the protectionist stance R. Eliezer b. Joel ha-Levi adopts in the closed alley case. The mainstream view, according to R. Breisch, rejects R. Joel ha-Levi's ruling.

Similarly, R. Joseph Ibn MiGash's explanation of the preserve rights of fishermen must be regarded as expressing a minority viewpoint since it is not in conformity with the mainstream interpretation of this right offered by R. Solomon b. Isaac (*Rashi*, France, 1040–1105) and Nahmanides (Spain, 1194–1270). What qualifies the first fisherman for a territorial preserve, according to *Rashi*, is not the deprivation effects of the interloper's action, as R. Joseph Ibn MiGash would have it, but rather the *anticipation of gain* he enjoyed prior to the arrival of the interloper. Casting bait in the fish's hiding place effectively assures the fisherman that he will be able to lure fish into his net. With his catch effectively assured (i.e., *matu le-yado*), another fisherman may not spread his net at the same spot, since doing so would deprive the former of an anticipated gain.[15]

Recall that the Talmud attempts to draw support for R. Huna from the fisherman case, but rejects the comparison by reason of "fish are different because they look about [for food]." *Rashi*'s understanding of the fisherman case makes the rejection, according to R. Breisch, pertain to even the ruinous competition case. The key here is that the former customers of a firm, even if the firm is a monopolist, cannot be regarded as *matu le-yado*. This is so because the original firm, even in R. Huna's view, could not prevent a competing firm from locating in an adjacent closed alley. Hence, customers who are patronizing the firm that arrived first could have, at any time, been lured away to a distant competitor. In contrast, casting bait at a safe distance from the first fisherman would in no way affect the latter's catch. Casting bait in a particular location, therefore, establishes for the fisherman a territorial preserve.

Another difference between the cases, according to R. Breisch, is that the anticipated gain of the fisherman, the catch of fish, exists at the time the intruder arrives on the scene. In contrast, the anticipated gain of the store-keeper, the patronage of his long-standing clientele, is nonexistent (*davar shelo ba la'olam*) at the time the rival competitor sets up shop. Because the anticipated gain in the latter case is nonexistent at the time of the intrusion, the established competitor is denied the right to treat his former clientele as his exclusive preserve.

Nahmanides offers a different rationale for the preserve rights of a fish-erman. The prohibition, according to Nahmanides, is rooted in the concern that fish already captured in the first fisherman's net could, at times, spring into the second fisherman's net. Hence, what is at issue here is violation of the law of misappropriation.[16] In sharp contrast, setting up a competing business cannot be viewed as taking away from the established firm cus-tomers that were already the entitlement of the established firm. The fish-erman case hence cannot serve as a model to confer monopoly rights to an established tradesman to block any new entrants.

Moreover, the fisherman case is omitted in the codes of R. Isaac b. Abraham Alfasi (Algeria, 1013–1103), Maimonides (Egypt, 1135–1204), R. Jacob b. Asher (Spain, 1270–1343), and R. Joseph Caro (Israel, 1488–1575).

Finally, an inconsistency is noted in the writings of R. Mosheh Isserles in regard to his adoption of the deprivation-generating rule. In his responsa work,[17] R. Isserles protected the right of R. Meir b. Isaac Katzenellenbogen (1473–1565) to disseminate Maimonides' work against the encroachment of a competing publisher. R. Joel ha-Levi's ruling is cited in support of the decision. Yet in his gloss in the *Shulhan Arukh* (*Rema*), R. Isserles rejects R. Joel ha-Levi's view.[18] Noting that R. Joel ha-Levi's ruling was only *one* of many factors in the R. Katzenellenbogen case and that *Rema* is a later work, R. Breisch posits that R. Isserles, in reality, rejects the deprivation-generating rule.

One final point on the luncheonette case. Although R. Breisch refused to enjoin the inside food vendor from competing with the luncheonette, he averred that it would be a matter of *lifnim mi-shurat ha-din* (i.e., beyond the letter of the law),[19] for the inside food vendor to refrain from expanding their menu so as to go into competition with the luncheonette.[20]

Israeli rabbinic courts have also followed the anti-protectionist school of thought. In this regard, the highest rabbinical tribunal in Israel expressed the view that it would not enjoin a religious school teacher from enrolling children from the neighborhood of a competitor, notwithstanding the ruinous impact on the rival religious school teacher.[21] Similarly, in a case involving an alleged breach of contract between a newspaper and a publisher of Talmud, the court refused to enjoin the newspaper from entering into a distributorship agreement with a competing publisher of Talmud, despite the deprivation effects the arrangement would generate for the first publisher.[22]

PREDATORY PRICE CUTTING

Although the free entry school does not protect a firm against ruinous competition per se, we offer the proposition that this school of thought agrees that a firm can be enjoined against selling below its own per unit costs. This tactic is referred to in the economic literature as *predatory price cutting*. An early authority that prohibited predatory price cutting was the nineteenth century Hungarian decisor R. Solomon Leib Tabak (1852–1908). Selling below cost makes the seller, in the opinion of R. Tabak, a *mazzik* (damager).[23]

In the United States, predatory pricing as a legal claim begins with the 1911 Standard Oil decision.[24] Prior to this landmark decision, predatory price cutting claims against competitors were brought by plaintiffs as a tort action in the common law courts. But these claims were usually thrown out on the rationale that the benefits to consumers from underpricing a rival outweighed the harm to the victim.[25]

The prohibition against predatory pricing, in the opinion of this writer, finds support in the rationale R. Meir b. Todros ha-Levi Abulafia (Spain, ca. 1180–1244) offers for the freedom of entry school of thought. Preliminarily let us note that the Talmud finds support for R. Huna b. Joshua's freedom of entry position in an earlier anonymous Tannaic opinion, recorded in a *Baraita*.[26] Commenting on this Tannaic position, R. Abulafia offers two different rationales as to why an established firm (S_1) cannot block a resident of his neighborhood (S_2) from setting up a competing business in the same neighborhood. One rationale is that S_2 can "turn the tables" on S_1 and say "You operate your business on your premises and I operate my business on my premises. Why should I be concerned about your livelihood and you should not be concerned about my livelihood?" In the second rationale R. Abulafia offers, S_2's argument begins the same way, but disarms S_1's claim of loss by saying that he takes away nothing from him: "Whatever Heaven has decided for each of us in the form of livelihood we will get [and no more]."[27]

S_2's conduct of underpricing S_1 by selling below his own cost meets neither of the two rationales R. Abulafia offers for freedom of entry. Consider that the basic premise operating in both rationales is that S_2's activity in his own premises can legitimately be called a livelihood activity. In making this judgment we should not consider as the relevant time period anything beyond the current year. This is so because a basic belief in Judaism is that God decides on *Rosh ha-Shanah* the income we will earn for that year.[28] Each year beginning on *Rosh ha-Shanah* is hence a new time period as far as livelihood is concerned. S_2's conduct of underpricing S_1 by selling below his own cost is therefore not a livelihood activity for the current year, notwithstanding S_2's plan to handsomely recoup his losses in the next time period on the back of S_1's destroyed business.

S_2's predatory conduct will also find no justification within the ambit of R. Abulafia's second rationale for freedom of entry. This is so because the pronouncement that God determines the distribution of customers between the two rival sellers and no one gets *more* than what God decided for him is no defense when the person who makes this pronouncement shows by his own actions that this dictum is not a part of his belief system. What constitutes prudent conduct for someone who *believes* that God decides his income for the year on *Rosh ha-Shanah*? The answer, *Rashi* tells us, is not to engage in *extravagant* expenditures, as the income God has decided for him might not cover such a standard of living.[29] S_2 compounds imprudence by deliberately planning *negative* income and positive consumption for the current time period. Moreover, if the contested livelihood pursuit is the *only* source of income for S_2, S_2 adds a measure of impudence and arrogance by inviting God to counterbalance his negative income plan with an adequate income stream from either a windfall (e.g., a winning lottery ticket) or the public purse. One final point: R. Abulafia's second rationale turns on S_2 with a vengeance if it is evident that S_2's tactic of selling below cost won't need a full year to do the job. To invoke R. Abulafia's second rationale here transmogrifies an otherwise pious declaration into something like the following: "Please God concentrate whatever income from livelihood activities You have in mind for me this year in the portion of the year that's left after I drive out S_1."

In its dealing with Goldfarb's law suits, *Bet Din* consistently adopted the deprivation-generating criterion.[30] Let us now describe the details of these cases.

GOLDFARB V. CARMEL

The first incursion against Goldfarb's turf came late in the second year of the opening of his business. Sidney Carmel, a resident of nearby Greenville, began to peddle fruit and vegetables to the doorsteps of Plainville residents. In respect to the entire vegetable and fruit line, Carmel undercut Goldfarb by twenty percent or more. Carmel was able to offer such low prices because he operated at a significant cost advantage over Goldfarb. One advantage was that Carmel eliminated the cost of the middleman by buying the produce directly from individual farmers, rather than from a wholesaler as Goldfarb did. Buying from individual farmers entailed quite a lot of extra toil and effort, but Carmel felt that he needed to do this to secure a competitive edge over Goldfarb. In addition, Goldfarb owned a home in Plainville and paid property taxes to the Plainville municipality. On the other hand, Carmel neither owned nor rented a home in Plainville. Consequently, Carmel did not pay property taxes to the Plainville municipality, either directly as a homeowner or indirectly as a tenant. In addition, Goldfarb operated his business from his store and paid an annual license fee to the municipality for this privilege. In contrast, Carmel operated his business out of his SUV and was therefore not subject to any licensing fee by the Plainville Municipality.

In the *Bet Din* proceeding, which Goldfarb summoned Carmel to, Goldfarb petitioned the court to order Carmel to stop selling fruits and vegetables in Plainville.

Recall that in all Goldfarb's legal skirmishes, *Bet Din* adopted the deprivation criterion as the rule of fairness for competition. The task before *Bet Din* in *Goldfarb v. Carmel* was therefore two-pronged. First, *Bet Din* had to decide whether Goldfarb was entitled to summary judgment against Carmel on the basis that Carmel was a nontaxpaying outsider. If *Bet Din* decides against summary judgment for Goldfarb, the issue then becomes whether Goldfarb is entitled to block Carmel based on the deprivation criterion.

Let us begin with the first prong in *Bet Din*'s deliberations. Consider that Carmel was an outsider, and operated his business as a nonlocal-taxpaying competitor in Plainville. Recall that R. Huna b. R. Joshua denies free entry to a nonlocal, nontaxpaying competitor.[31] Note that the exclusion applies even if the outsider is willing to pay the poll tax along with the established firm.[32] Perhaps, *Bet Din* need look no further and should give summary judgment to Goldfarb based on Carmel's nonlocal taxpaying status. But, before this judgment can be reached the rationale behind R. Huna b. R. Joshua's denial of free entry to a nontaxpaying outsider must be clarified. Perhaps the rationale here is that *taxes is a cost of doing business*. Competing for the patronage of the local residents without participating in local taxes confers to the outsider an unfair cost advantage. Accordingly, the outsider is denied entry. But, if this is the rationale, then entry should not be denied if the outsider can prove that his tax payment to the municipality of his residency is equal to or greater than the corresponding tax liability of the rival businessman in the local area in which he seeks entry.

To see why the poll tax issue is not about unfair cost advantage, we need only focus on the rationale of why the tradesman's movement is unencumbered if he pays the poll tax to the same *adon* (lord) as the rival tradesman. The explanation, according to Rabbenu Gershom b. Judah Me'Or ha-Golah (France, ca. 960–1040), is that paying the poll tax to the same *adon* makes it as if the two tradesmen reside in the same city. [33] What can be read into R. Gershom is that the poll tax is the *quid pro quo* the townspeople pay to get the *adon* to protect them. One benefit of this protection is that it fosters a stable and dependable marketplace for the townspeople. Accordingly, if the two towns pay the poll tax to the same lord, the marketplaces of the two towns become integrated into a single marketplace. Consequently, tradespeople from each town can move unencumbered from one town to the other and set up shop in the town of their choice. What follows from R. Gershom's explication is that conducting business in the town without paying the local poll tax amounts to free riding on the stable economic environment the *adon* of the town fosters. The nontaxpaying outsider should therefore be denied entry even if no cost advantage will result for him if he is allowed to enter without paying the poll tax.

What follows from the previous understanding of R. Gershom is that Carmel's fruit and vegetable business in Plainville should be blocked, even if Carmel can demonstrate that his payment of taxes to other governmental units is equal to or greater than Goldfarb's tax bill.

There is, however, more to this matter. Consider that there are exceptions to the rule that the outsider, non-taxpaying trader is denied entry into the local area.

Commenting on the rule that blocks an outsider from local entry, R. Joseph Ibn MiGash avers that the outsider is not barred when he offers to sell his wares at a lower price than the local vendors. Insofar as competition here decidedly benefits local consumers, the local merchant's pleas for protection must be resisted.[34]

Citing the following *Mishnah*, Nahmanides disagrees with the above ruling of R. Joseph Ibn MiGash:

> [R. Judah says] He may not lower the price of his goods below the market price. But the sages say: He is remembered for good.[35]
>
> What is the reason for the sages? Because he lowers the market price (*mirvah le-tar'a*)[36]

Though the sages regard price cutting as a fair business tactic, they would not permit a nontaxpaying outsider to employ this stratagem to gain entry into the town. How can such vendors be permitted to generate losses to local merchants? If the townspeople feel that local prices are too high, legitimate means to reduce them are readily available. Encouraging local merchants to compete with the high-priced local vendors would be one approach. Alternatively, price reductions could be mandated directly through the legislative process. Given that the community has the power to fix local prices, this body may not allow outside merchants to effectively usurp this function by causing local prices to go down.

Furthermore, argues Nahmanides, if out-of-town merchants were guaranteed entry whenever they offered to undersell the local competition, the community would *never* be able to block foreign entry. This follows from the fact that an increase in supply, (other things being equal) will always exert a downward pressure on price. Hence, regardless of whether foreign merchants initially offer to undersell local vendors, their competitive presence will nonetheless force prices down.[37]

Understanding the anti-protectionist stance of R. Joseph Ibn MiGash to refer only to the circumstance where the out-of-town merchants offer to undercut the local competition by a significant margin, R. Joseph Habiba (14th cent.) et al. find R. Joseph Ibn MiGash's view to converge closely with Nahmanides' position.[38] Other authorities, however, find the two views diametrically opposed: Nahmanides' protectionist view is advanced even when the proposed price is significant, and R. Joseph Ibn MiGash's view is held even when the price cut involved is slight.[39]

The implication of these conflicting views for Jewish law is that *Bet Din* would not enjoin out-of-town merchants when they offer to undercut the local competition by a significant margin. Accordingly, R. Hiyya Abraham b. Aaron di Boton (ca. 1560–1609) refused to issue an injunction against a local tailor who offered his service at 50 percent of the local price.[40]

The upshot of the above analysis is that *Bet Din* cannot summarily enjoin Carmel from entering Plainville on the basis that he is a non-local taxpaying businessman. If Carmel's twenty percent lower prices qualify halakhically as a significant price cut, good authority will support Carmel in his right to conduct his fruit and vegetable business in Plainville.

In extrapolating what constitutes a significant price cut, let us draw from the law of the prohibition to give or take interest on a loan (*ribbit*). One of the rabbinical extensions of the law of *ribbit*, called *avak ribbit*, is the prohibition for a seller to set a two-tier price system, consisting of one price that applies if the customer pays upon delivery of the merchandise and a higher price that applies if the customer pays on a deferred basis. Nonetheless, if the item at hand is a nonstandardized one, the seller enjoys some flexibility in setting a credit price higher than the cash on delivery price. As to what this flexibility consists of, R. Joseph Caro presents two opinions. In the first opinion cited, the seller is allowed to quote a higher price for a credit sale, provided he makes no explicit mention of what the cash on delivery price is. The second opinion is more stringent. Quoting just the credit price on the deal is acceptable only if the difference in price between the two modes of payment is not large (*lo harbe*).[41] In defining what is *harbe*, R. Jacob Moses Lorberbaum (Poland, 1760–1832) draws an analogy with the law of *ona'ah* (price fraud). The law of *ona'ah* entitles a market participant to transact at the market norm. Accordingly, if the transaction at hand was concluded at a price that varies from the market norm, the injured party may be entitled to either recover the differential or possibly to even cancel the original transaction, depending upon how severe the overcharge (under-charge) was. In any event, if the discrepancy was less than one-sixth no adjustment is made.[42] Because the one-sixth figure is the benchmark to define a *significant* price discrepancy, it should also be used to define what a *significant premium* above the cash on delivery price is.[43] (Note that in Talmudic parlance, the one-sixth figure in the law of *ona'ah* means 20 percent.[44])

Following R. Lorberbaum's line of reasoning, we propose that the size of the price reduction offer an outsider must make to qualify for entry into the local market even according to Nahmanides should also be identified with the twenty percent benchmark.

Based on this analysis, Goldfarb is not entitled to summary judgment against Carmel just because Carmel is a non-taxpaying outsider. But, per-haps, Goldfarb should be entitled to block Carmel based on the deprivation criterion. Let us look at the issue of cost differentials between the competi-tors more closely.

Bet Din duly noted that Carmel was selling his fruits and vegetables below the pro rata costs Goldfarb incurred in running the fruit and vegetable part of his business. What gave Carmel the edge here was that he paid no annual license fee and managed to pare overhead costs to almost nothing by operating his business from the back of his SUV. In addition, by eliminat-ing the wholesaler and going directly to the local farmers, Carmel was able to acquire the fruits and vegetables at a lower cost than Goldfarb.

In Goldfarb's mind, the broad cost advantage Carmel had over him strengthened considerably his case that the ruinous threat he faced was not a transitory phenomenon, but would continue in the long run and hence force him out of the fruit and vegetable line. To dramatize this point to *Bet Din*, Goldfarb couched his argument in the technical jargon of the econo-mist and said:

> My dear judges, the long-term significance of Mr. Carmel's cost advan-tage is that even if we assume that the major component of his differ-ential variable cost, namely the price of gasoline, increases sharply over time, Mr. Carmel will still enjoy considerable latitude to sell very prof-itably his fruits and vegetables below my cost bases.

Despite the superficial appeal of Goldfarb's argument, the opportunity cost concept told *Bet Din* that Goldfarb had not decisively proven that he was facing a ruinous competition threat. Let us see why. The opportunity cost concept teaches that the true cost of anything is the value we forego in acquiring what we get. To be sure, Carmel saved an explicit differential cost by eliminating the wholesaler, but this savings was assuredly somewhat offset by the extra time he needed to spend in acquiring the fruits and vegetables by traveling from one farm to another. *Bet Din* calculated that the extra time involved was at least five hours per week. What monetary value should be put on these five hours? To answer this question, *Bet Din* inquired as to what wage per hour Carmel would command if he worked for someone else instead of operating his peddling business. The wage rate *Bet Din* came up with was $10 per hour. The opportunity cost of extra time Carmel spent in acquiring the fruits and vegetables from individual farmers offset the explicit cost advantage Carmel secured by eliminating the wholesaler. Consequently, the cost advantage Carmel enjoyed from his enterprise was a lot smaller than it appeared at first.

Suppose we give credence to Goldfarb's ruinous competition claim, Goldfarb still loses the suit. Consider that the grocery business is by its nature a multi-product business. The issue, then, becomes not whether Goldfarb's fruit and vegetable business would go under on account of Carmel, but rather whether Goldfarb would be forced to *close shop altogether* on account of Carmel. In respect to this latter assessment, *Bet Din* determined that Goldfarb would not close shop on account of Carmel's competitive presence, even under the worst case scenario.

Based on these considerations, *Bet Din* refused to block Carmel from peddling fruits and vegetables in Plainville. In the aftermath of *Bet Din*'s ruling, Goldfarb discontinued his fruit and vegetable line.

In issuing its ruling, *Bet Din* felt compelled to draw out for Goldfarb a vulnerability he should be aware of. Suppose someone down the road opens a kosher appetizer store and the assessment is that the combined competitive presence of both a store specializing in appetizers and Carmel's fruit and vegetable business would exert a ruinous effect on Goldfarb's business. In that case, Goldfarb should not count on any help from *Bet Din*. Because neither of the specialty competitors *alone* exerts a ruinous effect on Goldfarb,

Bet Din will restrain neither of them. The prudent thing to do, *Bet Din* urged Goldfarb, was to take this scenario into serious consideration in his long-term planning.

Carmel's victory in *Bet Din* was short-lived. Several months after the *Bet Din* ruling, the Plainville City Council passed an ordinance that required all peddlers that operated in the municipality to register and pay an annual license fee for the privilege of doing business. The legislation recognized the inherent unfairness of the status quo wherein storekeepers paid an annual license fee and peddlers were not subject to any license fee. All this changed with the legislation. The license fee was designed to create a level playing field between storekeepers and peddlers.

Not surprisingly, the Plainville legislation gave a second wind to Goldfarb's fruit and vegetable business. In a short while, the marketplace of Plainville featured both Goldfarb and Carmel competing for the fruit and vegetable business.

PRICE DISCRIMINATION AND FAIR COMPETITION

Another early competitive threat for Goldfarb came when Jonathan Koller, the proprietor of the kosher grocery store in a nearby town, Greenville, decided on a price discrimination policy for baked goods. Plainville residents were charged a lower price than Greenville residents for the same items. With the aim of luring away Goldfarb's customers, Koller designed the discount to make it worthwhile for Plainville residents to travel the extra distance and make their purchases in his store.

In his treatment of a case of this type, R. Hayyim Sofer (Hungary, 1821–1886) prohibited S_1 from luring customers away from a rival in a different town by charging them a lower price than he charged local residents for the same item. R. Sofer based his prohibition on the assertion that the Sages who validate the distribution of "nuts" to children as a business tactic do so only in respect to the local marketplace, but not as a means of snaring the business of a rival that is located in a different marketplace.[45]

Invoking the authority of R. Hayyim Sofer, the Greenville *Bet Din* ordered Koller to end his price discrimination policy and instead charge local and non-local residents the same price.

GOLDFARB V. MILLSTEIN—ROUND 1

In the eighth year of the operation of his grocery store business, Goldfarb got wind of the plans of a local resident, Sidney Millstein, to lease a storefront in the main shopping district of the town and operate a kosher grocery store there. In anticipation of his "grand opening," Millstein had already circulated fliers throughout Plainville letting everyone know that he was opening a competing grocery store. Millstein followed up the fliers with personal telephone calls to his many friends and acquaintances in Plainville. Goldfarb petitioned the local *Bet Din* to block Millstein from setting up a competing grocery in Plainville.

In lodging his objection to the entry of Millstein, Goldfarb bemoaned that all his customers were long-standing customers. Indeed, over the years Goldfarb had invested much time, energy, and money to build a reputation of honesty, reliability, and professional courtesy. Often Goldfarb went out of his way to get a customer special items he did not carry in his regular inventory at little or no profit for himself. As far as Goldfarb was concerned, the customer base of Plainville was his domain and he was "poised" to get the repeated business of these customers. Goldfarb petitioned the court to look upon Millstein as nothing less than an interloper with designs on snatching away his anticipated gains.

Another argument Goldfarb raised was that the competitive presence of another grocery store in Plainville would significantly reduce his earnings. Goldfarb was also very worried that Millstein's game plan was to compete with him on a cutthroat basis. In that case, Goldfarb would have no recourse other than to respond in kind. In short order either Millstein or Goldfarb would go under. Given the certainty of the above scenario, *Bet Din* should respect the fact that Goldfarb opened his store first and block the entry of Millstein.

What Goldfarb found most objectionable was the aggressive solicitations Millstein was already making to secure what he could of the grocery store business in Plainville.

Bet Din refused to block the entry of Millstein. In rejecting Goldfarb's claim, *Bet Din* rejected the notion that Goldfarb was "poised" to receive the repeat business of the local residents and Millstein's competitive presence amounted to "snatching away his anticipated gain." The principle *Bet Din* clarified here was the parameters of the prohibition of *ani hamehapekh bahararah* (literally, the poor man (P_1) casting about [trying to take possession of a certain] cake and another person (P_2) comes and snatches it away from him; P_2's interloping conduct brands him a wicked person).[46]

Let us discuss the parameters of this principle and its relevance in deciding the merits of Goldfarb's argument. The circumstances *ani hamehapekh bahararah* speaks of is a matter of dispute. In R. Solomon b. Isaac's (*Rashi*, France, 1040–1105) view, P_1 seeks a "handout" in the form of a cake from *E*. Alternatively, P_1 seeks to acquire a cake from ownerless property. The "cake" the Talmud speaks of, according to *Rashi*, is hence a gift, and the gain P_1 seeks is akin to taking possession of *hefker* (ownerless property).[47] Disputing *Rashi*, R. Jacob Tam (Ramerrupt, 1100–1171) avers that the "cake" P_1 seeks from *E* is a job. P_1 cultivates *E* in the hope that someday *E* will offer him a job and provide compensation in the form of a "cake." In R. Jacob Tam's view, *ani hamehapekh* is suspended in the ownerless property case. Since the acquisition of a free good at hand cannot be said to be waiting for P_2 elsewhere, seizing the opportunity for himself and snatching it away from P_1 is not unethical.[48] Decisors generally follow R. Tam's view here.[49]

Following R. Tam's line, R. Mosheh Isserles understands *ani hamehapekh* in a commercial transaction to apply only when the parties reach agreement regarding price, and the only matter missing to make the agreement legally binding is the performance of a symbolic act (*kinyan*) by the buyer B_1. Here another interested buyer, B_2 may not interfere in this transaction by offering to purchase the item. Such action brands B_2 a *rasha* (a wicked person).[50]

Does *ani hamehapekh* prohibit seller S_2 from interfering with the efforts of seller S_1 to make a deal with buyer *B*. R. Yair Hayyim Bacharach (Worms, 1638–1702) addresses this issue. The particulars of his case are as follows: A government official indicated to horse dealer S_1 that he was interested in buying horses. As long as the negotiations have not progressed to the point just prior to *kinyan*, it is not unethical for S_2 to step in and offer his horses for sale to the government official.[51]

What this explication of the *ani hamehapekh* principle shows is that the long-standing repeat business Goldfarb enjoyed from the local residents does not make him *ani hamehapekh* in respect to their *future* business. The *ani hamehapekh* principle applies here only if a customer places items on the checkout counter and the cashier rings up the purchase and presents the customer with a bill. Since the only thing missing is for the customer to pay the bill and take possession of the items, Millstein may not interfere at this point.

Our conclusion that *ani hamehapekh* has no relevancy to *Goldfarb v. Millstein*—Round 1 proceeds from R. Tam's understanding of this concept. But, perhaps *Rashi's* understanding of *ani hamehapekh* does have application here. Consider that within *Rashi's* understanding of the dictum, the "cake" P_1 seeks is a handout. If so, there are no terms and price to negotiate. P_1's complaint against P_2's preemption is based solely on the "toil and effort" he expended to secure a "handout" from E. Now, if P_1's toil and effort imposes a duty on P_2 to walk away from the scene when the gain he seeks is not available elsewhere, the duty to walk away certainly should pertain when the gain P_2 seeks is available to him elsewhere. Analogously, Millstein's solicitations, whether in the form of the fliers he saturated the town with or the personal calls he made, should constitute interloping and be in violation of *ani hamehapekh*. But, if the above reasoning is valid, *the mere opening of a new store*, even if it is accompanied with no notification to the public whatsoever, should also constitute interloping and violate the *ani hamehapekh* interdict. The latter conclusion is, however, certainly incorrect. Consider that Nahmanides understands *ani hamehapekh*, as *Rashi* does, to apply even when the gain contested is ownerless property.[52] But, Nahmanides also rules in accordance with the free entry position of R. Huna b. R. Joshua.[53]

The conflicting rulings point to the proposition that the right to pursue a livelihood by any legitimate means is so basic that it suspends certain aspects of the *ani hamehapekh* interdict. This proposition proceeds from both of the rationales R. Abulafia offers for the freedom of entry school of thought. Recall that in his first rationale, R. Abulafia posits that S_2 can "turn the tables" on S_1 and say "You operate your business on your premises and I operate my business on my premises. Why should I be concerned about your livelihood and you should not be concerned about my livelihood?" In the second rationale R. Abulafia offers, S_2's argument begins the same way, but disarms S_1's claim of loss by saying that he takes away nothing from him: "Whatever Heaven has decided for each of us in the form of livelihood we will get [and no more.]"[54] In both rationales, R. Abulafia is telling us that the circumstance that S_1 exerted efforts *first* does not give him preferential status to restrain S_2 from entering into the same business and soliciting the public for their patronage.

An analogous case where all opinions agree that "first efforts" do not give the actor an edge in respect to *ani hamehapekh* is in connection with the law of *pe'ah* (the corner of the field). The law of *pe'ah* requires growers in the Land of Israel to leave the corner of their field for the poor to harvest for themselves.[55] If a qualified indigent P_1 throws himself or his garment over a piece of *pe'ah*, he does not thereby acquire the *pe'ah*, as what he did is not a valid mode of acquisition. Because P_1 has not acquired the *pe'ah* he or his garment is lying over, another qualified indigent, P_2, may come along and remove P_1 from the spot and acquire the *pe'ah* for himself.[56] This law presents a difficulty for *Rashi*. To be sure, falling over the *pe'ah* does not acquire for P_1 legal title to it, but P_1 is surely poised to take possession of the *pe'ah*. P_2 should therefore be regarded as an interloper and violate *ani hamehapekh*. Addressing this issue, R. Nissim b. Reuben Gerondi (Barcelona, ca. 1290–ca. 1375) posits that since *pe'ah* is the entitlement of *all* paupers, P_1 is no more poised to acquire the *pe'ah* than P_2. P_2 is therefore not in violation of *ani hamehapekh*.[57] What proceeds from R. Nissim's analysis is that once someone meets the minimum criterion of being regarded as "poised" to acquire something, the circumstance that another party is much closer to actually acquiring legal title of the desired item does not give the latter preferred status as a *mehapekh* (one who is casting about).

R. Nissim's principle provides elaboration for R. Abulafia's rationale of the freedom of entry school. Since everyone has a basic right to pursue a livelihood, S_2 must be regarded as "casting about" for the patronage of the town's business even *before* he actually begins solicitations for S_1's customers, and even *before* he opens his business. Accordingly, at the very moment Goldfarb is pitching someone to become his customer, Millstein has every right to solicit that same person to make the purchases in his store. That Goldfarb set up shop before Millstein entered the marketplace does not make him more of a *mehapekh* than Millstein.

The upshot of this analysis is that characterizing Millstein's new entry into the grocery business as "snatching away" Goldfarb's anticipated gain has no basis in Halakhah. Having "come first" and exerted himself with goodwill gestures in the past to keep the townspeople's business in the future does not earn for Goldfarb a monopoly license for the retail grocery business of Plainville.

Let us now turn to Goldfarb's concern that Millstein's competitive presence would quickly engender "cutthroat" competition between them. In the end, Goldfarb would have us believe, only one firm would survive. *Bet Din* rejected Goldfarb's assessment. To be sure, the competitive presence of Millstein would reduce Goldfarb's earnings, but Goldfarb is not entitled to a monopoly hold over the kosher grocery customer base. It was clear to the court that the Jewish customer base of Plainville had expanded sufficiently to allow two kosher product grocery stores to coexist and earn a livelihood. One strong indication of this was that the local synagogue was now moving into new and expanded quarters to accommodate its explosive growth. Another telltale sign that Plainville was ripe for another grocery store was the chronic long lines that one always encountered whenever shopping at Goldfarb's. To boot, many of the items customers wanted were constantly in short supply at Goldfarb's. Finally, the court noted that Goldfarb's business was so brisk that he could afford to close his business for the lunch hour. Goldfarb spent his lunch hour at the local synagogue attending the afternoon services and participated in a learning group there as well.

The above set of facts made *Bet Din* summarily reject Goldfarb's contention that allowing Millstein to compete with him would set in motion cutthroat competition between him and Millstein.

GOLDFARB V. MILLSTEIN—ROUND 2

The court ruling proved a watershed event for the grocery store market in Plainville. Millstein took the ruling as a license to compete aggressively with Goldfarb for the grocery store business in Plainville. Plainville residents soon found fliers under their doors advertising Millstein's prices on key grocery items. Because he was not accustomed to a competitive environment, Goldfarb became visibly annoyed when some of his customers complained that his prices were higher than Millstein on many items. Gladdened by the effectiveness of his fliers in forcing householders to engage in price comparisons, Millstein got carried away with this competitive tactic and had friends drop his fliers on the floor of Goldfarb's store.

Another competitive tactic Millstein used was to offer a free delivery service. Millstein, of course, advertised the free delivery service in his fliers. But, he did not rely on the fliers alone to do the job. Instead, to add a personal touch to this service, Millstein called up every number in the Plainville directory. Whomever he contacted on the telephone, Millstein introduced his local grocery store business and hawked the free delivery service he offered.

Millstein's aggressive tactics seriously hurt Goldfarb's business. No later than four months after the arrival of Millstein on the competitive scene Goldfarb was back in court. Goldfarb opened up his books to the court and showed the judges that he had experienced a precipitous decline in sales revenue. If the trend continued he would soon be bankrupt. The dire straights Goldfarb found himself in now vindicated in his mind the contention he made all along that Plainville could not support two grocery stores.

Bet Din took Goldfarb's complaint seriously. But, *Bet Din* found that Goldfarb's severe downturn was partly attributable to competitive tactics that he could match. In addition, some of Goldfarb's difficulties were of his own doing.

In its ruling, the most fundamental point *Bet Din* addressed was the ethics of price cutting as a competitive tactic: Recall that the ethics of price cutting as a business tactic is a matter of dispute between R. Judah and the sages. R. Judah prohibits the tactic, whereas the sages not only permit it, but praise the price cutter: "He is remembered for good."

Halakhah takes the view of the sages as normative,[58] but commentators differ as to how far the price cutting privilege goes.

One school of thought, led by R. Meir b. Isaac Eisenstadt (Poland, 1670–1744) understands the price cutter (A) of the *Mishnah* to be a retail grain dealer. A's price cutting is legitimate, according to R. Eisenstadt et al., only because it results in the reduction of the market price of essential commodities (i.e., grain).[59] This scenario is described by *Rashi* in his commentary *ad locum*: A's price cutting makes hoarders of grain believe that the market price of grain is on the way down. This leads them to dump their supplies on the market, with the result that the market price of grain goes down.[60] Suppose the commodity at hand was not grain, but instead beer. Here, avers R. Eisenstadt, A's price cutting will assuredly not set into motion market forces that will push down the market price of grain. Where the economy operates under government price controls, the above assertion is reinforced. When *A's* price cutting will not set into motion market forces that will push down the price of grain, *A's* conduct is regarded as an unfair competitive tactic.[61]

Sharply disputing this view, R. Shelomo Kluger (Brody, 1785–1869) avers that the sages legitimize price cutting even when it does not set into motion market forces that will drive down the price of grain. Moreover, the tactic is legitimate even when the conduct does not force rival sellers to match the price cut. A close reading of *Rashi's* remarks, referred to earlier, clearly demonstrates that his scenario involving a retail grain dealer is offered only as constituting the case where the sages would heap praise on the price cutter. But, price cutting is fundamentally a legitimate competitive tactic, even when it does not lower the price of grain or the price that rival sellers charge for the commodity at hand.[62]

Although Halakhah follows the view of the sages and interprets the permissibility of price cutting in liberal terms, one caveat should be mentioned. Recall the view of R. Sofer et al. that a firm is generally entitled to protection against ruinous competition. Applying this caveat to the case at hand limits the legitimacy of Millstein's price cutting to the magnitude where Goldfarb is capable of matching the price cut while still managing to earn his opportunity cost earnings. Accordingly, upon entry into the grocery store business, Millstein is not bound by the prevailing price structure. Since price competition is permitted, Millstein may send out his fliers to inform the public of the prices he charges. The same can be said of the free delivery service Millstein instituted. In respect to all these tactics, Goldfarb is capable of remaining competitive by offering the same price and the same service as Millstein.

In investigating the cause of Goldfarb's precipitous loss of business since the arrival of Millstein on the competitive scene, *Bet Din* identified a factor that Goldfarb himself must take responsibility for. Recall that before Millstein entered the marketplace, it was Goldfarb's practice to close his store during lunch hour and attend afternoon services at the local synagogue and participate in the learning group there as well. Well, Millstein chose to keep his store open during the lunch hour. Because Millstein was open during the lunch hour, Goldfarb felt that he had no choice but to be open during the lunch hour as well. Goldfarb, however, did not want to change his routine of going to the synagogue for afternoon prayer and classes. Goldfarb was therefore only too eager to take up his aunt Clara's offer to mind the store in the lunch hour. Aunt Clara was a retiree looking to fill up her days with something interesting to do; she happily undertook the chore without pay. Aunt Clara, however, proved to be an incompetent clerk. In particular, she was slow and inaccurate in taking down special orders from customers, such as orders for smoked fish for Shabbat. As matters turned out, Clara's incompetence caused a very significant shift in patronage from Goldfarb to Millstein.

Convinced that it was Goldfarb's imprudent decision to let his aunt mind the store during lunch hour that was the cause of the shifting of patronage to Millstein, *Bet Din* invoked the words of the free competition advocacy of the sages, referred to earlier: "Just as I make presents of nuts so you can make presents of prunes." What *Bet Din* inferred from this position was that it was within Goldfarb's power to get back on track by either minding the store himself at the lunch hour or hiring a competent clerk to do so.

Although the thrust of the court decision was to find no objection to Millstein's aggressive competitive tactics, the court ordered Millstein to end one his stratagems on the grounds that it was unethical. This was his practice of getting friends to slip Millstein fliers on the floor of Goldfarb's store. The rationale behind the objection is enunciated in the following *Baraita*:

> . . . a person may open a rival store next to the store of his fellow, or a rival bathhouse next to the bathhouse of his fellow, and [the established operator] cannot prevent him from doing so, because [the rival] can say to [the established operator]—"You do as you wish inside your property, and I do as I wish inside my [property]."[63]

Proceeding from the *Baraita* is that the legitimacy of competition is predicated on the notion that a rival uses its own resources and not the resources of rival firms to compete for the patronage of consumers. By planting fliers in Goldfarb's store, Millstein is using Goldfarb's premises to compete for the patronage of the consumer. Such action is prohibited.

R. Yaakov Yesha'yahu Bloi (Israel, 1929–) dealt with an analogous case: S_2 marketed his product by making use of S_1's trademark. Given that the trademark, though it is intangible, is an economic asset for S_1, S_2's infringement of the trademark makes him guilty of effectively conducting business on S_1's premises.[64]

PHILANTHROPY AND FAIR COMPETITION

An encroachment against both Goldfarb's and Millstein's turf occurred when a local philanthropist, Eitan Kramer, launched a program to subsidize families living on the margin of subsistence in Plainville. By means of discreet investigation, Kramer identified these households and mailed the following letter to the head of each of these families:

Dear . . .

Your economic well being is of great importance to me. I know you struggle hard to make ends meet. You deserve a break!

I am happy to make available to you a number of grocery items at cost. Please check off the items and quantities you desire and mail this coupon to the above address. Free delivery will be made.

With best wishes,
Eitan Kramer

Kramer's subsidy program took away some business from both Goldfarb and Millstein. In this instance Goldfarb formed an alliance with Millstein. Both proprietors complained that Kramer's philanthropy was taking away their business.

Bet Din ruled in favor of the complainants. In their decision, *Bet Din* invoked a responsa of R. Mosheh Feinstein. The case involved a group of householders who broke away from a particular private synagogue and established their own synagogue within the vicinity of the first synagogue. R. Feinstein condemned the action because it resulted both in the ruination of the livelihood of the rabbi of the first synagogue and in a significant reduction in the commercial value of the premises of his synagogue. Moreover, even if the breakaway action would not exert a ruinous impact on the rabbi but instead only reduce his earnings, the action should still be condemned. Consider that R. Huna b. R. Joshua permits S_2 to set up a store in the same alley where S_1 is located only because S_1 has no right to prevent S_2 from earning a livelihood by conducting business in his own premises. But, suppose S_2's action merely takes away business from S_1, but generates no earnings whatsoever for S_2 himself. S_2's action is prohibited. This is the case at hand because the breakaway people did not establish a new synagogue with a position for a rabbi. Instead, they merely established a new place to conduct prayer services, without creating a livelihood opportunity for another rabbi. The breakaway group's action is therefore prohibited even if it only reduces the livelihood of the first rabbi and does not exert a ruinous impact on him.[65]

In adjudicating Goldfarb's and Millstein's complaint against Kramer, the Plainville *Bet Din* heaped praise on Kramer for his worthy objectives but criticized his means: If A's charity giving is at the expense of encroaching upon B's livelihood, A's act of charity is prohibited. Accordingly, the Plainville *Bet Din* ordered Kramer to disband his subsidized grocery store. The implication the *Bet Din* drew from R. Feinstein's responsa was that if Kramer desired to subsidize the poor he should do so by means of a *cash subvention*.

GOLDFARB V. MILLSTEIN—ROUND 3

After a period of relative calm between Goldfarb and Millstein, another dispute broke out between these rivals. Several days before the Thanksgiving holiday, Millstein widely issued circulars that he was running a Thanksgiving special on raw turkeys. Millstein sold the turkeys below his *own cost* bases. The prices he advertised, $12 for a ten-pound turkey and $18 for a twenty-pound turkey, put his prices 45 percent below Goldfarb's prices on these items.

Millstein's Thanksgiving giveaway was a "loss leader" ploy. What Millstein was hoping for was that the "giveaway" on turkeys would draw many more customers to his store than usual. Given the enormous saving on turkeys, customers, in Millstein's mind, should be driven to splurge on the other food items they buy for the Thanksgiving meal. Accordingly, Millstein was expecting a booming demand for potatoes, cranberry sauce, and the various desserts he carried. Whatever Millstein would lose on the turkeys he would more than make up on the turkey accessories the increased customer base would snap up. To boot, perhaps some of the new customers would switch from Goldfarb to him on a permanent basis.

Goldfarb was far too conservative in his thinking to mimic Millstein's bold move. In Goldfarb's mind, Millstein's scheme was fraught with risk. Perhaps consumers would react to the sale by snapping up the turkeys, but not increase their demand significantly enough for the complementary goods to make the sale worthwhile. Whether Millstein succeeded or not, the ploy was surely going to ruin Goldfarb's Thanksgiving related-business. This made Goldfarb think—you got it—*Bet Din*. At first blush, Goldfarb thought that no legal recourse was open to him to stop Millstein's Thanksgiving give away on turkeys. In his litigation against Carmel, Goldfarb absorbed the lesson that the demonstration that a rival's practice would ruin a piece of his business was not enough to enjoin that practice. But, a saving factor for Goldfarb was that Millstein was selling the turkeys below cost. Perhaps *Bet Din* would regard selling below cost as an unethical business practice and enjoin it.

In Goldfarb v. Millstein—Round 3 the central issue for *Bet Din* was the ethics of selling below cost. Goldfarb's complaint apparently finds support in the position the sages take against R. Judah, who disallows a storekeeper from distributing nuts as a free gift to the children who come to the store on a parent's errand: "Just as I make presents of nuts so you can make presents of prunes." What apparently can be *inferred* from the free competition stance of the sages is that a competitive tactic is legitimate only if a rival is capable of counteracting it. Recall, however, that R. Huna insists that his *protectionist* view is *consistent* with the position of the sages. This tells us that limiting free competition to competitive tactics that one's rival is capable of counteracting is a view only R. Huna subscribes to. R. Huna b. Joshua, who, in opposition to R. Huna, adopts a free entry advocacy, subscribes to no such limitation. Recall, however, that the Plainville *Bet Din* subscribed to the school of thought that reconciles R. Huna's and R. Huna b. Joshua's views and defines unfair competition in terms of ruinous competition. The issue at bar, then, turns on the likely impact Millstein's loss leader tactic will have on Goldfarb's grocery store business.

Although there can be no doubt that Millstein's loss leader tactic will predictably knock out Goldfarb's Thanksgiving business, the ploy does not threaten ruination for Goldfarb's grocery store business. Accordingly, *Bet*

Din refused to enjoin Millstein from running his loss leader special for the Thanksgiving season.

A variation of this scenario occurs when the loss leader stratagem affects not just a peripheral aspect of the competitor's business, but the core of the business. Consider the following scenario: R_1 and R_2 are two competing fast-food takeout stores competing for the same local market. R_1 initiates a promotion consisting of a choice of three different meat sandwiches for only \$3, down from the regular price of \$7. R_1 combines the bargain price for sandwiches with aggressive marketing for soups, large drinks, french fries, and desserts. R_1's stratagem is to make up for the losses on the sandwiches with big gains on the complementary items the clerks hawk when consumers come to snap up the giveaway sandwich deal.[66]

R_1's loss leader stategem is at best a risky proposition. Consumers may well flock to R_1 to take advantage of the "giveaway sandwich" deal, but fail to respond enthusiastically enough in buying the side dishes and desserts to make the stratagem translate into a profit for R_1.

Although it is clear that an investment motive stands behind R_1's ploy, the stratagem carries the potential to ruin R_2. Here, *Bet Din* cannot tell R_2 that he is capable of counteracting the stratagem. To be sure, inability to counteract a rival's competitive move is not in and of itself sufficient for *Bet Din* to issue a cease and desist order against the use of the stratagem, but in the case at hand, the loss leader stratagem relates to the core of R_1's business. Because R_1's sandwich giveaway threatens R_2 with ruination, *Bet Din* would enjoin the stratagem on the petition of R_2.

GOLDFARB AND MILLSTEIN V. BIG LION

By the year 2000, both Goldfarb and Millstein faced a competitive force that threatened to destroy both their businesses. In that year, the local grocers learned that a group of people planned to rent space in the town's shopping district to set up a supermarket. Of all the competitive threats the local grocers faced in the past, this threat was the most serious. The supermarket was going to be part of the Big Lion chain.

Fearing that they would lose much business to Big Lion, Goldfarb and Millstein petitioned *Bet Din* to block the supermarket from entry on the grounds that they, the incumbent firms of Plainville, were catering well to the needs of the Plainville community. What Goldfarb and Millstein feared most, however, was that they would never survive the competition of a supermarket chain. Specifically, the cost advantages Big Lion enjoyed in the form of professional buyers, bulk discounts, and inventory control would drive it to engage in cutthroat competition as a means of capturing the entire market for itself. In light of the serious threat they faced, Goldfarb and Millstein decided to put their differences aside and present a united front against Big Lion in *Bet Din*. To their dismay, the court ruling was very adverse to their interests.

In its deliberations, the court noted that the Jewish population in Plainville had increased dramatically over the years. When Millstein first joined Goldfarb on the local grocery store scene, there were no more than 400 Jewish families living in the area. Now, the number had expanded to 1000. For the same reasons *Bet Din* had earlier welcomed the arrival of Millstein on the competitive scene, *Bet Din* felt the marketplace was now ripe for the entry of a third competitor. Predictably, the entry of Big Lion would dramatically reduce both Goldfarb's and Millstein's profits. Goldfarb and Millstein, however, had no claim for an exclusive right to the patronage on the grocery market in Plainville.

As to plaintiffs' prediction that Big Lion planned to deliberately adopt a price policy designed to drive both Goldfarb and Millstein out of business, *Bet Din* dismissed that contention as mere speculation, with no tangible evidence to back it up. Moreover, suppose, just for argument's sake, that Goldfarb and/or Millstein go under in close proximity to the arrival of Big Lion; does the juxtaposition of these events evidence that it was Big Lion's pricing policy that directly brought on this result? Not necessarily. Consider that the arrival of Big Lion puts pressure on the whole commercial food industry in Plainville. In their suit against Big Lion, Goldfarb and Millstein conveniently blocked out that they were not the only vendors of food in Plainville. The other food establishments that would be hurt by Big Lion included Carmel's fruit and vegetable peddling business, Saroka's appetizer store, Mermelstein's bakery, and Truffle's Roving Kosher Ice Cream Truck business. Both Goldfarb's and Millstein's product lines overlap with the product lines of these food vendors. To be competitive with Big Lion all the food vendors would be under pressure to reduce prices. If any of the food vendors, including Goldfarb and Millstein, go under after the arrival of Big Lion, what is *directly* responsible for this is not Big Lion's pricing policy, but rather the competitive pressures of the marketplace as a whole.

Although there is no basis to issue an injunction against the entry of Big Lion, once the company gets the green light to open for business, it will not be permitted to set price below its own cost. This is predatory price cutting and is prohibited in both Jewish and American law. Given that the owners of Big Lion are both law abiding citizens and observant Jews submissive to Jewish law, it is wrong to block the entry of the firm based on the fear that once in operation it will engage in predatory pricing as a means of driving out the competition. Blocking Big Lion's entry based on this concern violates the ethical imperative to judge one's fellow favorably. Called the *kaf zehut* (literally, righteous scale) imperative, this ethical norm is discussed elsewhere in this volume.[67]

GOLDFARB'S 15-YEAR TURF WAR AND AMERICAN LAW

In this section we will compare Halakhah and American law in the treatment of the various scenarios discussed in this chapter. In recognition of the two schools of thought in respect to the protection Halakhah affords an incumbent firm, our comparison with American law will encompass both these approaches. Before we proceed to make a comparative law study regarding the scenarios discussed in this case study, we offer the following brief outline of the treatment of anti-competitive behavior in American law.

Regulation of monopoly and restraint of trade have been part of the American legal system since the enactment of the Sherman Anti-Trust Act of 1890. This Act outlawed "conspiracies in restraint of trade." Although price-fixing agreements clearly constituted such a conspiracy, it remained for both subsequent legislature and court decisions to delineate specific illegal practices. Tied contracts, exclusive dealerships, price discrimination, predatory price cutting, and lessening competition by acquiring another firm's stock were included in the specific restraint of trade practices made illegal by the Clayton Act (1914). Acquisition of the assets of another firm when the effect is to lessen competition was prohibited by the subsequent Celler-Kefauver Anti-Merger Act of 1950.[68]

Most states have enacted antitrust statutes that are usually patterned after the counterpart federal law, often containing the same language. State antitrust laws are used to attack anticompetitive activity that occurs in intrastate commerce.[69]

GOLDFARB AND MILLSTEIN V. BIG LION AND AMERICAN LAW

Let us begin with the Big Lion scenario. Conceding to the pleas of Goldfarb and Millstein for protection would apparently make *Bet Din* guilty of a "conspiracy in restraint of trade." *Bet Din*'s ruling not to block the entry of Big Lion is therefore consistent with secular law. Although *Bet Din*'s ruling here is in conformity with secular law, the reasoning *Bet Din* furnished for their ruling contains the seeds for conflict with secular law. Consider that the crucial point for *Bet Din* in not blocking Big Lion was the configuration of the commercial food marketplace in Plainville. The marketplace consisted of many diverse food vendors whose product lines overlapped significantly with the product lines Goldfarb and Millstein carried. Because the entry of Big Lion puts pressure on all food vendors to lower prices, it becomes well nigh impossible for the plaintiffs to prove that the pricing policy of Big Lion *directly* caused them to go under. Accordingly, there is no basis to issue an injunction against Big Lion as a means of preventing it from entering the marketplace. The only possible action against Big Lion is a predatory price claim. This claim can, of course, be based only on *actual, observed conduct* and not on the plaintiffs' assertion of predictable conduct.

In showing why this reasoning contains the seeds of conflict with secular law, let us consider a variation of the scenario. In this scenario we assume a very simple marketplace that expands and develops in a linear direction. The story begins with Goldfarb as a monopolist grocer in Plainville. Next, the population expands to the point where it is evident that Goldfarb lacks the capacity to cater to the entire market demand. There are no other firms that sell overlapping product lines with Goldfarb. Seeing the prospects of a bright future for an expanding demand, Big Lion desires to enter Plainville. The combined factors of Goldfarb's limited capacity and the population growth in Plainville tell *Bet Din* that the marketplace is not a natural monopoly and there is room to accommodate two sellers, without anyone's livelihood becoming ruined. No doubt the competition from Big Lion will cause Goldfarb's income to go down, but the reduction in income will only represent his loss in monopoly profits and not push Goldfarb below his opportunity cost earnings. Once in operation, Big Lion sells above its own cost, but below the cost of Goldfarb. Goldfarb sees quick ruination for himself and sues *Bet Din* to issue an injunction against the pricing policy of Big Lion.

Within the framework of the deprivation-generating criterion, how is *Bet Din* to react to Goldfarb's petition? On the one hand, Goldfarb has a legitimate claim that the pricing policy of Big Lion will drive him out of business. Let us, however, not lose sight of the fact that the marketplace is big enough to accommodate two sellers. Accordingly, to take Goldfarb's side and exclude Big Lion from operating in Plainville is an overprotection for Goldfarb and, at the same time, deprives Big Lion of its legitimate rights. The solution here, in the opinion of this writer, is the imposition of a price guidepost for Big Lion that protects Goldfarb from ruination. Economists call a protective price of this sort an umbrella price. What we mean by umbrella pricing is not an invitation for Goldfarb and Big Lion to engage in collusion, consisting of Goldfarb setting his prices and Big Lion dutifully following Goldfarb's leadership. This arrangement is an outright price-fixing arrangement and it violates secular law.[70] Instead, *Bet Din* should signal the parties that it fully expects price competition. This is the way of the marketplace and it is not for *Bet Din* to decide what kind or degree of price competition between the parties is appropriate. What umbrella pricing says to Big Lion is that it should not adopt a pricing policy across the board that would put Goldfarb in the red for, say, any particular month. Big Lion could, however, sell below the cost of Goldfarb on particular items. Finally, if Goldfarb claims ruinous competition, the burden of proof is on him.

One more caveat. *Bet Din* must tell Goldfarb that umbrella pricing is only a temporary stop gap measure. The dynamics of the marketplace are such that an efficient low-priced firm will attract a wide customer base with a significant radius. Accordingly, suppose another supermarket opens along the commuter route Plainville residents use to get to work. Since this store is located in a different geographical area from Plainville, the Plainville *Bet Din* has no authority to regulate competition between like stores located in the two separate geographical areas. If Plainville residents are attracted to the turnpike supermarket on account of its low prices and other factors, *Bet Din* will do nothing to stop this. Moreover, once it is evident that the competition from the turnpike supermarket will cause Goldfarb to go out of business, there is no basis to continue with the umbrella price constraint on Big

Lion either; irrespective of whether *Bet Din* constrains Big Lion in its pricing policies, Goldfarb will go under.

Consider that the umbrella pricing agreement, whether ordered by a *Bet Din* or agreed to voluntarily, is a restraint of trade agreement. If umbrella pricing is part of the tool kit of the *Bet Din* that adopts the deprivation-generating criterion, a serious conflict between this school of thought and secular law has been identified.

Notwithstanding the theoretical possibility that the *Bet Din* that subscribes to the deprivation-generating criterion would, on occasion, resort to this procedure, the scenario that invites this solution is very rare. It can come up only if the marketplace develops in a linear fashion in the lock step formation we outlined earlier. In the real world, the marketplace does not develop in this simple fashion. Because the imposition of umbrella pricing by a Jewish court that subscribes to the deprivation-generating criterion is more a hypothetical construct than real world tool, this concept does not pose a serious conflict between Jewish and American law.

PREDATORY PRICE CUTTING AND AMERICAN LAW

In our presentation of the two schools of thought regarding the protection Halakhah affords an incumbent firm against the competitive pressures of the marketplace, we theorized that all opinions agree that *Bet Din* would enjoin a market participant from engaging in predatory pricing consisting of selling below cost. Elsewhere we have proposed that Halakhah would adopt the Areeda-Turner definition of predation, which identifies predation as consisting of selling below one's own long-run marginal cost.[71]

Although both schools agree on this matter, the rationale behind the opinions is different.

For the deprivation-generating criterion, the rationale is that predatory price cutting exerts a ruinous impact on rival firms and therefore should be enjoined. If the threat of ruination is the key here, aspects of the loss leader stratagem should also be prohibited. Specifically, a loss leader stratagem that impacts the core business of the industry should be a candidate for enjoinment. Illustrating this type of loss leader stratagem, described earlier in this chapter, is the offer by a restaurant to sell a variety of its sandwiches below cost, with the expectation that customers will stampede to the store to get the giveaway and, at the same time, splurge on the various side dishes and desserts that customers purchase along with their sandwiches.

In *Goldfarb v. Carmel*, the Jewish court, committed to the deprivation-generating criterion, ruled that Carmel's fruit and vegetable business could not be blocked. In this ruling the *Bet Din* was in agreement with American law. Although the conclusion is here the same, the philosophies behind the rulings are different. For the *Bet Din* the key consideration was that the grocery store business should be viewed as a single integrated business, rather than as a loose conglomerate of different lines of products. Since Carmel's entry is a threat only to Goldfarb's fruit and vegetable business, not to the viability of Goldfarb's grocery store business as a whole, there is no basis to block Carmel. But for American law, the judgment that Carmel's fruit and vegetable business is not a ruinous threat to Goldfarb's grocery store business is not critical to the *laissez faire* approach. Rather, the key is that Carmel has not priced below his own costs. Even if the assessment was that Carmel's competitive presence would force Goldfarb out of business, American law would not block Carmel's entry.

For the free entry school, selling below cost is also prohibited. But the rationale here is not simply that S_1 threatens S_2 with ruination. The threat of ruination alone will not suffice to enjoin a business tactic. What prohibits this conduct is the principle that S_1's license to implement a business plan that will inevitably put S_2 out of business is limited. If the tactic will also generate losses for S_1 in the current period, S_1's conduct is *an investment* and therefore cannot be looked upon as a *livelihood* activity for the current time period.

Extending the concept of predation to a prohibition against the loss leader stratagem is, however, unwarranted. To be sure, S_2's loss leader stratagem is potentially ruinous for S_1, but from the vantage point of S_2, the stratagem is not self-destructive, but rather a risky investment that has every prospect, as far as S_2 is concerned, of turning into a handsome return in the current period of time.

Prohibiting selling below cost but permitting all forms of the loss leader stratagem puts the free entry school in accord with federal law on these issues.[72]

At this juncture let us take note that twenty-five states have enacted statutes prohibiting sales below cost of a general nature. Even more states prohibit sales below cost of particular products such as cigarettes, milk, other dairy products and insurance. States began to enact these statutes in the early part of the twentieth century in order to alleviate "the hardships of 'cut throat' competition" caused by the growth of discount retailers.[73]

In 1959, the United States Supreme Court opined that "one of the chief aims of state laws prohibiting sales below cost was to put an end to 'loss leaders' selling."[74]

In respect to the loss leader stratagem, state law is hence more consonant with the protectionist school.

DISCRIMINATORY PRICING

In the scenario *Goldfarb v. Koller* the issue was price discrimination. Jonathan Koller, the proprietor of the grocery store in a nearby town, Greenville, set up a dual pricing system for his baked goods, charging the Plainville customers a lower price than the local residents. Based on the responsa by R. Hayyim Sofer, who dealt with a similar case, *Bet Din* extrapolated that Koller's pricing policy violated Jewish law. The prohibition is rooted in the assertion that the sages who validate the distribution of "nuts" as a business tactic do so only in respect to the local marketplace, but not as a means of snaring the business of a rival that is located in a different marketplace. Since Goldfarb's price discrimination complaint is rooted in Judaism's notion of "fairness" in the use of competitive tactics, it should be unnecessary for him to prove actual losses in revenues on account of Koller's policy. Moreover, since the practice is an unfair business tactic, *Bet Din* would order Koller to end his price discrimination policy even if the complaint against it came from consumers in Greenville.

One final point: If price discrimination is prohibited because it is not a "fair" competitive tactic, the freedom of entry school may very well also agree that a businessperson may not employ this tactic on the grounds that it falls short of Judaism's ethical norms of the marketplace.

In American Law, price discrimination is prohibited under section 2 of the Clayton Act, commonly referred to as the Robinson-Patman Act.[75]

Directed at protecting the independent retailer from chain store competition, the Act prohibits price discrimination only when the effect of the discrimination is to lessen competition or to create a monopoly. Robinson-

Patman does not prohibit a retailer from engaging in price discrimination among his customers.[76] To prove a violation of the act, at least one of the two transactions that generate discrimination when they are compared must cross a state line.[77] Consider Koller is a retailer who practices discrimination among his customers. In addition, Koller does not engage in interstate commerce. Robinson-Patman clearly does not prohibit Koller's brand of price discrimination.

PHILANTHROPY IN THE MARKETPLACE

Another area of apparent conflict between American and Jewish law is the cease and desist order *Bet Din* issued against Eitan Kramer's philanthropy when he made subsistence goods available to the poor at cost. Since the issue at hand was the proper means of carrying out the charity obligation, the freedom of entry school could very well be in agreement with the conclusion of the court.

Would American law view *Bet Din*'s action as a call for restraint of trade and therefore be prohibited under the anti-trust laws? Perhaps not. The analog in American law is *State of Missouri v. National Organization for Women (NOW)*.[78] In that case the issue was whether NOW's call to its members for a convention boycott against all states that had not ratified the proposed Equal Rights Amendment (ERA) constituted a restraint of trade practice. The affirmative argument stated that the impact of this call for a boycott were such that the state's motels and restaurants catering to the convention trade and its economy as a whole was suffering.[79]

In its ruling, the United States Court of Appeals focused on the circumstance that NOW was not in a competitive relationship with Missouri that suffered as a result of the boycott. Moreover, NOW was not motivated by any type of anticompetitive purpose. Rather, its scope was political and, accordingly, was not within the ambit of the anti-trust laws.[80]

Analogously, *Bet Din* is not in a competitive relationship with any of the retail grocery stores in Plainville. Its purpose in promulgating its ruling is merely to express an opinion on how the charity duty required in Jewish law for Jews should be carried out. *Bet Din*'s call for Kramer to put to an end his cost-based pricing subsidy to the poor, hence, does not violate anti-trust law.[81]

RECONCILING JEWISH AND AMERICAN LAW

We have identified a number of instances where Jewish and American law clash on the issue of fair competition. Two of these instances relate to the ethics of specific business practices. These are the stratagems for a retailer to charge nonlocal customers a lower price compared to local customers and to employ a loss leader pricing policy for a product that is a core item in a rival's business. Both schools of thought in Jewish law may prohibit these stratagems. The conflict between the two systems of law is somewhat mitigated in respect to the issue of the loss leader stratagem because many states prohibit this practice.

The second area of conflict is the issue of protecting an incumbent firm from ruinous competition. The latter issue is a problem only for the deprivation-generating criterion. But, the freedom of entry school does not protect an incumbent firm from ruinous competition. Hence, this school of thought is consonant with American law on this point.

Let us begin with the first two stratagems involved in the first area of conflict. If *Bet Din* prohibits the use of these stratagems, the Jewish court could perhaps be accused of imposing a restraint of trade agreement on rival businesses. But, in the Torah society, is the *Bet Din* the first venue that takes up business ethics issues? No. In the Torah society, moral training is an integral part of the parental duty, the responsibility of the educational system, and the Torah education of the businessperson.[82] If the family and school are a moral training ground, ethical conduct for the marketplace is part of that training. The circumstance that unethical conduct comes to an end only by means of demanding its removal in the context of a court proceeding manifests at least some degree of failure in the parental institution and/or educational system.

Can this argument be extended to the proposition that the issue of protecting an incumbent firm against ruination would also not usually come up in a Jewish court? Apparently not. Consider that how this issue is treated is a matter of dispute in Jewish law. How, then, can we rely on the parental and religious educational institutions to handle the issue so that it never reaches the Jewish court? The answer is, we contend, that the difference between the schools of thought on fair competition is closer than what first appears. Recall the luncheonette case, where R. Breisch allowed the inside vendor to compete with the luncheonette, despite the possibility that the insider would ruin the business of the luncheonette. R. Breisch averred that it would be a matter of *lifnim mi-shurat ha-din* (i.e., beyond the letter of the law), for the inside vendor not to expand his food service business beyond tea and sweets. What R. Breisch is telling us is that causing a ruinous impact on an incumbent firm is a very serious matter. Before embarking on this path, one should carefully consider an alternative course of action. On the other hand, recall the state of the Plainville grocery marketplace just before Millstein was poised to enter. Goldfarb was a monopolist. The market demand was expanding considerably beyond his capacity and as a result the quality of Goldfarb's service was rapidly deteriorating. Notwithstanding these conditions, Goldfarb's thinking was that *Bet Din* should protect his monopoly profits forever. Suing Millstein in *Bet Din* to keep him out borders on abusive conduct on the part of Goldfarb. The point of our contrast is that if the moral institutions of society were doing their job, neither the luncheonette case nor the original suit Goldfarb lodged against Millstein would have ended up in court. What the moral educational institutions should accomplish is the cultivation of the proper balance between pursuing aggressively one's livelihood, and passing up opportunities in this regard for the sake of allowing one's fellow to earn a livelihood.

Let us not be guilty of begging the question. In this chapter, we have identified several scenarios where Jewish law is at odds with American law. The argument that the importance of moral education in the Torah society makes it likely that the contested issues of fair competition would be handled at various levels before it would reach an adversarial procedure in a *Bet Din* is no more than a normative statement. The reality, however, is that *Bet Din* does deal with the issue of freedom of entry and the ethics of various business tactics. If *Bet Din*, for instance, denies a firm the right to enter a town and set up a competing business with a local tradesman, does this ruling violate American law? Perhaps not. One redeeming factor is that *Bet Din* is never in a competitive position with any of the affected commercial enterprises. In this regard, the cases entailing the issue of ruinous competition are akin to the NOW case cited earlier. But, the second extenuating factor present in the NOW case is, however, absent in the ruinous competition and unethical business tactic cases. Consider that *Bet Din*'s motive in issuing a restraint of trade order is nothing but their opinion of what constitutes "fairness" as far as competition in the marketplace is concerned. *Bet Din*'s notion of what constitutes fairness is in opposition to what American law has legislated for American society. Nonetheless, the First Amendment principles found in NOW should provide some protection for a well-meaning *Bet Din*.

Final judgment on this matter must, however, be reserved. Consider that what the anti-trust laws forbid is "combinations and conspiracies in restraint of trade." Should a proceeding of *Bet Din* be regarded as a "conspiracy" in restraint of trade? Such a characterization is warranted only if at the end of the day *Bet Din*'s ruling adversely affects third parties, namely consumers. But, suppose not just the competitors, but the affected consumers as well, voluntarily submit to the authority of *Bet Din* on this matter. In these circumstances, the *Bet Din* proceeding should not be regarded as a "conspiracy in restraint of trade." Let us take note that in all the court battles between Goldfarb and Millstein and in the suit in which they joined together against Big Lion, the affected consumers were synagogue-member Jews located in the same local community. To avoid being accused of ordering a restraint of trade agreement on Goldfarb and Millstein, *Bet Din* need only have the affected consumers join the plaintiff competitor as petitioners in the case. It does this by getting each of the synagogues to authorize someone to represent them at the court hearing for the purpose of declaring to *Bet Din* that the body he represents authorizes *Bet Din* to adjudicate the matter. Since the litigant competitors as well as the impacted consumers authorize the *Bet Din* to adjudicate the matter, the *Bet Din* proceeding should be free of any conspiracy characterization.

Realistically, this procedure can work only when the affected consumers are identifiable, are committed to Jewish law, and can agree on a specific *Bet Din* that will be authorized to adjudicate the matter. The larger the geographic area the consumer base encompasses, the more likely that the consumer base will not be a cohesive group, and thus one or more of the above factors will be missing. Accordingly, this procedure may work for ritual items such as the four species, *matzah*, and wine. Other than for these items, the prospects are, in all probability, nil.

Notes

1. *Bava Batra* 21a.
2. R. Isaac b. Jacob Alfasi (Algeria, 1012–1103), *Rif, Bava Batra* 21b; *Tosafot, Bava Batra* 21b; Maimonides (Egypt, 1135–1204), *Yad, Shekhenim* 6:18; R. Asher b. Jehiel (Germany, 1250–1327), *Rosh, Bava Batra* 2:12; R. Jacob b. Asher (Spain, 1250–1327),

Tur, Hoshen Mishpat 156; R. Joseph Caro (Israel, 1488–1575), *Shulhan Arukh, Hoshen Mishphat* 156:5; R. Jehiel Michel Epstein (Belorussia, 1829–1908), *Arukh ha-Shulhan, Hoshen Mishpat* 156:6.

3. Ibid.

4. *Piskei Din shel Botei ha-Din ha-Rabbaniyim bi-Yisroel*, vol. 6, no. 3 (Jerusalem, 1965), p. 90; see R. Nahum Rakover, *Halikhut ha-Mishar*, no. 42 (Jerusalem: *Misrad ha-Mishpatim*, 1976), p. 12

5. Designation of scholars who were active in the period from the eleventh to the middle of the fifteenth century.

6. R. Eliezer b. Joel ha-Levi (Bonn, 1140–1225), quoted by R. Mordecai b. Hillel (Germany, 1240–1298), *Mordecai, Bava Batra* 1:516 and by R. Meir ha-Kohen (fl. 13th cent.), *Haggahot Maimuniyyot, Shekhenim* 6:8.

7. R. Mosheh Isserles (Poland, 1527–1572), *Responsa Rema* 10; see also *Darkhei Mosheh, Tur*, op. cit., 156, no. 4.

8. R. Joseph Ibn MiGash, *Ri MiGash, Bava Batra* 2lb.

9. R. Mosheh Sofer, *Responsa Hatam Sofer, Hoshen Mishpat* 78.

10. Ibid, 118.

11. R. Mosheh Feinstein, *Iggerot Mosheh, Hoshen Mishpat* 1:38

12. *Bava Batra* 21b.

13. Yad, *Mekhirah* 18:4; *Tur*, op. cit., 228:16; *Sh. Ar.*, op. cit., 228;18: *Ar. ha-Sh.*, op. cit., 228:14.

14. R. Hayyim Halberstam, *Responsa Divrei Hayyim, Hoshen Mishpat* 1:20.

15. R. Solomon b. Isaac, *Rashi, Bava Batra* 21b.

16. Nahmanides, *Bava Batra* 21b.

17. Responsa *Rema* 10; see also *Darkhei Mosheh, Tur, Hoshen Mishpat* 156, n. 4.

18. *Rema, Sh. Ar.*, op. cit., 156:5.

19. For sources and the application of *lifnim mi-shurat ha-din* to various business contexts, see Aaron Levine, *Case Studies in Jewish Business Ethics* (Hoboken, NJ: Ktav Publishing and Yeshiva University Press, 2000), pp. 257–264, 269.

20. R. Yaakov Mordecai Breisch, *Helkhat Yaakov* 2:65.

21. *Piskei Din Rabbaniyim*, vol. 6, p. 90; see R. Nahum Rakover, *Halikhut ha-Mishar*, no. 4l (Jerusalem: *Misrad ha-Mishpatim*, 1976), pp. 1–27.

22. *Piskei Din Rabbaniyim*, vol. 6, p. 90; see *Halikhut ha-Mishar*, op. cit., pp. 1–27.

23. R. Solomon Leib Tabak, *Teshurat Shai* 2:4.

24. John S. McGee, "Predatory Price Cutting: The Standard Oil (N.J.) Case," *Journal of Law and Economics* 137, (October 1958).

25. Keith N. Hylton, *Antitrust Law Economic Theory and Common Law Evolution* (Cambridge: Cambridge University Press, 2003), p. 213.

26. *Tanna Kamma, Baraita, Bava Batra* 21b.

27. R. Meir b. Todros ha-Levi Abulafia, *Ramah, Bava Batra* 21b.

28. *Betzah* 16a.

29. R. Solomon b. Isaac, *Rashi, Betzah* 16a.

30. In the 1980s The Rabbinical Council of Bergen County (RCBC) commissioned a *Bet Din* to adjudicate disputes within their jurisdiction relating to claims of "unfair competition." In all the cases an established firm petitioned the court to block a new entrant on the grounds that the competitive presence of the new firm would either hurt or ruin its busi-

ness. The cases reflected the growing pains of a community coming into its own. Together with Rabbis Yosef Blau and Mordecai Willig of RIETS, Yeshiva University, I served on that *Bet Din*. The criterion we adopted for all cases was the deprivation-generating criterion as formulated by R. Mosheh Feinstein.

31. An exception to the rule that a nontaxpaying outsider is barred from entry is the case of the peddler of perfume and beautification aids for women. With the aim of making these items readily available for women, Ezra (Babylonia, early 5th century B.C.E. or late 4th century B.C.E.) legislated that these peddlers be allowed to peddle their wares door to door (*Bava Batra* 22a).

32. R. Mosheh Isserles, *Rema, Hoshen Mishpat* 156:7. In the instance where the outsider also offers to take up residence in the town, authorities dispute whether the townspeople can still block his entrance, see, *Rema*, op. cit.

33. Rabbenu Gershom b. Judah Me'Or ha-Golah, *Rabbenu Gershom, Bava Batra* 21b.

34. R. Joseph Ibn MiGash, *Ri MiGash, Bava Batra* 21b.

35. *Mishnah, Bava Metzia* 4:12.

36. *Bava Metzia* 60b.

37. Nahmanides, *Ramban, Bava Batra* 21b.

38. R. Joseph Habiba, *Nimmukei Yosef* at *Rif, Bava Batra* 21b; R. Abraham b. Moses Boton (ca. 1560–1609), *Lehem Rav* 216.

39. R. Joseph Caro, *Beit Yosef, Tur*, op. cit., 156, part 3; R. Mordecai b. Hillel on interpretation of R. Boton, loc. cit.

40. R. Abraham b. Moses Boton *Lehem Rav*, op. cit.

41. R. Joseph Caro, *Shulhan Arukh, Yoreh De'ah* 173:1.

42. For the sources of the basic laws of *ona'ah*. Please turn to pp . **???** of this volume.

43. R. Jacob Moses Lorberbaum, *Havvot Da'at*, 173, note 3

44. See the silk ribbons case discussed at *Bava Metzia* 51a.

45. R. Hayyim Sofer, *Mahaneh Hayyim, Hoshen Mishpat* 2:46.

46. *Kiddushin* 59a.

47. R. Solomon b. Isaac, *Rashi, Kiddushin* 59a and R. Nissim b. Reuben Gerondi (Barcelona, ca. 1290–ca. 1375) explication of *Rashi*'s view, *Ran, Kiddushin* 59a.

48. R. Jacob Tam, *Tosafot, Kiddushin* 59a. and R. Asher b. Jehiel's explication of R. Jacob Tam's view (*Rosh, Kiddushin* 3:2).

49. *Sh. Ar., Hoshen Mishpat*, 237:2 on interpretation of R. Jacob Moses Lorberbaum (Lisa, 1760–1832), *Nitivot ha-Mishpat*, ad. loc., note 2; *Rema, Sh. Ar.*, op. cit., 237:1; *Rema me-Pana*, 67; R. Joel Sirkes (Poland, 1561–1650), Responsa *Bah* 61; R. Mosheh Feinstein, *Iggerot Mosheh, Even ha-Ezel* 1:92.

50. R. Meir b. Barukh (Rottenburg, 1215–1293), quoted by R. Mordecai b. Hillel (Germany, 1240?–1298), *Mordecai, Bava Batra* 3:55; *Rema, Sh. Ar.*, op. cit., 237:1; *Ar. ha-Sh.*, op. cit., 237:1.

51. R. Yair Hayyim Bacharach, Responsa *Havvot Ya'ir* 41.

52. Nahmanides, *Ramban, Kiddushin* 59a.

53. Nahmanides, *Ramban, Bava Batra* 21b.

54. R. Meir b. Todros ha-Levi Abulafia, *Ramah, Bava Batra* 21b.

55. Leviticus 19:9–10; 23:22.

56. *Mishnah, Pe'ah* 4:2; *Bava Metzia* 10a.

57. R. Nissim b. Reuben Gerondi, *Ran, Kiddushin* 59a.

58. Yad, *Mekhirah* 18:4; *Tur*, op. cit., 228:18; *Sh. Ar.*, op. cit., 228:18; *Ar. ha-Sh.*, op. cit., 228:18.

59. R. Meir b. Isaac Eisenstadt, *Panim Me'irot* 1:78; *Ar. ha-Sh.*, loc. cit.; R. Judah Loeb Graubart (Szrensk, 1862–1937), *Havalim ba-Neimim* 2:113.

60. Ibid.

61. *Panim Me'irot*, loc. cit.; see also *Ar. ha-Sh.*, loc. cit.

62. R. Shelomo Kluger, *Hokhmat Shelomo* at *Sh. Ar.*, op. cit., 228:18.

63. *Baraita, Bava Batra* 21b.

64. R. Yaakov Yesha'yahu Bloi, *Pithe Hoshen, Hilkhot Geneivah ve-Ona'ah* 9:11 *ot* 26.

65. *Iggerot Mosheh*, op. cit., 1:38.

66. The scenario in the text is based on the "burger wars" that took place in recent years among the major fast-food chains. For a brief account of the burger wars, the reader is referred to Brian Horovitz, "Fast-food Battle Escalates Into Whopper Price War," *USA Today*, December 12, 2002, p. 3b.

67. Please turn to pp. 330–331, 340–345 of this volume.

68. William J. Baumol & Allan S. Blinder, *Economic Principles and Policies* 9th ed. (Mason, OH: Thomson-South Western, 2003), pp. 380–382.

69. Henry R. Cheeseman, *Contemporary Business and E-Commerce Law*, 3rd Edition (Upper Saddle River, NJ: Prentice Hall, 2000), p. 899.

70. W. Kip Viscusi, John M. Vernon, & Joseph E. Harrington, Jr., *Economics of Regulation and Antitrust*, 3rd ed. (Cambridge, MA: The MIT Press, 2000), pp. 125–134.

71. Aaron Levine, *Free Enterprise and Jewish Law* (New York: Ktav Publishing House Inc. and Yeshiva University Press, 1980), pp. 21–24.

72. For the legality of the "loss leader" stratagem see *United States v. Milk Drivers & Dairy Employees Union, Local No. 471*, 153 F. Supp. 803 (D. Minn., 1957).

73. William H. Jordan, "Predatory Pricing After Brooke Group: The Problem of State "Sales Below Costs" Statutes," 44 *Emory L. R.* 267, 305.

74. *Safeway Stores v. Oklahoma Retail Grocers Assn.*, 360 U.S. 334, 340 (1959).

75. 15 U.S.C. 13(a).

76. *Mayer Paving and Asphalt Co. v. General Dynamics Corp.*, 486 F.2d 763, 766 (7th Cir. 1973).

77. *Gulf Oil Corporation v. Copp. Paving Co.*, 419 U.S. 186, 200, 42 L Ed. 2d 378,95 S. Ct. 392 (1974); *Mayer Paving and Asphalt Co. v. General Dynamics Corp.*, 486 F.2d 763, 766 (7th Cir. 1983).

78. *State of Missouri v. National Organization for Women, Inc.*, 620 F.2d 1301 (8th Cir., 1980).

79. Ibid. at 1302.

80. Ibid. at 1309–16.

81. David Schwartz of Wachtell, Lipton, Rosen & Katz brought to my attention the relevancy of *State of Missouri v. National Organization for Women* and a number of similar cases for the issue of reconciling Halakhah with secular law. My gratitude to him for his insights on this matter.

82. For sources and the development of this theme, see Aaron Levine, *Case Studies in Jewish Business Ethics* (Hoboken, NJ: Ktav Publishing and Yeshiva University Press, 2000), pp. 1–32.

4

Employee Agreements Not To Compete

In a "post-employment restrictive covenant" an employee agrees, upon being employed, to conform to certain conditions following termination of employment with his or her present employer. Thus, for example, a restrictive covenant might include an agreement by the employee not to enter, post-employment, into the same business for a specified or unlimited time period within a specified geographic area. Other clauses of the covenant could relate to trade secrets, confidential business practices, and customer lists.

Our purpose here will be to investigate how employee agreements not to compete are treated from the perspective of American law, economic theory, and Halakhah.

AMERICAN LAW

American law, as John R. Boatright points out, regards noncompetition agreements as inherently unfair. These agreements are almost entirely for the benefit of the employer and inflict a burden on employees that is out of proportion to any gain. At least twelve states consider them so unfair that they prohibit such agreements. In states that permit the agreements, a court will nonetheless outlaw a given agreement if it determines that the agreement's purpose is merely to protect an employer against competition. To be valid, the agreement must minimally be designed to protect the employer's legitimate entitlements, such as proprietary information or customer relations. To be sure, other criteria must be satisfied as well. These are (1) the restrictions must not be greater than what is required for the protection of the employer's legitimate interests; (2) the restrictions must not impose undue hardships on the ability of an employee to secure gainful employment; and (3) the restrictions must not be injurious to the public.

In determining whether the restrictions in a particular agreement are greater than those required to protect the entitlement of the employer, the courts will focus on (1) the time period specified, (2) the geographic area, and (3) the type of work that is excluded.[1]

THE RATIONALE FOR EMPLOYEE NONCOMPETE AGREEMENTS IN ECONOMIC THEORY

Paul Rubin and Peter Shedd offer an economic analysis of the common-law treatment of employee contracts not to compete. These authors conclude that the common-law treatment of this phenomenon is efficient, in that it promotes an optimal amount of investment in human capital. Standing at the core of Rubin and Shedd's analysis is Gary Becker's pioneering work on the impact of on-the-job training in the labor market.

Becker's work stresses that there are two types of on-the-job training: general training and specific training. General training is the type of training that, once acquired, is equally useful in all firms. These general skills, which can include typing, learning to drive, and learning how to use a computer, are found frequently in the labor market. Specific training is the type of training that enhances productivity only in the firm where it is acquired; the value of the training is lost once the worker leaves the firm. An illustration of specific training is learning how to drive a tank in the Army or memorizing the hierarchical nature of a particular organization.

In reality, much on-the-job training is a mixture of general and specific training. Nonetheless, the conceptual separation into purely general and purely specific training is extremely useful.

The central issue Becker addresses is who pays for general and specific on-the-job training. Is it the worker or is it the employer? Preliminarily, let us note that both general and specific training increase the worker's productivity and result in the firm's earning higher total revenue. In technical terms, the training increases the value of the worker's marginal product (VMP) for the firm.

There is insufficient economic incentive for a firm to provide general training. Any firm that provides this training will be forced by competitive pressures to compensate the trainee in the post-training period in accordance with his or her higher VMP. But there is no guarantee that the recipient of the general training will choose to stay with the firm that provided the training. Investing in general training exposes the firm to the prospect of incurring the cost of the training, yet reaping none of its benefits.

This leads Becker to assert that a firm will not provide general training unless the worker pays for general training by accepting a lower "trainee wage" during the training period. Later on, workers get the returns from the training by receiving a wage that equals the value of their post-training marginal product. Firms provide general training, therefore, only if they do not pay any of the costs.

There are many examples of workers who pay for general training through lower wages. It is common for trainees in formal apprenticeship programs to receive low wages during their training period, and to receive much higher wages after the training is completed. Similarly, medical interns earn low wages and work long hours during their residency, but their investment pays off substantially once they complete their training.

Let us now turn to the issue of who pays for specific training. The salient consideration here is that the productivity gains resulting from the training vanish once the worker leaves the firm. This means that market forces will not compel the firm providing the training to raise the trainee's wage to his higher VMP once the training is completed. Accordingly, the firm could incur the cost of specific training and collect the returns by not raising the trainee's wage to his higher VMP in the post-training period. But, if the worker quits in the post-training period, the firm suffers a capital loss. The firm, therefore, would hesitate to pay for specific training unless it has some assurance that the trained worker will not quit.

Is there sufficient incentive for the worker to incur the cost of specific training? By making himself more valuable to a particular firm, the worker who invests in firm-specific training can count on earning a higher wage in the post-training period. But let us not lose sight of the fact that firm-specific training is not portable. If the worker is laid off, he loses his investment. The worker, therefore, will not be willing to invest in specific training unless he is confident that he will not be laid off.

The upshot of this analysis is that both the worker and the firm are reluctant to invest in specific training. However, specific training carries with it the potential for mutual gain for both worker and firm. Market forces will therefore work to produce a post-training wage that is higher than the worker's productivity elsewhere, but lower than his VMP at the firm providing the specific training. Because both the firm and the worker share the returns of the specific training, the possibility of job separation in the post-training period is eliminated.[2]

Within the framework of Becker's analysis, there is no need for any contractual term limiting the future market behavior of the worker, as market forces will generate solutions without contracts. Yet many employment contracts do contain clauses limiting the future behavior of employees, and such contracts are common sources of legal disputes. Thus, there must be some aspects of real-world labor markets that Becker's analysis does not fully capture. The lacuna in Becker's analysis, Rubin and Shedd point out, occurs in certain types of general training for which the worker will not pay.

Assume, for example, that it takes a firm one day to teach a worker the details of a trade secret valuable to many other firms, and worth $100,000. The value of the information is so great that the worker cannot pay for it by accepting reduced wages. Moreover, because of difficulties in borrowing with human capital as collateral, there may be no other way for the worker to finance the acquisition of human capital with sufficiently high value. Human capital cannot serve as collateral for loans because of the impossibility of compelling specific performance. In this circumstance, the firm would want the worker to sign a noncompetition clause, for such a clause would indicate that the worker could not use the training acquired elsewhere.

Once the worker has received this training, however, he has an incentive to behave opportunistically, by violating the contract and then profiting from the training—either by going to work for himself or by going to work for another firm, which will pay him a premium because of the value of his training. In this situation, the worker attempts to appropriate for himself the value of the training for which he did not pay. Thus, if the noncompetition clause is not binding, firms will be forced to use more costly methods of production in some circumstances in order to protect their proprietary information.

To be sure, court-enforced restrictive covenants forestall opportunistic behavior on the part of employees, but employers can use these covenants as an opportunistic device as well. Specifically, if the courts were to enforce these covenants in a blanket way, the employer would be encouraged to design the clause to maximally reduce the worker's future mobility. Against a background of severely limited alternative employment possibilities, the worker would be forced to agree to "overpay" for the general training he received by accepting a wage below the full value of his marginal product.[3]

The Economic Efficiency of Common Law

In their survey of the common-law treatment of restrictive covenants, Rubin and Shedd claim that the rules that have been adopted are economically efficient. Specifically, the rules operate to forestall opportunistic conduct on the part of both employer and employee, and hence promote an optimal investment in human capital.

One area Rubin and Shedd consider is the treatment of customer lists, regarding which the most important legal distinction is the amount of effort required for their development. If the list of customers is generally available to firms engaged in a particular business or is a list of one-time customers, the courts have refused to protect the firm's property in this list. For example, courts have held to be unreasonable covenants not to compete signed by real estate salespeople and desk clerks of car rental agencies. These covenants were not enforced because the courts found that these employees had no special knowledge of the employer's past, present, or potential customers. Furthermore, in the real estate and car rental industry, the clientele tend to be transient, rather than repeat customers.

Conversely, if a firm can show that it spent time and resources in developing its customer list, it is entitled to protect the list, and a restrictive covenant designed for this purpose is recognized and enforced by law. According to Rubin and Shedd, this approach operates on the assumption that if resources are required to establish a list of customers, but that list will not be protected, the incentive will be to invest too few resources in developing lists.

Recall that economic efficiency requires the courts to protect the interest of the employee against opportunistic behavior on the part of the employer. The courts have done this with respect to the geographic scope of restrictive covenants. Specifically, the courts will only enforce restrictive covenants that disallow W from competing for the customers he dealt with while employed by E. The courts will not enforce a noncompetition agreement against W when the latter is competing for customers of E outside the sales territory where W worked when he was employed by E. This criterion prevents opportunistic behavior on the part of E. Specifically, by forbidding competition with respect to former customers, the courts are probably preventing W from using capital for which he/she did not pay. By allowing competition in other geographic areas, the courts are allowing W to utilize the general skills he/she acquired during his/her employment that were not considered in the noncompetition covenant.[4]

POST-EMPLOYMENT AGREEMENTS NOT TO COMPETE AND *DINA DE-MALKHUTA DINA*

From the perspective of Halakhah, perhaps the most basic issue to consider with regard to post-employment agreements is whether Samuel's dictum of "the law of the kindgom is the law" (*dina de-malkhuta dina*)[5] applies. The dictum relates to disputes between Jews in matters of civil law. Four views regarding the scope of this rule can be identified.

1. Taking the narrowest view on the scope of *dina de-malkhuta dina* is R. Joseph Caro (Israel, 1488–1575). In his view, Halakhah recognizes *dina de-malkhuta* only with respect to matters in which the government has a financial stake, such as taxes and currency regulation.[6]

2. Adopting a much wider scope for *dina de-malkhuta* is R. Mosheh Isserles (Poland, 1525 or 1530–1572). In his view, *dina de-malkhuta* applies to civil law generally. Conflict between Halakhah and *dina de-malkhuta*, in his view, is generally decided in favor of *dina de-malkhuta*.[7] There are exceptions to this rule, however. It does not hold in relation to the law of inheritance,[8] nor does it give Jews the option of taking their dispute to secular courts.[9] Moreover, *dina de-malkhuta* is recognized only when the law involved either benefits the government or was enacted for the benefit of the people of the land.[10]

3. Disputing R. Isserles is R. Shabbetai b. Meir ha-Kohen (Poland, 1621–1662), who avers that in litigation between Jews, the law of the land

is valid only when the non-Jewish law does not contradict Halakhah, or in a case where the practical application of Halakhah is not clear.[11]

4. Reacting to R. Shabbetai b. Meir ha-Kohen, R. Abraham Isaiah Karelitz (Israel, 1878–1953) sharply disputes the notion that lacunae exist in Halakhah. For any issue, a halakhic position can be extrapolated from legal precedents and rules. But following R. Shabbetai b. Meir ha-Kohen, he agrees that, if *dina de-malkhuta* contradicts Halakhah, even if the Halakhah was derived by means of extrapolation, the law of the land must be set aside.[12]

Many decisors regard R. Isserles' position as normative.[13] If we adopt R. Isserles' view, secular law's treatment of post-employment covenants in a given state should prevail. The matter cannot, however, be resolved so simply. Currently, there is no legislation on this matter. Instead, the legal treatment of post-employment covenants not to compete is entirely a matter of common law. Judges use their discretion to decide how post-employment covenants not to compete should be treated. Common law often follows precedent, but judges are not bound by it. What, we must therefore ask, is the scope of *dina de-malkhuta dina*? Does it apply only to legislation, or does it extend even to common law? Addressing himself to this issue, R. Isserles rules, quoting R. Solomon b. Abraham Adret (Spain, ca. 1235–1310), that *dina de-malkhuta* applies only to laws of the government, but does not apply to the discretionary authority of judges who make use of their own books of laws to decide cases. Giving legitimacy to the law of judges is tantamount to nullifying the law of the Torah.[14] Following this line of thought, R. Jekhutiel Asher Zalman Zausmir (Poland, d. 1858) describes the law of judges as discretionary decisions based on Greek and Roman law and innovations required by new conditions. In disputes between Jews, the law of judges should not be followed; instead, the law of the Torah should prevail. *Dina de-malkhuta* has its application only in laws the king directly promulgates.[15] In his treatment of this issue, the contemporary scholar R. Shelomo Dikhovsky (Israel) points out that legislation is also subject to judicial interpretation. What sets common law apart is that common law is not an interpretation of the king's edict but instead gives the judge wide latitude to base his or her decision on other systems of law.[16]

The upshot of this analysis is that in a dispute between Jews in a matter relating to a post-employment covenant not to compete, *dina de-malkhuta* does not prevail. We therefore must proceed beyond trying to resolve the issue by appeal to *dina de-malkhuta dina*, and instead extrapolate the halakhic perspective on the post-employment covenant not to compete.

POST-EMPLOYMENT AGREEMENTS NOT TO COMPETE AND HALAKHAH

Addressing the issue of the legal status of a noncompetition labor agreement is the contemporary Israeli Talmudic scholar, R. Yisrael Grosman. The particulars of the case are as follows:

> *E* offered to train and hire *W* to work in his factory to produce good *X*. *E* stipulated further with *W*: "In the event you leave my employ, you may neither work for someone else to produce good *X* nor become yourself a manufacturer of this good. If you go into competition with me in the future, I don't want to train you now." *W* raised no objections to these stipulations and began working for *E*. Ten years later *W* left *E's* employ and desired to produce good *X*.

In assessing whether *W* has a right to breach his agreement with *E*, R. Grosman brings to bear a number of considerations.

One consideration is whether the noncompetition agreement is binding by virtue of contract law. Take note that in the event *W* violates *E's* stipulation and competes with him in the future, *E* has no power to undo the training he provided *W*. *E's* inability to vitiate his undertaking on behalf of *W* makes any condition he attaches to the provision of this undertaking invalid in the first place. R. Grosman draws support for this contention from a comment of R. Akiva Eger (Germany, 1761–1837) on the *Mishnah* at *Pe'ah* 7:11. One of the agricultural gifts to which the Torah entitles the poor in Israel in Temple times is *shikhhah* (forgotten produce). This refers to sheaves forgotten in the field during the moving of the sheaves to the threshing floor, as well as to standing produce that the harvester overlooked. With regard to the farmer's *shikhhah* obligation, the *Mishnah* rules, "If someone says, 'Behold, I am reaping on condition that what I forget I shall take,' he is [still] subject to the law of *shikhhah*."

The stipulation is invalid, explains R. Israel b. Gedalyah Lipschutz (Germany, 1782–1860) because of the principle that if one stipulates a condition that, if effective, would override the law of the Torah, the condition is not valid.[17]

Commenting on R. Lipschutz, R. Akiva Eger avers that one can adduce a more fundamental reason to invalidate the farmer's stipulation. Specifically, the farmer's declaration regarding the consequence of nonfulfillment of his stipulation makes no sense. If his condition is violated, the crop cannot revert to its state prior to the reaping; the reaping cannot be undone. Since the farmer cannot undo his action in the event his stipulation is not fulfilled, his stipulation is invalid from the outset.

A stipulation is valid, according to R. Akiva Eger, only when the undertaking at hand can be viewed as a legal status (*halot*) subject to change. In such a case, the obligator can stipulate that the legal status of his undertaking should change, in the event his condition is not fulfilled. To illustrate: *L* lends *B* $1000 and stipulates that the Sabbatical year should not cancel *B's* obligation to pay back the $1000. *L* further stipulates that in the event the Sabbatical year cancels the debt, the original capital transfer should retroactively take on the character of a trust, which the Sabbatical year does not cancel. Since the obligator here stipulates a retroactive change in the status of his capital transfer, the *halot* condition is satisfied. *L's* stipulation would be fully effective, but for the rule that any stipulation that overrides a prohibition of the Torah is not valid.[18]

It seems to follow from the above analysis that a post-employment agreement not to compete cannot be achieved by means of Jewish contract law.[19]

This conclusion, however, can be questioned. If a conditional agreement must satisfy the *halot* condition to be valid, then a post-employment agreement not to compete can be crafted so as to satisfy this condition.

Before we spell out the form the post-employment agreement could take so as to satisfy the *halot* condition, let us note parenthetically that a conditional agreement, to be valid, must satisfy the *tenai kaful* (literally, "double condition") requirement. This requirement of contract law makes a conditional clause unenforceable unless the stipulations expressly spell out the consequences of both fulfillment and non-fulfillment of the clause.[20]

With the aim of satisfying both the *halot* requirement and the *tenai kaful* condition, the post-employment agreement not to compete could be crafted in the following manner: *E* agrees to train *W* with a particular skill without charge. *E* further stipulates that in the event *W* goes into competition with him, a fee of a specific amount will retroactively be owed for the service provided. This mechanism retroactively changes the provision of the training from a gift into a service done for a fee.

Consider a variation of this formulation. *E* commits himself without charge to train *W* with a particular skill. *W* agrees that in the event he goes into competition with *E* he will pay a penalty of a specific amount to *E*. This formulation does not meet the *halot* condition because non-compliance with the condition does not retroactively change the legal character of the transaction. Instead, non-compliance merely generates a new obligation on the part of *W*, which becomes operative at the moment he violates the non-compliance clause.

If the noncompetition agreement must, as we have established, take on the character of a retroactive sales transaction in the event of non-compliance, the price terms of the agreement will be subject to review on the basis of the law of *ona'ah* (price fraud). This law confers upon a market participant the right to conclude his market transaction on the basis of the competitive norm. Depending on how widely the price of the subject transaction departs from the competitive norm, the injured party may have recourse to void or adjust the transaction.[21]

But the law of *ona'ah* has limited application for a post-employment noncompetition agreement, because *ona'ah* applies only to commodities and services that sell at a competitive price.[22] Accordingly, if the skill *E* trains *W* with is not sold on the marketplace, the price terms of the agreement will not be subject to a "fairness" review based on the law of *ona'ah*.

ASMAKHTA

Another matter to consider in evaluating the validity of a post-employment agreement not to compete is the issue of whether such an agreement falls short of Halakhah's standard for a binding commitment. For an obligation to become legally binding, two critical tests must be met. First, the commitment must be made with deliberate and perfect intent (*gemirat da'at*). Second, the commitment must generate reliance (*semikhat da'at*) on the part of the party to whom it was made.[23] Both of these related conditions may be absent in a transaction that projects the finalization of an obligation into the future, becoming operative only upon the fulfillment of a specific condition. Such a transaction is referred to in Talmudic literature as an *asmakhta*. Since the obligation becomes operative only when a condition is fulfilled, the person obligating himself may very well rely on the probability that the condition will not be fulfilled, and thus that he will not become obligated. Because the presumption of perfect intent is lacking, the presumption that the commitment generated reliance is equally lacking.

A transaction characterized as an *asmakhta* is invalid *ab initio*.[24] If a post-employment agreement not to compete is an *asmakhta*, any attempt on the part of the employer to enforce it is a form of extortion.

In the final analysis, the halakhic validity of the post-employment agreement not to compete hinges on whether it satisfies the various criteria *Rishonim*[25] have proposed as to what constitutes an *asmakhta* undertaking. In what follows we will present these various criteria and apply them to the post-employment agreement not to compete.

One school of thought, led by R. Solomon b. Isaac (*Rashi*, France, 1040–1105), takes the position that *asmakhta* obtains when A makes a conditional obligation to *B*, but can escape it altogether, because he partially controls the triggering condition that makes the obligation operative. Let us illustrate this principle with a case discussed in the Talmud:

A agrees to buy current vintage wine for *B* at the low price of the Zulshafet marketplace. Furthermore, *A* stipulates that in the event he misses the window of opportunity to buy the wine while it is still cheap, he will make good to *B* the price differential involved. Now, if *A* acts quickly he can obtain the wine at the low price. If, on the other hand, *A* is negligent and tarries, he will miss the window of opportunity and will be liable to *B* to make good on the difference in price. Since A relies on himself (*toleh be-da'at atzmo*) to act quickly and avoid liability to *B*, he lacks firm resolve to make payment to *B* when it turns out that he misses the window of opportunity and faces the higher price.[26]

In a variation of the above case, when it is entirely within the control of the obligator to prevent the triggering condition, the agreement is not an *asmakhta*. Illustrating this is the tenant farmer's (*T's*) stipulation to his landlord (*L*) that in the event he does not cultivate the field, he will make good on *L's* loss of a crop. Consider that whether the price of seed is high or low, it is still within *T's* power to cultivate his field and avoid paying *L* for a lost crop. Because *T* realizes that he has no one to blame but himself if he ends up being liable to *L*, *T* resolves firmly to meet his obligation if it becomes operative. Here, *T's* stipulation does not take on the character of *asmakhta* unless he specifies a sum to indemnify *L* that is clearly in excess of *L's* foregone income.

At the other extreme stands the case where the obligator has absolutely no control over the triggering mechanism. Illustrating this case is a wager in a game of chance. Since each player realizes that he has no control over the outcome of the game, each player fully and firmly resolves to turn over the pot to the winner.[27]

Application of *Rashi's* criterion to the post-employment agreement not to compete should render this agreement null and void. Preliminarily, let us note that *W's* post-employment agreement not to compete with *E* may entail a considerable hardship for *W* if it comes to bear. This would be the case, for example, if *W* is suddenly terminated and has no skills with which to enter an alternative profession. But it is partially within *W's* power to avoid the hardship the post-employment agreement not to compete entails. *W* can be an exemplary worker and never give *E* reason to fire him. In addition, *W* can acquire another skill in his spare time and thereby avoid the difficulties that separation from *E* would otherwise entail. Nonetheless, it is not entirely within *W's* power to save himself from adverse consequences in the event his employment is terminated by *E*. *W's* post-employment agreement not to compete should therefore fall squarely into *Rashi's toleh be-da'at atzmo* criterion for *asmakhta*.

Disputing *Rashi's* criterion, R. Jacob Tam (France, c. 1100–1171) considers an *asmakhta* to be, in its essence, an agreement in a circumstance in which it evident that both parties desire the completion of the underlying agreement, and the conditional commitment is given merely as an assurance of good faith.[28]

R. Tam's formulation of *asmakhta* is clearly satisfied in the post-employment noncompetition case. Both *E* and *W* desire that their business tie remain mutually satisfactory and continue indefinitely. As a matter of good faith, *W* agrees not to compete in the event he ends his employment tie with *E*.

R. Solomon b. Abraham Adret advances still another criterion as to what constitutes *asmakhta*. Formulating an undertaking in terms of a penalty, in R. Adret's view, is what makes a conditional commitment an *asmakhta*.[29] Recall that formulating a post-employment agreement in terms of a penalty clause in the event of non-compliance fails the *halot* condition and hence makes the agreement invalid. R. Adret's criterion hence adds no new legal impediment for the crafting of a valid post-employment agreement not to compete.

The broadest conceptualization of *asmakhta* is that of Maimonides (Egypt, 1135–1204). In his view, any conditional obligation is an *asmakhta*.[30] Application of Maimonides' criterion to the post-employment noncompetition agreement renders this clause null and void.

At this juncture, let us take note that an *asmakhta* can ordinarily be counteracted by means of incorporating the phrase *me-akhshav* (literally, "from now") into the agreement. To illustrate: *L* lends *B* $10,000 on the security of the latter's field, which has a value of $15,000. *L* stipulates with *B* that if he is not paid in full within three years, *L* will acquire possession of the field for the original capital transfer of $10,000 he made to *B*. This arrangement is an *asmakhta*. But if *B* obligates himself *me-akhshav* to sell the field for $10,000 if he does not repay the debt within three years, the agreement is fully valid. The logic of why *me-akhshav* counteracts *asmakhta* is that had *B* not unreservedly committed himself to *L's* condition, *B* would not have agreed to retroactively confer *L* title to his field, from the time the loan was made.[31]

Incorporation of the *me-akhshav* mechanism into the post-employment agreement not to compete is quite compatible with the form this agreement must take, in any case, in order to conform to the *halot* caveat for conditional agreements. Specifically, at the outset, *E* must agree to confer upon *W* a gift consisting of making him privy to his trade secret and/or furnishing him with job training. If *W* then violates the noncompetition covenant, *E's* gift retroactively reverts to a service for a specified fee.

What this analysis has demonstrated is that the mechanism of contract has the halakhic capacity to implement a post-employment agreement not to compete. To be valid, such an agreement would have to conform to the guideposts of *halot*, *tenai kaful*, *asmakhta*, and *ona'ah*.

What is legally possible is, however, not always the economically rational thing to do. Do the constraints Halakhah imposes on a post-employ-ment agreement not to compete leave room for E and W to strike a deal of mutual advantage? Consider that E would not want to enter into such a deal unless he felt that he was adequately protected in the event W breached the contract. Perhaps E would not be satisfied with W's *me-akhshav* commit-ment alone, and, instead, would insist that W deposit a specific sum in an escrow account so that, in the event W became non-compliant with the non-competition clause, this sum would automatically become the property of E. If E sought this type of protection, the agreement would not get off the ground unless W could supply the escrow account with the sum E desired. Certainly, from W's perspective, a post-employment noncompetition agree-ment is economically irrational unless E guarantees him long-term job secu-rity.

Finally, if E plans to teach W a trade secret, the two parties may encounter substantial difficulties in setting a value on that knowledge. Con-sider that E does not put the trade secret up for sale; the trade secret hence has no objective value. Instead, the negotiations between E and W alone determine the value of the trade secret. This situation is an example of the classical bilateral monopoly model. Because the parties to the negotiation are not equipped with the information they would like to know, coming to terms entails considerable difficulties.

What the aforementioned has demonstrated is that significant complex-ity surrounds the negotiation of a halakhically valid post-employment agree-ment not to compete. These obstacles may prove so formidable as to prevent the parties from reaching an agreement.

HIN TZEDEK AND THE POST-EMPLOYMENT AGREEMENT NOT TO COMPETE

Another principle R. Grosman brings to bear in evaluating a post employ-ment agreement not to compete is the *hin tzedek* or good faith imperative dis-cussed earlier in this work. This ethical norm requires of an individual that if he makes a commitment or offer, he should fully intend to carry it out.[32]

Recall R. Grosman's conclusion that a post-employment agreement not to compete is not legally binding because it fails to meet the *halot* criterion. Although the agreement lacks legal force, *hin tzedek*, contends R. Grosman, requires W on moral grounds to abide by his commitment not to compete.

Retracting from a verbal commitment brands the violator as untrustworthy, and the Jewish court will admonish and publicly reprove the offender for his misconduct.[33]

R. Grosman's contention can, however, be put to question. Breaking a promise is permissible in certain circumstances. Consider the following two scenarios:

1. *A* verbally commits himself to confer a large gift to *B*. Subsequently, *A* has second thoughts and wishes to retract his commitment. Provided *A* made his commitment in "good faith," his subsequent retraction is not unethical. Given the considerable expenditure involved, *B* presumably never relied on the promise, and hence *A's* retraction did not dash B's expectations.[34]

2. A buyer, *B*, and a seller, *S*, commit themselves to a sales transaction. Before the transaction proceeds either to the point of *B* making a deposit or to the parties becoming legally bound, the market price of the item rises. On account of the price rise, *S* wishes to retract. Authorities dispute whether *S's* retraction should be regarded as unethical.[35] In this matter, R. Jehiel Michel Epstein (Belarus, 1829–1908) holds that *S's* retraction does not brand him untrustworthy.[36]

Both of these exceptions to the *hin tzedek* rule have relevance to the case at hand. Preliminarily, let us not lose sight that in R. Grosman's scenario, *E* offers *W* neither job security nor a raise for the post-training period. If we assume that *W* earns no more than his opportunity cost earnings in the current period, *W's promise* to *E* not to compete with him in the post-training period is very much akin to *W* promising *E* that he will confer him with a significant gift in the post-training period. Retraction from such a "good faith" promise should not brand *W* as untrustworthy. Moreover, if the job market worsens in the post training period, *W's* retraction from the promise he made *E* in the pre-training period should also not brand *W* as untrustworthy.

Another consideration in evaluating the relevance of the *hin tzedek* principle to the case at hand is the moral force this imperative exerts on an agreement that is an *asmakhta*. This would be the case, as discussed earlier, when the *me-akhshav* clause was not inserted. Given that the essential feature of an *asmakhta* is that the obligator lacks firm resolve, entering into an *asmakhta* agreement violates *hin tzedek* immediately, at the moment the commitment is made. Now, if *asmakhta* violates *hin tzedek*, then the commitment is binding on neither a legal nor a moral level. An *asmakhta* agreement hence does not morally compel the obligator to make good on his commitment.

LO TA'ASHOK

Another legal principle R. Grosman invokes in evaluating the constraints Halakhah imposes on W in the period following his separation from E is Leviticus 18:13: "Do not [unjustly] withhold [*lo ta'ashok*] that which is due your neighbor." Included in the *lo ta'ashok* interdict is the prohibition against withholding compensation from someone who performed one a service.[37] Let us apply this principle to the case at hand. Suppose E commits himself to teach W a skill or trade secret and stipulates no fee for this service, other than that W not go into competition with him. Because the *halot* condition is not met here, contract law cannot impose the noncompetition clause on W. But the noncompetition clause should be viewed as E's stipulation of compensation for teaching W the trade secret or the skill at hand. W's non-compliance with the noncompetition clause would hence violate the *lo ta'ashok* interdict.

　　R. Grosman finds precedent for his ruling in a similar case dealt with by R. Mosheh Sofer (Hungary, 1762–1839): S_1 granted S_2 a certificate of qualification to engage in ritual slaughter (*shehitah*). S_1 and S_2 disputed whether S_2 had accepted upon himself an oath not to practice *shehitah* in S_1's territory. In adjudicating the dispute, R. Sofer pointed out that even if S_2 had never taken an oath not to compete with S_1, S_2 was nevertheless bound not to compete in S_1's territory, because notwithstanding that nothing explicit had been stipulated in this regard, it would have been understood that part of S_1's compensation for conferring upon S_2 his certificate of qualification was that S_2 not practice *shehitah* in a manner that would undermine S_1's livelihood. S_2's engaging in *shehitah* in S_1's territory hence violated the *lo ta'ashok* interdict. Disputing R. Sofer, R. Abraham Teomin (Poland, mid. 19th century) maintains that it was not the usual practice to take a fee for conferring a certificate of qualification for *shehitah*. Consequently, if S_2 went into competition with S_1, S_2 could not be said to violate *lo ta'ashok*. Nonetheless, it was customary, concedes R. Teomin, for S_1 to take compensation for teaching S_2 the skill of *shehitah*. Consequently, if S_1 taught S_2 *shehitah* and nothing was stipulated regarding where S_2 could practice his skill, S_2 would be prohibited from entering into competition with S_1 in S_1's territory, on the basis of the *lo ta'ashok* interdict.

The aforementioned leads R. Grosman to the assertion that avoidance of *lo ta'ashok* forces W to adhere to the terms of the post-employment agreement not to compete.[38]

R. Grosman's analysis can be put to question, as his analogy appears inapt. In the instance where S_1 teaches S_2 *shehitah* and takes no fee for his service, the *quid pro quo* character of the agreement is clear-cut: S_1 teaches S_2 the skill, and implicitly expects S_2 to practice his trade in a manner that will not undermine his own livelihood. But if W is employed by E and earns no more than opportunity cost earnings in the current period and is promised neither job security nor a raise in the post-training period, W gets no *quid pro quo* for his promise not to compete. Since W has every right to break his "good faith" promise and does not violate *hin tzedek*, for the same reason breaking his "good faith" promise does not violate for W *lo ta'ashok*.

HASSAGAT GEVUL AND COMPETING WITH A FORMER EMPLOYER

In this section we turn to a consideration of Halakhah's rules for fair competition in the marketplace (*hassagat gevul*). An examination of these rules will show that, even in the absence of any agreement between E and W regarding noncompetition in the post-employment period, W is, in any case, subject to a number of restraints based on the *hassagat gevul* law.

UNDISPUTED CASES OF PROTECTION

Recall from the previous chapter that the criterion Halakhah adopts regarding what constitutes fair competition is a matter of dispute. One school of thought generally protects a complainant firm from competitive tactics that exert a ruinous impact on it, provided, of course, that the complainant is not capable of counteracting the tactics and surviving. Another school of thought calls for judicial intervention against only predatory tactics. Because the marketplace is governed by rules of "fair play," W will be subject to these rules, even if no agreement whatsoever was made between E and W regarding the post-employment period. The following are a number

of scenarios in which E would be entitled to protection based on either of
the attitudes toward "fair competition" cited above.

1. Special Low Price Introductory Offer

The Minimax Corporation is a tax preparation firm for the very wealthy.
The company assigns a team consisting of a tax preparer and an investment
counselor to each client. The company charges a $1,000 fee for this service.
Industry analysts regard Minimax as operating in tier-one of the tax preparation industry.

Max Silvertone, a star employee at the firm, a wiz in both tax preparation and investment advice, decides to leave the firm and set up a similar
firm. To ensure name recognition, Silvertone calls his new firm Silvertone
and Associates, Tax and Investment Advisers. Silvertone's intention is to set
up a tier-one firm.

In setting up his competing enterprise, Silvertone sets his fee with the
aim of attracting as many clients as possible. Silvertone is quite willing to
take no salary for himself the first year of operations. Silvertone's only constraint is that he should not incur any out of pocket expenses in running the
business. Toward this end, Silvertone prices his service at $500. With the
low introductory price, Silvertone expects to capitalize on his sterling reputation and attract clientele from Minimax and possibly from other first tier
firms. The upside of this plan is that Silvertone's $500 fee might even
appear attractive to the clientele of second-tier firms who pay $350 and get
for their money only a tax preparation service and no investment advice. To
be sure, Silvertone deliberately budgets in no salary for himself for the first
year. But, once he has corralled a satisfied clientele, Silvertone's plan is to
raise his fees steeply and eventually make far more money than he could
ever hope to earn continuing his career at Minimax.

In this scenario the firm that is put most at risk by Silvertone's entry is
Minimax. Given the above figures, it becomes a matter of compelling self-
interest for Minimax to drop the investment advice component of its service,
and join the ranks of tier-two firms who offer only a tax preparation service
for the wealthy and no investment advice. Because Silvertone's business
plan puts Minimax in disarray, it may very well be an easy matter for the
owners of this firm to demonstrate that Silvertone's business plan will drive

their earnings below the earnings of their socioeconomic peer group. Recall that making a demonstration of this sort qualifies the complainant for protection under the deprivation-generating criterion.[39] Although Silvertone's business plan qualifies for enjoinment on the basis of the deprivation-generating criterion, should we view his stratagem as a predatory tactic as well? To answer this question we need to put the stratagem to the test of the two rationales R. Abulafia offers for the freedom of entry school, discussed in the previous chapter. Recall that the first rationale says that S_2 can "turn the tables" on S_1 and say "You operate your business on your premises and I operate my business on my premises. Why should I be concerned about your livelihood and you should not be concerned about my livelihood?" In R. Abulafia second rationale, S_2's argument begins the same way, but disarms S_1's claim of loss by saying that he takes away nothing from him: "Whatever Heaven has decided for each of us in the form of livelihood we will get [and no more]."[40]

Silvertone's cut-throat pricing consisting of including only his out of pocket expenditures and ignoring totally the value of his own labor services meets neither of the two rationales for the freedom of entry school. Consider that the basic premise operating in both rationales is that S_2's activity in his own premises can legitimately be called *a livelihood activity*. Recall the proposition we made that in making this judgment we should not consider as the relevant time period anything beyond the current year. Silvertone's pricing policy of not budgeting in a salary for himself in the current year is therefore *not a livelihood activity for the current year*, notwithstanding Silvertone's plan to budget for himself a handsome salary next year by steeply increasing his rates.

Silvertone's conduct will also find no justification within the ambit of R. Abulafia's second rationale. Telling his former employer that God determines the distribution of customers between himself and them and no one gets *more* than what God decided for them rings hollow in light of Silvertone's own actions. If Silvertone *really believed* in what he was saying, he would, as discussed in the previous chapter, deny himself extravagances out of fear that the pre-ordained income God has for him this year will not cover his expenditures. Instead, Silvertone takes reckless action to guarantee that his household will be run on a budget of zero current labor income. Silvertone's own conduct makes a mockery out of the pious pronouncement he utters.

One point remains to be clarified. Suppose it is evident that Silvertone's pricing deal is designed to earn him net income in the current year. For what level of income expectation does it become clear that Silvertone's pricing policy is not an investment scheme, but rather, a livelihood activity for the current year? Economic rationality helps us arrive at the answer. Would Silvertone deliberately abandon his livelihood activity at Minimax unless he assessed that working for himself represented a better livelihood activity? No. To be sure, pecuniary reward is not the whole story. Many people clearly place a high psychological value on being their own boss. The issue, then, becomes whether Silvertone's pricing offer generates sufficient net income to cover the basic living expenses of his family in terms of food, shelter, and clothing. If the answer is no, then Silvertone's pricing offer should not be regarded as a livelihood activity for the current year, but, instead, as an investment activity on his part for the purpose of securing his livelihood in the future. Although Silvertone is no more obligated to be concerned that Minimax earn a livelihood in the current year than the reciprocal duty the company owes him, Silvertone has no right to conduct himself in a manner that ruins Minimax's livelihood and, at the same time, is for him no more than an investment for the future.

2. Hiring the Labor Force of a Competitor

Ben Graboni worked as an associate editor for *Wellspring*, a monthly magazine on Jewish thought. All employees at *Wellspring* work without the benefit of a contract. After ten years on the job, Ben quit *Wellspring* and founded a similar magazine, which he called *Fountainhead*. In founding his own magazine, Ben induced the *Wellspring* business manager, Kevin Saroka, to come along with him. Because Graboni waited until he cleaned out his office to make the offer to Saroka, and conditioned the offer on Saroka's willingness to start the job immediately, Saroka left his job at *Wellspring* without giving the customary notice.

In assessing the ethics of Graboni's hiring away Saroka to start his own magazine, we must consider this stratagem's potential to put *Wellspring* in disarray. If the stratagem can potentially prove ruinous for *Wellspring*, it should be prohibited according to the deprivation criterion for fair competition. Is this stratagem objectionable even according to the predation criterion? Apparently not. If locating a business on the open side of a closed alley where a similar firm is already located at the extreme end of the closed side is not objectionable,[41] then starting a new business by hiring away key resources from an established firm should also not be objectionable. In the former case, the established firm is put at a disadvantage because the new firm visually blocks the customer base from the old firm. This disadvantage will not fade with time. In the latter case, the established firm is disadvantaged only because it cannot operate without first *replacing* the resource that the new firm lured away from it. This disadvantage, however, may be only temporary.

This analogy, however, ignores one element: whether it is ethical for Saroka suddenly to leave his job at *Wellspring*. Quitting without notice may disrupt the operation of *Wellspring* and cause Saroka's former employer a loss. If it is unethical for Saroka to quit suddenly, it will be unethical for Graboni to approach him with a job offer.

An analogous case[42] recorded in the Talmud relates to the notice requirement for a landlord or tenant to terminate a leasing arrangement that was entered into for an indefinite period. Here, by dint of a Talmudic ordinance, neither the landlord nor the tenant may terminate the agreement without thirty days notice.[43]

Taking note that the thirty day notice requirement applies to landlord and tenant alike, a Tel Aviv *Bet Din* concluded that the rationale for the requirement is that each party is entitled to protection against an interruption of their income flow. What follows, according to the *Bet Din*, is that an employee who was hired for an indefinite term should be entitled to thirty days notice.[44]

If the notice requirement the Talmud prescribes for landlords and tenants applies to the labor market, it should apply to the rights of the employer no less than it applies to the rights of an employee. Specifically, under the assumption that a firm realizes a net gain on each worker it hires, a sudden departure, at least until the worker is replaced, generates a loss for the firm. Given the disruption in income a quitting employee causes his employer, it should be incumbent on an employee to give thirty days notice before leaving his job.

It must be recognized that a thirty day notice is not always sufficient to ensure that the employer's income will not be disrupted; if it takes more than thirty days to replace a worker, then more notice must be given. Indeed, the notice requirements in the parent case of a leasing arrangement entered into for an indefinite period call for extended notice beyond the ordinary thirty day requirement when eviction imposes particular difficulties on the tenant. In recognition of the fact that apartment hunting is a much more onerous task in the winter season [from *Sukkot* to *Pesah*] than in the summer season [from *Pesah* to *Sukkot*], it was established that a landlord forfeits his right to evict a tenant during the winter unless the tenant is given a full thirty day notice of eviction *before* the winter season begins.[45] Moreover, in recognition of the fact that a housing shortage usually exists in a big city, the notice requirement for a tenant who has an indefinite lease in a large city is always twelve months, regardless of whether the landlord seeks eviction in the summer or the winter.[46]

Halakhic sensitivity to the deprivation that eviction engenders can also be seen in the expanded notice rights Halakhah grants in connection with commercial leases entered into for an indefinite period. In recognition that storekeepers usually extend credit to their customers for a year, a landlord must give at least a year's notice; less notice would subject the storekeeper to losses, as customers would come back to pay their debts, but find that the proprietor was not in his accustomed place. Conferring on the storekeeper a one-year notice right allows him to smoothly collect old debts as well as to inform new customers of his new location.[47]

In recognition that dyers and bakers usually extend credit to their customers over a three-year period,[48] the Talmud extends the notice requirements for these commercial leases to three years.[49]

To be sure, specific application of the above Talmudic rules to the modern scene is problematic, but the numerous exceptions cited do indicate that a notice requirement longer than the ordinary thirty days is in order when the disruptive impact of a sudden firing or resignation on the income flow of the forsaken party lasts for more than thirty days.

The upshot of this analysis is that it is unethical for Saroka to suddenly quit his job as business manager at *Wellspring* without giving proper notice. Since it is unethical for Saroka to quit his job without giving proper notice, it is unethical for Graboni to recruit Saroka with the condition that the offer of employment stands only if Saroka takes it up immediately. Couching the employment offer in these terms is tantamount to advising someone to commit a sinful act, and hence amounts to proffering ill-suited advice, a violation of *lifnei iver*, the injunction against the provision of ill-suited advice.[50]

Let us now consider a variation of the above case. Suppose that, in addition to Saroka, Graboni induces Claudia Weinstock, the administrative assistant at *Wellspring*, to join him at his new magazine. Graboni insists to both Saroka and Weinstock that they don't join him without first giving the thirty day notice required by *Wellspring*. Although no single employee who gives the required thirty day notice will put the operation of *Wellspring* into disarray, the combined effect of a number of key employees giving notice at the same time will surely do this.

In considering the ethics of Graboni's orchestrated plan, recall the rationale behind the freedom-of-entry position: *"You do* as you wish *inside your property, and I do* as I wish *inside my [property]."*[51] By raiding the key resources of *Wellspring* as a means of launching his own enterprise, Graboni is effectively invading *Wellspring*'s premises and orchestrating a transfer of resources from inside *Wellspring*'s premises to his own premises. Graboni's raiding action hence fails the standard for ethical competition and should be prohibited.

3. Exploiting the Customer Relations of a Former Employer

White Laundry Company provides a pick-up and delivery service to householders. The only contact customers have with the company is with Fred Rogin, an employee. Rogin makes pick-ups and deliveries and also takes payment and arranges terms with customers. Rogin ends his employment with White Laundry Company and sets up his own laundry pick-up and delivery service. Rogin solicits customers along his old route.

In assessing the ethics of Rogin's conduct, consider that Rogin earns a salary for performing his duties as a White Laundry Company employee. Under the standard assumption that Rogin's marginal revenue product is greater than the salary White Laundry pays him, the company gains also. Part of this gain, especially if Rogin does an exemplary job, consists of the enhancement of White Laundry's reputation for customer service, which provides the company with an intangible asset called goodwill. Although no exact value can be placed on this asset as long as the company is operating under its present owners, a value can be fixed when the company is sold. It will be equal to the excess the purchaser actually pays for the company over the fair market value of the net assets of the company.

Because Rogin was White Laundry's customer relations man, the good-will the company enjoys on account of its reputation for customer satisfaction is embodied in Rogin himself. Once Rogin leaves White Laundry's employ, he is in a unique position to exploit his former firm's reputation for customer satisfaction for his own commercial gain. Recall the rationale of the free-entry position in the Talmud: "You do as you wish inside your property, and I do as I wish inside my [property]." Soliciting customers along his old route makes Rogin guilty of effectively conducting his business on White Laundry's premises.

An analogous case, dealt with by R. Ya'akov Yeshayahu Bloi (Israel, 1929–), concerns S_2's infringement of S_1's trademark. Given that the trademark, though it is intangible, is an economic asset for S_1, S_2's infringement of the trademark makes him guilty of effectively conducting business on S_1's premises.[52] Similarly, for Rogin to exploit White Laundry's customer relations amounts to conducting his business on White Laundry's premises.

Another relevant principle in evaluating Rogin's conduct is the following dictum of R. Yosei:

> [If] one rents a cow from another and lends it to someone else, and it dies naturally, the renter must swear that it died naturally, and the borrower must pay the renter. Said R. Yosei: "How does that person do business with another's cow? Rather, the cow should be returned to the owner."[53]

According to the first opinion expressed, when the animal dies, the renter becomes exempt from paying and acquires the animal. Since the renter is not liable for accidents, he takes an oath merely to placate the owner. Therefore, the borrower—who is responsible for accidents—must pay the renter.[54] R. Yosei, however, regards the renter who lends out the deposit as an agent of the owner. Therefore, the payment for the cow should be given to the owner, not the renter.[55]

Although Talmudic decisors follow R. Yosei,[56] authorities are in disagreement regarding the conditions necessary to trigger the prohibition of doing business with someone else's property. The majority position in this matter is to call for disgorgement whenever *A* makes commercial use of *B's* property while having no right to do so. The fact that *B* suffers no loss thereby is not relevant, according to this school of thought.[57]

How broadly does R. Yosei define an asset? If he includes in his prohibition even the misappropriation of someone's intangible asset, Rogin's conduct is prohibited on these grounds as well. Specifically, exploiting White Laundry's customer relations amounts to expropriating someone else's asset for commercial gain, and is therefore prohibited.

In his analysis and critique of secular law's treatment of employee agreements not to compete, Professor Harlan Blake proposes a criterion for determining what constitutes a reasonable duration with respect to protecting customer relationships. In his view, the duration is reasonable only if it is no longer than necessary for the employer to put a new person on the job and for the new employee to have a reasonable opportunity to demonstrate his or her effectiveness to customers.[58]

From the perspective of Halakhah, an employer's customer relationships warrant protection even if the employer did not secure this restraint by means of a contractual agreement with his former employee. Nonetheless, Blake's criterion for what constitutes a reasonable duration for protection should be Halakhically acceptable. Let us relate the criterion to our case. Rogin is prohibited to solicit White Laundry customers along his old route not by a blanket prohibition not to compete with his former employer, but by a prohibition not to exploit his former firm's goodwill for his own commercial gain. Once enough time has elapsed for White Laundry to place a new man on the job and demonstrate his effectiveness to customers, the restriction against Rogin's solicitation of his former employer's customers should be removed. Lengthening the restraint beyond this period amounts to protecting White Laundry against competition *per se*. But no school in Halakhah protects an incumbent firm against competition *per se* unless it is determined that the competition will exert a ruinous impact on it.

4. Using a Former Employer's Customer Lists

Over the years, Emanuel Federbush, founder of a life insurance company bearing his name, developed an approach to solicit strangers to buy whole life insurance. In Federbush's mind, the most promising prospects to go after were career educators. Educational institutions, reasoned Federbush, cover their teachers with term life insurance policies for the entire time these teachers remain in their employ. Once the educators retire, their term life insurance policies come to an end, leaving them with no life insurance coverage. Given this sudden loss of coverage at retirement, it makes sense for a teacher to buy a supplemental whole life insurance policy early in his or her career. If a teacher does this, by the time he or she retires, the whole life insurance policy will have been paid for, and the educator will enjoy the resultant peace of mind. The challenge for Federbush was to convince educators that the extra expenditure for life insurance during their working life was well worthwhile.

As one successful cold call led at times to a series of referrals, Federbush's approach proved successful. His success inspired his administrative assistant, Bernard Klapper, to hit upon an idea to parley his boss' business plan into a lucrative opportunity for himself. Toward this end, Klapper quit his job at Federbush and became a freelance life insurance agent. Making use of the Federbush customer lists, Klapper made cold calls to these people. His sales pitch was:

> I represent many different whole life insurance companies. Let me take a look at what you have. I probably can offer you the same type of coverage you have now at a reduced annual premium. Let us make an appointment.

Klapper's conduct raises an ethical issue. Soliciting whole life policyholders to switch to a different company dashes the expectations of Klapper's former boss, Federbush, that his customers will continue with the original policy by paying him the periodic premiums. From the perspective of Halakhah, Klapper's conduct must be examined against the various nuances of the ethical norm to not interfere with someone else's anticipated gain.

One aspect of this prohibition is the *ani hamehapekh bahararah* norm, discussed in the previous chapter. *Ani hamehapekh* is, however, not a relevant factor here, because, as discussed in the previous chapter, the freedom-of-entry position is in basic conflict with the *ani hamehapekh* principle. Federbush's anticipation of gain alone is not sufficient reason to require Klapper not to bid for life insurance business, even if Federbush enjoyed the premiums from the policy at issue over an extended period of time.

What makes the life insurance policy case different from an ordinary *ani hamehapekh* case is that Klapper is not only snatching away Federbush's anticipated gain, but also is *free riding* on Federbush's toil and effort. Consider that the educators Klapper approaches have both term and whole life insurance policies. It is Federbush's "toil and effort" that convinces these people of the need to supplement term life insurance with whole life early in their careers. Klapper *builds on* Federbush's work by offering a better deal on the whole life policy.

Analogous is the Torah tutor case dealt with by R. Isaac b. Samuel (France, 1120–1200). Invoking the *ani hamehapekh bahararah* ethical norm, R. Isaac rules that T_2 may not offer his services as a home tutor for E's child while another tutor (T_1) is still employed in E's home.[59]

Addressing himself to the tutor case, R. Joseph Trani questions the applicability of *ani hamehapekh* to this case. Is it not possible that T_2 assesses that the tutoring job at E represents the best employment opportunity for himself with respect to both salary and working conditions? If this is indeed T_2's assessment, the benefit he seeks is akin to the ownerless property (*hefker*) case, and the prohibition against preemptive conduct should be suspended. Notwithstanding the similarity of T_2's quest for employment by E to the *hefker* case, the proper analogue here, according to R. Trani, is the case dealing with competition among indigents for the olives left unharvested by a farmer (these olives are the entitlement of the poor). Here, indigent P_1 climbs to the top of an olive tree to retrieve the forgotten olives. P_1 manages to make the olives fall to the ground. Before P_1 can take legal possession of the olives, another indigent, P_2, pounces upon the olives and takes legal possession of them. Because P_1 was poised to take legal possession of the olives and P_2 snatched away his anticipated gain, P_2's interloping action constitutes theft by dint of rabbinical decree (*gezel mi-divreihem*). P_2's action is morally repugnant, and he is therefore expected to restore the olives to P_1. Nonetheless, P_2's snatching conduct is not theft by dint of Torah law; a Jewish court (*Bet Din*) will not force P_2 to return the snatched olives to P_1.

Note that in the ordinary *ani ha-mehapekh* case, the consequence for the interloper is that he is branded a wicked person, but there exists no duty, even on a voluntary basis, for the interloper to restore what he acquired. To see why P_2's interloping action is treated so severely in the case of the olives, we need only recognize that P_2's preemptive conduct did not consist of following P_1 up and then down the olive tree, and pouncing on the olives before P_1 got a chance to take legal possession of them. Instead, P_2 positioned himself on ground level, and sprung into action only after P_1's toil and effort dislodged the olives and caused them to fall to the ground. Because P_2 snatches away P_1's anticipated gain by free riding on P_1's toil and effort, P_2's interloping is regarded as *gezel mi-divreihem*. Similarly, T_2's offer to E to hire himself as tutor in place of T_1 amounts to a maneuver to free ride on T_1's toil and effort. This is so because T_1's successful tutoring makes his pupil a better student and more receptive to learning in the future. Because T_2's offer free rides on T_1's toil and effort, T_2's conduct is morally repugnant.[60]

Viewing interloping conduct in the tutor case as a compounded *ani ha-mehapekh* violation carries with it several stringencies. One stringency, already mentioned, is that if T_2 manages to displace T_1, T_2 should, on a voluntary basis; offer to give back the position to T_1.

Another point of stringency: in the ordinary *ani ha-mehapekh* case, the inability of the interloper to find employment elsewhere is a mitigating factor. Recall Rabbenu Tam's view that the *ani ha-mehapekh* interdict is suspended in the *hefker* case.[61] According to R. Mosheh Feinstein, in the modern labor market, this translates into a suspension of the *ani ha-mehapekh* interdict when the interloper cannot find employment elsewhere. In the latter instance, as long as the first applicant has not actually entered into a contract with the employer, a second applicant may offer himself for hire to that employer. But if the case entails free riding on someone else's toil and effort, the relevant prohibition is *gezel mi-divreihem*. Accordingly, inability to secure employment elsewhere should not permit interloping action.

Let us now apply R. Trani's insight—that free riding on someone else's toil and effort constitutes *gezel me-divreihem*—to the case at hand. Offering better deals to Federbush's whole life policy holders solicits business from people who own whole life insurance policies only on account of the toil and effort Federbush exerted to convince them that they needed such a policy on top of the very adequate term life insurance coverage they already had. Klapper's solicitations therefore amount to snatching away Federbush's anticipated gain by free riding on the latter's toil and efforts. Such conduct hence violates *gezel me-divreihem*.

Suppose Klapper goes into business on his own by making use of Federbush's general approach, but without actually making use of his former boss' customer lists. In this scenario, Klapper uses as his source for cold calls the Rabbinical Council of America (RCA)'s registry. The operative assumption here is that term life insurance, but not whole life insurance, is part of the compensation package of the pulpit rabbi. Because many of these rabbis will, in all probability, find themselves suddenly without life insurance coverage at retirement, they are prime targets for Klapper's argument that they need to purchase supplemental whole life insurance early in their rabbinical careers. Here, Klapper mimics Federbush's business plan, but does not free ride on his former boss' toil and effort. Accordingly, there should be no objection here to Klapper's business plan.

But let us take note of one qualification. Suppose Klapper learns from the rabbi he is speaking to that the rabbi already has both term life and whole life coverage. Now, if this portfolio came about through the toil and effort of some whole life insurance agent, it becomes unethical for Klapper to outbid for the whole life policy, and gain it for himself. To avoid violation of *gezel mi-divreihem*, Klapper must exert caution before he continues. Klapper should say something like, "rabbi, you have a portfolio of life insurance policies that whole life insurance agents exert much time and energy to convince people to own. Did you arrive at this decision on your own, or did some professional convince you that this is the way to go?" If the rabbi responds that he arrived at this decision without the benefit of the salesmanship of a whole life insurance agent, there should be no ethical problem in Klapper's attempt to gain the business for himself.

In the above variant, additional latitude may open up for Klapper to shift business to himself. Consider that once a whole life insurance policy is sold, it will automatically generate income for the salesperson whenever the policyholder pays his annual premium. The salesperson will earn this commission even if he provides no additional services, and, for that matter, even if he makes no additional contact with the policy holder subsequent to entering into the contract. Having convinced B to buy a whole life policy, S_1 thus anticipates a flow of commissions beginning in the current year and extending until the policy is paid up. Consider, however, that with the passage of time, B's increased family size, special circumstances and increased family income may render the original policy suboptimal or even a matter of ill-suited advice for him to keep. Unless S_1 maintains, at the very least, yearly contact with B regarding his possible changed conditions, S_1 may be guilty of destroying, albeit in a passive way, the value of the policy he originally sold B. If S_1 has, in fact, been remiss in servicing B's account, the benefit S_1 originally conferred B by convincing him to buy whole life insurance has dissipated, or worse still, has become a negative value by dint of it becoming ill-suited advice to keep the policy in its original form.

Let us apply this proposition to the case at hand. Suppose that in going about drumming up business, Klapper comes across a rabbi who has both a whole life and a term life insurance policy. Further conversation reveals that S_1 convinced the rabbi a number of years ago to get whole life insurance on top of the term life policy that his synagogue had already provided him with. At this juncture, Klapper should say something like, "I suppose S_1 is on top of things and is still in touch with you to see if your needs have changed as far as whole life is concerned." If the rabbi's answer is "no," Klapper should have license to shift the whole life insurance business to himself by offering a better deal.

SUMMARY AND CONCLUSION

Common law regards most employee agreements not to compete as inherently unfair. Such agreements are generally almost entirely for the benefit of the employer, and inflict a burden on employees that is out of proportion to any gain on their part. To be valid, an agreement must minimally satisfy the following: (1) it must be designed to protect the employer's legitimate entitlement, such as proprietary information or customer relations; (2) the restrictions must not be greater than what is required for the employer's legitimate interest; (3) the restrictions must not impose undue hardship on the ability of an employee to secure gainful employment; and (4) the restrictions must not be injurious to the public.

Rubin and Shedd conclude that the common law treatment of employee agreements not to compete is efficient in that it promotes an optimal amount of investment in human capital. The role of the courts is to enforce the restrictive covenant in a manner that minimizes opportunistic behavior on the part of both parties.

In disputes between Jews, many decisors do not apply *dina de-malkhuta dina* to rules developed by judges using their discretionary authority to draw upon the precedents set in various legal systems, rather than merely interpreting what the relevant statute says. Thus, in extrapolating the halakhic perspective on post-employment covenants not to compete, one cannot simply invoke the principle of *dina de-malkhuta*, because formal government legislation on this matter does not currently exist; the treatment of such agreements is entirely a matter of common law.

From the perspective of Halakhah, many technicalities must be overcome in crafting valid employee agreements not to compete. To be valid, the contract must meet the requirements of *halot* and *tenai kaful*. It must also be free of *asmakhta* and not violate the law of *ona'ah*. The cumulative effect of these technicalities is to make the creation of noncompetition agreements through the mechanism of halakhic contract cumbersome and probably economically irrational.

In the absence of an agreement, the commercial conduct of a former employee is governed by Halakhah's rules for fair competition. There are two schools of thought regarding fair competition. One generally protects a complainant firm from competitive tactics that exert a ruinous impact on it, provided, of course, that the complainant is not capable of counteracting the tactics and surviving. The other calls for judicial intervention only against predatory tactics. Because the marketplace is governed by rules of fair play, a former employee will be subject to these rules, even if no agreement whatsoever was made between employer and employee with respect to the post-employment period.

Within the context of Halakhah's concept of fair play in the marketplace, there is a balance between the economic interests of an established firm and the legitimate rights of a former employee of that firm to compete in the same business. Although the parameters of the conduct that a former employee may engage in hinge on which of the two schools of thought we adopt, certain forms of conduct fail the standards of both approaches.

One form of this conduct is for S_1 to engage in a business plan that ruins S_2's business and at the same time generates no livelihood for himself in the current period, but merely constitutes an investment on his part to secure future livelihood. This prohibition should make it unethical for a former employee to launch his own business by offering clients a "low introductory" fee that is so low that it threatens the viability of the former employer and, at the same time, offers the former employee no current prospect of earning anything that could pass as a livelihood.

Another prohibited stratagem is for the former worker (W) to launch his own business by hiring away the key employees of his former employer (E). Such action disrupts E's business, threatening E with ruin. In this context, a number of scenarios were identified. In one scenario, W induces key employees to leave E and makes his job offer contingent upon these employees' immediate resignation, without giving E notice. If a sudden resignation disrupts E's business, leaving E's employ without proper notice constitutes unethical conduct. Accordingly, W's act of inducing E's key employees to quit without giving notice violates *lifnei iver*. Moreover, even if W insists that E's key employees give E proper notice before joining him, the tactic will still be prohibited if the coordinated resignations have the effect of disrupting E's business. The rationale here is that W's orchestration amounts to *effectively* opening his own business by setting up shop on E's premises.

Finally, Halakhah prohibits W from engaging in various forms of opportunistic conduct.

One such form is for W to free ride on goodwill that rightfully belongs to E; for example, if W was the only customer relations person employed by E and now goes out on his own and solicits for himself the accounts he previously handled for E. Since as far as customers are concerned, E and W are one and the same, W's solicitation of E's customers amounts to "doing business with E's asset."

Another form of opportunistic conduct by W occurs when W snatches away E's anticipated gain by free riding on E's toil and effort. Illustrating this is a scenario entailing W's use of E's customer list. If it is E's toil and effort that is responsible for the customer's contracting for a particular service (e.g., whole life insurance), W may not offer this customer to provide the same service on more advantageous terms. Such conduct makes *W* guilty of snatching away *E's* anticipated gain by free riding on the toil and effort *E* exerted to convince the customer to contract for the services in the first place.

In summary, the protection common law is willing to accord an employer, *E*, against his employee, *W*, once *W* leaves *E's* employ becomes operative only if *E* contracts for it in the form of a noncompetition agreement. From the perspective of Halakhah, the mechanism of contract is, for all intents and purposes, useless for achieving that result. But, in any case, *E* is entitled to broad protection against *W* out of concern for fair competition. This protection certainly encompasses the very limits of what *E* could achieve in common law by means of a restrictive covenant with *W*.

NOTES

1. John R. Boatright, *Ethics and the Conduct of Business*, 2nd ed. (Upper Saddle River, NJ: Prentice Hall 1997), 140–141.
2. The exposition of Gary Becker's work in the text draws from George J. Borjas, *Labor Economics* (New York: McGraw Hill Company 1996), 250–257.
3. Paul H. Rubin, & Peter Shedd, "Human Capital and Covenants Not to Compete," *Journal of Legal Studies* 10 (1) 1981: 93–110.
4. Rubin & Shedd, 102–104.
5. Samuel, *Gittin* 10b.
6. R. Joseph Caro, *Shulhan Arukh, Hoshen Mishpat* 369:6–11.
7. R. Mosheh Isserles, *Rema, Hoshen Mishpat* 369:11.
8. Ibid.
9. R. Joseph Caro, *Sh. Ar.*, op. cit., 26:1; R. Mosheh Isserles, *Rema*, op. cit., 26:1.
10. *Rema*, op. cit., 369:11.
11. R. Shabbetai b. Meir ha-Kohen, *Siftei Kohen, Shulhan Arukh, Hoshen Mishpat* 73, note 39. In litigation between Jew and non-Jew, *dina de-malkhuta* is operative (*Siftei Kohen*, ad loc.).
12. R. Abraham Isaiah Karelitz, *Hazon Ish, Hoshen Mishpat, Likkutim* 16:1.
13. R. Moshe Feinstein (New York, 1895–1986), *Iggerot Mosheh, Hoshen Mishpat* 2:62; R. Yosef Eliyahu Henkin, *Teshuvot Ivra*, vol. 2, p. 176. See also list of authorities cited by Professor Shmuel Shilo, *Dina de-Malkhuta Dina* (Jerusalem, 1974), 157, no. 26.
14. R. Mosheh Isserles, *Darkhei Mosheh, Tur, Hoshen Mishpat* 369, note 3.
15. R. Jekutiel Asher Zalman Zausmir, *Responsa Mahariaz* 4.
16. R. Shelomoh Dikhovsky, "*Hilkhot ha-Shittuf—ha-Im Dina de-Malkhuta?*," *Tehumim* 18 (1998): 18–21.
17. R. Israel b. Gedaliah Lipschutz, *Tiferet Yisrael, Mishnah, Pe'ah* 6:11, note 51.
18. R. Akiva Eger, commentary at *Mishnah, Pe'ah* 6:11, note 69.
19. R. Yisrael Grosman, Responsa *Nezah Yisra'el*, 42.

20. For the *tenai kaful* condition and related requirements, see Maimonides (Egypt, 1135–1204), *Yad*, Ishut 6:1–6 and 6:14; R. Asher b. Jehiel (Germany, 1250–1327), *Rosh, Gittin* 6:9; R. Jacob b. Asher (Spain, 1270–1340), *Tur, Even ha-Ezer* 38; R. Joseph Caro, op. cit., 207:1; R. Jehiel Michel Epstein (Belarus, 1829–1908), *Arukh ha-Shulhan, Even ha-Ezer* 38:26–27, 38:46. A minority view holds that in monetary matters, a conditional agreement is binding without a *tenai kaful* (see *Arukh ha-Shulhan*, op. cit., 38:46).

21. For the sources and details of the law of *ona'ah* please turn to pp. 188, 206–207 of this volume. See also Aaron Levine, "*Ona'ah* and the Operation of the Modern Marketplace," *Jewish Law Annual*, Hebrew University, vol. xiv, 2003, pp. 225–258.

22. For the development of this point, please turn to pp. 48, 256 of this volume.

23. For a development of sources from the Talmud and *Rishonim* dealing with both *gemirat da'at* and *semikhat da'at* conditions, see Shalom Albeck, *Dinei ha-Mamonot ba-Talmud* (Tel Aviv, Devir 1976), 112–143.

24. R. Jacob b. Asher, *Tur*, op. cit., 207; R. Joseph Caro, op. cit., 207:9–13; R. Jehiel Michel Epstein, *Ar ha-Sh*, *Hoshen Mishpat*, 207:22–53.

25. Designation of scholars who were active in the period from the eleventh to the middle of the fifteenth century.

26. *Bava Metzia* 73b and *Tosafot*, ad loc., s.v. "*hatam be-yado hakha lav be-yado*."

27. *Rashi, Sanhedrin* 24b, s.v. "*kol ki hai gavna lav asmakhta hi*," according to the interpretation of *Tosafot*, ad loc., s.v. "*kol ki hai gavna lav asmakhta hu*;" Rashi's view is also held by *Tosafot, Bava Metzia* 74a, s.v. "*hakha lav be-yado*;" Nachmanides (Spain, 1194–1270), *Ramban, Bava Batra* 168a; *Rema*, op. cit., 207:13.

28. R. Jacob Tam, quoted in *Tosafot, Bava Metzia* 74a, s.v. "*hakha lav be-yado*" and in *Tosafot, Sanhedrin* 24b, s.v. "*kol ki hai gavna lav asmakhta hi*."

29. *Rashba*, quoted in *Shittah Mekubbetzet, Bava Batra* 168a.

30. *Yad, Mekhirah* 11:2.

31. Ibid., 11:2, 7.

32. Please turn to pp. 395–396 of this volume.

33. Responsa *Nezah Yisra'el* 42.

34. R. Yohanan, *Bava Metzia* 49a; *Rif*, ad loc.; *Yad, Mekhirah* 7: 8–9; *Rosh, Bava Metzia* 4:12; *Tur*, op. cit., 204; *Sh. Ar.*, op. cit., 204: 7–8; *Ar. ha-Sh.*, op. cit., 204:8–9.

35. See R. Mosheh Isserles, *Rema, Sh. Ar.*, op. cit., 204:11. R. Isserles himself rules stringently in this matter.

36. R. Yehiel Michel Epstein, *Ar. ha-Sh.*, op. cit., 204:8. In this case R. Epstein opts for the view that not to retract would be a matter of *middat hasidut* (pious conduct). Note that *Tosafot (Bava Metzia* 24b, s.v. *lifnim mi-shurat ha-din)* rules that *lifnim mi-shurat ha-din* (conduct beyond the letter of the law) pertains only to making a claim on one's toil and effort, but not to the requirement of incurring financial loss. R. Epstein's mention of *middat hasidut* here should, therefore, be understood as saying no more than that not to retract is praiseworthy conduct. A requirement not to retract does not, however, obtain here even on a *lifnim mi-shurat ha-din* level.

37. *Yad, Gezeilah* 1:4; *Tur*, op. cit., 359; *Sh. Ar.*, op. cit., 359:9; *Ar. ha-Sh.*, op. cit., 359:7.

38. R. Yisrael Grosman, Resp. *Nezah Yisra'el* 42.

39. Please turn to pp. 96–99 of this volume.

40. R. Meir b. Todros ha-Levi Abulafia, *Ramah, Bava Batra* 21b.

41. For a discussion of this case, please turn to pp. 100–106 of this volume.
42. The discussion in the following section draws from my previous work *Case Studies in Jewish Business Ethics* (Hoboken, NJ: Ktav Publishing, Yeshiva University Press, 2000), pp. 250–257.
43. *Mishnah, Bava Metzia* 8:6; *Baraita Bava Metzia* 101b; *Rif, ad loc.*; *Yad, Sekhirut* 6:7–8; *Rosh, Bava Metzia* 8:24; *Tur*, op. cit., 312; *Sh. Ar.*; op. cit., 312:4,7; *Ar. ha-Sh.*, op. cit., 312:13, 17.
44. *Piskei Din Rabbaniyim* 3:282–3.
45. *Bava Metzia* 101b; *Rif, ad loc.*; *Yad*, op. cit., 6:7; *Rosh*, op. cit.; *Tur*, op. cit.; *Sh. Ar.*, op. cit., 312:4; *Ar. ha-Sh.*, op. cit., 312:13.
46. *Mishnah, Bava Metzia* 8:6; *Yad*, op. cit., 6:7; *Tur*, op. cit., 312; *Sh. Ar.*, op. cit., 312:6; *Ar. ha-Sh.*, op. cit., 312:15.
47. *Mishnah, Bava Metzia* 8:6 and R. Solomon b. Isaac (Troyes, 1040–1105), *Rashi*, ad loc. s.v. *u-bahanuyot*; *Rif*, ad loc.; *Rosh*, op. cit.; *Yad*, op. cit.; *Tur*, op. cit.; *Sh. Ar.*, op. cit.; *Ar. ha-Sh.*, op. cit., 312:15.
48. *Baraita, Bava Metzia* 101b; R. Joseph Caro, *Beit Yosef, Tur*, op. cit., 312; R. Joshua ha-Kohen Falk (Poland, 1555–1614), *Sefer Meirat Aniyyim, Sh. Ar.*, op. cit., 312 note 10; *Ar. ha-Sh.*, op. cit., 312:16.
49. Rabban Shimon b. Gamliel, *Mishnah, Bava Metzia* 8:6; *Rif*, ad locum; *Rosh* op. cit.; *Tur*, op. cit.; R. Mosheh Isserles, *Rema, Sh. Ar.*, op. cit., 312:6; *Ar. ha-Sh.*, op. cit., 312:16.
50. For sources and discussion of the *lifnei iver* interdict, please turn to pp. 257, 400, 412–413 of this volume.
51. *Baraita, Bava Batra* 21b.
52. R. Ya'akov Yeshayahu Bloi, *Pithei Hoshen, Hilkhot Geneivah ve-Ona'ah*, 9:11, at 26.
53. *Mishnah, Bava Metzia* 3:2
54. *Bava Metzia* 34b and *Rashi* ad loc., s. v. *ve-ha-shoel*.
55. *Rosh, Bava Metzia* 3:5.
56. *Rif, Bava Metzia* 34b; *Yad. Sekhirut* 1:6; *Rosh, Bava Metzia* 3:5; *Tur*, op. cit. 307:5; *Sh. Ar.*, op. cit., 307:5; *Ar. ha-Sh.*, op. cit., 307:5.
57. R. Solomon b. Abraham Adret, *Hiddushei ha-Rashba, Bava Kamma* 21a; R. Joseph Habib, *Nimmukei Yosef, Bava Kamma* 2. A minority interpretation of R. Yosei's dictum is expressed by R. Ephraim b. Aaron Navon, *Mahaneh Efrayim, Sekhirut* 19. Disgorgement, in R. Navon's view, is called for only when the following two conditions obtain: (1) the defendant's commercialization of plaintiff's property was unauthorized; and (2) the plaintiff suffers a loss in conjunction with the unauthorized use of his property.
58. Harlan Blake, "Employee Agreements Not to Compete," *Harvard Law Review* 73 (1960): 625, 677–678.
59. R. Isaac, *Tosafot, Kiddushin* 59a.
60. R. Joseph Trani, *Hiddushei Maharit, Kiddushin* 59a.
61. Please turn to pp. 114–115 of this volume.

5

Leverage Is The Thing

Parties to a mutually advantageous transaction rarely meet on equal terms. Often, one party has leverage or an advantage over the other. If the leverage consists of market power, the stronger party will walk away from the transaction with the lion's share of the gains. This is the way of the marketplace.

Halakhah does not always accept the way of the marketplace. Within the context of an inter-Jewish loan transaction, the exercise of leverage by the lender runs afoul of the prohibition of _ribbit_, the charging and payment of interest on loans. In nonloan transactions, however, the exercise of market power to get the lion's share of the potential benefits of the transaction is rarely an ethical issue. We have dealt with this issue elsewhere.[1]

The focus of the case studies of this chapter is on the ethics of exploiting an existing leveraged situation for further gains. Indeed, the distinction between negotiating a lopsided deal and unilaterally changing the terms of that deal once it has been negotiated may become blurred or even lost entirely in the mind of the advantaged party.

In what could be called reverse _leverage_, the _weaker party_ maneuvers to escape an obligation in the hope that the obligation will go unnoticed. Alternatively, the _weaker_ party can maneuver to escape payment because on a cost-benefit basis it is not worthwhile for the advantaged party to pursue his or her claim through legal channels.

LEVERAGE IS THE THING

Ivan Frier is the CEO of the Palisade Department Store chain. His dynamic and energetic leadership built a modest variety shop into a national chain of more than 500 department stores. Industry observers see in the young Frier shades of his grandfather, I.M. Frier. The elder Frier earned a reputation as a tough, hard-nosed "mean boss."[2] As a youth, Ivan spent much time at his grandfather's business, the I.M. Frier Novelty Company. It was there that Ivan got an education in the hard knocks of the business world and formed his own *weltanschauung* for how to succeed in it.[3] In Ivan's way of thinking, the key to success in business is to "understand the concept of leverage and make it work for you."

IVAN FRIER'S FIRST VENTURE IN LEVERAGE—THE ICED TEA LOAN

With a gleam in his eyes, Ivan recalls his first triumph in the exercise of leverage:

> I was only 14 years old. It was a hot summer day at camp. My friend Eitan Kramer was parched and desperate to borrow $1 to purchase a bottle of iced tea at the canteen vending machine. With an expression of hesitancy and reluctance, I reached into my pocket for the $1 bill. However, before I put the bill in Eitan's outstretched hand, I blurted out: "O.K., but you must buy the mint-flavored one and give me a gulp as well." Because I had Eitan over the barrel, he agreed to my terms. A number of my friends were on hand. They were all impressed by how I handled the deal.
>
> In similar circumstances, Eitan's brother, Erez, approached me for a $1 iced tea loan. Here, I was careful not to attach any conditions to my loan, as I knew that if I did Erez would turn elsewhere for the loan. I made no stipulations whatsoever when I put the $1 bill in Erez's hand. However, when Erez returned from the vending machine, I asked him to get an extra cup and pour me a "swallow's worth." I guess Erez did not want to feel like an ingrate. He begrudgingly complied with my request.

GIVING LEVERAGE TO CUSTOMERS—FRIER'S GENEROUS RETURNS POLICY

Before describing the various deals Frier made with the use of leverage, it is only fair to point out that Frier believed that the best way to earn customer goodwill was to *give* customers leverage. Frier did this by devising a very generous return policy. The policy told customers that as long as the merchandise was not damaged, they could return it anytime within seven days of purchase and have the sale *retroactively* canceled. Frier believed that the word *retroactively* had a powerful emotional appeal for customers. It said to them that they could erase a purchase as if it never happened.

Let us now go on to describe the various ways Frier imposed leverage on those he interacted with in business and social circles.

REVERSE LEVERAGE

In the fledgling years of the operation of his business, Frier exploited the fact that he was a very insignificant customer to some of his suppliers. Frier recognized that this was a reverse leverage setting, and took measures so that his obligation became either unnoticed or too much trouble to pursue through legal channels.

One such incident involved Frier's dealings with the Oriole Brothers Company. In those early years, Frier obtained much of the inventory for his store by entering into consignment arrangements with a number of suppliers. One such agreement was with Oriole Brothers, a publisher of nonfiction paperback books. The agreement called for Palisade to pay, at the end of the quarter, an agreed-upon price for each book sold. In addition, the agreement called for Palisade to return the unsold books at the time payment was remitted. Oriole Brothers agreed to give Palisade credit for any books that either arrived or became damaged during the relevant accounting period. When Frier received the Oriole Brothers quarterly invoice, he responded by claiming a 6 percent credit for damaged and defective merchandise. Frier was fully aware that his claim was partially false, but hoped that because the amount in question was so small, it would somehow fall through the cracks of Oriole Brothers vast bureaucracy.

Frier was wrong! Before long Oriole Brothers sent Frier a request that he return all the damaged books to validate his claim for credit. Because he knew that the wheels of a vast bureaucracy turn very slowly, Frier simply ignored the Oriole Brothers' request. However, Oriole Brothers followed up its written request with telephone calls. Initially, Frier instructed his secretary to respond that he was not available. Subsequently, Frier took the calls but brushed aside the caller by claiming either that the computers were down or that the accounts payable man was out sick. Frier's dilatory tactics managed to prolong the dispute between the companies for another two months. In its last correspondence with Frier, Oriole Brothers threatened to initiate legal action against him. Frier's response to the threat of legal action was to simply plead that the damaged books had been misplaced and could not be sent back. Oriole Brothers' threat to take legal action turned out to be a bluff, just as Frier had predicted.

While the correspondences between Frier and the accounts receivable department of Oriole Brothers'went back and forth, the consignment agreement between Palisade and the Oriole Brothers' marketing department was renewed at the initiative of Oriole Brothers. Frier was right after all! Oriole Brothers was indeed a huge bureaucracy, and one part of the organization apparently was unaware of what a different part of the same organization was doing. Accounting did not communicate with marketing at Oriole Brothers. During this period, the publisher raised his price for some of the books Frier held unlawfully in inventory from the first consignment period. Accordingly, Frier not only kept books that he should have returned, but ended up selling these books in the next accounting period at a premium price.

I'LL TAKE MY BUSINESS ELSEWHERE

On the way to building up his empire, Frier dealt with more than 1000 suppliers, ranging from obscure soft drink companies to colossal pharmaceutical companies. In negotiating price, credit, and other terms with many of the suppliers, Frier exploited to the hilt the leverage he wielded in ordering for 500 stores. In the heat of negotiations, Frier could frequently be heard to threaten a supplier, the small obscure ones in particular: "If you can't give me my terms, I'll take my business elsewhere."

Because threatening to take his business elsewhere proved to be an effective negotiating tactic, Frier occasionally employed this approach to deny a supplier a payment that was due. A case in point was Frier's dealings with the Silvan Watchband Company. In setting up terms with Silvan, Frier got the company to agree to give him credit for damaged goods. When Frier received an invoice from Silvan, he claimed a hefty 6 percent of the money owed as a deduction for damaged goods. Silvan balked at Frier's claim and demanded documentation. An irate Frier wasted no time in replying: "You'll have to trust me on this. If we can't trust each other, I'm afraid we can't do business in the future."

Another situation that was ripe for the exercise of leverage occurred when Frier discovered that a particular supplier gave more favorable terms to a store or chain that Palisade had just acquired. If Frier discovered that the company he acquired was treated more favorably by the supplier even in respect to a single feature of the terms of sale, Frier would demand that Palisade be given that same advantage *retroactively*.

A case in point was Frier's dealings with Amerchee Ltd. For a number of years, a clothing design company named Amerchee Ltd. had been giving Center Brothers, a rival department store chain, a generous return policy on new creations for the first two weeks of the season. In this period, Center Brothers was given the right to return all unsold new creations at 40 percent of their invoice price. In Amerchee's written contract with Palisade, no such provision appeared. To be sure, the Palisade contract had other advantageous provisions that the Center Brothers contract did not have. Nonetheless, when Palisade acquired Center Brothers and Frier discovered the return policy Center Brothers had with Amerchee Ltd., he demanded that the same terms be given to Palisade for the current season, and that they be awarded a credit of $10,000 to make up for the fact that Palisade *did not but should have had* this arrangement over the past two years. The basis for this demand was that Center Brothers was now part of the Palisade chain and negotiations between the companies for the merger had been ongoing for two years. In Frier's thinking, fairness dictated that the two companies be considered as *one entity* throughout that two-year span and that the same deal should have been offered to Palisade. Amerchee Ltd. initially balked at Frier's demand, but eventually came around when Frier threatened to move his business elsewhere.

ENHANCING EXISTING LEVERAGE WITH INSIDER INFORMATION

As an artful practitioner of leverage, Frier understood that the better the information he had on his opposite number, the more mileage he could expect from his asymmetric economic power. Frier's appreciation of the value of quality information, on occasion, drove him to conduct that was clearly beyond the boundaries of legal activity. There is no gainsaying that Ivan Frier is, basically, a law-abiding individual. He is certainly no mobster. But, when an easy opportunity to get valuable private information presents itself, Frier just grabs it. A case in point is the story of how Frier got insider information from Eugene Gold. The particulars are as follows:

Fairmount, a large manufacturer of toys, is Frier's main supplier of toys for his department store chain. When Frier learned that Eugene Gold, a passing acquaintance of his son, Bolton, had been hired fresh out of college by the accounting department of Fairmount, Frier was driven to get insider information from Gold. Gold was young, very ambitious, and morally weak, attributes that made him easy prey for Frier's overtures. Frier wanted to know the per-unit cost of each toy Fairmount produced, and to identify the best-selling toys in the northeast. Frier was also interested in Fairmount's cash flow position. For a pair of tickets to the World Series, Gold was only too eager to supply this information to Frier.

Equipped with this information and the threat to take his business elsewhere, Frier had the wherewithal to negotiate very advantageous deals with Fairmount.

GETTING GOOD MILEAGE FROM A LOAN TO THE SYNAGOGUE

For Frier the exercise of leverage was not just a way of doing business, it was an important strategy that he employed in all aspects of his life. A case in point is the conduct Frier engaged in while his $50,000 bridge loan to his synagogue, Beth Kodesh, was still outstanding. The purpose of the loan was to keep the building project going despite the cost overruns the project encountered. Frier felt that because he "came through" for the synagogue he was entitled to demand reasonable favors, especially while his loan was not paid up. In one instance, he asked the rabbi of the synagogue, Aryeh Samson, to tutor his son, Bolton, for the geometry regents exam he took that

year. At the synagogue's annual dinner, the honoree couple was always presented with a gift. Frier successfully persuaded the committee to present the
honorees with a $250 gift certificate redeemable in his department store,
Palisade.

We now turn to a consideration of the ethics of the various stratagems
that Ivan Frier employed.

IVAN'S $1 LOAN TO EITAN

Ivan's first venture into the world of leverage got him caught up in a serious
violation of *ribbit* law. *Ribbit* is the Torah's prohibition against both receiving and making interest payments.[4] The prohibition applies only to inter-
Jewish transactions.[5] The essence of the *ribbit* prohibition entails
demanding a *premium for waiting* (*agar natar*) for the return of one's capital.[6] On a biblical level, *ribbit* is violated only if the extra payment is
requested within the context of a loan. *Agar natar* takes place when the premium above principle is prearranged (*ketzutzah*) either as a precondition for
the loan or later as a condition for extending the due date.[7] The biblical violation of *ribbit* is called *ribbit ketzutzah*. By rabbinical enactment, the *ribbit*
interdict is considerably expanded and extended. These extensions are
called avak *ribbit* (literally, the dust of *ribbit*.)[8]

Before granting Eitan the $1 loan he sought, Ivan got him to agree to use
the money to buy a mint-flavored iced tea drink and to give him a gulp as
well. Since these stipulations are made as a precondition to the loan, Ivan's
deal amounts to a violation of *ribbit ketzutzah*. Both parties to the transaction, Ivan and Eitan, violate this prohibition.[9] Moreover, since the transaction violates *ribbit* law on a biblical level, Ivan must compensate Eitan for
the monetary value of the gulp he took from his drink. A Jewish Court (*Bet
Din*) will compel this payment.[10]

In his loan transaction with Erez, Ivan violated no biblical law. Consider that Ivan's demand for a "swallow's worth" of the drink was neither
made as a precondition for the loan nor made later as a condition for extending the due date of the loan. Ivan hence did not violate *ribbit ketzutzah*.
Nonetheless, Ivan's demand and Erez's acquiescence to give him a portion
of the drink violates *avak ribbit*.

Since Ivan had no right to shame Erez into giving him a swallow's worth of his drink, Ivan is ethically bound to compensate Erez for the monetary value of the portion of Erez's drink that he consumed. Nonetheless, since Ivan's infraction of *ribbit* law is only on a rabbinical level, a *Bet Din* will not compel Ivan to make this compensation.[11]

FRIER'S GENEROUS TRIAL-PERIOD POLICY

Frier generated much goodwill from his seven-day money back guarantee. The key phrase in Frier's advertisements for his generous trial period was the word *retroactive*: If a customer was not happy with the purchase, all that was needed to get a refund was to bring back the proof-of-purchase slip and a Palisade clerk would stamp it: "Sale retroactively void from date of purchase." This properly stamped slip gave the customer the right to a full refund. To maximize the mileage out of his return policy, Frier loved to hang around the returns department and gleefully boast to customers: "How many things in life can you *retroactively* undo? Only here at Palisade."

Although there can be no doubt that Frier's return policy was a generous one, it runs afoul of *avak ribbit* law. Ironically, what is objectionable here is the retroactive feature of the policy. Empowering the customer to retroactively void the sale creates the possibility that the original purchasing price will end up taking on the character of a loan. This will happen if the customer opts to return the item within seven days. If this option is taken, giving back the customer anything more than the original purchasing price amounts to the payment of *ribbit*. But, this is what Frier is doing. The customer gets his money back, but also ends up using the product without charge for as much as seven days. The free use of the article for the trial period should therefore constitute a prohibited interest payment.

In his discussion of the money-back free-trial-period offer, R. Yisroel Reisman (New York, contemp.) points out a number of surprisingly simple solutions to this *ribbit* problem. One solution is for the seller to phrase the free trial period as an offer by the company to *buy back* the item within, for example, seven days of the purchase. By avoiding the use of the word *retroactively*, the purchase price will never assume the status of a loan.

Another approach to ensure that the purchase price Frier gets on a trial period sale never assumes the character of a loan is to make the sale a conditional one. This can be accomplished by maintaining a policy that the sale is made on condition that the customer be permitted to return the merchandise within *x* number of days. Because it is the conditional basis of the original sale that requires the seller to exchange the item of purchase for the price the customer originally paid, the return of the item in no way makes the original transaction into a loan. Indeed, when the conditional sale phraseology is employed, the original sale becomes retroactively void if the seller *does not* honor the customer's demand for a refund.

Finally, the *ribbit* problem can be avoided by requiring the customer to keep the item for a specified time before the company honors its money-back guarantee. The waiting period requires that the merchandise remain in the customer's irrevocable control for some specified time. This ensures that the money back-offer will not confer loan status on the original purchase price, but instead, will be viewed as a new sale from the customer to the company.[12]

WITHHOLDING PAYMENT

In the opening vignette, Frier exercises reverse leverage by deftly maneuvering to avoid meeting his obligation to the Oriole Brothers, all along hoping that the big company would forget about him and that he would fall through the cracks. Frier's conduct violates an aspect of the law against misappropriation, called *oshek*. *Oshek* entails the misappropriation of property that came into one's possession with the consent of the owner. Maimonides (Egypt, 1135–1204) formulates *oshek* in the following manner:

> Who is deemed guilty of unlawful withholding (*oshek*)? One who, having come into possession of another person's money with the latter's consent, withholds it forcibly and does not return it upon the other's demand. Such is the case if one who has a loan or wages due him from another claims his due but cannot get it from his debtor because he is an overbearing and hardhearted person. It is of this that Scripture says, "You shall not oppress (*lo ta'ashok*) your neighbor" (Leviticus 19:13).[13]

Note that in Maimonides' formulation, *lo ta'ashok* is not violated on a biblical level unless the party that misappropriates (*M*) is overbearing or hardhearted in resisting the original owner's (*O's*) efforts to obtain what is lawfully his. In their formulations of *lo ta'ashok*, R. Jacob b. Asher (Germany, 1270–1103),[14] R. Joseph Caro (Safed, 1488–1575),[15] and R. Jehiel Michel Epstein (Belorussia, 1829–1908)[16] all include the above caveat.

M violates Halakhah even if he is not overbearing, but instead resists *O*'s demands that he is capable of meeting by telling him to go away and return. Such conduct violates a rabbinical prohibition as opposed to a biblical one. This rabbinical prohibition is alluded to in the verse: "Say not to your neighbor, 'Go and come back (*lekh ve-shuv*), and tomorrow I will give, when you have [it] with you'" (Proverbs 3:28; henceforth the rabbinical prohibition will be referred to as *lekh ve-shuv*).[17]

The *lekh ve-shuv* prohibition is recorded in the Talmud and proscribes an employer from stalling his worker when the latter demands his wage.[18] R. Jehiel Michel Epstein takes the view that the employer violates *lekh ve-shuv* only if he was both not preoccupied and had the capacity to pay when his worker made the wage demand on him.[19] The prohibition of *lekh ve-shuv* is also mentioned as a prohibition for a debtor to stall his creditor when the latter demands payment. The debtor violates *lekh ve-shuv* only if he has the capacity to pay up his debt and instead of meeting the legitimate demands of the creditor, chooses to deflect the payment demand with *lekh ve-shuv*.[20] In the opinion of R. Yaakov Yeshayahu Bloi (Israel, 1927-), the *lekh ve-shuv* prohibition applies to anyone (*M*) who unlawfully withholds someone else's property and resists the demands of that person (*O*) to get his due by means of using *dilatory* tactics. Nonetheless, if *M* was preoccupied at the time *O* made his demand upon him, *M* does not violate *lekh ve-shuv*.[21]

In his dealings with the Oriole Brothers, Frier was guilty of *oshek*. Frier begins by making a fraudulent damaged book claim, and never retreats from this position. Indeed, Frier's final word on the matter was that the damaged books were misplaced and could therefore not be returned to Oriole Brothers. Frier's use of dilatory tactics along the way should therefore be viewed as a mechanism to make him inaccessible, rather than an indication on his part that he eventually might pay what he owed. This leads to the judgment that Frier violated *oshek* on a biblical level.

Frier's *oshek* violation generates potential liability beyond the price Oriole Brothers billed him for at the time he denied his obligation to the company. Recall that Oriole Brothers renewed the consignment agreement with Palisade and raised the price of the titles that Frier unlawfully held over from the previous accounting period. Selling the unlawfully held books in the second accounting period increases Frier's liability for these books to the new, higher price Oriole Brothers now charges for these books. The scenario just described is very much akin to a case recorded in the codes. Maimonides' treatment is typical:

> If one robs another of a cask of wine worth a *dinar* at the time of the robbery, and its value goes up to four while it is in his possession, the rule is as follows: If the robber breaks the cask, or drinks the wine, or sells it or gives it away as a present after it has increased in value, he must pay four *dinars*, its value as of the time it vanished, since the *wine itself* would have to be restored had he let it alone. If, however, the cask breaks through no fault of his, or is lost, the robber need pay only a *dinar*, its value as of the time of the robbery.[22]

There is a great irony here. If Frier had acknowledged his debt to Oriole Brothers, then any accidental loss or accidental damage (*ones*) of the books would not have been Frier's responsibility. Instead, the contractually arranged returns policy would have been operative for the *bailment* that Frier held. Frier's lie that the books were damaged *converts* the bailment into the category of *stolen goods*. Frier therefore bears the responsibility for them, even in the face of unavoidable circumstance.

In his dealings with Silvan, Frier also was guilty of *oshek*. Consider that Frier knew full well that the representation he made regarding the amount of defective merchandise his company received was an outright lie. Invoking the return policy clause as a reason for not paying the money that he owed Silvan was therefore nothing but a shallow attempt to put a veneer of legitimacy on a false representation. Deflecting Silvan's demand for documentation by threatening to take his future business elsewhere compounded Frier's wrongdoing by adding an element of coercion to his denials of the debt owed to Silvan. Frier's conduct meets the criteria for *oshek*.

In other dealings with suppliers, Frier was guilty of the lesser offense of *lekh ve-shuv*. This occurred when he chose not to deny a claim, but instead to stall the inevitable by making up excuses for not paying such as "the computers were down" or "the accounts payable person was out sick."

ABOVE SUSPICION

From the perspective of Halakhah, Frier's approach of fending off demands to validate his claim of damaged goods is morally wrong. Indeed, Frier should not make a damaged goods claim in the first place without accompanying his claim with the return of the damaged goods. The operative moral principle here is "And you should be guiltless before the Lord and before Israel" (Numbers 32:22). Moses made this statement to the descendants of Gad and Reuben in the aftermath of their request to be given their inheritance on the eastern bank of the Jordan in the cities of Gilead. In their initial approach to Moses, the petitioners failed to clarify their request. Specifically, they failed to signal their commitment to join forces with the rest of the nation and cross the Jordan to conquer the land of *Cana'an*. Although their intent was to rejoin their families in the cities of Gilead only after the conquest of the land of *Cana'an* was completed, the petitioners spoke initially only of their desire to take up their inheritance on the East Bank. Moses misunderstood their intent and immediately launched a tirade against them, drawing parallels with the episode of the spies. *To avoid drawing suspicion on themselves* the petitioners should have immediately clarified their intent by signaling their commitment to join forces with the rest of the nation before returning to their families in Gilead. The requirement for the petitioners to clarify their intent is read by the sages into the words of Moses: "And you should be guiltless before the Lord and before Israel." For purposes of brevity, we will refer to the aforementioned moral imperative as the "above suspicion" principle.

Applications of the above suspicion principle abound in the Talmudic literature.[23] One application relates to the conduct prescribed for charity wardens.

In *Mishnaic* and *Talmudic* times, copper coins were considered unsuitable for extended storage because they were liable to tarnish and mold. Thus, when copper coins accumulated, they were typically exchanged for silver coins. To avoid suspicion, charity wardens were not permitted to exchange copper coins in their trust for their own silver coins. Instead, they were required to exchange the coins with outsiders only. Similarly, when surplus food accumulated in the soup kitchen the overseers could not buy the food themselves, but instead had to sell it to others.[24]

The application of the above suspicion principle to the opening vignette is clear-cut. To avoid suspicion that a false claim is being made, Frier should not use his leverage to override the supplier's policy to give credit only when the damaged goods claim is accompanied with the return of the damaged goods. The ethical principle of above suspicion should go further. Consider the following scenario: Suppose Silvan never told Frier in advance what kind of proof it would require if he made a damaged goods claim. Given that Frier is a big customer, there is a good chance the company will swallow Frier's unsubstantiated claim for a credit for damaged goods. Let us assume that Frier's damaged goods claim is an honest one. Perhaps it is morally acceptable for Frier to put in a claim for a credit for damaged goods without accompanying his claim by returning the damaged goods. If Silvan reacts to the unsubstantiated claim by insisting the damaged merchandise should be returned, Frier will, of course, comply. But, in the meantime, Frier can spare himself the effort and expense of taking the initiative to accompany his claim with the return of the damaged goods. With the aim of objectively demonstrating his honesty, the above suspicion principle tells Frier not to play games with Silvan and wait for the company to demand that he substantiate his damage claim. Instead, Frier should take the initiative and accompany his damaged goods claim with the return of the damaged goods.

Ordinarily, in the scenario just described, fulfillment of the above suspicion imperative would not require the company making the damaged goods credit claim to actually return the damaged goods along with their claim for credit. Accompanying the claim with a *mere offer* to validate the claim with the return of the damaged goods should suffice. However, for the case at hand the *mere offer* to return the damaged goods would not suffice. Given the leverage Frier has over Silvan and the brutal way he always exercises it, Silvan is likely to take Frier's *offer* to return the damaged merchandise as a *test* as to whether they trust him. The situation at hand is clearly an *intimidating* one for Silvan. Because it is predictable that Silvan will not take Frier up on his offer, Frier demonstrates his honesty openly only by actually taking the initiative and providing proof that the damaged merchandise credit he claims is an honest one. Although Frier is free to choose the least costly method of proving the honesty of his claim, proving the claim in an unconvincing manner, as for example sending Silvan a photograph of the damaged goods, runs the risk of making a mockery of the above suspicion imperative.

LEVERAGE AND ASYMMETRIC BARGAINING POWER

The huge orders Frier made for his 500 stores gave him leverage over many of the suppliers with which he dealt. Nowhere was this leverage greater than with Silvan Watchband Company. Frier's large order of the watchbands kept the fledgling manufacturer at high gear for the entire year. Operating at high capacity allowed the company to reduce per unit costs in various ways, including achieving an optimal capital-to-labor ratio and securing better credit terms from their bank. What Silvan liked best was that having its product displayed in Frier's 500 stores amounted to a free promotion of its merchandise. For some of the company executives, winning a supply contract with Frier meant that brand-name status for their product was around the corner. Frier's keen grasp of all the advantages his big customer standing meant for Silvan made him drive a hard bargain. At some point in the negotiation Frier would predictably rant "if you can't give me my terms, I'll take my business elsewhere." Following the tirade, Silvan would come up with the further concessions Frier desired.

Does Frier's hard-nosed bargaining with Silvan breach halakhic ethics? One issue is whether Frier is bound by some reference price in his bargaining with Silvan. In Halakhah the price terms of a commercial transaction are usually subject to a fairness test when a competitive market price exists for the article at hand. This is called the law of *ona'ah*. Depending on how widely the price of the subject transaction departs from the competitive norm, the injured party may have recourse to void or adjust the transaction.[25] Although the law of *ona'ah* applies to a differentiated product market, it does not apply when the product at hand is sold under monopoly conditions.[26]

Let's apply the parameters of the law of *ona'ah* to Frier's bargaining with Silvan. Most fundamentally, it must be noted that the reference price in an *ona'ah* claim is the competitive norm. By definition a competitive norm is not a speculative matter. It is not a price that one could theoretically achieve by means of negotiating skill and/or economic leverage. Rather, the competitive norm is a clearly identifiable price that *already* exists and is *available to anyone for the asking*. For the law of *ona'ah* to work for Silvan, it is not enough for the company to claim that it could have negotiated a better deal with some other department store chain; rather, Silvan must show that the deal it hammered out with Frier is a *standard package* that had ready takers in the same marketplace at a higher price than Frier paid. This is certainly not the case here.

The upshot of this analysis is that the more a deal departs from the standard transaction for the commodity at hand, the more likely that the law of *ona'ah* will not govern that transaction.

Another issue to consider is that Frier's hard-nosed negotiations may violate the biblical prohibitions of ". . . And you shall not covet" (*lo tahmod*) and ". . . shall not desire" (*lo tit'avveh*, Deuteronomy 5:18.) Elsewhere in this volume we have discussed at length the parameters of these prohibitions.[27] One aspect of these interdicts is the prohibition for *G* to exert pressure on *S* to confer him a gift of an article he owns. By extension, *G* should be prohibited from pressuring *S* to sell him an item he owns at a discount. Given that Silvan's watchbands have a clearly defined price when they are sold in the standardized way, Frier's pronouncement "if you can't give me my terms, I'll take my business elsewhere" should be viewed as a pressure tactic designed to get a discount from Silvan.

However, one can question the premise that the negotiation should be conceptualized as Frier's push for the deepest discount he can squeeze out of Silvan for his big order. Conceptualizing Frier's conduct in this manner implies that within the context of the negotiation at hand, the watchbands have a fixed, objective market value and that Frier is wielding leverage to achieve a discount. This is not the case. Given that a competitive price does not exist for the package deal that Frier is negotiating with Silvan, the economic value of the watchbands within the context of the deal is indeterminate. Instead, the economic value of the watchbands will be determined by the outcome of the negotiations themselves. Frier's hard nose negotiations are not pushing to transfer an article of *definite* economic value to himself at a discount; rather, the deal the parties discuss transforms the watchbands into nonstandardized items with no determinate value. As a result Frier's negotiation tactics do not violate *lo tahmod*.

Scenarios that have some affinity to the Silvan case include monopoly pricing under various conditions of demand elasticity[28] and the bilateral monopoly model.[29]

The Amerchee Scenario and the Prohibition Against Extortion

In the Amerchee scenario Frier uses his leverage to get a benefit that amounts to unilaterally changing the terms of the existing contract between Frier and Amerchee. Frier accomplishes this by threatening to cut off Amerchee unless he is *retroactively* given the same concession or advantage that a recent Palisade acquisition enjoyed.

Using leverage to change contractual terms with a supplier is a form of extortion. The model case in Halakhah is called *teluhu ve-zavin* (literally, he was [threatened] to be hanged and [because of this] sold)[30]: Buyer *B* coerces Seller *S* to sell him property he owns at its "fair market value." Considering both the duress *S* is subject to and his receipt and acceptance of the cash representing the "fair market" value of the property, it is evident that the latter desires to transfer the article to *B*.[31] The sale, although immoral,[32] is nevertheless legally binding.[33] To this, the Talmud adds that to be valid *S* must in the end declare, "I am willing" (*rotzeh ani*).[34] Decisors regard *S*'s acceptance of the purchase price *without protest* as equivalent to declaring *rotzeh ani*.[35] A variation of this case occurs when *B* snatches away *S*'s article but leaves him with its fair market value. Here, *S*'s acquiescence to the exchange does not become objectively evident until *S* explicitly verbalizes his consent.[36]

A variant of this scenario has direct relevance to the Amerchee situation described in the opening vignette. In this variant, *B* coerces *S* to make him a gift or sell his property below fair market value. The transaction, according to R. Jacob b. Asher and R. Joseph Caro, is invalid and *B* is guilty of extortion.[37] These decisors define coercion in terms of either physical duress or monetary threats.[38] In opposition to the school of thought that regards monetary threats as a form of coercion, R. Joseph Colon would not invalidate a commercial transaction on this basis.[39]

Recall that when Frier discovered that Amerchee Ltd. gave Center Brothers a 40 percent credit on new creations returned the first two weeks of the season, he demanded that the same terms be given to Palisade for all new creations purchased over the last two seasons. Frier's proposition amounts to a demand that Amerchee confer Palisade with a gift. Consider that Amerchee initially balked at this proposition and only eventually conceded because of the economic pressure applied by Palisade. The concession

Amerchee eventually gives should therefore amount to a violation of *gezel* by Frier. If we, however, take the view, along with R. Colon, that economic pressure does not constitute extortion, the above judgment does not hold.

Regardless of the position we take on whether economic pressure constitutes extortion, Frier's dealings with Amerchee violate the biblical prohibitions of ". . . And you shall not covet" (*lo tahmod*) and ". . . shall not desire" (*lo tit'avveh*, Deuteronomy 5:18). Elsewhere in this volume we have discussed at length the parameters of these prohibitions.[40] Falling in the ambit of these interdicts is the prohibition for *A* to exert pressure on *B* to confer him with a gift. The economic pressure Frier uses to induce Amerchee to confer him an advantage that clearly does not proceed from their contractual arrangement with him violates *lo tahmod* and *lo tit'avveh*.

SECURING PRIVATE INFORMATION FROM GOLD

Frier's drive to enhance his leverage led him to acquire private information from Eugene Gold, who worked in the accounting department of Fairmount. The information Frier obtained included Fairmount's current cash flow position and the company's per unit cost of various toy items that his company bought from Fairmount for his department store chain. Is Eugene Gold guilty of misappropriating Fairmount's property when he hands over to Frier the information on these items? Two scenarios present themselves. In one scenario the information Frier seeks is readily available to Gold because as one of the company's accountants he compiles this sort of data in the course of executing his routine daily duties. In the second scenario, Gold must "steal" the data because the information Frier seeks is compiled and/or recorded by other employees in the organization. In the opinion of this writer, in both instances Gold is guilty of misappropriation because once a labor agreement is struck, the output of the worker is automatically the legal property of the employer. This principle is expressed in the form of the Talmudic dictum: "The hand of the worker is like the hand of the employer" (*yad po'el ke-yad baal ha-bayit*)[41] In a market economy, *yad po'el* translates into the worker's obligation to hand over the entire *value* of his output to his employer. By handing over the Fairmount accounting data to Frier, Gold decidedly diminishes the value of this information and hence is guilty of misappropriation.

In the industrial espionage caper, Gold is also guilty of *unlawful dissemination* of the private information of his employer. Such conduct violates

Jewish privacy law and is an aspect of the prohibition for *A* to make an evil but true report (*lashon ha-ra*) about *B* to *C*. This prohibition is derived from the verse: "You shall not go as a talebearer . . ." (Leviticus 19:16.) Maimonides formulates this prohibition as follows:

> Who is a gossiper? One who collects information and [then] goes from person to person, saying: "This is what so and so said;" "This is what I heard about so and so." Even if the statements are true, they bring about the destruction of the world. There is a much more serious sin than [gossip], which is also included in the prohibition: *lashon ha-ra*, i.e., relating deprecating facts about a colleague, even if they are true.[42]

Maimonides teaches us here that if *A* conveys *private information* about *B* to *C*, even though the information is *truthful and not derogatory*, *A* violates "You shall not go as a talebearer. . . ."[43]

Another general principle in Jewish privacy protection law emerges from an analysis of Rabbenu Gershom b. Judah Me'Or ha-Golah's (France, ca. 960–1040) edict against reading another person's mail without permission.[44] Standing at the basis of this edict, according to R. Jacob Hagiz (Jerusalem, 1620–1674), is the admonition: "You shall not go as a talebearer among your people" (Leviticus 19:16). The verse prohibits the bearing of someone's private information, whether it is for self-consumption or for the purpose of revealing it to someone else.[45]

It proceeds from the above source that Gold violates Leviticus 19:16 when he hands the report to Frier. But, suppose Gold has a change of heart and decides not to turn over the accounting data to Frier. Does Gold's change of heart extricate him from violation of Leviticus 19:16? The answer to this question will hinge on the means by which Gold obtained the data. If recording the data that Frier requires is in any case part of the duties of Gold at Fairmount, then assembling the data in comparative form cannot be said to amount to *bearing* the private information of Fairmount for his own self-consumption. But, if Gold had to look in a coworker's files to compile the report, Gold should remain guilty of "bearing" his employer's private information for self-consumption, even if he ends up not giving the report to Frier.

Once it is recognized that handing over the accounting data to Frier constitutes a violation by Gold of the prohibition against unlawful dissemination of private information, Frier is in violation of this prohibition as well. This follows from the consideration that by dint of the verse "Do not accept a perverse report," (*lo tisah shamea shav*, Exodus 23:1), the prohibition against *lashon ha-ra* extends beyond the speaker to the one who accepts the evil report as well.[46] Since the prohibition against *lashon ha-ra* includes the interdict against disseminating someone's private information, accepting a report that reveals private information about someone should also be prohibited.

Another ethical principle Frier violates when he accepts Gold's report is Bar Kappara's dictum: "What [is the meaning of what] is written, 'You must also keep a spike with your implements . . . ?' [Deuteronomy 23: 14]. Do not read 'your implements' but upon your ear; [this means to say] that if a man hears an unworthy thing he shall plug his finger into his ears."[47]

Let's now return to Gold's moral lapse in the industrial espionage caper. Another ethical debit against Gold is that Frier will use the report he produces to the detriment of Fairmount. Gold either knows or should know this. To be sure, the link between Gold's action and the harm Fairmount later suffers is too indirect to saddle Gold with any financial responsibility for the loss involved. Nonetheless, consider that the rightful owner of the information is Fairmount. Gold is therefore forbidden to hand over the information to anyone who will use the information to cause some detriment or disadvantage to Fairmount. R. Aryeh Loeb b. Joseph ha-Kohen Heller's (*Ketzot*, Galicia, 1745–1813?) principle of *gorem de-gorem* (remotely indirect harm) is relevant here. The specific case dealt with by the *Ketzot* involves an individual, *A*, who hires two witness to bear false testimony that *B* owes $100 to *C*. The witnesses testify in court and *B* pays $100 to *C*. Notwithstanding that *A* indirectly caused *B* a loss of $100, *bet din* (the Jewish court) will not order *A* to compensate *B* for his loss. The principle here is that credence is given to *A*'s argument that the witnesses should never have obeyed his instruction to commit a sin: "If you must choose between the words of the Master [i.e., God, Who commands you not to sin] and the word of the disciple [*A*, who instructs you to sin], whose word should you obey? (*divrei ha-rav ve-divrei ha-talmid divrei mi shomin*).

The above logic prevents *Bet Din* from issuing a judgment against *A*. But to fulfill his obligation to the Heavenly court (*dinei shamayyim*), *A* should voluntarily compensate *B* for his loss.

Suppose that instead of *hiring* the false witnesses, *A* merely induces them to bear false testimony that *B* owes $100 to *C*. Here, *A* bears no obligation whatsoever to *B*, even in respect to *dinei shamayyim*. Nonetheless, there is no gainsaying that *A*'s conduct played a role, albeit a very indirect one (*gorem de-gorem*) in causing the witnesses to sin. *A*'s conduct is hence immoral.[48] Several earlier rulings follow *Ketzot*'s line.[49]

The *gorem de-gorem* principle dictates that Gold's conduct is classified as that of a tortfeasor (*mazzik*). Notwithstanding that Gold bears no financial responsibility for the weakened bargaining position Fairmount is put into on account of his making the company's private information available to Frier, handing over the information is morally wrong.

The upshot of the above analysis is that in the industrial espionage caper both Gold and Frier are guilty of misappropriation. Both are regarded as tortfeasors for taking action that financially hurts Fairmount. Finally, both Frier and Gold are guilty of infractions of Jewish privacy law.

Strictly speaking, in this scenario, a case for making defendants liable to Fairmount for a specific monetary penalty cannot be made. Nonetheless, Frier and Gold conspired to financially hurt Fairmount. To fulfill their duty to the Heavenly court, the defendants should, therefore, make monetary payment to Fairmount sufficient to compensate the company for its loss.

LEVERAGE EXERTED ON A SYNAGOGUE AND IT'S RABBI

Because Frier came through for his synagogue with a bridge loan, he felt he was entitled to make certain reasonable demands on the synagogue's policy and on the time of the synagogue's rabbi. Frier's conduct here may run afoul of *avak ribbit* law, *lo tahmod*, and the rules of proper conduct for citizens of a communal organization,

Let us begin with Frier's demand that the synagogue break with its tradition of purchasing a gift for its honorees at the annual dinner and instead present the honorees with a $250 gift certificate, redeemable at his variety store. Frier's demand apparently violates *avak ribbit* law. Consider that while a loan agreement between lender *L* and borrower *B* is operative, *L* may not demand a favor from *B*, even if the favor is costless from the standpoint of *B*.[50]

Perhaps, the *avak ribbit* issue can be dismissed in consideration that the loan was made to a synagogue and a synagogue is one of the categories of exemptions[51] as far as *avak ribbit* law is concerned.[52] The exemption status of a synagogue is, however, not a saving factor here. This is so because the rabbis established the exempt categories for the purpose of monetarily benefiting the funds in these categories. For this reason the rabbis of the Talmud urged us to go out of our way to find someone who is willing to incur the *debits* of *avak ribbit* as the counterparty for these transactions.[53] However, in the case at hand, Frier, who is the counterparty for the synagogue transaction, seeks to turn the tables and obtain extra benefits for himself.

In addition to violating *avak ribbit*, Frier should be bound by the rule that in synagogue policy matters, self-interest must defer to what is best for the community as a whole. This principle can be extrapolated by the guidepost R. Mosheh Isserles (*Rema*, Poland, 1525 or 1530–1572) lays down for communal legislation: "In communal decision-making, everyone should cast his vote in the matter at hand *le-shem shamayyim*, i.e. for the sake of Heaven. Once the majority has spoken, its decision is binding on the minority."[54] *Le-shem shamayyim* means, as a matter of certainty, that self-interest must give way to what is in the best interest of the majority. *Rema*'s guidepost for legislation of a community-wide scope should equally apply to community organizations of narrower scope and, in addition, not just to monetary matters, but to policy decisions generally.

The upshot of the above analysis is that before Frier puts in his request for changing the synagogue's procedures for the honoree gift, he should ask himself whether his proposal is just self-serving or it would enhance the welfare of the synagogue. If Frier's request is costless from the standpoint of Beth Kodesh, there should be nothing objectionable about his request.

Another concern here is that Frier's loan to the synagogue naturally creates a feeling of indebtedness to him on the part of the members of the organization. Because lending money to the shul is a *mitzvah* (religious duty), it is not proper for Frier to seek any personal benefit from his *mitzvah*.[55] Nonetheless, Frier is in a position to exploit this feeling of indebtedness, especially when a shul policy issue comes up. One could argue that the typical member of the synagogue would not oppose Frier's proposal to change the synagogue's long-standing procedure relating to the gift for the honorees at the annual dinner. Despite resentment at Frier for using the synagogue dinner for his own economic advantage and prestige, people generally will fear that rebuffing Frier risks losing his good-will and financial support in the future. Honest self-appraisal should tell Frier that people would go along with his idea in a reluctant manner, and even possibly with a sense of coercion. The analogue here is R. Jonah b. Abraham Gerondi's (Spain, ca. 1200–1264) ruling in respect to the *lo tahmod* prohibition. R. Jonah writes that if a distinguished person (*D*) feels that his request to *P* to either sell or offer him as a gift a particular item will be acceded to only on account of the pressure *P* will feel to comply with his will, *D* should not make the request. Making the request violates *lo tahmod*.[56] Analogously, Frier should not exploit the indebtedness people feel toward him because of the loan he gave the shul. Making the proposal for the gift certificate hence may violate for Frier *lo tahmod*.

GETTING RABBI SAMSON TO TUTOR BOLTON FOR THE REGENTS

Let us now turn to the ethics of Frier demanding that Rabbi Samson tutor Bolton for the geometry regents exam. Frier's request for the rabbi's time may run afoul of *ribbit* law. Consider that one of the stringencies of *avak ribbit* law is the prohibition for the lender to request favors from his debtor while the loan he extended him is outstanding.[57] In the opinion of R. Joshua b. Alexander ha-Kohen Falk (Poland, 1555–1614), the prohibition against asking for favors applies even if the favor would entail only insignificant toil and effort for the borrower.[58] However, Frier's request for the rabbi's time *is not* an *avak ribbit* violation in the context of the loan he extended Beth Kodesh. Frier's loan to the synagogue is made to the synagogue *qua* organization. The loan is made to Beth Kodesh as a collective institution, not to the members of the organization as individuals. Is it imaginable that by entering into a loan arrangement with the shul, all restrictions in conduct between lender and debtor prescribed by *ribbit* law becomes operative between Frier and *each and every* member of the synagogue for the entire period the loan is outstanding? Certainly not. Moreover, given that the loan arrangement was all along between Frier and the synagogue, there should be no objection for the synagogue to take the initiative and offer to reimburse Rabbi Samson for the time he spent tutoring Bolton.

Although the tutor request does not violate *avak ribbit* law, it may entail other ethical infractions. We take it as a given that Frier's request here strays beyond what any reasonable man would consider to be the contractual duties of a rabbi. Since the request does not fall under the reasonable man's concept of rabbinical duties, the request may divert the rabbi from attending to the needs and/or requests of other congregants and from the study of Torah.

Consider also that R. Jonah b. Abraham's rule against making inherently coercive requests may be operative here. Frier is a big supporter of the synagogue. In recognition of Frier's importance, Rabbi Samson may feel that he has no choice but to accede to Frier's request, even if it is very burdensome and unrelated to his duties as rabbi.

SUMMARY AND CONCLUSION

We have investigated the ethics of exercising leverage in a variety of business and social settings. For the practitioner of leverage, perhaps the most natural setting that is ripe for exploitation is the loan transaction. *Ribbit* law prohibits the lender from exploiting his or her debtor's feelings of gratitude by either requiring favors as a precondition for making the loan or imposing favors while the loan remains intact.

The artful student of leverage knows how to neutralize the leverage his opposite number has on him. One example of this is when a debtor maneuvers to make it not worthwhile for his creditor to pursue him. Such conduct runs afoul of the law against *oshek*.

Pragmatic considerations tell the practitioner of leverage that empowering customers with leverage generates a significant return in the form of goodwill. But, a free trial period policy that has a retroactive feature to it violates *ribbit* law.

The exercise of leverage has its legitimate realm. This occurs when the sale of a commodity takes place against the backdrop of no competitive norm to assess the fairness of the price and other terms of the transaction. To be sure, absent the negotiations between the parties, the commodity at hand has an objective market value. But, the bargaining process itself determines the value of the commodity at hand. Because the negotiation assigns market value, the asymmetric power one party brings with him to the negotiations does not wrest away value that was in the legitimate possession of the other party. Accordingly, the outcome achieved by means of asymmetric power does not constitute a violation by the gainer of the *lo tahmod* interdict.

The obsessive drive to exercise leverage in as many settings as possible blurs moral boundaries. One cannot, for instance, equate taking the lion's share of the possible gains from a negotiation with the use of economic leverage to make one's opposite number give up his contractual rights. The latter use of leverage is simply extortion, notwithstanding that the party that wrests away the right does so with a veneer of legitimacy. Similarly, securing private, nonpublic information to enhance the mileage one can get from economic leverage violates the law of theft and the law of privacy.

NOTES

1. In the sale of *hayyei nefesh* (essential foodstuff) items, the seller, by dint of a Talmudic ordinance, is constrained from charging whatever the market will bear. Instead, the rabbis imposed a 20 percent profit rate constraint. For the relevance of this ordinance today, see Aaron Levine, "Price Controls in Jewish Law-An Efficiency Analysis" (*Dine Israel*, Tel Aviv University Law School, vol. 23, forthcoming). Selling an item at whatever the marketplace will bear is also an ethical issue when the buyer's very life depends on getting the item. For treatment of this and related cases, see Aaron Levine, " *Ona'ah* and The Operation of the Modern Marketplace," *Jewish Law Annual*, Hebrew University, vol. XIV, 2003, pp. 225–258.

2. See Aaron Levine, *Case Studies in Jewish Business Ethics* (Hoboken, NJ: Ktav Publishing, Yeshiva University Press, 2000), pp. 237–248 and pp. 272–276 this volume. Please take note that the two works just mentioned described different aspects of meanness of the same person. The meticulous reader will also notice the variant names by which I.M. Frier's company is called. Let me clarify matters. The company in the early years was called the I.M. Frier Greeting Card Company. However, the name was later changed to the I.M. Frier Novelty Company. Why Frier changed the name of his company remains a mystery.

3. *Case Studies in Jewish Business Ethics*, op. cit.

4. Exodus 22:24; *Mishnah, Bava Metzia* 75b; R. Isaac b. Jacob Alfasi (Algeria, 1012–1103), *Rif* ad loc; Maimonides (Egypt, 1135–1204), *Yad, Malveh* 4:2; R. Asher b. Jehiel (Germany, 1250–1327), *Rosh, Bava Metzia* 5:80; R. Jacob b. Asher (Toledo, 1270–1340), *Tur, Yoreh De'ah* 160; R. Joseph Caro (Israel, 1488–1575), *Shulhan Arukh, Yoreh De'ah* 160:1; R. Abraham Danzig (Prague, 1748–1820), *Hokhmat Adam* 130:1.

5. Deuteronomy 23:21; *Yad*, op. cit., 5:1; *Tur*, op. cit., 159; *Sh. Ar.*, op. cit., 159:1.

6. Rav Nahman, *Bava Metzia* 63b; *Rif* ad loc; *Rosh*, op. cit., 5:10; R. Mosheh Isserles (Poland, 1525–1592), *Rema, Sh. Ar.*, op. cit., 161:1

7. C.F. *Hokhmat Adam* 131:1–3.

8. R. Mosheh Isserles, *Rema, Sh. Ar.*, op. cit., 161:1.

9. *Mishnah, Bava Metzia* 5:1; *Rif*, ad loc; *Yad*, op. cit., 4:2; *Rosh, Bava Metzia* 5:80; *Tur*, op. cit., 160; *Sh. Ar.*, op.cit., 160:1.

10. R. Elazar, *Bava Metzia* 61b; *Rif*, ad loc; *Yad*, op. cit., 4:3; *Rosh*, op.cit., 5:5; *Tur*, op. cit., 161; *Sh. Ar.*, op. cit., 161:5.

11. R. Elazar, *Bava Metzia* 61b; *Rif*, ad loc; *Yad*, op. cit., 4:6; *Rosh*, *Bava Metzia* 5:8; *Tur*, op. cit., 161; *Sh. Ar.*, op. cit., 161:2.

12. R. Yisroel Reisman, *The Laws of Ribbis* (New York: Mesorah Publications, 1995), pp. 39–41. See also R. Jacob Moses Lorberbaum (Poland, 1760–1832), *Havvot Da'at* 174:1 and R. Joshua Alexander ha-Kohen Falk (Poland, 1565–1614), *Sema, Hoshen Mishpat* 207:11.

13. Maimonides, *Yad, Gezeilah ve-Aveidah* 1:4

14. R. Jacob b. Asher, *Tur*, op. cit., 359.

15. R. Joseph Caro, *Sh. Ar.*, op. cit., 359:8.

16. R. Jehiel Michel Epstein, *Ar. ha-Sh.*, op. cit., 359:7.

17. Rav Yosef, *Bava Metzia* 110b.

18. *Bava Metzia* 110b; *Rif*, ad loc.; *Yad*, Sekhirut 11:5; R. Asher b. Jehiel, *Rosh*, *Bava Metzia* 9:43; R. Jacob b. Asher, *Tur*, op. cit., 339; R. Joseph Caro, *Sh. Ar*, op. cit,. 339:8; *Ar. Ha Sh.*, op. cit., 339:9.

19. *Ar. ha-Sh.*, op. cit.

20. *Tur*, op. cit., 339; *Sh. Ar.*, op. cit., 339:8; *Ar. ha-Sh.*, op., cit. 339:9.

21. R. Yaakov Yeshayahu Bloi, *Pithe Hoshen, Hilkhot Geneivah ve-Ona'ah*, p. 19 note 11.

22. *Yad, Gezeilah ve-Aveidah* 3:1.

23. See *Pesahim* 13a; *Yoma* 38a; *Mishna Shekalim* 3:2; *Ta'anit* 11b.

24. *Pesahim* 13a; *Yad, Mattenot Aniyyim* 9:11; *Tur, Yoreh De'ah* 257; *Sh. Ar.*, *Yoreh De'ah* 257:2 and *Rema* ad loc.; *Ar. ha-Sh.*, *Yoreh De'ah* 257:9. See also *Bava Batra* 8b.

25. Rava, *Bava Metzia* 50b; *Rif*, ad loc.; *Yad, Mekhirah* 12:1–4; *Rosh, Bava Metzia* 4:15; *Tur*, op. cit., 227; *Sh. Ar.*, op. cit., 227:1–6; *Ar. ha-Sh.* op. cit., 227:1–6.

26. *Mishnah, Ketubbot* 13:7; *Bava Metzia* 58b. For the development of this thesis, see Aaron Levine, "*Ona'ah* and the Operation of the Modern Marketplace," in the *Jewish Law Annual*, Hebrew University, vol. XIV, 2003, pp. 225–258.

27. Please turn to pp. 234–244 of this volume.

28. See Aaron Levine, *Case Studies in Jewish Business Ethics* (Hoboken, NJ: Ktav Publishing, Yeshiva University Press, 2000), pp. 157–160.

29. Please turn to pp. 47–48, 61–63 of this volume.

30. *Bava Kamma* 62a.

31. R. Samuel b. Meir, *Rashbam, Bava Batra* 48a, s.v. *ad she'yomar*.

    A "fair market value" duress sale, according to R. Isaac Alfasi, on the interpretation of R. Abraham b. David of Posquières (quoted in *Beit Yosef, Tur*, op. cit., 205:1, and *Rema, Sh. Ar.*, op.cit., 205:1) is valid only if the buyer makes *full* payment at the time the transaction is entered into. Absent this feature, the duress sale is not recognized, notwithstanding that it was both formally legally consummated (e.g., *kinyan shetar*) and called for a "fair market" price.

32. The pressure tactics *B* uses to acquire *S's* property violates for *B* the *lo tahmod* interdict. See R. Ezra Basri, *Dinei Mamonot* vol. 2 (Jerusalem: Sucath David, 1976); 70, note 1.

33. R. Huna, *Bava Kamma* 62a; *Rif, Bava Batra* 48a; *Yad*, op. cit., 10:1; *Rosh, Bava Batra* 3:51; *Tur*, op. cit., 205; *Sh. Ar.* op.cit., 205:1; R. Jehiel Michel Epstein, *Ar. ha-Sh.*, op. cit., 205:2.

34. *Bava Kamma* 62a.

35. R. Joseph Caro, *Beit Yosef, Tur*, op. cit., s.v. *mi she'ansuhu*; *Bah, Tur, Hoshen Mishpat* 34 s.v. *ha'over*; *Rema, Sh. Ar*, op. cit., note 2; R. Eliyahu b. Solomon Zalman, *Ha Gra, Sh. Ar.*, op. cit., note 1.

36. R. Jacob Moses Lorberbaum, *Netivot ha-Mishpat, Sh. Ar.*, op. cit., 205 note 1; *Sema, Hoshen Mishpat*, 205 note 2.

37. *Tur*, op.cit.; Sh. Ar., op. cit., 205:4.

38. *Tur*, op.cit.; *Sh. Ar.*, op. cit., 205:7.

39. R. Joseph Colon, quoted in *Rema, Sh. Ar.*, op. cit., 205:7.

40. Please turn to pp. 234–244 of this volume.

41. *Bava Metzia* 10a.

42. *Yad, De'ot* 7:2.

43. R. Joseph Caro (Safed 1488–1575), *Kesef Mishneh* at *Yad*, loc. cit.

44. R. Moses b. Naphtali Hirsch Rivkes (Lithuania d. ca. 1671/72), *Be'er ha-Golah, Sh. Ar., Yoreh De'ah* 334, note 123.

45. R. Jacob Hagiz, *Resp. Halakhot Ketannot* 1:276.

46. *Rashi* at Exodus 23:1; R. Pinhas ha-Levi (Barcelona, 1235–1300), *Sefer ha-Hinnukh* 74.

47, *Ketubbot* 5a.

48. R. Aryeh Loeb b. Joseph ha-Kohen Heller, *Ketzot, Shulhan Arukh, Hoshen Mishpat* 32, note 1.

49. See R. Yair Hayyim b. Moses Samson Bacharach (Germany, 1638–1702), Responsa *Havvot Yair* 166; R. Zevi Hirsch b. Jacob Ashkenazi (Germany, 1660–1718), Responsa *Hakham Zevi* 139.

50. *Yad, Malveh ve-Loveh* 5:13, according to interpretation of R. David b. Samuel ha-Levi (Poland, 1586–1667), *Taz, Sh. Ar., Yoreh De'ah* 160:12 note 5; *Sh. Ar.*, op. cit., 160:12 on interpretation of *Taz*, ad loc.

51. The exempted categories are: orphan funds, funds designated for the poor, funds designated to support the study of *Torah*, and funds designated for the needs of a synagogue. See *Sh. Ar.* op. cit., 160:18.

52. *Yad, Malveh ve-Loveh* 4:14; *Rosh, Bava Metzia* 4:50; *Tur*, op. cit., 160; *Sh. Ar.*, op. cit., 160:18. R. Solomon b. Abraham Adret (*Rashba*, Spain, ca. 1235–1310), raises a doubt as to whether the exemptions included all *avak ribbit* transactions, or was, perhaps, narrower in scope (see, *Beit Yosef, Tur*, op. cit., 160).

53. See Rabbah and Rav Ashi in opposition to Rav Yosef, *Bava Metzia* 70a. The specific case refers to an orphan fund, but should apply equally to all the exempt categories.

54. *Rema, Hoshen Mishpat* 163:1.

55. *Avot* 1:3; *Avodah Zorah* 19a.

56. R. Jonah b. Abraham Gerondi, *Sha'arei Teshuvah* 3:43. See also R. David Ariav, *Le'Reakha Kamokha* (Jerusalem: Ariav, 2000), vol. 1, p. 53.

57. *Yad*, op. cit., 5:13; *Tur*, op. cit., 160; *Sh. Ar.*, op. cit., 160:12.

58. R. Joshua b. Alexander ha-Kohen Falk, *Perishah, Tur*, op. cit., 160 note 19.

III. Marketing
And Salesmanship

6

Girard's Law of 250— The Case for Moral Education

The Guinness Book of World Records lists Joe Girard as the world's greatest salesman. In a fifteen-year career, from 1963–1977, Joe sold 13,001 automobiles, all retail. In his peak year, 1976, Girard earned gross commissions in excess of $300,000.[1]

One does not become the world's greatest salesman without developing and perfecting a repertoire of sales techniques and stratagems. Joe describes the contents of his sales "toolbox" in his best-selling book, *How to Sell Anything to Anybody*.[2] Of greater interest than the specific techniques themselves is the philosophy that both energizes Joe and gives shape to the stratagems he employs. Joe dubs the philosophy behind his phenomenal success "Girard's Law of 250." This philosophy begins with the observation that the average attendance at a funeral is 250; at a wedding, 500. This told Joe that an average person interacts in a socially meaningful way with approximately 250 people. A satisfied customer could therefore potentially spread goodwill toward a businessman to 250 people, and a dissatisfied customer could potentially "badmouth" him to as many as 250 people. Any customer therefore really represented 250 people wrapped up together in one.

Because Girard's Law of 250 was Joe's guidepost, he treated *all* the customers that came his way with the same dignity, enthusiasm, and respect and never let his dislike for a particular customer show outwardly. Ever aware of the potentially ruinous impact of a dissatisfied customer, Joe did not take his success as a license to make short shrift out of the customers he disliked. Girard's Law of 250 drove Joe to do everything he could to ensure that each of his customers would be happy not only at the closing of the deal, but also later on, when the customer looked back and reflected on it.[3]

Our purpose here will be to examine Joe's philosophy not in terms of how it promoted success, but rather in terms of whether it resulted in virtuous and ethically acceptable behavior in the marketplace. As we shall see, Joe's commercial conduct is a mixed bag. Some aspects of Joe's conduct should be characterized as no less than supererogatory with respect to his customers. Others of Joe's stratagems serve his self-interest while doing his customers no harm. At times, though, Joe's conduct generates at best illusory gains for his customers and reflects a self-serving paternalism on his part. Girard's Law of 250 seems to turn a blind eye to the impact of Joe's stratagems on his rivals. Some of the conduct Joe describes is, in fact, downright brutal to his competitors, and Jewish law would brand the conduct as wicked.

GIRARD'S LAW OF 250: THE UPSIDE

At the outset, high praise should be lavished on Girard's Law of 250 for elevating the civility of the business climate. Whether on his way up or already at the zenith of commercial success, Joe never "turned off" a customer with rude or insulting treatment. Moreover, if Joe heard that a customer was in the hospital, he would send a get well card.[4] What salesman does that?!

In theological terms, Joe clears his end of the business climate from the sin of *sinat hinnam* (unwarranted hatred).[5] Likewise, the respect and courtesy Joe shows his customers in his interactions with them is a positive fulfillment of the biblical mandate, "You shall love your fellow as yourself" (Leviticus 19:18).

With respect to elevating the level of civility, it is worth mentioning the impact of Girard's Law of 250 on negotiations for credit the customer receives for trading in his old car. Negotiation between auto salesperson and customer on this matter is potentially explosive. Engaged in a difficult battle with the customer over the amount of credit to be awarded for the trade-in, the salesperson may be tempted to bark, "Your old car is a piece of junk!" Once one party parries an insult, the potential for further ugliness in the dialogue increases dramatically. In theological terms, the negotiations for the trade-in may prove fertile ground for violation of the biblical prohibition against causing someone needless mental anguish (*ona'at devarim*).[6] Joe avoids all this by prefacing his trade-in offer to the customer with a remark like this: "You're some driver to get 120,000 miles out of this car."[7] This comment disarms the customer and avoids the usual ugliness that accompanies negotiations for the trade-in price.

Girard's Law illustrates the power of self-interest to generate conduct that fellow market participants regard as uplifting and ennobling. Unlike the typical car salesman, who makes himself scarce and unavailable to customers after the closing, especially in the event of problems, Joe tries his best to endear himself to his customers. Because Joe desperately wants repeat business and recommendations, he is sure to send out a thank-you card to his customer on the same day that the sale is completed. Joe calls a few weeks later to make sure that the customer is not experiencing any problems with the car, and to remind him or her to bring the car in for the checkups necessary to ensure that the warranty will remain intact.[8] With an eye to winning future business, Joe will even spend money out of his own pocket to give the car a free service job that is not covered in the warranty.[9]

Here again, we must praise Girard's Law of 250. It propels Joe to transcend his contractual obligations. In theological terms, Joe sometimes acts vis-à-vis his customers *lifnim mi-shurat ha-din* (i.e., beyond the letter of the law).[10] Note, however, that only the expenditure of "toil and effort" falls within the ambit of *lifnim mi-shurat ha-din*. *Lifnim mi-shurat ha-din* does not generally require the incurring of an added expense.[11] Joe's conduct of spending money out of his pocket to give the car a free service job that is not covered in the warranty is hence supererogatory. It goes beyond the parameters of *lifnim mi-shurat ha-din*.

Girard's Law of 250 reaches its pinnacle in inducing uplifting and ennobling conduct when Joe inadvertently sells his customer a lemon. Though very rare, a car can roll off the assembly line and have multiple problems that were not caught and fixed in the factory. People, Joe tells us, talk more about their cars than about the weather. If someone buys a lemon, you can be sure that 250 people will hear about the experience in all its minutiae. Joe realizes that how he handles such a case will have an explosive impact on his reputation, either positively or negatively. Accordingly, Joe goes all out to correct the situation for the customer. His goal, he tells us, is nothing short of transforming the lemon into a peach. It is in these moments of crisis that Joe's *investment* in buying the goodwill of the people in the service department pays off. Joe expects these people to come through for him and go the extra mile to make things right for his customer.[12] Joe's drive to transform the lemon into a peach undoubtedly entails conduct that goes beyond the parameters of *lifnim mi-shurat ha-din.* The power of Girard's Law of 250 is working again to drive Joe to virtuous conduct.

One final example of the virtue inherent in Girard's Law of 250 is that Joe will not let a customer do himself in. Hardly anyone, Joe tells us, pays the sticker price for a new car. If Joe encounters a customer who does not bargain with him and is ready to pay the sticker price for the car, Joe will refuse to allow the customer to do so. Instead, he will, without any prodding, offer, say, a $250 discount, or throw in some optional equipment at no extra charge. It is self-interest, not generosity of spirit, that drives Joe to do this. Don't forget, people talk a lot about their cars. Joe's greatest nightmare is that this naive customer will show off his new car at a lodge meeting to a large collection of his 250 friends. To make sure that they believe him that the car is indeed new, this customer will be sure to keep the sticker on the car. What will happen when the inevitable question comes up as to how much he paid and he says *not one penny more than the sticker price?* This man will become a colossal fool in the eyes of his friends. You can be sure that this man will go about badmouthing Joe in the most vicious way to his circle of 250, to say nothing of the aftershocks. Letting a customer do himself in is hence nothing less than disastrous for business in the long run.[13]

Joe's conduct here is not just prudent from a business standpoint. It is virtuous from an ethical standpoint as well. From the ethical point of view, the issue turns on what constitutes a "fair price" in a competitive marketplace. Preliminarily, let's note that the ethics of the price terms of a transaction are governed in Jewish law (Halakhah) by the law of *ona'ah,* which states that it is unethical for parties involved in a transaction to conclude it at variance with the market price. Depending on how much the transaction price departs from the market price, the plaintiff may have the right either to cancel or to modify the transaction.[14] From the standpoint of the law of *ona'ah*, is the retail new car market bound by the manufacturer's sticker price? Addressing himself to the issue of *ona'ah* in the retail market when the product involved displays a manufacturer's sticker price, R. Yaakov Yeshayahu Bloi (Israel, 1929–) posits that the reference price for adjudicating *ona'ah* claims is the sticker or manufacturer's suggested price.[15] Any deal concluded below the sticker price is apparently looked upon as a *discount* from the operative market price. If we follow R. Bloi's line of thought, Joe is under no obligation to offer a discount from the sticker price if the customer volunteers to pay that price. Yet offering a discount when the customer does not force it upon Joe saves the customer from large-scale future embarrassment at a significant financial cost to Joe. The gesture hence manifests supererogatory conduct on the part of Joe, but is also consistent with Joe's long-term business interests.

GIFTS OF OBLIGATION

In the first moments of contact with a customer, it is crucial for the salesperson to relax his prospect and make him feel indebted for having taken up the salesperson's time. An effective way to accomplish this task is to confer upon the prospect "gifts of obligation." The idea is for the customer to believe that the salesperson will do anything to make him happy. Joe loses no opportunity to convey this impression. To illustrate: As part of his work attire, Joe is partial to polka dot sport shirts. If a prospect compliments him on the shirt, Joe makes a motion to take off the shirt, saying, "You like it? Here. It's yours." Joe is serious about this offer. He keeps an extra shirt in his office in case a customer ever takes him up on his gesture (one customer once did!).

If a prospect begins to pat his pocket for a cigarette, Joe quickly offers the prospect a cigarette before the prospect gets a chance to reach for one of his own. Moreover, Joe surprises the customer by offering him a selection of brands and nonplusses him by giving him a whole pack of his favorite brand to keep. It should come as no surprise that Joe's office is well stacked with wine, scotch, and vodka, and that the customer is offered his choice of drink.

If the prospect brings along her child, Joe will comment that the child is cute, even if he really feels the child is a monster. Joe's office is well stocked with balloons, lollipops, and buttons that say simply, "I like you."[16]

There can be no doubt that Joe's "gifts of obligation" generate him a favorable bias in the eyes of his customers. Favorable bias may, in turn, inveigle the customer into discontinuing his market search, thereby depriving him of the opportunity to strike a better deal. Moreover, Joe's royal treatment may lead the customer to the illusion that he is getting a better deal than he really is. From a Halakhic perspective, therefore, the moral issues involved here are the parameters of fair competition and the legitimacy of capturing an advantage on account of a favorable bias.

Before delving into these issues a few preliminary remarks are in order. We take it as a given that the goodwill Joe derives from the expertise, patience, courtesy, and reliability he demonstrates to his customer is his rightful entitlement. Joe need not be concerned that these qualities attract customers to him and away from competing salespeople. But "gifts of obligation" *are extrinsic to the sales presentation itself*. It is the edge Joe derives from this practice that is, perhaps, unfair to competing salesmen, and it is this tactic that may potentially qualify as unethical manipulation of the customer.

The ethics of making use of "gifts of obligation" to lure customers is discussed in the *Mishna* (*Bava Metzia* 4:12):

A storekeeper may not distribute toasted grain or nuts to the children, because he accustoms them to come to him. But the sages permit this.[17]

Halakhah follows the view of the sages, who do not regard the handing out of treats as an unfair competitive tactic.[18] The Talmud explains the sages' reason: One who makes use of this ploy can validly argue to his rival, "Just as I distribute nuts to attract customers, so you can distribute prunes."[19]

Joe's practice of conferring "gifts of obligation" to his customers hence enjoys solid ethical backing by the majority view of the sages. Since competing salesmen are capable of engaging in the same practice, the stratagem should not be viewed as an unfair competitive tactic.

The sages' view requires further elaboration. Consider that the sages analyze the ethics of the tactic only from the perspective of rival sellers. Why do they not consider it from the customer's perspective? Distribution of treats to a patron assuredly curries the favor of that person and may leave her with the false belief that the item at hand is a better buy than is actually the case. Causing a customer to conclude a deal with the false sense of having gotten a bargain violates the prohibition against creating a false impression (*geneivat da'at*).[20] The pertinent Talmudic precedent here is Samuel's case involving the sale to a non-Jew of meat originating from an organically defective animal (*nebelah*). Duping the customer into believing that he is getting a bargain by misrepresenting the meat as originating from a healthy animal constitutes *geneivat da'at*.[21] Although price fraud may not be involved, as the non-Jew may be charged a fair price for what he actually receives, the transaction is nonetheless prohibited, since it leaves the customer with a feeling of obligation to the storekeeper, which is undeserved.[22]

The analogy between the cases is, however, inapt. Consider that Joe does nothing *affirmative* to misrepresent the car he is selling. The monetary value of the cigarettes, liquor, and balloons is very clear-cut. If the provision of these amenities is regarded by the customer as a welcome gesture within the context of the sales transaction, the customer will in fact assign them additional value above and beyond their objective market value. Joe's conduct hence does not generate a *false* sense of having received a bargain. Similarly, if Joe's royal treatment moves the customer to end his market search, this is the *decision* of the customer and is not the *direct* result of Joe's proddings or representations.

Supporting the above defense of the "gifts of obligation" stratagem is the following case, discussed in the Talmudic literature:

[The vendor] may not sift crushed beans to sift out the refuse; these are the words of Abba Shaul. But the sages permit it.[23]

Whose view is identified as that of the sages? It is the view of R. Aha, as it was taught in a Baraita: "R. Aha permits enhancing the appearance of merchandise through something discernible."[24]

Removing the refuse from crushed beans can be accomplished at a definite cost. The buyer knows this cost. The dispute between Abba Shaul and the sages, according to R. Solomon b. Isaac (*Rashi*, France, 1040–1105), is whether the enhanced appearance of the sifted beans inveigles the customer into paying more for the sifting than is warranted. In Abba Shaul's opinion, the enhanced appearance of the beans allows the seller to overcharge the customer by raising the price of the beans far beyond the value of the effort involved in sifting. Disputing Abba Shaul, the sages feel that since the enhancement is plainly discernible to the customer, the seller's conduct does not inveigle him to pay more for the sifting than is warranted.[25] Halakhah adopts the opinion of the sages as normative.[26]

What follows from this discussion is that one need not be concerned that "gifts of obligation" lead the customer to believe that she has received greater value for her money than is actually the case. In the case at hand, the value of the various treats Joe offers his customer in the course of a sales presentation is *evident* to the customer. If the treats plant a false belief in the mind of the customer regarding the value of the deal Joe offers, it is the customer, not Joe, who is responsible for the misconception.

GIRARD'S LAW OF 250: THE DOWNSIDE

Let us now turn to the negative consequences of Girard's Law of 250. To this end, we will examine a number of Joe's techniques, including his use of the cold call, the use of birddogs, comparison shopping by invitation, and various nuances of his policy regarding honesty.

The Cold Call[27]

The fundamental challenge for the cold caller is to attract attention in the first twenty seconds of the call, thereby preventing the potential prospect at the other end of the line from hanging up before the caller can deliver his message. Joe draws his potential prospects more or less randomly from the telephone directory. He sustains the interest of the person on the other end of the line by saying that the car he or she "ordered" is ready for pickup. Illustrating how this conversation opening can be productive in lining up a prospect was Girard's experience with the Kowalskis. When Mrs. Kowalski predictably reacted to Joe's opening line by telling him that he must have dialed the wrong number, as she did not order any car, Joe quickly apologized for his mistake. However, he kept Mrs. Kowalski on the phone long enough to ask her if she was in the market to buy a new car. When she responded that she did not know, Joe got her permission to call back to get her husband's answer to the question. Joe subsequently learned from Mr. Kowalski that he might be interested in a new car in six months, and so he called Mr. Kowalski again after five months to make a sale.[28]

Note that Joe launches his cold call with a *lie*. On the face of it, Joe violates the biblical injunction against lying: "Distance yourself from a false word" (Exodus 23:7).[29] One might argue that the lie Joe employs, namely, informing the person on the other end that his or her car is ready for pickup, is innocent and harmless. It hurts no one and serves only to keep the conversation alive long enough for Joe to impart mutually advantageous information to the potential prospect. From the perspective of Halakhah, however, this argument is not acceptable. To be sure, a lie used as a vehicle to deceive is more egregious an offense than a lie that merely expresses an untruth but does not deceive. But the prohibition against lying, according to R. Israel Meir Kagan (Radin, Poland, 1838–1933)[30] and R. Abraham Y. Karelitz (Israel, 1878–1953)[31] applies even when the falsehood does no harm to anyone. Halakhah would hence object to the approach Joe takes in making his cold calls.

Birddogs

Let us now move to Joe's use of birddogs to drum up business. In its vanilla variety, the technique consists of offering a $25 reward to someone who brings in a new customer. But Joe makes this offer not only to satisfied customers, but also to almost everyone he comes in contact with. To make it easy to collect the fee, Joe instructs the birddog to write his name on the back of a Girard business card, and to make sure that the prospect hands him the card when he comes to the lot to buy the car. If the prospect ends up buying a car, Joe will make good on his word to send the birddog a $25 check.[32]

From an ethical perspective, it must be noted that without proper disclosure, the birddog could be guilty of either proffering ill-suited advice or projecting his opinion of Joe in an overly favorable manner. The value of the referral to the prospect depends critically on whether the referrer had first-hand experience with Joe as a satisfied customer, or got his information second-hand, or, worse still, knows absolutely nothing about Joe's service other than that he will get a commission for a successful referral. Ethical considerations therefore demand that the birddog disclose both the *basis* of his recommendation and what he stands to gain from a successful referral.

As far as the disclosure of the fee is concerned, there should be no requirement to specify its exact amount. Referring to the fee as a "small commission" should suffice to alert the prospect to the favorable bias the birddog presumably has, and to the consequent need for extra caution in taking his advice.

The above disclosure requirement makes it *useless* for Joe to enlist a stranger as a birddog. If the disclosure obligations are adhered to, the bird-dog's pitch to the prospect amounts to saying:

> Girard is a new car salesperson. He claims that he has many happy cus-tomers. I have no independent verification of his claim. All I know is that if I give him a successful referral, I'll get a small commission.

Given the disclosure duties of a birddog, it becomes unethical for Joe to enlist the services of total strangers as birddogs. Offering a stranger $25 for a successful referral effectively encourages that person to lie or deceive in various ways in order to transform an otherwise useless exercise into a con-vincing recommendation. Enlisting a person as a birddog who can only suc-ceed by lying or misleading creates for that person a setting for veiled misconduct, which is an aspect of the prohibition against facilitating a sin (*lifnei iver lo titen mikhshol*, Leviticus 19:14).[33]

Joe's referral technique assumes a particularly objectionable form when he enlists bank officers who handle automobile loans to become his bird-dogs. In Joe's mind, it pays to invest in the goodwill of such people by buying them expensive bottles of whiskey or taking them out for lunch in a restaurant they cannot normally afford to patronize. Take note of the follow-ing incident. For expositional convenience, we will call the loan officer Green, the original seller Sardy, and the customer Carmel. In this scenario, Carmel had already come to terms with Sardy, a salesperson who worked for a different dealership. Carmel came to Green to arrange financing. Green happened to be one of Girard's "birddogs." Before approving the loan, Green excused himself for a moment and left Carmel to call Joe. Convinced by Green that Carmel would not switch to him unless offered the same car for $50 less, Joe quickly absorbed the details of the deal and decided that he could "beat" the price by $50. Green returned and told Carmel that the bank would approve the loan, but quickly added that Joe had the same deal for him, and that it was his to be had for $50 less than the Sardy deal. All Carmel had to do to get the cheaper Girard deal was to sign a second piece of paper. Carmel decided to switch, lose his deposit with Sardy, and give his business to Joe. Joe was particularly proud of that sale. As Joe put it:

> What I have done by making that loan officer a birddog is to put him in a position where he can send me business I could not have possibly gotten in any other way. He got me a sale that was already sold by another salesman. He helped his loan customer by saving him money, he earned $25 for himself, and he got me a sale I had no way of getting. Even with the birddog fee and the price cut I gave the customer, I am still going to earn some commission. Even if I net only $50 for myself on that sale, that is still $50 I could not have got in any other way.
>
> That was found money, right from the sky into my pocket. Think about that. Think about how I created that extra money for myself. And think about how you can do things like that in your business.[34]

There can be no doubt that the conduct described in the above scenario violates Halakhah. Carmel, Green, and Joe are, in fact, all guilty of infractions of Halakhah. Let's begin with Carmel.

Preliminarily, let's note that a transaction does not generally become legally binding in Halakhah unless it is consummated by means of a symbolic act (*kinyan*).[35] Nonetheless, if the seller (*S*) and buyer (*B*) reach oral agreement regarding all the details of their deal, it is generally unethical for either party to retract. Retraction at this juncture brands the reneging party as "untrustworthy" (*mehusrei emunah*).[36]

Suppose *B* and *S* make their commitments in good faith, but one of the parties desires subsequently to renege because a better market opportunity now presents itself. Is the reneging party called "untrustworthy"? Authorities quoted by R. Mosheh Isserles (Poland, 1525 or 1530–1572) dispute whether retraction under these circumstances brands the reneging party as untrustworthy.[37]

Addressing himself to this issue, R. Jehiel Michel Epstein (Belorussia, 1829–1908) maintains that retraction under these circumstances does not brand the reneging party untrustworthy. Nonetheless, he writes, keeping to the original agreement constitutes *middat hasidut* (pious conduct).[38] Let us take note that *Tosafot* ruled that the category of obligations called *lifnim mi-shurat ha-din* (conduct beyond the letter of the law) encompasses only additional expenditure of toil and effort, but almost never involves the requirement of incurring financial loss.[39] R. Epstein's mention of *middat hasidut* here means, therefore, merely that not to retract is praiseworthy conduct. There is no *requirement* not to retract, however, even on a *lifnim mi-shurat ha-din* level.

The ethical breach of the reneging party increases in severity if the verbal agreement has advanced to the point where *B* has paid *S* the purchasing price or a deposit for the item at hand, without actually effecting a change in *legal title*.

One case of this sort is the transfer of movable property. By dint of Pentateuchal law, the transfer of *kesef* (money), whether the entire purchase price or only a deposit, effects the transfer of legal title over such property. Out of fear that *S* would be less than diligent in extricating from fire and other dangers merchandise on his premises previously sold to *B*, the sages decreed that *kesef* does not effect this transfer.[40] Nonetheless, in recognition of the heightened anticipation on the part of both *B* and *S* that the transaction will be legally finalized, retraction by either party at this juncture has more severe consequences than being branded untrustworthy. The reneging party is subject to the curse of "He who exacted vengeance from the generation of the Flood and the generation of the Dispersion will exact payment from the one who does not stand by his word." The curse is referred to in rabbinical literature as *mi she-para* (literally, "He who exacted").[41]

Let's apply the above rules to the case at hand. Recall that Carmel reached agreement with Sardy regarding all the particulars of their auto deal. In addition, Carmel had given Sardy a deposit. Green tells Carmel that the bank loan is approved. Carmel's deal with Sardy hence advanced to the point where retraction by either party would be subject to the consequence of *mi she-para*. The fact that an opportunity presented itself for Carmel to enter into a very similar deal at a lower price does not change the above moral judgment.

Joe's scheme to inveigle Carmel into switching to him is particularly reprehensible. The operative halakhic principle here is the prohibition against snatching away another's anticipated gain, called *ani hamehapekh bahararah*, a reference to a case in which *A*, a "poor man" (*ani*) is "casting about" (*mehapekh*), trying to take possession of a certain "cake" (*hararah*), and another person (B) comes and snatches it away from him. *B's* interloping conduct brands him a wicked person.[42] Elsewhere in this volume we discuss the details of this prohibition.[43]

Joe's interloping action snatches away from Sardy his anticipated gain—a commission on a car sale to Carmel. Now, recall R. Jacob Tam's (Ramerrupt, 1100–1171) view that *ani hamehapekh* is suspended in the case of ownerless property. Should the sales commission Joe seeks be regarded as a free good, unavailable elsewhere, and therefore "fair game" for Joe to go after? No. Clearly, Joe's livelihood as a car salesperson is not predicated on getting loan officers to divert business to him. Moreover, consider that at the moment Joe hatches his scheme, Carmel had not only reached terms with Sardy, but also had given him a deposit. Given that under these conditions, Carmel may not on his own accord renege on the deal without incurring *mi she-para*, Joe's interloping action amounts to *facilitating* Carmel's sin of *ani hamehapekh*. Guilty of the same sin is the bank officer, Green. Facilitating the commission of a sin violates the biblical prohibition of "Do not place a stumbling block before the blind" (*lifnei iver lo titen mikhshol*, Leviticus 19:14).[44]

Let's now consider a variation of this case. Suppose Carmel agreed only on terms, but did not give Sardy a deposit. Recall R. Epstein's position that Carmel would not be branded as untrustworthy for retracting from the deal at this juncture in order to take advantage of a lower price or better terms. In the opinion of this writer, this judgment should hold only if Carmel becomes aware of the better opportunity through his own *initiative*. But a different judgment is in order if Joe, a competing salesperson, takes the initiative and offers Carmel better terms and urges him to get out of his deal with Sardy. Since Joe's interloping action inflicts a clear injustice upon Sardy and brands him a *rasha* (wicked person), Carmel is prohibited from switching to Joe. Switching would make Carmel guilty of facilitating Girard's sin.

Comparison Shopping By Invitation

When Joe encounters difficulties in closing a deal, he will, on occasion, urge his prospect to shop around for a better deal and return in hand with the best deal he can find. Joe promises the prospect that he will undercut the best deal by $500. When the customer returns with the best deal he discovered in his comparison shopping, Joe may either refuse to offer a better deal or bid only $50 lower than the competing bid. Joe will refuse the opportunity for business only when he feels that underbidding the comparison bid will not leave him with even a meager commission. This circumstance, Joe tells us, signals that the competing salesman is also not making money on the deal, and that in making the offer, the competing salesman is not motivated by profit, but instead by envy, wishing to "beat Girard's deal."

Joe feels no qualms about reneging on his promise to beat the competing deal by $500. According to his way of thinking, beating the competing bid by $50 still offers the customer the best deal on the car, and therefore leaves her satisfied and better off than before.[45]

Such conduct on Joe's part is ethically unacceptable. Joe's deal transforms a sales transaction into a setting for veiled misconduct for the customer. To collect on Joe's promise the customer must approach competing salespeople and pry price terms and even bargain with them *only* for the purpose of presenting that price information to Joe, so that Joe can make good on his promise to give him the same deal, minus $500. The customer therefore ends up pricing articles with no intention to buy. Such conduct is specifically mentioned in the *Mishna* as an example of the prohibited act of causing one's fellow needless mental anguish (*ona'at devarim*).[46] R. Menahem b. Solomon Meiri (Perpignan, 1249–1316) explains that pricing an article creates anticipation on the part of the seller that he will make a sale. This expectation is then dashed when the inquirer decides not to pursue the matter further.[47] Although the prospective buyer need not concern himself with the disappointment a vendor may experience should his *serious* price inquiry not result in his making a purchase, pricing an article he has no intention of buying causes the vendor *needless* distress and is hence prohibited.[48] Joe's offer to "beat the deal" hence entices his customer to veiled misconduct, and violates *lifnei iver*.

Additionally, of course, consider that at the very moment Joe promises his prospect that he will beat the competition by $500, he has no intention of carrying it out. Verbalizing a commitment without the resolve to carry it out is a commitment made in "bad faith" and constitutes unethical conduct.[49]

Recall that Joe would have us focus on the $50 his ploy saves the customer and not take him to task for reneging on the $500 differential he promised. This attitude amounts to nothing more than a rationalization for a self-serving lie. Moreover, the lie is by no means harmless. It encourages the prospect to engage in the unethical conduct of insincere comparison shopping, and inflicts harm and injustice on competing salespeople. Moreover, dashing the expectation of the customer undermines the value of trust in society.

HONESTY IS THE BEST POLICY

Girard's Law of 250 is, from the perspective of Halakhah, fundamentally flawed, because Joe feels that his law gives him a license to engage in veiled misconduct. Take note of Joe's attitude on "honesty is the best policy":

> When I say that honesty is the best policy, I mean exactly that: It's a policy and the best one you can follow most of the time. But a policy, as I mean it, is not a law or a rule. It is something that you use in your work when it is in your best interests. Telling the truth usually is in your best interests, of course, especially if it is about something that a customer can check up on later. Nobody in his right mind would dream of telling a customer he had bought an eight-cylinder car when what you sold him was a six-cylinder model. The first time he opened the hood and counted the wires coming out of the distributor cap, you would be dead, because he would bad-mouth you to a lot more than 250 people.[50]

As this passage indicates, Joe is terrified of being caught telling a lie. But if Joe assesses that a customer will not detect a particular lie, he will not hesitate to use it to move along a sale. To illustrate: Suppose a customer asks Joe if the car he is interested in has a 3.25 rear axle ratio. Joe will respond in the positive and compliment the customer for his knowledge of cars. Joe will confirm that the car at hand has the rear axle ratio the customer is looking for, even though he does not know this to be fact. Joe's research indicates the savings in gas from such a ratio amounts to pennies, indicating that the lie is harmless. Besides which, taking the time to find out the answer to the customer's question interrupts the flow of his sales presentation.[51]

In this scenario, Joe makes use of a lie to move along a sales presentation. Joe rationalizes the lie with an element of self-serving paternalism. Someone more desperate than Joe to close the deal might be willing to take a chance on a bigger lie and rationalize it with the same logic that Joe uses.

Let us take another example. Suppose a customer, Hans Weinstock, calls in to inquire if Joe has a certain car equipped in a certain way. Joe's response will invariably be, "I have one out on the lot and you can pick it up today." Joe says this even though he knows positively in advance that he cannot provide one of the features Hans requested. Once Hans takes the trouble to come down to the lot, Joe relies on his persuasive powers to convince Hans to agree to take whatever he actually does have in stock that is a close match with the specifications Hans gave him over the phone.[52]

Joe's stratagem here is a sophisticated version of the bait-and-switch tactic. In its basic form, bait-and-switch involves the advertising of a popular item at a bargain price simply for the purpose of luring customers into the store. The deception becomes apparent when the bargain bait cannot be purchased, on one pretext or another, and the salesperson, after disparaging the advertised product, attempts to convince the customer to switch to a higher-priced substitute.

Since the vendor has no intention of selling the bait item, the advertisement is clearly an insincere offer and hence violates the good faith imperative discussed earlier. Moreover, because the offer is insincere, the disappointment the customer experiences when he is informed that the advertised item is unavailable should be categorized as *needless* mental anguish. The tactic thus violates the *ona'at devarim* interdict.[53] To be sure, use of the bait-and-switch tactic may lead *eventually* to the satisfaction of the customer. The fact remains, however, that the customer is filled with disappointment at the moment he is advised that the item is not available.

In the scenario described above, Joe promises over the phone to provide Hans with a car meeting his *exact* specifications. In actuality, no such car is available. If Joe were playing out the vanilla variety bait-and-switch routine, he would apologize to Hans when he arrives at the lot and tell him that the car with the specifications he had described over the phone was not available, but that he had something very similar to show him. Instead, Joe pretends all along that what Hans wants is available, and only when he is ready to *close* does he let Hans know that the exact specifications he seeks are not available on the lot. Consider that Hans has already made a considerable investment of time in listening to Joe's presentation and negotiating various details with him. Consider also that Joe may have conferred upon Hans some "gifts of obligation." All this works to soften the blow when Hans hears from Joe that a particular feature he wants is not available.

Because the car Hans described over the phone was, in fact, not available for pick-up on the lot, and Joe knew this, Joe's misrepresentation of the facts is a violation of the good faith imperative. Moreover, the disappointment Hans feels when Joe tells him that the particular feature he was counting on is in fact not available must be categorized as *needless* mental anguish, and Joe is responsible for it. Joe hence violates the *ona'at devarim* interdict as well. Joe not only dashes Hans' legitimate expectations, but his assurances over the telephone induce Hans to make a special trip to the showroom. Because Hans might not have come to the showroom altogether had Joe been truthful to him in their telephone conversation, Joe's deception hence violates *geneivat da'at law* as well. Elaboration on this can be found elsewhere in this volume.[54]

Joe's brand of bait-and-switch illustrates the concept of the slippery slope as it relates to the moral sphere. Suppose Hans enumerates a number of features he is looking for in a car, including a pushbutton radio in powder blue. Joe knows he has on the lot everything the customer wants, except that he has the pushbutton radio only in gray. Now, suppose further that Joe tells Hans that he has the *exact* car Hans seeks, and invites Hans to come down to the lot. In this instance, some might be sympathetic with Joe and regard his conduct as only a trifling example of the "bait-and-switch" tactic. Some might even insist that Joe violated no ethical norm in his response; after all, no two cars are exactly alike in every detail, and Hans presumably never took Joe's assurance at face value: he only expected a close match. But, once we give Joe license *not* to respond to his client, "I have everything you want except that I have the pushbutton radio *only in gray*," where do we stop? Specifically, at what point does Joe's assertion that "I have one out on the lot and you can pick it up today" turn into unethical conduct given what Joe actually has available? Giving each salesperson the license to make his or her own subjective judgment here leaves the ethical norm in shambles.

A variation of the previous scenario obtains when Joe can get Hans what he wants by special order from the factory, but has at hand a close match. Here, Joe will not disclose to Hans that he can get exactly what he wants by putting his specifications on order. Ordering the car from the factory introduces a delay. During this delay, unavoidable circumstances or other reasons for canceling the deal could set in, and the sale may be lost.[55]

Joe thus finds his own financial interest in conflict with the best interests of his customer. Revealing to Hans that he can have his preferred bundle of amenities by means of special order from the factory makes Hans happy but, in Joe's mind, puts the entire deal up in the air, as it affords Hans the possibility of changing his mind before the car arrives. Is this perceived conflict of interest a valid reason to maneuver Hans into making a deal on the basis of what is available for immediate delivery?

Joe's initial contact with Hans may come in response to Hans's telephone inquiry as to whether Joe has available in the showroom a certain car equipped in a certain way. Joe responds that he does, but knows that a car meeting the exact specifications the inquirer seeks is not at hand and can only be obtained through special order from the factory. In this case, Joe's initial contact with Hans gets him involved in a bait-and-switch tactic. Maneuvering Hans into choosing from the stock he has on the lot makes Joe guilty of following through on his original unethical plan from when he first made contact with Hans. This judgment holds even if Joe does not have to lie in response to Hans's *direct* question as to whether the exact specification he wants can be ordered from the factory.

Alternatively, suppose Hans comes to Joe's lot and asks for certain specifications. Joe shows Hans the closest match he has, without revealing to him that he can get exactly what he wants by means of special order. Now suppose Hans asks Joe whether he can get his exact specifications by means of special order, and Joe answers that he cannot. Joe hereby makes use of a lie to promote his own interests against the interests of his customer, which is prohibited.

One final variant. With no prior contact with Joe, Hans arrives at the showroom to purchase a car, and chooses a car from among the vehicles on display in the showroom. Before finalizing the deal, is Joe obliged to apprise Hans that if the car he chose does not *exactly* meet what he had in mind, it might be possible to put on special order a number of variations on the models he saw in the showroom? This issue turns on whether the salesperson is obliged to assume the role of counselor in his dealings with the customer, as the next section will discuss.

THE SALESPERSON AS COUNSELOR[56]

The following case, recorded in the halakhic codes, provides evidence that Halakhah does not inherently impose the role of counselor on the salesperson in his or her dealings with customers. The essential elements are the following:

S sells B an ox, but does not inform him that the ox is vicious (*naghan*). Because the ox is a menace to society, it must be destroyed and may not be used for plowing.[57] When the transaction is completed, B discovers that the ox is a *naghan*. B's intention all along was to purchase an ox for plowing, but he was silent on this point in his negotiations with S, who claims he reasonably sold B an ox that can be slaughtered and eaten. B sues for a refund on the grounds that most customers purchase oxen for plowing, and not for butchering. Because majority practice cannot be used as the deciding factor in a monetary dispute,[58] B will not prevail on the basis of this argument. B needs to demonstrate that the circumstances of his transaction with S manifested that S was *aware* that he wanted the ox for plowing.

One way of proving this is to refer to the purchasing price. Specifically, suppose the fair market value of an ox suitable for plowing is higher than the corresponding value of that same ox when it is suitable only for butchering. If B agreed to a price in the higher range, that fact should have clearly communicated to S that B intended to plow with his ox, not slaughter it.

Another way for B to validate his claim is to show that he is a long-standing customer of S, and has an established track record of purchasing oxen for plowing. Notwithstanding that B was silent in the disputed transaction regarding his plowing intent, S should have reasonably understood this intent by assuming B would follow his normal pattern.[59]

The legal treatment of the *naghan* case seems astonishing. To be sure, majority practice cannot be decisive in a monetary dispute, and thus, indeed, B cannot succeed in overturning the original transaction based on S's nondisclosure. But since the *majority* of people purchase oxen for the purpose of plowing, how can S *knowingly* sell B a *naghan* without first eliciting from *B* that his intent is to buy the ox for consumption? What follows is that Halakhah does not *inherently* conceptualize the role of a salesperson as a counselor. To be sure, *S* must disclose up front to *B* all defects in the ox he is selling him. But if the market price of an ox suitable only for consumption rises until it is the same as that of an ox also suitable for plowing, *naghan* status is not inherently a defect. It is so only if the ox is intended for plowing.

In the same vein, R. Yom Tov Lipmann b. Nathan ha-Levi Heller's (Moravia, 1579–1654) explains that the transaction is not overturned because the *onus* is on *B* to inform *S* of his intent to plow.[60] R. Heller's assertion, in generalized form, is that Halakhah imposes upon *S* the responsibility of being a counselor only when either *B* asks for *S*'s opinion or advice, or *S* takes this role upon himself by making a recommendation to *B*. On his own, however, *S* is not required to assume the role of counselor in his dealings with his customers.

Given that Halakhah does not inherently assign a salesperson the role of counselor, Joe has no duty to volunteer to Hans the special order option when Hans does not arrive with specifications that are not available on the lot. Moreover, given that Joe perceives the disclosure of the special order option to be inimical to his own economic interests, disclosure of this option is not required even on the level of *lifnim mi-shurat ha-din.*

The foregoing discussion has highlighted the implications of Joe's attitude that honesty is not an absolute, but only a policy that should be followed when a lie will explode in your face. Giving license to make a self-serving lie that will not be discovered makes truth and integrity a subjective matter. Within a moral climate where there are no objective standards for truth and integrity, trust and harmonious relations are dealt a lethal blow. Without objective standards and well-defined duties, morality in the marketplace sinks to the lowest common denominator.

GIRARD'S LAW OF 250 AND THE HALAKHIC CODE FOR THE MARKETPLACE

From the perspective of Halakhah, Girard's Law of 250 is fundamentally flawed. For Joe, the name of the game is to make customers happy. But what about the impact of Joe's conduct on competitors? Girard's Law of 250 totally ignores the ethics of fair competition. Joe's use of a bank loan officer as a birddog illustrates how his brand of ethics can result in a commercially satisfied customer but, at the same time, lead to moral infractions on the part of both the customer and Joe for taking business away from a competitor. True, Girard's Law has the capacity to propel Joe to the very heights of virtue in his treatment of his customers. But the incentives Girard sets up make it likely that these customers will, at times, engage in veiled misconduct.

Veiled misconduct will not be overcome by means of a philosophy or guidepost rooted in self-interest. Only the spiritual force of a God-fearing person can counteract the magnetic attraction of veiled misconduct. This is indicated by the Torah's exclusive use of the warning phrase, "And you shall fear your God," in connection with prohibitions[61] of actions that one could convince himself he could commit without detection, hence avoiding loss of social standing.[62] The Torah suggests that only proper fear of God can prevent such transgressions from taking place.

It is noteworthy that some of the Torah's references to veiled misconduct are made specifically in the context of marketplace conduct. These contexts include (1) the prohibition against offering ill-suited advice (Leviticus 19:14); (2) the injunction against causing someone needless mental anguish (Leviticus 15:17); and (3) the interdict against charging interest[63] (Leviticus 25:36).[64]

Similarly, the Torah's puzzling reference to the Exodus in connection with certain of its precepts is explained by the sages to amount to the following warning from God to the smug practitioner of veiled misconduct: "Don't imagine that just because your misdeeds go undetected by your fellow man you will escape punishment. Remember that it was *I* who distinguished in Egypt between the first-born and those who were not first-born." Not surprisingly, one of these precepts is the prohibition against false weights and measures.[65]

CULTIVATING THE ETHICAL PERSONALITY AND HALAKHAH

From the perspective of Halakhah, the most basic requirement for the cultivation of the ethical personality is moral education, which begins in one's youth. In the formative years, responsibility for inculcating moral education is in the hands of the parents and the religious educational enterprise. At the center of moral education is a reward punishment system that stresses truth-telling and provides training against selfishness and greed.

In this system, fostering the character trait of gratitude is crucial. Its essential role is to make an individual equate failing a test of piety with letting down (betraying) his parents and/or moral educators. The challenge is therefore to put the family and school system on solid financial footing so that these institutions can maximize their impact on the moral climate of society. Finally, government is given a vital role in deterring and ferreting out instances of veiled misconduct.

Elsewhere we have described the details of this program along with the rabbinic sources on which it is founded.[66]

POSTPRANDIUM

PROBLEM 1

A number of colleges throughout the United States administer their examinations on the basis of the honor system. The two most salient features of the honor code are unproctored examinations and written pledges from students that they have completed their work honestly. In this system students have majority or complete control over the judicial system that deals with infractions. Many traditional codes also place some level of obligation on students to report incidents of cheating they may observe among their peers, although such clauses are infrequently enforced.[67]

What ethical issues does the honor code represent from the perspective of Halakhah?[68]

PROBLEM 2

Professor Zevulin Einhorn, chairman of the economics department at Brickmire College, gave a sigh of relief when he filled the last adjunct position for the fall economics schedule in late May. The professor could now turn to his research for the summer ahead without distraction. But, this was not to be. One month before the start of the fall term, Professor Andre Arden, one of the adjuncts slated to teach in the fall, called Einhorn and informed him that he was unable to meet his commitment to teach the two courses he was slated to teach in the fall. Although Arden had a good excuse for reneging on his commitment and was very apologetic about quitting so soon before the start of the fall term, the call left Einhorn in a state of near panic. Through frantic networking efforts Einhorn did find a replacement for Arden, but the pressure to replace Arden in such a short time frame forced Einhorn to agree to pay the adjunct $400 a course more than the rate Arden was slated to get.

With the aim of preventing an Arden type of incident in the future, Einhorn felt he needed a pool of resumés to draw from in the event it suddenly became necessary to fill an adjunct position. Toward this end, Einhorn came up with the idea of placing an ad in the Sunday *New York Times* in May that the economics department of Brickmire College was seeking to hire adjunct faculty for the coming fall semester. The ad would be placed even if all the adjunct positions were already filled. In the latter case, the ad would serve the useful purpose of generating resumés for Einhorn's file cabinet. If a vacancy would suddenly develop, Einhorn would then seriously look through the resumes to find a suitable candidate.

Running the ad entails a moral dilemma. Consider that at the time the ad is run, *no* position for the fall is available and the only way a position could open up is by means of the totally unexpected circumstance that one of the already hired adjuncts reneges on his or her commitment for the fall. Given that the ad is not a serious offer for the fall, is it unethical to run the ad? What moral principles does running the ad possibly violate?

Could the language of the ad be formulated in a manner that will avoid violation of any ethical principles?

PROBLEM 3

Shimroni and Shalhevet Berkowitz are a Kollel couple. They live with their two small children in a modest home within walking distance of the Kollel. The Berkowitzs bought a new home in a nearby housing construction project. It will take approximately 16 months for their new home to be ready. For the couple, the ideal situation is for them to sell their old home immediately, with the right to remain as tenants of the new owner until their new home is ready for occupancy. Shimroni's brother Alon is single and very well to do. Alon is willing to buy his brother's home as an investment and allow his brother and family to remain on the property as tenants until their new home is ready for occupancy. Alon's only problem is that he is willing to pay only the actual market value of the home and he does not want to overpay.

Alon comes up with the following plan. He tells Shimroni to put up his home for sale through a broker, but not to give the broker an exclusive for the home. "Let's wait three weeks," Alon says, "and see what the highest bid the broker comes up with. I'll give you the highest bid minus the portion of the price that represents the broker's commission."

Evaluate the ethics of Alon's scheme. What ethical principles are violated? Is there a way for Alon to accomplish his objective without violating ethical norms?

NOTES

1. Joe Girard, *How to Sell Anything to Anybody* (New York: Warner Books, 1977), p. 11.
2. loc. cit.
3. *How to Sell Anything to Anybody*, op. cit., pp. 47–50.
4. op. cit., p. 179.
5. For the severity of the sin of unwarranted hatred and the untoward consequences this sin has on society, see *Avot* 2:1; *Kallah* 8; *Shabbat* 32b; *Yoma* 9b.
6. Leviticus 25:17; *Mishnah, Bava Metzia* 4:10; R. Isaac b. Jacob Alfasi (Algeria, 1012–1103), *Rif,* ad loc.; *Yad, Geneivah* 14:12; R. Asher b. Jehiel (Germany, 1250–1327), *Rosh, Bava Metzia* 4:22; R. Jacob b. Asher (Spain, 1270–1343), *Tur, Hoshen Mishpat,* 228; R. Joseph Caro (Safed, 1488–1575), *Shulhan Arukh, Hoshen Mishpat* 228:1; R. Jehiel Michel Epstein (Belorussia, 1829–1908), *Arukh ha-Shulhan, Hoshen Mishpat* 228:1.
7. *How to Sell Anything to Anybody,* op. cit., p. 112.
8. op. cit., p. 164.
9. op. cit., p. 158.
10. For the parameters and sources of the *lifnim mi-shurat ha-din* duty in the context of the modern business setting, see Aaron Levine, *Case Studies in Jewish Business Ethics* (Hoboken, NJ: Ktav Publishing, Yeshiva University Press, 2000), pp. 257–264, 314.
11. See *Tosafot, Bava Metzia* 24b.
12. op. cit., pp. 160–164.
13. op. cit., pp. 113–115.
14. For a general discussion of the law of *ona'ah* as it pertains to the modern marketplace, see Aaron Levine, "*Ona'ah* and the Operation of the Modern Marketplace," *Jewish Law Annual,* Hebrew University, Vol. xiv, 2003, pp. 225–258.
15. R. Yaakov Yeshayahu Bloi, *Pithe Hoshen, Hilkhot Geneivah-ve-Ona'ah,* 299.
16. *How to Sell Anything to Anybody,* op. cit., pp. 119–121.
17. *Mishnah, Bava Metzia* 4:12.
18. *Yad, Mekhirah* 18:4; *Tur,* op. cit., 228; *Sh. Ar.,* op. cit., 228:18; *Ar. ha-Sh.,* op. cit., 228:14.
19. *Bava Metzia* 60a.

20. For an explication of the sources and various nuances of the prohibition of *geneivat da'at* please turn to pp. 8–17, 389–391 of this volume.
21. *Hullin* 94a.
22. R. Joshua b. Alexander ha-Kohen Falk (Poland, 1555–1614), *Sema* to *Sh. Ar.*, op. cit., 228, note 7; *Ar. ha-Sh.*, op. cit., 228:3.
23. *Mishnah, Bava Metzia* 4:12.
24. *Bava Metzia* 60b.
25. R. Solomon b. Isaac, *Rashi, Bava Metzia* 60b; *Tur*, op. cit., 228; *Ar. ha-Sh.*, op. cit., 228:13.
26. *Yad*, op. cit., 18:4; *Tur*, op. cit., 228; *Sh. Ar.*, op. cit., 228:17; *Ar. ha-Sh.*, op. cit., 228:13.
27. For a discussion of various ethical issues relating to cold calling, turn to pp. 230–238, 241–253 of this volume.
28. op. cit., pp. 59–61.
29. While the Talmud explicitly connects this verse only to engaging in falsehood in a *Bet Din* setting (*Shavuot*, 31a), R. Israel Meir ha-Kohen Kagan (Radin, 1838–1933, *Hafetz Hayyim, Essen sief* 13) understands *sheker* to be violated on a biblical level, whether the falsehood was uttered in *Bet Din* or outside *Bet Din*.
30. R. Israel Meir ha-Kohen Kagan, *Sefat Tamim, perek* 6.
31. R. Abraham Y. Karelitz (Israel, 1878–1953), *Emunah u-Betahan* Chapter 4, *at* 13.
32. *How to Sell Anything to Anybody*, op. cit., pp. 83–97.
33. *Bava Metzia* 75b and Rashi ad locum. For a treatment of the prohibition against creating for a fellow a setting for veiled misconduct, see *Case Studies in Jewish Business Ethics*, op. cit., 185–187.
34. *How to Sell Anything to Anybody*, op. cit., pp. 91.
35. C.F. Maimonides, *Yad, Mekhirah* 1
36. R. Yohanan, *Bava Metzia* 49a; *Rif*, ad loc.; *Yad*, op. cit., 7:8–9; *Rosh, Bava Metzia* 4:12; *Tur*, op. cit., 204; *Sh. Ar.*, op. cit., 204:7–8; *Ar. ha-Sh.*, op. cit., 204: 8–9.
37. R. Mosheh Isserles (Poland, 1525 or 1530–1572), *Hoshen Mishpat* 204:11.
38. *Ar. ha-Sh.*, op. cit., 204:8.
39. *Tosafot, Bava Metzia* 24b.
40 R. Yohanan, *Bava Metzia* 46b; *Rif*, ad loc., *Rosh*, op. cit., 4:8; *Yad*, op. cit., 3:5; *Tur*, op. cit., 198; *Sh. Ar.*, op. cit., 198:1; *Ar. ha-Sh*, op. cit., 198: 1–6.
41. *Mishnah, Bava Metzia* 4:1; *Rif*, ad loc.; *Rosh*, op. cit., 4:13; *Yad*, op. cit., 7:1–6; *Tur*, op. cit., 204; *Sh. Ar.*, op. cit., 204, *Ar. ha-Sh.*, op. cit., 204: 1–7.
42. *Kiddushin* 59a; *Rif*, ad loc., *Rosh*, Kiddushin 3:2; *Tur*, op. cit., 237; *Sh. Ar.*, op. cit., 237:1–2; *Ar. ha-Sh.*, op. cit., 237:1–5.
43. Please turn to pp. 114–116, 165–166.
44. For sources and explication of the *lifnei iver* principle, please turn to pp. 304–305, 514.
45. *How to Sell Anything to Anybody*, op. cit., pp. 153–155.
46. *Mishnah, Bava Metzia* 4:10.
47. R. Menahem b. Solomon Meiri (Perpignan, 1249–1316), *Beit ha-Behirah, Bava Metzia* 59a. Pricing an article with no intention to buy it is prohibited, according to R. Samuel b. Meir (ca. 1080–1174), *Rashbam, Pesahim* 112b, on account of the possible financial loss this behavior might cause the vendor. While the vendor is preoccupied with the insincere inquiry, serious customers may turn elsewhere.
48. See commentary by *Rashi* at Leviticus 25:17.
49. For the derivation of this prohibition, please turn to pp. 152–154, 395–396 of this volume.

50. op. cit.,110.
51. op. cit., 115.
52. op. cit., 111.
53. For a discussion of the details of the *ona'at devarim* interdict, please turn to pp. 7–8, 259–263, 291–292, 396 of this volume.
54. Please turn to pp. 8–13, 389–391 of this volume.
55. op. cit., 111
56. The following section draws upon my previous work *Case Studies in Jewish Business Ethics* (Hoboken, NJ: Ktav Publishing House Inc., Yeshiva University Press, 2000), pp. 122–124.
57. R. Joshua ha-Kohen Falk (Poland, 1555–1614), *Sema, Sh. Ar.,* op. cit., 232, note 57.
58. Samuel, *Bava Batra* 92b; *Rif,* ad loc., *Rosh, Bava Batra* 6:2; *Tur,* op. cit., 232; *Sh. Ar.,* op. cit., 232:23; *Ar. ha-Sh.,* op. cit., 232:36.
59. *Tur,* op. cit.; *Sh. Ar.,* op. cit.; *Ar. ha-Sh.,* op. cit.
60. R. Yom Tov Lipmann b. Nathan ha-Levi Heller, Filpula Harifta, *Rosh, Bava Batra* 5, note 2.
61. The Torah makes use of the phrase "And you shall fear God" in connection with the following moral imperatives: (1) the prohibition against offering ill-suited advice (Leviticus 19:14); (2) the duty to bestow honor to a talmudic scholar (Leviticus 19:32); (3) the injunction against causing someone needless mental anguish (Leviticus 15:17); (4) the interdict against charging interest (Leviticus 25:36); and (5) the prohibition against working an Israelite bondsman oppressively (Leviticus 25:43).
62. *Kiddushin* 32b and R. Solomon b. Isaac (France, 1040–1105), *Rashi,* s.v. *davar ha-masur la-lev.*
63. It should be noted that the prohibition against interest (*ribbit*) applies only to inter-Jewish transactions. Moreover, loan agreements can sometimes be restructured into partnership agreements and avoid violation of the prohibition against *ribbit.* The mechanism is called *hetter iska.* For an excellent work on the laws of *ribbit,* see R. Yisroel Reisman, *The Laws of Ribbis* (New York: Mesorah Publications), 1995.
64. The prohibition against veiled misconduct in the form of working an Israelite bondsman oppressively, referred to in note 61, also has implications for the modern labor market. For a discussion of this application, see *Case Studies in Jewish Business Ethics,* op. cit., pp. 144–146.
65. *Bava Metzia* 61b.
66. See *Case Studies in Jewish Business Ethics,* op. cit., pp. 1–18.
67. Donald McCabe, Linda Klebe, "Honesty and Honor Codes," *Academe,* vol. 88, Issue 1, January 1, 2002, pp. 37–42.
68. For a legal and ethical analysis of the honor code from a secular standpoint, see Larry A. DiMatteo, Don Weisner, "Honor Codes: A Legal and Ethical Analysis," 19, Southern Illinois University Law Journal 49, Fall 1994.

7

Ethical Dilemmas in The Telemarketer Industry

The telemarketing industry expanded rapidly over the last decade.[1] Currently employing 4.2 million people, the telemarketing industry has generated about \$200 billion in annual sales in recent years.[2]

Both the business practices of this industry and the way consumers have reacted to these practices present a number of serious moral dilemmas. These include the use of pressure tactics, pricing policies, conduct consumers engage in to thwart the telemarketer, and using the information the telemarketer offers without compensating him or her for the provision of that information.

We will explore the above issues using the case study method. This will show that moral dilemmas that have their origin in the interaction between cold caller and customer spill out into society at large.

THE COLD CALLER

Ted Arrow: Hello, Mr. Oak, my name is Ted Arrow. I'm calling with an offer you will never regret accepting. It entails only a small amount of money.

Sidney Oak: By your own admission, you're a telemarketer. I don't speak to telemarketers. This conversation is over. Have a good—

Ted Arrow: Please don't hang up. Give me 20 seconds. I'm not your run of the mill telemarketer. My call is about how to prevent identity theft. One of five families today is a victim of identity theft. You'll bless me every day of your life for the invaluable information I give.

Sidney Oak: I told you I don't speak to telemarketers. Besides, I have no need for your service. No one will steal my wallet. I protect it well. Have a wonderful-

Ted Arrow: Please, please, just another 15 seconds.

Sidney Oak: OK. The clock is running.

Ted Arrow: Give me two minutes and I'll show you how vulnerable you are to identity theft. If you're not convinced, I promise that you'll be rid of me instantly. OK. Thanks! I take your silence as a yes to proceed. Just think how easily we give away our social security number. When we visit a doctor for the first time, we fill out a questionnaire. One of the items is our social security number. Our student and employee identification numbers are often the same as our social security number. Once you give out your social security number, you lose control of it. You may trust the person that you directly give your social security number to, but other people employed by the organization will also have easy access to this piece of private information. Herein lies your vulnerability. Once someone has your name, address, and social security number, that person can apply for and get a credit card in your name and charge it to the maximum. Because the identity thief can arrange a billing address that is different than your real address, you may not get wind of the fraud until you are already living in an irreversible nightmare.[3] Identity fraud is now the fastest growing crime in America, striking more than 2000 people per day. To date, victims who have reported this crime have spent more than 175 hours and more than $10,000 per incident just to resolve these problems.[4]

Sidney Oak: OK. You have convinced me. I can especially relate to the questionnaires doctors ask you to fill out. So what are you selling and how much will it cost me?

Ted Arrow: Our company, called Identity Shield, has put together an audiocassette. In palpable form you will learn all the practical things you can do to prevent identity theft and minimize the damage to you if you ever are victimized by this crime. Learning was never made so painless. The cost to you is only $35.

Sidney Oak: Your offer sounds good. Tell me how to order.

Oak proved to be a very satisfied customer. The audiocassette actually changed his lifestyle. For one, he became extremely circumspect in releasing his social security number and obsessively tried to retrieve it from those to whom he already gave it. Oak made all the doctors he visits replace his social security number in their files with coded letters.[5] Oak prevailed upon his employer to issue him a new employee identification number that bore no resemblance to his social security number. The audiocassette made Oak aware that identity thieves sift through the garbage to retrieve pre-approved credit lines that are discarded by the people who receive these offers in the mail. These pre-approved credit lines contain much valuable personal data. To thwart this practice, called dumpster diving, Oak purchased a shredder and used it as an efficient tool to destroy documents containing personal data that he wanted to discard. Finally, to get an early warning of identity theft, Oak took up the audiocassette's $45 deal to have Identity Shield arrange to have three monthly credit reports sent to him. Oak planned to examine these reports closely for irregularities.

At his high school reunion dinner six months later, Sidney Oak was seated at the same table as Mark Besser, whom the graduation yearbook dubbed as the class "know-it all." The conversation turned to telemarketers. Besser expressed an antipathy for telemarketers:

What gall these companies have invading our privacy, often at the dinner hour, with useless offers. You know I was once awakened at five in the morning by a telephone ring. Thinking it was a call about a death in the family or worse, my heart sank as I answered the phone. Adding to my anticipated horror was that there was an agonizing pause of thirty seconds before I heard a voice. It turned out to be a pre-recorded auto dial from a telemarketer hawking a chemical treatment for my lawn. No matter how much I tried, I could not fall back to sleep after I hung up the phone. That experience was a wake-up call for me. I have resolved to take revenge against telemarketers. I started my campaign by hunting down the personal telephone numbers of the officers of the company that called me. Believe me, it took some nifty detective work to get these numbers. I can't describe to you the glee I felt when I called each of these culprits at five in the morning. and asked them whether they used the company's chemical treatment product on their own lawns. My short-term goal is to get the telemarketer to hang up on me. My long-term goal is to do my part in encouraging telemarketers to exit the industry and to choose a job that doesn't entail pestering people.

I'll tell you some of the things I do. Let me start with a relatively civilized response. As soon as I get the feeling I'm talking to a telemarketer, I demand to be connected to a supervisor. When the supervisor gets on I say immediately: "I want to be put on your do not call list." I then firmly say "If you call again I'm going to exercise my right to sue you in small claims court for $500."[6] As you can well imagine, it's not worth my time to keep a record of which telemarketers called and it goes without saying that I'm not prepared to incur the opportunity cost involved in pursuing a repeat call telemarketer in small claims court. But, I think my bluff works well and the supervisor will actually make sure I'm not called again.

When I'm in a whimsical mood, I have fun with the telemarketer. I quickly interrupt the sales pitch and advise my caller that I'm eating dinner, but request a number I can call back because I'm really interested in the chemical lawn treatment or whatever. If I get a number to call back, I save it on my Palm Pilot. When I get a call from the next telemarketer I ask him to call me at another number in my den, and give him the previous telemarketer's number.[7]

Although Oak shared Besser's bias against telemarketers and was entertained by Besser's tactics on how to take revenge against telemarketers, Oak felt compelled to say the following:

Sure, telemarketers are generally an annoyance, but I would not tune off and respond in a robotic, disconnected manner when a telemarketer calls. I just had a very satisfying experience with a telemarketing company called Identity Shield.

Because Oak felt that he was one up on the class "know-it-all," he went on to display what he learned from the audiocassette about how to prevent identity fraud. Instead of getting a nod of approval from Besser for his investment in the audiocassette, Oak got an earful of criticism:

> Friend, you were ripped off. Everything you picked up on the audio-cassette on how to prevent and minimize damage from identity theft could have been culled free of charge from a booklet the Federal Trade Commission puts out called "ID Theft: When Bad Things Happen to Your Good Name."[8] Sorry to tell you, this publication can even be downloaded as a PDF from the FTC Web site.

The revelation that the information he bought from Identity Shield was available free of charge made Oak feel foolish. Oak's feeling of foolishness quickly turned into anger when Besser went on to express surprise that Oak needed Identity Shield to order credit reports. Using Identity Shield as a middleman, Besser exclaimed, unnecessarily inflated your expense. "You can order credit reports yourself directly from any of the three major credit reporting agencies. Sorry to tell you, the first report, as far as I know, is free."

Apparently not noticing the devastating impact his critique had on Oak, Besser took Oak's experience with Identity Shield as an invitation to provide a matching experience with salespeople:

> I think it's always a good practice to try to bargain with a salesperson whenever possible. The other day, I went shopping with my wife, Claudia, for a double stroller at the Child Emporium. We found the double stroller we were looking for. It had a $185 price tag attached to it. When the salesperson, Mr. Simmons, came towards us and noticed how our two kids, Erez and Shalhavet, age 16 months and 3 years, respectively, were wandering all over the place, he must have sized us up that we desperately needed the stroller and therefore closing the deal would be a cake walk. Boy was he surprised when I blurted out, "This stroller is overpriced. I'm sure I can get it cheaper at the Wunderkind department store." With a noticeable tone of annoyance, Simmons replied, "No, its not cheaper elsewhere and it's not our practice to bar-gain with customers. That's why we put a price tag on everything." At this juncture, Claudia weighed in and said, "Mr. Simmons, excuse my husband's curtness. Let me tell you, we absolutely love this stroller and

as you can see we desperately need it. Without it my sanity will be threatened daily. You see our problem is that our budget is very tight. How about a ten percent discount from the price tag? If you can manage that, we'll think of you and bless you every day we use the stroller. What do you say? You'll be making our day." Simmons scratched his head and rolled his eyes, but closed the deal on *our* terms.

THE USE OF PRESSURE TACTICS

In the opening vignette, both Arrow and Besser succeed in their commercial transactions by engaging in pressure tactics. Their conduct may run afoul of the biblical prohibitions against coveting (*lo tahmod*) and against desiring (*lo tit'avveh*): "You shall not covet your neighbor's house. You shall not covet your fellow's wife, his manservant, his maidservant, his ox, his donkey, nor anything that belongs to your fellow" (Exodus 20:14). "You shall not covet your fellow's wife, you shall not desire (*lo tit'avveh*) your fellow's house, his field and his slave and his maidservant, his ox and his donkey, and anything that belongs to your fellow (Deuteronomy 5:18).

Before the prohibitions of *lo tahmod* and *lo tit'avveh* can be related to the case at hand, the parameters of these prohibitions must be defined. These parameters are a matter of dispute between Maimonides (*Rambam*, Egypt, 1135–1204) and R. Abraham of Posquières (*Rabad*, 1125–1198). We begin with Maimonides' formulation of these prohibitions:

If one [B] covets the male slave or the female slave or the house or goods of another [S], or anything that it is possible for [B] to acquire from [S], and [B] weighs down [S] with friends or importunes [S] until he allows him to buy it, even though [B] gives [S] a high price for the item, [B] transgresses the negative commandment, "You shall not covet your fellow's house" (Exodus 20:14). No flogging is incurred for breach of this prohibition, since it does not involve action. Nor does [B] transgress this prohibition until he buys the object that he covets, as is exemplified by Scripture when it says, "the carved images of their gods you shall burn in the fire; you shall not covet and take for yourself the silver and gold that is on them, lest you be ensnared by it, for it is an abomination of *Hashem*, your God" (Deuteronomy 7:25). Thus implying that the transgression of coveting is effected only when accompanied by action.

If [B] desires [S']s house or [S']s wife or [S]'s goods or any similar thing that [B] might buy from [S], [B] transgresses a negative commandment as soon as he thinks in his heart how he is to acquire the desired object and allows his mind to be seduced by it. For Scripture says, "[Y]ou shall not desire. . . ." (Deuteronomy 7:25).[9]

In his gloss on Maimonides' text, *Rabad* makes three comments. First, *Rabad* finds it astonishing that Maimonides' regards *lo tahmod* as a prohibition not involving action. How can this be when the prohibition is not violated unless B actually takes possession of the article he covets? Can there be any greater action than taking legal possession? Nonetheless, *Rabad* agrees that B does not incur flogging for violating *lo tahmod* because B must return the object of his coveting to S. Finally, *Rabad* postulates that in the event S declared *rotzeh ani* "(I am willing) before B took legal possession of the article, B becomes free of the *lo tahmod* violation.[10]

The dispute between *Rambam* and *Rabad*, according to R. Vidal Yom Tov of Toloso (*Maggid Mishneh*, flourished 14th cent.), turns on the fundamental matter of what constitutes the essence of the *lo tahmod* prohibition. *Rabad* regards *lo tahmod* as prohibiting B from obtaining an object from S by means of coercion. *Lo tahmod* is hence an aspect of the prohibition against theft (*gezel*). Given that *lo tahmod* is an aspect of *gezel*, B is required to reverse the transaction he conducted with S. Because S's declaration of *rotzeh ani* removes the coercive element in the transfer, the transaction becomes free of *lo tahmod*. *Rambam*, on the other hand, regards B's efforts to overcome S's resistance (*hishtadlut*) as constituting the essence of the *lo tahmod* prohibition. *Lo tahmod* is hence not an aspect of *gezel*. Moreover, the circumstance that *lo tahmod* is not violated unless B acquires the object of his coveting does not categorize this prohibition as one involving the commission of an action. Given that S's declaration of *rotzeh ani* in no way cancels the *hishtadlut* B has already done, the *lo tahmod* prohibition remains intact. Now, if S declared *rotzeh ani* before the transaction was completed, B violates only *lo tahmod*, but is not in violation of *gezel*. Accordingly, B is under no obligation to reverse his transaction with S. Nonetheless, absent S's declaration of *rotzeh ani*, B compounds his *lo tahmod* violation with an infraction of *gezel* as well. Here, *Rambam* is in agreement that *B* must reverse his transaction with *S*. But, what requires *B* to return *S* his article in exchange for the money he paid is not *lo tahmod*, but rather the prohibition against *gezel*.[11]

In clarifying *Rambam*'s position, one question remains: What role does acquisition of the object of coveting play in the *lo tahmod* interdict. Is it merely a technicality of law that must be satisfied, or is it a measure of the degree of coveting that is necessary for the interdict to be violated? Addressing this issue, R. Yaakov Yisrael Kanievsky (Israel, 1899–1985) posits that *lo tahmod* in *Rambam*'s formulation is a transgression of the heart and the condition that *B* does not violate *lo tahmod* unless he acquires the object of his coveting conduct should be looked upon as the measure of the degree of coveting *B* must have in order to violate *lo tahmod*. It is because *lo tahmod* is a transgression of the heart that *Rambam* characterizes the interdict as involving no action when it is violated.[12]

If we accept R. Kanievsky's formulation *B* may very well violate *lo tahmod* without committing any pestering action whatsoever. Consider the following scenario: *B* makes a $200 bid for *S*'s article. *S* refuses *B*'s offer. *B* then asks *C* to bid *S*, say, $300 for the article and instructs him not to reveal to *S* that he is acting as *B*'s agent. *B* continues to use fronts until he acquires the article he wants. The salient feature of this scenario is that *B* goes about acquiring *S*'s object without subjecting *B* to any pestering action whatsoever. Here, *B*'s hishtadlut consists of an orchestration he sets up to overcome *S*'s initial resistance to sell him the article. Given that *B* has succeeded in acquiring the article of his coveting, his coveting has reached the requisite level to violate the *lo tahmod* interdict.[13]

LO TAHMOD AND THE COMMERCIAL STATUS OF THE ITEM

Another fundamental issue to clarify in respect to *lo tahmod* and *lo tit'avveh* is the commercial status of the item *B* seeks to acquire. Is the item at hand something *S* put up for sale, or does the prohibition basically apply to an item that *S* did not put up for sale? Addressing this issue R. Solomon b. Joseph Ganzfried (Hungary, 1804–1886) posits that *lo tahmod* and *lo tit'avveh* refer only to an item that was not up for sale.[14]

Support for R. Ganzfried's position can be seen from the following. Consider that lumped together with the various commercial items mentioned in connection with *lo tahmod* and *lo tit'avveh* is the prohibition of coveting and desiring a neighbor's wife. Consider also that at Deuteronomy 5:18 where the prohibition is formulated as *lo tit'avveh*, the Torah switches to *lo tahmod* in connection with a fellow's wife. Hence, the only setting where *lo tahmod* is repeated both at Exodus 20:14 and at Deuteronomy 5:18 is in connection with a non-commercial case. The prohibition against coveting a neighbor's wife should therefore be taken as the model to define both *lo tahmod* and *lo tit'avveh* as referring to the seeking of an item that is not accessible to the one who seeks to acquire it. Just as the woman *B* covets is a woman that is married and is not on standby to be divorced and become accessible to him, so too the commercial items mentioned at Exodus 20:14 and Deuteronomy 5:18 refer to items *S* owns but has not put up for sale.

Consider also that putting an item up for sale signals on the part of *S* a desire to part with the item provided the price is right. Now, if *lo tahmod* and *lo tit'avveh* apply even when *S* puts up the item for sale, *B* should be in violation of *lo tahmod* only if he exerts pressure on *S* to accept his original bid, but not if he increases his bid for the item. Expanding the ambit of *lo tahmod* to include the instance when *B* offers a higher bid is understandable only in the instance where *S* did not initially put up the item at hand for sale. Here *S*'s flat rejection of *B*'s initial offer should be taken as an implicit affirmation of what *B* already knows, namely, that the item at hand is not for sale. Because we have no signal from *S* that he wants to put the item up for sale, we should view *B*'s higher bid for the item as a form of pressure to change *S*'s attitude toward the item and put it up for sale.

What the above conceptualization does is to make *lo tit'avveh* and *lo tahmod* into prohibitions to plot and exert pressure on *S* to stop looking at the item at hand in terms of personal attachment and, instead, to look upon it merely as a commodity that can be traded in the marketplace.

LO TAHMOD, *LO TIT'AVVEH*, AND ITEM PUT UP FOR SALE

Does the above analysis lead to the conclusion that *lo tahmod* has no application at all to the instance where *S* puts up the article for sale? No. A number of different scenarios can be identified. Let's look first at a scenario that involves only persuasion: *S* puts up an article for sale with no asking price. Because no specific price demand accompanies *S*'s offer, *S*'s notice amounts to an invitation to the public to enter into a negotiation with him.

Accordingly, if *B* increases his bid or sends friends to convince *S* to accept his initial bid, these tactics should all be viewed as forms of negotiation and therefore not violate *lo tahmod*.

Let's now turn to a number of scenarios that may entail coercion: Suppose *S* sets a specific price for his article. Does *S*'s specific asking price amount to a preemptive message to *B* that he will not accept less? If the specific asking price amounts to an advance "no" in respect to a lower bid, *B*'s lower bid should be viewed as a form of pressure on *S* to change his mind and therefore violate *lo tahmod*. Our basic assumption as to what the specific asking price conveys can, however, be questioned. Consider that when *S* puts up an article for sale, he cannot expect the item to sell on the spot, as every commercial item has its own inventory cycle. Accordingly, when *B* offers a price lower than the asking price, two alternative strategies are open to *S*. One tack is to reject the low offer in favor of waiting for the customer that will pay the price that is indicated on the price tag. Alternatively, *S* can take the lower offer and seize upon the opportunity to liquidate his inventory at a faster rate than he could normally expect. If *S*'s liquidity needs are great he may find it quite rational to take the second course. Since *B*'s lower bid speaks not only of his own needs, but also to *S*'s self-interest, *B*'s lower bid should not be viewed as pressure he exerts on *S* to change his mind.

EXERTING PRESSURE TO GET A DISCOUNT

A variant of the above case produces a scenario where *B*'s conduct may well constitute pressure or coercion: *S* puts up his article for sale at a specific price. *B* offers to buy the article at a lower price. *S* rejects *B*'s lower price offer and goes on to say: "I'm confident that there are many customers around that will pay the price marked on the price tag. I know you'll be happier with the ten percent discount you propose, but I'm here to make money. My store is not a mechanism for income redistribution." Reacting to *S*'s rejection, *B* says: "I really love this item and I would like to buy it now, but the price you ask strains my budget, could you please give it to me at a ten percent discount." Consider that *S* has already informed *B* that he does not want to make the item available at a discount. *B*'s subsequent plea for a discount should therefore be characterized as exerting pressure on *S* to change his mind and hence violates *lo tahmod*.

The legitimacy for *B* to pressure *S* for a discount, as it appears to this writer, turns on the issue of whether *lo tahmod* is violated when the pressure the object seeker exerts is not to make the owner sell the object to him, but rather confer the item to him as a gift. Addressing the issue of the applicability of *lo tahmod* in the gift case is R. David Ariov (Israel, contemp.). R. Ariov marshals a number of authorities that adopt a strict view here.[15] Counted in this group is R. Israel Meir ha-Kohen Kagan (Radin, 1838–1933), who cautions a bridegroom not to exert pressure on his future father-in-law to increase his dowry.[16] If exerting pressure on *S* to give up his article as a gift is a violation of *lo tahmod* and *lo tit'avveh*, then so too is exerting pressure on him to sell the article at a discount.

LO TAHMOD, LO TIT'AVVEH, AND THE SELLER'S CONDUCT

The prohibition against coveting is formulated in the codes in terms of the behavior of the buyer. By logical extension, posits R. Yaakov Yeshayahu Bloi (Israel, 1929–), the interdict should prohibit the seller from coveting the money of the buyer. Accordingly, the use of pressure tactics by the seller to make a sale is prohibited conduct.[17]

If the basic model for *lo tahmod* is the setting where the item at hand is not up for sale, *S* should have wide latitude in the conventional commercial setting to overcome *B*'s resistance by offering him or her better terms or a better price. Walking into a store, for example, signals on the part of *B* that he or she is interested in buying the item provided the price and other terms are right. Similarly, if *B* grants an appointment to *S*, the appointment signals that *B* is interested in buying provided the price and terms are right. In both these instances there should be no ethical issue for *S* to overcome *B*'s initial rejection by making a better offer.

Suppose, however, *S* barges in on *B* and makes a sales pitch to him. Here *lo tit'avveh* and *lo tahmod* should prohibit *S* from offering a more favorable price as a means of overcoming *B*'s initial rejection of the offer. If *S* wants to continue his sales pitch he must first secure *B*'s explicit permission to do so.

The application of the prohibition of *lo tahmod* to the conduct of the seller requires further clarification. Consider that the salesperson (*S*) is an employee. Who violates *lo tahmod*? Is it the employer (*E*), *S*, or, perhaps, both? The issue entails a number of scenarios. We'll initially assume that *S* acts on his or her own and the high pressure sales pitch is not part of the protocol of *S*'s training.

We begin with the case where *S* works on a straight salary basis. Here, the revenue from the high pressure sale goes to the company and not *directly* into *S*'s pocket. Accordingly, *S*'s sales pressure should not be characterized as coveting the customer's money for himself. Reinforcing this judgment is the possibility that the high pressure tactic will get *S* into trouble. This will be the case when success at the task at hand in no way is predicated on the need to engage in high pressure tactics and the practice of such conduct brings on complaints against *S* to his or her boss. In the scenario just described *S* is not guilty of coveting the customer's money. But, consider, if the customer does not declare at the conclusion of the deal, *rotzei ani*, the sales transaction must be characterized as *gezel*. Now, if *S* consummates the transaction by taking the customer's credit card number, *S* is guilty of effecting a transaction that is *gezel*. Accordingly, *E*, as the proprietor of the business, is obligated to cancel the transaction and give the customer a refund. Although *S* does not violate *lo tit'avveh* and *lo tahmod*, *S* is, nonetheless, guilty of facilitating a prohibited transaction.[18]

In a variation of the above scenario, *E* instructs *S* to engage in high pressure tactics whenever customer resistance is encountered. Since *S* is *E*'s employee, *E*'s instruction should be viewed as "sending a friend to overcome the buyer's resistance." Accordingly, *E* violates *lo tit'avveh* and *lo tahmod*. *S* is here, too, guilty of facilitating *lo tahmod*. If the customer does not declare *rotzei ani* at the conclusion of the transaction, *S* will be guilty of facilitating the prohibition of *gezel* as well.

Let's now consider the scenario where *S* works on a commission basis. The most serious infraction in this scenario occurs when *E* trains *S* in high pressure tactics and instructs him to use these tactics to overcome customer resistance. Given that any sale concluded by *S* generates revenue *directly* for both himself and for *E*, *S*'s use of high pressure tactics violates for him both *lo tit'avveh*, and *lo tahmod*. In addition, for every successful high pressure sale, *E* violates *lo tahmod*. Moreover, if the customer does not declare *rotzei ani* at the conclusion of the deal, *S* will be guilty of affecting a transaction entailing *gezel*. As the proprietor of the business, the onus will be on *E* to cancel the deal and give the customer a refund. Finally, in the instance where *S* engages in high pressure tactics on his own and not at the behest of *E, S* alone violates *lo tit'avveh, lo tahmod* and the prohibition of *gezel*. Although *E* is entirely disconnected from the high pressure tactics, the deal is *gezel* and, as the proprietor of the business, the onus is on *E* to cancel the deal and give the customer a refund.

TED ARROW AND THE ETHICS OF SALES PRESSURE

The most salient feature of the Arrow-Oak incident is that Oak never invited Identity Shield to call him. Arrow's cold call is therefore tantamount to barging into Oak's home. Once Oak tells Arrow that he never speaks to telemarketers, Arrow's maneuvering to get Oak's attention should be regarded as both *lo tit'avveh* and *lo tahmod* conduct. A saving factor here is that Oak interrupts Arrow's sales pitch before he gets a chance to articulate a specific offer. Oak's initial resistance to hear out Arrow is therefore a refusal to grant Arrow a favor to present his offer, and not a rejection of any specific offer. Because Oak did not reject any specific offer, Arrow's push to gain Oak's attention should not violate *lo tahmod*.

Provided his call is made at a reasonable hour, there is nothing wrong with Arrow trying to overcome Oak's initial resistance and pleading to be heard out. But, once Oak refuses to continue the conversation, Arrow's persistence runs the risk of violating the prohibition of causing someone needless mental anguish (*ona'at devarim*).[19] It goes without saying that insulting Oak as a desperate means of getting his attention to continue the sales pitch violates the *ona'at devarim* interdict. Consider that no minimum amount of unnecessary aggravation is required for violation of *ona'at devarim*.[20] Accordingly, if Arrow's call comes in at the customary dinner hour (5–7 P.M.), and Oak, in fact, interrupts his dinner to pick up the call, the call is inherently *ona'at devarim* conduct, irrespective of whether Oak ends up buying the product as a result of the call.

TELEMARKETING FOR A CHARITABLE CAUSE

A variation of the above case occurs when Arrow is a charity solicitor. R. Bezalel Sthern dealt with an analogous case: A Rabbi (*R*) had in his possession *matzah* for the night of Passover in excess of his own religious requirement (*mitzvah*) needs. His friend (*F*) had no *matzah* to fulfill his *mitzvah* need and therefore requested *R* to either sell or give him the excess supply. Here, *F*'s efforts to overcome *R*'s initial resistance to make the *matzah* available to him violates neither the *lo tit'avveh* or the *lo tahmod* interdicts. This is so because absent *F*'s pleadings and exertions, *R*, is, in any case, obligated to make the *matzah* available to *F* so that he can fulfill his *mitzvah* need.[21] Similarly, in the case at hand, Oak is obligated to give charity as a religious duty.[22] Making use of persuasion of all sorts to overcome Oak's initial rejection to contribute to the charitable cause should therefore not entail a violation of *lo tit'avveh* and *lo tahmod* on the part of Arrow. Similarly, Arrow's persistence and persuasion to overcome Oak's resistance should not amount to causing him needless mental anguish and should therefore not violate *ona'at devarim*. One caveat, however. To be sure, Oak has a religious duty to give charity. But, Oak may feel that he is not obligated to support the particular organization Arrow is soliciting funds for. Accordingly, Arrow does not have an unlimited license to push his cause on Oak. At some point, Arrow's persistence and pestering become a violation of *ona'at devarim*.

OVERCOMING A REFUSAL WHEN THE REFUSAL IS BASED ON ERRONEOUS INFORMATION

With the aim of clarifying another point in the law of *lo tahmod*, let's change the opening vignette a bit. Instead of having Oak interrupt Arrow before Arrow gets a chance to make a specific offer, let's assume that Oak is silent until Arrow makes a specific offer. Recall that Oak offers two different reasons for rejecting the offer. One reason is his belief that he has no need for the audiocassette because identity theft occurs mainly in the context of a stolen wallet. The second reason is that he never deals with telemarketers. Since Arrow's cold call barges in on Oak and the conversation reaches the point where Oak rejects Arrow's specific offer, pressing on with his sales pitch amounts to *lo tahmod* conduct for Arrow. But, there is a saving factor here. Consider the first reason Oak gives for not being interested in the offer. Oak's understanding of identity fraud is very naïve. Setting him straight on this matter and showing him how vulnerable he is to falling victim to this crime should not amount to *lo tahmod* conduct and should not violate the *ona'at devarim* interdict. This is so because both coercion and pestering conduct should be defined in terms of inducing someone to coop-

erate with you by *reducing* that person's options. Inducing someone to cooperate with you by *expanding* that person's options is neither coercion nor
pestering conduct. It is *persuasion* and hence permissible conduct.[23]

But, Oak also mentions that his practice is never to deal with a telemarketer. Should Arrow take the two reasons Oak cites as independent reasons for his rejection? Or, does Arrow have a right to treat the two objections
as intertwined. If the reasons are indeed intertwined, then perhaps Arrow
can continue with his sales pitch based on the further assumption that Oak
does not deal with telemarketers only because he has had disappointing
experiences with them in the past. This will surely not be the case this time.
Arguing against pushing on with the sales pitch is the Talmudic principle
that a man never sees a disability when it comes to his own interests (*ein
adam ro'eh hova le-atzmo*).[24] Given the possibility that pressing on with the
sales pitch violates *ona'at devarim* and constitutes *lo tahmod* conduct,
Arrow must say to Oak something to the effect "Sir, may I very briefly show
you why you *are* vulnerable." For Arrow to continue with the sales pitch, he
must get an affirmative response from Oak.

CUSTOMER PRESSURE ON A SALESPERSON

In the opening vignette, we find Mark and Claudia Besser exerting pressure
on Mr. Simmons to sell them the double stroller at a lower price than the
$185 price tag. Recall the proposition we made earlier that a price tag does
not amount to an implicit preemptive rejection of a lower bid on the part of
a customer. This is so because every item has an inventory cycle and the
seller cannot therefore expect to liquidate an item the minute he puts it up
for sale. The customer therefore has a right to regard his lower bid as an
offer to the salesperson to liquidate the item sooner than his normal
expectancy. The offer to buy the item below the price tag price therefore
does not violate *lo tahmod*. But, Mark Besser did not content himself merely
to offer a lower price. Instead, he claimed that the stroller was cheaper in
the same marketplace at Wunderkind's. Besser had not actually identified
the cheaper price. Rather, his assertion "I'm sure this stroller is cheaper at
Wunderkind" was done merely to rattle the salesperson. Because he makes
a claim without first investigating whether the assertion is rooted in fact,
Mark Besser's assertion is a lie and violates the prohibition against lying

(*lo teshakkeru*).[25] Recall that this tactic did not succeed in securing the stroller at a lower price. Mark hence does not violate *lo tahmod* with his lie. Nonetheless, since Mark uses a lie as a means of exerting pressure on Simmons to lower the price, Mark does violate *lo tit'avveh*. Claudia's conduct is, however, a different matter. Her stratagem of flattery and invoking pity succeeded. Claudia hence violates *lo tahmod*.

In securing the double stroller at the discount price, the couple may also be in violation of the prohibition against creating a false impression (*geneivat da'at*).[26] Consider that the pressure Claudia exerts in the form of flattery and a plea for kindness is enhanced because she apologizes for the rude conduct of her husband. Perhaps, it is Claudia's apology that makes the difference and pushes Simmons over the edge to give the discount Claudia requests. Now, if the interaction between Mark and Claudia with Simmons is spontaneous and Claudia's apology is sincere, Claudia's conduct does not create a false impression and hence it violates only the law of *lo tahmod*. But, suppose the interaction of the couple with Simmons is the "acting out" of a preconceived plan designed to get the stroller at a discount. The game plan calls for an initial attack of nastiness by Mark to be followed by an effusive apology by Claudia for her husband's shameful conduct. The apology is, of course, not sincere, and instead is but a component of the scheme to get the discount. Once having taken the side of the salesperson, the script calls for Claudia to go into her desperate-ingratiating routine to get the discount. The idea is to plant in Simmons's mind the image that Claudia is a wonderful gentle soul that is always suffering from the nastiness of her husband. Here's a chance to help out a battered wife and an overwhelmed mother! If, in the final analysis, it is the false impression created by the "team script" that induces Simmons to give a discount he would not otherwise give, the couple compound *lo tahmod* with an infraction of *geneivat da'at*.

THWARTING THE TELEMARKETER

In the opening vignette, Mark Besser describes various tactics he uses to end a telemarketer call quickly. There can be no doubt that the telemarketer's cold call amounts to an invasion of Besser's privacy, and Mark therefore has no duty to hear out the telemarketer. Bolstering this judgment is that since 1991 the recipient of a telemarketer call has had the legal right to disconnect the telemarketer in the future by demanding to be put on a "do not call" list.[27] Interrupting the telemarketer and demanding that he should be put on the "do not call" list efficiently accomplishes for Besser the dual goals of minimizing the current invasion of privacy he suffers and ensuring that the invasion of privacy will not be repeated in the future. The tactics Besser describes generally go beyond these goals and are designed to induce the telemarketers to quit their jobs or at least hang up on him.

What is at issue here is identifying the legitimate boundary for exercising one's entitlements. Perhaps most fundamental here is the minimum harm rule for self-defense. This principle states that if *A* seeks to harm *B*, *B* may take action to avoid this harm but must do so in a manner that minimizes harm to *A*.

Let's explicate the minimum harm principle with the prototype case, called the *rodef* case. In this case *H* pursues (*rodef*) *V* with the intent to kill him. Here, everyone is duty bound to save *V* from being killed, even to the extent of killing *H*. Now, if the threat to *V* can be neutralized by means less drastic than killing *H*, the lesser means must be utilized.[28] If a rescuer (*R*) kills *H*, when it is evident that he could have affected the rescue by applying less than lethal force to *H*, *R* is put to death on account of taking *H*'s life.[29] This principle is called *yakhol le-haziloh be-ahad ma-avorov* (literally, he could have saved him [the victim] with one of his [the pursuer's] limbs; henceforth, *yakhol le-hazilo*). Note that the Talmud calls for, if possible, the issuance of a warning to *H* to desist.[30] Some authorities take the warning to desist requirement to be an application of the principle of *yakhol le-hazilo*.[31]

Perhaps the mandate of *yakhol le-hazilo* applies only to a bystander. But, as far as the would-be victim is concerned, consider that he is engulfed in a life and death struggle with the perpetrator. We should therefore have no right to expect him to have the presence of mind to remove the threat against his life with anything less than lethal force. R. Isaac b. Sheshet Perfet (Spain, 1325–1408) invokes this line of reasoning to exempt the would-be victim from any duty to warn the *rodef* to desist before taking action to defend himself.[32] By logical extension, argues R. Judah Rosanes (Turkey, 1657–1727), the same line of reasoning should be used to exempt the would-be victim from the *yakol le-hazilo* requirement.[33] Other authorities that take this line are R. Eliyahu Mizrahi (*Tur*key,1440–1525)[34] and R. Mordecai b. Abraham Jaffe (Prague, ca. 1535–1612).[35] R. Solomon b. Isaac (France, 1040–1105)[36] and R. Meir b. Todros ha-Levi Abulafia (Spain, ca. 1170–1244)[37], however, lump together the bystander and the would-be victim. In his analysis of the issue of *yakhol le-hazilo*, R. Rosen (Israel, contemporary) musters support for Mizrahi's view and proposes that *Rashi's* and Maimonides' comments on this issue can be read to be consistent with *Mizrahi's* view.[38]

The principle of restraint in self-defense applies, according to R. Asher b. Jehiel (Germany, 1250–1327), not only to a case where the victim faces a potentially lethal threat, but also to a simple assault case. In this regard, R. Asher rules that if *A* assaults *V*, *V* may respond only with the minimum force necessary to neutralize the threat he faces. If *V* responds with more force than is necessary, *V* becomes liable for his attack no less than *A* bears responsibility for initiating the attack on *V*. The principle that informs *V*'s liability in the latter case, according to R. Asher, is the *yakhol le-hazilo* principle.[39]

We take it as a given that the minimum harm principle is a rule of conduct for any victim regardless of the type of harm he faces, whether it is monetary, bodily injury, or abuse. Recall the opinion in the prototype *rodef* case that the *yakhol le-hazilo* constraint applies only to a bystander who assumes the role of rescuer, but not to the would-be victim himself. Would this school of thought suspend the minimum harm rule for the victim himself regardless of the type of harm he faces? No. Recall that the rationale for suspending the *yakhol le-hazilo* protocol is the recognition that a would-be victim lacks the presence of mind to operate on the level of rationality to use just enough force to neutralize the threat. Suspension of *yakhol le-hazilo* is understandable, therefore, only when the would-be victim finds himself engulfed in a life and death struggle. But, when the situation confronting the victim is not even remotely life threatening, we expect the victim to have the presence of mind to neutralize the threat he faces by means of the method that will exert the least harm to the one who unlawfully threatens his interests.

The operativeness of the *yakhol le-hazilo* constraint for the victim when the attack he faces entails no lethal threat to him whatsoever, either directly or indirectly, can be seen from a point in law relating to *avid inish dinai l'nafshai* (literally, a man may enforce the law for himself; henceforth *avid inish dina*): *H*'s ox attacks *V*'s ox and lodges itself on top of *V*'s ox. Two options are open to *V* to save his ox from injury. One possibility is for *V* to pull away his own ox. Another possibility is to push away *H*'s ox. The latter stratagem is clearly potentially more damaging for *H*. In this situation *V* is entitled to enforce the law for himself and take action to rescue his animal from injury. But, *V* is expected to use the least harmful method from the perspective of *H*. Accordingly, suppose *V* rescues his animal by pushing away *H*'s animal and as a result *H*'s animal is killed. *V* bears responsibility for the loss.[40]

At this juncture, let's note that the type of monetary loss *V* faces depends on the past record of the aggressor ox. *H*'s ox can be categorized as either a *tam* (literally, ordinary) or *mu'ad* (literally, forewarned). The first three times the ox gores it is called a *tam*. The liability of the owner is limited to a responsibility to make good for only one half the damage inflicted. This sum is collectible only from the asset of the goring ox itself. If a bull gores three times and the owner was duly warned after each incident, the owner must pay full damage for the fourth and all subsequent incidents. The law that makes *V* responsible for the death of *H*'s ox if *V* pushed away *H*'s ox instead of pulling away his own ox makes no distinction whether the aggressor ox is a *tam* or *mu'ad*. What this lack of distinction in law between the two cases shows, according to R. Solomon b. Abraham Adret (Spain, ca. 1235–1310), is that the owner of the lower ox is expected to think calmly and save his animal by means of the method that entails the least potential damage for the owner of the upper ox. Rescuing his animal by means of pushing away the upper animal therefore makes *V* liable for the upper animal's death.[41]

What can be generalized from the *avid inish dina* case is that the *yakhol le-hazilo* protocol is operative even for the victim, provided that the detriment the victim faces entails no threat whatsoever to his life.

Let's now apply the minimum harm self-defense doctrine to how Mark Besser should handle the cold call from a telemarketer. Since Besser has no duty to hear out the telemarketer, cutting him off and insisting that he be put on the "do not call" list is no more than exercising his legitimate rights. To be sure, such treatment will faze the telemarketer and cause him mental anguish, but this response is a minimum self-defense response and hence does not violate for Besser the *ona'at devarim* interdict.

Recent federal legislation has changed what constitutes the minimum self-defense response to a telemarketer. On June 27, 2003, the Federal Trade Commission launched a national do not call registry. Telemarketers who call listed people could be fined up to $11,000 for each violation. Not all telemarketing is covered by these rules. Polling, surveys, and calls from political and charitable organizations are exempt. In addition, the rules allow calls from firms with existing business relations with consumers.[42] Now, if Besser is certain that he does not want any contact whatsoever with telemarketers, his minimum self-defense strategy consists of registering, in advance of receiving any calls, on the national do not call list. Waiting to receive a telemarketer's call and only then demanding to be put on the do not call list violates the minimum defense principle because registration avoids the unpleasant encounter with the telemarketer altogether.

BLUFFING TO SUE THE TELEMARKETER

The significant number of complaints governmental bodies receive that telemarketers are ignoring their own do not call lists makes for the judgment that for Besser to just request the cold caller to put his name on the do not call list is not always sufficient to stop future calls by the same telemarketer. Accordingly, Besser may legitimately feel that he needs an "additional edge" to ensure that the telemarketer will actually abide by his wishes and not call again. Consider that under current Federal statute, if a telemarketer calls Besser after he has requested the company to place him on its own do not call list, Besser has the right to sue in small claims court for actual monetary damages or $500 per violation (whichever is greater). Suing a telemarketer for ignoring its do not call list may entail for Besser a significant opportunity cost in terms of both time and out-of-pocket expense. Given Besser's right to stop an unwanted cold call, is it permissible for him to bluff the telemarketer with an idle threat to sue if the unwanted call is repeated? Making a commitment to do something with no intention to carry it out is ordinarily unethical conduct. Such conduct violates Abaya's (4th century) dictum of *hin tzedek* (literally, [Your] yes [should be] righteous).[43] But, in the case at hand, Besser's bluff is intended only to thwart unethical conduct toward him.

An analogous case involves the hiring of a worker to perform a task that requires immediate attention on the part of the worker. If the worker abandons the work before completion the employer will suffer material loss. These circumstances are referred to in the Talmud as the *davar ha-avud* (literally, something is lost) case. In the *davar ha-avud* case, the employer has the right to cajole the reneging worker to stay on the job by offering him a raise. If the tactic succeeds, the employer bears no responsibility to make good on his promise for a raise. Moreover, if the worker demands the extra fee up front, the differential pay is recoverable in a *Bet Din* (Jewish Court). This tactic is referred to as *mat'an* (literally, he deceives them).[44] Likewise in the case at hand. Since Besser's bluff to sue is directed only to thwart the telemarketer from violating his privacy, which is protected by the federal statute, bluffing the telemarketer with the aim only that the telemarketer should not call again does not constitute unethical conduct.

Mocking the Telemarketer

Clearly falling outside the pale of minimum harm self-defensive conduct is Besser's prank to waste the time and aggravate the telemarketer by either initially feigning interest in the product or engaging in deliberately idle conversation. Because the conduct exceeds the boundaries of reasonable self-defense, Besser is guilty of causing needless mental anguish and violates *ona'at devarim*. Taking *ona'at devarim* to a more blatant level of violation is Besser's conduct of mocking the telemarketer to the point that his caller hangs up on him.

The Cold Call Entailing *Ona'at Devarim*

An essential component in making the case that the telemarketer is entitled to be treated with a minimum harm self-defense response is that, provided the call is placed at a reasonable hour, there is nothing unethical about making the cold call. The case for the minimum self-defense response is hence predicated on the dual premises that there is nothing unethical about making the call, but, at the same time, there is nothing unethical about the recipient handling the call in a manner that will ensure that both the conversation is as short as possible and the call is not made again.

The aforementioned holds true if the telemarketer calls between 8 A.M. and 9 P.M. But suppose the telemarketer calls at a time that is outside this

window. Within the current legal environment, federal law prohibits telemarketers to call outside the 8 A.M.–9 P.M. window, and some states have
legislation pending that would forbid calls during the dinner hour, 5–7
P.M.[45] Given the illegality of telemarketing calls outside the 8 A.M.–9 P.M.
window, a telemarketing call placed in this illegal time window should
inherently be regarded as an abuse of the recipient and hence be treated as
a violation by the telemarketer of the *ona'at devarim* interdict. If the cold
call is inherently a violation of *ona'at devarim*, is the recipient still bound
by the minimum harm self-defense? Relevant here is the following ruling of
R. Pinhas ha-Levi (Barcelona, 1235–1300) in respect to the ethics for *V* to
insult *H* in response to *H's* initial insult of him. In the opinion of R. Pinhas
ha-Levi, *V* violates *ona'at devarim* only if he *initiates* an insult to *H*. But, in
the instance where *H* insults *V*, the Torah does not expect *V* to react with
silence and be ". . . a stone that has no one to turn it over." Instead, *V may*
save himself ". . . from the words of the other's mouth which is filled with
cunning and deceit, with every means by which he can rescue himself."[46]

Analogously, if Besser receives a telemarketer call outside the
8 A.M.–9 P.M. window, he would not be ethically at fault if he either hung up
on the telemarketer or expressed outrage for receiving a call at an unreasonable hour.

From the standpoint of conducting oneself with the highest standards of
piety, the curt responses just described apparently meet only an acceptable
behavioral standard, but fall short of the ideal in piety. Consider that in the
instance where H initiates an insult to *V*, the ideal for *V*, according to
R. Pinhas ha-Levi, is not to get upset and lash out at *H*. Instead, it is praiseworthy for *V* to hear his disgrace and not reply.[47]

Besser's ideal response to a telemarketer that calls outside the reasonable time window should not, however, be derived from R. *Pinhas* ha-Levi's
case. To be sure, silence is the admirable response for *V* when the pain *H*
inflicts on him is directed at and confined to him alone. It is quite a different matter when Besser receives a call from a telemarketer at 5 A.M. The call
Besser receives at this unreasonable hour should not be viewed as an isolated incident, but rather as reflecting industry practice. Because the harm
Besser experiences will affect others as well, silence is not an option here.
Besser must do his share to ensure that this practice will be stopped. The
proper reaction is therefore to speak to the telemarketer's supervisor and

vigorously protest the practice and, at the same time, report the infraction to the appropriate regulatory body.

REVENGE AND GRUDGE BEARING AGAINST THE TELEMARKETER

Besser's response to the 5 A.M. telemarketer call went considerably beyond berating the supervisor for the practice and reporting the infraction to the appropriate regulatory authorities. Besser set out to take revenge on the policy makers of the firm that bear ultimate responsibility for the pain he experienced. Toward this end, Besser hunted down the personal telephone numbers of the culprits and called each at 5 A.M. to ask them whether they used the company's chemical treatment product on their own lawns. Besser's tit for tat response raises the issue of whether he violated the biblical infraction against revenge: "You shall not take revenge (*lo tekom*) . . ." (Leviticus 19:18).

The prototype case of *lo tekom* is elucidated in the Talmud as follows:

[B] said to [L], – "lend me your sickle, and – [L] said to [B], " No." – The next day, – [L] Said to [B], – "Lend me your hatchet," and – [B] said to [L], – "I am not lending it to you – just as you did not lend me your sickle." – This is taking revenge.[48]

Nahmanides (Spain, 1194–1270) takes note that the salient feature of the prototype case of *lo tekom* speaks of the instance where *A* has no monetary duty to *B*. But, suppose *A* owed *B* money, caused him damage, or stole something from him. *B* has every right to seek satisfaction of his legitimate claim against *A*. Doing so is not a violation of *lo tekom*.[49]

What proceeds from Nahmanides is that Besser's stratagem of cutting off the telemarketer and requesting that his number (Besser's) be put on the "do not call" list does not raise an issue of *lo tekom*. Such conduct amounts to no more than the pursuit of his legitimate rights. But, hunting down the personal telephone numbers of the culprits and calling each at 5 A.M. to ask them whether they used the company product on their own lawns violates *lo tekom*.

Another objectionable aspect of Besser's conduct is his attitude. Besser's actions are not driven entirely by a desire to protect his and other people's privacy rights. Mixed into Besser's motivation is a desire for revenge. Besser is in violation of the biblical prohibition against bearing a grudge: "... [Y]ou shall not bear a grudge (*lo tittor*) against the members of your people" (Leviticus 19:18). *Rambam* formulates *lo tittor* in the following manner:

> [W]hat is bearing a grudge? Reuben says to Shimon: Rent me this house or lend me this ox and Shimon refuses. Subsequently, Shimon comes to Reuben to borrow or rent from him and Reuben replies: Here it is, I am willing to lend you; I am not like you, I shall not pay you back in your own coin. Whoever behaves like this is guilty of violating the prohibition of "You shall not bear a grudge." But he should eradicate the matter from his heart and not harbor a grudge. For so long as he harbors a grudge and remembers it, he is in danger of taking vengeance.[50]

Note that Maimonides understands *lo tittor* not only to prohibit Reuben from engaging in "I'm not like you" conduct vis-à-vis Shimon, but also to prohibit Reuben from guarding the resentment he has against Shimon. Instead, Reuben should "eradicate the resentment from his heart." What can be inferred from Maimonides, avers R. Avrohom Ehrman (Israel, contemp.), is that there is no moral objection against Reuben's initial feeling of resentment against Shimon. This is so because it is only a normal human reaction for Reuben to resent Shimon for rebuffing him in his request for a favor. Since the Torah never legislates on involuntary feelings, the spontaneous feeling of resentment that Reuben has for Shimon cannot be prohibited. But, on matters that depend on the free will the Torah does legislate. Accordingly, what *lo tittor* prohibits is for Reuben to guard or harbor his resentment against Shimon. Instead of fostering the resentment he has for Shimon, Reuben should take action to eradicate the ill feeling he has for Shimon.[51]

Maimonides' dictum speaks directly to Besser. At first, it offers him solace. Specifically, Besser should not be criticized for his initial feeling to take revenge on the policy makers responsible for his getting the 5 A.M. call. Given the outlandish hour of the call, the smoldering feelings for revenge that lodge within his heart are understandable and he therefore bears no moral blame for them. However, getting his revenge by actually calling the policy makers of the telemarketing firm at 5 A.M. violates *lo tekom*. But, to carry out his tit for tat plan Besser must expend much time and energy to unearth the names and home telephone numbers he needs. Suppose Besser never gets the information he needs. Because he does not implement the plan Besser is free of *lo tekom*. Notwithstanding the failure of the plan, Besser is guilty of guarding his grudge while he desperately scampers about for the information he needs. Besser is therefore guilty of keeping alive and even possibly magnifying his initial feeling for revenge, and is hence guilty of *lo tittor*. As a means of extricating himself from *lo tittor*, Besser should abandon his original plan of revenge and instead resolve that he will take action only to exercise his legitimate rights. The minute Besser abandons the plan of revenge and moves in the direction of asserting his rights with a minimum harm self-defense strategy, Besser fulfills Maimonides' mandate of "eradicating the resentment from his heart."

YOU GOT "RIPPED OFF" AND PRICE FRAUD (*ONA'AH*)

In the opening vignette, Mark Besser reacts to Sidney Oak's recounting of a satisfying experience with Identity Shield by telling Oak that he was ripped off. Why pay $35 for an audiocassette on how to prevent identity theft when the FTC publishes the same information free? Besser's diatribe presents two issues. One issue is the ethics of charging any price whatsoever for the audiocassette when the information it conveys is available free elsewhere. If charging a price is legitimate, then the second issue of fair pricing comes to the fore.

We begin with the recognition that Besser's assessment that "you were ripped off" is valid only for those who are well read and sophisticated in the art of information gathering. Such a person will not need a call from a telemarketer to convince him that he is vulnerable to identity theft. Moreover, such a person will also be already somewhat familiar with the information Identity Shield seeks to sell or at least knows that the relevant information can be obtained free from any a number of sources. Consequently, this category of person will not take up Identity Shield on its offer in the first place. But, for the person who is not aware of the serious problem of identity theft, Identity Shield provides a definite benefit. The benefit consists of showing the person that he needs the information on how to prevent identity theft. The analogue here is the matchmaker (*shadhan*) and the commercial broker (*sirsur*). Identity Shield is an information broker. Its service is to persuade the customer that he needs information on how to prevent identity theft, and then it goes on to offer access to that information in a palatable form. The service Identity Shield provides goes beyond the minimum criterion Halakhah (Jewish law) sets for a *shadhan* or a *sirsur* to be entitled to a fee. Let's examine this criterion and relate it to Identity Shield.

Perhaps the most fundamental point to be made is that the *sirsur* earns his fee for recommending to either a buyer (*B*) or seller (*S*) a counterpart for his transaction. If it is, however, assessed that the recommended counterpart is so obvious that *S* or *B* would have made their connection without the *sirsur*'s efforts, the *sirsur* is not entitled to any fee.[52]

To get his fee the *sirsur* need not have been commissioned by one of the principals to pursue the deal. His services are analogous to the one who enters a neighbor's field and plants it without permission. If the field is suitable for planting the planter is entitled to the customary wages of a contracted planter.[53] The *sirsur*'s fee is hence rooted in the certainty that his service is a definite benefit (worth money) for the parties involved.

It should be noted that the fee the *sirsur* earns is for the connection he makes, and is not predicated on the provision of any minimal amount of toil and effort to push the deal through. Demonstrating this is the allocation of the *sirsur* fee when a number of brokers are involved in making the transaction happen. Here, the lion's share of the *sirsur* fee goes to the person whose efforts bring the transaction to a successful conclusion. This person is called the *gomer* (closer). Also due a part of the *sirsur* fee is the *mathil*, (the person who gets the transaction started). The *mathil* is entitled to his fee even if the principals cut him off immediately and work out all the details themselves. Exerting the smallest claim for a portion of the *sirsur*'s fee is the person who is neither *mathil* nor *gomer*, but, nevertheless, expended toil and effort to move the transaction forward.[54]

What proceeds from this discussion of the law of *sirsur* is that Identity Shield is entitled to charge Oak for its audiocassette on how to prevent identity theft even though the information the cassette conveys is available free from the FTC. Absent the call from Arrow, Oak would not seek out this information on his own nor would this information fall into his hands. Identity Shield's *sirsur* service consists, therefore, in persuading Oak that he has a need for this information.

Let's now turn to the issue of fair pricing. For the purpose of exposition simplicity we will initially assume that Identity Shield's product consists not of an audiocassette, but rather a copy of the FTC booklet. In assessing the "fairness" of Identity Shield's price of $35, the relevant legal principle here is the law of *ona'ah* (price fraud). The law of *ona'ah* prohibits an individual from concluding a transaction at a price that is more favorable to him than the competitive norm. Depending on how widely the price of the subject transaction departs from the competitive norm, the injured party may have recourse to void or adjust the transaction.[55]

In applying the law of *ona'ah* to the case at hand, consider that Identity Shield incurs no expense other than postage and handling in connection with the FTC booklet it sends out. Its charge therefore is almost entirely for its *sirsur* service of convincing customers that they need the information on how to prevent identity fraud. Identity Shield's profit therefore amounts to a return on the owner's labor services, consisting of the research they did to conceive the business plan and the time they put into training the telemarketers on how to convince customers that they need the information on how to prevent identity fraud. The issue of "fair" pricing for the case at hand, then, turns on whether the law of *ona'ah* applies to the price of labor services.

Before relating the law of *ona'ah* to the labor market, we take note that Halakhah classifies a worker as either a per-diem worker (*po'el*) or a piece-worker (kabbelan). What distinguishes the *po'el* from the *kabbelan* is the provision for fixed working hours. Whereas the *po'el*'s contract obligates him to perform work for his employer at specified hours over a given period of time, no such clause is included in the *kabbelan's* agreement.[56] Given the controlling nature of the fixed-hour factor, the absence of this provision retains *kabbelan* status for an employee even when her contract calls for her to complete the project by a specified date.[57]

In his treatment of the law of *ona'ah* as it pertains to the labor market, *Rambam* rules that *ona'ah* applies only to a *kabbelan* and not to a *po'el*.[58]

Proceeding from the above discussion is that the law of *ona'ah* should theoretically govern the pricing policy of Identity Shield. To be sure, the company is essentially selling a *sirsur* service, but it does not fall into the category of *po'el*. The return on the owner's "toil and effort" that is factored into the price Identity Shield charges for its audiocassette is a finished output at the juncture when the firm's telemarketers call potential customers and therefore should be regarded as the sale of *kabbelan* labor services to the public.

Although Identity Shield's pricing policy is theoretically governed by the law *ona'ah*, it must be recognized that the reference price in an *ona'ah* claim is the competitive norm. If Identity Shield is the only firm that performs the *sirsur* service of persuading people that they need the information about how to prevent and deal with the problem of identity theft, then Identity Shield enjoys monopoly status and its pricing policy is not regulated.

A variation of this case occurs when another firm, say, Identity Protection Services, offers the same or a superior product compared to Identity Shield but charges a lower price. Here, Identity Shield is in violation of *ona'ah*. A complication arises when two or more firms are in the industry. Each firm offers a differentiated service and charges a different price. Since a reference price cannot be identified here, an *ona'ah* claim is not honored.

IDENTIFYING THE COMPETITIVE PRICE WHEN NOT-FOR-PROFIT FIRMS ARE IN THE INDUSTRY

Suppose not-for-profit companies are reaching out and actively educating the public on the problem of identity theft. Other firms hence provide *gratis* the same *sirsur* service performed by Identity Shield. Does this make the reference price for Identity Shield's service a zero price and make it unlawful for Identity Shield to charge any price for its audiocassette?

The issue, as it appears to this writer, turns on whether a zero, and for that matter, a below market price, can serve as the reference price in an *ona'ah* claim. Elsewhere, we have shown that the reference price in an *ona'ah* claim is the price the marketplace commands for the item in question. Accordingly, a discount price, whether it is rooted in an investment or philanthropic motive, does not serve as a reference price in an *ona'ah* claim.[59] Objecting to Identity Shield's $35 fee based on the circumstance that other entities are actively promoting public awareness of the problem of identity theft and charging no fee for this service does not automatically delegitimize Identity Shield's fee. Calling the fee into question would have to be based on evidence that public awareness of the problem of identity theft was so pervasive that Oak would have easily picked up that he has a "need" for the information to prevent identity theft without the call from Identity Shield.

DOUBLE DIPPING ON THE *SIRSUR* FEE

One final variant. Let's use the opening vignette to illustrate it. Recall Identity Shield's audiocassette recommended Oak pay the company $45 up front to arrange to have three monthly credit reports sent to him. In this aspect of its business, Identity Shield is guilty of a "rip off." The company is "double dipping" on its *sirsur* fee. Consider that Identity Shield has already collected a *sirsur* fee of $35 from Oak. To be sure, the legitimacy for collecting this fee is compensation for convincing Oak that he needs information on how to prevent identity theft. But, Oak is also paying the fee to actually get the information he needs on what he should do to prevent identity theft. Once Oak receives the audiocassette, he should be viewed as actively searching the marketplace to get the best deal on purchasing his own credit report. Given that Oak could order the credit reports directly from one of the three credit bureaus at a cost of, say, $9 per report (the first report is free), the audiocassette's advice to buy the credit reports through Identity Shield for a $45 upfront fee is decidedly ill-suited advice and violates for Identity Shield the prohibition against proffering ill-suited advice (*lifnei iver*).[60] Since Identity Shield has already collected a *sirsur* fee for advising Oak that one of the things he needs to do to prevent identity theft is to obtain his credit reports, the company has no right to charge a second fee for the same advice again. Accordingly, any price Identity Shield charges above the price that was available to Oak by obtaining the credit reports directly from any of the credit bureaus should be governed by the law of *ona'ah*.

EXPLOITING THE TELEMARKETER

The law of *sirsur* provides the backdrop for a moral dilemma entailing exploiting the telelemarketer by making use of the information he offers and not compensating him for it. A variation on the opening vignette illustrates this dilemma. Suppose that Oak in the course of his conversation with Arrow experiences a rude awakening and realizes that he indeed is very vulnerable to becoming a victim of identity theft and therefore needs the information to prevent it. But, why take Arrow up on his offer when the information Oak needs can probably be obtained free of charge by visiting the FTC's

Web site and surfing the Net for articles in the popular literature on identity theft? To exploit the valuable insight regarding vulnerability Arrow gave
him, Oak thanks Arrow for his time and for the information he provided him
and politely tells him that he does not want to take up Identity Shield's offer.
Oak then proceeds to research the information he needs, which entails no
out of pocket expense. Does Oak owe Identity Shield anything for the information imparted?

R. Jehiel Michel Epstein (Belarus, 1829–1908) dealt with a similar
case: S is in the market to sell his house. A_1 offers S his *sirsur* services to
induce B to buy the house. S refuses A_1's offer, giving A_1 various excuses why
he does not want to deal with B. S then proceeds to pursue B on his own as
a customer to buy his home and concludes the deal without the benefit of a
sirsur. Alternatively, S enlists the *sirsur* services of A_2 to make a deal with B
for the sale of his home. In both these instances S owes A_1 the *sirsur* fee due
a *mathil*. Moreover, suppose A_1's suggestion makes S resolve immediately to
sell his home to B, but he pushes off A_1 because he sees an opportunity to
get his friend A_2 involved in the deal as a *sirsur*. S prefers to have A_2 conclude the deal and have A_2 collect the lion's share of the *sirsur* fee as the
gomer. In this scenario S owes A_1 the entire *sirsur* fee. Nonetheless, if S
insists that the excuses he offered A_1 as to why he did not want to sell his
house to B were truthful at the time and circumstances forced him to recon-
sider and sell to B through a different *sirsur*, A_1 will not have recourse in a
Bet Din to collect more than the fee of a *mathil*. Moreover, *Bet Din* will not
even require S to affirm his side of the story by means of oath. Nonetheless,
if A_1's assertion is true, S is morally obligated to pay A_1 the entire *sirsur* fee.[61]

R. Epstein's ruling finds ready application to the case at hand. There
can be no doubt that Arrow's insight on vulnerability and the statistic he
provided on the average cost of fixing an identity theft problem is valuable
information for Oak. Being persuaded that he has a need for the information
is a benefit worth money to Oak. Accordingly, as soon as Oak resolves to *get*
the information on how to prevent identity theft, he owes Identity Shield a
sirsur fee. To be sure, Arrow is hawking the audiocassette and not a *sirsur*
service. But, recall that a *sirsur* earns a fee for providing a definite benefit
and he is entitled to that fee even if he was not commissioned in advance to
perform the service. Oak therefore owes Identity Shield the value of the service he received. But, how do we calculate the value of this fee? If there is

an organized market in respect to persuading people that they need information on how to prevent identity theft, the competitive fee for this service will reflect supply relative to demand forces. Because the competitive fee reflects the interaction of market forces, the norm would neither equal the maximum sum someone would pay for this benefit nor the minimum fee someone would demand to provide this service. Instead, the competitive norm would be somewhere in between these two values. In the case at hand, there is no competitive norm to refer to. Accordingly, the fee must be set equal to the *minimum* price Identity Shield would charge for tying up a telemarketer for, say, the ten minutes Arrow spent with Oak. This amounts to no more than the pro-rated hourly wage Identity Shield pays its telemarketers. For argument sake let's assume that this amounts to $2.

Once it is recognized that Oak owes Identity Shield $2 for their *sirsur* service, Oak cannot get away with just thanking Arrow for the information and hang up. Instead, Oak should say, "Thanks for the information. I owe you money for your time. Give me an address."

"YOU GOT RIPPED OFF" AND *ONA'AT DEVARIM*

Irrespective of the ethics of Identity Shield's pricing policy, if Oak can do nothing to cancel or modify the deal he entered into, perhaps Besser's revelation to Oak that he was ripped off amounts to causing Oak needless mental anguish and violates for Besser the *ona'at devarim* interdict. Relevant here is the following Talmudic passage, recorded at *Ketubbot* 17b:

> Our rabbis taught: How does one dance (what does one sing or recite) before the bride? Bet Shammai say: "the bride as she is." And Bet Hillel say: "Beautiful and gracious bride!" But Bet Shammai said to Bet Hillel: "If she was lame or blind, does one say to her: 'Beautiful and gracious bride'? Whereas the Torah said: Distance yourself from falsehood" (Exodus 23:7). Said Bet Hillel to Bet Shammai, "According to your words, if one [*B*] has purchased a "bad purchase" from the marketplace (*ha-shuk*), should one [*F*] praise it in his eyes or deprecate it? Surely [*F*] should praise it in his eyes." Therefore, the sages said: "Always should the disposition of man be pleasant with *ha-beriyyot* [literally, fellow man]."

Talmudic decisors follow Bet Hillel's view.[62] Identifying the parameters of the "bad purchase" case is therefore critical in judging the propriety of Besser telling Oak that his purchase of the audiocassette from Identity Shield was a rip off.

One basic issue for clarification is whether B has recourse to cancel or modify the sale. R. Samuel b. Joseph Strashun (Lithuania, 1794–1872) rejects this possibility. If the "bad purchase" is reversible in some manner on the basis of defect or overprice, lying to B that he did well is ethically wrong. R. Strashun draws support for his thesis by pointing out that the Talmud refers to the "bad purchase" as having come not from any specific seller, but rather from the marketplace (*ha-shuk*). The indication is that B has no recollection from whom he bought the article. Since returning the item to get a refund or adjustment on account of defect or overprice is not open for B, it is permissible for F to lie and praise B for his selection.[63]

Understanding the "bad purchase" case in the same manner as R. Strashun is R. Israel Meir ha-Kohen Kagan (Radin, 1838–1933).[64]

The "bad purchase" case requires further clarification. Perhaps the directive to praise the purchase is limited to the instance where the person who is asked for an opinion, F, is a bystander who is a stranger. Given the reasonableness of the assumption that the two will have no further contact, F's goal should be to help B make the best of his situation. Praising the purchase is therefore the indicated course of action. But, suppose B shows the purchase to a closely connected person such as his parent, spouse, or good friend. Perhaps the response here should be geared with the aim of maximizing B's long-term interest. To be sure, B has no recourse now to fix his mistake, but the purchase manifests irresponsible marketplace conduct on his part. With the aim of setting B straight, the closely connected person should tell the truth. By telling the truth, B will not *repeat* his mistake in the future.

Support for restricting the response of praise for the "bad purchase" case to the instance where F is a stranger can be drawn from the nuance of expression the Talmud chooses to employ in connection with the aphorism it quotes: "Always should the disposition of man be pleasant with *ha-beriyyot* (literally, fellow man)." Note that the Talmud describes the connection between B and F as *beriyyot* (i.e., fellow human beings). Other expressions such as friends (*re'im, haverim*) or neighbors (*shekhenim*) could just as easily have been used. The use of the phrase *ha-beriyyot* indicates that the prototype case for the response of "praise" is the instance where the connection between parties is that they are strangers.

Further support for the above distinction can be seen by an examination of the rationale behind the permissibility for F to lie in the "bad purchase" case. Commentators have offered a number of rationales.[65] We take R. Yom Tov Ishbili's (Seville, ca. 1250–1330) understanding as expressing the mainstream rationale here. In his view, Bet Hillel espouse the *darkhei shalom* (literally, ways of peace) principle.[66] What this principle asserts is that falsehood is legitimate conduct when its purpose is to end conflict and/or to avert the outbreak of discord. But, the ending of what conflict is referred to here? If we take the "bad purchase" case to refer to the instance where B has no recollection of where he bought the item, B's doubts about his purchase are producing ill feeling toward no particular seller. If the *darkhei shalom* principle is invoked here, it must, therefore, refer to ending B's inner torment that he made a bad purchase and hence wasted his money. By telling B that he did well with his purchase, F brings B into a state of inner peace.[67]

Once it is recognized that it is the *darkhei shalom* principle that is the basis for allowing and even recommending F to lie to B and tell him that he did well with his purchase, consideration of the impact of the lie on B's long-term inner peace or welfare must be taken into account. Consider that B's bad purchase may just be a fluke, but, on the other hand, it may manifest irresponsible marketplace conduct. If the latter is the case, then the mistake will be repeated again and again unless it is corrected. What should F make of the mistake? Now, if F is a stranger, why should he be concerned with possible adverse long-term ramifications of his lie? Consider the bad purchase may be nothing but a fluke that will be corrected in the future. Assuming the worst, F should have the right to rely on those that are closely connected to B to take on the responsibility to correct his ways. Consideration of possible adverse effects on B becomes, however, decidedly relevant if F is closely connected to B. Now, if F is B's parent or someone in charge of his guidance or education, responsibility devolves upon that person to set B straight. "Wounds of a lover are faithful, whereas kisses of an enemy are burdensome" (Proverbs 27:6).

Several additional scenarios can be identified: Suppose F is a close friend of B but can reasonably assume that B's parent or teacher will tell him the truth about the purchase at hand. Here, F's false compliment will surely explode in his face. Since *darkhei shalom* does not permit a lie that will be exposed,[68] the close friend has no choice but to tell *B* the truth. Finally, suppose *F* has reason to believe that there is no one around that will straighten out *B*. Here, since *F* has a long term close relationship with *B*, responsibility devolves upon him to do the job. Setting *B* straight involves much more than just criticizing *B* for the purchase he made. Pride may cause *B* to deflect the criticism and focus only on the hurt *F* inflicts on him. If *B* reacts in this way, *F* may very well violate the *ona'at devarim* interdict. Rather, *F* should couple his criticism with a remark like, "That candelabrum is overpriced. Next time you're in the market for a silver item, be sure to check out Zlomowitz and Sander on Eden Commons Boulevard."

Let's now apply the various scenarios of the "bad purchase" case to evaluate the propriety for Besser to pronounce to Oak that he was ripped off. Consider that Oak has no legal recourse to cancel or modify the deal he made with Identity Shield. Accordingly, if Besser is not Oak's close friend, it is permissible for him to nod approvingly at the purchase. If Besser cannot bring himself to do this even in a "feebly polite" way, silence would be the appropriate reaction. Going to the other extreme and telling Oak that he was ripped off and explaining to him exactly why may run afoul of the *ona'at devarim* interdict. This is so because the judgment that Oak's purchase was a rip-off is valid only from the perspective of people like Besser who are well read and sophisticated in the art of comparison shopping. If Oak is neither well-read or sophisticated in the art of comparison shopping, the "overcharge" Oak suffered from the deal he made with Identity Shield cannot be said to reflect irresponsibility in engaging in market search before making a purchase. Because the rip-off is all rooted in Oak's ignorance and lack of sophistication in information gathering, telling him he was ripped off and explaining to him why will serve no useful purpose in the future unless Oak can count on someone to help him in comparison shopping in the future. Besser should ask himself why Oak still thinks he did well with his purchase from Identity Shield a full four months after the purchase. Surely, Besser is not the first one to whom Oak is relating his satisfactory experience with Identity Shield. The reasonable judgment is that no one from Oak's inner circle was prepared to say to him something like the following: "you were ripped off. The next time you want to take up an offer, run it by me. I'll show you how to check it out." Accordingly, unless Besser is willing to couple his criticism of the purchase with an offer of assistance in comparison shopping in the future, his comment: "You were ripped off because . . ." runs afoul of the *ona'at devarim* interdict.

ELEVATING ONE'S SELF AT THE EXPENSE OF SOMEONE ELSE'S DEGRADATION

In voicing his criticism of Oak's purchase, Besser does not content himself in telling Oak he was ripped off and explaining why, but takes Oak's story as an invitation to provide a "matching story" from his own experience. Besser goes on to relate how he and his wife teamed up to masterfully pressure the salesperson at the Child Emporium to give them the best deal possible on a double stroller. By contrasting his own prowess in making a good deal with the rip-off Oak fell into in his deal with Identity Shield, Besser rubs in for Oak the bad purchase more poignantly and hence violates the *ona'at devarim* interdict on an aggravated level. Moreover, the contrast of stories projects Besser's shrewdness in getting the best deal possible in a more flattering light than he would otherwise obtain. *Magnifying* one's self at the expense of someone else's degradation runs afoul of R. Yose b. Hanina's dictum: "Anyone who elevates himself at the expense of his friend's degradation has no share in the world to come (*mitkabbed bi-klon havero ein lo helek l'Olam ha-Ba*)."[69]

SUMMARY AND CONCLUSION

The salient feature of the telemarketing industry is the uninvited or cold call. This feature creates a natural tension between the commercial strivings of the industy's practitioners on the one hand and its targeted customers. The ethical pitfall for the telemarketer is not to fall prey to *lo tahmod, lo tit'avveh*, and *ona'at devarim*. In trying to thwart the designs of the telemarketer, the pitfall for the targeted consumer is not to go beyond the boundaries of the minimum harm principle. At the other extreme, feigning noninterest in the telemarketing product, but all along listening carefully to the information with the aim of using it advantageously, may well deprive the telemarketer of his entitled *sirsur* payment.

From the standpoint of Halakhah, regulation of the telemarketing industry to reduce the inherent tension between the cold callers and the targeted customers is desirable. One favorable development towards this end began in 1985 with the self-regulating initiatives the industry took to maintain "do not call" lists at the request of its customers.[70] Since 1991, federal legislation requires telemarketers to maintain these lists. Within the current legal environment, federal law prohibits telemarketers from calling outside the 8–9 P.M. window, and some states have legislation pending that would forbid calls during the dinner hour, 5–7 P.M.

The most recent development of great significance that should reduce the inherent strain between the telemarketer and the target consumer is the launching of a national do not call registry. The Federal Trade Commission launched this registry on June 27, 2003. Telemarketers who call listed people could be fined up to $11,000 for each violation. The new law does not cover nonprofits, politicians, and survey-taking organizations. In addition, the rules allow calls from firms with existing business relations with consumers. Registration on the national do not call list hence does not stop these firms from calling.

The free service, intended to block most telemarketing calls, grew to more than 10 million phone numbers in the four days following its launch.[71] The FTC reported that in the first year of the operation of the registry more than 62 million telephone numbers were put into the list.[72] There are about 166 million residential phone numbers in the United States.[73]

The telemarketing industry estimates that the do not call list could cut its business in half, costing it up to $50 billion in sales each year.[74] One expert was more optimistic: "consumers who don't sign the national registry may be more responsive to phone pitches."[75] The effect of the new law, then, may be to give the telemarketing industry a radical face-lift and transform it into a "kinder and gentler" industry.

Notes:

1. Perry Bacon Jr., and Eric Rosten, *Time*, vol. 17, No. 17, April 28, 2003, p. 6.
2. Jonathan Krim, "Do Not Call Registry to Begin Today; Industry Faults FTC on Steps to Block Unwanted Telemarketing," *Washington Post*, June 27, 2003, p. E01.
3. Federal Trade Commission, Nov. 2003, "ID Theft: When Bad Things Happen to Your Good Name," http://www.consumer.gov/idtheft/info.htm.
4. http://www.creditnexus.com/index.html.
5. Oak had his doctors replace his social security number with the corresponding Hebrew letters. Just for good measure Oak interchanged each corresponding Hebrew letter with its counterpart in the *at bash gar dak gematria* system.

6. National Fraud Information Center, "Taking Action Against Telemarketers Who Won't Take No for an Answer," http://www.fraud.org/telemarketing/teletips/action.htm.

   On June 27, 2003, the Federal Trade Commission launched a national do not call registry. To register the consumer need only call the toll-free number 1–888–382–1222 or visit the Web site at www.donotcall.gov. Telemarketers who call listed people could be fined up to $11,000 for each violation. (See David Ho, "FTC Launches Do Not Call List," Associated Press, June 27, 2003).

7. Besser got this and other whimsical ideas on how to make telemarketers hang up on you from Mike Quinn, *Telecom-Digest*: vol. 16, No. 130, Message 3 of 6.

8. See note 3.

9. Maimonides, *Yad*, *Gezel* 1:9–10.

10. R. Abraham of Posquieres, at *Yad*, loc.

11. R. Vidal Yom Tov of Toloso, *Maggid Mishneh*, *Yad*, loc.cit.

12. R. Yaakov Yisrael Kanievsky, *Birkat Peretz*, *Parshat Yitro*. With significant additional nuances, R. Michael Rosensweig (*Beit Ytizhak*, Rabbi Isaac Elchanan Theological Seminary, vol. 19, 1987, 215–227) arrives at the same understanding of *Rambam*'s position.

13. The notion that it is possible to violate *lo tahmod* without committing any pestering action whatsoever is a novelty. Consider that *Rambam*'s formulation of *lo tahmod* conduct describes various forms of pressure, e.g., vexing [*hiftsir*]; sending friends to exert influence [*hikhbid alav re'im*]; and increasing one's bid [*natan lo damim rabbim*]. Perhaps, the issue turns on the philosophical underpinning of the *lo tahmod* prohibition. In his explication of *Rambam*'s position on the *lo tahmod* interdict, R. Michael Rosensweig (*Beit Yitzhak*, ad loc.) points out that a number of views on this matter have been expressed. Nahmanides (*Ramban*, Spain, 1194–1270, Leviticus 19:1) avers that the various prescriptions between man and man appearing in *Parsshat Kedoshim* correspond to the Ten Commandments. Along this line, ". . . [Y]ou shall love your fellow as yourself . . ." (Leviticus 19:19) corresponds to the *lo tahmod* interdict. R. Abraham Ibn Ezra (Spain, 1089–1164, Exodus 20:14), however, finds the philosophical roots of the prohibition of *lo tahmod* in the Torah's mandate to be "one who rejoices in his lot." What this entails is to believe that no efforts and maneuvering will be successful in acquiring something God does not want us to have. Now, if *lo tahmod* is rooted in ". . . love your friend as yourself. . . ." then as long as *A* ensures that in the process of acquiring *B*'s article, no one, including himself, pesters *B*, *A* should be free of the *lo tahmod* interdict. But, if the basis of *lo tahmod* is the mandate to be joyous in the lot God gives us, any orchestration *A* sets up to overcome *B*'s initial refusal to sell him the article should violate for *A* *lo tahmod*, notwithstanding that *A* insures that no one pesters *B* along the way.

14. R. Solomon b. Joseph Ganzfried, *Kitzzur Shulhan Arukh* 182:5.

15. R. David Ariav, *Le'Reakha Kamokha* (Jerusalem: Ariav, 2000), pp. 49–50. See also R. Bezalel Sthern, *Be-zel ha-Hokhmah*, 3:45.

16. R. Israel Meir ha-Kohen Kagan, *Ha-Mitzvot ha-Katsar*, *lo ta'asseh* 40.

17. R. Yaakov Yesha'yahu Bloi, *Pithe Hoshen*, *Hilkhot Geneivah ve-Ona'ah*, p. 30, note 26. See also *Le-Reakha Kamokha*, op. cit., pp. 48–49.

18. R. David Ariov dealt with an analogous case: *A* makes use of high pressure tactics to convince *B* to sell his home to *C*. *C* is entirely unaware of *A*'s efforts on his behalf. In addition, *A* concludes the transaction with *C*'s money. Given that *A* is not exerting high

pressure tactics to acquire the home for *himself*, *A*, in the opinion of R. Ariov, does not violate *lo tahmod*. Because *C* is entirely unaware of what A is doing on his behalf, *C* also is not in violation of *lo tahmod*. (See, *Le'Reakha Kamokha*, op. cit. p. 61). R. Ariov's conclusion can be put to question. To be sure, A is free of *lo tahmod*. But, if *B* did not declare *rotzei ani* at the conclusion of the transaction, the transaction must be characterized as *gezel*, with the consequence that *C* has no right to take possession of the home.

19. *Mishnah, Bava Metzia* 4:10; R. Isaac b. Jacob Alfasi (Algeria, 1012–1103), *Rif, Bava Metzia* 4:10; R. Asher b. Jehiel (Germany, 1250–1327), *Rosh, Bava Metzia* 4:22; R. Jacob b. Asher (Germany, 1270–1343), *Tur, Hoshen Mishpat.*, 228:3; R. Joseph Caro (Israel, 1488–1575), *Shulhan Arukh, Hoshen Mishpat* 228:4; R. Jehiel Michel Epstein, (Belarus, 1829–1908), *Arukh ha-Shulhan, Hoshen Mishpat* 228:2.

20. *Mekhilta* Exodus 180:22.

21. R. Bezalel Sthern, *Be-zel ha-Hokhmah* 3:43.

22. Leviticus 25:35; Deuteronomy 15 7–8, 10. In respect to agricultural produce, the Torah prescribes a ten percent obligation (Deuteronomy 14:22). Talmudic decisors differ as to whether the ten percent benchmark applies to income as well. Opinions in the matter range from an income tithe requirement arising from biblical law to one established by rabbinical edict. In his survey of the Responsa literature, R. Ezra Basri concludes that the majority opinion regards the ten percent level as a definite obligation, albeit by dint of rabbinical decree. In any case, devoting less than ten percent of one's income to charity is considered by the rabbis to reflect an ungenerous nature. (R. Ezra Basri, *Dinei Mamonot* vol. 1, p. 405).

23. The distinction between persuasion and coercion made in the text is taken from Paul Heyne, *The Economic Way*, 6th ed. (New York: Macmillan, 1991), p. 367.

24. *Shabbat* 119b.

25. R. Jonah b. Abraham Gerondi (Spain, ca. 1200–1264), *Sharei Teshuvah, sha'ar* 3; R. Israel Meir ha-Kohen Kagan, *Sefat Tamim*; R.Hillel Litwack, *M'Devar Sheker Tirhak*, p. 47.

26. The biblical source of the *geneivat da'at* interdict is disputed by Talmudic decisors. Maimonides (*Yad*, De'ot 2:6) and R. Jonah b. Abraham Gerondi (*Sha'arei Teshuvah, sha'ar* 3, ot 184) place such conduct under the rubric of falsehood (*sheker*). R. Yom Tov Ishbili (Seville, ca. 1250–1330, *Ritvah, Hullin* 94a), however, subsumes it under the Torah's admonition against theft (*lo tignovu*, Leviticus 19:11). What *lo tignovu* enjoins is both theft of property and "theft of the mind" by means of deception.

27. Federal Telephone Consumer Protection Act, Public Law 102–243.

28. R. Yonatan b. Shaul, *Sanhedrin* 74a; *Yad, Rotzeah* 1:7; *Rosh, Sanhedrin* 8:1; *Sh. Ar.*, op. cit., 425:1; *Ar. ha-Sh.*, op. cit., 425:6.

29. R. Yonatan b. Shaul, loc. cit.; *Rosh*, op. cit.; *Sh. Ar.*, op. cit.; *Ar. ha-Sh.*, op. cit. Maimonides (*Yad*, op. cit. 1:13) understands the punishment to be "in the hands of Heaven," as opposed to being meted out by *Bet Din*. For an explanation of Maimonides' view, see *Ar. ha-Sh.*, loc. cit.

30. *Sanhedrin* 72b.

31. R. *Pinhas* ha-Levi (Barcelona, 1235–1300), *Sefer ha-Hinnukh* 601; R. Joseph Rozin (Poland, 1854–1936), *Tzafenat Pa'ne'ah, Sanhedrin* 72b.

32. R. Isaac b. Sheshet Perfet, Responsa *Ribash* 238.

33. R. Judah Rosanes, *Mishneh le-Melekh* at *Yad, Hovel U-Mazzik* 8:10.

34. R. Eliyahu Mizrahi, *Mizrahi*, Genesis 32:8.

35. R. Mordecai b. Abraham Jaffe, *Levush*, Genesis 32:8.

36. R. Solomon b. Isaac, *Rashi, Sanhedrin* 57a, 74a.

37. R. Meir b. Todros ha-Levi Abulafia, *Ramah, Sanhedrin* 57a.

38. R. Israel Rosen, "Killing a Pursuer in Self-Defense," *Tehumim*, vol.10, pp. 76–89.

39. R. Asher b. Jehiel, *Bava Kamma* 3:13.

40. *Bava Kamma* 28a; *Yad, Hovel u-Mazzik* 6:6–7; *Tur*, op. cit., 382:2; *Sh. Ar.*, op. cit., 382:2; *Ar. ha-Sh.*,op. cit., 383:6.

41. R. Solomon b. Abraham Adret, *Rashba, Bava Kamma* 28a.

42. "Do Not Call Registry to Begin Today; Industry Faults FTC on Steps to Block Unwanted Telemarketing," op. cit., E1.

43. Abaya derives his prohibition against making an insincere promise at *Bava Metzia* 49a in the following manner: In connection with the biblical prohibition against false weights and measures, the Torah writes: "Just (*tzedek*) balances, just weights, a just *ephah*, and a just *hin* you shall have" (Leviticus 19:36). Since the *hin* is a measure of smaller capacity than the *ephah*, its mention is apparently superfluous. If accuracy is required of a large capacity, it is certainly required in measures of small capacity. This apparent superfluity leads Abaya to connect *hin* with the Aramaic word for "yes," *hen*, giving the phrase the following interpretation: Be certain that your "yes" is *tzedek* [sincere] and [by extension] be certain that your "no" is *tzedek* [sincere]. If an individual makes a commitment or an offer, he should fully intend to carry it out. The duty to ensure that a commitment is made in a sincere manner is referred to as the *hin tzedek* imperative.

44. *Rosh*, op. cit., *Yad*, op cit., *Tur*, op. cit., *Sh. Ar.*, op. cit; *Ar. ha-Sh.*, op. cit., 333:19.

45. "Telemarketers Face Pressure, Do Not Call Lists Put Jobs at Risk", The Morning Call, October 20, 2002, http://www.gryphonnetworks.com/press/articles/2002 10 20.asp.

46. R. Pinhas ha-Levi of Barcelona, *Sefer ha-Hinnukh* 338.

47. *Sefer ha-Hinnukh*, op. cit., 338.

48. *Yoma* 23a.

49. Nahmanides, *Ramban*, Leviticus 19:18.

50. Maimonides, *Yad, De'ot*: 7:7–8.

51. R. Avrohom Ehrman, *Journey to Virtue* (New York: Mesorah Publication, 2002), pp. 62–68.

52. *Ar. ha-Sh.*, op. cit., 185:12.

53. R. Meir b. Barukh of Rothenburg (1215–1293) quoted by R. Elijah b. Solomon Zalman (Vilna, 1720–1797), *Bi'ur ha-Gra* to *Sh. Ar., Hoshen Mishpat* 185 *ot* 13.

54. *Ar. ha-Sh.*,op. cit., 185:10,12.

55. For details and sources for the law of *ona'ah* and how it applies to the modern marketplace, see Aaron Levine, " *Ona'ah* and The Operation of The Modern Marketplace," *Jewish Law Annual*, Hebrew University, vol. XIV, 2003, pp. 225–258.

56. R. Meir b. Barukh of Rothenburg, *Responsa Maharam* 477; R. Isaac b. Moses of Vienna (ca. 1180–1250), *Or Zaru'a* 3, *Bava Metzia*, *piska* 242; R. Meir ha-Kohen (end of 13th cent), *Haggahot Maimuniyyot, Sekhirut* 9:4.

57. R. Jekuthiel Asher Zalman Zausmir (d.1858), Responsa *Mahariaz, siman* 15, *amud* 14, *tur* 1.

58. Maimonides, *Yad*, Mekhirah 8:15. For a discussion on how Maimonides derives the principle that the law of *ona'ah* does not apply to a *po'el*, see Aaron Levine, *Economic Public Policy and Jewish Law* (Hoboken, NJ: Ktav Publishing, Yeshiva University Press, 1993), pp. 41–42.

59. See Aaron Levine, *Case Studies in Jewish Business Ethics* (Hoboken: Ktav Publishing House Inc. and Yeshiva University Press, 2000), pps. 133–135.

60. *Torat Kohanim*, Leviticus 19:14; Maimonides, *Yad*, *Rotzeah* 12:14.

61. *Ar. ha-Sh.*, op. cit., 185:10.

62. R. Jacob b. Asher, *Tur*, *Even ha-Ezer* 65:l; R. Joseph Caro, *Sh. Ar.*, *Even ha-Ezer* 65:1; R. Jehiel Michel Epstein, *Even ha-Ezer* 65:1.

63. R. Samuel b. Joseph Strashun, *Rashash*, *Ketubbot* 17a.

64. R. Israel Meir ha-Kohen Kagan, *Hilkhot Issurei Rekhilut K'lal* 9:12.

65. For two alternative explanations, see R. Judah Lowe b. Bezalel, *Maharal*, *Ketubbot* 17a and R. Nethanel b. Naphtali Levi Weil, *Korban Netanel* at *Rosh*, *Ketubbot* 2:2, note 4.

66. R. Yom Tov Ishbili, *Ritvah*, *Ketubbot* 17b.

67. For an explicit application of the notion that the *darkhei shalom* principle can refer to inner peace, see R. Jacob b. Joseph Reicher (Austria, d. 1733), *Iyun Yaakov*, commentary on *Ein Yaakov*, *Sanhedrin* 43a.

68. R. Jacob b. Joseph Reicher, *Iyun Yaakov*, commentary on *Ein Yaakov*, *Yevamot* 63a.

69. *Jerusalem Talmud*, *Hagigah* 8a. For application of the prohibition of *mitkabbed bi-klon havero* to negative comparison advertising, please turn to pp. 399-400 of this volume. See also Aaron Levine, *Case Studies in Jewish Business Ethics* (Hoboken, NJ: Ktav Publishing, Yeshiva University Press, 2000), pp. 60–67.

70. "Telemarketers Face Pressure; Do Not Call Lists Put Jobs at Risk," *The Morning Call*, October 20, 2002, op. cit.

71. "Do Not Call Registry to Begin Today; Industry Faults FTC on Steps to Block Unwanted Telemarketing," *Washington Post*, June 27, 2003, op. cit., p. E1.

72. Caroline Mayer, "In 1 Year, Do-Not-Call List Passes 62 Million," *Washington Post*, June 24, 2004, p. E05.

73. "Do Not Call Registry to Begin Today, Industry Faults FTC on Steps to Block Unwanted Telemarketing," op. cit.

74. "Do Not Call Registry to Begin Today; Industry Faults FTC on Steps to Block Unwanted Telemarketing," op. cit.

75. Brian Steinberg, Suzanne Vranica and Yochi J. Dreazen, "Do Not Call Registry Is Pushing Telemarketers to Plan New Pitch," *The Wall Street Journal*, July 2, 2003, p. A1.

IV. Labor Relations

8

The Mean Boss

A salient feature of modern labor relations is that contract negotiations are generally silent on work rules. Instead, workers will first discover their employers' work rules on the job. Springing a work rule on a worker is legitimate only when the particular rule amounts to nothing more than an enforcement of the employer's right against misappropriation or protection against harm. When this is not the case, springing the rule on the worker may amount to prohibited conduct as it unilaterally generates negative psychic income for the employee. Had the employee known the intention of the employer regarding the work rule before negotiating the labor contract, the outcome of the negotiation might very well have been different.

Our purpose here will be to identify work rules that are designed to maximize productivity and to discourage idleness and shirking. Because these rules both put a strain on the worker and severely constrain his or her freedom, we will call these rules the "rules of the mean boss." By means of the case study method we will examine the halakhic validity of these rules. We will show that both economic theory and economic analysis are important tools for Halakhah in resolving these issues.

Before presenting our case study a preliminary remark is in order. One issue we will investigate here is the ethics for an employer E to prohibit employees to use the office equipment for personal communications. Elsewhere[1] in this volume we deal with the ethics for E to *monitor* the electronic communications coming in and going out of the office. We consider the two issues separately because in this chapter E is satisfied to enforce his or her prohibition without actually reading the *content* of the communications.

In respect to incoming messages, the policy is easy to implement. For telephone messages all that is needed is to install caller ID and an electronic device that tells E to which extension the incoming call is directed as well as the duration of that call. E puts the burden on the worker W to show that *all* incoming calls relate to the business of the firm. For calls that come through the switchboard, E instructs the operator to inquire both who the caller is and the nature of the caller's business. If the call does not relate to the business of the firm, the operator will refuse to put the call through. In respect to e-mail messages, only mail from approved e-mail addresses are allowed into the company system.

Within this system of monitoring, outgoing communications are treated in a similar way. It goes without saying that the banning of cell phones in the office is an essential component of this system.

Naturally, if E is concerned with the leaking of confidential information, monitoring W's incoming and outgoing communications in respect to addresses and numbers will not suffice. The system just described will also not suffice if E's concern is that W will use the office equipment to engage in sexual harassment or to abuse co-workers with racial slurs. If these issues are E's concerns, a more invasive monitoring system will be necessary. In Chapter 9, which deals with privacy issues in the workplace, we take up the ethics for E to monitor electronic communications in ways that are much more intrusive than the method of monitoring assumed in the current chapter.

WORK RULES AT THE FRIER NOVELTY COMPANY

I. M. Frier, CEO of the Frier Novelty Company, interviews all candidates for employment at his company. Anyone hired will readily confirm that the duties Frier assigns a hire match well with what he discussed with the candidate at the interview. The same would be said about salary and fringe benefits. But, employees are always in for a big surprise when it comes to the work rules that they will find themselves subject to. There can be no doubt that Frier designs his work environment to maximally discourage idleness and shirking. Let's take a glimpse at this environment.

At the Frier Novelty Company relatively few employees have private offices. Most of the staff is stationed in cubicles equipped with a desktop computer, a telephone, and assorted office supplies. The first rule Frier communicates to a new hire is what he calls his *face time* requirement: "I expect you to be at your work station at all times during the work day." One quickly learns that Frier's face time requirement translates into an expectation that each employee should be practically "glued" to his or her workstation for the entire workday. How else could one be in a state of readiness to receive an assignment at any time?

Frier tells each new hire that he does not permit employees to go out for lunch. Instead, employees are expected to bring lunch in a brown paper bag and eat lunch in their cubicle at a designated time. This rule ensures that "out for lunch" will never be used as an excuse for not being present in the cubicle when Frier makes his three daily inspection tours of the cubicles. To thwart discovery of a pattern for these inspection tours, Frier, of course, conducts these tours on a random schedule basis. If Frier finds a worker missing from the workstation, he immediately pages that worker with the instruction to report to his secretary. In the meantime, Frier quickly positions himself opposite the restrooms. This stratagem prevents the employee from claiming that he was using the facility at the time, when, in fact, this was not the case.

With the aim of minimizing the shock effect of his work rules, Frier strategically waits to inform a new hire of his policy regarding coffee breaks until the new hire absorbs the details of his lunch policy. Surprise! At the Frier Novelty Company there is no coffee break.

Frier's concern goes beyond taking measures to ensure that no one abandons his or her post during the course of the workday. Near the top of what Frier would call a direct assault on the work ethic he is trying to foster is catching an employee playing a card or video game on his or her computer. For this offense, Frier docks the employee one hour of pay and records the misdeed in his "critical incident"[2] notebook.

Another matter Frier comes down hard on is when an employee makes use of the office equipment for personal communications. Toward this end, Frier checks the telephone numbers and e-mail addresses an employee sends his or her communications to against the contact numbers and e-mail addresses of the businesses the company deals with. If an employee's communications are not going to approved listings, he or she will have a lot of explaining to do.

Frier is also particular that his employees should not make personal use of the office copier. If Frier catches an employee making personal use of his copier, he will typically snarl at the offender. Although Frier has never been known to dock the pay of an employee for this offense, he does not hesitate to record the offense in his critical incident notebook if the culprit was a repeat offender.

When Frier negotiates salary with an employee he is sure to have his "critical incident" notebook handy. It takes little imagination to see that Frier uses his dreaded notebook as a wedge to beat down salary increment demands by his employees.

One employee who found Frier's work rules particularly tormenting was George Pines. In his previous job at a large publishing firm, Pines was not monitored nearly as closely as he was now. In his previous job, no one said anything to him the first time he came late. Because he escaped with impunity on his first offense, Pines led himself down the slippery slope in respect to tardiness and before he knew it he found himself testing the waters to see how often and by how much he could get away with lateness. It was essentially the same story in respect to appropriating office supplies for personal use. The first time Pines was guilty of this offense it involved only a box of paper clips. His attitude then was that he would replace the half-empty box he took with a new box ASAP. In fact, Pines never replaced the paper clips. Because no one ever noticed that the paper clips were missing, Pines was emboldened, in time, to take home more valuable supplies for his personal needs, including an adding machine and a large stapler.

In observing the operation of Frier's work rules one is struck by the stark contrast between the harshness and decisiveness by which Frier promulgates his rules and the manner in which he goes about enforcing them. For some rules Frier makes no apparent attempt at enforcement; for others, selective enforcement is the order of the day.

The largest gap between promulgation and implementation can be seen in respect to Frier's prohibition against personal use of office supplies. In reminding everyone of his interdict in this matter, one could often hear Frier bark, "I mean *anything and everything* is off limits for personal use, including bent paper clips and half-used number two pencils." When someone makes a pronouncement with such ferocity, the expectation is that draconian enforcement procedures will ensue. This was not the case. Office supplies were located in a large closet that was easily accessible to everyone.

The closet was always open and anyone who needed supplies, from paper clips to an assortment of computer mouses, could help himself to what he needed. Imagine, no requisition forms and no red tape whatsoever! But, you all know Frier. There must be a catch. Frier had a video camera concealed in an inconspicuous spot in the ceiling of the closet. Frier reviewed the videotapes periodically. If someone's face turned up too often for his liking, Frier took it as very suspicious and indicative that the party involved was stealing. This person had no future in the company. Unbeknownst to the culprit the supply closet served as a screening device and determined his or her suitability for continued employment or promotion.

Frier's implementation of his sick days policy shows that Frier *selectively* tolerated shirking. Frier's contract allows employees up to five days' sick pay. To qualify for this benefit, the employee must call in sick and later verify his or her illness by bringing in a medical note. If an employee fails either to call in sick or to verify the sickness with proper documentation, his or her pay will be docked for that day. In practice, Frier never enforces the documentation requirement. If an employee calls in sick, he or she will get paid for the day provided the sick days for the year do no exceed five days. To boot, if an employee comes up with a nonmedical, really good excuse for his or her absence, the employee might be surprised to find that no pay deduction was made. Frier feels that this practice is a worthwhile investment. In his words, "Taking a sick day when it is really a personal day is outright theft. I'm sure it's accompanied with a sense of guilt. When I let it go by, I'm sure that the employee feels that he or she owes me something. Some day I'll call in the IOU to my great advantage."

Frier's policy of *selectively* tolerating shirking is further seen by the following two incidents involving two employees, Ben Green and Leonard Sunshine.

Ben Green is the chief financial officer of Frier's company. The first time Frier caught Ben making personal use of the company's copier, Ben dreaded that he had just lost his job. To his great surprise, Frier neither snarled nor berated him, and the critical incident notebook was nowhere to be seen. Frier's silence emboldened Ben to repeat the offense two weeks later. But when the ubiquitous Frier caught him again and reacted with a type of silence that did not even send out "bad vibrations," Ben spontaneously developed the attitude that Frier did not mind at all that he made use of the copier for personal use. In fact, the next time Frier caught him in the act, Green felt not even a twinge of guilt about using the copier. Eventually, *just before he was fired*, Ben considered making use of the company's copier for his personal needs an implicit fringe benefit.

Leonard Sunshine is the company's chief designer of trinkets. In a meeting with Sunshine and the company's artist, Manfred Olemark, Frier stumbled on the fact that Sunshine had appropriated a 54 crayon box of Crayolas for his son Eric's arts and crafts school project. As soon as Frier got wind of this he turned to Sunshine and exclaimed, "You should have taken Olemark's *pastels* for Eric's project." Sunshine took this comment to mean that Frier had no objection to what he had done and perhaps was even pleased that the company's inventory could be drawn upon to help along Eric's school project.

UNILATERALLY IMPOSING RULES AFTER THE CONTRACT IS SIGNED

One basic issue Frier's work rules raises is the legitimacy of springing these rules on a new hire without first properly informing him or her of the rules in the negotiating stage of a contract. The issue revolves around how we should categorize these rules. Should the work rules be regarded as enforcements of Frier's rights against misappropriation and protection against harm? If the rules are viewed in this manner, springing them on a new hire does not deprive the worker of an amenity that might otherwise be legitimately expected. Or, perhaps Frier's rules deprive his employees of actual amenities. Since the denied amenities translate into negative psychic income, a candidate is entitled to know about these rules in weighing Frier's employment offer, no less than being entitled to know of the wages, pension, and health benefits Frier is offering before signing on.

FACE TIME AND HALAKHAH

Let's begin with face time. Frier's strict rules regarding face time are apparently consistent with the duty Halakhah imposes on someone hired to work at fixed hours not to idle on the employer's (E) time.[3] This type of worker is called a *po'el* (henceforth, P). Idling on E's time forfeits for P the wages he/she would have earned for this period.[4] The conduct of the biblical

Jacob as he went about tending the sheep of his father-in law, Laban, is relevant here. The sages regard Jacob as the model of the worker of integrity.[5] Recounting to his wives, Rachel and Leah, the manner in which he tended the flocks of their father, Laban, Jacob proclaims: "I was there, by day the heat consumed me, and frost by night; my sleep drifted from my eyes" (Genesis 31:40).

Indicative of the stricture the sages took regarding idling on E's time is the abbreviated version of the benedictions after meal formula as well as the shortened version of the daily prayers they prescribed for P.[6]

Frier's insistence that his staff should at all times be at their work stations is apparently well grounded in Halakhah. He can even point to the biblical Jacob as a model for his staff to emulate. There is, however, more to the story here. Consider that despite the institution of shortened benedictions and prayers for P, E eventually developed a liberal attitude in this matter. It took the form of voluntarily allowing P to recite the *standard* texts prescribed for these religious duties. The consequence of this liberalization of attitude was that the right to recite the standard formulae for these religious duties became an *implicit* condition of employment for P.[7] Moreover, once P's reciting the standard formulae became established, an explicit stipulation on the part of E to disallow it, according to R. Jehiel Michel Epstein (Belarus, 1829–1908), was no longer recognized.[8]

What the above development regarding the right of P to recite *standard* prayer and benedictions on the job illustrates is the role that prevailing practice (*minhag*) plays in labor relations. If a clear-cut *minhag* can be identified for a particular condition of employment, that practice will become operative for the labor agreement at hand if the labor contract was silent on that matter. The length of the workday provides a case in point. By dint of Torah law, P must leave his home for the workplace at sunrise and continue to work at the workplace until nightfall.[9] But, suppose the labor agreement was *silent* on the issue of the workday and local practice was for P's workday to extend only, say, from 9 A.M. to 5 P.M. Here, local custom prevails and P's workday will be set from 9 A.M. to 5 P.M.[10] The shorter workday of local custom will set for P his daily schedule even if E agreed to give him a higher than competitive wage and claims that he did so only with the implicit understanding that the work day should extend to the Torah law work day.[11] One final point here. If P agreed in advance with E's explicit stipulation that the workday should be the Torah law workday, the stipulation is binding even if local custom calls for a shorter workday.[12]

Let's apply the rule of *minhag* to Frier's face time regulations. Can there be any doubt that both Frier's rule against a coffee break and his insistence that everyone remain "glued" to their work stations throughout the entire workday run against prevailing practice in labor relations across America? Reinforcing this judgment is the widespread societal outrage against "sweatshop" conditions in the labor market.[13] Because Frier's rules effectively create "prison-like" conditions for his workforce, many would condemn him for running a "sweatshop" type of operation. These rules hence certainly run counter to the prevailing norm.

The upshot of this analysis is that Frier's rules that disallow a coffee break and his prohibition for a worker to leave his or her work station other than to use the facilities deprives his workforce of amenities that enjoy just about *universal* currency in the *legal* labor market in the Unites States. Because Frier makes no mention of these rules in the negotiating stage of the labor contract, he has no right to unilaterally impose these rules on a captive labor force. This judgment holds even in respect to the portion of his labor force he pays above competitive wages to.

We now turn to an assessment of Frier's prohibition against making a personal local telephone call even when P places the call when he is in between assignments. Consider that by dint of Torah law P is duty bound to apply himself to the task at hand on a *continuous* basis.[14] Breaking away from the task at hand even for a short interval makes P guilty of misusing E's time and should be regarded as an act of misappropriation (*gezel*). If Frier's rule is objectionable, it must therefore be demonstrated that a limited privilege of making personal local calls is not *gezel*. In making this case, the net benefit principle will be crucial. What follows is an explication of this principle.

THE NET BENEFIT PRINCIPLE

Explication of the net benefit principle begins with an examination of the rights of a service worker or craftsman (W) to keep residual portions of the material he is supplied with by E. In this regard, the rule is that the launderer may keep the small shreds that fall out while he is rinsing the garment. Likewise, the fine shavings that fall off the board the carpenter planes belong to him.[15] Why these insignificant materials belong to *W* cannot be explained simply on the basis of their trivial value. We should not ignore the fact that these insignificant materials are inherently the property of *E*. The law pertaining to the stealing of an item worth less than a *perutah* must here be invoked. A *perutah* is equal in value to an amount of silver weighing a half-grain of barley.[16] If *A* steals from *B* an item worth less than a *perutah*, *A* is not obligated to return the item to *B*.[17] Because the item has no monetary value we presume that *B* waives his claim to recover the item.[18] But, misappropriating *B's* property even if it has no monetary value for the owner is prohibited conduct.[19] This is so because the owner assuredly experiences pain and anguish at the moment he discovers that his property has been misappropriated, even if the said property is not worth a *perutah*.[20] To be sure, given the insignificant value involved, this pain quickly dissipates. *B*, therefore, comes around to waive his claim in the matter. The presumption that *B* eventually waives his rights in the matter does not, however, legitimize *A's* theft in the first place!

Further supportive of the notion that the right of *W* to keep the residual portion of the material supplied him is not based on looking at the value of these materials alone is the ruling that the particles that the wool comber pulls out of the garment in doing his job are the property of *E*. Compared to the launderer, the comber pulls out more particles from the garment. Because the amount of particles involved is substantial, *E* presumably wishes to retain ownership of the material.[21] Now, if the right of *E* to keep the residual portion of the material he was supplied with is based solely on the insignificant value involved, why doesn't the wool comber keep the same number of particles the law allows the launderer to keep?

Another difficulty of labor law dealing with the residual portion of the material *W* is supplied with is the ruling that if *W* performs the job on *E's* premises, even the sawdust belongs to *E*.[22] Now, if *W's* right to the residual materials is based solely on their insignificant value, why should the circumstance that the job is performed on *E's* premises result in *W* losing his rights to the residual materials entirely?

These difficulties lead to the thesis that the issue of who has the property right in the residual materials should be analyzed in terms of whether *E* reaps a *net gain* if we assign the property right to *W*. We take it as a given that when E enters into a labor contract with W, E desires that W should produce for him the finest workmanship possible. Toward this end E is always in a state of readiness to offer W a goodwill gesture that *costs him nothing* to assure that W will apply himself with his utmost diligence to the task at hand. Consider that in many instances the residual materials from the job will be more valuable to W than they are to E. A case in point is the particles W removes when he launders E's garment. Given that the quantity involved is small, these particles have no monetary value for E. Not so for W. Because W is constantly plying his trade, the particles he accumulates on this job will *combine* with particles he will accumulate on his next job. For E to deny W something that is of no monetary value to himself but has value for W smacks of a meanness of spirit. Denying W the right to keep the particles hence can only work to adversely affect W's productivity. Allowing W to keep the particles, on the other hand, does no less than generate a goodwill gesture to him.

Standing at the basis of W's right to keep the residual materials in the above cases, according to R. Mosheh Isserles (Poland, 1525 or 1530–1572), is the presumption that E is not particular (*eino makpid*) about retaining ownership of the materials involved.[23] Note that in R. Isserles' understanding the basis of W's right to keep the residual material is not the *trivial value* of these materials *per se*, but rather the presumption that E is not *makpid*. What the above analysis has done is to put concreteness into the word *makpid* and define it in terms of whether E expects to realize a *net benefit* in the matter. Specifically, if E expects to realize a net benefit in the matter, he is not *makpid* that W should retain the residual materials. If, on the other hand, E does not expect to realize a net benefit in the matter, he is *makpid* that W should retain ownership in his property regardless of the value involved.

At this juncture let's take note that R. Solomon b. Isaac (*Rashi*, France, 1040–1105) understands the launderer's right to the insignificant shreds to be true even if E has made it known before W took on the job that he is particular about retaining the particles. Notwithstanding that E has expressed in no uncertain terms that he is particular about this matter, we simply do not reckon with E's attitude, and W is permitted to keep the particles.[24] Why we don't reckon with E's protest can be explained on the basis that E's attitude runs in the face of the presumption that allowing W to keep the particles generates a net benefit for E.

The net benefit criterion explains why a wool comber is not entitled to even *a portion* of the shreds he removes while performing his service. Since the quantity of particles the wool comber removes is something of value, we cannot presume that E is willing to forego this value in order to generate a goodwill gesture to W.

Another point that the above thesis clarifies is why performing the job on E's premises changes the law and makes even sawdust the property of E.[25] This is so because the gain for E in all the residual material cases is the prospect that allowing W to keep the residual materials will increase his productivity and denying him this amenity will sharply reduce his productivity. This all makes sense if W operates on his own premises and hence is unsupervised. Here, E has a vested interest that W should not be resentful or petty and subconsciously fall short of his best effort. This, however, is not the case when W performs the job on E's premises and is under E's supervision. Here, E relies on his own supervision to ensure that he gets top value for his money. Consequently, we have no right to presume that E is willing to give up anything that is rightfully his, regardless of its value, in order to make a goodwill gesture to W.[26]

The notion that A has a license to misappropriate B's property when it is *objectively evident* that B will derive a net benefit from the action finds support in R. Judah's dictum that a bystander may take away the cress plants that grow among the flax plant. Such action does not constitute misappropriation.[27] Expounding on R. Judah's dictum, *Rashi* avers that the action of the bystander actually generates a net benefit to the owner, as cress cause more damage to flax than the cress plants are worth.[28]

Prohibiting the Use of Office Equipment For Personal Communications On a Blanket Basis

We move now to apply the net benefit criterion to analyze the issue of whether it is ethical for W, in the absence of an *explicit* rule prohibiting the conduct, to appropriate for himself/herself the use of company equipment for personal communications on company time. In exploring this issue we begin with the more fundamental question of whether it is ethical for E to promulgate in advance a blanket prohibition against such conduct.

We begin with the principle that by dint of Torah law W has a right to withdraw without penalty from his contract to work.[29] Let's illustrate the nature of this right by means of an arithmetic example:

E hires P_1 to work for him for eight hours at $10 an hour. At the end of four hours P_1 tells E that he is quitting. At this juncture the wage rate has gone up to $15 an hour. Hiring a replacement worker, P_2, requires E to expend an additional $60 to complete the job. Because P_1 has a right to withdraw from work without penalty, P_1 is entitled to the entire $40 prorated wages he earned up to the point of his withdrawal, and is not docked $20 to compensate E for the *extra cost* resulting from his withdrawal.[30]

Why P_1 has a right to withdraw in the middle of the workday without penalty is discussed at *Bava Metzia* 10a:

> A worker can withdraw from his employment even in the middle of the day—For the children of Israel are servants unto Me (Leviticus 25:42) – In effect, God says, "they are My servants, and not servants to other servants!"

In his explication of the above Talmudic text, R. Yom Tov Ishbili (Seville, ca. 1250–1330) contends that the retraction right is conferred to ensure that the worker should not be bound to his employer against his will. Without the retraction right, the labor contract will be akin to servitude. Following this line of reasoning, R. Ishbili goes on to say that the retraction right is conferred only on a worker who contracts to work at specific hours (*po'el*, henceforth P). Absent the retraction right, obligating oneself to work at specific hours is akin to servitude. But, the retraction right is not conferred on a worker who is paid for finished work and who does not obligate himself to work at specific hours (*kabbelan*). Because the *kabbelan*'s undertaking carries with it the liberty to withhold work at any specific time, the sages did not confer the *kabbelan* the retraction right.[31]

R. Ishbili's exposition requires further clarification. Conferring P with a retraction right, in R. Ishbili's thinking, is what frees the labor agreement from being akin to servitude. But, consider that the labor agreement generates only a commitment on the part of P to undertake E's assignment but generates for E no lien on the person of P.[32] P's contract is, hence, *inherently not akin to servitude*. It is for this reason, R. Ishmael b. Abraham Isaac ha-Kohen (Italy, 1723–1811) points out, that there is no objection for P to agree voluntarily to a no retraction clause. This clause does not violate: "They are My servants, and not servants to other servants."[33] Why, then, is it necessary to confer to *P* a retraction right? This difficulty leads to the proposition that the retraction right is rooted in a psychological need of the worker. Because he obligates himself to work at specific hours, the agreement naturally generates for the worker a feeling of losing his independence. This feeling is not rooted in the *legal* status that becomes operative for him as a result of the agreement, but rather is purely psychological in nature. Giving *P* a retraction right removes the psychological burden of loss of independence.

It follows from this analysis that the Torah's definition of *servitude* in connection with the prohibition of, "They are My servants – and not servants to other servants" does not simply relate to the legal realm, but consists of a psychological element as well.

Once it is recognized that contracting to work for fixed hours is psychologically debilitating and akin to servitude for *P*, the retraction right can be viewed as not only preserving the independence of *P*, but as generating a *net benefit* for *E* as well.

In developing the thesis that conferring *P* with a retraction right generates a net benefit to *E* we note, preliminarily, that *P's retraction* right is not recognized when leaving the work scene will generate a material loss to *E*. This circumstance is referred to as the *davar ha-avud* case.

An example of *davar ha-avud*, cited in the Talmud, is the hiring of a worker to remove flax from its steeping. If the task is not performed immediately, *E* will suffer material loss. Another example is the hiring of a worker to bring litter-carriers and pipers to a wedding ceremony. Since the litter-carriers and pipers are sent with the purpose of enhancing the ceremony, delay in their dispatch will defeat the purpose of the sender because they will arrive after the ceremony is already over.[34] Another circumstance where *P's* retraction right is not recognized occurs when the motivation for withdrawing is to secure a higher paying job elsewhere.[35]

Taken together, these exceptions have the effect of severely limiting the operational significance of the retraction right for *P*.[36]

The flip side of the coin is the contention that *P's* retraction right works only to minimally harm *E*. But, before making this judgment call, the impact of *P's* retraction right on the *transaction costs* of *E* to hire replacement workers must be considered. In one scenario the labor force is low-skilled and homogeneous, and the usual duration a worker hires himself out for is either for a number of hours or on a per-diem basis. Here, quitting in the middle of the day, other things being equal, may not be disruptive. This is so because the *supply side* of the marketplace features an abundant number of workers who are both capable and willing to fill in the gap E faces as a result of P's retraction. Here, P's retraction is minimally disruptive for E and entails *no* cost other than the toil and effort involved in hiring replacement workers. This situation probably describes the labor market in the time of the Talmud. But consider that in modern times, workers, other than temps, rarely hire themselves out for *only* one day. Accordingly, P's suddenly quitting may entail considerable search and training outlays by E to replace him. Does Halakhah recognize the right of P to quit even when the quit will be both costly and disruptive for E as far as the future operation of his business is concerned? Relevant here is the modern-day discussion regarding the notice requirement the employer owes an employee who was hired for an indefinite term. This type of worker is commonly referred to as an employee-at-will.

In Halakhah, the requirement to give an employee-at-will notice is a matter of contract law. Various views have been advanced regarding the *length* of the notice requirement. Underlying all the formulations is the recognition that a sudden firing disrupts the income flow of the employee-at-will and/or saddles him with the market search costs of getting reabsorbed into the workforce.[37]

Likewise, an employee-at-will suddenly quitting disrupts the income flow of the employer and/or saddles him with the search and orientation costs associated with hiring a replacement worker. If notice is an implied condition of employment for the employer, the same logic puts this responsibility on the employee. This makes it unethical for the employee-at-will to quit without giving notice.

Although P's retraction right entails little downside for E, the operation of the rule may very well generate a considerable upside for him. Consider that in the judgment of the sages working at fixed hours psychologically depresses P to the point of making him feel that he has lost his freedom and is *chained* in a servitude relationship with E. Conferring P with the right to withdraw from the work scene without penalty, even though this right is by no means absolute, restores *P's* mindset to the extent that he no longer equates working at fixed hours to a status of servitude. The retraction right hence cultivates in *P* a more *positive* attitude toward his job. Because *P's* retraction right makes him feel less encumbered, the rule can only work to induce *P* to apply himself to the task at hand more energetically. The upside for *E* therefore is that the retraction right actually works *to increase P's productivity*.

One could argue that *P's* retraction right is meaningful only in the context of a labor marketplace where both employers demand labor and workers supply their labor on a *day-to-day* basis. Within this milieu, *P's* knowledge that he can quit at any time without forfeiting any portion of the prorated wages he has already earned is psychologically comforting. This is so because tomorrow, *P* can offer his services again on a *day-to-day* basis and latch on to a different employer more to his liking. What meaning does *P's* retraction right have, however, on the modern work scene where *E* demands labor and *P* supplies his services on a long-term basis? One could argue that in the modern work scene *P's retraction right* is reduced to a vapidity. Consider that suddenly quitting his job will incur for *P* significant job search costs. It is for this reason, as discussed above, that Halakhah protects *P* against sudden discharge and requires *E* to give him proper notice. If the modern work scene renders *P's* retraction right meaningless, then nothing rubs in *P's* dependency status more than a work rule that chains *P* and at the same time generates no tangible benefit for *E*. This would be the judgment if *E's* prohibition on *E* to use a cell phone on company property is combined with a prohibition to use office equipment for personal communications even when the communications is very short and is done in between assignments. The same judgment holds when the cell phone prohibition combines with a *blanket* prohibition on *P* to accept outside personal messages through the office equipment. In respect to telephone calls, two variations can be identified here. If the call comes during a lull in the work flow, denying *P* the right to accept the call and minimally converse with the caller has the effect of making *P* totally inaccessible to the outside world, and hence chaining him to the workplace. If the call does not come at a lull, *P* may, nevertheless, feel the same way if he is denied even the opportunity to ascertain, at least, what the call is about.

The upshot of this analysis is that a rule that denies *P* even a minimal personal communications right with the outside world undermines the mindset of liberty *P* is entitled to feel while on the job. This rule is hence *halakhically problematic* because it *interferes* with a basic entitlement of *P*.

ALTERNATE UNSHACKELING MODES AND THE RETRACTION RIGHT

The modern workplace affords *P* with the capacity to communicate with the outside world in various ways, including telephone, facsimile, and e-mail. *E's* duty not to create a work environment that makes *P* feel shackled argues only that *P* should be allowed some amount of personal communications with the outside world. But the mode *P* is given to exercise his right to feel "unshackled" should, perhaps, be the prerogative of *E*. Accordingly, one might argue that *E* "unshackles" *P* by conferring him with a minimal privilege to send and receive personal e-mails through the company's equipment, even though *P* is denied personal telephone privileges. However, of the three modes of communication mentioned, only the telephone privilege resembles the *freedom P* enjoys if he retracts. Communicating through facsimile and e-mail allows *P* to *transmit and receive messages*, but only the telephone affords *P* the opportunity to engage in a *personal conversation*. If we are looking for a mode of personal communication with the outside world that gives substance to *P's* retraction right in the modern marketplace, then the only viable candidate, as a practical matter, is the personal telephone privilege. Moreover, if going with the e-mail option upsets *P's* inherent preference on how he wants to "unshackle" himself, getting a consolation prize breeds nothing but resentment by *P*.

APPROPRIATING FOR ONESELF A MINIMAL PERSONAL COMMUNICATIONS PRIVILEGE

Let's now consider a variation of the above case. Suppose *E* never promulgated any rules relating to the office equipment for personal communications. Does *P* enjoy some minimal latitude here? Arguing in the affirmative is that *appropriating* for oneself this amenity in a minimal way is a basic entitlement. It is *P's* way of giving *minimal substance* to his retraction right in the modern work scene. If *P* wants to be strict about this matter and *deny* himself this privilege entirely, he will soon regard his job as akin to servitude. Moreover, because appropriating for himself a minimal privilege frees *P* of a shackled mindset, *E* benefits in the form of higher productivity from *P*. *P*'s appropriation of a minimal personal communications privilege hence generates a *net benefit* for *E*.

The net benefit argument is reinforced when one considers that *P*'s retraction right confers *P* with leverage over *E*. We will proceed to analyze the nature of this leverage and show that drawing out its implication legitimizes the presumption that *E implicitly agrees in advance* to allow *P* to use the office equipment, including the telephone, in a minimal manner for personal communications. Consider the following scenario: *P* comes to *E* and *proposes* that he be allowed to quit his job without pay for a brief interlude of say fifteen to twenty minutes during a lull in the workflow. *P* explains that he plans to use this chunk of time to make a few personal calls outside the premises of the business. *P* goes on to propose that *E* should rehire him at the conclusion of the twenty-minute period and restore his lost pay. *P*'s quitting is legitimate. But *E* is under no obligation to accede to the *second part* of *P*'s request, namely, that he should rehire him at the conclusion of the twenty-minute interlude. Nonetheless, as a practical matter, *E* will, in all probability, find it in his own self-interest to rehire *P*. This is so because hiring someone else incurs for *E* market search, retraining, and transaction costs. Rehiring *P* after the personal time interlude is over avoids these costs.

Once we concede that *P* can make *E* agree to the personal telephone break, it is but a small step to show that *P* may appropriate this amenity for himself on the grounds that *E implicitly* agrees to it in advance. To make this argument we need only show that *E* prefers self-appropriation to direct talks with *P*. Let's see why. Consider that *P* can bring up his quit-rehire proposal as often as he likes, even on a daily basis. If *P* would not actually quit, but instead remain at his workstation, then, the time necessary to make the personal calls would be cut in half. Cutting the personal time interlude in half is not only important for *E* time-wise, but also has the additional advantage of reducing the risk that a *davar ha-avud* assignment would not unexpectedly come up for *P* in his absence. *E* would therefore be far better off if *P* would not bring up his quit-rehire proposal at all and instead just take matters into his own hands and appropriate for himself a minimal personal telephone privilege.

In the final analysis, *P*'s license to appropriate for himself minimal personal telephone privileges is predicated on the presumption that such conduct generates a *net benefit* for *E*. Let's take a moment to spell out what the loss and gain for *E* consist of. The loss for *E* consists of the opportunity cost he incurs for the time *P* spends on the personal telephone calls. Counted on the benefit side for *E*, however, is not only *P*'s increased productivity, but also the *marginal opportunity cost P*'s quit-hire scheme *could have* imposed on him had *P* chosen to bring it up in direct talks.

People differ widely in respect to what liberties they feel they must have in order not to regard their jobs as akin to servitude. In this regard, some might include in their wish list a need to keep abreast with the local, national, and international news; checking up on one's financial portfolio; and keeping up on the sports news. To get this information, *P* will undoubtedly want to use the company computer to visit various Web sites. Does *P*'s right not to feel shackled while on the job for *E* allow him to seek this above information during the workday? No. To be valid the privilege must pass the net benefit criterion. The issue therefore is what benefit can *E* expect from each new thrust by *P* into new dimensions of experiencing liberty. Each self-permitted extension of the privilege runs the risk that *E* will no longer realize a net benefit from the conduct. One strongly suspects that the benefit side of the calculation is given to sharply diminishing returns as the time *P* spends on expanding his horizons of liberty increases. Accordingly, *P* must exercise caution in this matter and not test the waters to see if he can get away with going beyond the minimal level of privilege without drawing *E*'s protest. In respect to making personal calls, *P*'s license is to *communicate* so much so that he should not feel shackled. However, *P* enjoys no right to *socialize* with anyone on company time in a non-job-related context. In respect to outside calls, *P* should bear the responsibility to tell anyone to whom he gives his number that the number should only be used to contact him in an emergency.

THE TELEPHONE PRIVILEGE AND *LIFNIM MI-SHURAT HA-DIN*

The net benefit argument is somewhat attenuated when the workplace has only one telephone line shared by many employees. Add to this the complication involved for a firm such as a medical practice. Within this context, making personal telephone calls in between assignments blocks incoming calls and may cause considerable harm.

Arguably the above-described scenario is a rare instance, as even small businesses find it to the advantage of their bottom line to operate with more than one telephone line, or at least to install the call-waiting feature in their communications system. Let's, however, consider the halakhic ramifications of the above scenario. If the communications system of the firm lacks the capacity to handle more than one call at a time, the net benefit argument is weakened and *P* would have no license to make his personal call between assignments. Moreover, by the strict letter of the law *E* would have the right to prohibit the conduct outright. The only thing standing in the way of making the personal telephone privilege a win-win proposition is *E's* refusal to equip his communications system to handle more than one call at a time. Given the *insignificant marginal cost* involved in setting up his communications system with this capacity, *E's* duty to act *lifnim mi-shurat ha-din* (beyond the letter of the law)[38] *urges* him to make this expenditure. To be sure *lifnim mi-shurat ha-din* generally makes a claim only on an individual's toil and effort, but does not make a demand on him to incur an expense.[39] Nonetheless, when the expense involved is trivial, the expense should be incurred. Not incurring the expense is regarded as very petty conduct.[40]

ABBA HILKIAH—THE RIGHTEOUS *PO'EL*

The Talmud cites Abba Hilkiah, the grandson of the famous Honi the Circle-maker, as the paragon of the righteous *po'el*.[41] What follows is an episode in the life of Abba Hilkiah.[42] Analysis of the story will have a bearing on the issue of the ethics for *P* to interrupt his work and respond to an outside caller.

> Abba Hilkiah was a grandson of Honi the Circle-Maker-and when the world needed rain, the rabbis would send [a request] to him, and he would pray for mercy, and the rains would come. Once, [when] the world needed rain, the rabbis sent a pair of rabbis to him [to ask him] to pray for mercy that the rains come – They went to his house but did not find him- They went [out] to the fields and found him hoeing–they greeted him, *ve-lo asbar-le-hu appeih* [he did not turn his face to them, *Rashi*].

In the evening- when he gathered up [some] wood [he carried the wood and hoe on one shoulder], – and his cloak on [the other] shoulder. – The entire way [home], he did not wear shoes; [but] when he came to [a stream of] water, he put on his shoes [to cross it]. – When he came to [an area of] thorns and thistles, -he lifted [the hem of] clothing, [thereby exposing his legs to the thorns]. When he reached the town, his wife came out to meet him adorned [with jewelry]. – When he reached his house, his wife entered first, – then he entered, – and the rabbis [were] then [invited to] enter. – He [then] sat down and ate bread, – without saying to the rabbis, "come [and] eat," [i.e., he did not invite them to join in the meal]. – He apportioned bread to the children; – to the older [child he gave] one [bread to eat], and to the younger [child he gave] two. – He [then] said [quietly] to his wife: "I know that the rabbis have come [to ask me to pray] for rain. Let us go up to the roof and pray for mercy; – perhaps the holy One, blessed is He, will accept [our prayer], and rain will come, – and we will not [have to] take credit for ourselves [for bringing the rain] – They went up to the roof. – He stood at one corner- and she [stood] at [another] corner, [and they prayed and were answered.] – [When the rain came], the clouds arrived earlier from that corner where his wife [stood in prayer]. – When he came down [from the roof], he said to them: "Why have the rabbis come?"-They said to him: – "The Rabbis have sent us to ask you to pray for mercy for rain." – He said to them: – "Blessed is the Omnipresent, Who did not require you [to depend] upon Abba Hilkiah. – They said to him: "We know that the rain has come on account of [the prayer of] the master, –but would the master [please] explain to us–these things that puzzle us. –Why, when we greeted the master, *lo asbar lan mar appeih* [the master did not turn his head toward us, *Rashi*]- He said to them: "I was [hired as] a day worker, and I said to myself [that since I am being paid by the day], *lo eipagar*."

Abba Hilkiah's initial reaction to the rabbinical delegation bears directly on the issue of whether it is ethical for *P* to *take* time to respond minimally to a visitor or caller. The narrative says that when the delegation arrived *lo asbar lehu appeih*. R. Samuel Eliezer b. Judah ha-Levi Edels (Poland, 1555–1623) understands this phrase to mean that Abba Hilkiah did not *return* the greeting of the rabbis' altogether.[43] *Rashi*, however, interprets the phrase to mean that Abba Hilkiah did not turn his face toward the rabbis in response to their greeting.[44] In this understanding of the phrase, Abba Hilkiah could very well have returned their greeting. Apparently following *Rashi*'s line, R. Joseph Hayyim b. Elijah al-Hakham (Baghdad, 1834–1909) theorizes that Abba Hilkiah did respond to the rabbis' greetings, albeit in a very perfunctory manner, (i.e., without the warmth and enthusiasm one usually greets people of stature with). In R. Joseph Hayyim's view Abba Hilkiah did not interrupt his work of hoeing while he returned the greeting of the delegation of rabbis.[45]

In speculating whether Abba Hilkiah briefly interrupted his work to return the rabbis' greeting, it is instructive to focus on the key phrase *lo eipagar* he used in explaining why he was unresponsive to them. Note that the root *pgr* means either laziness[46] or weakness.[47] Consider that Abba Hilkiah could have responded *lo eibatal*, (i.e., "I [decided] not to interrupt [my work]"). Instead, he said, "I [decided] not to be lazy or display weakness." Now, there is a basic difference between interruption versus weakness or laziness. Interruption is evident even if it occurs ever so briefly, but weakness or laziness is evident only if it is manifested over a *significant stretch of time*. What Abba Hilkiah conveyed to the delegation was therefore essentially that his status as *po'el* disallowed him from breaking off from work and *spending a significant chunk of time with them*.

Another relevant matter in the narrative for the issue at hand is the circumstance that Abba Hilkiah did not ask the rabbis the purpose of their mission until after he traveled home and had a meal with his family. Making the rabbis wait so long without attending to them entails a possible violation of the prohibition of causing someone needless mental anguish (*ona'at devarim*).[48] Relevant here is the following text at *Mekhilta* Exodus 180:22:

Said R. Shimon to R. Ishmael: Master! I cannot for the life of me understand what I have done to deserve execution. Whereupon R. Ishmael replied: Have you ever kept a man who came to you for a lawsuit or consultation waiting until you had a drink, put on your shoes and cloak? The Torah stated: If afflict you afflicted (Exodus 22:22) – whether a grievous affliction or a trivial one. He answered him: You have consoled me, O master.

Proceeding from *Mekhilta* is that R. Shimon violated *ona'at devarim* by means of his inaction or passivity. Specifically, by not immediately giving his attention to an anxiety-ridden person, he effectively prolonged that person's state of anxiety and hence violated *ona'at devarim*.

In evaluating Abba Hilkiah's conduct in respect to the *ona'at devarim* interdict, let's note that the rabbis came to him without a prior appointment. Moreover, because the rabbis found Abba Hilkiah busy at work hoeing in the field, they had no reasonable expectation that he should interrupt his work to give them attention. To be free of the *ona'at devarim* interdict, Abba Hilkiah should, however, let the rabbis know *immediately* when he will see them. To tell the rabbis when he first encountered them that he would be finished with his work at nightfall, but to delay in giving them an audience until he first traveled home, ate a meal with his family, and went up together with his wife to the attic to pray for rain, amounts to *putting off* anxiety-ridden people and hence violates *ona'at devarim*. Could Abba Hilkiah give the rabbis a precise appointment? No. Consider that Abba Hilkiah desperately wanted to hide from the rabbis his power to make the rain come through his supplication. To accomplish this he could not let the rabbis know why he and his wife went up to the attic after the conclusion of the meal. Abba Hilkiah could therefore not simply spell out for the rabbis a sequence of activities he would be involved in after work, culminating with the attic prayer session with his wife, and tell them that he would see them then.

What the above discussion has done is to uncover yet another aspect of Abba Hilkiah's conduct that must be called mysterious. Given the long delay between his initial contact with the rabbis and when he finally got around to asking them why they had come to see him, how did Abba Hilkiah avoid violating *ona'at devarim*? We theorize that Abba Hilkiah must have told the rabbis that they would be free to follow him about after he completed his work and when he was ready he would attend to them.

Recall the proposition we offered earlier that a *po'el* is inherently entitled to break off from his work and *minimally* respond to an outside call to determine if it is an emergency situation, requiring his immediate attention. Providing support for this proposition is the Abba Hilkiah incident. Why Abba Hilkiah is cited as the model of the righteous *po'el* is now clear-cut. Abba Hilkiah was given this distinction because he is the paragon of the individual who exercises an inherent right *without abusing the privilege involved*. Perhaps the most important thing Abba Hilkiah did to ensure that his break from work would be minimal was not turning his face to the rabbis in returning their greeting. By doing this, Abba Hilkiah immediately signaled to the rabbis that his interaction with them at this time would be minimal.

TAKING OUTSIDE PERSONAL CALLS AND HALAKHAH

An examination of the prohibition for *P* to stand up for a Talmudic scholar (*hakham*) will show that the right of *P* to receive outside personal calls is limited. Moreover, it will also show that *P* has a duty to inform his relatives and friends that they should not call him at work unless the message is urgent and is necessary as the only way to avoid significant aggravation or loss.

The biblical verse, "You shall rise in the presence of an old person and you shall honor the presence of an elder and you shall have fear of your God—I am Hashem" (Leviticus: 19:32) sets out the duty to rise in the presence of a *hakham* (rabbinical scholar).[49] The sages, however, prohibited *P* from standing up for a *hakham*.[50] Unlike the ordinance that disallowed *P* from reciting the standard texts for prayers and benedictions, referred to earlier, this prohibition was not eventually swept away by the development of generous employer attitudes towards workers. Accepting an outside call is apparently analogous to reacting to the arrival on the work scene of a *hakham*. If standing up for a *hakham* is prohibited, accepting outside calls should also be prohibited. Moreover, how is the prohibition for *P* to stand up for a *hakham* reconciled with the Abba Hilkiah incident discussed earlier? The implication of this incident is that *P* is permitted a minimal response to an unexpected surprise outside caller. Why, then, did the sages establish a prohibition for *P* to stand up for a *hakham*?

Reconciliation between the conflicting points is achieved by focusing on some of the technical aspects of the law of standing up for a *hakham*. First, let's look at the definition of *hakham*. In R. Mosheh Isserles' view, *hakham* is understood to include not only one's teacher or one of the prominent Torah scholars of the generation, but also includes one's superior in Torah scholarship.[51] This expansive definition of *hakham* creates the possibility that someone who warrants a show of respect from a *po'el* will visit the work scene many times a day.

Another point of law that makes the obligation to stand up for a *hakham* a time consuming enterprise is the requirement that one should stand up for him in a manner that allows the *hakham* to perceive that the "standing up" is in his honor. This translates into the requirement that A should not stand up for the *hakham* until the *hakham* reaches within four *amot* (approximately eight feet) of him. If A would get up sooner, it would not be evident that getting up was in honor of the *hakham*, but instead would be understood as motivated by A's own needs.[52] To fulfill this obligation properly, A must hence watch the movements of the *hakham* very carefully. In addition, once A stands up for the *hakham*, he must remain standing until the *hakham* passes by him.[53]

Let's also consider the possibility that the duty to stand up for a *hakham* may be thrust on P at a time that is inconvenient or even disruptive from the standpoint of the employer.

We now can see why employers never decided that it would be proper for them to absorb the costs of allowing their employees to comply with the duty to stand up for a *hakham*. These costs are neither trivial nor predictable. In sharp contrast, allowing P to accept a short outside call during business hours ordinarily entails but a trivial cost for E in both outlay and time and, in addition, is usually not disruptive.

The upshot of this analysis is that the right of P to accept outside calls is very limited. The sages understood that the employer is very particular that the work scene should not be disrupted. What follows is a duty for P to inform his relatives and friends that they should not call him at work unless the message is urgent and delivering it immediately is the only way to avoid significant aggravation or loss.

THE RIGHT OF THE *PO'EL* TO WITHDRAW AND PRODUCTIVITY THEORY

In this section we will place the halakhic right of P to withdraw from his job in the context of productivity theory in the current economic literature. We will show that our thesis that the right of P to withdraw generates for E a net benefit is consistent with both modern economic theory and the empirical record that tests that theory. We begin with an explication of the efficiency wage theory.

The efficiency wage hypothesis states that some firms might be able to improve worker productivity by paying a wage that is *above* the wage paid by other firms. The reasoning here is that higher wages will elicit increased effort and reduced shirking by employees. Higher wages may also allow the firm to attract a more qualified pool of candidates to choose from. Other possible benefits include lower turnover costs, improved morale, more easily facilitated teamwork, and greater feelings of loyalty by workers to the firm.[54]

The attractiveness of the efficiency wage model is that the theory provides an explanation for large and persistent "noncompetitive" wage differentials across firms and industries for workers with similar productive characteristics. The theory also explains why equilibrium is consistent with persistent involuntary unemployment.[55]

Professor George J. Borjas cites the example of how the efficiency wage policy works to the advantage of the firm in less developed economies. At the subsistence competitive wage, workers might not get the nutrition necessary to maintain a healthy lifestyle. If firms pay the competitive wage, they attract a workforce composed of undernourished workers who are not very productive. As a result, it is possible for a firm to enhance worker productivity and increase its profits by paying workers a wage above the competitive wage.

The empirical record supports the notion that there is a link between the nutrition of workers and their productivity. A 10 percent increase in caloric intake among farm workers in Sierra Leone, for example, increases productivity by about 3.4 percent.[56]

The efficiency wage hypothesis apparently has predictive value even when the competitive wage the worker initially enjoys is above subsistence. The Raff–Summers study on why Henry Ford introduced the $5 day in 1914 bears this out.

The $5 day proved a phenomenal success. Between 1914 and 1915 the Ford Company produced fifteen percent more cars per day, with 2000 or fourteen percent fewer workers and a reduction in the number of hours worked per worker. These figures, supplied by Henry Ford himself in testimony before the Industrial Relations Commission, suggest a close to thirty percent productivity increment. The figure Raff and Summers come up with based on their statistical technique is a forty to seventy percent productivity gain.[57]

From an objective standpoint, Ford's introduction of the $5 day was a risky proposition. The cost of introducing this wage increase was $10 million. This sum represented as much as one-half of the projected profits of the company for 1914.[58] Efficiency wage factors Raff and Summers found plausible in explaining the motivational force behind the $5 wage were a desire to reduce turnover, to elicit greater work effort, and to improve worker morale.[59]

The theoretical link between a supracompetitive wage and productivity, as Borjas points out, becomes weaker as the wage rises too high above subsistence. At some point the increase in the firm's labor costs will probably exceed the value of the increased productivity of its workforce. There will exist a wage, however, called the efficiency wage, where the marginal cost of increasing the wage exactly equals the marginal gain in the productivity of the firm's workers.[60]

The Sierra Leone and Ford studies lend support to the proposition that a morale lifting measure introduced against an initial condition of extremely low morale will be effective in raising productivity.

In the thinking of the Talmudic sages, agreeing to work at fixed hours creates for *P*, other things being equal, *an inherently low morale condition*. It is no less than a shackled condition akin to servitude. What rescues *P* from this otherwise shackled condition is his theoretical right to withdraw from his work at any time without incurring a penalty for the time he has worked up to that point. But, in the modern work scene, *P's* retraction right is effectively reduced to a vapidity. Consider that suddenly quitting his job will incur for *P* significant job search costs. It is for this reason, as discussed above, that Halakhah protects *P* against sudden discharge and requires *E* to give him proper notice. If the modern work scene renders *P's* retraction right meaningless, nothing underscores *P's* dependency status more than a *work rule* that chains *P* and at the same time generates no tangible benefit for *E*. This would be the judgment for a *blanket* prohibition on *P* to place a personal call even when the call is very short and is placed between assignments. The same judgment holds for a *blanket* prohibition on *P* to accept outside calls. Conferring *P* with minimal telephone privileges hence "unshackles" him and at the same time boosts his morale. If conferring the minimal telephone privilege boosts *P's morale*, his *productivity* will increase as well. It is therefore in *E's self-interest* to confer *P* with the minimal telephone privilege. What follows as a corollary is that in the absence of an explicit prohibition against telephone privileges, *P* has the right to appropriate these privileges for himself. The argument here is that taking these privileges generates a net benefit for *E*.

CONTRACTING AGAINST THE USE OF OFFICE EQUIPMENT FOR PERSONAL COMMUNICATIONS

The thrust of the discussion thus far relates to why it is halakhically problematic for *E* to spring a blanket prohibition on *W* in respect to the use of office equipment for personal communications. Given that the entire issue revolves around the prohibition for *E* to impose servitude-like conditions in his workplace, there should be no halakhic impediments for *E* to put a no personal use clause in *W's* contract. If there is no objection to having *W* to agree in advance to waive his right to withdraw without penalty, then, there should also be no problem to get *W* to agree in advance not to use company equipment or a personal cell phone to engage in personal communications on company time. We take it, however, as a given that workers have a very strong preference for the amenity of having a minimal personal communications privilege. If so, it becomes empirically possible to put in quantifiable terms just how much the minimal telephone privilege is worth to workers in various professions. To make this determination we need only conduct a controlled experiment and find out by how much *E* must increase his offer at the negotiating stage to get *W* to agree to a no personal telephone or electronic communications clause.

If our intuition is correct and getting *W* to agree to the no personal telephone or electronic communications clause requires *E* to offer an additional wage premium, then the case against *springing* the no personal telephone or electronic communications rule is enhanced. This is so because the trade-off demonstrates that in the absence of the advance mention of the no personal telephone privilege the minimal personal telephone call privilege is a fully expected amenity among workers. Self-appropriation of a minimal personal telephone privilege is hence not unethical.

PLAYING COMPUTER GAMES BETWEEN ASSIGNMENTS

Let's now turn to the ethics for Frier to prohibit his staff from playing computer games in between assignments. The ethics of Frier's conduct here revolves around both how *P* accesses the computer game and Frier's motivation in prohibiting the conduct. Let's look at several scenarios.

The most objectionable scenario occurs when P wants to download computer games from the Internet. Since P's action slows down the Internet connection for the entire office staff, P's action might adversely affect the productivity of workers who are not between assignments. Frier is within his rights to object to the downloading, and in the absence of an explicit prohibition P has no right to appropriate the privilege for himself.

In another scenario, P does not make use of the Internet to access the computer game. Instead, he merely turns on the game application on his computer desktop. Here, we need to focus on Frier's motivation in prohibiting the computer games between assignments. In one scenario Frier believes that playing video games between assignments *adversely* affects P's productivity during working hours. The passion and excitement some people have for these games creates the possibility that a worker who plays a game during a lull in the workflow will continue to replay the game again and again in his mind when he should be devoting his full concentration to the assignment at hand. If this attitude is behind Frier's objection to the games, it should be prohibited for P to turn on the game application on his desktop computer. Consider that the computer is Frier's property and he has every right to object to misappropriation of his property.

Now, if the above concern rings true for a particular P, the conduct should be prohibited for that person even if there is no explicit rule against it. The basis of prohibiting this conduct is the obligation of P to exert himself on behalf of E with his *utmost* energy.[61] On the basis of this requirement, P may not work at night while under contract during the day.[62] Similarly, P may not refuse to use his wages to provide himself with minimal nourishment, even if the money saved is used toward the support of his family.[63] Similarly, a schoolteacher may not stay up late at night or rise very early.[64] In all these instances, the conduct reduces P's productivity while performing his contracted work and is therefore prohibited.[65] If "moonlighting" is prohibited for P because it adversely affects his productivity during his daytime job, then playing video games during a lull in the workflow should be prohibited for the same reason.

Another reason why Frier might object to video games on company time is that the conduct may drag down the work ethic at his place of business. Consider that most of the staff works in cubicles. The appearance of a video or card game on the screen of one of the desktop computers in one cubicle is therefore easily visible from the vantage point of many of the other cubicles. Now, if everyone has a license to entertain him-or-herself with a video or card game during a lull in the workflow, the simultaneous appearance of these games on more than one computer screen may very well create the false impression that not much work is done at the Frier Novelty Company. Such a false impression can do no less than drag down the work ethic at Frier's company.

If the concern not to undermine the work ethic is what stands behind Frier's rule against computer games, running the computer game on the company machine would be an act of misappropriation by *P*.

A variation of the above cases occurs when Frier sees no harm in the video games, but prohibits the conduct anyway. He does so because as principal owner and CEO of the company, he feels he is entitled to *control* the lives of his employees, at least during working hours. Any rule that rubs in *P*'s state of dependency heightens Frier's sense of control and enhances his sense of satisfaction.

If the rule against computer games is all about control and no more, the halakhic validity of Frier's prohibition can be put to question. In this scenario, turning on the game application on Frier's computers cannot be summarily categorized as an act of misappropriation. Consider that at a moment's notice *P* can switch off the game program and return to the software applications he uses in his work. What loss, therefore, does Frier suffer if *P* entertains himself by running the game program between assignments? The principle in Halakhah is that if *A* benefits from *B*'s property when the benefit involved costs *B* nothing, *A* bears no compensation responsibility to *B*. Denying a fellow a benefit when it costs one nothing is regarded by the sages as reflecting the character trait of the people of Sodom.[66] In some instances, *Bet Din* (a Jewish court) will coerce (*kofin*) an individual not to act in the manner of Sodomites.[67]

Would *Bet Din* order Frier to accede to *P*'s request to allow him to turn on the game application between assignments when Frier cannot identify any loss this conduct would entail for him? Perhaps not. The *kofin* principle has its limitations. In the opinion of one school of thought, led by *Tosafot*, *kofin* is only an *ex post* liability exemption rule, but does not work to allow someone to *affirmatively* make use of another's property. A case in point is the squatter case discussed at *Bava Kamma* 21a: *A* settles on *B*'s property without the latter's knowledge. *B* had not put up the said property for rent. When *B* discovers that *A* is squatting on his property, he exerts a rental claim against *A* for the period of occupancy. Since *A*'s action entails no loss for *B*, *A* bears no compensation responsibility for his period of occupancy. Nonetheless, discovery of *A* on his premises allows *B* to evict him. *B*'s right to do so obtains, according to *Tosafot*, even if he has no intent to either rent or to use the property himself.[68]

Let's apply the above conceptualization of the *kofin* principle to the case at hand. To be sure, *P*'s request to turn on a computer game application when he is between assignments entails no expense or disadvantage for Frier, but the request entails allowing *P* to make use of Frier's property. Frier is hence apparently within his rights to refuse *P*'s request.

Rejection of the *kofin* principle here should, however, be reserved. Let's consider the rationale behind *Tosafot*'s conceptualization of the *kofin* principle.

In his analysis of *Tosafot*'s view, R. Shimon Shkop (Lithuania, 1860–1940) points out that ownership fundamentally manifests itself with the element of *control*. The squatter's plea not only confronts the owner with a request to make use of the land gratis, but also demands the owner relinquishes his control of the property for the period of occupancy. Since the great majority of people harbor a preference to retain control of their property, denying the squatter's request does not reflect a Sodomite character.[69]

Applying R. Shkop's rationale of *Tosafot*'s view to the case at hand would call for Frier to accede to *P*'s request. Given that *P* has the facility to turn off the game application and use the computer to do his work at a moment's notice, his request to play games on the computer in a lull in no way wrests the computer from Frier's control. Denying the request therefore amounts to Sodomite behavior.

Another school of thought, led by R. Mordecai b. Hillel (Germany, 1240–1298), conceptualizes the *kofin* principle more broadly. In this formulation, *A*'s request to make affirmative use of *B*'s property is not always illegitimate. The request is illegitimate only when *B* either intends to use the property himself or has at least the *possibility* to rent it out to someone else, if he so desires, at the time the request was made. If *B* neither intends to use the property himself nor has possibility to rent it out at the time the request was made, denying *A*'s request reflects on the part of *B* a Sodomite character. Here, *Bet Din* will direct *B* to allow *A* to make use of the property.[70]

Application of the above formulation to the case at hand should make it mandatory for Frier to accede to *P*'s request. Consider that it is impossible to predict in advance the time of day and the amount of time P will be between assignments. Accordingly, it is impossible for Frier to rent out in advance P's idle computer time to anyone. Because Frier can identify no loss P's request entails for him, *Bet Din* will force him to accede to it.

The upshot is that if Frier has no bottom line concerns about his employees either downloading or turning on computer games when they are between assignments, he should not prohibit this conduct.

Given that bottom line concerns about playing the video games between assignments is legitimate, P has the responsibility to be alert to the possible harm playing these games could have on the work ethic of his company. In the absence of express permission to play these games, P is hence prohibited from doing so.

Many scenarios have been described. What is Frier's *real* attitude toward video games? You guessed it; the answer is *all of the above*. Specifically, Frier is concerned that allowing employees to play these games will drag down the work ethic he desires to create. But, absent any bottom line concern, he would, in any case, prohibit these games because *exerting control for the sake of control* is a fundamental need in his life. Given that Frier's bottom line concerns are legitimate, he should not be barred from implementing his rule just because he also loves to control people. Can Frier promulgate the rule and tell all concerned that the rule is rooted in productivity concerns? Consider that Frier's declaration is not a lie because bottom line considerations independently motivate his rule against video games. The answer here will depend on how Frier generally comports himself in the workplace. If his treatment of subordinates is generally demeaning and debasing, then the workforce will take the productivity motive he openly declares as a sham. Because the declaration accomplishes nothing to placate subordinates regarding the need for the rule and serves only to heap mockery on top of the resentment they feel toward the rule, Frier's explanation for his rule *exasperates* ill feeling and hence causes needless mental anguish. Accordingly, Frier's public relations ploy to put a positive spin on his rule violates the *ona'at devarim* interdict.

EXPROPRIATING OFFICE SUPPLIES FOR PERSONAL USE

From the perspective of Halakhah, making use of office supplies for personal use is an act of misappropriation. Legitimacy for this conduct cannot be given even if the item involved has only trivial monetary value. Recall that misappropriating an item of even less than a *perutah* is prohibited conduct. Misappropriating someone's property even with the *intention* to replace it with a more expensive item does not free the offender (*O*) from the prohibition against theft.[71] The only exception here is the instance where we are certain that the misappropriation leaves the victim (*V*) with a net advantage. Net advantage obtains when the following conditions are met: (1) The misappropriated property consists of a nonhousehold item;[72] (2) *O* leaves a more expensive item for *V* in exchange for the item he took; and (3) at the same time that *O* takes possession of *V's* item he confers ownership of the more expensive item to V through a third party.[73]

Stealing office supplies generates no gain for *E*. This conduct should therefore be prohibited even if *E* does not promulgate any explicit prohibition against this conduct.

PROMULGATING A RULE AGAINST MISAPPROPRIATION BUT DOING NOTHING TO ENFORCE IT

Recall the opening vignette involving Ben Green. Green was well aware of Frier's prohibition against making personal use of the company copier, but violated the interdict anyway and was caught red-handed doing so. Frier chose not to reprimand Green for the infraction. Does Frier's silence in the face of observing an open violation of his interdict license Green to conclude that Frier was never serious about the interdict in the first place and proceed in the future to treat personal use of the copier as an implicit fringe benefit he had all along? No. Frier's non-enforcement of his rules should be taken as saying to his employees "if you think you can steal from me and get away with it, go ahead and try." A similar case was dealt with by R. Joseph Trani (Italy, 1568–1639): *A* said to *B*, "if I don't do such and such for you, then, you can go ahead and *steal* from me." Since *A* made no arrangement to transfer his property to *B* as a *gift*, his statement amounts to no more than *an invitation to B to steal from him*. Since stealing is prohibited conduct, *B* may not take up *A* on his invitation. Moreover, if *B* goes ahead and takes something from *A*, the article he took must be regarded as a "stolen object" and must be returned to *A* (*hashavat gezeilah*).[74] Similarly, in the case at hand, non-enforcement of rules is not an implicit gift transfer statement. It is, at most, an invitation to steal. Since stealing is a prohibited act, P may not violate Frier's rules even though Frier makes no attempt to enforce them. Moreover, whatever is taken is regarded as an article of theft and must be returned.

Reinforcing this judgment is the consideration that Frier's silence in the face of his discovery of misappropriation may reflect no more than economically rational behavior not to protest. Professor Paul S. Carlin's explanation of why some employers tolerate non-serious forms of shirking provides the logic here. Carlin defines nonserious shirking to consist of behavior that is indisputably *improper*, but is tolerated by E because it imposes only relatively modest current period costs on him. Examples of this conduct offered by Carlin include occasional slight tardiness, taking "sick days" when not really sick, excessive numbers of coffee breaks, and occasional personal use of an office copier. In deciding whether to discipline P for the instances of nonserious shirking he observes, E will balance the quasi-fixed costs of dismissing and hiring replacements against the costs the shirking imposes on him in the current period.[75]

What follows from this analysis is that far from signaling approval, *E's silence* should be taken as communicating no more than his conviction that the course of action that minimizes losses for him at this juncture in time is not to punish or even protest the misdeed.

If silence does not signal retroactive approval, perhaps an explicit statement by E can accomplish this. In this regard, let's turn to Frier's exchange with Leonard Sunshine, referred to in the opening vignette. Recall that Sunshine took a box of company crayons for his son Eric's arts and crafts project. When Frier got wind of it he blurted out apparent approval to Sunshine by saying "you should have taken Olemark's *pastels* for Eric's project."

An analogous case is dealt with in the Talmud in connection with the law of betrothal. The law states that one can effect betrothal with a woman by giving her money or an item worth at least a *perutah*. This money or item must be the property of the groom. If the money or item he gives the woman is not his, the betrothal does not take affect. Against this backdrop, the Talmud relates that a brewmaster betrothed a woman by giving her date remnants. These date remnants were the property of the owner of the brewery. In the manufacturing process, it was common practice to use one bunch of dates to produce several runs of beer. Because the dates would lose more and more of their flavor in successive runs, each round produced a progressively inferior grade of beer. Date remnants of various grades were lying about in the factory and the brewmaster took one of them and betrothed a woman with it. When the owner of the brewery discovered what the brewmaster had done, he said to him "Why did you not give [her some] of these [more] flavorful [remnants instead]." The issue at hand was whether the owner's declaration should be construed as his approval of what the brewmaster did. If the owner's remarks are to be interpreted in this way, the brewmaster's action effected betrothal. On the other hand, if we don't read approval into the words of the owner, the brewmaster effected betrothal with the owner's money and the betrothal was not valid. In resolving this issue, the most basic point the Talmud makes is that the owner of the brewery was under no obligation to give up any of his date remnants to the brewmaster. Accordingly, instead of reading approval into his words, we should interpret them as being said because he was *embarrassed* (*mishum kisufa hu d'avid*) to insist to the brewmaster that he return the date remnants. Because his *ex post* statement should not be taken as approval, we have no basis to assume that if the owner had been consulted initially he would have approved.[76]

Proceeding from this analogy is that Sunshine should not take Frier's statement, "You should have taken Olemark's *pastels* for Eric's project" as an indication that the boss actually approved of what he did. Sunshine should certainly not take Frier's comment as a revelation that making personal use of company property was a fringe benefit he had all along.

FRIER'S OFFICE SUPPLY CLOSET AND HALAKHAH

In the opening vignette we encounter Frier's *harsh* prohibition against the personal use of office supplies. Yet, he not only makes no apparent attempt to enforce his interdict, but also actually *inveigles* his employees to misappropriate the office supplies for their personal use.

Frier's conduct runs afoul of the prohibition to create for a fellow a setting for veiled misconduct. Such conduct is an aspect of the interdict against facilitating a sin (*lifnei iver lo titan mikhshol*). The prototype case in the Talmud is the prohibition for *L* to lend money to *B* without the benefit of witnesses. Such an arrangement effectively *tempts B* to repudiate the loan, as no one other than the lender can testify that the loan actually took place.[77]

Frier's comportment in respect to his prohibition against the personal use of office supplies amounts to creating a setting for veiled misconduct for his employees. Frier does this by making the office supply closet *directly* accessible to everyone *without accountability*. Because the hidden camera is a secret, employees imagine that taking the office supplies for personal use represents an opportunity to engage in veiled misconduct. Frier's conduct hence *inveigles* his employees to engage in veiled misconduct.

In his treatment of the ethics of testing the honesty of a worker (W), R. Joseph Hayyim b. Elijah al-Hakham invokes the *lifnei iver* interdict as a basis to prohibit an employer (E) from subjecting W to an honesty test that inveigles him into thinking that his dishonesty will go undetected. Moreover, even if E eliminates in advance for W the problem of theft by conferring him title to the money involved without W's knowledge, the test remains prohibited conduct. R. Joseph Hayyim's source is *Nazir* 23a:

> "Her husband has annulled [her vows] and Hashem will forgive her" (Numbers 30:13). – Scripture speaks of a woman whose husband has revoked [her vow] for her, but she was unaware [that he had done so, and it teaches] that she needs atonement and forgiveness. – When R. Akiva would reach this verse, he would weep [and say:] – "If someone intended that pork should come into his hand, but [instead] lamb's meat came into his hand-is in need of atonement and forgiveness, – [then] someone who intends that pork should come into his hand, – and [indeed] pork came into his hand, – how much more so [is he in need of atonement and forgiveness]!"[78]

SHIRKING AS TREATED IN THE ECONOMIC LITERATURE

In the economic literature, a number of theories have been offered to show that it is economically rational for E to tolerate shirking. One theory, advanced by Professor Carlin, referred to earlier, makes E's reaction to P's shirking a matter of balancing the quasi-fixed costs of dismissing P and hiring a replacement for him against the costs P's shirking imposes on him in the current period.

The organizational model implicit in Carlin's theory, as Professor Thomas R. Ireland points out, is a model of antagonism between E and P.

In Ireland's thinking, it is economically rational for E to set up rules against specific forms of shirking, but to deliberately be selective in enforcing the rules. In opposition to Carlin, E *selectively* tolerates shirking not because doing so minimizes his costs in the current period, but rather because selectively tolerating the conduct generates benefits for himself. Consider that selective tolerance of shirking conduct creates for P a more pleasant work environment and hence can be envisioned as a fringe benefit that can be offered in lieu of somewhat higher wages. P also benefits in the form of receiving nontaxable psychic income. The tax liability that would have accrued if the benefits to P were taken as wages represents a positive sum to be divided between E and P if taken in the form of selective tolerance of shirking.

Another advantage for E to announce rules against shirking, but to deliberately only selectively enforce these rules, is that selective tolerance of shirking serves well as a screening device for promotion. Consider that the potential cost of shirking is much higher at higher levels of management than at lower levels. It is therefore in the best interests of E to determine P's reliability now as a gauge for his promotability at some time in the future. The more liberties P takes in flaunting the specific forms of shirking conduct E prohibits him from engaging in, the more he will be demonstrating his unsuitability to be promoted.[79]

SELECTIVE TOLERATION OF SHIRKING AND VEILED MISCONDUCT

The prohibition to create for a fellow a setting for veiled misconduct, referred to earlier, casts doubt on the ethics of Ireland's scheme for E to use selective toleration of shirking as a screening device to determine an employee's suitability for promotion. This scheme is objectionable even if E takes proper legal action beforehand to free P of misappropriation for any shirking he engages in. Because P is *unaware* that his shirking is permissible conduct at the moment he engages in it, E's screening device is ethically unacceptable.

Ireland's theory creates the setting for the following moral dilemma: Suppose Frier neither explicitly issues a directive against various forms of shirking nor reprimands anyone for engaging in such conduct. Does P have the right to assume that Ireland's scheme is operating in the workplace?

Specifically, suppose P, in the absence of any directive against it, engages in shirking in full view of Frier and faces no consequences from the boss for the liberties he takes. Does P have the right to read into Frier's comportment that he is being awarded a fringe benefit in the form of a shirking privilege? Alternatively, may P interpret Frier's comportment as reflecting a deliberate investment on the part of Frier to determine whether his current employees are candidates for continued employment and for promotion? No. The most fundamental point to be made here is that Ireland's analysis produces no more than a theory. In the absence of explicit permission from E to engage in what is otherwise an act of misappropriation against him, P has no right to ascribe attitudes and motives to E that effectively license him to engage in the conduct. Frier's nonenforcement of his rules should be taken as saying to his employees "if you think you can steal from me and get away with it, go ahead and try." Recall R. Trani's point that B is forbidden to take up A's invitation to steal from A. Taking up the invitation makes B guilty of misappropriation. Recall also that even when E catches P red-handed in an act of misappropriation and reacts in a seemingly approving manner, P remains guilty of misappropriation. Ireland's theory therefore cannot be said to *definitively identify* E's attitude toward P's specific act of misappropriation. From the vantage point of P, Ireland's theory is no more than a rationalization to engage in prohibited conduct.

Man's drive to put a veneer of legitimacy on prohibited conduct as a means of relieving his sense of guilt is a phenomenon well understood by the Talmudic sages:

> R. Huna said: Once a man has committed a sin once or twice, it is permitted to him. Permitted? How could that occur to you? –Rather, *nassit lo ke-hetter*, i.e., it *appears* to him as if it were permitted. (*Yoma*, 86b)

Invoking Ireland's theory to put a veneer of legitimacy on an otherwise prohibited act provides a modern example, in the context of labor relations, of the principle of *nassit lo ke-hetter*. Where does *nassit lo ke-hetter* lead? The answer, R. Avraham Grodzinski (Poland, ca. 1882–1944) tells us, is a slippery slope, culminating in the rationalization that the forbidden conduct is actually a *mitzvah* (i.e., virtuous conduct).[80] Indeed, embracing Ireland's thesis leads us down this slippery slope. For one, the distinction he draws between serious and non-serious shirking leaves the dividing line between these spheres subjective and imprecise. Moreover, if we are to take Ireland seriously, *P* should not only not feel a sense of guilt in engaging in nonserious forms of shirking, but should also feel that the conduct he engages in is a matter of *entitlement*. We are already perilously approaching the mindset that the prohibited conduct at hand is actually virtuous behavior. We hit the bottom of the slippery slope when *P* feels a sense of self-congratulatory pride for being smart enough to unmask the boss's selective toleration of nonserious forms of shirking to be nothing more than the operation of a screening mechanism for promotion. By being smart enough to recognize "the true intentions" of the boss, the boss's investment will not go wasted!

SUMMARY AND CONCLUSION

This chapter has examined a number of issues relating to work rules that an employee first discovers on the job, as opposed to rules that he or she agrees to in advance of the labor contract. The rules that we dealt with are the kind that are designed to discourage idleness and various forms of shirking. Springing a work rule on a worker is legitimate only when the particular rule amounts to nothing more than an enforcement of the employer's right against misappropriation or protection against harm. When this is not the case, springing the rule on the worker may amount to prohibited conduct as it unilaterally generates negative psychic income for the employee.

A rule that is sprung on the worker that runs counter to *minhag* is not valid. Frier's rules against both a coffee break and his insistence that everyone remain "glued" to their workstations throughout the entire workday effectively create "prison-like" conditions for his workforce, akin to a sweatshop operation. These rules certainly run counter to *minhag*, and are hence invalid even in respect to the portion of Frier's labor force that he pays above competitive wages to.

In the Torah's way of thinking, the *po'el* (P) labor contract is psychologically akin to servitude. This is so because agreeing to work *at fixed hours* makes *P* feel that he has entered into a "shackled" relationship with his employer (*E*). To remove this feeling of dependency, the Torah empowers *P* with a *theoretical* right to withdraw in the middle of the day without incurring penalty for the time he has already worked.

P's theoretical retraction right is an important factor in evaluating the ethics for E to impose a work rule and also in evaluating P's right to appropriate a privilege for himself in the absence of an explicit prohibition by E for P not to take this privilege.

In relating the retraction right to work rules, we argued that the retraction right is meaningful only in the context of a labor marketplace where both employers demand labor and workers supply their labor on a *day-to-day* basis. Within this milieu, P's knowledge that he can quit at any time without forfeiting any portion of the prorated wages he has already earned is comforting. One could argue that in the modern work scene P's retraction right is reduced to a vapidity. Consider that suddenly quitting his job will incur for P significant job search costs. It is for this reason that Halakhah protects P against sudden discharge and requires E to give him proper notice. If the modern work scene renders P's retraction right meaningless, nothing underscores P's dependency status more than a work rule that chains P and at the same time generates no tangible benefit for E. This would be the judgment for a *blanket* prohibition on P to use office equipment in between assignments for personal communications. The same judgment holds for a *blanket* prohibition on P to receive outside personal communications through the company equipment.

In evaluating the ethics for P to appropriate for himself an amenity not explicitly awarded to him in the labor contract, we offered the "net benefit" criterion. This criterion requires that it be objectively evident that P's appropriation of the privilege will generate a net benefit for E. P's theoretical right to retract plays a vital role in making this calculation. Specifically, if taking the privilege *unshackles* P, taking the privilege also increases P's productivity and hence benefits E as well. Moreover, P's retraction right gives him a certain amount of *leverage* over E to make him agree to a quit-rehire scheme. Because the quit-rehire proposal imposes greater costs on E than the costs E would incur if P would appropriate the privilege for himself without consulting E, E presumably agrees with the appropriation. Still another factor for the calculation of the "net benefit" criterion is efficiency wage theory.

One final point. The argument for self-appropriation of a minimal personal telephone privilege is enhanced if a controlled experiment shows that P demands a premium in extra wages if he or she is asked in advance to forego any personal telephone privileges. The demonstration of this trade-off shows that in the absence of an advance prohibition of a personal privilege, a minimal personal use of the office phone is the reasonable expectation of P.

These various strands of analysis lead to the proposition that in the absence of E's explicit prohibition, P may appropriate a minimal personal telephone and electronic communication privilege when he or she is between assignments. Relatedly, the thrust of the analysis leads to the permissibility for P to respond *minimally* to an outside call. To be sure, it is P's duty to inform his friends and family to call him only when not making the call would cause considerable aggravation or disruption.

The "net benefit" criterion leads to the clear-cut *prohibition* for P to appropriate for himself the privilege to make personal use of office supplies. In the many variations of this case discussed, we demonstrated that E's silence or even apparent statements of approval in the face of his discovery of shirking does not signal his approval of the conduct.

In the contemporary scene, the notion that an employer has the right to *control* subordinates on the job enjoys some currency. From a Torah perspective, this attitude is unacceptable. Proceeding from the Torah's concern that the labor contract should not leave P feeling shackled is that entering into a labor contract creates for P only the duty to energetically apply himself without interruption to the tasks and obligations proceeding from the labor contract. The labor contract does not, however, entitle E to *control P*. In this chapter, we related the above principle to the issue of whether E is within his rights to prohibit P to turn on the game application on his company computer when he finds himself between assignments. To be sure, there is valid reason for E to object to the practice. Legitimate concerns include the fear that P will mentally keep on replaying the game again and again and hence adversely affect his productivity on the job. E may also be concerned that allowing the practice will drag down the work ethic of his place of business. If P wants to download the game from the Internet there may be the additional concern that this action will slow down the Internet connection for co-workers. But suppose E can identify no debit for his business in this practice, but begrudges that he loses *control* over P while the game is being played. Because disallowing the practice is all about *control* and nothing more, it should be unethical for E to promulgate a rule against this practice. Various nuances of this case were considered.

Finally, the ethics for E to entrap P to engage in shirking is considered. Such conduct is prohibited because it *inveigles* the subordinate to engage in veiled misconduct.

The prohibition to create for a fellow a setting for veiled misconduct puts to question the notion that E may use selective toleration of shirking as a screening device to determine P's suitability for promotion. This scheme is objectionable even if E takes proper legal action beforehand to free P of misappropriation for any shirking he engages in. Because P is unaware that his shirking is permissible conduct at the moment he engages in it, E's screening device is ethically unacceptable.

POSTPRANDIUM

Reading up on the phenomenon of the operation of the sweatshop makes the term *mean boss* a relative term.

Let us take a glimpse at the operation of such a sweatshop, the Chun Si Enterprises Handbag Factory, located in southern China. Making handbags sold by Wal-Mart, the company attracted a labor supply by advertising that it pays a "fair salary" and provides decent working conditions. But, once a worker signed up with the company, he or she was in for a number of surprises. First, the company required the new arrival to give up his or her personal identity card for an expired temporary resident permit. Because the local police knew that all workers in the factory had expired temporary-resident cards, the workers faced certain arrest if they left the employ of the company. Becoming an employee of Chun Si Enterprises hence made the employee a virtual captive. Another surprise for the new arrival was that he/she was charged a fee of $15 a month for food and lodging in a crowded dorm. This is a crushing sum as workers didn't clear more than $22 a month working for the company. Because workers typically put in a 90-hour work week, their hourly wage amounts to one-half cent per hour. Guards regularly punched and hit workers for talking back to managers or even for walking too fast, and workers were fined up to $1 for infractions such as taking too long in the bathroom. One final point: At Chun Si, the 900 workers were locked in the walled factory compound for all but a total of 60 minutes a day for meals.[81]

Consider that the essence of the prohibition against entering into a status of servitude, according to *Tosafot*, is that the arrangement inherently gives the worker no possibility to retract.[82] At Chun Si the company created prison-like conditions for a worker once he or she was hired. The coercion and intimidation Chun Li utilized to get the workers to put in extra time and tolerate conditions never stipulated in advance makes working for this company no less than a prohibited servitude arrangement.

Moreover, given the coercion involved, the workers have a valid claim for the overpayment they were charged for room and board at the factory, to say nothing of the overtime they put in without getting any differential compensation whatsoever. An analogous case is discussed by R. David b. Samuel ha-Levi (Poland, 1586–1667). The elements of the case are as follows: *E* hired *P* to transport on his shoulders a load of a stipulated weight. In actuality, *E* put on *P's* shoulders a larger weight than he specified. Notwithstanding that *P* raised no protest regarding the extra weight, *E* must pay *P* for the extra weight he imposed on him.[83] R. David ha-Levi's approach should be applied to the case at hand. Specifically, when workers become employees at Chun Si they have every legitimate expectation to the entitlements of Chinese labor law and the rule of law generally. Accordingly, if Chun Si violates the law by imposing overtime without differential pay and overcharges for room and board, the worker's silence should not be taken as a waiver of his or her entitlements. Quite to the contrary, the intimidation and coercion Chun Si subjected its workers to makes the terms and conditions nothing more than forced labor.

The circumstance that Wal-Mart only contracted for the *purchase* of the finished product and was not the employer of record of the exploited workers does not disassociate them from responsibility in this matter. To be sure, Wal-Mart eventually terminated its relationship with Chun Si. Among other abuses, Chun Si was found guilty of setting up a bogus factory on one of the floors of the plant to throw off the inspectors. But, through its audits, Wal-Mart was aware early on of violations and opted to continue its contract with Chun Si. What did Wal-Mart do about the abuses when it became aware of them? One could argue that unless Wal-Mart made continuation of the contract contingent upon making monetary amends to the workers for past abuses and agreed to put an independent audit in place to insure against future abuses, Wal-Mart is guilty of abetting these transgressors. To boot, continuing the contract without taking the firm actions just outlined makes Wal-Mart guilty of directly profiting from the sins of Chun Si. We should, therefore, invoke the Talmudic dictum that the "sinner should not be at an advantage."[84]

The policy of "chasing after the cheapest labor supply" on a *global level* also does terrible injustice to the Divine blessing "be fruitful and multiply and fill the earth and subdue it" (henceforth, *kibbush*, Genesis 1:28). In the thinking of R. Joseph B. Soloveitchik, *kibbush* is a mandate to man for self-actualization as a creative being. Man fulfills this mandate by breaking away from a state of dependency and using the power and freedom obtained to discharge his responsibilities to God and fellow man.[85] Understanding *kibbush* in these terms makes this mandate within the reach of every man. It is achieved by the pursuit of ordinary livelihood activities accompanied by a rarefied sense of duty and responsibility to God and fellow man.

Now, if the starting point of the "chase after the cheapest labor supply" is the production of the good where workers are given a livable wage and decent working conditions, but switches to places where workers are treated worse and worse, even to the extent they receive less than subsistence earnings and are abused in various ways, the pursuit of a livelihood is accompanied by a deteriorating sense of responsibility toward fellow man. This was the case for Nike, as it moved its operation from country to country. Nike first moved production out of the United States to Taiwan and then to South Korea when American workers organized to demand a reasonable wage. Then, when democracy took hold in Taiwan and South Korea, Nike moved production again, this time to China, Indonesia, and Vietnam, where the governments violently suppress workers' rights.[86] In *kibbush* terms, if the profit motive drives firms to locate where wages are below subsistence and to where workers enjoy no rights, then economic activity is devoid of any sense of rarefied responsibility.

In some countries local labor law, even on paper, does not measure up to the most minimal internationally agreed upon standards. A case in point is Indonesia, Malaysia, and Thailand in which several core labor conventions of the International Labor Organization have gone unratified—including the right to organize. Minimum wages in these countries are well below the poverty line.[87] The *kibbush* mandate gets its severest thrashing when the profit motive drives companies to locate in these countries.

For some commentators, the abysmal earnings by western standards of the unskilled workers employed by the multinationals is not a debit for globalization. The proper comparison to make is what earnings these unskilled workers would earn if the multinationals were to choose to locate in a different country. A case in point is the earnings of the workers at the Nike plant in Vietnam. In 2002 workers there earned only $670 a year. By western standards this is an appalling sum. But, consider that the minimum annual wage in Vietnam at the time was a mere $134. In other words, Nike workers in Vietnam were earning *five times* the minimum wage.[88] I question very much the above sanguine interpretation of this data. Consider that the differential just cited is a conundrum for economic theory. If workers at Nike are really so much better off than their local counterparts, why are unskilled workers not camping out to get hired by Nike? If market forces are working, the wage differential should bring a huge increase in supply relative to demand, and in the process wipe out the differential. But, there is no stampede to work for Nike. Why not? The persistence of the differential gives additional credence to the well-documented phenomenon that unskilled workers in the international sweatshops have suffered terrible abuses.[89] Nike's own record is a case in point. The company voluntarily agreed to an industry-wide agreement known as the Workplace Code of Conduct and hired former UN Ambassador Andrew Young to review how its Code of Conduct was working in practice. Young's conclusion was that it was his "sincere belief that Nike [was] doing a good job in the application of its Code of Conduct." But, Young himself criticized the company for not having in place some kind of third-party monitoring. Criticism of the Young Report was widespread. The report failed to pick up on such issues as poverty level wages, excessive overtime, minimum wage violations, corporal punishment, and a militaristic management style to control workers.[90]

In recent years the anti-sweatshop movement has gained much momentum. Its main source consists of the White House Apparel Industry Partnership, implemented by the Clinton Administration in 1999. This partnership consists of a voluntary task force of 18 members. These members include clothing and footwear manufacturers, consumers, corporate social responsibility advocates, human rights organizations, and Labor Unions. Another important component of the anti-sweatshop movement is the various student organizations.

The anti-sweatshop movement is pushing hard to get apparel manufacturers to accept a code of what constitutes decent and humane working conditions. This code would be formulated in specific terms of acceptable labor practices (ALP). Companies would commit to this code and agree to have independent auditors monitor compliance with the code. Finally, companies would be rated on a scale of one to five in terms of ALP. Along with other information, currently required by law, such as fiber content and country of origin, this rating would appear on the label of apparel sold by these companies.[91]

There can be no doubt that getting an ALP rating onto apparel labels is an objective the *kibbush* mandate would cheer. What the ALP rating does is *empower* the consumer to connect the company's bottom line to conducting its operations with ethically acceptable labor practices.

In Judaism, the guidepost for interpersonal conduct is the duty to emulate God's attributes of mercy and compassion. This behavioral norm is called *imitatio Dei* ("imitation of God"). For Nike, the relevant Divine attribute to emulate can be found in R. Yohanan's dictum: "Wherever you find the greatness of the Holy One Blessed is He, there you find His humility" (*Megillah* 31a). Where does Nike's grandeur shine more than when it begins operations in a country such as Vietnam? Because Nike and companies like it make substantial investment in plant and equipment and are major employers, their operations impact substantially in raising the GDP of the host country. But what about the plight of the downtrodden, unskilled workers Nike hires to staff it operations? To be sure, since 1992 Nike has voluntarily adopted "codes of conduct." The key provisions of Nike's Code of Conduct include a maximum of sixty hours and at least one day off in seven; minimum wages; zero tolerance of corporal punishment and abuse; and a minimum worker's age of fifteen. But, these high sounding principles can easily become a sham unless an independent audit system is in place to ensure enforcement of the codes. When adequate enforcement procedures are in place, Nike's display of grandeur in the form of impacting in a perceptibly favorable manner on the aggregate level of output of the host country combines with a meaningful concern to elevate and dignify the downtrodden workers that it employs.

NOTES

1. Please turn to pp. 358–361, 362–365 of this volume.
2. In the critical incident performance appraisal approach, a supervisor observes employee behavior and documents negative incidents of observed performance. Instead of providing the employee with negative feedback, the supervisor continues to record negative incidents until a case for dismissal can be made. For a discussion of this method of performance appraisal from the standpoint of Halakhah, See Aaron Levine, *Case Studies in Jewish Business Ethics* (Hoboken,NJ: Ktav Publishing., Yeshiva University Press, 2000), pp. 304–320.

3. Maimonides (Egypt, 1135–1204), *Yad, Sekhirut* 13:7. The prohibition of idling on *E's* time, according to R. Isaac b. Moses (Vienna, late 12th cent. -mid–13th cent., *Or Zaru'a*, vol. 3, *Bava Metzia* 77a, *piska* 242), applies only to the *po'el* (per diem worker), but not to a *kabbelan* (piece worker). What legally distinguishes a *po'el* from a *kabbelan* in Halakhah is that the former is either hired for a specific block of time or is required to work at fixed hours. The *kabbelan*, in contrast, is hired to perform a specific task, with no provision made regarding fixed hours. Since the *kabbelan* is paid for the completed job, rather than by the hour, breaking off the job whenever he so desires should be his prerogative.

For the legal distinction between the *po'el* and the *kabbelan*, see *Rashi, Bava Metzia* 112a; R. Menahem b. Solomon Meiri (France,1249–1316), *Beit ha-Behirah, Bava Metzia* 112a ; R. Meir b. Barukh of Rothenburg (Germany, ca. 1215–1293), *Responsa R. Meir b. Barukh* 477; R. Joshua b. Alexander ha-Kohen Falk (Poland, 1555–1614), *Sema, Shulhan Arukh, Hoshen Mishpat* 333, n.16.

4. Shillem Warhaftig, *Dinei Avodah ba-Mishpat ha-Ivri*, vol. 1 (Jerusalem: *Moreshet*, 1968), p. 324.

5. *Yad*, op cit., 13:7.

6. *Berakhot* 16a.

7. R. Meir ha-Kohen (Germany, fl. 13th cent.), *Haggahot Maimuniyot, Yad, Berakhot* 1; R. Joseph Caro (Israel, 1488–1575), *Shulhan Arukh, Orah Hayyim*) 110:2, 191:2; R. Jehiel Michael Epstein (Belarus, 1829–1908), *Arukh ha-Shulhan, Orah Hayyim* 110:7, 191:4.

8. *Ar. ha-Sh.*, op. cit.,

9. R. Jacob b. Asher (Spain, 1270–1340), *Tur, Hoshen Mishpat* 331; R. Mosheh Isserles (Poland, 1525 or 1530–1572), *Rema, Sh. Ar., Hoshen Mishpat* 331:1; *Ar. ha-Sh.*, op. cit., 331:2.

10. *Bava Metzia* 83a; R. Isaac b. Jacob Alfasi (Algeria, 1013–1204), *Rif*, ad loc; Maimonides (Egypt, 1135–1204), *Yad, Sekhirut* 9:1; R. Asher b. Jehiel (Germany, 1250–1327), *Rosh, Bava Metzia* 7:1; *Tur*, op. cit., 331; *Sh. Ar*, op. cit., 331:1; *Ar. ha-Sh.*, op. cit., 331:4.

11. *Bava Metzia* 83a; *Rosh*, op. cit.,; *Tur*, op. cit., *Sh. Ar.*, op. cit., *Ar. ha-Sh.*, op. cit.,

12. *Rema*, op. cit.

13. C.F. Charles Kernaghan, "Sweatshop Blues," *Dollars and Sense*, March/April 1999, pp. 18–21.

14. *Yad*, op. cit., 13:7.

15. *Mishnah, Bava Kamma* 10:10; *Rif*, ad locum, *Yad, Geneivah* 6:6, 8; *Rosh, Bava Kamma* 10:35; *Tur*, op. cit., 358; *Sh. Ar.*, op. cit., 358:7, 10; *Ar. ha-Sh.*, op. cit., 358:8, 9.

16. Maimonides, commentary to *Mishnah, Kiddushin* 1:1. The amount of silver weighing a half-grain of barley, according to R. Abraham Y. Karelitz (Israel, 1878–1953, *Hazon Ish, Yoreh De'ah* 182: 19), translates into approximately one-fortieth of a gram of silver.

17. *Yad, Gezeilah* 1:6; *Tur*, op. cit., 360:1; *Sh. Ar.*, op. cit., 360:1; *Ar. ha-Sh.*, op. cit., 360:8.

18. *Ar. ha-Sh.*, op. cit.,

19. *Yad, Gezeilah* 1:1; *Tur*, op. cit., 359:1; *Sh. Ar.*, op. cit., 359:1; *Ar. ha-Sh.*, op. cit., 359:1.

20. *Sanhedrin* 57a.

21. *Mishnah, Bava Kamma* 10:10; *Rif*, ad loc *Yad*, op. cit., 6:6; *Rosh*, op. cit.; *Tur*, op. cit., 358; *Sh. Ar.*, op. cit., 358:7; *Ar. ha-Sh.*, op. cit., 358:8.

22. *Mishnah, Bava Kamma* 10:10; *Rif,* ad locum; *Yad,* op. cit., 6:8; *Tur,* op. cit., 358; *Sh. Ar.,* op. cit., 358:10; *Ar. ha-Sh.,* op. cit., 358:9.

23. *Rema, Sh. Ar.,* op. cit., 358:7,10.

24. R. Solomon b. Isaac, *Rashi, Bava Kamma* 119a.

25. *Mishnah, Bava Kamma* 10:10; *Rif,* ad loc; *Yad,* op. cit., 6:8; *Rosh,* op. cit., *Tur,* op. cit., 358; *Sh. Ar.,* op. cit., 358:10; *Ar. ha-Sh.,* op. cit., 358:9.

26. See, however, R. Yom Tov Lipmann b. Nathan ha-Levi Heller (Moravia, 1579–1654), *Tosafot Yom Tov, Mishnah, Bava Kamma* 10:10.

27. *Bava Metzia* 107a.

28. R. Solomon b. Isaac, *Rashi, Bava Metzia* 107a.

29. *Bava Metzia* 10a; *Rif, Bava Metzia* 77b; *Yad, Sekhirut* 9:4; *Rosh,* op. cit., 6:6; *Tur,* op. cit., 332; *Sh. Ar.,* op. cit., 333:3; *Ar. ha-Sh.,* op. cit., 333:6.

30. *Yad,* op. cit., *Tur,* op. cit., 333 *Sh. Ar.,* op. cit., 333:4; *Ar. ha-Sh.,* op. cit., 333:16. How P's right to withdraw works itself out if the wage rate went down is a matter of dispute. In this scenario, P, according to R. Jacob b. Asher (ad loc.), is entitled to collect more than his prorated wage for the time he actually put in. Let's use the example in the text to illustrate this: Suppose the wage rate went down to $5 an hour. The cost to hire P_2 to complete the job is hence only $20. Since E agreed to pay P_1 $80 for an eight-hour work day and P_2 is paid only $20, P_1 is entitled to wages of $60. Disputing R. Jacob, R. Shabbetai b. Meir ha-Kohen (Poland, 1621–1662, *Siftei Kohen,Sh. Ar.* loc. cit., note 19) finds no basis to allow P to parlay his withdrawal right into a profit. In his view, P's entitlement here is no more than what he would get if the wage rate went up and hence P is due only $40. R. Aryeh Loeb Joseph ha-Kohen (Poland, 1745–1813) rules in accordance with R. Jacob b. Asher's view (*Ketzot ha-Hoshen, Sh. Ar.,* op. cit., n. 8).

    The right to withdraw without penalty was not given to a worker who is paid for the finished product and is not required to work at fixed hours. This type of worker is called a *kabbelan.* Accordingly, in the illustration of the text, if the wage rate went up to $20 an hour, the *kabbelan* faces a penalty of $20 and has his earnings reduced to $20. (See sources cited in the beginning of this footnote.)

31. R. Yom Tov Ishbilli, Ritva, *Bava Metzia* 76b.

32. In his analysis of the nature of the claim an employer acquires of the *po'el* as a result of the labor contract, R. Mosheh Feinstein (*Iggerot Mosheh, Hoshen Mishpat* 1:81) identifies three approaches: (1) R. Aryeh Loeb b. Joseph ha-Kohen (*Ketzot ha-Hoshen, Sh. Ar., Hoshen Mishpat* 333, note 5) regards the claim to take the form of a lien on the person of the *po'el*; (2) *Tosafot* (*Kiddushin* 17a, s.v. *halla*) explicitly rejects this approach. Instead, *Tosafot,* in R. Feinstein's view, conceptualize the labor contract as generating reciprocal claims for the parties involved. Specifically, the employer has a claim on the *po'el* that the agreed-upon assignment should be done and the *po'el* has a claim on the employer to provide the work and compensate him upon completion of the job; and (3) R. Jacob Moses Lorberbaum (Lisa, 1760–1832, *Netivot ha-Mishpat, Sh. Ar.,* op. cit., 333, note 6) regards the labor contract as generating only *self-requirements* for the parties involvement. Reciprocal claims do not, however, proceed as a result of the *po'el* contract. R. Feinstein regards the third view as normative. For an extensive identification of the view of the rishonim on this issue, see R. Menahem Shelomo Levi, *Me-Shel Soferim Hilkhot Sekhirut Po'elim,* pp. 18–21.

33. R. Ishmael b. Abraham Isaac ha-Kohen, *Resp. Zera Emet*, Vol. 2, *Yoreh De'ah* 97.

34. *Bava Metzia* 77b; *Rif* ad locum; *Yad*, op. cit.; *Rosh*, op. cit.; *Tur*, op. cit., 333; *Sh. Ar.* op. cit., 333:5; *Ar. ha-Sh.*, op. cit., 333:18–24.

35. *Tur*, op. cit., 333:2; *Rema, Sh. Ar.*, op. cit., 333:4; R. Joseph b. Mosheh Trani (1568–1639), *Responsa Maharit, Yoreh De'ah* 50; *Ar. ha-Sh.*, op. cit., 333:17

36. For discussion of additional exceptions to *P's* withdrawal right, see Aaron Levine, *Free Enterprise and Jewish Law: Aspects of Jewish Business Ethic*s (New York: Ktav Publishing., Yeshiva University, 1980), pp. 44–49.

37. For a discussion of the notice requirement, see Aaron Levine, *Case Studies in Jewish Business Ethics* (Hoboken, NJ: Ktav Publishing, Yeshiva University Press, 2000), pp. 250–257.

38. The *lifnim mi-shurat ha-din* behavioral imperative is derived from Exodus 18:20 and Deuteronomy 6:12. See *Bava Kamma* 99a and Nahmanides at Deuteronomy ad locum.

39. *Tosafot, Bava Metzia* 24b.

40. R. Judah, *Bava Metzia* 33a and *Ar. ha-Sh.*, op. cit., 264:1.

41. *Makkot* 24a.

42. *Ta'anit* 23a, b.

43. R. Samuel b. Judah ha-Levi Edels, *Maharsha, Ta'anit* 23b.

44. R. Isaac b. Solomon, *Rashi, Ta'anit* 23b.

45. R. Joseph Hayyim b. Elijah al-Hakham, *Ben Yehoyada, Ta'anit* 23b.

46. R. Solomon b. Isaac, *Rashi, Shabbat* 129b.

47. *Tosafot, Shabbat* 129b.

48. Leviticus 24:17; *Mishnah, Bava Metzia* 4:10.

49. *Kiddushin* 32b; *Rif*, ad loc; *Yad, Talmud Torah* 6:9; *Rosh, Kiddushin* 1:53; *Tur, Yoreh De'ah* 244; *Sh. Ar., Yoreh De'ah* 244:1; *Ar. ha-Sh., Yoreh De'ah*, 244:1.

50. *Baraita, Kiddushin* 33a; *Rif*, ad loc; *Yad*, op. cit., 6:2; *Rosh*, op. cit., 1:53; *Tur*, op. cit., 244:5; *Sh. Ar.*, op. cit., 244:5; *Ar. ha-Sh.*, op. cit., 244:7.

51. R. Mosheh Isserles, *Rema, Sh. Ar.*, op. cit., 244:1.

52. *Baraita, Kiddushin* 33b, *Yad*, op. cit., 6:6; *Tur*, op. cit., 244; *Sh. Ar.*, op. cit., 244:9; *Ar. ha-Sh.*, 244:4.

53. Ibid.

54. George J. Borjas, *Labor Economics* (New York: McGraw-Hill), pp. 425–427; Lawrence F. Katz, "Efficiency Wage Theories: A Partial Evaluation," in Stanley Fisher, ed., *NBER Macroeconomics Annual 1986* (Cambridge: The MIT Press, 1986), pp. 235–276.

55. "Efficiency Wage Theories," op. cit., p. 236.

56. *Labor Economics*, op. cit., and p. 422.

57. Daniel M. G. Raff and Lawrence H. Summers, "Did Henry Ford Pay Efficiency Wages?" *Journal of Labor Economics*, 1987, vol. 5, no. 4, pt. 2, pp. S76-S77.

58. Loc. cit., p. S75.

59. Loc. cit., pp. S78–S86.

60. *Labor Economics*, op. cit., p.422.

61. *Yad, Sekhirut* 13:7; *Tur, Hoshen Mishpat* 337; *Sh. Ar., Hoshen Mishpat* 337:20; *Ar. ha-Sh., Hoshen Mishpat* 337:26.

62. *Tosefta, Bava Metzia* 8:2; *Talmud Jerusalem, Demai* 8:3; *Rif, Bava Metzia* 90b; *Yad*, op. cit., 13:6; *Rosh, Bava Metzia* 7:3; *Tur*, op. cit., 337; *Sh. Ar.*, 337:19; *Ar. ha-Sh.*, op. cit., 337:25.

63. Talmud Jerusalem, *Demai*, loc. cit., *Rif*, loc. cit., *Sh. Ar*, op. cit., *Ar. ha-Sh.*, op. cit.

64. R. *Mordecai* b. Hillel (Germany, ca. 1240-ca. 1298), *Mordecai, Bava Metzia* 6:343.

65. *Yad*, op. cit.; *Tur*, op. cit., *Sh. Ar.*, op. cit., *Ar. ha-Sh.*, op. cit.

66. C.F. *Ketubbot* 103a; Eruvin 49a; *Bava Batra* 59a, 168a.

67. For an extensive taxonomy of cases drawn from the Rishonic and Responsa literature where *Bet Din* applies *kofin*, see Professor Aaron Kirschenbaum, *Equity in Jewish Law* (Hoboken, NJ: Ktav Publishing Yeshiva University Press, 1991), pp. 185–236.

68. *Tosafot, Bava Kamma* 20b; R. Aaron ha-Levi quoted by R. Joseph Habiba (early 15th cent.), *Nimmukei Yosef* at *Rif, Bava Kamma* 8b; see also R. Abraham Hirsch b. Jacob Eisenstadt (Bialystok, 1813–1868), *Pithei Teshuvah* to *Sh. Ar.*, op. cit., 363, note 3.

69. R. Shimon Shkop, *Hiddushei Rabbi Shimon Yehudah ha-Kohen, Bava Kamma* 19, part 3.

70. R. *Mordecai* b. Hillel, *Mordecai, Bava Kamma* 20b. Ruling in accordance with *Mordecai* is R. Moses Isserles, *Rema, Sh. Ar.*, op.cit., 363:6 and R. Jehiel Michel Epstein, *Ar. ha-Sh.*, op. cit., 363:16.

71. *Baraita, Bava Kamma* 60a; *Rosh, Bava Kamma* 6:12; *Tur*, op. cit., 359:3; *Sh. Ar.*, op. cit., 359:2; *Ar. ha-Sh.*, op. cit., 359:2.

72. Decisors dispute the meaning of this condition. One view is that if the item is *not a houshold item*, we may presume that the owner is willing to exchange it for a more expensive item. This is the position of R. David b. Samuel ha-Levi (Poland, 1586–1667, *Turei Zahav, Sh. Ar.*, op. cit.,) and R. Aryeh Loeb b. Joseph ha-Kohen Heller (Poland, 1745–1813, *Ketzot, Sh. Ar.*, op. cit., note 2). A stricter view here is taken by R. Shabbetai b. Meir ha-Kohen (*Siftei Kohen, Sh. Ar.*, op. cit., note 4) and R. Eliyahu b. Solomon Zalman (Poland, *Biur Ha-Gra, Sh. Ar.*, op. cit., note 3). This school of thought does not allow the exchange to be done unless we are reasonably certain that the nonhousehold article is up for sale.

73. *Rosh*, op. cit., *Tur*, op. cit., *Sh. Ar.*, op. cit., *Ar. ha-Sh.*, op. cit., R. Solomon Luria (Poland, 1510–1573) expresses a minority view in this matter. In his view, conferring *O* with a more expensive item than the one at hand does not legitimize the taking of his inferior item. Anything taken without the knowledge of its owner is *misappropriation*, as we may not do business with someone else's asset without that person's knowledge. (*Yam Shel Shelomo, Bava Kamma* 6:27)

74. R. Joseph Trani, *Mabit* 306.

75. Paul S. Carlin, "Why the Incidence of Shirking Varies Across Employers," *Journal of Behavioral Economics*, 18:2, pp. 61–73.

76. *Kiddushin* 52b and *Rashi* ad loc.; *Rif*, ad locum; *Yad, Ishut* 5:8; *Rosh*, 2:30; *Tur, Even ha-Ezer* 28:17; *Sh. Ar., Even ha-Ezer*, 28:17; *Ar. ha-Sh., Even ha-Ezer* 28:71–73.

77. *Bava Metzia* 75b and *Rashi, ad loc.* For a treatment of the prohibition against creating for a fellow a setting for veiled misconduct, see *Case Studies in Jewish Business Ethics*, op. cit., 185–187.

78. R. Joseph Hayyim b. Elijah al-Hakham, *Torah le-Shemah* 407.

79. Thomas R. Ireland, "How Shirking Can Help Productivity: A Critique of Carlin and 'Shirking as Harm' Theory," *Journal of Behavioral Economics*, 18:2, pp.75–79.

80. R. Avraham Grodzinski, *Torat Avraham*, p. 458.

81. Dexter Roberts and Aaron Bernstein, "A Life of Fines and Beatings," *Business Week*, October 2, 2000, pp. 122–126.

82. *Tosafot, Bava Metzia* 10a.

83. R. David b. Samuel ha-Levi, *Turei Zahav, Sh. Ar,. Hoshen Mishpat* 308:7.

84. C.F. *Pesahim* 50b.

85. R. Joseph B. Soloveitchik, *The Lonely Man of Faith* (New York: Doubleday, 1965), pp. 16–20.

86. Nadeem M. Firoz and Caren R. Ammaturo, "Sweatshop Labour Practices: The Bottom Line to Bring Change to the New Millennium Case of the Apparel Industry," *Humanomics*, vol. 18, no.1/2, 2002, p. 32.

87. John Miller, "Why Economists Are Wrong About Sweatshops and the Anti-sweatshop Movement," *Challenge*, January-February 2003, p. 97.

88. Assaf Sagiv, "Globalization: Just Do It," *Azure*, 19, Winter / 2005, p. 93.

89. Robert Pollin, Justine Burns, and James Heinz, "Global Apparel Production and Sweatshop Labour: Can Raising Retail Prices Finance Living Wages?" *Cambridge Journal of Economics*, vol. 28, no. 2, 2004, pp. 153–171.

90. Ryan P. Toftoy, "Now Playing: Corporate Codes of Conduct in the Global Theatre. Is Nike Just Doing It?" 15, *Ariz. Journal of International and Comparative Law*, 905.

91. "Sweatshop Labour Practices: The Bottom Line to Bring Change to the New Millennium Case of the Apparel Industry," op. cit., pp. 29–45.

V. Privacy Issues

9

Privacy Issues in the Workplace

Our concern here is the issue of privacy in the workplace. By means of the case study method, we will investigate whether Halakhah validates pre-hiring screening for drug, tobacco, and alcohol abuse. Is the issue of screening job applicants with pencil and paper integrity testing and handwriting analysis treated the same way? What is Halakhah's attitude toward the use of the polygraph in the workplace? If pre-hiring screening for some purpose is halakhically valid, once a candidate is hired, does the employer have the right to retest? Or, may the employer only periodically elicit the employee's self-declaration that he or she is not in violation of the policy the employer seeks to enforce? Is privacy in the workplace all a matter of contract between the employee and employer? Finally, we take up the issue of the extent and manner in which an employer may monitor the electronic communications coming into and going out of the office.

Privacy Issues at the I. M. Frier Novelty Company

It's no easy job to change a corporate culture. This was the type of daunting challenge Justin Frier faced when he took over as CEO of the I. M. Frier Novelty Company. Under the helm of his grandfather, I. M. Frier, the founder of the company, all but the most timid employees never stayed with the company more than a few years. No wonder. The old Frier was obsessed with a need to *control* his workers, at least while they were on the job. His *sine qua non* was to spring work rules on a captive employee. The rules were designed to maximize productivity and to discourage idleness and shirking. Old man Frier's reputation as a "mean boss" was well deserved.[1]

Unlike his grandfather, Justin Frier believed that it was inherently unfair to "spring" work rules on captive employees. Ideally, a labor contract should deal with all contingencies that will come up during the term of employment that the contract covers. Much energy should be expended to ensure that all contingencies are fully anticipated before the contract is written up. Whenever Justin felt an employee owed the company a particular duty, the only argument one would hear him invoke was that the labor contract either explicitly or implicitly required it. For Justin, the word "contract" was imbued with a certain degree of sanctity.

In the young Frier's mind, every labor-management issue was reducible to a negotiation about a commodity. Privacy issues were no exception. Frier put much energy into anticipating many productivity issues that touch upon the privacy of workers. His approach was to put these issues up front as part of negotiations before a contract was signed. To each new hire Frier explained the following policies:

Integrity Testing

"I'm sure you can appreciate that we don't want people around here that will hurt us by either stealing from the firm or depriving us of potential profits because of their dishonest behavior. Just put yourself in my position. If you had the ability to ferret out potential trouble in advance, I'm sure you would do it. We therefore ask all applicants to take a pencil and paper integrity test.

I'll also require you to leave a handwriting sample as part of the application process. I believe in the science of graphology. Much can be learned about the character of a person by studying that person's handwriting. I can't say that I'm going to actually submit your handwriting for analysis, but I reserve the right to do so before I make my decision whether I should hire you or not. Be sure that if I do hire you, I'll keep your writing sample on file. Let's hope I'll never have occasion to refer to it."

When Frier speaks to an applicant about integrity testing, he makes a point to tell the potential hire that his own preference is for the polygraph. But, Frier explains that this is not possible because federal law since 1988 generally prohibits the use of the polygraph as a screening device for employment.[2] However, he goes on to caution the applicant that in the event an incident of theft occurs in the firm, all employees will have to submit to a polygraph to ferret out the culprit. Administering a polygraph test to employees under these circumstances is legal under the 1988 law.[3]

Drug Abuse

"If you do drugs we don't want you here. I'm sure you can appreciate our concerns. Doing drugs, whether on or off the job, adversely affects performance on the job. Moreover, anyone doing drugs might be tempted to steal from the firm or from co-workers as a means of supporting his or her habit. Drug use hence threatens the safety and the quality of our work environment.

Our attitude toward drug use is not just an ideal. We put this policy in every labor contract and your signature on your contract commits you to this policy.

In addition, we won't hire anyone without that person first passing a drug test. The way it works is that we'll refer you to a designated lab and ask you to submit a specimen for urinalysis. Don't worry, we'll take note of the prescription drugs you are now taking and take other measures to ensure against false positives. Rest assured, we'll give you the greatest privacy compatible with ensuring that the specimen belongs to the person being tested."

Nonsmokers

"If you're a smoker, we don't want you here, even if you agree not to smoke on the job. Medical science has amply demonstrated the serious health risk that smoking entails. Hiring only nonsmokers will minimize our productivity losses, turnover expenses, and other out-of-pocket expenses associated with employee sick leave days and extended medical leaves of absence brought on by smoking. Moreover, the company can get a better deal from a provider of a group health insurance plan if all employees in the plan are non-smokers. By hiring only non-smokers the company can reduce its medical health insurance costs.

We put our tobacco policy in every labor contract, and your signature on your contract commits you to this policy.

In addition, we won't hire anyone without that person first passing a tobacco test. The same urine test you will be taking to test you for drugs will also test for traces of nicotine."

Annual Drug and Tobacco Testing

Once hired, an employee will get notice once a year to report to an independent lab for urine analysis to test for drug and tobacco use. To minimize the chance for employee manipulation, the notice for the test arrives suddenly on the job and consists of an order to immediately get into a company car. This car whisks the employee to the laboratory for the test. These annual tests provide the same care against false positives and sensitivity for privacy as the pre-employment test. In the event someone fails the annual drug and tobacco tests, a reconfirmation test is ordered. If the reconfirmation test again turns up positive, the employee is summarily dismissed.

In going through the annual ordeal of the drug and tobacco testing, many employees grumble with resentment. George Pines's attitude on this matter is typical:

My signed contract is my commitment not to "do drugs" and not to smoke. My promise alone was not enough to get the job. I had to pass the lab test as well. When will the company start trusting me? Asking me to take an annual lab test to detect drug and tobacco use tells me that they trust me only until the next test. The ordeal of the annual test impugns my integrity. In my mind, circulating an annual memo reminding us of the company's drug and tobacco policy should more than suffice. And I'll tell you something else. At the job interview I was never told that there would be annual testing for drugs and tobacco. Imposing the lab test on me after I have already signed the contract is nothing but exploitation.

Electronic Communications Monitoring

Frier routinely monitors both telephone and e-mail transmissions coming into and going out of the office. He makes no distinction between business and personal messages. In respect to this invasion of privacy, Frier feels no ethical duty to inform employees up front that this monitoring will take place. No advance notice, according to Frier, is necessary for business correspondences. These messages are the property of the firm and anything going out in the name of the firm is subject to supervision and quality control. Frier is particularly interested in interoffice e-mails. Monitoring these e-mails provides an instant pulse on office politics and a good sense of the intensity of employee loyalty to the firm. This revealing picture would be considerably compromised, if not entirely lost, if employees were given advance notice of the practice.

Another concern for Frier is that by means of electronic communications, an employee may inadvertently or even deliberately leak confidential information about the firm. In Frier's mind, if an employee desires to make confidential information available to a competitor, he or she will most likely do so in the guise of a personal e-mail correspondence. It is for this reason that Frier finds it necessary to intercept and read all employee e-mail correspondence, even if the message appears to be unrelated to the business of the firm and is purely personal in nature.

Still another concern for Frier is that one of his employees might send another employee an e-mail containing sexual harassment or a racial slur. By monitoring and reading all employee e-mails, Frier will become immediately aware of the misconduct and take prompt action against the offender, all along ensuring that he will not be accused of fostering a hostile work environment.

Finally, even if the employee does nothing pernicious in his or her personal telephone and e-mail use, sending a personal message on company time is, in Frier's mind, a breach of contract. Monitoring e-mail to ascertain the amount of time an employee spends away from his or her job is, in Frier's mind, no more than an enforcement of his right to get the productivity he deserves. Moreover, if an employee sends out an attachment with his or her e-mail, the entire network connection will be slowed down.

All of these considerations led Frier to believe that he had every right to monitor and read all employee telephone and electronic correspondences without giving them any advance notice of his policy.

THE VAULT CAPER AT THE I. M. FRIER NOVELTY COMPANY

The trust and goodwill Justin Frier had for his staff was delivered a crushing blow when he discovered one day that $10,000 was missing from the company vault. As soon as Justin discovered the pilferage, he ran out to the balcony outside his office suite and shouted at the top of his lungs "inside job." The outburst was understandable. There was no sign of forced entry. To accomplish the theft the culprit had only to twirl the sequence of numbers that opened the vault. Who was the culprit? Only five people, including Frier himself, knew the combination to the safe. They were Claudia Weinstock, his administrative assistant; Avery Green, the company's CFO, Leonard Sunshine, the company's computer graphics specialist and Adir Singer, the firm's resident poet.

With the aim of narrowing down the list of suspects, Frier asked the four suspects to give him a written account in their own handwriting of their contact with the vault room during the two-day window of time in which the burglary could have occurred. Frier then called in a graphologist to analyze the handwriting samples. Recall that Frier requires job seekers to submit handwriting samples as part of the application process and tells the aspirants that the company reserves the right to have the samples analyzed by a graphologist before making the decision to hire them or not. Because graphologist fees run very high, Frier did nothing until now with the handwriting samples of employees he had on file. The time to analyze these samples had unfortunately arrived. Frier handed the handwritten accounts of the four suspected employees together with the writing samples of these people he had on file to Dr. E. Edgar Gottfried, the highly recommended graphologist he hired.

In short shrift Dr. Gottfried was ready to make his report. Clutching Claudia Weinstock's handwritten account of her contact with the vault room on January 12, Gottfried presented his findings. Though he tried his best to put a professional tone and inflection to his voice, Gottfried could not camouflage his glee and excitement:

Mr. Frier, one of the packets of handwriting samples is sounding an alarm in my head. It's Claudia Weinstock's material. Take a close look at this sentence ... "at   2:30 P.M. I left the office to make a deposit in the bank. I returned about 3:30 just in time to take minutes at Mr. Frier's meeting with Leonard Sunshine and staff."

Mr. Frier, take notice of the exaggerated space between the word at and 2:30 P.M. Claudia obviously hesitated before writing 2:30. You have to ask yourself why Claudia would stop before writing 2:30 P.M. Consider the possibility that she is lying. I found the same type of exaggerated space between words in the writing sample Claudia submitted as part of her job application. She wrote, "I'm 36   years old." [hearty laughter].

Mr. Frier, let us now take a look at how the slant of Claudia's writing jumps from left to right. In my opinion that indicates that the writer has an unstable mind. I think it reflects stress and untruthfulness in the accounting Claudia gave of herself for the relevant period.

One more troubling point. Note how Claudia writes her lowercase *a*. It has an open top. An open top is *like an open mouth*. It means that Claudia can't keep confidences and is overly talkative. Who knows, someone bent on evil might have overheard Claudia blurt out the sequence of numbers as she twirled the combination lock to open the vault.

Frier was so impressed with Gottfried's presentation that he decided on the spot that Claudia was the likely culprit. With the knowledge that federal law permits use of the polygraph as an investigative tool to ferret out fraud, Frier demanded of Claudia that she take a lie detector test. Claudia's reaction was no less than ballistic. In her mind it was inconceivable that a trusted and valuable employee like herself should be put to the humiliation of a polygraph test. Claudia's pain was that much more unbearable because she knew that it was the results of the analysis of her handwriting that led Frier to request that she take the polygraph test. Rather than submit to the indignity of the polygraph, Claudia quit on the spot.

Claudia's tantrum and resignation did not faze Frier. Regarding Claudia as an unfortunate casualty in his press to get to the bottom of the vault caper, Frier took inventory on what his investigation came up with so far. It didn't take Frier much time to decide that his next move would be to request Avery Green to take the polygraph test. Analysis of Avery's handwriting samples also came up with some red flags. Because Avery was hardworking and fiercely loyal to Frier, he felt deeply hurt when the request to take the polygraph test filtered down to him through the hierarchy. Unlike Claudia, Avery swallowed his pride and took the test. Unfortunately, Avery failed the test.

Frier's instinct was to fire Green on the spot. But, legal obstacles apparently stood in the way. Recall that the Employee Polygraph Protection Act of 1988 allows polygraph use during internal investigations of suspected employee theft. But, no employee who fails the test can be fired on account of that alone. Other evidence must be found that is sufficient to warrant dismissal.[4] As Frier cautiously assessed how to proceed with Green, he decided that the "red flags" Gottfried had found in Green's handwriting constituted sufficient corroborating evidence. Confident that he was not violating federal law, Frier fired Green and handed over the dossier he had on him to the police for further investigation. Professing his innocence all along, the case against Avery Green went nowhere, and in a short while the police decided that no charges would be brought against Green.

FRIER'S SCREENING PROCESS AND HALAKHAH

Frier desires to hire people who are honest, nonsmokers, and nondrug users. An applicant's (A) declaration that he meets these criteria is not sufficient, however. Instead, *A* will have to submit a handwriting sample and submit to and pass a pencil and paper integrity test as well as a drug and tobacco test. By doubting *A*'s self-declaration, and instead, requiring him to verify his declarations by means of examination, perhaps Frier violates the imperative to judge a fellow favorably. The duty to judge a fellow favorably applies even when the conduct involved is questionable is derived from the verse . . . [W]ith righteousness (*tzedek*) shall you judge your fellow" (Leviticus 19:15). In the rabbinic literature this requirement is called the *kaf zehut* (literally, scales of merit) imperative.[5] Relatedly, if Frier is wrong to doubt the self declarations of the candidates then the loops he puts the candidates through in the form of integrity, drug, and tobacco testing and handwriting samples amounts to causing someone needless mental anguish. The prohibition to cause someone needless mental anguish is derived from the verse: ". . . *Lo tonu ish et amito* [do not harass one another]" (Leviticus 25:17).[6] This prohibition is referred to in the rabbinic literature as *ona'at devarim* (literally anguish of words).

Does Frier's screening process inherently violate the *kaf zehut* imperative and the *ona'at devarim* interdict? No. Notwithstanding that the screening process generates mental anguish for the candidates, the aggravation generated cannot be characterized as needless. Consider that Frier has *a right* to tell a potential hire (*A*) that he will check out his or her references. If *A* does not check out to Frier's satisfaction, Frier is under no moral obligation to hire *A*. Ordinarily, *B* is prohibited from speaking ill of *A*, even if what he has to say about *A* is the truth. This interdict, called the prohibition against *lashon ha-ra* (literally, evil talk), is derived from the verse "You shall not go about gossiping among your people" (Leviticus 19:16).[7] The prohibition applies to both speaker and listener.[8] But, suppose *B* becomes aware that Frier is considering hiring *A* and has firsthand knowledge of *A's* dishonesty, *B* then must take the initiative and inform Frier of what he knows. Because *B's* motivation is to provide Frier with a clear-cut benefit, the prohibition against *lashon ha-ra* is suspended here. The duty that compels *B* to act is the verse, "Do not stand idly by the blood of your neighbor" (Leviticus 19:16). Exegetical interpretation of this verse understands the interventionist duty the verse speaks of to apply to a monetary matter as well.[9] Specifically, if *B's* intervention can save a fellow (C) from a loss, *B* must take timely action to extricate *C* from the loss.[10]

Proceeding from the same logic is the right for Frier to take the initiative and check out *A* by making inquires about him to *B*. Because Frier tells *B* that inquiries are a requirement for making a hiring decision, *B* must candidly respond. If *B's* report turns out to be damaging for *A*, Halakhah will not regard *B's* declarations as *lashon ha-ra*. Now, if Frier's inquiry regarding *A* does not entail an infraction of *lashon ha-ra*, his inquires should not entail violation of either the *kaf zehut* imperative or the *ona'at devarim* interdict.

PENCIL AND PAPER INTEGRITY TESTING AND HALAKHAH

The most basic reason Halakhah would object to the use of pencil and paper integrity testing as a hiring screening device is that the scientific community regards this test as useless in predicting honest behavior on the part of employees.[11]

Given that what legitimizes the use of a screening device for hiring is that it gives an employer a basis to *predict* relative performance among competing candidates, using a device that has no predictive value generates only *ona'at devarim* for the candidate that is rejected on the basis of the test. To be sure, the candidate may never find out why he or she did not get the job, but not getting the job assuredly generates dashed expectations for the rejected candidate. If the rejection turns out to be *arbitrary* because the employer relied on a *useless test*, the dashed expectation of the rejected candidate is the responsibility of the employer.

A second reason to object to the test is that a substantial[12] part of the theory of honesty standing behind the questions runs counter to basic Jewish values. Placing faith in the examination by basing hiring decisions on it is therefore tantamount to demonstrating a lack of belief in the basic Jewish values the test denies. In this regard, let us take a look at the underlying philosophy behind two of the groupings of questions and see why Halakhah rejects the underlying philosophies.

One assumption is that only people who have punitive and authoritative attitudes towards dishonesty are themselves honest and trustworthy. Let's illustrate this point by referring to the following questions taken from a sample integrity test:

1. As a rule, I almost always try to give people a second chance. Y/N

2. If I were the boss, I'd be more apt to overlook a minor incident of shoplifting if the employee were a single mother.   Y/N

3. If you were the boss, would you treat a long-term employee differently from a new hire if both were caught punching the time clock for friends?   Y/N

4. I think some crimes are so awful that they require the death penalty.   Y/N

5. An employee who takes home damaged merchandise without permission should be treated just as if the merchandise were not damaged.   Y/N

6. I believe in the phrase "An eye for an eye and a tooth for a tooth." Y/N

7. Do you think that a person should be treated like a criminal if she steals something her family really needs?   Y/N

Someone of integrity, according to the designers of the test, is supposed to give an answer of N for 1–3 and an answer of Y for 4–7. Each incorrect answer moves the candidate in the direction of being categorized anywhere from medium to high-risk in terms of dishonest behavior.[13]

The punitive and authoritative attitude toward dishonesty that emerges from the answers the test designer is looking for is an attitude Halakhah does not subscribe to. As a means of demonstrating this, let us see how Torah sources would react to some of the specific questions in this section.

In the mindset of the integrity test designer, the belief in an "eye for an eye" system of justice scores points for the respondent in the integrity exam for having the right punitive attitude. The notion of an "eye for an eye," however, runs counter to basic Jewish values on several counts. For one, in Judaism justice is never equated with retribution and/or revenge.[14] Second, rather than understanding the biblical phrase an "eye for an eye" literally, the sages interpret the assailant's liability to consist of a monetary payment.[15]

In the mindset of the integrity test designer, "giving someone a second chance" indicates a tendency toward dishonesty. But, the circumstance the questionnaire refers to is vague on a number of levels. This makes the answer the test maker is looking for anything but compelling. First, we need to consider the nature of the offense as well as who is impacted by the offense. If the offense is not a tort and consists of an insult and the only one impacted is P_1, it would be a matter of supererogatory conduct for P_1 to tolerate the insult without protest.[16] Moreover, suppose the offense consists of a monetary harm P_2 committed against P_1 or P_3 and P_1 has firsthand evidence that implicates P_2, P_1 enjoys no *carte blanche* right to present his evidence to the authorities. Instead, Halakhah subjects P_1's disclosure to the fulfillment of a number of conditions. If these conditions are not in place, the disclosure should not be made.[17] Because the absence of these conditions tells P_1 not to make his disclosure, P_2 will, at times, effectively "get a second chance."

Another problematic area for the integrity test is the section dealing with a series of admissions regarding past conduct in respect to dishonesty and the use of illegal drugs. Respondents were asked to either deny or affirm the following admissions:

1. There are times when I like to get away from everything and be by myself.   T/F

2. I sometimes have thoughts that I wouldn't want my supervisor to know about.   T/F

3. Like most people, I have occasionally broken a minor traffic law. T/F

4. Have you ever used a company photocopying machine without permission?   Y/N

5. Have you ever destroyed company property in a fit of anger?   Y/N

6. If someone has hurt me, I'll make sure that I get even.   T/F

7. If I knew that a coworker was stealing company property, I would probably keep my mouth shut.   T/F

8. Have you ever punched a friend's time card when he or she wasn't at work?   Y/N

9. Have you ever had a friend punch your time card when you were not at work?   Y/N

10. I occasionally like to have an alcoholic drink at breakfast.   T/F

11. I have smoked marijuana while on the job.   T/F

12. I have used cocaine, crack, or other illegal drugs while on the job. T/F

13. Have you ever sold cocaine, crack, or any other illegal substance? Y/N

For each of the above questions, the examiner is looking for an F or N answer. The underlying theory is that anyone who makes admissions regarding dishonest, illegal, or corrupt conduct in the past is a risk for continuation of the objectionable behavior in the future.

The reason for rejecting an applicant on account of past misdeeds is simply that a record of dishonesty in the past creates a concern that the dishonest conduct will continue in the future. But, the questionnaire provides no follow-up opportunity for the test taker who confesses a past offense to say that he or she has made amends for the offense. No distinction is made between the repentant and the non-repentant offender. This notion is contrary to the basic Jewish value that one who has transgressed but makes amends to the victim and demonstrates contrition should be given a "second chance." Let us relate this cardinal principle to the labor market. Preliminarily, we note that if employer E suspects that worker W is stealing from him, E is within his rights to terminate W, even if W was under contract and the term of the contract had not yet expired.[18] Suppose, however, that W confesses to the theft, makes amends, and promises to turn over a new leaf. Should E retain W and give him a second chance? A relevant source here is Rav Hai Gaon's (Babylonia, 938–1038) ruling regarding the job tenure of a cantor who was suddenly discovered to be a thief. In this case Rav Hai Gaon ruled that if the cantor repents, the community should not discharge him from his position. Similarly, E should retain a repentant thief that makes the firm whole on the theft he was guilty of.[19]

The underlying theory behind denying someone a position based on his or her admissions of past misconduct, hence, runs counter to a basic doctrine of Judaism that we accept with open hands and without prejudice the contrite repentant.[20]

DRUG TESTING AND THE SECULAR BUSINESS ETHICS LITERATURE

From the perspective of the secular business ethics literature, the issue drug testing presents is the resolution of conflicting rights. From the standpoint of the employer (E), drug use leads to lower productivity and harm on the job. Drug testing allows E to increase productivity and prevent harm on the job.[21] Moreover, E has a right and even duty to create a drug free environment. From the standpoint of the worker (W), drug testing violates his privacy in several ways. One aspect of this invasion is the right of W to do as he/she sees fit off the job.[22] Another concern is that the testing procedure itself may violate W's physical privacy.[23] The issue goes beyond pre-employment drug testing. Requiring annual testing for drugs puts W on notice that E basically does not trust him. This amounts to an assault on W's integrity and dignity.[24]

In their treatment of the issue of drug testing in employment, Des-Jardins and Duska argue generally against this practice.

One reason of objection is that drug testing subjects W to coercion. At the pre-employment screening level, coercion is taking place because W is made to choose between giving up his privacy and giving up his chance to land the job. Because passing up the employment opportunity is often not a viable option, agreeing to drug testing to get the job cannot be characterized as a bonafide consent situation. Relatedly, drug-testing policies that are unilaterally imposed by *E* on *W* amount to coercion.

DesJardins and Duska raise another objection. Drug use may very well reduce *W's* productivity. But *E* has no claim to the maximum or optimum level of productivity *W* is capable of. Instead, *E* has a legitimate expectation for an acceptable standard of performance. If *W* is a very talented person, drug use may drive his productivity level below his maximum capable level, but his performance may still remain above or at least at the expected standard. Provided *W's* performance level remains at par, there should be no objection for him to "do drugs" off the job.

If *W's* drug use drives his performance below par, *E* will have *prima facia* grounds for warning, disciplining or releasing *W*. But the justification for this is *W's* unsatisfactory performance, not *W's* use of drugs. Accordingly, drug use information is either unnecessary or irrelevant and consequently there are not sufficient grounds to override the right of privacy.

DesJardins and Duska also attack the argument that drug testing is justified because employees under the influence of drugs can pose a threat to the health and safety of themselves and others. In the opinion of these commentators, the issue of danger to others arises only when unsatisfactory job performance presents a "clear and present danger" to others. In DesJardin's and Duska's opinion, the only jobs that clearly fit into this category are airline pilots, school bus drivers, public transit drivers and surgeons.

Moreover, if *E* has just cause in believing that *W* presently poses a real threat of causing harm more effective and less intrusive technologies are available than drug testing to prevent the harm. In this regard, what should be used are dexterity tests that gauge eye-hand coordination, balance, reflexes, and reasoning ability. These tests have also the advantage of giving instant results.

DesJardin and Duska concede that regular or random testing of all employees will prevent harm by deterring drug use by those who are occasional users and those who do not wish to be detected. But, these benefits do not override the harm that this policy inflicts on the workers who don't use drugs at all or whose use of drugs present no danger of harm.[25]

DRUG TESTING AND HALAKHAH

In this section we will examine DesJardins' and Duskin's thesis from the perspective of Halakhah. Let us begin with their proposition that E is entitled only to an acceptable productivity standard from W but not W's best effort. Provided W meets the acceptable standard, he should be free to do as he likes off the job. There can be no doubt that this proposition is at odds with Halakhah. From the perspective of Halakhah, W must give his best effort and exert himself maximally on the job. Moreover, W is constrained from engaging in any activity off the job that would adversely affect his performance level on the job. These aforementioned duties find expression in Maimonides' treatment of labor law:

> ... [B]ut a worker may not do his work at night and hire himself for the day, or thresh with his cow in the evening and hire her out for the day; nor may he starve himself, giving away his own food to his children, because by doing so he weakens himself physically and mentally and renders himself incapable of exertion in his work, thus depriving the employer of what is due to him.
>
> Just as the employer is enjoined not to deprive the poor worker of his hire or withhold it from him when it is due, so is the worker enjoined not to deprive the employer of the benefit of his work by idling away his time, a little here and a little there, thus wasting the whole day deceitfully. Indeed the worker must be very punctual in the matter of time, seeing that the sages were so solicitous in this matter, that they exempted the worker from saying the fourth benediction of grace.
>
> The worker must work with all his power, seeing that the just Jacob said "And you know that with all my power I have served your father," (Gen. 31:6), and that he received his reward therefore in this world, too, as it is said "And the man increased exceedingly." (Gen. 30:43).[26]

Now, if a labor contract *automatically* requires W to give his best effort and not to engage off the job in activities that diminish his performance on the job, explicit stipulation by E for this productivity standard cannot be said to amount to *coercing* W to agree to certain conditions of employment. Accordingly, prohibiting W from using drugs off the job amounts to no more than concretizing both E's entitlement and W's obligation into specific terms.

Moreover, the policy of pre-employment drug screening should not be put to question on ethical grounds even if W proposes that he will control his use of drugs in off hours so that his productivity on the job will not at all be adversely affected. Consider that one who *uses* illegal drugs breaks the law whether his productivity on the job is affected or not. The issue therefore is not whether E must take W on his word. Even if E is willing to take W on his word, E is within his rights to insist that he hires only law abiding citizens. If pre-employment drug testing is not improper intrusion, this policy cannot be said to amount to effectively coercing W to agree to deprive himself of an entitlement as a means of getting the job.

DRUG TESTING DESIGNED TO FERRET OUT MANIPULATIVE DRUG USERS

Once it is recognized that E's policy of not hiring drug users is not an improper intrusion into W's private domain, checking out the veracity of W's claim that he does not "do drugs" is no less legitimate than E's right to verify the veracity of the educational credentials, the skills and work experience W puts down on his resume. Given the legitimacy of checking out W's non-drug use claim, the issue becomes the selection of the proper method of checking out the claim. Since urinalysis under proper controlled conditions is helpful in ferreting out drug users, E should not be denied this method of verifying W's non-drug use claim. To be sure, the devious and resourceful drug user will find ways to "beat the system," but E should not be denied use of this pre-employment test just because certain violators will engage in manipulative conduct and escape detection.

To ensure maximum reliability for the test, E should require an applicant to produce a specimen under *observed conditions*. But, this feature is necessary only if the objective is to thwart an applicant *who is a drug user and is ready to engage in manipulative conduct to escape detection*. For an applicant who is drug free this precaution is an unnecessary humiliation. May E implement his test for drugs with the aim of ferreting out even manipulative drug users? No. The principal here is *ahazukei inish b'reshiei lo mahazikinan*, i.e., we make no *presumption* of wickedness. Let's illustrate this principle with a case in connection with an aspect of the rabbinical extension of the prohibition of *ribbit* (prohibited payment in connection with a loan transaction) called *mehezei keribbit* (lit. the "appearance" of *ribbit*):

B requests *L*: "Lend me money and live in my courtyard." Until now *B* did not put up his courtyard for rental. If *L* wants to take up *B's* proposal, he should, in the first instance, do so only by offering *B* to pay rent for the time of his occupancy. Given that *L's* occupancy will be a matter of public knowledge, taking up residency in the apartment without paying rent gives the "appearance" that *L* is taking *ribbit* for the loan he extends *B*. But, suppose *L* takes up *B's* offer without offering in advance to pay rent, and, in addition, does not want to pay rent for his occupancy? Does *L* bear any responsibility here to pay the rent, at least on a supererogatory level (*losat yedei shamayyim*)? Addressing himself to this issue, Nahmanides' (Spain, 1194–1270) answers in the negative. Consider that until now *B* did not put up his apartment for let. Given this circumstance, *L's* occupancy causes *B* no loss. If *L's* rent-free occupancy entails no loss for *B*, then, *L's* rent-free occupancy should not be regarded as *ribbit*. This judgment should not change even if *L* is the type of fellow that usually rents apartments and the free occupancy he gets in *B's* apartment saves him rent he would otherwise be paying another landlord. Nonetheless, a gain for *L* is not deemed *ribbit* unless it is simultaneously an earning (*marbit*, lit. an increment) for *L* and a loss (*nosheh*, lit. a bite) for *B*.[27]

Commenting on Nahmanides' analysis, R. Asher b. Jehiel (Germany, 1250–1327) queries, perhaps, *L* does, after all, bear responsibility for rental? Granted that until the time *B* proposed that *L* lend him money and take up residence in his courtyard, *B* had not put up his courtyard for rent. But, perhaps, *B* had a change of heart, and the courtyard was up for rent at the time *B* made his proposal to *L*. Now, if, in fact, *B* was incurring an opportunity cost in the form of foregone rental by proposing that *L* take up occupancy of his courtyard, then, avoidance of violation of *ribbit* law requires *L* to pay rent to *B* for his period of occupancy. In the final analysis, *L*, avers R. Asher, bears no financial responsibility here even on a supererogatory level. This is so because we may not read into *B's* original proposition intent to contract into a *ribbit* arrangement. The principle here is *ahazukei inish b'reshiei lo mahazikinan*.[28]

Let's now apply the prohibition not to presume wickedness to the issue at hand. Because Frier's financial interest are at risk if he takes an applicant on his word that he does not "do drugs," Frier is within his rights to verify the applicant's self-declaration by means of a drug test. To be sure, *maximum* reliability of results requires that the drug test should require an applicant to produce his specimen under observation. But, implementing the test in this humiliating fashion is only necessary if we presume that the applicant is a drug user and stands ready to engage in manipulative conduct to avoid detection. Since we may not presume wickedness implementing the test in this fashion is prohibited. Instead, the test may be implemented only with the aim of allowing a non-drug user to verify his word.

DRUG TESTING AND COERCION

Recall DesJardin's and Duska's argument that requiring W to submit to drug testing as a condition for hiring amounts to coercion because this requirement makes W choose between giving up his privacy and giving up his chance to land a job. Halakhah would disagree with this characterization. Rather, drug testing as a screening device is E's legitimate means to validate W's self-declaration that he is drug free. The ethics of springing a drug test on W is, however, a different matter. Once W has already established a track record for credibility, E should rely on W's periodic self-declarations that he or she is drug free. If, instead, E insists on continuing the pre-hiring drug test with annual repeat tests, E violates the *kaf zehut* imperative. Moreover, consider that W's job security will be compromised if he fails to acquiesce to the annual repeat drug test. Accordingly, even though the policy offends W and W feels that E has no right to impose on him what was not set out in advance of his hiring, W will go along with it anyway. Springing a repeat drug requirement on W, hence, amounts to coercion.[29]

Another context where coercion becomes an issue occurs when E demands that the test should consist of producing a specimen under observed condition. Preliminarily, let us take note that Jewish law entitles an individual to protection of his privacy against the visual trespass of a neighbor. This form of harm is called *hezek re'iyah* (lit. injury inflicted by viewing or prying).[30] One application of this principle is the prohibition to install windows facing the courtyard of a neighbor.[31] *Hezek re'iyah* is regarded as a tort in Halakhah, with the consequence that the party who stands to be injured can get a restraining order to prevent the visual trespass.[32] What the law of *hezek re'iyah* tells us is that *springing* a drug test on W that calls for him or her to produce a specimen under observed conditions compounds the coercion that is present when an ordinary drug test is imposed on *W*. It is coercion because *W* wants to be trusted and instead is forced to take the drug test. It is also coercion because the invasive drug test forces *W* to give up his privacy rights.

Moreover, if *E* promulgates his policy in the *pre-hiring* screening stage, *W* should not agree to it. This is so because going along with the request not only constitutes for *W* a waiver against invasion of his privacy, it also says that it is legitimate for *E* to regard him as a *manipulating* drug user *until proven otherwise*. By going along with the policy, *W* is giving *E* permission to violate the *kaf zehut* imperative. But, it is improper for one to waive his right to be judged favorably. R. Joshua Judah Leib Diskin's formulation of the *kaf zehut* imperative shows that there is an important *social* component to the *kaf zehut* imperative. The implication of R. Diskin's analysis is that no one should not waive his right to be judged favorably.

Preliminarily, R. Diskin notes that when the community is solidly committed to religious law, a moral climate is created. The climate consists of the shame one would feel if he breaks away from the norm. Shame hence is a powerful deterrent against sin. In a group of, say, ten, the deterrent of shame is undermined even if only one person breaks away and sins. The deterrent shame creates is even more exasperated when the new sinner is not the first to break away from the *norm but rather joins forces with a group that has already broken away*. What the aforementioned shows is how vitally important it is for each member of the community to have an attitude that everyone in the group is fully committed to religious law. It's this attitude that makes *A* feel a sense of shame if he sins. What follows is a rationale of why we are bidden to judge a fellow favorably. *A* is deterred from sinning only because he assesses that everyone else is righteous. But, if *A* has a license to judge everyone unfavorably on the basis of a suspicion he has, the moral climate *A* imagines surrounds him and is already weakened. The more an individual is forced to regard everyone around him as *righteous*, the greater deterrence exists for *A* against sin.[33]

What emerges from R. Diskin's rationale of the *kaf zehut* imperative is that one who is entitled to favorable judgment should not waive his rights in the matter. Doing so undermines the deterrence effect of shame both for the accuser and for society as a whole. Application of this principle to the issue at hand disallows an applicant to waive his right to take the drug test under conditions of observation. Doing so legitimizes *E*'s operating presumption that the applicant before him is a drug user and a manipulative one at that. Because consenting to the humiliating test undermines the moral climate of society, *W* should not acquiesce to take the test in this manner.

Recall that employees at the Frier Novelty Company complained bitterly of the company policy that required them to repeat the drug test once a year. Halakhah would surely find sympathy with the complaint. The principle here again is the *kaf zehut* imperative. To be sure, in the initial hiring stage, Frier has every right to protect his financial interest and not rely on the word of *W* that he is not a drug user. But, once *W* establishes a track record of honesty, the *kaf zehut* imperative tells Frier to judge *W* favorably and not show distrust by requiring him to repeat the drug test. Instead, Frier should periodically ask *W* to sign an affidavit that he/she is committed to his policy of maintaining a drug free workforce.

Several caveats on repeat testing are, however, in order. One caveat relates to the situation where an unsatisfactory performance by *W* presents a "clear and present danger" to others. Recall that in DesJardin's and Duska's opinion, the only jobs that clearly fit into this category are airline pilots, school bus drivers, public transit drivers and surgeons. If *W* falls into any of these categories, an unsatisfactory performance on his part carries the potential of generating an irretrievable loss and even death to the consumers of his services. Anyone contracting for *W's* services presumably implicitly demands that *W's* fitness to perform his service be periodically checked. This presumption is self-evident to the point of creating a *quasi-contract* with *E* to take proper measures to ensure that *W* is fit. In the *quid pro quo* of the quasi-contract, consumers are saying to *E* "in respect to safety, don't cut corners. Make sure *W* is fit. Whatever this necessary cost is factor it into our bill." Consumers' implicit demand for safety does not, however, allow us to question the integrity of *W*. If *W* initially passed the drug test, requiring him to periodically repeat it, violates *kaf zehut*. Nonetheless, the public's implicit demand for optimal safety precautions requires *E* to ensure that *W* has the adequate dexterity and motor skills before putting him on assignment. Requiring *W* to take a periodic motor skill and dexterity test is certainly in order. The latter approach reconciles the public's demand for safety with the prohibition against questioning *W's* integrity once *W* has already established a track record for his veracity.

What the aforementioned has demonstrated is that Halakhah's attitude toward drug testing in the "clear and present danger" case is *similar* but not identical to the approach DesJardin and Duska adopt. In opposition to Des-Jardin and Duska, who would do away with drug testing altogether in the work scene, Halakhah would allow drug testing in the initial employment screening process. But, once W passes the initial drug test, his self-decla-ration that he does not "do drugs," may not, other things being equal, be questioned. Requiring him to take periodic drug tests even in the "clear and present" danger case violates the *kaf zehut* imperative. Nonetheless, E is bound by a quasi-contract with the public to subject W to periodic motor skill and dexterity tests to ensure that he is fit for the job.

Another caveat for repeat testing relates to the instance where a rash of petty thefts hits the work scene. Here, the indication is that one of the employees is the culprit and the possibility must be taken into account that it is drug related. Specifically, we must consider the possibility that one or more of the employees are engaging in petty theft at the office to support a drug habit. Given the suspicious circumstances and concern for financial losses and physical harm in the future, reconfirming that each of the employees is not a drug user does not violate *kaf zehut*.

DRUG TESTING IN A HIGH RISK DRUG USER WORKPLACE

Drug abuse in the workplace is rampant today. Over 74% of all current ille-gal drug users work. The overall cost of illicit drug abuse is estimated to have been $160.7 billion in 2000, and 69% of these costs are from produc-tivity losses due to drug-related illnesses and deaths.

Small businesses bear the greatest burden of substance abusers. This is because larger employers usually participate in drug-free workplace prac-tices. As a result small and medium employers are adversely selected in terms of the employees that are left to hire.

Recent statistics show that about 8% of all full-time workers aged 18–49 used illicit drugs. But the rates showed considerable variation across profes-sions. At the low end, workers in administrative support and protective ser-vice reported illicit drug use of only 3.2% and 3%, respectively. On the high end, construction, other service occupations and transportation, and material moving, reported rates of 12%, 11.4% and 10.8%, respectively.

Indicative of the pernicious effects drug abuse has for the entire workplace is the following two statistics: 80% of drug abusers steal from their workplaces to support drug use. Substance abuse is the third leading cause of workplace violence.[34]

If the labor force of a firm falls into one of the high risk categories for drug abuse, E may feel that the model we described above falls short of adequately protecting himself as well as his workforce from the pernicious effects of drug abuse. Perhaps, in the instance when E is operating in a high risk drug environment, it is legitimate for him to institute a repeat drug testing policy. R. Isser Zalman Meltzer's (Russia, 1870–1953) analysis of a point in law of the judicial procedure for notes of indebtedness bears on this issue:

Preliminarily, let us take note of the following judicial procedure that governs the collection of a note of indebtedness: L produces in court a note of indebtedness signed by two witnesses that B owes him $1,000. B is dead. Accordingly, L's claim is against either B's heirs or against C who bought land from B subsequent to the date the debt with L was entered into. Notwithstanding that no one is claiming forgery, *Bet Din* will put L's claim on hold until it verifies the authenticity of the signatures of the witnesses. If the hold on collection would not be done, *Tosafot* tell us, "no one would survive" as the floodgates would open up for every forger.[35]

This procedure, queries R. Meltzer, is in apparent conflict with the principle that "people don't have the impudence to forge documents."[36] Since the procedure of requiring verification of the signatures of the witnesses *impugns* the integrity of L, and the claim of forgery never came up in the court proceeding, no barrier should be put in the way of L to collect his debt. R. Meltzer's answer is that the procedure *Bet Din* establishes does not directly impugn the integrity of the claimant that stands in front of us. But, there is no denying that "forgers" exist and if the procedure of signature verification were not required, someone over time would be victimized.[37]

What can be generalized from R. Meltzer's thesis is that a testing practice for drug abuse that does not directly impugn the integrity of the worker that stands in front of us, but, instead, is, in place only to *deter* the *statistical* man from engaging in drug abuse conduct, is a permissible practice.

Within the high risk drug use environment, a policy of supplementing the initial pre-hiring drug screening with *random* drug testing should not violate for E the *kaf zehut* imperative. This is so because random drug testing in no way casts aspersions on any particular W. Instead, the policy merely puts in place a *deterrent* against drug use. Perhaps, within the high risk drug environment, *universal repeat drug testing* also does no violence to the *kaf zehut* imperative. The rationale is that the drug testing here is not instituted because we doubt the self-declaration of any particular *W*, but only to build up a strong deterrence *culture* against drug use.

One caveat should, however, be noted. A high risk drug use environment does not justify a policy that requires *W* to produce a specimen under observed conditions. Such a policy goes beyond creating an anti-drug culture and says that each *W* tested is suspected of being a drug user and a *manipulative* one at that.

THE VAULT CAPER INVESTIGATION—AN HALAKHIC ANALYSIS

Halakhah would find much fault and criticism in how Frier went about investigating the vault caper. Let us begin with his use of graphology.

Graphology is for many American employers an increasingly popular tool for making employment decisions. In a recent survey, about six thousand American companies, including many large and prominent ones, reported using graphology in personnel decisions.[38] Despite its popularity, graphology's validity and reliability have not been scientifically established. In their meta analysis of more than 200 graphology studies, Dale and Barry Beyerstein conclude that graphology is neither valid nor reliable enough to be useful. Those slight positive effects in validity that come up in the studies are attributed to the *content* of the handwriting sample rather than to graphology per se.[39]

Given that the scientific community places no credence in graphology as an instrument for ascertaining the character traits of the subject, Frier should not request a job seeker to submit a handwriting sample for possible analysis. Rejecting a job seeker on the basis of graphology amounts to rejecting the person on the basis of a false and or useless test and makes Frier guilty of discrimination and causing needless mental anguish. Use of graphology in the screening process hence violates the *ona'at devarim*[40] interdict.

Frier compounds violation of *ona'at devarim* by resorting to graphology as an investigative tool to flush out the culprit responsible for the vault caper. Because graphology has no validity, making an accusation on the basis of it violates the *kaf zehut* imperative.

THE POLYGRAPH AND TRUTH TELLING

We move now to Frier's use of the polygraph. The polygraph records a subject's perspiration and heart rate as an investigator poses questions. The subject's reactions are traced onto a paper tape and then analyzed. The theory behind polygraphs is that when the subject lies his or her physiological response is different from when the subject tells the truth.[41]

THE POLYGRAPH AND SECULAR BUSINESS ETHICS

In his treatment of the ethical issues involved in the use of the polygraph, Professor Richard T. De George identifies three ethical concerns.

One concern is the reliability of the test. Since the polygraph measures physiological reactions, it is possible to learn how to control those reactions and so "fool" the machine. Dishonest people, precisely the type the firm does not want to hire, are the likely candidates to manipulate the results. At the other end of the continuum, we must recognize that innocent but very nervous people often react in a way that can be interpreted as lying. Finally, different polygraph experts will disagree whether the subject was lying in response to a particular question.

Another concern is the nature of the so-called innocuous questions the examiner puts to the subject for the purpose of establishing a base for the subject's physiological responses. There is a concern that these questions may be entirely out of bounds and invade the private sphere of the subject. Firms have the right to ask questions that are job related; they do not have the right to probe into one's personal life about non job-related activities.

The third issue relates to control over the results of the polygraph test. Subjects taking the exam have a right to guarantees and safeguards that the results of the test will be kept private and will not be made available to third parties.

It was the above three concerns that led Congress to pass the Employee Polygraph Protection Act in 1988. This Act prohibits pre-employment polygraph testing, and random post-employment polygraph testing.

The law allows polygraph use during internal investigations of suspected employee theft or economic loss and in a number of exempt industries.

An employee has the right to refuse to take the test and cannot be fired for such refusal. No employee who fails the test can be fired because of that;

other evidence must be found that is sufficient to warrant dismissal. No questions on sex, politics, or union activities may be asked, and all questions must be furnished in advance. Individual states may pass more restrictive measures with respect to polygraph use.[42]

THE POLYGRAPH AND HALAKHAH

The halakhic literature on the polygraph deals with the admissibility of and possible role for this instrument in criminal law, civil litigation and in a divorce proceeding.[43]

Let us begin with a divorce proceeding case that was taken up by the Haifa Rabbinic Court. In this case, a husband petitioned the court for a divorce, based on alleged immoral conduct of his wife. However, all that was proven was that the woman had been secluded in private, during daylight hours, with her employer, in a house situated among other inhabited buildings. Since the accepted law is that seclusion is not sufficient grounds for prohibiting a woman to her husband, the majority decision of the court was that there was no basis in this case for a prohibition. The minority opinion of the court was to accept the husband's demand that the woman be given a polygraph test, and only afterwards should a final decision be reached. The husband appealed the majority decision to the Rabbinic Supreme Court of Appeals (RSCA) and requested that the Supreme Court accept the minority opinion and order the polygraph test. The RSCA rejected the appeal.

The rabbinic discussions surrounding the RSCA decision has much relevancy for the use of the polygraph as a screening device in hiring and as an investigative tool in discovering responsibility for theft and fraud in the workplace. Some of the discussion relates to judicial and evidentiary procedure in a Jewish court. We will not be concerned with that aspect of the discussion. Instead, we will confine ourselves to the discussion that is germane to the issue at hand.

In rejecting the husband's petition that the court should order his wife to take the polygraph test, R. Eliezer Yehudah Waldenberg averred *inter alia* that the polygraph test is incapable of proving anything conclusively.

In a respectful challenge to the court, Professor Elihav Shochetman contends that the polygraph would serve well as an investigative tool in the case at hand. Consider that if the woman passed the polygraph test, her husband might become convinced that she was innocent of his charge of adultery. Given that the evidence does not, in any case, support prohibiting the woman to her husband, requiring the woman to take the polygraph might produce the result of reconciling the couple. This would be the case if the woman would pass the polygraph test.

In pushing his advocacy of the polygraph as an investigative tool, R. Shochetman cites the approval the 1981 Israeli Government Polygraph Commission gave for the polygraph as a "useful means of advancing an investigation, especially a criminal one." In this report, the Commission cited research findings that for the purpose of advancing an investigation "polygraph tests are accurate in over 90% of the cases."[44]

If the legitimacy of the use of polygraph turns on its dependability, there should be no question that Halakhah would reject its use as a screening device for hiring. Relevant here is the strong opposition of the scientific community against the use of the polygraph as a screening device for hiring.[45]

Given that the scientific community does not regard the polygraph as a valid test to identify deceptive people, rejecting an applicant based on this test causes that person needless mental anguish and hence violates for the employer both the *ona'at devarim* interdict and the *kaf zehut* imperative.

In his friendly critique of the RSCA decision, Professor Shochetman avers that when the day comes that improvements in polygraph testing make the results dependable, the results of these tests should be treated on the level of *umdana demukhrah*, i.e. circumstantial evidence. In civil litigation, circumstantial evidence is admissible in a Jewish court.[46]

R. Shochetman's optimistic attitude regarding the future of the polygraph in Jewish law is, in the opinion of this writer, unwarranted.

Preliminarily, let's note that the issue of the accuracy of the polygraph turns on both its reliability and its validity. Reliability refers to the consistency of the exam and is determined by the level of agreement between repeated tests, or between independent evaluations of the same test. The validity of the test is the extent to which the test measures what it claims to measure, and is determined by the level of agreement between the test results and the "ground" or actual truth. On the one hand, a test can be highly reliable but have low validity; on the other hand, a test with low reliability cannot have high validity. Finally, an exam's reliability serves as the upper limit on its validity.[47]

If a competent examiner under proper conditions conducts the polygraph test, the reliability factor should improve. But, the validity issue remains.

From the perspective of Halakhah, the issue of the validity of the polygraph begins with an investigation into the design of the test. Most basic to understanding how the polygraph works is the concept of relevant and control questions.[48]

Let us explain these terms in relation to Justin Frier's criminal investigation of the vault caper. Recall that Avery Green was subjected to a polygraph test. Relevant questions relate specifically to the vault caper incident itself. In this regard, Avery was asked: Did you take the money from the safe? Are you withholding any information that you know about the robbery? In contrast, control questions don't relate to the criminal incident under investigation, but rather only to related criminal incidences in the past. In this regard, Avery was asked the following questions. Over the last five years, have you ever deliberately cheated the government out of more than $100 on your income tax? Between high school and two years ago, have you ever stolen anything worth more than $25? Between high school and two years ago, did you ever tell a lie to someone in authority in order to stay out of trouble?

Control questions are designed to induce the subject to lie. In the case at hand, Avery is expected to answer "no" to the control questions. This is so because the specific misconduct the control question speaks of, for example, the stealing of something worth more than $25 over a long period of time, is presumably a crime many people are guilty of, including Avery. But, for Avery to admit to the crime would severely compromise his credibility in claiming his innocence of the vault caper at I. M. Frier. Accordingly, if Avery answers no to the control question, the examiner will *privately* take his answer as a lie.

Suppose, Avery surprises the examiner and admits to a theft amounting to more than $25. Avery's answer has not "spoiled" the control question. To get back on track, the examiner need only *incrementally* increase the amount of money he mentions in the control question. When the sum reaches an amount, say $75, that Avery answers "no," the examiner will privately take Avery's response as a lie.

The assumption behind the polygraph examination is that the subject's "no" answer to a control question is a lie. Accordingly, the physiological responses of the subject the polygraph records for the control questions gives the physiological responses the subject makes when he is lying.

The scoring of the polygraph examination is now straightforward. If the polygraph responses to the relevant questions are systematically larger than those elicited by the controls, the subject is considered to have been deceptive in his answers to the relevant questions. If his responses to the controls are the larger, then he is classified as truthful. The test is declared to be inconclusive if there is minimal difference in size between the two sets of responses.

With the aim of encouraging Avery to lie in respect to the control questions, the examiner said the following to Avery just before the polygraph test began:

> "All right, Mr. Green, now whoever took this money, it's unlikely that it was the first dishonest thing that person ever did. Therefore, during the test, I'm going to ask you some questions to find out what kind of person you are, whether in the past you have ever done anything that might indicate you're the sort of person who would steal money from the office safe. For example, take your income tax returns. I suppose most people make mistakes on their income tax now and then, forget to put something down or exaggerate their expenses. But, you haven't been deliberately cheating on your tax returns, have you? If I ask you, over the past five years, have you ever deliberately cheated the government out of more than $100 on your income tax? You could answer that 'no,' couldn't you?" After some hesitation and breaking eye contact with the examiner, Avery answered "yes, my answer is 'no.'"

The examiner made the same type of prefatory remarks in respect to the other control questions. In respect to the question relating to lying to someone in authority in order to get out of trouble, Avery spoiled the designs of the examiner by admitting to such an incident. Unfazed, the examiner recorded Green's misdeed and asked him that aside from that one incident were there any others? When Green responded no, the examiner rephrased the control question: "aside from the incident that you just described of lying to someone in authority to get out of trouble, were there other incidences in your life of this sort? When Avery responded no, the examiner privately took the response as a lie and went on to the next control question.

In his authoritative work on the uses and abuses of the polygraph, David T. Lykken takes strong exception to the above assumption. Reacting more strongly to the relevant questions may merely indicate that the relevant questions have greater immediacy or are more threatening to the subject than the control questions. Because the relevant questions are more stressful, they naturally produce in the subject greater arousal in the form of physiological reactions. The greater physiological reaction should therefore not be taken as an indication that the subject is lying. A rape case illustrates this point: suppose *F* accuses *M* that he raped her. *M* does not deny the liaison but claims it was consensual. To determine the truth in the matter, authorities administer a polygraph test for *F*. *F* fails the polygraph test. One possible explanation is that *F* was lying. She lied to either mollify her parents or her husband. But, *F* could have been telling the truth. Her strong physiological response was simply that the question evoked in her a vivid recall of the brutal and violent incident of rape that she was put through. Naturally, the incident of the rape should evoke a stronger response on the polygraph than the incidences the control question evokes.[49]

In the opinion of this writer Halakhah would be in agreement with the basic thrust of Lykken's attack on the validity of polygraph results. Let's see why.

One reason for rejecting the underlying theory of the polygraph is the principle of indirect responsibility. The Talmud explicates this principle in connection with the biblical case dealing with the instance where a murder victim is found and there are no witnesses to the crime. Here, the Torah prescribes a ritual called *eglah arufah* (beheaded heifer). In the first step, the elders measure to find which city is closest to the spot where the murdered victim was found. Next, the elders of the nearest town are instructed to take a heifer that was not yet pulled with a yoke and break the back of its neck in a dry, craggy valley.[50] The elders of the city are then bidden to wash their hands over the broken head of the heifer and say:

> "Our hands have not spilled this blood, and our eyes did not see. Atone for the people of Israel whom You have redeemed, O Hashem: Do not place innocent blood in the midst of Your people Israel! Then the blood shall be atoned for them" (Deuteronomy 21:8).

The need for the elders of the nearest town to make the above declaration indicates that the elders themselves are suspects in the crime. But, is it imaginable that we should regard them as suspects so as to necessitate this declaration of innocence? Because it is nothing but astonishing to take the elders protestation at face value, the Talmud reads into the declaration: "Our hands have not spilled this blood..." a *disavowal of being even indirectly responsible for the murder*. The exact nature of the disavowal is disputed in the Talmud. One opinion has it that the disavowal of indirect responsibility refers to the slayer. Within this understanding, the elders are saying, in essence, that they were not remiss in their duty to deter, ferret out and punish crime. In another opinion, the disavowal refers to the victim. In this understanding, the rabbis are saying that they let no one who came in their jurisdiction leave without providing that person with an escort (so as not to go alone in a place of danger).[51]

If we read into the declaration: "Our hands did not shed this blood" a disavowal of indirect responsibility for the murder, indirect responsibility becomes equated in some manner with shedding the blood of the victim. The equality is, of course, not on the level of legal liability. Only the murderer and the accessories bear actual punishment. If the equality means anything, as it appears to this writer, it must be in the emotional dimension, on the level of guilt. If the elders were remiss either in their responsibility to create the proper hospitable climate for strangers or in fostering the proper detriment against crime, they should feel *guilt* for the snuffing out of the life of the victim on the same level as the guilt the murderer should feel for actually shedding the blood of the victim. One who is overcome with guilt on account of indirect responsibility for the crime will be driven to take measures to ensure that the crime will not repeat itself. Guilt hence produces beneficial consequences.

Let us apply the doctrine of indirect responsibility to the operative assumption behind polygraph testing. Avery Green had nothing to do with the robbery of the safe. Nevertheless, the needle on the polygraph machine went wild when Green responded "no" to the question of whether he took the money and other valuables from the safe. But, this can be easily explained. Because Green, as CFO of the company, held a position of authority and influence, Frier would certainly have given a suggestion from him serious thought, especially if the idea did not require an expenditure to implement. At the time the theft occurred, those who were entrusted with the combination of the vault had free access to it. Green realized how precarious and imprudent that arrangement was. It was so simple to make it right. All that was needed was to allow no one in the vault room without first logging in and out. To boot, Green was planning to propose that he be in charge of the logging in and out, as his desk was located adjacent to the vault room. It was these thoughts that raced through Avery's mind as the examiner asked him on the polygraph test if he (Avery) had taken the money. "Had I only taken this simple initiative, a proper deterrent against robbery would have been in place and I would not be now strapped down to this contraption." As Avery reflected on this last thought, he was overcome with a need for self-infliction for his lapse. Wallowing in self-anger, Avery bit his tongue and suffered silently all through the repeat of the same question, in different word order. Unbeknown to Avery, the needle of the polygraph went ballistic as he silently wallowed in pain over his bitten tongue.

Another reason to reject the underlying theory of the polygraph is that questioning someone about a crime while strapping the subject to a polygraph machine amounts to *accusing* that person of the crime. Instead of interpreting a strong physiological reaction as a indication of guilt and hence a telltale sign that the subject is lying, the strong response may say no more than the subject is indignant of wrongly being accused of committing the crime.

Consider, however, that polygraph theory claims that the guilty *always* react with a strong physiological response to the relevant questions of the polygraph examination. If we can say no more than that the falsely accused will, *on occasion*, react with an emotion of indignation to the implicit accusation inherent in the relevant questions, the underlying theory of the polygraph remains essentially intact. But, this is not so. From the perspective of Halakhah's theory of human behavior, the *ordinary and normal* reaction to a false accusation is indignation. The above proposition emerges from an analysis of an incident recorded at Samuel 1:1–18:

But, Hannah, she was speaking in her heart, only her lips were moving, and her voice was not heard, and Eli thought her to be a drunken woman. And Eli said to her: Until when will you be drunk? Throw off your wine from upon yourself. And Hannah answered and said: No, my master, I am a woman of sorrowful spirit, and neither new wine nor old wine have I drunk, and I poured out my soul before the Lord. Deliver not your bondswoman before the unscrupulous woman, for out of abundance of my complaint and my vexation have I spoken until now. And Eli answered and said: Go in peace, and the God of Israel will grant your request, which you have asked of Him. And she said: may your bondswoman find favor in your eyes; and the woman went on her way and ate, and her face was not (sad) anymore (I Samuel 1:13–18).

Commenting on the accounting Hannah gave of herself to Eli in response to his accusation of drunkenness, the Talmud avers that Halakhah required Hannah to clear her name. Why keeping silent with the knowledge that her actions were proper in the eyes of God was an option not open to her, is explained by the commentaries in various ways. One approach, advanced by R. Solomon b. Isaac (*Rashi*, France, 1040–1105) is that an individual is required to remove himself (herself) from suspicion.[52] *Rashi's* approach makes Hannah's conduct an application of the behavioral imperative to conduct oneself in a manner that one will be "vindicated" both in the eyes of God and in the eyes of man.[53] Alternatively, the requirement to speak up and clear one's name is based on the dictum that anyone who suspects the innocent is vulnerable to suffer Divine retribution in the form of physical punishment. To prevent this harm to his accuser, the option of silence is not open to the accused.[54]

Let us take note, however, that in response to Eli's accusation, Hannah gave much more than an accounting of herself. Consider Hannah could have begun her response with the words *"My master."* Instead, she uses the phrase "no, my master." Taking note of this, the Talmud reads into Hannah's response harsh words directed at Eli. What Hannah said to Eli was: *"You are not a master in this matter*—and the Divine spirit does not rest upon you-that you suspect me of this thing (i.e., of praying while intoxicated).[55] Do not these harsh words constitute an overreaction on the part of Hannah and show disrespect to the spiritual leader of the generation? No. Consider that the Talmud derives from the Eli-Hannah incident the requirement that if one wrongly accuses a fellow, the accuser is required to pacify the one he wrongly suspected. This lesson can be seen by analyzing Eli's parting words to Hannah: "Go in peace, and the God of Israel will grant your request, which you have asked of Him." Peculiarly, the salutation "Go in peace," appears in the beginning of Eli's comment. Instead, these words of greeting should have been his concluding words. More than the usual salutation is therefore read into the words "Go in peace." What these words convey is the opening salvo of words of pacification to Hannah for wrongly accusing her.[56] Now, if Hannah's reaction to Eli's accusation was excessive and showed therefore disrespect for the sage of the generation, Hannah should have also apologized to Eli. Because no such apology is recorded and the Talmud is not, in any way, critical of Hannah for overreacting to Eli's accusation, the conclusion must be drawn that there was nothing improper in Hannah's reaction. If reacting in a more than measured way to an accusation is not morally improper, then, reacting to a false accusation with a strong physiological response is, from the perspective of Halakhah, quite normal, ordinary and expected.

Let us apply the above principal to the case at hand. Green's strong physiological responses to the relevant questions on the polygraph test should not be taken as an indication that he was lying in respect to his protestations of innocence in the vault caper. What, then, should we make of Green's strong physiological reactions to the relevant questions? As a long-time, hardworking and fiercely loyal employee of the I.M. Frier Novelty Company, Green felt a deep resentment against Justin Frier for putting him through the humiliation of validating his protestation of innocence by taking a polygraph test. Add to this the guilt Green felt for not proposing a security plan for the vault. These emotions of indignation, resentment, and guilt for indirect responsibility, to say nothing of the pain he felt from biting his tongue, manifested itself in strong physiological responses in responding to the relevant questions put to him by the examiner. Green failed the polygraph test, but failing the test in no way indicated that he was a liar.

The upshot of the previous analysis is that Halakhah does not agree with the underlying theory of the polygraph. The use of the polygraph in a *Bet Din* proceeding should be denied even if the reliability factor improves dramatically over time. Because Halakhah denies the validity of the polygraph, improvements in the reliability of this device should not legitimize its use.

FRIER'S E-MAIL POLICY AND SECULAR LAW

In this section we will describe the latitude secular law that affords an employer (E) to monitor the electronic communications of his employees on the job. This examination will lead us to the conclusion that Frier's electronic communications policy violates American law.

In 1986, Congress, amending an earlier piece of legislation, enacted the Electronic Communications Privacy Act (ECPA). This Act prohibits carriers of electronic communications from engaging in unauthorized interception of electronic messages in transmission and storage. Violators may be subject to fines or imprisonment.[57]

The ECPA includes three exceptions to its prohibition: (1) an exception if one of the parties consents;[58] (2) an exception allowing providers of wire or electronic communication services to monitor their lines to ensure adequate services;[59] and (3) an exception if done by a device provided by the communications provider or subscriber and done in the interceptor's ordinary course of business.[60]

In assessing whether Frier's e-mail policy violates secular law, the most salient point to note is that Frier did not even inform, to say nothing of getting the consent of his employees in advance, that he would be monitoring their electronic communications. Because the employees had no advance notice of Frier's monitoring policy, the legitimacy of Frier's practice hangs on how broadly the other two exceptions are interpreted.

In respect to the provider exception, many commentators interpret it very broadly. Alexander I. Rodriguez, for instance, points out that under the provider exception an employer who provides his company with e-mail networks could always justify an intrusion into employee communications to protect against breaches in confidentiality, trade secret theft, or system maintenance. The same justifications could be used by the provider employer for accessing employee e-mail saved on the company server.[61] In this vein, another commentator, Ruel Torres Hernandez claims that the provider exception gives many private employers almost "unfettered discretion" to read and disclose the contents of even their employees' personal e-mail messages.[62]

Other commentators, however, point out, that the provider exception may not apply altogether if the employer merely provides a common carrier's e-mail service to its employees. In providing e-mail service for his company, Frier merely provided an intranet system and made no use of public phone lines. It is therefore questionable for Frier to rely on the provider exemption to legally justify his policy of reading all employee e-mails without announcing his practice in advance.[63]

We now turn to the last exemption. In making the judgment whether an employer has met the "ordinary course of business" criterion, courts have taken two approaches. One approach, called the content approach, permits an employer to monitor "business related" communications but does not allow monitoring of personal communications. In deciding the legitimacy of the employer's interest in the content approach, courts analyze the purposes behind the monitoring and whether the content of the communications is reasonably related to the proffered purposes. While legitimate business interests will not justify a general practice of extensive e-mail content monitoring, the scope of the acceptable monitoring generally corresponds to the employer's business interests.

The second is the context approach. In this approach the Court looks to the employer's reason for monitoring his employees' communications to determine whether he had a legitimate business justification for the monitoring. The courts determine the reasonableness of the employee's expectations in the context approach by analyzing the employer's notification procedures.[64]

Let us take note that forty-eight states and the District of Columbia have statutes similar to the federal ECPA. Thirteen states require, however, that prior consent must be given by all parties to the communications. Twenty-two states and Washington, D.C. have no "business extension" exception or restrict the "provider" exception to communication common carriers. In thirty-one states and D.C., therefore, the electronic communication privacy statutes seem to provide protection for employees superior to the ECPA, as long as the interception occurs within their jurisdiction.[65]

Frier's policy of surreptitiously monitoring employee e-mails is not unlike the general practice in the United States today. One national survey, for instance, found that 66.2% of the employer respondents who monitor their employees stated that they do not inform their employees in advance that they may be monitored.[66] Frier's practice of surreptitiously *reading* all employee e-mails, both personal and business correspondences, undoubtedly invades the privacy of his employees beyond the general practice. Because Frier does not articulate a business need in advance of the monitoring he does, his practice apparently runs afoul of the ECPA.

From the standpoint of American law, Frier need only make slight adjustments to ensure that his e-mail policy does not run afoul of the ECPA. All that he needs to do is to promulgate in advance his business interest in monitoring and reading employee e-mails. The stated objectives of quality control, preventing the leaking of confidential information and the prevention of the contamination of the work environment should give Frier free reign to monitor and read both the business and personal e-mails of his employees that are transmitted and received by the office intranet system.

To ensure that employees don't claim ignorance of the policy, Frier should program the office computers to flash a warning that greets anyone who logs on. The warning would say:

> "The Company computing and communication resources are provided for business related purposes. The Company will monitor system use and inappropriate activity will subject users to appropriate disciplinary action, which may include termination."

With the aim of gaining an extra measure of confidence that his telephone use and e-mail policy will not run afoul the ECPA, Frier should craft a document that clearly articulates his *business interests* for recording telephone conversations and monitoring and reading e-mails. The document would include a consent form. Upon becoming a hire, each employee would be asked to sign this document consent form.

EMPLOYEE COMMUNICATIONS MONITORING AND HALAKHAH

For analytical simplicity we will initially assume that Frier allows his employees some freedom to engage in personal electronic communications during the course of the workday. We make a further initial assumption that Frier trusts his employees to self-identify the communications they make using the company equipment as either business related or personal. In respect to the telephone, these two categories are easily identified as some telephone lines are designated exclusively to be used for business and others exclusively for personal use. In respect to e-mails, Frier instructs employees to use headers as a means of identifying their correspondences as either personal or business related.

We proceed now to extrapolate the monitoring rights Halakhah confers Frier in respect to both business and personal employee office communications equipment.

Business Messages

In respect to the business communications that come through the company equipment, Frier has every right to monitor them. Note R. Yohanan's dictum: If one's father left him a great sum of money [as an inheritance], – and he wishes to lose it, let him. . . . hire workers and not sit with them [to supervise].[67] Implicit in R. Yohanan's statement is that the right of an employer to supervise his worker is self-evident. Since it is the duty of the worker *W* not to idle on the job and to exert himself with his full energies, monitoring the work *W* does is the employer's way of insuring he gets maximum productivity out of *W*.[68] Monitoring the business communications of employees should therefore be viewed as an aspect of quality control of the way the firm transacts business. Because monitoring the performance of a worker is Frier's right, he need not secure from his employee permission to do so in advance.

Given Frier's right to monitor business communications coming in and out of his workplace, does he have a license to surreptitiously monitor these communications, without giving notice of his practice in advance? No. Consider Frier plans to use the information gathered to gauge employee productivity. If Frier uses the information gathered to make personnel decisions, his surreptitious monitoring runs afoul of Jewish law's performance appraisal requirements. This standard requires Frier to set performance goals in *advance* and provide an employee with *feedback* so that corrective action can be taken before an adverse personnel decision is rendered.[69]

Making an adverse personnel decision based on the surreptitious monitoring may also make Frier guilty of dashing the reasonable expectations of his employee and hence put him in violation of the prohibition of causing someone needless mental anguish (*ona'at devarim*).[70] Consider that estimates show that workers with on-line access spend five to ten hours per week searching the World Wide Web for non-work-related sites or sending e-mails of a personal nature.[71] Now, suppose that Frier's monitoring shows that a particular worker at his company falls into this mould, but Frier fires his worker by telling him that at his firm he expects a higher productivity standard. Because the fired worker falls into the national productivity standard and Frier *failed* to stipulate in advance that he was expecting a higher standard, the firing *dashes* the reasonable expectations of the worker and hence violates the *ona'at devarim* interdict.

Personal Messages

We now turn to a consideration of Frier's monitoring rights in respect to his worker's (*W's*) outgoing and incoming personal electronic communications. Whether or not *W* is granted a limited *personal* electronic communications privilege, once Frier *realizes* that the conversation he is recording or the e-mail he is reading is a personal matter, he must immediately break off the monitoring. Not doing so apparently puts Frier in violation of Rabbenu Gershom b. Judah Me'Or ha-Golah's (France, ca. 960–1040) edict against reading another person's mail without permission.[72] Standing at the basis of this edict, according to R. Jacob Hagiz (Jerusalem, 1620–1674), is the admonition: "You shall not go as a talebearer among your people" (Leviticus 19:16). What the verse prohibits is the bearing of someone's private information, whether it is for self-consumption or for the purpose of revealing it to someone else.[73]

One could, however, argue against the applicability of R. Gershom's dictum to the monitoring of an employee's personal electronic communications in the work scene. The objection here is that the work scene is a setting for diminished expectations on the part of *W* for privacy. Consider that *W's* electronic communications are stored in the company's server. *W* should therefore anticipate that in the event a security breach occurs, a *Bet Din*, under a certain set of conditions, might allow Frier to examine the electronic records he has as a means of ferreting out the culprit. If Frier could not invoke this right under certain conditions, the personal e-mail privilege he grants *W* would amount to setting up *W* for a veiled misconduct opportunity to leak confidential information. All *W* needs to do to leak the confidential information is to send it off with a header marked with the word *personal* and Frier would have no right to ever look at it.

The work scene is not only *inherently* a place for diminished expectations of privacy for *W*, but there is considerable room for a boss to diminish *W's* expectations for privacy by design. Let us see why. Suppose Frier's policy is to inform *W* in advance that he plans to monitor his e-mail and other business related electronic communications. This monitoring will be done, Frier explains, as an aspect of the company's performance appraisal system. In addition, Frier grants *W* a limited personal electronics communications privilege. While Frier says nothing about his intentions to monitor *W's* personal electronics communications, he continuously warns *W* not to abuse this privilege by engaging in sexual harassment via e-mail or sending out e-mails containing racial slurs. On the basis of these warnings should not *W* conclude that Frier will be doing some sort of monitoring of his personal electronic communications? If *W* expects some sort of monitoring in respect to his personal electronic communications, as for example, a key word scan, then, perhaps R. Gershom's dictum does not apply for his entire personal electronic communications at the office.

While the business scene is a setting for diminished privacy expectations for *W*, R. Gershom's dictum should still apply. This is so because R. Gershom's prohibition against reading someone else's mail is operative not only when the letter is contained in a sealed envelope, but also when the message is written on a postcard.[74] If the edict applies to reading a postcard addressed to someone else, diminished expectation of privacy is not enough to suspend the prohibition. What is needed is no less than an explicit or implicit waiver by both the sender and receiver of the private message.

DIMINISHING PRIVACY EXPECTATION IN AMERICAN AND JEWISH LAW

The aforementioned discussion points to a fundamental difference between American and Jewish Law in respect to privacy. In American law, there is nothing to stop *E* from adopting policies that *diminish W's* expectations for privacy in respect to personal electronic communications.

No more evidencing this is that American courts don't regard *E's* breach of promise not to monitor *W's* e-mail as a tort and therefore the breach of promise cannot be the basis for a wrongful discharge suit. The oft quoted case is the 1996 case Smyth v. Pillsbury Co. In this case, a U.S. District court ruled that even if a company assures its employees in advance that the company will not intercept their e-mail messages, the company is within its rights to access these messages and to fire an employee if it finds the content of the messages harmful to the company. The particulars of the case were the following: An employee of Pillsbury and his supervisor were sending "inappropriate and unprofessional comments" over Pillsbury's e-mail system. These messages got into the hands of their boss, and both men were fired. One of the fired employees, Michael A. Smyth sued, claiming he had lost his $62,500 a year job as a regional manager due to invasion of privacy. In rejecting Smyth's claim, the court advanced two arguments.

One point was that the e-mail was sent over an e-mail system that the entire company utilized. Accordingly, notwithstanding the company's prior assurances of privacy, *any reasonable expectation of privacy was lost.*

Morereover, even if Smyth had a reasonable expectation for privacy, the right of privacy is not an absolute right, but rather must be balanced against the company's interest in preventing inappropriate and unprofessional comments or even illegal activity. In the case at bar, the court felt that a reasonable person would not consider the interception of his e-mail that is sent in the company's e-mail system to be a substantial and highly offensive invasion of his privacy. The company's interest must therefore be regarded as paramount here.[75]

We have already seen that as far as Jewish law is concerned the prohibition against reading someone's private correspondences applies even when the person whose privacy is invaded has diminished expectations of privacy.

In his treatment of Jewish privacy law, R. Norman Lamm adds an additional element by positing that privacy is not only a *legal right* but also a *moral duty*. This duty consists of a responsibility to safeguard one's own intimacies from the inquisition of his neighbors.[76] The duty to protect one's own privacy also proceeds from the *imitatio Dei* (lit. imitating God) principle. This principle is the guidepost for interpersonal conduct. It consists of a duty to imitate God's Attributes of Mercy in our interpersonal conduct: "as He is compassionate and gracious, so you must be compassionate and gracious."[77] Just as God's Essence and Absoluteness are forever unknown to man, so too, man must also have a private side to himself. Concealment in human form translates, according to R. Lamm, in a duty on the part of man not to be in unlimited communication. There must be a side in man that manifests itself in a desire to remain "unknown, puzzling, enigmatic, and a mystery."[78]

ELECTRONIC COMMUNICATIONS MONITORING POLICY AND HALAKHAH

The implication of the stringencies of Jewish privacy law for the monitoring of electronic communications in the workplace is that an employer E does not have *carte blanche* to focus solely on his business needs and, then, set out to craft policies that *diminish* W's privacy expectations consistent with these business needs. Instead, E must tax his creativity by balancing his business interests with a policy that is as *least* invasive as possible of the privacy of his employees. What follows is that the type of monitoring system E *should* adopt will be a function of the size of the firm, the nature of social and personal ties *E* has with the individual members of his firm, and finally will depend on the nature of the business itself.

Let us begin with a simple model. The employees of the firm consist of a small number of workers. All members of the firm are either *E's close* family or have close social and personal ties with him. The firm's ordinary course of business is not trade secrets.

In this simple model, *E* has no basis to impose any monitoring whatsoever on the personal electronic communications of his workers. Accordingly, *E* should inform his workers in advance that only their business related electronic correspondences will be monitored. In respect to this monitoring, they will receive regular feedback as part of the firm's performance appraisal system. In regard to personal telephone calls, a particular line will be designated for personal calls. No one will listen in on these calls, but these calls will be automatically recorded. To prevent abuse of the personal call privilege, the use of a password will be required to initiate the call. In addition, the company will keep tabs on the identity of the caller as well as the length of the call. But, in the event of an internal investigation to ferret out the source of misconduct, fraud or theft, the company reserves the right to listen in on these personal conversations. Similarly, in respect to e-mail transmissions, to avoid company monitoring *W* need only mark the word *personal* on the header of the message. The word *personal* will ensure that the privacy of these messages will be respected. Naturally, *E* might want to make it clear to *W* that his right to engage in personal electronic communications on company time is very limited. Accordingly, to ensure that *W* does not abuse this privilege, *E* informs *W* that he will be monitoring both the frequency and the bandwidth of his messages. Though e-mail messages marked personal will not be read for content in the ordinary course of business, these messages will be stored on the company server and, in the event of an internal investigation to ferret out the source of misconduct, fraud or theft, the company reserves the right to comb through these messages.

One final point. Since recording and storing electronic personal messages for possible future listening violates R. Gershom's dictum, *W* may not commence telephone conversations and personal e-mail correspondences with anyone until the outside party signs a consent form. Halakhah's consent requirement is hence more strict compared to the ECPA and conforms to the stricter criterion required by some of the states, as mentioned earlier.

If the firm's stock and trade consists of trade secrets and other confidential information, conferring W with the privilege to send out unmonitored personal electronic communications might be regarded by E as a sure fire formula to put him out of business in short shrift. Similarly, even if leaks of confidential information is not a significant concern, E may have a very large labor force that mostly have no personal relationship with him. With this type of labor force, E may have legitimate concern that the company's electronic equipment might be used by a few employees to contaminate the work environment. Given these concerns, it should not be objectionable for E to promulgate a policy that forbids W to use office equipment for anything other than business related matters. The policy also says that the company will monitor all outgoing messages to ensure that no one uses office equipment to send out personal messages. In explaining the policy to W, E should say that it is rooted in the past record of industry wide behavioral patterns, rather than suspicions he has of *any particular* W. Because this rationale avoids impugning the integrity of W in any direct way, this policy does not do violence to the *kaf zehut* mandate.

The *advance stated* policy that the company equipment should only be used for business related purposes allows the company to monitor all communications that come through the office equipment, both business related and personal. With respect to business communications, the company monitors *content* and includes a feedback feature as part of a performance appraisal system. But, for personal correspondences the company has no right to monitor content other than the minimum necessary to reach a determination that W violated company policy with his electronic message.

The above policy may run afoul of Jewish labor law. Springing a comprehensive communications monitoring policy on a captive employee informs the hire that he/she is expected to abdicate entirely the freedom to *communicate privately* with the outside world for the entire daily routine at the office. Because these policies transform the workplace for W into "electronic sweatshop,"[79] E runs afoul of the prohibition against imposing on W "servitude" like conditions. Elsewhere in this volume, we have elaborated on the nature of this prohibition and its application for the modern marketplace. The gist of that discussion is that entering into a labor contract to work at fixed hours (i.e., *po'el*) is an agreement akin to servitude. With the aim of psychologically relieving the *po'el* from feeling "shackled" to his employer, the Torah confers the *po'el* with a limited right to retract from the labor agreement with no penalty. Given that workers today don't switch jobs from day to day, the right to retract is rendered a vapidity as far as the typical modern employee is concerned. Accordingly, what is necessary to "psychologically unshackle" the modern *po'el* is to give him the freedom to minimally communicate with the outside world. Giving the *po'el* the right to minimally communicate with the outside world, but at the same time informing the *po'el* that all his/her communication will be monitored and recorded *denudes the po'el of any sense of freedom* in his communications with the outside world.

If *E* is bent on implementing a comprehensive communications monitoring communications, he can, however, overcome the above barrier in Jewish labor law by introducing the policy as a condition of employment item before the labor contract is signed. Recall that there is no halakhic objection for a *po'el* to voluntarily agree to give up his right to retract before the labor agreement is entered into. Because the right to retract was voluntarily given up in advance, working under a no retraction clause is not akin to servitude. Likewise, if *E* introduces the electronic communications monitoring policy upfront before the labor negotiation is finalized, his electronic communications policy cannot be said to impose servitude-like conditions on *W*.

It is in the latter scenario where Halakhah taxes the ingenuity of the firm to come up with creative solutions that would minimize the harm to *W's* privacy. Instead of forbidding all personal telephone calls and electronic communication, perhaps there is a way to achieve the desired result with less invasion of *W's* privacy. To come up with alternatives, the company must be abreast of the latest technology. Perhaps there is a solution. By installing a security device in the company computers, the firm can prevent the electronic transfer of its documents. Combining this method, called the firewall approach, with subjecting electronic transmissions to a key word scan, might accomplish *E's* goal with much less invasion of *W's* privacy than under the comprehensive consent approach.

SUMMARY AND CONCLUSION

From the standpoint of Halakhah, entering into a labor contract automatically requires the worker to put out his best effort and not to engage in outside activities that diminish performance on the job. This makes the employer's goal to hire a trustworthy workforce and one free of substance abuse a legitimate enterprise. Because an employer is free to validate the self-declarations of candidates regarding their credentials and qualifications for the job, getting candidates to agree to drug testing as a precondition to hiring is not unethical.

Several caveats should, however, be noted. For one, the privacy of the candidate must be respected. This means that the tests must be administered with the greatest privacy consistent with insuring the reliability of the tests. Second, the legitimacy of the goal of achieving the highest possible productivity standard does not justify the administration of tests that the scientific community regards as worthless.

One clear-cut example is the handwriting test to predict the honesty of the employee. This test is utterly worthless.

Another case in point is the widely used pencil and paper honesty test. The scientific community regards this test as useless in predicting honest behavior on the part of employees. Accordingly, the pencil and paper honesty test effectively mocks the job applicant and hence violates both the *kaf zehut* imperative and the *ona'at devarim* interdict.

The productivity standard the employer is entitled to says no more than that the employer has every right to check out a job applicant's resume and by extension to have the candidate agree to drug testing. But, once the candidate passes the tests and is hired, the *kaf zehut* imperative tells the firm to trust the employee and rely on the latter's periodic declarations that he or she is drug free.

Several exceptions to this general procedure can be identified. One exception obtains when the work scene is hit by a rash of petty thefts and an employee is suspected as the culprit. Now, if it is feared that the thefts are drug related and were done to support a drug habit, drug testing is justified as a means of ferreting out the culprit.

Relying on the worker's self-declaration after he initially passes the pre-hiring drug test is also not in order for a job where unsatisfactory performance puts the public's safety at risk. Because a quasi-contact exists between the public and the employer not to rely on the employee's periodic self-declaration alone, periodic testing to ensure the public's safety is in order. Insuring the public's safety concerns need not, however, take the form of requiring the employee to go through with periodic drug testing. Instead, the employee's word need not be directly doubted and the same objective for the public's safety can be achieved with periodic dexterity and motor skill tests.

If the labor force of a firm falls into one of the high risk categories for drug abuse, E is justified to augment his pre-hiring drug testing with additional measures with the aim of creating an environment of deterrence against drug use. Continuing the initial pre-hiring drug testing with a system of random testing qualifies as a supplemental measure that does no violence to the *kaf zehut* imperative. With the aim of creating a strong anti-drug culture to combat the high-risk drug abuse environment, a system of universal repeat drug testing is, perhaps, also justified. But, requiring W to submit specimens under observed conditions directly assaults the *kaf zehut* imperative and is therefore prohibited.

Given that the scientific community does not regard the polygraph as a valid test to identify deceptive people, rejecting an applicant based on this test causes that person needless mental anguish and hence violates for the employer both the *ona'at devarim* interdict and the *kaf zehut* imperative.

Does the polygraph have any future prospect for acceptability in the evidentiary procedures of the Jewish Court? The answer lies in the assessment of why the polygraph is in disrepute in the scientific community today. For some scholars the problem lies in the reliability of this test. Specifically, the test is not *reliable* because the same exam administered by different examiners gets different results. Consider, however, that in the current state of affairs polygraph tests are often administered by examiners who are overworked or who are inexperienced. When the day comes that improvements in polygraph testing make the results dependable, the results of these tests should, according to some scholars, be treated on the level of *umdana demukhrah*, i.e., circumstantial evidence. In civil litigation, circumstantial evidence is admissible in a Jewish court.

Based on the authoritative work of David Lykken, we have rejected the above assessment of why the polygraph suffers from a poor reputation in the scientific community today. What's wrong with the test is not on the level of consistent results when different examiners administer the same test, but rather the problem is that the test does not measure what it purports to measure. In the design of the test, the answers the subject gives to the questions the examiner uses as control questions are taken by the examiner to be lies. The stress level the polygraph shows for these questions is therefore taken as a measure of the stress the subject feels when he or she lies. Now, if the subject produces greater stress for the relevant questions than he does for the control questions, the subject's response to the relevant questions is taken as a lie. But, the relevant questions may produce more stress for the subject than the level of stress the control questions elicit, even though the subject is innocent of the crime accused. Consider that from a Torah perspective an individual should feel guilt, not only if he commits a crime, but also if he could have taken timely action that *might have prevented* the crime from happening. Consider also that from a Torah perspective an employee who has established his loyalty and trustworthiness to his company over a long period of time, has every right to feel an outrage for being falsely accused of a crime, say, stealing from the company. This outrage can be that much stronger when the false accusation is coupled with the requirement to submit to the humiliating experience of the polygraph test. Accordingly, instead of measuring the stress one has when lying, the stress the relevant question produces could be of an innocent type, namely the guilt of indirect responsibility for the crime and or the outrage of being accused falsely.

Finally, on the issue of company monitoring of the worker's electronic communications, we found major differences between Halakhah and American law. In American society, The ECPA and the court interpretations of this law constitute the main guideposts for the restraints imposed on E to monitor the electronics communications of his workplace. But, this law provides a number of exceptions. In the opinion of many commentators, one particular exception, called the "provider exception" gives an employer who provides his company with an e-mail network almost "unfettered discretion" to read and disclose the contents of even their employee's *personal* e-mail messages. To be sure, even if E does not want to rely on this lenient interpretation of the provider exception, other means are available to him to achieve a comprehensive electronic communications monitoring policy. One approach is to clearly articulate and promulgate in advance a business interest that rationalizes the monitoring policy he wants to implement. Another route for E is to get the advance consent of the employees for the monitoring policy he desires to implement. Under the ECPA one party consent is sufficient.

In state law, thirty-one states and D.C. protect the privacy of a worker's electronic communications more than the ECPA.

The treatment in Halakhah of privacy protection for the electronic communications of an employee at the work scene begins with the distinction between business related and personal communications. As far as business communications are concerned, an employer is entitled to monitor them. Since it is the duty of the worker not to idle on the job and to exert himself with his full energies, monitoring the work is the employer's way of insuring he gets the most productivity possible out of his worker. Nonetheless, monitoring *W*'s work must be made part of, and not separate from, the performance appraisal system *E* is required to set for *W* for the purpose of rendering personnel decisions. Properly setting up a performance appraisal system requires *E* to set goals for *W* and provide him with periodic feedback in respect to how effectively he is accomplishing these goals. Finally, an adverse personnel decision cannot be made against *W* unless he is given a chance to correct the deficiencies the negative feedback provided him with. To surreptitiously monitor *W*'s business communications and make personnel decisions based on the observation eliminates the feedback process of performance appraisal. Still worse, firing a worker on the basis of surreptitious monitoring may dash the reasonable expectations of *W* and hence violate *ona'at devarim*.

As far as personal correspondences are concerned, by dint of R. Gershom's dictum, *E* has no right to read or monitor them. The circumstance that the work scene is a place for diminished expectations of privacy for *W* does not make R. Gershom's dictum inoperative. Consider that R. Gershom's prohibition against reading someone else's mail is operative not only when the letter is contained in a sealed envelope, but also when the message is written on a postcard. If the edict applies to reading a postcard addressed to someone else, diminished expectation of privacy is not enough to suspend the prohibition. What is needed is no less than an explicit or implicit waiver by both the sender and receiver of the private message.

If the type of business the firm deals in and or the size and composition of its labor force make the leakage of confidential information and the contamination of the workplace a legitimate concern, it should not be objectionable for *E* to promulgate a policy that forbids *W* to use office equipment for anything other than business related matters. The policy also says that the company will monitor all outgoing messages to ensure that no one uses office equipment to send out personal messages. In explaining the policy to *W*, *E* should say that it is rooted in the past record of industry wide behavioral patterns, rather than suspicions he has of any particular *W*. Because this rationale avoids impugning the integrity of *W* in any direct way, this policy does not do violence to the *kaf zehut* mandate. Promulgating this policy does not give the company *carte blanche* to examine the contents of all messages sent out. If the message is business related, the firm has, of course, every right to examine its contents. The right to do so goes to the very essence of the labor contract. But, if the monitoring tells the firm the message is personal, the contents of the message may not be scrutinized and the reading of the message must stop as soon as its personal nature is realized.

A caution must here, however, be sounded. An all comprehensive monitoring policy that calls for *W* to abdicate all his private communications with the outside world amounts to caging *W* into an electronic sweatshop and violates Jewish labor law. If a comprehensive monitoring policy is deemed essential, as it might be, if the firm is a member of the government intelligence or counterintelligence community, management should put its monitoring policy up front in the negotiating stage of the contract, rather than coming later as a consent form it pushes on *W* after the labor contract has already been agreed upon.

The comparison between American and Jewish law points to a basic difference in philosophy. In American law, nothing stops *E* from achieving greater control by means of promulgating policies that diminish *W's* expectations for privacy. In Jewish law, it is, however, morally wrong to pursue business interests without giving careful consideration as to how these goals can be achieved with the least invasion of *W's* privacy. Moreover, even if *E* manages to reduce *W's* expectations of privacy, this factor alone does not confer *E* with a right to breach *W's* privacy.

POSTPRANDIUM

Large firms use in-house Employee Assistance Programs(EAP) to combat drug use in the workplace. We will describe how these programs work and show a basis for these programs in Halakhah. We will proceed to deal with the issue of considering EAP as an alternative to drug testing in the workplace.

EAP address the personal problems of an employee. The aim of these programs is to help employees solve problems affecting their job performance. While the objective is providing assistance, the goal is to keep the good employee working and free of problems that could affect job satisfaction and performance.

Deteriorating job performance is usually the basis for referring an employee to an EAP. It is then the function of the EAP practitioner to determine what the underlying problem may be. Once the problem is assessed, the employee is referred to an outside provider service for assistance. The majority of referrals in these programs turn out to be for alcoholism or drug abuse.[80]

The success of EAP's is indicated by the estimated recovery rates of 65 to 85 percent among employees who accept a referral for help rather than face disciplinary action for deteriorating job performance. This means that at least 65 percent of all employees receiving EAP services will be returned to "full" productivity within one year.[81]

Cost-benefit analysis argues persuasively to the large employer that he should implement EAP in his workplace.[82] The moral case for such a program is the requirement of an individual to conduct himself/herself *lifnim mi-shurat ha-din* (beyond the letter of the law). Discussed earlier in this chapter, the relevant aspect of this behavioral imperative is the following case dealing with a damage claim an employer has against his worker:

> Some porters broke a barrel of wine belonging to Rabbah b. Bar Hannan. Thereupon he seized their garments; so they went and complained to Rav. "Return their garments to them," he ordered. "Is that the law?" he inquired. "Yes," he rejoined, "that you shall walk in the way of good men (Proverbs 2:20)." Their garments having been returned, they observed, "We are poor men, have worked all day, and are hungry. Are we to get nothing?" "Go and pay them," he ordered. "Is that the law?" he asked. "Yes," he rejoined, "and keep the path of the righteous (Proverbs 2:20)."

Preliminarily, let us take note that, according to *Tosafot, lifnim mi-shurat ha-din* generally makes a claim only on an individual's toil and effort, but does not make a demand on him to incur an expense.[83]

Under the assumption that the wine barrels were broken through the negligence of the porters,[84] Rabbah b. Bar Hannan had a legitimate damage claim against them. While the behavioral expectation to act *lifnim mi-shurat ha-din* did not require Rabbah b. Bar Hannan to forego his damage claim, Rav urged him to do so on the basis of the moral principle "that you shall walk in the way of good men." Upon learning that the porters were indigent, Rav even urged Rabbah b. Bar Hannan to pay them their wages on the basis of the ethical imperative "and keep the path of the righteous." These latter ethical teachings evidently demand of man an even more generous and selfless nature than the *lifnim mi-shurat ha-din* imperative.[85]

While the *Tosafot* understand the ethical principles proceeding from the verse in Proverbs as constituting a moral principle distinct from the *lifnim mi-shurat ha-din* behavioral expectation, R. Solomon b. Isaac (Rashi, Troyes, 1040-1105) and others regard these teachings as forming an integral part of the latter concept.[86]

The dispute between Rashi and *Tosafot* points up a large difference in opinion as to how far the *lifnim mi-shurat ha-din* duty goes. This gap is somewhat narrowed by R. Mosheh Feinstein's (New York, 1895–1986) understanding of the Rabbah b. Bar Hannan incident discussed above. R. Feinstein's thesis begins with an explanation of how the duty to forego a damage claim can be read into: "that you shall walk in the way of good men" (Proverbs 2:20). His answer: A good person will not press his debtor to pay when he knows that the latter has no ability to do so. Such conduct violates the biblical prohibition: "When you lend money to my people, to the poor man among you, *do not press* him for repayment" (Exodus 22:24). Relying on the Talmudic presumption that a poor person is not likely to become a person of means, Rav ordered Rabbah b. Bar Hannan to forgive the damage claim he had against the poor workers. Given the unlikelihood that the poor workers would ever afford to make good on this debt, forgiving the debt amounts to no more than relieving them of a psychological burden. Now, once Rabbah b. Bar Hannan had canceled the workers debt to him, Rav felt that the workers were due their wages not merely as a matter of charity but as a matter of legal entitlement.[87]

Proceeding from R. Feinstein's analysis is that Rashi is in basic agreement with *Tosafot*: *Lifnim mi-shurat ha-din* conduct generally makes a claim only on the toil and effort of an individual. If the sought after benefit entails a financial outlay, *lifnim mi-shurat ha-din* does not, as a general matter, require it.

Rashi's understanding of the porter case serves as a model for the requirement for an employer to set up an EAP. If the *lifnim mi-shurat ha-din* imperative tells the employer to forego a damage claim against his worker and treat that worker as a priority charity case, the same principle tells the employer to tolerate a deterioration of his worker's job performance and help rehabilitate[88] the troubled worker by referring him to appropriate help.

For the large employer, the expense involved in setting up an EAP is trifling. Given the minimal expense involved, it would be petty on the part of the employer not to set up the EAP. Accordingly, for the large employer, the ethically right thing to do is to set up an EAP in his workplace.[89]

CHOOSING BETWEEN DRUG TESTING AND EAP

Professor Jennifer Moore, a critic of drug testing in the workplace, proposes that firms should make use of broadbrush educational and rehabilitative programs as an alternative to drug testing.[90] Moore's proposal is not persuasive. Although EAP's can effectively combat many of the consequences of illicit drug use by employees, they are limited in scope because they depend on the willingness of employees who need assistance to come forward. However, most employees who are chemically dependent deny their drug problems and are not motivated to seek help from an EAP. A drug testing program can identify employees who have used illegal drugs and thus provide the necessary evidence to confront the chemically dependent employee who is in denial.[91] Drug testing provides a deterrent against the use of illegal drugs. Since the halakhic argument for drug testing is based on the employer's right to protect his property as well as his duty to protect the work place, Halakhah would not tell the employer to rely entirely on EAP and deny himself the option of making use of drug testing.

Walter F. Scanlon theorizes that an in-house program is cost effective only if the workforce consists of 1,000 employees or more. This is especially true where the employee turnover is not significant. A program that reaches 2 percent of its population, for example, might get 20 referrals in the first year. After that, the referral rate would be reduced to a trickle. Since most workers in America work for small companies with a total population of less than 500, most companies will find EAP not to be cost effective. Subscribing to the services of an outside EAP or forming a consortium with other small companies is an alternative to an in-house program. But, these alternatives may also not prove cost effective for the small firm.[92]

Scanlon's thesis has important implications for Halakhah. It tells an employer of 500 workers or less that from a purely investment perspective, EAP will not be cost effective; rather, implementing the program will entail a significant expenditure. Since *lifnim mi-shurat ha-din* conduct generally makes a claim only on toil and effort, but does not require a *significant* expenditure, Halakhah would not require a small employer to implement EAP. Given the right of an employer to protect himself and the work environment from drug use, the alternative of implementing an EAP does not preclude the small employer from implementing a policy of comprehensive drug testing as a screening device and random drug testing for the existing labor force.

What the above analysis says is no more than that the small employer is not required to set up an in-house EAP. The *lifnim mi-shurat ha-din* imperative is not, however, an all or nothing proposition. *Rashi's* treatment of the porter case tells us that *lifnim mi-shurat ha-din* should operate for the employer on some level even vis-à-vis a worker that has caused him damage. To be sure, *lifnim mi-shurat ha-din* conduct will not require the employer to retain a worker who is found to be chemically dependent. Nonetheless, this behavioral imperative tells the employer that he should deal with the troubled worker he is about to terminate with dignity and humanity. At the very least, the employer should be prepared to offer his worker sound advice regarding where to seek help and where to get financial assistance, if needed.

Let us make one final point regarding *lifnim mi-shurat ha-din* conduct. One cannot deal with the problem of chemical dependence on a spontaneous basis. If the employer is to deal with his troubled employee with compassion and dignity, the employer must do the necessary research in advance and be prepared for the eventuality.

NOTES

1. The reader is referred to pp. 272–276 of this volume.
2. 102 STAT. 646 Public Law 100-347, Sec 3(1),(2),(3), June 27, 1988.
3. 102 STAT. 646 Public Law 100-347, Sec 7,8, June 27, 1988.
4. 102 STAT. 646 Public Law 100-347, Sec 7,8, June 27, 1988.
5. *Shevu'ot* 30a; R. Isaac b. Jacob Alfasi (Algeria, 1012–1103), *Rif*, ad locum; R. Asher b. Jehiel (Germany, 1250–1327), *Shevu'ot* 4:3; R. Isaac b. Sheshet Perfet (Spain, 1325–1408), *Responsa Ribash* 446, 447.

6. Leviticus 25:17; *Mishnah, Bava Metzia* 4:10; R. Isaac b. Jacob Alfasi, *Rif, Bava Metzia* 58b; R. Asher b. Jehiel, Rosh, Bava Metzia 4:22; R. Jacob b. Asher (Spain, 1270–1343), *Tur, Hoshen Mishpat* 228; R. Joseph Caro (Safed, 1488–1575), *Shulhan Arukh, Hoshen Mishpat* 228:4; R. Jehiel Michel Epstein (Belorussia, 1829–1908), *Arukh ha-Shulhan, Hoshen Mishpat* 228:2.

7. Maimonides, *Yad, De'ot* 7:2.

8. *Erkhin* 15b; *Yad,* op. cit. 7:3.

9. *Sifra,* Leviticus 19:16.

10. R. Israel Meir ha-Kohen Kagan (Poland, 1828–1933), *Hafetz Hayyim, Hilkhot Issurei Rekhilut* 9:1, *Be'er Mayyim Hayyim* 1.

11. The Use of Integrity Testing for Preemployment Screening, OTA-SET-442 (Washington, D.C.: U.S. Government Printing Office), p. 10.

12. One section of the examination deals with questions that attempt to ascertain whether the respondent's attitude and perceptions regarding honesty conform to socially responsible behavior. The theory behind this component of the test, it appears, is that one who views the world surrounding him as pristine and fiercely honest is likely to conform to the high standards of honesty everyone else has. This aspect of the underlying theory of the integrity test is in conformity with Jewish values. See discussion later in this chapter on R. Joshua Leib Diskin's rationalization of the *kaf zehut* imperative.

13. Charles Clifton, *Preemployment Integrity Testing: How to Ace the Test and Land the Job,* (Boulder, Colorado: Paladin Press, 1993), pp. 60–93.

14. *Baraita Yoma* 23a; *Yad, De'ot* 7:7.

15. *Baraita Bava Kamma* 83b; *Baraita Bava Kamma* 84a; *Yad, Hovel u-Mazzik* 1: 1–6.

16. For sources and discussion of this point, please turn to p. 250 of this volume.

17. For discussion of this point, please turn to pp. 438–440 of this volume.

18. R. Mosheh Isserles, *Rema, Hoshen Mishpat* 421:6.

19. Rav Hai Gaon, *Sha'arei Teshuvah* 50.

20. C.F *Yad, Teshuvah,* 7:4–8.

21. Joseph R. DesJardins, Ronald Duska, "Drug Testing in Employment," in W. Michael Hoffman, Robert E. Frederick and Mark S. Schwartz, Eds., *Business Ethics Readings and Cases in Corporate Morality,* fourth edition (New York: McGraw Hill, 2001), pp. 274–276.

22. Michael Waldholtz, "Drug Testing in the Workplace: Whose Rights Take Precedence," in *Business Ethics Readings and Cases in Corporate Morality,* op. cit., p. 282.

23. Richard T. De George, *Business Ethics,* fifth edition (Upper Saddle River, New Jersey: Prentice Hall, 1999), pp. 403–405.

24. Waldholtz, op. cit., pp. 283–284.

25. Joseph R. DesJardins, Ronald Duska, op. cit., 276–281.

26. *Yad, Sekhirut* 13:6–7

27. *Nahmanides,* quoted by *Rosh, Bava Metzia* 5:16, 17.

28. *Rosh,* op. cit. 5:16, 17.

29. For the halakhic parameters of coercion, please turn to pp. 190, 235, 238 of this volume.

30. *Bava Batra* 3a; *Rif, ad locum; Yad, Shekhenim* 2:14; *Rosh, Bava Batra*1:1; *Tur,* op. cit. 157; *Sh. Ar.,* op. cit. 157:1; *Ar. ha-Sh.,* op. cit. 157:1.

31. *Bava Batra* 59b; *Rif, ad locum; Yad, Shekhenim* 7:6; *Rosh,* op. cit. 3:75; *Tur,* op. cit. 154; *Sh. Ar.,* op. cit. 154:3; *Ar. ha-Sh.,* op. cit. 154:7.

32. *Bava Batra* 3a; *Rif, ad locum*; *Yad, Shekhenim* 2:14; *Rosh, Bava Batra* 1:1; *Tur*, op. cit. 157; *Sh. Ar.*, op. cit. 157:1; *Ar. ha-Sh.* op. cit. 157:1

33. R. Yehoshua Leib Diskin, Responsa *Maharal Diskin*, appended at the end of the work. Why there is a need for a special verse: "[W]ith righteousness shall you judge your fellow" (Leviticus 19:15) to establish the *kaf zehut* imperative requires explanation. The duty to judge one's fellow favorably should be *subsumed* in the general mandate of "Love your friend as yourself" (Leviticus 19:18). R. Diskin's rationale for *kaf zehut* clarifies this point. His explanation makes judging one's fellow favorably a *hesed* (loving kindness) duty to *oneself* as well as a *hesed* duty to the *Jewish community as a whole* in the form of strengthening the deterrence of shame against sin. "Love your friend as yourself" conveys a duty only to perform acts of *hesed* to a fellow as an individual. "[W]ith righteousness shall you judge your fellow" directs us to perform an act of *hesed* to a fellow because doing so will strengthen the bonds of the Jewish Community and hence uplift the moral climate of society.

34. National Drug-Free Workplace Alliance, http://www.ndfwa.org/statistics.htm.

35. *Tosafot, Gittin* 2a.

36. R. Solomon b. Isaac, *Rashi, Gittin* 3a.

37. R. Isser Zalman Meltzer, *Even ha-Ezel, Yad, Avadim* 6:7.

38. Richard J. Klimosky, "Graphology and Personnel Selection," in Barry l. Beyerstein and Dale F. Beyerstein, *The Write Stuff: Evaluation of Graphology, The Study of Handwriting Analysis*, (Buffalo. New York: Prometheus Books, 1992), 232–244.

39. Geoffrey A. Dean, "The Bottom Line: Effective in Size, in *The Write Stuff*, op. cit., p. 301.

40. Leviticus 25:17; *Mishnah, Bava Metzia* 4:10; *Rif*, ad locum; *Yad, Geneivah* 14:12; *Rosh, Bava Metzia* 4:22; *Tur, Hoshen Mishpat*, 228; *Sh. Ar.*, op. cit. 228:1; *Ar. ha-Sh.*, op. cit. 228:1.

41. Richard T. De George, op. cit., pp. 400–401.

42. Ibid, pp. 401–403.

43. For an incisive early work on this topic, see R. Yehoshua Baumol (New York, 1880–1948), Responsa *Emek Halakhah* 14.

44. Professor Eliav Shochetman, "The Polygraph in Jewish Law," in *Crossroads Halacha and the Modern World*, vol.3 (Alon Shvut, Israel: Zomet Institute), pp. 203–215.

45. Statement of The American Medical Association to the House Subcomm. On Employment Opportunities of the Comm. On Education and Labor (March 5,1987); American Psychological Association, APA Resolution Says Reliability of Polygraph Test Unsatisfactory (press release, Feb. 1, 1986).

46. "The Polygraph in Jewish Law," op. cit., pp. 206–215.

47. David T. Lykken, *A Tremor in the Blood Uses and Abuses of The Lie Detector* (New York: Plenum Trade, 1998), p. 76.

48. For an extensive discussion on the concepts of relevant and control questions in relation to polygraph testing, see Lykken, op. cit., pp. 76–88.

49. Ibid., pp. 119–136.

50. Deuteronomy 21:1–7.

51. Jerusalem Talmud, *Sotah* 9:6; See also R. Meir Yehudah Leibush b. Yehiel Michel (*Malbim*, Russia, 1809–1880), *ha-Torah ve-ha-Mizvah*, Deuteronomy 21:7.

52. R. Solomon b. Isaac, *Rashi, Berokhot* 31b.

53. CF. *Pesahim* 13a; *Yoma* 35a.

54. *Otzrot ha-Agadah, Ein Yaakov, Berokhot* 31b.
55. *Berokhot* 31b.
56. Ibid.
57. 18 U.S.C. § 2510–2520.
58. 18 U.S.C. § 2511.
59. Ibid.
60. Ibid.
61. Alexander I. Rodriguez, "All Bark, No Byte; Employee E-Mail Privacy Rights in the Private Sector Workplace," 47 *Emory Law Journal* 1439, 1451,(1998).
62. Ruel Torres Hernandez, "ECPA and Online Computer Privacy," 41 FED, COMM. L. J. 17, 39 (1988).
63. Julia T. Baumhart, "The Employer's Right to Read Employee E-Mails: Protecting Property or Personal Prying," 8 *Lab. Law.* 923, 925 (1992).
64. Larry O. Natt Gantt, 11, "An Affront to Human Dignity: Electronic Mail Monitoring in the Private Sector Workplace," 8 *Harvard J. Law & Tec* 345, 364, (Spring, 1995).
65. Lawrence E. Rothstein, "Privacy or Dignity? Electronic Monitoring in the Workplace," *New York Law School Journal of International and Comparative Law*, vol. 19, no. 3, 2000, p. 404.
66. Charles Pillar, "Bosses With X-Ray Eyes," MacWorld, July, 1993, pp. 118, 123.
67. *Bava Metzia* 29b.
68. *Maimonides, Yad, Sekhirut* 13:7. For a discussion of the productivity requirements a worker owes his employer, please turn to pp. 276–277, 298, 427 of this volume.
69. For a treatment of performance appraisal in Jewish law, see Aaron Levine, *Case Studies in Jewish Business* Ethics (Hoboken, New Jersey: Ktav Publishing Co. Inc., Yeshiva University Press 2000), pp. 304–320.
70. For sources and details of this prohibition, please turn to pp. of this volume.
71. Amy Rogers, "You got Mail But Your Employer does Too: Electronic Communications and Privacy in the 21st Century Workplace," 5 J. Technical Law and Policy, Spring, 2000, p. 2.
72. R. Moses b. Naphtali Hirsch Rivkes (Lithuania d. ca. 1671/72), *Be'er ha-Golah, Sh.Ar., Yoreh De'ah* 334, note 123.
73. R. Jacob Hagiz, *Resp. Halakhot Ketannot* 1:276.
74. R. Meir Yehudah Leibush b. Yehiel Michal Malbim, quoted by R. Aharon Yaakov Greenberg, *Iturei Torah*, vol. 3, Exodus 21:23.
75. *Smyth v. The Pillsbury Co.*, 914 F. Supp. 97 (E.D. PA, Jan. 18, 1996).
76. *Yoma* 86b.
77. *Shabbat* 133b.
78 R. Norman Lamm, *Faith and Doubt* (New York:Ktav Publishing House Inc., second edition, 1986), pp. 290–309.
79. The term "electronic sweatshop" was coined by Laurie Thomas Lee, "Watch Your E-Mail! Employee E-Mail Monitoring and Privacy Law in the Age of the "Electronic Sweatshop," 28 J. Marshall L. Rev. 139, 143 (1994).
80. Walter F. Scanlon, *Alcoholism And Drug Abuse in The Workplace*, (New York: Praeger Special Studies, 1986), pp. 17–19.
81. *Alcoholism And Drug Abuse in the Workplace*, op. cit., p. 96.
82. Ibid, pp. 96–103.

83. *Tosafot, Bava Metzia* 24b.

84. Most commentaries (Rashi, *Bava Metzia* 83a s.v. *shekula'i; Tosafot, Bava Metzia* 24b; and *Tur, Hoshen Mishpat* 304:1 on interpretation of Beit Yosef, ad loc.) interpret the incident to refer to the circumstances where the barrels were broken through the negligence of the porters. R. Samuel Eliezer b. Judah ha-Levi Edels (Poland, 1555–1631, *Maharsha,* ad loc.), however, understands Rabbah b. Bar Hannan to have instructed the porters to transport the barrels over an incline. The porters could therefore not be held responsible for the subsequent breakage. Rav wryly indicated this to Rabbah b. Bar Hannan by quoting to him the verse "That you shall walk in the way of good men." A play on the word *way* was meant. Since Rabbah b. Bar Hannan instructed the porters to transport the barrels over an incline instead of a *good way* (i.e., a smooth and even road), the porters cannot be held responsible for the breakage.

85. In the understanding of R. Joseph Hayyim b. Elijah al-Hakham (Baghdad, 1834-1909, *Ben Yehoyada, Bava Metzia* 83a), the higher moral standard proceeding from Proverbs 2:20 is directed only to the ethical elite of society. See also R. Eliezer Yehudah Waldenberg (Israel, contemporary), *Responsa Tzitz Eliezer* 8:3 *ot* 8.

86. Rashi, *Bava Mtezia* 83a, s.v. *baderekh; Tur,* loc.cit., R. Joel Sirkes (Poland, 1561–1640), Bah, Tur, op. cit., 304:1; R. Menahem Mendel Krochmal (Moravia 1600-1661), *Responsa Tzemah Tzedek* 89; R. Mosheh Teitelbaum (Hungary, 1759–1841), *Responsa Heshiv Mosheh, Yoreh De'ah* 48.

87. R. Mosheh Feinstein, *Iggerot Mosheh, Hoshen Mishpat* 1:60.

88. The highest level of charity is to put the needy person on his own feet, see *Torat Kohanim* at Leviticus 25:35; *Yad, Mattenot Aniyyim,* 10:7; *Ar. ha-Sh., Yoreh De'ah* 249:15.

89. For the expectation to incur a trifling expense and discharge an opportunity of *hesed,* rather than to rely on one's exemption in the matter, see R. Judah, *Bava Metzia* 33a and *Ar. ha-Sh.,* op. cit. 264:1.

90. Jennifer Moore, "Drug Testing and Corporate Responsibility: The 'Ought Implies Can' argument," *Journal of Business Ethics,*vol. 8 (1989), pp. 279-287.

91. Daily Lab Rep. (BNA) No. 170, at A-1 (Sept.3,1987).

92. *Alcoholism And Drug Abuse in The Workplace,* op. cit. p. 101.

VI. Public Policy Issues

10

Regulation of Advertising

The theme of this chapter is government regulation of advertising. We will draw a comparison between how secular society and a society governed by Jewish law (Halakhah) deal with this issue. We will refer to a society governed by Halakhah as a Torah society.

From the standpoint of secular society, two areas of regulation can be identified. One is in the area of deception. Playing a central role in determining the criterion for deception is the approach the Federal Trade Commission (FTC) takes in this matter. Besides delineating the FTC's approach, we will also consider what critics of the FTC have to say about this issue. Most prominent here is the approach of economic efficiency advocates.

The second issue is the treatment of negative commercial speech.

We will show that there is a very significant difference between the approaches of the secular and Torah societies to advertising regulation, which widens considerably when we take into account what economic efficiency has to say about government regulation of advertising. We will show that for secular society, government regulation of advertising revolves essentially around the issue of deception, whereas, in addition to the fact that Halakhah's concept of deception is far stricter, Halakhah is also concerned with the promotion of truth as a positive value and life force in society. Furthermore, Halakhah lays out prohibitions in connection with negative commercial speech.

THE FTC'S CRITERION FOR FALSEHOOD AND DECEPTION

In 1983, in response to a Congressional request, the FTC promulgated the criterion it uses in evaluating complaints of falsehood and deception in advertising. The commission defined deception as "a representation, omission or practice that is likely to mislead the consumer acting reasonably in the circumstances."[1]

Giving concreteness to this criterion is the FTC's standard for substantiation and its policy of materiality. The substantiation requirement tells the advertiser that before disseminating a claim it must have a reasonable basis for supporting the claim. A firm's failure to possess and rely upon a reasonable basis for objective claims constitutes a deceptive act.[2]

In regulating advertising, the FTC does not see a public interest in ferreting out all forms of falsehood. The FTC is concerned only with falsehood that is detrimental to the consumer.[3] The detriment criterion is referred to as the materiality condition.

In his historical review of the materiality condition, Professor Ivan Preston shows that the FTC understood it in very broad terms. To be deceptive, according to the FTC definition, it is not necessary to make a claim that is judged likely to induce a purchase that would not otherwise have taken place. Rather, detriment exists if the deceptive claim is "likely to affect a consumer's choice of or conduct regarding a product."[4] To illustrate, suppose a firm misrepresents its product in the print media, but corrects the misrepresentation when the consumer comes to the showroom. The ad is, nonetheless, deceptive. Though the deception may have no direct bearing on the ultimate purchase decision, the claim may unfairly attract business to the seller's store, thereby enabling the salesperson to apply persuasive techniques that otherwise would not have been possible.[5] This broad conceptualization of materiality will be evident in the manner in which the FTC handled the Kraft complaint, which is discussed later in this chapter.

By incorporating the element of materiality into its definition of deceptive advertising, the FTC has explicitly given notice that its goal is not to obliterate deception entirely; rather, it objects only to harmful deception.

NEGATIVE COMPARATIVE ADVERTISING IN AMERICAN LAW

Comparative advertising has enjoyed legitimacy in the United States since 1972, when the FTC began advocating this form of marketing. This stratagem entails advertising in which a named competitor's product is unfavorably compared to the advertiser's own product. A particularly widely criticized variety of this tactic, called negative puffery, occurs when the disparagement takes the form of half-truths or misleading opinion about a competitor's product.

Currently, the only recourse open to a target of comparative advertising is to sue under the common-law tort action of injurious falsehood. But the law of injurious falsehood, as Professor Paul T. Hayden points out, is inadequate in combating disparagement in modern comparative advertising, for two reasons. First, in bringing action in such cases, the plaintiff must prove that the disparaging representation is false. Many courts, however, have concluded that only *factual* misrepresentation meets this test. The second difficulty is the requirement that the plaintiff in tort law prove special damages in the form of pecuniary loss in order to obtain compensation.

With the law of injurious falsehood the only defense against comparative advertising, it is no surprise that negative puffery flourishes virtually unchecked by common law as a legally accepted means of marketing.

In his critique of the present legal treatment of comparative advertising, Hayden argues that negative puffery should be regulated as a possible violation of both deceptive advertising and unfair competition. If the representation is "likely to deceive or mislead" a significant number of prospective purchasers, it should be disallowed.

He asserts, moreover, that in bringing a suit against the negative advertisement of a competitor, a plaintiff should not be burdened with the responsibility to prove special damages. Rather, demonstration of "likely commercial detriment" should suffice. This entails no more than a demonstration that the negative ad would likely influence the conduct of prospective buyers, and, in consequence, results in harm for the plaintiff, in the form of either customer loss or damage to reputation. Indeed, the above-mentioned elements constitute the standard embodied in the new Restatement of Unfair Competition.[6]

PUFFERY AND AMERICAN LAW

Another area in which American law tolerates deception of sorts is puffery. In this regard, American law recognizes the right of a seller to express an opinion regarding his or her product. This opinion, the law presumes, will naturally be favorable. Prospective buyers are therefore expected to understand that they should not rely literally upon the seller's assertions. Since an opinion makes no assertion of fact, it cannot be characterized as misrepresentation.

Commenting on the present state of affairs, Preston argues the current legal approach to puffery is misguided. Statements of opinion or value often *imply* fact and thus should be considered as factual representation. To illustrate, a beer manufacturer's assertion that his product is "Milwaukee's finest" *implies* that beer production quality standards exist, and that the advertised beer is superior to the competitors on the basis of these standards. Given that no such quality standards exist, the manufacturer's assertion is misleading and deceptive.

Preston submits that instead of approaching the issue of puffery by making semantic distinctions between fact and opinion, advertising messages should be examined on the basis of their behavioral-psychological impact. Whether the claim is fact, opinion, or value, the legal test should be whether the message deceives (i.e., creates untrue expectations that influence purchasers).[7]

Following Preston's line of thought, Professor Richard L. Oliver suggests that whenever consumers overrate a product relative to its actual merits as a result of puffery, the advertising message should be regarded as deceptive. To illustrate: If an advertiser states that detergent X gets clothes "cleaner than clean" or "whiter than white," this statement is likely to cause the consumer to expect that X cleans in some superior sense. If the appropriate disclaimer is not made, the puffery will influence the consumer to regard the cleaning power of X more favorably than would be the case had the advertiser simply said "clean" or "white."[8]

THE ECONOMIC EFFICIENCY CRITERION

We will now set out to show that the philosophy inherent in the FTC's definition of deception is consistent with the economic efficiency approach to government regulation, and that if we adopt economic efficiency as the relevant criterion in the promotion of truthfulness in advertising, a certain measure of harmful deception will be tolerated.

The economic efficiency criterion makes the maximization of wealth the goal of economic public policy and government regulation. A restrictive form of this approach to social choice is the Pareto optimality criterion, which dictates that government action is not justified unless it offers the reasonable prospect of improving the economic well-being of at least one person without reducing anyone else's well-being. If improvement for A can be accomplished only by reducing the welfare of B, the status quo condition must remain intact.

Since government action will almost invariably entail gains for some but losses for others, the Pareto rule is too austere to be of any operational use. A less stringent efficiency criterion, called the Kaldor-Hicks rule, has accordingly been advanced as an appropriate guidepost for government actions. This rule dictates that decision makers assess a proposed change in terms of what value gainers would assign to their gains and what value the losers would assign to their losses. If the gains exceed the losses in monetary value, the proposal enhances society's wealth and should therefore be adopted.

Kaldor-Hicks does not require the gainers to compensate the losers. Nevertheless, any proposal that meets this criterion carries with it the potential of enhancing the well-being of the losers in the long run even if compensation was not given to them at the time the action was taken. This result obtains because the increase in *aggregate* income that Kaldor-Hicks makes possible sets into motion a whole series of rounds of spending and income creation. Called the multiplier effect, this expansionary process results regardless of how the original gainers choose to divide their new-found increment in income between saving and spending. Suppose G, the gainer, decides to spend the increment on P_1's product. Then, G's spending increases P_1's income, which, in turn, triggers an increase in income for P_2, when P_1 spends his new-found income on a purchase from P_2. Since in each successive round of income creation, some portion of the increment is saved, the expansionary process must eventually come to a halt. Suppose, however, that G opts to save the new increment in his income. Because G's action, other things equal, increases the supply of loanable funds relative to the demand, G's saving lowers the borrowing cost for P_1. P_1's consequent increased borrowing will then enable him to make his extra purchases from P_2, setting into motion the multiplier effect described above.[9]

Kaldor-Hicks would say that there is no public interest in the government's prohibiting and ferreting out the non-material variety of deceptive advertising. Since consumers are not harmed, the FTC should not waste its resources on this type of deception.

Although the FTC incorporates the element of materiality into its definition of deception, Kaldor-Hicks would likely be in agreement with the following critique Professor Ivan Preston offers on how the FTC handles the materiality issue in practice.

In the current legal environment, the FTC regards every explicit claim in an advertisement as material.[10] Accordingly, if an explicit claim is found to be false, the ad will be declared deceptive. Currently, the FTC provides no methodological guidance to firms on how they can disprove that an explicit claim they make is not material.

Professor Preston is very critical of the FTC's approach in this matter. He argues that a claim should not automatically be presumed material, simply because it is explicit. Indeed, some claims are made simply to distinguish identities of parity products, even though the claimed feature has no bearing on consumer decision making. Moreover, he asserts, the burden of proving materiality should be shifted to the FTC. In Preston's opinion, unless a claim is proven to be deceptive and material, advertisers should be permitted to make it, without fearing that simply because they use the claim it must be material. Short of shifting the burden of proof regarding materiality, Preston feels the FTC should, at the very least, provide firms with methodological guidance on how to disprove materiality.

Preston suggests the contours of a test that would determine materiality. He proposes that the issue is not whether the deceptive claim is likely to affect consumer behavior, but whether it is more likely than a true claim to have such an effect. If consumers will take the same action regardless of whether the claim is true or false, the deceptive claim should not be regarded as material. To illustrate: Suppose *S* sells an item that is displayed in a showroom and advertises its price at $80. When customers come to the showroom they are told that the print ad is a mistake and the price is really $90. If the same number of consumers will visit the showroom regardless of which of these two prices is advertised, the falsely advertised price should not be regarded as material. Certainly, Preston tells us, there would be little "public interest" in regulating this false claim.[11]

Kaldor-Hicks bears on another consideration in advertising regulation, one raised by Professor Richard Craswell. Because Kaldor-Hicks is essentially a cost-benefit criterion, it would, perhaps, endorse Professor Craswell's notion that a materially false advertising claim is sometimes acceptable.

In this regard, Craswell points out that an advertising message that makes a misleading claim may at the same time convey useful information to the consumer. To illustrate: A manufacturer claims that its storm windows can save homeowners "up to 85 percent" of their heating bill. The evidence shows that this may be literally true, in the sense that 85 percent may be the upper limit on the savings attainable by a consumer with an extremely poorly insulated house. However, the evidence also shows that most consumers can expect to save only 40–50 percent at the very most. Within the current regulatory environment, the storm window ad will be regarded as misleading because the ad incorrectly implies that an average consumer has a reasonable likelihood of obtaining the 85 percent savings.[12]

In Craswell's opinion, the judgment that the ad is misleading should not be the end of the story. Instead, it should be recognized that the ad contains some useful information about the savings in fuel bills one can expect if one installs storm windows. Correcting the ad so that the false impression is eliminated might create new false impressions or obscure entirely the message that the installation of storm windows will lead to savings. In deciding what to do with the ad, the criterion the FTC should use, according to Craswell, is:

> An advertisement is legally deceptive if and only if it leaves some consumers holding a false belief about a product, and the ad could be cost effectively changed to reduce the resulting injury. This involves comparing the ad with possible alternatives.

The most important factor is not the aggregate level of injury, but the extent to which that injury can be reduced. If 10 percent of a product's consumers hold a false belief about the product, but the evidence shows that at least 10 percent would hold that same false belief regardless of what the ad said, there is no point in ordering that the ad be changed. Similarly, if one advertisement currently deceives 20 percent of its audience and the addition of some qualifying language would reduce that figure to 10 percent, while a second ad currently deceives

30 percent but 25 percent would still be deceived even after the proposed correction, the first advertisement presents the stronger case for intervention (assuming the two false beliefs are equally serious), even though its injury is smaller in absolute numbers.[13]

One more proposition: Let us consider the possibility that Kaldor-Hicks would embrace Professor Paul H. Rubin's proposition that allowing deceptive advertising to go unchallenged can, at times, result in a clear-cut long-term gain for the consumer. Rubin provides a number of illustrations:

1. Suppose a firm advertises "Regularly $50, now $25." Now, if $50 was not the common transaction price, the ad is deceptive. Notwithstanding the possible deception here, the FTC rarely brings deceptive pricing cases because it recognizes that any advertisement that stresses prices are likely to lead to lower prices. Consumers hence gain in the long run from the deceptive ad.

2. In 1986–87, fierce competition began in the food industry regarding claims of low cholesterol level. Some firms who were claiming that their products were low in cholesterol were, in fact, producing food low in cholesterol, as they claimed, but their products were made with palm and coconut oils that had the same harmful effects as cholesterol. To be sure, drawing attention to the food's low cholesterol level, while at the same time hiding their tropical oil content, was a deceptive health claim, but the deception worked to foster a long-term gain in welfare for the consumer. Competition for the patronage of health-conscious consumers led other firms to advertise that their products were not only low in cholesterol, but also did not contain tropical oils. Indicative of the substantial benefit society reaped in the long term from the original deceptive claim of the low cholesterol/high tropical oil producers was that imports of palm oil fell 44 percent from 1986 to 1987.[14]

REGULATION OF ADVERTISING AND HALAKHAH

Our purpose here will be to show that Halakhah's concern in the regulation of advertising is not only to root out deception, but also to prohibit what it regards as "unfair" commercial speech. Towards this end, we will describe the various prohibitions in Halakhah that relate to both deception and negative commercial speech. What will emerge from this presentation is that compared to the corresponding secular approach, Halakhah's approach to regulation of advertising is both far more exacting and extensive. We will then make the case that an FTC-like institution should be set up in the Torah society. Our contention is that reliance on the family, the educational system and the local courts *alone* to educate the public about acceptable advertising standards will not achieve the desired results.

PROHIBITIONS RELATING TO DECEPTION

1. *Geneivat Da'at*

The pivotal prohibition involved in regulating the advertising industry is the prohibition against creating a false impression (*geneivat da'at*). Discussed in detail in the first chapter of this book, our purpose here will be to relate the *geneivat da'at* prohibition to issues specifically germane to deceptive advertising. Let us first turn to the materiality issue.

Most crucial to the materiality issue is the treatment of a mass communications message that conveys its intended point by implication, rather than explicitly. Recall the discussion regarding the formula the rabbis devised to inform the townspeople that the day's supply of meat was not kosher. The dilemma the rabbis faced was how to make the announcement in a manner that would not repel non-Jewish customers. In this regard, the rabbis had to walk a tightrope. On the one hand, proclaiming explicitly that the meat supply for that day was *terefah* (i.e., not kosher), would, in the opinion of the rabbis, unnecessarily repel the non-Jewish customers, because the word *terefah* communicates directly to the non-Jews that the vendors themselves would not consume the meat they were selling. To avoid offending non-Jews, a more subtle way of informing them that the meat was not kosher was necessary. On the other hand, given that kosher meat was regarded as of higher quality by the non-Jews, the rabbis had to be careful not to create a false impression that the meat was kosher. If the formula created a false impression, the vendor would be guilty of *geneivat da'at*. The rabbis had to determine how far the limits of creative advertising could be stretched before crossing the line into deceptive conduct. The rabbis settled on the formula, "Meat for the army has fallen into our hands" (*nafla bisra li-bnei heila*). Because *no announcement* was made on the days when the meat was kosher, the Rabbis relied on their intuition that the absence of the word *terefah* (non-kosher) in the announcement would not dupe the non-Jews into thinking the meat was kosher. Anyone who made this mistake would be guilty of self-deception.

The notion that the designer of a message containing an implicit statement has license to determine that anyone who does not correctly understand his intended point is guilty of self-deception is surely a novelty. Since the prototype case in which such conduct serves as a defense against charges of *geneivat da'at* is the *nafla bisra* announcement, the application of this license must be limited. Consider that in the *nafla bisra* case, the target audience was local and homogeneous, and therefore quite familiar to the rabbis who crafted the text of the announcement. Consider also that if the judgment of the rabbis had proven wrong, and the *nafla bisra* announcement had duped the non-Jewish customers into thinking the meat was kosher, complaints of fraud in the marketplace would have proliferated. Jewish butchers would have earned the reputation of being swindlers and the name of God would have been profaned. Because these very untoward consequences would surely have ensued if the judgment of the rabbis had been wrong, it may be expected that they were extra careful in ensuring that they made the right judgment regarding the mindset of the marketplace. Add to all of this that the designers of the message were *not* the Jewish butchers, who would have had a vested interest in not repelling non-Jewish customers with an explicit statement that the meat they were selling was not kosher, but rather, the rabbis of the Talmud, who had no financial interest in the marketing effect of the message, and who, because of their piety and integrity, could be counted on to be as objective as possible regarding how the marketplace would understand the message. The necessary conclusion is that there is a very limited license to classify as self-deception interpretations of an implicit message that differ from what the message designer himself intended. The leniency should certainly not apply when the target audience is large and heterogeneous, or when the seller himself commissions the ad and faces only minor consequences if only a small minority of those exposed to it are duped.

What emerges from this discussion is that disseminating a message that includes implied claims is fraught with halakhic danger. Unbeknownst to the seller, a portion of the target audience may be misled by the message.

Given that the prohibition to mislead applies not only when one knows in advance that one's words or actions will mislead, but also if one realizes that they *may*,[15] avoidance of the *geneivat da'at* prohibition requires the seller to pilot test an advertisement involving implied claims before it is released to the public. Elsewhere we have discussed what the general contours of the pilot test should be. Given that some mistaken interpretations can be halakhically defined as self-deception, as per the *nafla bisra* case, one who crafts a mass consumption message need only worry about the misperceptions of the "reasonable man." In quantitative terms, we have proposed that the "reasonable man" translates into a 15–20 percent threshold, meaning that if a message containing an implied claim deceives less than 15–20 percent of the targeted audience, it should not be regarded as deceptive.[16]

What proceeds from the above discussion is that, like secular law, *geneivat da'at* law has a materiality condition. But there is a basic difference in how materiality is handled in the two systems of law. In secular law, where there is no requirement for the advertiser to pilot test an ad to ensure that it is free of deception, the issue of materiality comes into play only after the ad is released and challenged on the basis of its deceptiveness. It is at this juncture that the FTC will apply the materiality test to determine whether it will pull the ad. In the Torah society, it is the responsibility of an advertiser to pilot test his mass communication message, to determine whether it has the capacity to deceive, *before* exposing it to the public. If the ad passes the 15–20 percent test, it is not considered capable of deceiving the "reasonable man." Once the 15–20 percent threshold is met, the ad becomes immune to challenge.

On a related matter, the *geneivat da'at* interdict tells us that Halakhah would find ready sympathy with the Preston-Oliver critique of puffery. Instead of approaching the issue of puffery by making semantic distinctions between fact and opinion, advertising messages should be examined on the basis of their behavioral-psychological impact. Whether the claim is fact, opinion, or value, the legal test should be whether the message deceives (i.e., creates untrue expectations that influence purchasers).

2. *Sheker*

The biblical sources and many of the nuances of the prohibition against falsehood (*sheker*) have been discussed in Chapter 1 of this book. Our concern here is with the aspects of this prohibition that are specific to and germane for the advertising industry.

The unproven claim. In relating *sheker* to the advertising industry, perhaps the most fundamental point to make is that the prohibition against *sheker* is violated not only through a statement the speaker knows to be false or misleading, but also with a statement the speaker knows may be false.[17] The implication for the advertising industry is that a seller should make no claim unless he has verified its truthfulness beforehand. This aspect of the law of *sheker* is hence in conformity with FTC policy on misleading advertising.

The harmless lie. One aspect of the stringency of the prohibition against *sheker* is that it is violated even when the lie does harm to no one. In the thinking of R. Israel Meir ha-Kohen Kagan[18] (Radin, Poland, 1838–1933) and R. Abraham Y. Karelitz (Israel, 1878–1953),[19] the harmless lie violates the biblical prohibition against falsehood. A minority position is expressed by R. Eliezer b. Samuel of Metz (*Yere'im*, ca. 1175). In his view a falsehood that generates no harm or damages to someone else does not violate biblical law.[20] In R. Eliezer Judah Waldenberg's (Israel, contemp.) opinion, *Yere'im* would be in agreement that a harmless falsehood is, nevertheless, prohibited by dint of rabbinical decree.[21]

The stringency with which Halakhah treats a harmless lie tells us that the prohibition of falsehood is violated even when the materiality condition is absent.

The transparent lie. In his authoritative work, *Niv Sefatayyim*, R. Nahum Yavruv (Israel, contemp.) posits that if a false statement is understood by everyone as false and deceives no one, the statement is *inherently* not false and hence does not violate the prohibition against *sheker*. Nonetheless, basing himself on Jeremiah 9:4—"They train their tongue to speak falsehood . . ."—R. Yavruv cautions that even a lie of this sort should be avoided, as speaking even such a lie could accustom one to lying.[22]

R. Yavruv's caution for the habituating effect of a transparent lie appears to be particularly apt when the *same* lie is repeated again and again. This is what we are dealing with in the advertising industry, where success of an advertising message depends upon the repetition of the message again and again over a period of time.

Recall that R. Yavruv invokes Jeremiah 9:4 as the basis for the concern for habituation in lying, even when the lie spoken is a permissible one. R. Solomon b. Jehiel Luria (Poland, 1510–1573) also understands Jeremiah 9:4 as referring to circumstances in which a permissible lie is repeated again and again. R. Luria's analysis of the following passage at *Yevamot* 63a bears this out.

> Rav's wife would aggravate him.–When he would tell her, "Prepare me lentils,"–she would instead prepare peas.–If he said, "Prepare me peas,"–she would instead prepare lentils.–When his son, Hiyya, grew up and would relay his father's requests to his mother,–he would reverse them to her, so that his father would end up receiving exactly what he had requested.– Upon receiving the desired dish, and not realizing Hiyya's subterfuge, [Rav] said to him, "Your mother has improved her ways!" – [Hiyya] replied to him, – "It was actually I who reversed your request to her," [Rav] replied to him,– "this bears out the popular saying:–[the child] who comes from you will educate you." I, too, should have thought of this trick!–However, you should not do this,–for it says: "They train their tongue to speak falsehood. . . ." (Jeremiah 9:4).

Rav's objection to Hiyya's conduct requires explanation. Insofar as Hiyya made use of lies to promote domestic harmony between his parents, his conduct should have been regarded as an application of the *darkhei shalom* principle (the duty to promote peace in society), and hence praise-worthy.[23] Addressing himself to this issue, R. Luria understands Rav's objection to Hiyya's conduct to be rooted in the habituating effect of a lie. To be successful, Hiyya would have to engage in his ruse for an indefinite period of time. Because habitual lying even for a permissible purpose debil-itates one's character, Rav objected to Hiyya's conduct.[24]

Truth telling as a positive value. Beyond the prohibition against *sheker*, Judaism teaches that there is a *positive* duty to embrace the value of integrity and truth-telling. As a proactive force in life, truth telling (*emet*) is an integral part of Judaism's guidepost for interpersonal conduct called *imi-tatio Dei* (imitation of God),[25] the duty to emulate God's Attributes[26] of Mercy.

One aspect of God's Mercy is His Attribute of truth (*emet*). To understand how the Divine Attribute of *emet*, which ordinarily evokes the notion of strict, uncompromising justice, provides guideposts for *kindness* in interpersonal relations, it is necessary to identify the *mercy* aspect of God's Attribute of *emet*. R. Solomon b. Isaac (*Rashi*, France, 1040–1105) provides the key here by telling us that *emet* in the context of the thirteen Attributes of Divine Mercy means "to pay a good reward to those who perform His will."[27] Rashi's interpretation clarifies the *mercy* element in *emet*. Preliminarily, consider that God endows humankind with free will. This means that neither virtue nor the avoidance of sin is for us compelling. If doing God's will would be compelling, we would deserve neither a reward for virtue nor a reward for resisting sin.[28] The reward God promises us for doing His will—"so that you will benefit and you will live long"—is infinite[29] and consists of a delight beyond the imagination of a human being.[30] This reward can be experienced only in the infinite world of the afterlife.[31] But, let us not deny the reality that human beings have a positive time preference. This means we are quite willing to trade an infinite reward that is deferred for us indefinitely for a lesser reward that we can enjoy here and now. Our eagerness and even desperation to make this trade-off, however, is the result of our ignorance of the nature of the infinite reward that is awaiting us. Here, God displays His mercy element in *emet* and does *not accept* the trade-off we offer. Instead, God is faithful in fulfilling His promise. Everyone who performs God's will gets his or her due in the form of an infinite reward.

The Attribute of *emet* speaks against Craswell's and Rubin's notion that deception should be a permissible tool for the seller if it promotes wealth maximization for society now or in the long-run. The notion is theologically wrong because the cost-benefit calculus is deficient. Comparing the debit of those who are deprived of their expected quid pro quo with the gain for the marketplace in the form of better information and/or lower prices is not the whole story. What is missing in this calculation is how deception undermines the value of trust in society. The assault is, of course, greatest for the victims of the deception. These duped individuals feel a sense of betrayal. But, the damage to the value of trust goes considerably beyond those who are the victims of a false promise. Expectations have now become lowered. A promise coming from *anyone* is now less reliable. If trust and integrity are not embraced as positive values in society, we will be headed down a slippery slope where less and less "beneficial deception" is tolerated in the name of promoting wealth maximization now and in the future. If the slippery slope goes unchecked, the goal of wealth maximization itself will, at some juncture, become severely undermined. This happens through increased transaction costs. Because distrust is so prevalent, parties to a deal will feel a need to protect themselves more and more against breach of contract. This same distrust will make the parties unwilling to enter into long term agreements.

Since the promotion of trust in interpersonal relations is an *imitatio Dei* duty in the Torah society, there can be no tolerance for deception in the name of long term wealth maximization.

Another mandate for commercial speech that proceeds from the *imitatio Dei* duty of *emet* is that advertisers should formulate their claims in objectively verifiable form. This requirement can be derived by the conduct of the patriarch Jacob, who in Jewish tradition is regarded as personifying the ideal of *emet*.[32] Consider the method of compensation Jacob proposed for himself to his father-in-law, Laban: All of the spotted and mottled animals would be removed from Laban's flock, leaving in Jacob's care only the uniformly colored animals. Jacob's wage was to consist of the mottled and spotted animals born from the uniformly colored herd, which he would separate out into a flock of his own. This method of compensation would make any departure by Jacob from the stipulated conditions immediately evident to Laban. As Jacob put it, "Thus my honesty will tell. When you come to look into my wages with you, any goat in my lot that is not speckled and spotted, any sheep that is not dark, you may consider to have been stolen" (Genesis 30:33).

3. *Hin Tzedek*

Another relevant ethical principle for the advertising industry is the *hin tzedek* (good faith), imperative, which says that if an individual makes a commitment or offer, he or she should fully intend to carry it out.[33]

An application of *hin tzedek* for the advertising industry is the "bait and switch" scheme. In its basic form, bait and switch involves the advertising of a popular article at a bargain price simply for the purpose of luring customers into the store. The deception becomes apparent when the bargain bait cannot be purchased, on one pretext or another, and salesmen, after disparaging the advertised product, attempt to convince customers to switch to higher priced substitutes. Since the vendor has no intention of selling the bait item, the advertisement is clearly an insincere offer and hence violates the "good faith" imperative.

If the bait and switch ad induces people to come to the store, the seller violates the *geneivat da'at* prohibition as well.

4. *Ona'at Devarim*

The prohibition against causing someone needless mental anguish (*ona'at devarim*)[34] has a number of applications to the advertising industry.

One application is a variant on the bait and switch stratagem just described. Suppose *B* reads the "bait and switch" ad and plans to make a trip to the store to purchase the "bait" item, but before he gets a chance to visit the store, a friend of his informs him of the scam. Because the ad did not *induce B* to do something he would not otherwise have done, the seller has not violated *geneivat da'at* with respect to *B*. But *B* assuredly experiences disappointment when his expectations are dashed. An analogous case, one of the examples of *ona'at devarim* conduct cited in the *Mishna* at *Bava Metzia* 4:10, entails the prohibition of pricing an article that one has no intention of buying. What is objectionable, according to R. Menahem b. Solomon Meiri (France, 1249–1316), is that pricing an article creates the anticipation on the part of the seller that he will make a sale, which is dashed when the inquirer decides not to pursue the matter further. Although the prospective buyer need not concern himself with the disappointment a vendor may experience should his *serious* price inquiry not result in his making a purchase, pricing an article he has no intention of buying causes the vendor *needless* distress and is hence prohibited.[35]

Recall that Meiri understands that the creation of *dashed expectations alone* constitutes a violation of the *ona'at devarim* interdict. Accordingly, violation of the prohibition occurs even if the seller is not induced to spend any significant amount of time in giving attention to the insincere customer. Likewise, *B*'s dashed expectation, upon learning from his friend that the ad he was planning to follow up on is a sham, should be sufficient to indicate that the advertiser has violated the *ona'at devarim* interdict.

Negative Commercial Speech and Halakhah

From the perspective of Halakhah, the regulation of advertising goes beyond deterring deception and promoting truth-telling as a positive value in society. In the Torah society, freedom of speech is by no means an absolute right. A firm does not have license to bring to the public's attention flaws, defects, and other disadvantages of a rival's product. Bringing negative, though true, information about a rival's product to the public's attention may violate a number of ethical directives. These are the prohibitions against (1) talebearing (*lashon ha-ra*); (2) proffering ill-suited advice (*lifnei iver*); (3) elevating oneself at the expense of another's degradation (*mitkabbed bi-klon havero*); and (4) causing someone needless mental anguish (*ona'at devarim*).

Let us take up each of these prohibitions and show how they relate to the advertising industry.

1. *Lashon ha-ra*

Delivering an evil but *true* report about one's fellow violates the biblical interdict against tale-bearing, "You shall not go about as a talebearer among your people" (Leviticus 19:16). The essence of what this prohibition forbids, according to Maimonides (Egypt, 1135–1204), is delivering an evil report and thereby causing one's fellow anguish or financial loss.[36] Maimonides' formulation puts negative commercial speech within the ambit of the laws of *lashon ha-ra*. In his analysis of the interdict against tale-bearing, R. Israel Meir ha-Kohen Kagan specifically includes under the prohibition the deprecation of the product of a merchant.[37]

The prohibition against *lashon ha-ra* is not absolute. If the motive behind the evil report is to produce a clear-cut benefit (*toelet*) in the form of righting a wrong or preventing a harm, the prohibition may under certain conditions be suspended. To be sure, disclosure is not valid unless a large number of conditions are satisfied. In the chapter dealing with whistleblowing (Chapter 11), we discuss this issue at length. In the context of comparative negative advertising, it is doubtful whether the fundamental condition of *toelet* even gets off the ground. Consider that if S_1's product is superior in all respects to rival S_2's product, market forces will ordinarily put S_2 out of business in short shrift. Why, then, does S_1 incur the expense of engaging in a negative comparison advertising campaign against S_2? Perhaps, the reason is that the rival products have offsetting advantages and disadvantages and S_1 incurs an expense to get an opportunity to point out the flaws in S_2's product. If this is the case, S_1's disclosure generates no *toelet* for the public unless he at the same time makes the public aware of the flaws in his own product. Informing the public of the flaws in S_2's product, without at the same time informing the public of the flaws in his own product, amounts to *deprecating* S_2's product and violates for S_1 the prohibition against *lashon ha-ra*.

2. Lifnei iver

Another prohibition relevant for negative commercial speech in the advertising industry is "Do not place a stumbling block before the blind" (*lifnei iver lo titen mikhshol*, Leviticus 19:14). In the exegesis of the sages, this prohibition is taken out of its literal meaning and understood to refer to two aspects of conduct: facilitating a sin committed by someone else, and proffering someone ill-suited advice.[38]

The *lifnei iver* interdict has particular relevance for the advertising industry with respect to the comparative merit stratagem. To be sure, there is nothing inherently unethical about making a claim of superiority. If a company really believes that its product beats the competition, advancing a claim of superiority does not render the company guilty of proffering ill-suited advice. But if the comparison goes beyond making a superiority claim and, instead, actively dissuades the target group from looking into the merits of the rival product, the ad amounts to proffering ill-suited advice and violates *lifnei iver*.

Within the context of negative comparison advertising, the seller may very well violate *lifnei iver* with respect to even those people who do not buy the product as a result of being exposed to the ad. Recall that one aspect of the *lifnei iver* interdict is the prohibition against A's aiding or abetting B in the commission of a sin. With respect to this aspect of *lifnei iver*, authorities dispute as to whether A violates *lifnei iver* when the sin he encourages B to commit is, in actuality, not committed by B.[39] One school of thought, led by R. Malachi b. Jacob ha-Kohen (Italy, d. ca. 1785), takes the view that *lifnei iver* prohibits A from setting up B with an *opportunity* to sin. Whether B ends up committing the sin or not is immaterial as far as A's infraction is concerned.[40] Another school of thought, led by R. Isaac Blaser (Russia, 1837–1907), relieves A of the *lifnei iver* violation unless the sin he encourages B to do is actually committed by B.[41] This same dispute should apply to the second aspect of *lifnei iver*, namely, the prohibition to proffer someone ill-suited advice.

3. *Mitkabbed bi-klon havero*

Negative commercial speech may run afoul of R. Yose b. Hanina's dictum, "Anyone who elevates himself at the expense of his friend's degradation has no share in the world to come" (*mitkabbed bi-klon havero ein lo helek la-olam ha-ba*).[42] R. Yose b. Hanina's dictum does, however, not prohibit negative comparison advertising on a blanket basis. Let us see why.[43]

1. Note that the key word in R. Yose b. Hanina's dictum is degradation (*kalon*). Elevating oneself at the expense of someone else is not obnoxious per se. It becomes so only when the elevation is achieved at the expense of someone else's *degradation*.

Relatedly, R. Hayyim Hezekiah Medini (Russia, 1832–1904) ruled that voicing the opinion that *A* is a greater Talmudic scholar than *B* does not amount to degrading *B*, and is therefore a permissible statement.[44]

R. Yose b. Hanina's dictum hence does not lead to a blanket prohibition of comparison advertising. Negative advertising comes into question only when a seller magnifies the attractiveness of his product by pointing out *defects* or *flaws* present in a rival's product. Promoting his product by pointing out that it has features that are not offered in rival products does not violate R. Yose's dictum.

2. Another consideration in identifying the parameters of what constitutes *kalon* is the difference in price between the rival products. Suppose the inferior product sells at a lower price. Here, the undesirable feature of the inferior product should be regarded as a limitation rather than as a defect. This is so because consumers, to a certain extent, trade off quality for a price reduction. Accordingly, provided the superior product clearly communicates in its negative comparison ad that the competing product is *cheaper*, pointing out the rival product's defects does not violate *mitkabbed bi-klon*.

3. Finally, *mitkabbed bi-klon* should not apply in the context of defensive advertising. To illustrate: Suppose Spotless Carpet and Vanish Dust are competing vacuum cleaners. Spotless Carpet sells for $230 and Vanish Dust sells for $200. Spotless Carpet advertises that its model has an expected

useful lifetime of six years, whereas Vanish Dust has an expected useful lifetime of only four years. The ad conveniently does not mention that users of Spotless Carpet will have to tolerate the vacuum's bulkiness and annoying noise level. Because Spotless Carpet's ad is misleading, it is morally acceptable for Vanish Dust to defend itself by pointing out the aforementioned defects in the rival's higher priced Spotless Carpet model. Within the context of defending itself against a misleading ad, pointing out the defects of Spotless Carpet should not be viewed as *mitkabbed bi-klon* conduct on the part of Vanish Dust, but rather only as correcting the marketplace's misconceptions about its product.

4. *Ona'at Devarim*

Recall that *ona'at devarim* is one of the prohibitions that relate to deceptive practices in the advertising industry. Let us take note that the *Mishna*, at *Bava Metzia* 4:10, provides a number of examples of *ona'at devarim*, such as pricing an article with no intention to buy. Yet, in his commentary on the biblical source of this prohibition, "And you shall not hurt the feelings of one another" (Leviticus 25:17), Rashi gives his own example of what this interdict prohibits, one not cited in the *Mishna*: proffering someone self-serving ill-suited advice.[45] Understanding the *ona'at devarim* prohibition to forbid this type of conduct raises a difficulty, in that such conduct is already prohibited by dint of the prohibition of *lifnei iver* at Leviticus 19:14. This difficulty is readily resolved with the proposition that the prohibition against proffering someone ill-suited advice comes in two varieties. One aspect obtains when the advisee either relies on the ill-suited advice or at least treats it as valuable enough to warrant further investigation. Here, the adviser violates *lifnei iver*. The second aspect obtains when the advisee immediately recognizes the advice as ill-suited. Because the advice mocks the intelligence of the advisee, the adviser violates the *ona'at devarim* interdict.[46]

What proceeds from this discussion is that one aspect of the *ona'at devarim* interdict is the prohibition against causing someone needless aggravation in the form of mocking conduct. This type of conduct finds ready application in the context of negative comparison advertising. An ad that Orajel ran in *Parents* magazine[47] illustrates this issue. In this ad, two babies were depicted, one the Orajel baby, the other the Tylenol baby. The Orajel baby was depicted as smiling. The caption under this baby read, "Within one minute after Baby Orajel." The Tylenol baby was depicted as miserable, and the caption under this baby read, "Teething baby. Up to thirty minutes after Children's Tylenol."

The ad, as Professor Hayden points out, is misleading, because Tylenol has an advantage that Orajel does not: Tylenol is long-lasting, whereas Orajel is not. Accordingly, the captions under the two babies could just as easily have been reversed.[48]

For educated consumers, the Orajel ad is a sham. Orajel's omission of the fact that Tylenol has the offsetting advantage of being long-lasting mocks their intelligence. Given that a segment of the target group that is exposed to the ad feels that Orajel mocks their intelligence, the company, perhaps, violates the *ona'at devarim* interdict.

THE FTC IN THE TORAH SOCIETY

Our purpose here will be to demonstrate the need to set up an FTC-like institution in the Torah society. Making this case requires a demonstration that the institutional arrangements in the Torah society without an FTC in place will prove inadequate to achieve the desired standards.

We begin the argument with a consideration of the educational and legal environment in a Torah society. Religious education and training for youth is compulsory.[49] The community is required to set up a judicial system based on religious law.[50] One aspect of the judicial system is the ad hoc court of law. In the ad hoc procedure, each litigant nominates one member of the judicial panel, and the two judges designated in this manner choose the third member of the tribunal.[51] If the parties agree, they can select a single judge to adjudicate their dispute.[52] The ad hoc procedure, especially if the one-judge option is used, makes adjudication of disputes very cost-effective.

These institutional arrangements can be expected to formulate abstract legal principles for marketplace conduct and a mechanism for resolution of disputes as they arise. But will they prove adequate for addressing the legal and moral issues that come up in a mass communications industry? This is a formidable challenge.

In the following paragraphs, we will demonstrate that complex issues relating to rule setting, investigative capabilities and leadership in scholarly research surround the implementation of the "reasonable man" standard for a mass communications message. Their resolution requires uniform rules, widely recognized expertise and moral authority, and adequate funding. Reliance on the local courts and isolated rabbinical experts to deal with these matters will fall far short of the desired results. To protect the marketplace from becoming vulnerable to confusion and discord, the Torah society must set up an FTC-like institution to address these issues. This panel would issue guideposts for ethical advertising. What follows is a sample of the issues and guideposts the authority would deal with:

1. One challenge for the FTC of the Torah society would be to set guideposts for the methodology that must be used in designing pilot testing. Clearly the same standard should not apply regardless of whether the target audience is local and homogeneous or diverse and spread out over a large geographic area.

2. Does the same standard apply to material in an ad that clearly plays no role in affecting the consumer's conduct? Perhaps the standard should be more lenient regarding deception of the nonharmful variety. At the other end of the continuum, consider that Halakhah takes a stricter stance when human life is at stake than it does in protecting against violation of a prohibition.[53] Accordingly, the "reasonable man" should be defined more strictly in relation to health claims.

How variables 1 and 2 translate into a quantifiable measure above and below the 15–20 percent standard for the ordinary case of harmful monetary deception would be for the FTC of the Torah society to determine.

3. A related issue that needs clarification is the treatment of a transparent lie in an advertising message, an issue that goes to the very heart of modern advertising. In modern advertising, advertisers demonstrate great creativity in making consumers associate a product with a fantasy. The fantasy can be in the form of a jingle or of some ludicrous image that the consumer finds to be entertaining. The fantasy-inducing ad transforms an otherwise humdrum product into one that the consumer gets some measure of fun from. Let's illustrate the nature of the dilemma the FTC of the Torah society faces regarding this issue with the following ad that appeared in the work of Professor Ivan Preston:

With the aim of eliciting a few laughs, the Pittsburgh Brewing Company produces its Iron City Beer under a special label during the holiday season. The beer's name changes to Olde Frothingslosh, and the label proclaims that Olde Frothingslosh is the "only beer in which the foam is on the bottom."

A customer bought some Olde Frothingslosh to amuse friends at a party and was disturbed to find that the claim was nothing but a *big lie*. The foam was up there on top where it always is! She wanted her money back from the beer distributor.[54]

In confronting the Olde Frothingslosh ad, Halakhah must grapple with how to treat a transparent lie in a mass communications message. To be sure, the vast majority of the targeted group recognizes that the claim the Frothingslosh ad makes is false. For this group, the perception of reality is in no way altered, and the use of the product is actually enhanced because of the entertainment value of the transparently false claim. But, at the same time, a small percentage of the targeted audience will take the claim that the foam is on the bottom seriously and fail to see that it is an obvious lie made for entertainment purposes. It may be that the "reasonable man" standard applies only when the issue is deception via *implication*, in which case, if less than 15–20 percent of the targeted group is deceived, the message cannot be said to *impose* harm on anyone; anyone who is misled by the message is guilty of *self-deception*. But if the message is explicitly false, the circumstance that less than 15–20 percent of the targeted group is misled by it may not define the claim as a transparent falsehood for everyone, and such an outright falsehood may still be prohibited. Nonetheless, there is a Talmudic principle that states that we need not be concerned with *meutei de-meutei* (i.e., a minute minority).[55] Accordingly, perhaps some stricter quantitative standard than the 15–20 percent rule would be sufficient to characterize an explicitly false statement as being both *harmless* and *transparent*.

4. Let's look at one more issue relating to the survey requirement. Economists have pointed out that most products have three relevant traits: search, experience, and credence. Search traits are those that are apparent to a buyer before making the purchase, such as the price of an item, its color, and its other observable attributes. Experience traits are those that manifest themselves only after purchase, including such factors as the taste

of toothpaste and the durability of a washing machine. Finally, credence traits are those that never manifest themselves to the buyer, such as repair service. A buyer who has a product repaired will never learn whether certain specific repairs were actually necessary.[56] The standard the seller should be subject to in relation to claims made with regard to these three traits should not be the same. It would be the task of the FTC to set appropriate standards in each case.

5. Can the FTC of the Torah society limit its role to rulemaking and rely on the private sector to do its job in engaging in the requisite type of research to ensure that the reasonable man would not be misled by its claims? Likely not. The cost-benefit calculus of self-interest will always incline human beings to resolve moral dilemmas in their own favor. Creating a moral society requires an investment in objective data, without which its moral codes languish in neglect. To be sure, development of this objective data is the responsibility of market participants; but these formulations, if left to the sellers themselves, will be riddled with subjective bias.

If the FTC of the Torah society is to place truth-telling in advertising on a pedestal, it must sponsor independent and unbiased research on scientific methods of designing consumer surveys, and on the interpretations and inferences consumers draw from claims formulated in various ways.

This analysis points to the need for a highly trained and specialized authority to regulate advertising. Expertise in Halakhah combined with worldly knowledge would be essential for anyone sitting on this panel. The FTC of the Torah society would hence revive the Talmudic personality called *adam hashuv* (i.e., the distinguished person).[57]

THE REGULATION OF ADVERTISING AND THE PUBLIC INTEREST

Given that materiality is not a component of the definition of *sheker*, the FTC of the Torah society could conceivably get bogged down in cases involving deception of the nonharmful type. But this need not be the case. Consider that the FTC is not the *only* authority that deals with the issue of truth-telling in a commercial setting. Most fundamentally, in a Torah society, moral education is an integral part of the educational responsibility of parents and the school system. Elsewhere, we have shown that moral education entails a reward-punishment system centering on truth-telling.[58] One tenet of moral education, a point that is so fundamental that it is worthy of repetition, is that an individual should not make a claim unless he has already verified it. To the extent that moral education is successful, the rule against making unsubstantiated claims in advertising messages will generally be observed, and the number of challenged ads will not be alarming.

Another factor working to reduce the number of challenged ads is the subsidy the government (specifically the FTC) would give to foster ethical advertising. Wide dissemination of findings regarding the inferences consumers draw from various advertising messages would identify pitfalls for advertisers to avoid.

Finally, the ad hoc courts that may be set up to adjudicate financial disputes can serve well as screening devices for the FTC of the Torah society. If an advertiser is found to have made an unsubstantiated or false claim, but the judgment of the court is that the falsehood or deception involved is of the nonmaterial variety, the court can issue an appropriate reprimand to the guilty party. But if, in its preliminary investigation, the court uncovers a prima facie case involving material deception, the case can then be sent up to the FTC for adjudication. This system, wherein the ad hoc courts serve as the initial jurisdiction for complaints against advertisers, can ensure that the resources of the FTC are used to investigate and mete out penalties to the most egregious offenders.

As a means of dramatizing the differences in approach between the halakhic and American (secular) society approaches to the regulation of advertising, we present Kraft's "Skimp/Brown Eyes" advertisement. After presenting the wording of the ad, we will describe why the FTC regarded it as deceptive. We will then proceed to discuss what is objectionable about the ad from the perspective of Halakhah.

KRAFT'S "SKIMP/BROWN EYES" AD

Lady (Voice Over): I thought of skimping. I admit it. But could you look in those big brown eyes and skimp on her? So I buy Kraft *Singles*. Imitation slices use hardly any milk. But Kraft has five ounces per slice. Five ounces. So her little bones get calcium they need to grow.

No, she doesn't know what that big Kraft means. Good thing I do.

Singers: Kraft *Singles*. More milk makes 'em, more milk, makes 'em good.

Lady (Voice Over): Skimp on her? Not me.

Two changes were made in the text of the challenged ads in the approximately two-and-a-half years during which they were disseminated. In January 1986, the statement "Kraft has five ounces per slice" was changed to "Kraft is made from five ounces per slice." Also, in March 1987, the disclosure that "One 3/4-ounce slice has 70 percent of the calcium of five ounces of milk" was added as a superscript in the television advertisements and as a footnote in the print advertisements.

The FTC found the Kraft advertisement to be false and misleading. Recall that a challenged representation must be *material* for deception to occur. The FTC assumes all *express claims* to be material. Implicit claims are judged material if there is evidence that the advertiser *intended* to imply them.

Kraft's Singles promotion featured both an explicit and an implicit claim. The explicit claim was that each Singles was made from five ounces of milk, and hence contained the same amount of calcium as five ounces of milk. In its television ads, Kraft reinforced its equivalency claim by showing milk poured into a glass up to a five-ounce mark, with the glass then transferred by animation onto a cover of a Singles package. Kraft's implicit claim was that its Singles contained more calcium than imitation cheese slices.

The FTC found Kraft's explicit claim—that Singles had as much calcium as five ounces of milk—to be false. In actuality, only 70 percent of the milk used in cheese-making gets into the cheese, and hence Singles contain only 70 percent of the calcium of five ounces of milk. The FTC also found false Kraft's implicit claim that Singles have more calcium than most imitation slices. To be sure, imitation slices don't derive their calcium from milk, but the amount of calcium they contain is not less than the amount found in Kraft's Singles.

Kraft's principal defense was to argue that its challenged claims were *immaterial* in the consumer's decision to buy its product. Accordingly, even if its ad did convey false claims, as the Commission contended, it should still not have been regarded as meeting the legal definition of deception.

In pursuing this line of defense, Kraft produced a survey that showed that consumers ranked calcium only seventh among nine factors that might affect whether they would buy Singles. Kraft interpreted the survey results as showing that calcium was not *material* in the consumer's decision to buy Singles. Moreover, 96 percent of those surveyed said that they "would continue" to buy Kraft Singles after they were told the truth—that each Singles slice had only 70 percent of the calcium of five ounces of milk.

Rejecting Kraft's contention that the challenged claims it made in its ads were non-material, the FTC questioned both the methodology of Kraft's survey and the company's interpretation of the data. One basic objection, for instance, was that none of the people surveyed were exposed to Kraft's challenged ad. The only relevant issue, as the commission saw it, was whether calcium was material to consumers *as Kraft advertised it*. The advertisement might itself have created materiality that would otherwise have been absent; by raising the public's awareness of the importance of calcium in their daily diet, the company might have created a demand for *Singles*.

Another objection the commission raised was the company's interpretation of the phrase "would continue to buy" in the survey. The survey restricted people to answering only "continue buying" or "stop buying." Other legitimate answers could have been that they would buy less than before, or buy the same amount but also drink more milk, or switch to competing brands that were cheaper or that contained more calcium. Had consumers been able to choose these other answers, calcium might have proven much more *material* than Kraft claimed.[59]

The commission duly noted the superscription that appeared in the Kraft commercial that "One 3/4-ounce slice has 70 percent of the calcium of five ounces of milk." The commission, however, felt that this disclosure was too weak to dispel the net impression that Kraft Singles contained the same amount of calcium as five ounces of milk. Given the distracting visual and audio elements and the brevity of the appearance of the complex superscript in the middle of the commercial, the Commission concluded that it was unlikely that the visual disclosure was effective as a corrective measure.[60]

"Skimp/Brown Eyes" and Halakhah

From the standpoint of Halakhah, perhaps the most basic point to make regarding the Kraft case is that the company should have pilot tested the

"Skimp/Brown Eyes" ad before making commercial use of it. In light of the FTC's arguments in its challenge of the ad, there can be no doubt that a scientifically designed pilot test would have shown that more than the 15–20 percent threshold level was deceived by the ad. The pilot test would have also put the spotlight on Kraft's explicitly false claim that Singles had as much calcium as five ounces of milk.

We will now proceed to critically evaluate the Kraft ad from the perspective of Halakhah's criteria for deception and falsehood, as well as its prohibition of negative commercial speech.

DECEPTIVENESS

From the standpoint of Halakhah, Kraft's survey evidence purporting to show that calcium is not an important factor in people's decision to purchase Singles is a non-sequitor. The issue is whether Kraft's commercial speech, specifically its "Skimp/Brown Eyes" ad, has the capacity to deceive the reasonable man. Since the people surveyed were not exposed to the ad in question, the survey does not bear on the issue of whether the ad has the capacity to deceive.

"Skimp/Brown Eyes" was not designed to convey information that people already knew. Rather, the ad was designed to raise people's awareness that calcium was, in fact, an important reason to buy Singles. By saying that imitation cheeses contained hardly any milk, Kraft conveyed a claim of superiority over imitation cheese, implying that Singles had more calcium than most imitation slices. Because that implication was false, Kraft's "Skimp/Brown Eyes" ad created a false impression of superiority. Kraft hence violated the prohibition against creating a false impression (*geneivat da'at*).

Another *geneivat da'at* infraction involves Kraft's milk equivalency claim. Recall that originally the ad stated, "Kraft has five ounces per slice." In January, 1986, this statement was changed to, "Kraft is made from five ounces per slice." The second version states nothing explicitly false, but its reasonable implication is that a slice of *Singles* has the same calcium content as five ounces of milk. In actuality, since only 70 percent of the milk used in cheese-making gets into the cheese, *Singles* contains only 70 percent of the calcium of five ounces of milk. Kraft's claim hence creates a false impression.

What of Kraft's claim that this false implication was adequately *neutral-*

ized by the superscription that appeared in its ads? Bearing directly on this question is the following case dealing with a hospitality incident, discussed at *Hullin* 94a.[61] Here we are told that a host (*H*) should not delude his guest (*G*) into believing that he has acted toward him with magnanimous hospitality when in fact he has not done so. Opening a barrel of wine in honor of someone usually constitutes a gesture of magnanimous hospitality, as the wine remaining in the barrel may deteriorate as a result of its exposure to the air.[62] The magnanimity of the gesture is considerably reduced, however, when *H* happens to have sold the barrel of wine to a retailer just prior to the arrival of *G*. (A price adjustment will, of course, be made with the retailer.)

What constitutes proper conduct for *H* in the latter circumstances is a matter of dispute between *Rashi* and *Tosafot*. In *Rashi's* view, *H* is prohibited from telling *G* that he is opening the barrel especially for him. Since *G* will reasonably assume that the barrel was not sold prior to his arrival, *H's* declaration will win him an undeserved sense of indebtedness.[63]

However, *Tosafot* argues that if *G* is assuming that the wine is owned by *H*, he will just as assuredly be misled even if *H* says nothing while pouring out the wine for him. For this reason, *Tosafot* disagrees with *Rashi*, requiring *H* to disabuse *G* of his erroneous assumption and inform him that the barrel was sold prior to his arrival. Such disclosure will leave no doubt in *G's* mind that *H's* gesture of hospitality entailed no extraordinary expense.[64]

Rashi's position here is puzzling. To be sure, there is nothing inherent in *H's* opening of the barrel that directly communicates to *G* that he is the recipient of generous hospitality. But given the reasonableness of *G's* assumption that the barrel was not sold prior to his arrival, *H's* action does generate a false impression of magnanimity. Why should *H* not therefore be obliged to set *G* straight?

Perhaps the key to understanding *Rashi's* position is that the case at hand takes place in a social setting. Gestures of friendship, according to Talmudic dictum, must be made openly, in a manner that will result in the recipient's associating the friend with the gift: "One who bestows a gift on a friend is obligated to inform him of it."[65] Underlying this rule of etiquette is the rabbis' conviction that open gestures of friendship promote pleasant and harmonious interpersonal relations.[66]

Let us assume that this rule of etiquette is operative for both parties in the wine barrel hospitality case. Now, if *H* intends to bestow a generous gesture of hospitality on *G*, proper protocol requires him to tell *G* forthrightly that the barrel is being opened in his honor, rather than rely on *G*'s reaching the same conclusion on his own. *H*'s silence in the face of his having made an apparently magnanimous gesture should itself shake *G*'s assumption that the opening of the barrel entailed considerable expense for *H*.

One could argue that if *G* is a reasonable person, he should interpret *H*'s silence as a gracious way of telling him that no particular expense was involved in the hospitality gesture. Openly informing *G* runs the risk of offending him, as he might infer that the barrel would certainly not have been opened for him if an expense had been involved. Depending upon *H*'s exact use of words, his tone and his voice inflection, *G* might find additional reason to take offense, concluding, for example, that *H* regards him as unworthy of a magnanimous gesture of hospitality. Hence, noting the lack of expense involved in opening the barrel simply via a gracious silence may represent the most diplomatic approach to resolving an awkward situation, a good application of the Talmudic dictum *milla be-sela mashtuka bi'trein* ("A word is worth a *sela*; silence, two *selas*" [*Megillah* 18a]).

The foregoing discussion allows us to better understand the dispute between *Rashi* and Tosafot. In *Rashi's* view, *H* is saddled only by a responsibility to clarify his intent. The silence with which he performs an apparently magnanimous gesture communicates to *G* that the gesture does not entail any particular expense. Given the awkwardness of the situation, silence is the most gracious way of making *G* understand this. *Tosafot*, on the other hand, regards *H*'s silence as an inadequate means of disabusing *G* of his erroneous impression. There may be several reasons for this. *Tosafot* may believe that a false impression cannot be undone unless the force that attempts to remove it is at least as strong as the force that created it. Since the false impression was created by *H*'s action, *H*'s silence, notwithstanding its communicative power, cannot remove it; only an explicit statement can. Furthermore, the false impression here is not merely a conceptual error. It relates to personal worth, as it involves *G*'s sense of *H*'s regard for him. Since *G* wants to believe that *H* holds him in high regard, cognitive dissonance may set in and prevent him from recognizing the message inherent in *H*'s silence.[67] *Tosafot* may thus maintain that nothing less than an explicit statement is required.

The above explanation makes *Rashi*'s position tenable only for a social setting, where *etiquette* gives silence its communicative power. In a commercial setting, *Rashi* could very well be in agreement with *Tosafot*. Indeed, *Rashi* explicitly espouses the position that silence is not an adequate disabusing mechanism in connection with the sale of nonkosher meat to a non-Jew. Preliminarily, let's note that a non-Jew regards kosher meat as of higher quality than nonkosher meat of the same type. In a case in which the butchers of a town are all Jewish and the townspeople are informed in an acceptable manner[68] when the supply of meat on a particular day is not kosher, the reasonable assumption of a shopper is that the meat is kosher when no announcement is made. Accordingly, if a Jewish butcher wants to sell nonkosher meat to a non-Jew on a day when no announcement has been made, the butcher has an obligation to tell his non-Jewish customer explicitly that the meat she is buying is nonkosher. Only this explicit disclosure will disabuse the non-Jew of her reasonable assumption that the meat is kosher. Without this explicit disclosure, *Rashi* believes, the butcher is guilty of *geneivat da'at*.[69]

Proceeding from the above discussion is an analytic framework Halakhah would adopt in evaluating Kraft's defense that the false impression the ad created was adequately neutralized by the superscript the company inserted in its ad. Let's compare the *force* of Kraft's false claim against the *force* of the caveat it offered in the superscript. Consider that Kraft's false claim of 100 percent milk equivalence was made lucidly in the beginning of the commercial without the distraction of audio and visual elements. In sharp contrast, the caveat it offered appeared only briefly, in complex form and amidst audio and visual distractions. Because the *force of the false implication* was much greater than the *force of the caveat* that was designed to neutralize it, Halakhah would be in agreement with the FTC's judgment that Kraft's caveat did not serve as an effective corrective measure. Halakhah would hence conclude that the ad's calcium claims constituted *geneivat da'at*.

FALSITY AND MATERIALITY

The issue of materiality assumed center stage in the battle between the FTC and Kraft. Kraft's defense was essentially that even if it had conveyed false claims, as the commission contended, those claims were nevertheless harmless, as the calcium factor was not an important reason for the purchase of Singles. The FTC said in its rebuttal that Kraft's survey technique was flawed and that the company had not shown that calcium was immaterial in the purchases and conduct of consumers vis-à-vis Kraft Singles. All sides agreed, however, that a harmless lie should not be legally regarded as deception. Recall that from the standpoint of Halakhah, a harmless lie is also prohibited. Secular law here is fundamentally at odds with Halakhah.

NEGATIVE COMMERCIAL SPEECH

What is remarkable about the FTC's analysis of the Kraft case is the narrowness of its concerns. The issue with "Skimp/Brown Eyes" is deceptiveness, and deceptiveness alone. Consider, however, that the Kraft ad is an exercise in negative comparison advertising. It tells the public that buying imitation cheese is "skimping."

From the perspective of Halakhah, Kraft's negative comparison ad violates the rules against negative commercial speech. The relevant ethical principles the ad violates are (1) the prohibition against proffering ill-suited advice (*lifnei iver*); (2) the prohibition against deprecating a competitor's product (*lashon ha-ra*); and (3) the prohibition against elevating oneself at the expense of someone else's degradation (*mitkabbed bi-klon havero*).

1. "Skimp/Brown Eyes" and *Lifnei Iver*

Kraft's use of the comparative merit stratagem transforms its message from a mere representation into a claim of superiority. As stated previously, there is nothing inherently unethical about making a claim of superiority; if a company really believes that its product beats the competition, advancing a claim of superiority does not make the company guilty of proffering ill-suited advice. But Kraft's "Skimp/Brown Eyes" ad goes beyond making a superiority claim. By associating Singles with a mother who tenaciously refuses to *skimp* on the nutritional needs of her developing child, Kraft *shames* the public into not investigating the merits of imitation cheese. Because Kraft's ad amounts to *active dissuasion* from becoming informed of the merits of imitation cheese, the ad amounts to ill-suited advice and violates *lifnei iver*.[70]

Recall the ruling of R. Malachi b. Jacob ha-Kohen that *lifnei iver* prohibits *A* from setting up *B* with an *opportunity* to sin. Whether *B* ends up
committing the sin or not is immaterial, as far as *A*'s infraction is concerned.
This same stringency should apply to the other aspect of *lifnei iver* conduct,
namely, the prohibition against proffering someone ill-suited advice. It follows that "Skimp/Brown Eyes" violates *lifnei iver* even with respect to those
people who don't rely on the ad, and end up buying imitation cheese after
learning that imitation cheese has as much calcium per slice as Singles, and
is cheaper, to boot.

Another point to consider is whether Kraft violates *lifnei iver* with
respect to consumers who encounter the company's ad but are already aware
of the merits of imitation cheese slices. Consider that this group does not
take the company's claim as advice, even on the level of information that
warrants further investigation. Instead, the informed consumer immediately
recognizes the company's claim as misleading. With respect to the informed
consumer, the company cannot be said to be guilty of proffering ill-suited
advice.

2. "Skimp/Brown Eyes" and *Ona'at Devarim*

Recall that one aspect of the *ona'at devarim* interdict is the prohibition
against causing someone needless mental anguish by means of mocking
conduct. "Skimp/Brown Eyes" may constitute mocking conduct toward the
well-informed consumers who are exposed to the ad. This group knows the
merits of imitation cheese before they encounter the Kraft ad. Because they
immediately recognize that the Kraft ad is misleading, they may feel that the
ad mocks their intelligence. Does this necessarily mean that Kraft violates
ona'at devarim with respect to this segment of the population? Perhaps not.
We must not lose sight of the fact that the Kraft's "Skimp/Brown Eyes" ad is
an impersonal, mass communication message. Perhaps, the great majority
of the targeted audience relate to the message only on an informational
basis, but not on a personal and emotional level. If so Kraft is guilty only of
advising the target group not to look into imitation cheese as an alternative.
But, the company is not guilty of *shaming* people not to look into alternatives. Consider that Halakhah regards those who unreasonably read unintended claims into an advertising message as being guilty of *self-deception*.

Likewise, if only an insignificant percentage of those who are exposed to a mass communications message feel that the message mocks their intelligence, the hurt feelings of these people should be regarded as *self-inflicted*. To put this proposition in concrete terms: suppose 30 percent of the target group is fully aware that imitation cheese is also a source for calcium and therefore are not misled by the Kraft ad. Suppose further that within this *informed group*, less than 15 percent relate to the ad on a personal and emotional level and feel that the Kraft ad mocks their intelligence. What the survey tells us is that anyone who feels the Kraft ad mocks them is guilty of *self-inflicted* anguish. Kraft, therefore, does not violate *ona'at devarim* in respect to the contingent that feel the Kraft ad mocks their intelligence.

3. "Skimp/Brown Eyes" and *Mitkabbed Bi-klon Havero*

By use of the comparison technique, Kraft's "Skimp/Brown Eyes" ad manages to *magnify* the virtues of its product at the expense of imitation cheese slices. This promotional device may run afoul of the prohibition, discussed earlier, against elevating oneself at the expense of another's degradation.

In its "Skimp/Brown Eyes" commercial, Kraft obliquely refers to the fact that imitation cheese slices are cheaper, by having the mother in the commercial say, "I thought of skimping. I admit it. . . . Skimp on her? Not me." We take it as a given that lower price is a definite advantage from the standpoint of the consumer. Kraft's sneering reference to the lower price of imitation cheese slices amounts, therefore, to a compounding of the company's infraction of R. Yose's dictum.

SUMMARY AND CONCLUSION

The overriding theme of this chapter is that the FTC of a society governed by Halakhah would adopt a standard of truth-telling that is much higher than the standard the FTC sets for American society today. The centerpiece in illustrating this difference is that materiality is officially an integral component of the definition of deception for the FTC. The FTC assumes all *express claims* to be material. Implicit claims are judged material if there is evidence that the advertiser *intended* to imply them. For Halakhah, however, a lie is unacceptable even if it imposes harm on no one.

If maximizing society's wealth becomes the sole guidepost for government regulation of advertising, the gap between Halakhah and the FTC will widen regarding the types of deception in advertising that ought to be prevented. For one, as Preston argues, the burden of proving materiality should fall on the FTC. In the current state of affairs, it is the firm that runs the challenged ad that must prove that the misleading claim was not material in affecting consumer conduct.

Adoption of wealth maximization as the criterion for the regulation of advertising results in additional leeway for advertisers, even when a material misleading claim is made. Craswell suggests that cost-benefit analysis be given primacy in deciding if such an ad should be removed or modified. Moreover, Rubin asserts that short-term deception should be tolerated if a long-term benefit is foreseen.

From the standpoint of Halakhah, an advertiser must not make a claim unless he has already objectively verified it to be accurate. Because he cannot rely on his own judgment that his mass communication message will not mislead anyone, the advertiser must generally pilot test the message before it is released to the public. Pilot testing should be required regardless of whether the claim is in the form of fact or opinion, because opinion often *implies* facts.

Materiality is a halakhic consideration with respect to an implicit claim. There is, however, a basic difference between the approach of the two systems of law to materiality in implicit claims. In secular law, where there is no requirement for the advertiser to pilot test his ad to ensure that it contains nothing deceptive, the issue of materiality comes into play only after the ad is released and is challenged on the basis of its deceptiveness. It is at this juncture that the FTC will apply the materiality test to determine whether to pull the ad. In the Torah society, it is the responsibility of the advertiser to pilot test his mass communication message to ensure that it is not deceptive, *before* exposing the public to it. If the ad passes the 15–20 percent test, it is not considered capable of deceiving the "reasonable man."

Although the mission of the FTC of the Torah society would be to champion truth-telling, this authority would also have the daunting challenge of applying the various principles of truth-telling to a mass communications message. This task would require the development of a set of standards different from those that apply to small-scale interaction.

This FTC would have to set guideposts for the methodology to be used in designing pilot testing. The rigor, formality, and other requirements for these tests would naturally vary, depending on the size and heterogeneity of the target group.

The FTC would also have to put the "reasonable man" in quantifiable terms for a wide variety of different settings and contexts.

We proposed that the FTC of the Torah society would not be able to limit itself to rule making, relying on the private sector to do its job in engaging in the requisite type of research to ensure that the reasonable man would not be misled by its claims. Creating and maintaining a moral society requires an investment in objective data, without which its moral codes fall into disuse. To be sure, development of this objective data is the responsibility of market participants, but it will be riddled by subjective bias if left to the sellers themselves to generate. In concrete terms, the FTC of the Torah society must subsidize consumer research to ensure an adequate level of expenditure, and the integrity of the research process itself.

Another sharp contrast between Halakhah and the American FTC is the scope of government regulation of advertising. In American society, comparative negative advertising is permitted, and the focus and thrust of governmental regulation of advertising is in the area of deception. What constitutes fair competition in comparative negative advertising is left to the law of injurious falsehood. Within the framework of this doctrine, advertisers enjoy wide latitude to express whatever opinion they like about competing brands. In sharp contrast, commercial speech is severely restrained by Halakhah.

As far as commercial speech is concerned, firms governed by Halakhah would be under a number of constraints. If a firm ventures beyond representing its product and opts to assume the role of counselor to its potential customers, the advertising text must not violate the prohibition against ill-suited advice. Shaming the consumer into not investigating the competition is an example of a violation of this dictum. Similarly, if negative imagery with which the rival is associated in the ad induces some people in the targeted group to think less of the rival's product, the advertiser becomes guilty of deprecating the rival's product and hence violates *lashon ha-ra*. Finally, the prohibition against negative commercial speech requires the advertiser to refrain from presenting his product alongside a rival's product in a manner that effectively elevates his product while degrading the rival's.

Let's take note that constraints on commercial speech are just one aspect of the rules for fair competition. Because fair competition is essentially a different area of law, the authority in charge of this sphere in the Torah society, as is the case in American society, would be a body separate from the FTC.

If materiality is not a component of the definition of deception, the FTC of the Torah society could theoretically become bogged down in cases involving deception of the non-harmful type, but this need not be the case. The moral education provided by familial and educational institutions, government subsidization of ethics-oriented advertising research, and the ad hoc courts could combine both to prevent much unethical advertising from occurring and to address many problems that still present themselves without requiring FTC intervention.

POSTPRANDIUM

The secular business ethics literature has advanced a number of definitions for deceptive advertising. Critically evaluate each of the following definitions from the standpoint of Halakhah.

- Professor David M. Gardner defines deceptive advertising as follows:

  If an advertisement (or advertising campaign) leaves the consumer with an impression(s) and/or beliefs(s) different from what would normally be expected if the consumer had reasonable knowledge, and that the impression(s) and/or belief(s) is factually untrue or potentially misleading, then deception is said to exist.[71]

- Professors Thomas L. Carson, Richard E. Wokutch, and James E. Cox define deceptive advertising as follows: An advertisement is deceptive if it causes a significant percentage of potential consumers (i.e., those at whom it is directed or whose consumption behavior is likely to be influenced by it) to have false beliefs about the product.[72]

- Professor John R. Boatright defines deceptive advertising as follows: Deception occurs when a false belief, which an advertisement either creates or takes advantage of, substantially interferes with the ability of people to make rational consumer choices.[73]

NOTES

1. FTC Policy Statement on Deception, Oct. 14, 1983, Summary.
2. 48 FR 10471, March 11, 1983; http://www.ftc.gov/bcp/guides/ad3subst.htm
3. FTC Policy Statement on Deception, Oct.14, 1983, Summary.
4. Deception Statement, 103 F.T.C. at 182; Novartis Corp., slip op. at 11–12; Kraft, Inc., 114 F.T.C. at 134.
5. Ivan L. Preston, "The Definition of Deceptiveness in Advertising and Other Commercial Speech," 39 *Catholic University Law Review*, 1990, p. 1047.
6. Paul T. Hayden, "A Goodly Apple Rotten at the Heart: Commercial Disparagement in Comparative Advertising as Common-Law Tortuous Unfair Competition", 76 *Iowa Law Review*, 1990, p. 83.
7. Ivan L. Preston, The Great American Blow-Up: Puffery in Advertising and Selling (Madison, WI: University of Wisconsin Press, 1996), pp. 68–89.
8. Richard L. Oliver, "Interpretation of the Attitudinal and behavioral Effects of Puffery," *Journal of Consumer Affairs* 13, no.1 (March, 1979): pp. 8–27.
9. The exposition of the Pareto and Kaldor-Hicks criteria as they apply to social choice follows Richard A. Posner, *Economic Analysis of Law*, 4th edition (Boston: Little, Brown and Company, 1992), pp. 3–19. The explanation of why Kaldor-Hicks works to maximize society's wealth in the long-run, even if the gainers don't actual give the loser's compensation is the author's.
10. FTC Policy Statement on Deception, October 14, 1983.
11. Jeff I. Richards, Ivan L. Preston, "Legal Treatment of Deceptive Advertising," *Journal of Public Policy and Marketing*, vol. 11, no. 2, Fall, 1992, pp. 45–57.
12. Richard Craswell, "Interpreting Deceptive Advertising," *Boston University Law Review*, vol. 65, July, 1985, p. 674.
13. Ibid. p. 688.
14. Paul H. Rubin, "The Economics of Regulating Deception," 10(3) *CATO Journal*, Winter 1991, pp. 667–691.
15. For this point please turn to pp. 13–16 of this volume in regard to the discussion on self-assessment and the disabusing obligation.
16. See Aaron Levine, *Case Studies in Jewish Business Ethics*, (Hoboken, New Jersey: Ktav Publishing House Inc., Yeshiva University Press, 2000), pp. 33–48.
17. R. Nahum Yavruv, *Niv Sefatayyim*, 3rd edition, *helek alef*, p. 14.
18. R. Israel Meir ha-Kohen Kagan, *Sefat Tamim, perek* 6.
19. R. Abraham Y. Karelitz (Israel, 1878–1953), *Emunah u-Bitahon*, chapter 4 to 13.
20. R. Eliezer b. Samuel, *Yere'im* 235.
21. R. Eliezer Judah Waldenberg, *Resp. Tzitz Eliezer* 15:12.
22. R. Nahum Yavruv, *Niv Sifatayyim*, op. cit. *helek alef*, p. 94.
23. For an explication of this principle please turn to pp. 17–18, 49 of this volume.
24. R. Solomon b. Jehiel Luria, *Yam Shel Shelomo, Yevamot* 6:46.
25. *Sotah* 14a; *Sifrei* at Deuteronomy 10:12.
26. In the opinion of R. Naftali Zevi Yehudah Berlin, *imitatio Dei* extends beyond a duty to emulate those Attributes of God's mercies explicitly enumerated at Exodus 34:67. By the exegesis of Joel 3:5, a duty to emulate God in every manifestation of His mercy is established (*Emek Netziv, Sifrei* at Deuteronomy 10:2, *piska* 13).

27. R. Solomom b. Isaac, *Rashi*, Exodus 34:6.

28. Maimonides (Egypt, 1135–1204), *Yad, Teshuvah* 5:1–5

29. Let us take note that the *Torah* in various places does promise that adherence to the Divine commandments will be rewarded with physical and material recompense and disobedience of the *Torah* will be followed by punishment in this world. Addressing this issue, Maimonides (loc. cit., 9:1) avers that the material and physical rewards and punishments mentioned are not for compliance and disobedience. Rather, if we desire with gladness to perform God's will, God will remove all obstacles to the performance of *mitzvot*. These obstacles include war, disease and poverty. If we fail to show alacrity for the *mitzvot*, we may not merit to have these obstacles removed. But, the reward for performing God's will and the punishment for disobedience are infinite in nature and therefore reserved for the world of the infinite.

30. The exception to this rule is that the person who is called "God's enemy" is given reward for his good deeds in this world: "And He pays His enemy to his face to destroy him. He does not delay for his enemy-to his face does He pay him" (Deuteronomy 7:11). See *Rashi* ad loc.

31. *Yad*, op. cit., 8:7–8, 9:1; Nahmanides (Spain, 1194–1270), *Kitvei Ramban*, Vol.1 *hakdamah*, 23, 24.

32. Micah 7:20; *Makkot* 24a; *Tanna debei Eliyahu Rabbah* 6.

33. For the derivation of the *hin tzedek* imperative, please turn to p. **???** of this volume.

34. Leviticus 25:17; *Mishna, Bava Metzia* 4:10; Rif, ad locum; Yad, *Geneivah* 14:12; *Rosh, Bava Metzia* 4:22; *Tur, Hoshen Mishpat*, 228; *Sh. Ar. Hoshen Mishpat* 228:1; R. Jehiel Michel Epstein, *Ar. ha-Sh., Hoshen Mishpat* 228:1.

35. R. Menahem b. Solomon Meiri (Perpignan, 1249–1316), *Beit ha-Behirah, Bava Metzia* 59a. Pricing an article with no intention to buy it is prohibited, according to R. Samuel b. Meir (ca. 1080–1174), *Rashbam, Pesahim* 112b on account of the possible financial loss this behavior might cause the vendor. While the vendor is preoccupied with the insincere inquiry, serious customers may turn elsewhere.

36. *Yad, De'ot* 7:5.

37. R. Israel Meir ha-Kohen, *Hafez Hayyim, Hilkhot Issurei Lashon Ha-Ra, Mekor ha-Hayyim* 5:7.

38. Leviticus 19:14; *Torat Kohanim* at Leviticus 19:14; Maimonides, *Yad, Rotzeah* 12:14.

39. For an extensive discussion on this point, see R. Jeroham Fishel Perla's commentary on *Sefer ha-Mitzvot of R. Saadia Gaon, Minyan ha-Lavin* 54. He traces the issue to the Geonic period.

40. R. Malachi b. Jacob ha-Kohen, *Yad Malakhi* 367.

41. R. Isaac Blaser, *Peri Yitzhak* 2:49.

42. R. Yose b. Hanina, *Jerusalem Talmud, Hagigah* 8a.

43. The following section draws from my previous work *Case Studies in Jewish Business Ethics*, op. cit., pp. 63–65.

44. R. Hayyim Hezekiah Medini (Russia, 1832–1904), *Sedei Hemed*. IV, K'lal 86. p. 524

45. Rashi at Leviticus 25:17.

46. Several considerations support the contention that the ill-suited advice *Rashi* reads into the *ona'at devarim* interdict is not the same category of ill-suited advice the *lifnei iver* interdict speaks of. For one, *Rashi* illustrates the *ona'at devarim* interdict with the example of *A* offering *B* self-serving, ill-suited advice only *after* first making the general

statement that *ona'at devarim prohibits verbal harassment.* Now, if the self-serving, ill-suited advice that *Rashi* speaks of is not *transparently ill-suited,* then, *A's* conduct would not be characterized as verbal harassment. Moreover, the phraseology *Rashi* employs to convey the notion of ill-suited advice in the context of his explanation of *ona'at devarim* is not the same phraseology he employs in his explication of *lifnei iver.* In the context of *lifnei iver, Rashi* defines ill-suited advice as advice that is not appropriate for the advisee (*B*) (*she-einah hogenet lo*); but, in connection with the *ona'at devarim* interdict *Rashi* adds to the phrase *she'eno hogenet lo,* the phrase "but is in accord with the mode of life and the benefit of the *adviser* [A] (*lefi darko va-hanna'ato shel yoetz*). In this regard, note the specific example *Rashi* gives in connection with *lifnei iver*: "sell your field, and buy yourself a donkey." *A's* intention, *Rashi* tells us, is to acquire the field himself once *B* puts it up for sale. But, when proffering the advice *A* does not let on that he himself will be an eager bidder for the field. Because *A's* self- serving motive is *hidden* from *B* at the point when *A* proffers his ill-suited advice, *A* cannot be said to be guilty of *harrassing B* and hence in violation of *ona'at devarim.* Rather, *A's* sin is *lifnei iver.* But, if *A* puts his self-serving interest in the matter *up front,* as for example, when *A* offers the advice to *B* "*sell me* your field and buy yourself a donkey with the proceeds," the overture may, at times, be regarded by *B* as nothing but verbal harassment or mockery. This occurs when *A's* self-serving interest in the advice opens *B's* eyes to the inescapable judgment that the advice is ill-suited. In the latter instance, *B* never takes *A's* advice seriously and, instead, takes the overture as nothing but verbal harassment. In the latter instance, *A's* sin is hence *ona'at devarim.*

Both the above variants of ill-suited advice are examples of veiled misconduct, but for different reasons. In the instance where *A* does not let on up front his self-serving interest in the matter, *A* imagines that he will end up with the field and *B* will never catch on that his own welfare was all along caverlierly disregarded by *A.* In the second variant, *A* is so self-centered that he imagines that if *B* possesses something that he wants, *B* will always find it in his *own self-interest* to give the item up on *A's* terms.

47. *Parents Magazine,* November 1989, p. 111.
48. Paul T. Hayden, "A Goodly Apple Rotten at the Heart: Commercial Disparagement in Comparative Advertising as Common-Law Tortuous Unfair Competition," op. cit.
49. *Bava Batra* 21a; *Rif* ad locum; Maimonides, *Yad, Talmud Torah* 2:1; R. Asher b. Jehiel, *Rosh, Bava Batra* 2: 6; R. Jacob b. Asher, *Tur, Yoreh De'ah* 245; R. Joseph Caro. *Sh. Ar,. Yoreh De'ah* 245: 7–8; R. Jehiel Michel Epstein, *Ar. ha-Sh., Yoreh De'ah* 245:6–11.
50. *Sanhedrin* 16b; Maimonides, *Yad, Sanhedrin* 1:1.
51. *Mishna Sanhedrin* 3:1; *Rif, Sanhedrin* 23a; Maimonides, *Yad, Sanhedrin* 7:1; R. Asher b. Jehiel, *Rosh, Sanhedrin* 3:1–2; R. Jacob b. Asher, *Tur, Hoshen Mishpat* 13; R. Joseph Caro, *Sh. Ar., Hoshen Mishpat* 13:1; R. Jehiel Michel Epstein, *Ar. ha-Sh., Hoshen Mishpat* 13:1–6.
52. R Shabbetai b. Meir ha-Kohen, *Siftei Kohen, Sh. Ar., Hoshen Mishpat* 3 note10. In R. Shabbetai's opinion a single judge is acceptable in a monetary case only when the Torah law in the matter at hand is straightforward as far as the judge is concerned. Alternatively, a single judge is valid when the judge gets the litigants to accept his ruling even if it will not conform to the Torah law, notwithstanding his best efforts to achieve that result.
53. *Hullin* 10a.

54. Preston, op. cit., p. 114.

55. *Yevamot* 119b.

56. For a discussion of the notion of search and experience goods, see Philip Nelson, "Information and Consumer Behavior," *Journal of Political Economy* 78 (March 1970): 311–329; Philip Nelson, "Advertising as Information," *Journal of Political Economy* 82 (July 1974): 729–755. For a discussion of the notion of a credence good, see Michael R. Darby, and Edi Karmi, "Free Competition and the Optimal Amount of Fraud," *Journal of Law and Economics* 16 (April 1973): pp. 67–88. For the application of these concepts to the regulation of advertising, see Ellen R. Jordan, and Paul H. Rubin, "An Economic Analysis of the Law of False Advertising." *Journal of Legal Studies* 8 (June 1979): 116–155.

57. In Talmudic times, communal legislation was linked to religious law by the requirement that all communal enactments must be approved by the locally recognized religious authority and communal leader (*adam hashuv*). This person combined expertise in Halakhah with worldly wisdom. Should an individual blessed with these attributes not be present locally, communal legislation is fully valid without any outside approval. (For sources and discussions of these points see Aaron Levine, *Free Enterprise and Jewish Law: Aspects of Jewish Business Ethics* [New York: Ktav and Yeshiva University Press], p. 135).

58. *Case Studies in Jewish Business Ethics*, op. cit., pp. 1–32.

59. Ivan L. Preston, *The Tangled Web They Weave* (Madison: University of Wisconsin Press, 1994), pp. 47–51.

60. Ibid.

61. The following section draws upon my previous work, *Case Studies in Jewish Business Ethics*, op. cit., pp. 118–121.

62. R. Solomon b. Isaac, Rashi, *Hullin* 94a.

63. Ibid.

64. *Tosafot, Hullin* 94a.

65. *Betzah* 16a.

66. R. Solomon b. Isaac, Rashi, *Betzah* 16a.

67. Illustrating the phenomenon of cognitive dissonance is the Kassarjian and Cohen study which investigated the effect the Surgeon General's Report had on smoker's attitudes and behavior. The findings showed that 36.5 percent of the surveyed smokers did not believe that the report had established a linkage between smoking and cancer. Moreover, the figure among heavy smokers was 41 percent suggesting that the more committed one is to a product, the greater the dissonance and the less likely one is to admit the product's adverse effect. Study cited in Richard L. Oliver, "An Interpretation of the Attitudinal and Behavioral Effects of Puffery," 13(1) *Journal of Consumer Affairs*, March 1979, pp. 8–27.

68. For the wording of the formulation the rabbis used, see *Hullin* 94b.

69. *Rashi* at *Hullin* 94a. See, however, R. Gershom b. Judah Me'Or ha-Golah (*Hullin* 94a) who follows Rashi's line in his understanding of the wine barrel case, but interprets the case to refer to a *commercial* setting.

70. Leviticus 19:14; *Torat Kohanim* at Leviticus 19:14; Maimonides, *Yad, Rotzeah* 12:14.

71. David M. Gardner, "Deception in Advertising: A conceptual Approach," 39 *Journal of Marketing*, January 1975, 40–46.

72. Thomas L. Carson, Richard E.Wokutch, and James E. Cox, Jr., "An Ethical Analysis of Deception in Advertising," 4 *Journal of Business Ethics*, 1985, 103, note 6.
73. John R. Boatright, *Ethics and the Conduct of Business*, 2nd ed. (Upper Saddle River, NJ: Prentice Hall, 1997), pp. 259–283.

11

<u>*Whistleblowing*</u>

Whistleblowing is an attempt by a member or former member of an organization to disclose wrongdoing in or by the organization. If the whistleblowing is reported only to those higher in the organization it is called *internal* whistleblowing. When the wrongdoing is reported to external individuals or bodies such as government agencies, newspapers, or public interest groups, the disclosure is called *external* whistleblowing.[1]

Our purpose here will be to draw a comparison between the treatment of whistleblowing in secular society and Halakhah (Jewish Law). We begin with a presentation of the general approaches secular business ethics and Halakhah take on this issue. We will then relate these general approaches to case studies, drawn from the secular business ethics literature.

We then turn to a consideration of the protection the whistleblower enjoys under the law today and the critique of these laws from the standpoint of Halakhah.

Finally, we turn to the moral challenge of creating both an organizational structure and a corporate culture that preclude the problem of whistleblowing in the first place.

THE TREATMENT OF WHISTLEBLOWING IN SECULAR SOCIETY

For the treatment of whistleblowing in secular society we draw upon both the legal and the business ethics literature. Our first task will be to put the challenge of the would-be whistleblower within the context of a moral dilemma. What legal principle urges the whistleblower to disclose wrongdoing and what legal principle informs him not to disclose the wrongdoing? Next, we turn to the steps the whistleblower should take in making his or her disclosure.

Dealing with the phenomenon of the corporate whistleblower (*W*), Professor Leonard M. Baines, of St. Johns University Law School, proposes that the tension for *W* is how to reconcile the duty of loyalty with the duty of care he owes his firm. Consider that indiscriminate external whistleblowing puts the company and members of the firm at maximum legal exposure for any wrongdoing committed. Keeping the incriminating documents and other evidence within the firm, however, gives the company the opportunity to come up with a strategy that minimizes its potential liability and maximizes its profits. However, the duty of care tells *W* that he must do everything reasonable to stop the wrongdoing from continuing.[2]

We now turn to a consideration of the steps the whistleblower should take in making his or her disclosure. For this aspect of our study we turn to the work of Professor Richard T. De George, of the University of Kansas. Professor De George has written very incisively on the ethics of whistleblowing. We take his work as an authoritative view on this topic in the secular business ethics literature.

At the outset, let us note that De George intended his following criteria and series of steps to apply only to nongovernmental, impersonal, external whistleblowing. Although Professor De George feels that the steps and insights he provides are useful in giving guidance to the whistleblower in other contexts, additional argument would be necessary to make the analysis complete.[3]

De George specifies five conditions that, if satisfied, make whistleblowing morally acceptable, and even obligatory. If the first three are satisfied, the act of whistleblowing will be morally justified and permissible. If the additional two are satisfied, the act of whistleblowing will be morally obligatory. Whistleblowing will be morally permissible if:

1. "The firm, through its product or policy, will do serious and considerable harm to employees or to the public, whether in the person of the user of the product, an innocent bystander, or the general public."[4]

Illustrating a nonserious harm is the public disclosure by an auto plant worker that his suggestion to make a particular model slightly safer by modifying a part was rejected by his firm. This disclosure should not be made. Why? Because it is not immoral not to make the safest automobile possible. There is always a trade-off between safety and cost. Moreover, if serious harm is not threatened, then the slight harm that is done by the use of the product can be corrected after the product is marketed (e.g., as a result of customer complaint).

2. "Once employees identify a serious threat to the user of a product or to the general public, they should report it to their immediate superior and make their moral concerns known. Unless they do so, the act of whistleblowing is not clearly justifiable."

De George defends this disclosure procedure on several levels: (a) Most basically, this procedure represents the quickest route to the desired change. This follows from the reasonable assumption that most firms do not want to cause death or injury, and do not willingly or knowingly set out to harm the users of their products in this way; (b) Because the employee has a duty of loyalty to his or her firm, the firm must be given the chance to rectify its action before it is charged in public; (c) Harm to the firm is generally minimized if the firm is informed of the problem and is allowed to correct it.

3. "If one's immediate superior does nothing effective about the concern or complaint, the employee should exhaust the internal procedures and possibilities within the firm. This usually will involve taking the matter up the managerial ladder, and, if necessary—and possible—to the board of directors."

To say that whistleblowing is morally permitted does not impose any obligation on an employee. Unless two other conditions are met, the employee does not have a moral obligation to blow the whistle. These conditions are:

4. The whistleblower must have, or have access to, documented evidence that would convince a reasonable, impartial observer that his or her view of the situation is correct, and that the company's product or practice poses a serious and likely danger to the public or to the user of the product.

5. The employee must have good reasons to believe that by going public the necessary changes will be brought about. The chance of being successful must be worth the risk he or she takes and the danger to which he or she is exposed.[5]

DE GEORGE ON INTERNAL WHISTLEBLOWING

In his treatment of the ethics of whistleblowing, De George also considers the instance where a worker observes wrongdoing by either a co-worker or a superior. The type of wrongdoing he considers in this category of cases is, for example, padding an expense account, taking kickbacks, or accepting large gifts from suppliers. Although it is clearly in the interest of the firm to know of this type of wrongdoing by their employees, informing on a co-worker or superior in regard to this misconduct is not morally obligatory. Making the disclosure can surely jeopardize the informer's position or his or her prospects for promotion. Moreover, reporting such wrongdoing does not fall within the purview of the duties the would-be whistleblower was hired for. Nor is it clear that asking employees to act in that capacity would make for a productive corporate atmosphere. Such a requirement would turn a normal society into a police state or cultivate a police state mentality among its citizens.

Although De George concludes that internal whistleblowing is never obligatory, he posits that it is permissible for a worker to report the wrongdoing of the co-worker or superior to the appropriate person within the firm. Because the perpetrators of the prohibited actions in question are acting against the good of the firm, they can claim no right to privacy with respect to those actions and no immunity from being reported. It is for this reason that De George sees no requirement to inform the wrongdoer before reporting him or her.[6]

THE WHISTLEBLOWER AND HALAKHAH

In this section we will set out to identify the horns of the whistleblower's dilemma from the perspective of Halakhah.

We begin with the ethical case against disclosure. Recall that within Baines's formulation the ethical value of loyalty is invoked to argue that the discoverer of the wrongdoing should not protest the misdeed or try to stop it. In Halakhah loyalty plays no role in making a case that the worker (W) should take no action if he discovers his supervisor (S) or employer (E) engaged in wrongdoing. To be sure, the labor contract creates obligations for W, but these obligations say no more than that W must not idle on company time and is required to energetically apply himself to the task at hand.[7] But, if S or E instructs W to engage in either unethical or illegal activity for the good of the firm, W is prohibited from following the instruction. The principle here is "If you must choose between the words of the Master [i.e., God, Who commands you not to sin] and the word of the disciple [who instructs you to sin], whose word should you obey [*divrei ha-rav ve-divrei ha-talmid divrei mi shomin*]?[8] This principle conveys that God's law not to engage in wrongdoing supersedes E's instruction that is contrary to that law. The *divrei ha-rav* principle remains operative even when W otherwise owes a *religious* duty to S or E to honor them and respect their wishes, as would be the case when S or E is W's parent.[9]

Given that the workplace does not change the character of a practice that would otherwise be categorized as immoral, W may not ignore the conduct when he observes it. Ordinarily, if A observes B engaged in wrongful conduct, A is obligated to approach B and reproach him for engaging in this conduct. This is called the religious duty of *tokhahah* (reproof).[10] Accordingly, if W observes wrongdoing in the workplace, he may not ignore the conduct. Instead, he must confront the wrongdoer and remonstrate with him regarding the prohibited conduct. How far does the *tokhahah* obligation go? R. Mosheh Isserles (Poland, 1525 or 1530–1572) regards the *tokhahah* duty as remaining intact even when it will not be heeded. In public, a single protest will suffice; but in private, the admonisher must persist until the transgressor either begins to curse or to assault him.[11]

Fulfilling R. Isserles's standard may very well get W fired. Does W's *tokhahah* duty extend, if necessary, to getting fired? The issue turns around the financial obligation one must incur to avoid violating religious duties. Obligatory religious duties dichotomize into positive commandments (*mitzvot aseh*) and negative prohibitions (*mitzvot lo ta'aseh*). The rule for the extent of financial obligation that pertains to these two categories is a matter of dispute. R. Mosheh Isserles formulates the rule as follows: To fulfill a *mitzvat aseh*, an individual is required, if necessary, to expend up to one-fifth of his net worth. But, to avoid violation of *mitzvat lo ta'aseh*, an individual must lose, if necessary, his entire net worth.[12] Disputing R. Isserles, R. Mosheh Sofer (Hungary, 1762–1839) argues that the stringency for the *lo ta'aseh* category applies only when the negative commandment will be violated in an *active manner* (*kum va-as'eh*). When the negative commandment will, however, be violated only in a passive manner (*shev-ve-al ta'aseh*), the one-fifth rule applies.[13]

Consider that the positive duty of *tokhahah* is violated by the *inaction* of the party who observes the misconduct. Following R. Sofer's line, if *W* assesses that engaging in *tokhahah* with the wrongdoers at the work scene will put his job in jeopardy; *W* should be free of the *tokhahah* duty.

Several leniencies regarding the application of the *tokhahah* obligation should be noted. One leniency, mentioned by R. Isserles himself, is that if the prohibition involved is not explicitly recorded in the Torah, there is no obligation for *A* to remonstrate with *B* for violating the prohibition if *A* assesses that *B* will not adhere to his admonishment.[14] Moreover, if *A* assesses that his admonishment will cause *B* to either hate him or take revenge against him, *A*, according to R. Judah b. Samuel he-Hasid (Regensberg, ca. 1150–1217), is relieved of his *tokhahah* duty.[15] Similarly, R. Jehiel Michel Epstein (Belarus, 1829–1908) rules that if the object of the admonishment is someone who is a heretic, the *tokhahah* duty does not apply against him.[16]

The aforementioned discussion regarding *tokhahah* makes it clear that the whistleblower's duty becomes potentially operative even when the harm he or she observes impacts only on the firm and does not impact on the public. Halakhah hence rejects De George's distinction between internal and external whistleblowing.

Given that *tokhahah*, at least on a theoretical level, is operative for *W* if he observes wrongdoing in the work scene, the principle of loyalty cannot play a role in arguing the case against whistleblowing.

FREEDOM OF SPEECH AND WHISTLEBLOWING

In searching for an ethical principle that argues against whistleblowing, let's take note that freedom of speech is by no means an absolute right in Halakhah. Maligning a fellow violates the biblical prohibition against slander (*motzi shem ra*).[17]

Delivering a true but evil report about a fellow violates the biblical interdict against talebearing "You shall not go about as a talebearer among your people" (Leviticus 19:16). Talebearing comes in two varieties. If a speaker's (S's) evil report on a perpetrator (P) to a listener (L) relates to misconduct P has done or is planning to do to L, it is called *lashon ha-ra*. If the misconduct relates to harm not threatening L, but rather someone else, the talebearing is called *rekhilut*. Depending upon the circumstances, talebearing may involve the violation of a total of 31 Pentateuchal positive commandments and prohibitions.[18] Proceeding from the above is that the ethical principle behind the argument against whistleblowing is the prohibition against talebearing.

While freedom of speech is not an absolute right, there are circumstances when reporting wrongdoing is mandatory. One example of such a scenario is if the wrongdoing is not stopped, certain loss of human life will result. W's disclosure can avert this loss of human life. W's obligation to take timely action proceeds from the biblical injunction: "Do not stand idly by the blood of your neighbor" (*lo ta'amod al dam rei'akha*, henceforth *lo ta'amod*, Leviticus 19:16). On the basis of this verse, if A's life is in danger and a bystander (B) is in position to extricate him from this danger, B must take timely action to do so.[19] But, how extensive is B's obligation here? Must B take action to extricate A even when the life threatening danger facing A is only remote? Addressing this issue, R. Nissim b. Reuben Gerondi (Barcelona, ca. 1290–ca. 1375) answers in the affirmative. Let's examine how R. Nissim arrives at this conclusion.

R. Nissim begins his analysis by pointing out that *lo ta'amod* is not the only biblical source for the duty of a bystander to save someone from a life-threatening situation. This duty is also derived from a point in the law of rape. The specific point in law concerns the rape of a betrothed woman that took place in a field far removed from a public thoroughfare. Under these circumstances we may assume that the woman called for help to fend off the attack but nobody heard her and she was forcibly violated. Because of the presumption that the liaison was not consensual on the part of the woman, the woman is exempt from execution. The biblical source for this law is: "But you shall do nothing to the *na'arah* (girl), the girl has committed no capital crime; for like a man who rises up against his fellow and murders him, so is this thing" (Deuteronomy 22:26). Note that the verse compares the crime of rape to the crime of murder. The purpose of this analogy is apparently to establish the law that we do not punish the betrothed girl for having relations against her will, as her situation is analogous to becoming a murder victim. But, queries the Talmud, the analogy appears to be superfluous, as the woman's exemption from execution is already communicated by the phrase in the same verse: "But you shall do nothing to the girl. . . ." The intention of the verse, avers the Talmud, is therefore not merely to make a simple analogy, but rather to establish a technical correspondence (*hekkesh*) between the cases of rape and murder. The analogy should therefore be understood to *run both ways* (i.e., there is a law regarding murder that applies to rape as well, and there is a law regarding rape, which can be applied to cases of murder). The analogy that runs from the case of rape to the case of murder teaches us that saving the victim is paramount. Just as the passerby is required, if necessary, to kill someone pursuing a betrothed girl in order to save her from being violated,[20] so too, the passerby is required, if necessary, to kill someone poised to commit an act of murder in order to save the victim.[21]

Consider that the duty for a bystander to take timely action to extricate a fellow from a life-threatening situation is already established on the basis of *lo ta'amod*. What does the *hekkesh* between the cases of rape and murder add to this obligation? The answer, posits R. Nissim, is that *lo ta'amod* expands the duty to take timely action to save the potential victim, even when the life-threatening dangers he faces is not certain, but only probable.[22]

Must the passerby take timely action to save a life when doing so puts his own life in peril? A number of views on this matter have been advanced. The following is a summary of these views.

One school of thought is led by R. Meir ha-Kohen (fl. 13th cent.). This authority, basing himself on the Jerusalem Talmud, states that an individual is obligated even to put his own life in peril in order to save a fellow.[23]

R. David b. Solomon ibn Abi Zimra (*Radbaz*, d. 1573), following the line of the Jerusalem Talmud,[24] offers guidance as to what amount of danger a would-be rescuer (*R*) must subject himself to in order to save a fellow. In the opinion of *Radbaz*, the duty applies only when *R* enjoys a better than even chance to return from his rescue operation without serious injury.[25]

Radbaz's understanding of the Jerusalem Talmud is shared by R. Mosheh Schick (Hungary, 1807–1879), R. Ovadiah Yosef (Israel, contemp.), and R. Eliezer Yehudah Waldenberg (Israel, contemp.). All these authorities, however, take the position that the Babylonian Talmud disputes this ruling. Accordingly, these authorities aver that if saving a fellow's life entails a substantial danger it is prohibited for R to attempt the rescue.[26]

When saving a fellow entails only inconsequential danger, R is *required* to undertake the rescue mission and not be overly concerned with his own safety.[27]

A variation of the above case occurs when the threat to life is not to an individual but rather to the public. Authorities dispute what the duty of the would-be-rescuer (R) is here. In the opinion of R. Meir Simha ha-Kohen (Latvia, 1843–1926), if the rescue mission would put R's life in peril, R is prohibited from undertaking the mission, regardless of the number of people that might be saved by his efforts. R. Jehiel Yaakov Weinberg (Switzerland, 1885–1966), however, disputes this view. In his opinion, if more than one person stands to be saved by the rescue mission, R is required generally to undertake the mission.[28]

LO TA'AMOD AND MONETARY LOSS

Another point to consider is whether the obligation for the bystander to take timely action to extricate a potential victim from harm applies only when the harm involved is a danger to human life. What if the harm involved is only a monetary loss? While *lo ta'amod* speaks of the prohibition for a bystander not to take timely action in a life-threatening situation, *Safra* extends the interdict to the prohibition of withholding testimony in a monetary matter.[29] Basing himself on *Safra*, R. Israel Meir ha-Kohen Kagan (Radin, 1838–1933) understands the monetary application of the *lo ta'amod* interdict in broad terms: A's failure to supply B with timely information that would avert a financial loss for B is a violation of the *lo ta'amod* interdict.[30]

One final consideration: Does the *lo ta'amod* interdict apply even when the disclosure is against the financial interests of the informer? Let's address this issue in relation to the three cases we have dealt with.

We begin with the case where the harm the victim stands to suffer is only a financial loss. The duty of the bystander here consists of no more than a duty to promote the well-being of his fellow (*gemilut hasadim*). Confronted with a *hesed* opportunity, the situation may warrant a response in the form of personal attention and/or financial outlay. In respect to toil and effort, Halakhah sets no upper limit on what is expected of an individual in fulfilling a *hesed* opportunity. But as far as financial outlay is concerned, the sages established an upper limit consisting of one-fifth of one's net worth.[31]

This rule, according to R. Zalman Nehemiah Goldberg (Israel, contemp.), applies only when the object of the *hesed* is a poor person. When this is not the case, modification of the rule applies. In respect to the toil and effort component of the *mitzvah*, it makes no difference whether the target of the *hesed* is poor or not. Accordingly, suppose a rich man is sick— the *mitzvah* of *bikkur holim* (visiting the sick) requires people to visit him with no limits placed on this duty in respect to time expended. But, there is no obligation to either incur an expense or sustain a loss in connection with attending the needs of the well-off. The paradigm here is the *mitzvah* of restoring lost property to its rightful owner (*hashavat aveidah*). This *mitzvah* consists of both a positive and a negative duty. The positive duty is set out at Deuteronomy 22:1–3 and the negative duty consists of *lo ta'amod*.[32] Now, consider that an individual is not required to engage in the task of *hashavat aveidah* when it would be at the expense of restoring his own property or losing time on his job. This exemption is exegetically derived from the verse, "Except when there shall be no needy among you" (*efes ki lo yehiyeh bekha evyon*, Deuteronomy 15:4). The word *efes* is interpreted to mean "end" or "prevent," with the meaning being, "Be careful not to engage in conduct that might result in causing poverty for you."[33]

Hashavat aveidah provides a model for all religious duties falling into the category of *gemilat hasadim*. The operative principle, with few exceptions,[34] is that the bystander has no duty to take action to avert financial loss for a potential victim when taking such action runs counter to his own financial interest. Taking action on behalf of the potential victim under these circumstances is not a duty; rather, it is a supererogatory act.[35]

Let us now move to the case where the harm involved is a possible loss of life. Here, the bystander faces much more than a *gemilat hasadim* opportunity. By dint of the *lo ta'amod* interdict *R* must get involved. The extent of *R*'s duty is explicated at *Sanhedrin* 73a:

> From where do we know that if one sees his fellow drowning in a river, or [if he sees] a wild beast ravaging him or bandits coming to [attack]

him—that he is obligated to save [the fellow]?—Scripture [therefore] teaches: "You shall not stand by the blood of your friend" (Leviticus 19:16). [But rather save him from death].—But is it [indeed] from here [that this law is] derived? [Surely not]—[for according to the following *Baraita*,] [the law] is derived from a verse [Deuteronomy 22:2]: From where do we know [that one must return] a lost body, [e.g., the individual is drowning, there is an obligation to save him]—Scripture [therefore] teaches [a superfluous phrase:] . . . "And you shall return it to him." [If we would derive the obligation] from there [i.e., the verse "And you shall return it to him"]—I would have said that this [obligation] applies only when [a person] himself [has the opportunity to save a fellow's life.]—But *mitrah* ([with regard to] *bothering*) *u-magar agurei* (and *hiring* [a rescuer]) I would say [that one is [not] required to do so] —[the verse "You shall not stand by the blood of your brother" therefore] informs us [that he is required even to hire] someone [to rescue] the fellow.

What apparently proceeds from the Talmudic text is the obligation for the rescuer to expend all his resources, if necessary, to extricate the potential victim (*V*) from the life-threatening danger. This understanding of the text is reinforced by the comment R. Solomon b. Isaac (*Rashi*, France, 1040–1105) makes ad locum in explaining how the language of Leviticus 19:16 points to the bothering and hiring obligation: "Do not stop yourself from saving a fellow under any circumstance; you must even hire help, if necessary, in order to save his life."

Recall R. Sofer's view that an individual is not required to expend more than one-fifth of his resources to avoid violating a negative proscription of the *Torah*, if this proscription is violated in a passive way. The monetary parameters proceeding from the above passage for *lo ta'amod* apparently contradict R. Sofer's position. R. Eliezer Yehudah Waldenberg (Israel, contemp.), a proponent of R. Sofer's view, sees no contradiction, however. In defending R. Sofer's position, R. Waldenberg cites the interpretation R. Yair Bacharach (Worms, 1638–1701) offers for the "bothering and hiring obligation" the Talmud mentions in connection with *lo ta'amod*. Consider that the Talmud could have simply stated that the superfluous verse of *lo ta'amod* expands the rescue obligation to include *agurei migar* (hiring). Why add the word *mitrah* (bothering)? The answer: *mitrah* tell us that when there is danger to life, the would-be rescuer's (*R*'s) obligation extends beyond effecting the rescue by means of his *personal involvement*. Accordingly, if he is incapable of effecting the rescue personally—as for example, when he is not a swimmer, *R*'s obligation expands to a responsibility to *exert the necessary toil and effort to find rescuers and hire them to do the job*.

In contrast, when the loss the victim stands to lose is merely a financial loss, *R*'s obligation extends only to personal involvement. If *R* is incapable of averting the loss by means of his personal involvement, *R* bears no further responsibility in the matter. In any case, *V* is responsible to reimburse *R* for any expenses he incurred in effecting the rescue. *Rashi's* comment, cited earlier, avers R. Bacharach, can also be understood in this vein.[36]

Another early authority that understands *lo ta'amod* in the limited responsibility manner described above is R. Meir ha-Levi Abulafia (Spain, c.1180–1244). In his view the responsibility proceeding from *lo ta'amod* is for *R* to *exert the necessary toil and effort to find rescuers and hire them to do the job*. *V*, however, bears the responsibility to reimburse *R* with the expenses he incurred to effect the rescue.[37]

R. Waldenberg's conceptualization of the parameters of *lo ta'amod* is disputed by R. Mosheh Feinstein (New York, 1895–1986). In R. Feinstein's view, absent any mention of the *lo ta'amod* interdict in Scripture, *R* would, in any case, be obligated to take timely action to extricate *V* from the threat to his life. *R*'s charity obligation compels action here. To be sure, the duty to save *V* is not *R*'s alone, and must be shared by everyone. But if no one else is willing to do anything, then, *R* must shoulder the burden alone. The limit of *R*'s financial obligation here is defined by the one-fifth rule. *Lo ta'amod*, avers R. Feinstein, clearly takes *R* to an even higher level of financial responsibility. This responsibility is to expend *all his resources*, if necessary, in order to extricate *V* from the danger to his life. R. Feinstein understands *Rashi's* comment at *Sanhedrin* 73a, referred to earlier, to say exactly this. Why does *Rashi*, however, find it necessary to show us that the language employed by *lo ta'amod* points to the requirement to expend all one's resources, if necessary, in order to save *V*? Suppose for a moment that the language of *lo ta'amod* did not clearly point to this stringency. Would that make a difference? Consider that *lo ta'amod* is a negative prohibition. Recall R. Isserles's rule that in order to avoid violating a negative prohibition, one must, if necessary, expend all one's resources. The answer, avers R. Feinstein, is that the negative prohibition of the *Torah* is violated by *one's failure to act*. Because moral failure here is a result of *inaction*, we might think that the one-fifth rule applies. To dispel the notion that the financial duties that apply to a negative command that is violated by means of inaction should be equated with the financial duties laid out for a positive commandment, *Rashi* goes to pains to demonstrate that the *language* of *lo ta'amod* indicates an all-encompassing financial obligation.[38]

In his treatment of the one-fifth rule as it applies to the charity obligation, R. Israel Meir ha-Kohen Kagan avers that the one-fifth rule does not apply when failure to take immediate action might result in the death of the supplicant. R. Kagan dubs this case the instance of *pikuah nefesh mamash* (a real and tangible threat to life). In support of his position, R. Kagan cites the following Talmudic text at *Bava Metzia* 62a:

> Two people were traveling along the way—and one of them had in his possession a flask of water—if both drink [from it], they will [both] die [because there is not enough water to sustain both of them until they can reach more water.]—However, if [only] one of them drinks, he will [be able to] reach a settlement, [where more water is available].—Ben Petura preached [concerning the above case]—It is better that both should drink and die—than that one should witness the death of his fellow.—[Ben Petura's teaching was accepted] until R. Akiva came [along] and [taught]—[The Torah states] "And let your brother live with you." (Leviticus 25:36)—This implies that [your] life takes precedence over your fellow's life.

Preliminarily, let's take note that R. Akiva's position is the normative view in Halakhah.[39] What can be derived from the above text, avers R. Kagan, is no more than that it *is* legitimate for *A to* save his own life before taking action to save *B's* life. But, it would be unconscionable for *A* to fail to take action to save *B's* life in order to avoid a financial loss for himself.[40]

Another scenario to consider is the instance where *A* threatens *B* with death unless he agrees to cooperate in either an active or passive manner in the murder of *B*. We begin with the following teaching at *Sanhedrin* 74a regarding the severity of the prohibition against murder:

R. Yohanan said in the name of R. Shimon b. Yehozadak:– They took a vote [on the matter] and decided in the attic of Niszah's house in Lod: —[concerning] all prohibitions in the Torah,– [the law is that] if they tell a person: "Transgress [such and such a prohibition] and you will not be killed, [but if you refuse to do so, we will kill you,"]—he should transgress [the prohibition] and not allow himself to be killed—except for [when he is told to engage in] idol worship, liaison with a married woman, or murder. [A person must give his life rather than commit any of these three sins].

. . . . [And] from where do we know this [law] itself, [that a would-be] murderer [must sacrifice his life rather than commit murder?]—It is [based on] logic, as [we can see from where] that man came before Rabbah and said to him—"The governor of my town told me—'Go kill so and so—and if [you do] not [kill him], I will kill you,' [What shall I do?"] [Rabbah] said to him:—Let him kill you—and do not kill [anyone—for] who says (*mai hazit*) that your blood is redder [than that of your victim?]—Perhaps the blood of that man [whom they want you to kill] is redder [than yours!].

Referred to in the rabbinical literature as the *mai hazit* principle, Rabbah's dictum speaks only of the instance where *A* can save his own life only by *actively* participating in the murder of *B*. But, suppose to save his own life *A* needs only to *passively* participate in the murder of *B*. Does the *mai hazit* principle require *A* to forfeit his life here as well? Addressing himself to this issue, R. Hayyim Soloveitchik (Russia, 1853–1918) posits that authorities are in dispute on this matter. The specific case discussed is: *B* confronts *A* with the threat that "if you don't allow me to hurl you on top of a little child, I will kill you." In this case, R. Isaac b. Mordecai (Germany, ca. 1170) rules that *A* is not required to sacrifice his life in order to save the child from death. In his treatment of the *mai hazit* principle, Maimonides makes no mention of the passive case. This omission leads R. Solevitchik to propose that in Maimonides's view *A* must give up his life even when the demand placed on him is only to assume a passive role in the murder of *B*.[41]

In his analysis of the *mai hazit* principle, R. Mosheh Feinstein avers that *A* must, if necessary, submit to death at the hands of *C* rather than go along with *C's* demand to cause *B's* death, even indirectly. Accordingly, if *C* threatens to kill *A* unless he removes a ladder from the pit in which *B* is trapped, *A* must resist *C's* demand, and instead, submit to death. R. Feinstein bases this ruling on *Rashi's* interpretation of the *mai hazit* dictum. The logic of this dictum, according to *Rashi*, is that it directs us to do the lesser evil. If *A* accedes to *C's* death demand, *A* is guilty of committing murder. In addition, a life is snuffed out. If, on the other hand, A resists *C's* demand, *A* will lose his own life, but will commit no transgression. Since regardless of what *A* does, *one life* will be snuffed out, *A* must submit to death to avoid the compounding of the loss of *one* life with the committing of a sin on his part.[42] Since it is the calculation of what constitutes the *lesser evil* that drives the *mai hazit* dictum, the duty for *A* to submit to death rather than carry out *C's* death demand should apply whether the demand consists of murdering *B* or indirectly causing his death. In both instances *C's* demand on *A* is the commission of a transgression. Resisting *C's* death demand hence avoids the compounding of the loss of *one* life with the commission of a *sin* on the part of *A*. In the opinion of R. Feinstein, R. Isaac b. Mordekhai agrees with the rationale *Rashi* offers for the *mai hazit* dictum. Accordingly, R. Isaac would also agree that *A* must submit to death rather than indirectly cause *B's* death by removing the ladder from the pit where *B* finds himself trapped.[43]

At this juncture, let's summarize our findings regarding the financial obligation associated with *lo ta'amod*. If the harm involved is only a financial loss for *V*, and taking timely action on behalf of *V* would entail a loss for *R*, *R* is not obligated to make the disclosure to *V*. If the harm *V* faces is a threat to his life, *lo ta'amod* requires *R* to take timely action to extricate *V* from the danger he faces. Because *R's* inaction is what makes him guilty of violating *lo ta'amod*, some authorities would excuse *R* if he assessed that taking action would cause him to lose his job. Other authorities dispute this point of leniency. If more than one life is in mortal peril, *R*, according to R. Jehiel Yaakov Weinberg, must take action to save the endangered people, even at risk to his own life. If we follow this line, consideration of possible financial losses for *R* is certainly not a reason to excuse him from engaging in the rescue operation. Finally, concern for loss of job is not an exculpating factor when *R* himself is party to the harm *V* faces.

The discussion regarding the limits of the financial duty of *R* has much relevancy for whistleblowing cases. Consider that whistleblowers usually fare very poorly at the hands of their company. Most are fired. In some instances, they have been blackballed in the whole industry. If they are not fired, they are frequently shunted aside at promotion time and treated as pariahs.[44] It is therefore legitimate for a would-be whistleblower to consider that he will lose his job as a result of his disclosure.

THE HORNS OF THE WHISTLEBLOWER'S DILEMMA IN HALAKHAH

Proceeding from the above analysis is an identification of the horns of the moral dilemma for the whistleblower (*W*). Arguing in favor of whistleblowing is the *lo ta'amod* interdict. Arguing against whistleblowing, on the other hand, is the prohibition against talebearing. How is this conflict between ethical principles resolved? Does *lo ta'amod* suspend the talebearing interdict in a blanket way? Addressing himself to this issue, R. Israel Meir ha-Kohen Kagan, in his classical work *Hafetz Hayyim*, answers in the negative. *Lo ta'amod*, in the opinion of *Hafetz Hayyim*, does not suspend the talebearing interdict unless *W* satisfies a number of restrictive conditions:

1. Disclosing wrongdoing is permissible only if the objective of the whistleblower is to achieve a legitimate benefit (*toelet*). The *toelet* may consist of making whole a victim, including himself, of some wrong suffered at the hands of an offender, such as theft, fraud, or injury. Also qualifying as *toelet* is a disclosure made for the purpose of "degrading the evil in the eyes of the public."[45] The *toelet* here consists of the deterrent effect that the disclosure will have on would-be evil-doers.[46]

2. The whistleblower (*W*) must be *certain* in his own mind that the subject of his report (*S*) has committed the crime or transgression. If *S* is not guilty as accused, *W's* report to the potential victim (*V*) amounts to *motzi shem ra*.

3. Unless *W* is certain that *S* will not accept his complaint, *W* must seek satisfaction by first approaching *S* directly to desist from the conduct and make the necessary amends.

4. *W* must be reasonably certain that *V* will take his report on *S*'s misconduct seriously. If this is not the case, the disclosure should not be made. Moreover, without the prospect of credibility, the disclosure could very well prove counterproductive. Consider the following likely scenario: *V* initially rejects *W*'s report. But, subsequently, *V* becomes disenchanted with *S* and regrets that he rejected *W*'s report. When *V* confronts *S* with an accusation of wrongdoing, he tells him that he should have heeded *W*'s report all along. Invoking *W*'s report in his confrontation with *S* violates the variant of the talebearing prohibition called *rekhilut*. *V*'s *rekhilut* infraction is indirectly brought on by *W*'s initial report.

5. In informing on *S*, *W*'s objective should be for *V* to summon *S* to a *Bet Din* (Jewish court), which will determine the disposition of the case.

6. The damaging report must be known to *W* firsthand. If *W* does not know the objectionable conduct firsthand, *Hafetz Hayyim* is unresolved as to whether the disclosure should be made. In any event, *W*, in this case, may not present his report as fact, but may merely disclose what he has heard and advise the concerned party to exercise caution on the basis of the information.

7. Since exaggeration is falsehood, *W* must exercise caution not to magnify or embellish the offense he is reporting.

8. If *W* assesses that his report will result in *S* suffering penalties more severe than what is due him by dint of Halakhah, the disclosure should not be made.

9. In reporting against *S*, *W*'s actions should be entirely motivated by a desire to secure what is rightfully his and/or to show zealousness for truth and justice. However, if the motivation behind the revelation is a long-standing grudge against the offender or a desire to ridicule or degrade him for his present misdeed, the disclosure should not be made.

10. If *W's* legitimate objectives can be achieved by other means, *lashon ha-ra* should not be resorted to. Similarly, in seeking remedy against *S*, *W* must make every effort to see to it that *S's* degradation is minimized. Indeed, if minimizing *S's* offense in his report to *V* does not compromise *W's* objective, this must be done.[47]

CASE STUDIES

In this section we present a number of case studies dealing with the issue of whistleblowing. These case studies are drawn from the secular business ethics literature. We will then analyze these case studies from the perspective of both De George's criteria and Halakhah.

Fairway Electric

Fairway Electric designs nuclear reactors for public utility companies. Jim Bowen, a lower-level employee at the company, accidentally discovered a 15-year-old report of a flawed construction plan Fairway Electric made for a public utility client. The report revealed that management at that time investigated the matter and found that the flaw was not a safety problem but would predictably result in significant cost overruns for the public utility client. Fearing for its own reputation and financial ruination, top management at Fairway Electric decided against sharing the information on the flaw with the public utility client. Further research by Bowen discovered that, indeed, several years later the public utility client that used Fairway Electric's design had to pay large sums to have the flaw repaired. The utility company was, however, able to pass on the expense of repairing the flaw to the ratepayers.

Standing up for integrity and motivated by a desire to ensure that Fairway Electric would not repeat the corrupt practice he discovered, Bowen pressed his supervisor to have the company make a public disclosure of this matter. Bowen's supervisor, along with top management, refused to do anything about this "mistake" of the past.

Because the company gave him no support, Bowen disclosed what he knew to a newspaper reporter and the story appeared two days later. In making the exposé, the newspaper reporter didn't even look at the Fairway report. It was therefore no surprise that the exposé blew the matter out of proportion. The headline was: FAIRWAY SOLD DEFECTIVE REACTORS-REPORT WARNED OF HAZARD.[48]

The Aircraft Brake Scandal

In 1967, B. F. Goodrich won a contract with the LTV Aerospace corporation to produce wheels and brakes for the new A7D light attack aircraft that LTV had been commissioned to build for the U.S. Air Force. The Goodrich design was appealing to LTV because the brake prototype was relatively small, containing only four disks and weighing just over 100 pounds. The weight of any aircraft is extremely important; the lighter a part is, the heavier the plane's payload can be.

As the A7D brake design underwent preliminary testing at Goodrich, it was readily apparent to Searle Lawson, one of the engineers, that the brake was flawed and that the design would have to be scrapped. Yet despite clear indications that use of the brake in flight-testing would result in brake failure and cause injury or death, the project manager, Robert Sink, insisted that testing continue as if no problem had been detected. Sink ignored Lawson's warnings because Goodrich had already assured LTV that the brake was nearly ready for flight testing, and Sink was not prepared to take the blame for this critical error.

In the end Lawson cooperated with the fraud by describing the results of the qualifying tests with fabricated data. Lawson knew that the false data would be used by the company to certify that the air brake was safe.

Before the certifying report was issued, several B. F. Goodrich personnel were in position to stop the fraud, but they fell short of the mark.

One of those people was the test lab supervisor, Ralph Gretzinger. At various stages, before the certifying report was issued, Gretzinger declared that his lab would under no circumstances issue a false report. However, Gretinzinger's protesting fell short of assuming the role of whistleblower.

Another person who tried to stop the fraud but fell short in accomplishing this goal was the technical writer, Kermit Vandivier. From the beginning of his involvement in the project, Vandivier realized the fraud and vigorously protested it by bringing it to the attention of various supervisory personnel. In the end, Vandivier also reluctantly cooperated by producing the certifying report, complete with various false engineering curves and graphic displays. To alleviate his nagging conscience, Vandivier wrote in the conclusion of the report that the A7D brake "does not meet the intent or the requirements of the applicable specification documents and therefore is not qualified." At no surprise to Vandivier, the negative conclusion was changed to a positive one in the final report.

Within a week after the qualification report was published, flight tests began at Edwards Air Force Base in California. In short shrift, several near crashes during landings forced the Air Force to cancel further flight testing.

Soon after the abortive testing at Andrews, both Vandivier and Lawson resigned their positions and went to the Federal Bureau of Investigation. Several months later, B. F. Goodrich recalled the qualification report and the four-disk brake and announced that it would replace the brake with a new, improved five disk-brake at no cost to LTV.[49]

The Ill-Fated *Challenger* Launch

On January 28, 1986, in sub-freezing weather, the space shuttle *Challenger* was launched from the Kennedy space center. Just 73 seconds into its flight the shuttle exploded. The explosion killed all seven astronauts aboard the flight. The Rogers commission, formed to investigate the tragedy, concluded that the explosion occurred due to the seal failure of a solid rocket booster joint. The tragedy could have been avoided. Morton Thiokol, Inc., the company that manufactured solid fuel boosters for *Challenger*, had previously warned the National Aeronautics and Space Administration (NASA) of the dangers of a cold weather launch. Data from previous launches indicated that the rubbery O-rings designed to seal the boosters' segments lost their resiliency as temperatures decreased. At low temperatures, this problem could cause the shuttle to explode.[50]

On the night before the launch, the forecast for the lift-off was 18 degrees fahrenheit. This forecast led NASA officials to confer with Morton Thiokol via teleconferences regarding the safety of the launch the following morning. In this teleconference, the engineering staff at Morton Thiokol, led by Russell P. Boisjoly, recommended against the launch. Initially, Vice President for Engineering Bob Lund supported his staff's judgment, but after NASA's strong objection, Senior Vice President Jerry Mason allegedly told Lund to "take off your engineering hat, and put on your management hat." At that juncture, Lund reversed himself and recommended that the launch take place as scheduled the following morning.[51]

After the disaster, project supervisor Allen McDonald and Boisjoly "blew the whistle" on Morton Thiokol and testified before the Rogers commission about their objections against the launch. Almost immediately thereafter, Morton Thiokol reorganized its booster design operations and placed McDonald and Boisjoly out of contact with NASA. This realignment move by Morton Thiokol was regarded as retaliation against McDonald and Boisjoly.

Although Congressional pressure eventually led to the restoration of both McDonald and Boisjoly to their former assignments, a major rift had developed within the corporation. Some co-workers believed Boisjoly's testimony had hurt the company's image. Boisjoly and his cohorts had become pariahs. Boisjoly's emotional anguish following the *Challenger* disaster and its aftermath became so great that he eventually requested long-term disability leave for stress-related conditions.[52]

A Whistleblower Makes a Deal

As head of corporate audits for Omicron Pharmaceutical Company, one of Steven Grey's duties was to answer questions FDA auditors had about Omicron's applications for approval of new drugs. In the interview FDA auditors conducted with Grey on Omicron's application for approval for its high blood pressure drug Pepsodine, auditors had some tough questions regarding the company's research data. Grey felt he answered the questions to the satisfaction of the FDA auditors, but the session with the auditors raised doubts in his own mind regarding the reliability of the data he defended. To assuage his own conscience, Grey asked a staff member to bring him photocopies of the original research reports. It took no more than a quick glance at the photocopies for Grey to realize that the raw data in the research department on Pepsodine was entirely different from the data the company filed on its application for approval at the FDA.

Omicron sets out its whistleblowing policy in a handbook the company distributes to all its employees. The policy calls for the whistleblower to report the misconduct to the next highest level above the person who committed the wrongdoing. Grey meticulously followed this procedure and sent his report on the discrepancies he found to Omicron's legal department. On the basis of Grey's complaint, the legal department launched an investigation, which culminated in a report to Omicron's Board of Directors. The report stated that Pepsodine was not only ineffectual, but could be fatal for the patient if taken in combination with other drugs. Acting on the report, the board took decisive action and asked the project coordinator for Pepsodine to tender his resignation. But, to avoid embarrassment and public exposure, the company wanted to move forward and get final approval for Pepsodine from the FDA. The company promised Grey that no harm to the public would result from this course of action because it would never sell a single pill of Pepsodine to the public. Toward this end, the plan called for the company to inform the FDA, shortly after getting final approval for Pepsodine, that it wanted to withdraw its application for approval of the drug because of the discovery of errors it made in marketing projections.

Grey accepted the deal. The board kept their word, and the drug was kept off the market. After the "deal," however, other changes were instituted at Omicron. Corporate policy was revised so that Grey's department no longer had ready access to company records. Under the new policy, audits had to be prearranged with the department involved, and the department could stop an audit and reschedule it at any time. Finally, the department was allowed to review the audit before it was submitted. The effect of these changes was to severely limit the ability of Omicron's audit department to uncover wrongdoing.[53]

Better Late Than Never

Ken Dryden is an ombudsman at Rockland International. This means that Dryden is the contact person for whistleblowers at the company, as he has direct access to Jeremy Flint, Rockland International's CEO.

Dryden got Rockland International to set out its whistleblowing policy in the handbook the company distributes to all its employees. One aspect of the company's policy is the promise that "no employee will suffer any adverse personnel action as a result of making a report in compliance with this policy."

One of the whistleblowing complaints, lodged by Art Holmes, came to Dryden against the backdrop of a downsizing operation the company was undertaking. Rumors were adrift that Flint was planning to eliminate some of the jobs in the purchasing department. Art Holmes was frequently mentioned as a possible casualty. The timing of Holmes's complaint was, to say the least, uncanny. Holmes came to Dryden and claimed that Philip Pines, the head of the purchasing department, was guilty of taking "kickbacks."

Holmes had plenty of documentation to back up his accusation. It consisted of photocopies of dozens of cancelled checks and invoices. A comparison of the invoices with shipments received revealed convincingly that payments had been made for goods not delivered, and that Pines had made the authorization for the checks in every instance. Notwithstanding the solid documentation Holmes came equipped with, Dryden was very troubled by the fact that the checks and invoices in the photocopies were *more than a year old*. Dryden surmised that Holmes had surreptitiously photocopied the evidence as a form of "insurance," and now that he feared being laid off, he was seeking the protective cover provided by the whistleblowing policy. Holmes denied such motives and contended that he feared retaliation from the wrongdoer, who was his immediate boss. Now that he had less to lose, he felt safer in doing his duty. "Better late than never," he quipped.[54]

DE GEORGE ON THE CASE STUDIES

1. Fairway Electric

In extrapolating how De George would deal with Fairway Electric, the most basic point to make is that De George's criteria do not address a case of the genre of Fairway Electric. In De George's formulation, whistleblowing is morally acceptable only when society as a whole can expect to reap a clear-cut net gain from the disclosure. Since whistleblowing will always financially harm the firm that is the target of the informer's report, De George informs us that the above criteria are met on a clear-cut basis only when the harm entails danger to human life or compromises health standards. If the harm is only financial, the case for whistleblowing is much harder to make, especially if the financial loss is spread over many people and from an individual standpoint the monetary loss is slight.

De George bolsters his argument against whistleblowing for the nonserious harm case with the observation that if whistleblowing becomes commonplace, the whistleblower would lose his hero image and, consequently, the public would take whistleblowing less seriously.

Finally, we must recognize that whistleblowers don't always make accurate assessments and are not always morally motivated. If the disclosure of even nonserious harm were morally acceptable, then whistleblowing might become too widespread and would therefore be rendered an ineffective vehicle for change.[55]

The above considerations argue against Bowen's whistleblowing in the Fairway Electric Case. Final judgment on what the De George criteria would recommend in the Fairway case must, however, be reserved. Consider that De George's criteria are designed to maximize the good for society. De George's approach is hence clearly a utilitarian approach.[56] In the utilitarian approach an expected consequence is evaluated in terms of whether it will be *instrumental* in bringing about a good that is valued for its *own sake*.[57] Will Bowen's disclosure bring about a clear-cut social gain? Viewed very narrowly, one could argue in the negative. Consider that the fraud was committed 15 years ago and the public utility suffered no loss in the long run because it passed on the cost overruns to the ratepayers in the form of higher rates. From the perspective of the public the cost of the fraud was spread over a huge customer base. Each individual ratepayer therefore suffered inconsequential monetary loss. But, perhaps a broader perspective is in order. Exposing the fraud offers the prospect of deterring such behavior in the future. To let the fraud slip through the cracks would only encourage bolder varieties of this type of fraud in the future. Indeed, Bowen's motive in pushing for public disclosure of the fraud was clearly for the deterrence effect it would have. Consider, however, that cost overruns that result from faulty construction designs are not an infrequent occurrence. Accordingly, the deterrent effect Bowen was seeking would not be accomplished unless disclosure of the scandal resulted in the implementation of *new procedures* for companies in the business of selling construction designs for nuclear plants. Is Bowen's documentation sufficient to induce reform in the construction design industry? The assessment that the good proceeding for society in making the disclosure outweighs the harm to Fairway's reputation is therefore open to challenge.

Moreover, in evaluating whether Bowen met De George's first condition, let's consider the careless manner in which he went public. Because there was no immediate danger to the public, Bowen should have handed the report to the Nuclear Regulatory Commission (NRC). Putting the matter in the hands of this agency would have confined the issue to monetary fraud, rather than inaccurately portraying the issue as one of public safety. Instead, Bowen went to the local newspaper. The newspaper reporter apparently never even read the document and the subsequent exposé injected a false issue of safety that sullied Fairway's reputation far more than was warranted by the actual facts. To be sure, Bowen scrupulously took his concerns up the corporate ladder and hence satisfied De George's second and third conditions. But, Bowen's act of external whistleblowing may have violated De George's first condition.

2. The Aircraft Brake Scandal

There can be no doubt that Vandivier was dealing with an objectively serious threat to human life. Vandivier's obligation to take action to prevent the harm is therefore firmly established. Consider that before Vandivier went to the FBI, he pushed Gretzinger, Lawson, and Sink to scuttle the A7D project. Before resorting to external whistleblowing, Vandivier hence exhausted the internal mechanism of the firm. Consider also that Vandivier was himself party to the crime of fraud against LTV and the Air Force, and had firsthand knowledge of who his co-conspirators were. Vandivier's story was hence very credible, and exposure of the scandal offered every prospect of resulting in a change of procedures that would prevent debacles like this from occurring in the future. Having met all five of De George's criteria, Vandivier's whistleblowing was mandatory.

One point of criticism is Vandivier's conduct: To be sure, Vandivier's disclosure served society well as far as preventing future debacles, but Vandivier had a more fundamental and immediate duty to inform the Air Force in a timely manner that the air brake was not safe and testing the air brake under flight conditions would endanger the lives of its personnel. In respect to averting danger to the flight pilots and runway personnel, Vandivier's disclosure was not timely.

3. *Challenger* Launch Case

The case involves government and therefore does not fall explicitly within the scope of De George's five-step procedure. Nonetheless, the case easily lends itself to De George's utilitarian approach. Consider that Boisjoly was dealing with an objectively serious threat to human life. Because he had both the expertise and the documentation to make his concerns credible,

Boisjoly had the duty to take action to prevent the harm. Boisjoly voiced his objections to the launch to his superiors at Morton Thiokol, but his protests turned on deaf ears. By exhausting the internal procedures of Morton Thiokol there can be no doubt that Boisjoly proceeded in a manner designed to minimize harm to his company's reputation. Boisjoly's duty to testify to the Rogers commission was hence well-established, notwithstanding the harm his company's reputation suffered thereby.

Boisjoly's actions can, however, be criticized. To be sure, Boisjoly had a duty to society to prevent the *Challenger* debacle from repeating itself. But, Boisjoly's more immediate concern should have been the safety of the seven astronauts aboard *Challenger* on the day of the launch. Because Boisjoly's protests fell on deaf ears, he should have gotten to the astronauts before the launch and warned them of the impending danger they faced.

4. A Whistleblower Makes A Deal

The central issue in this scenario is the ethics for a would-be whistleblower, Grey; to accept a deal. Consider that Grey discovered that Pepsodine represented a definite danger to human life. Since every one of the five criteria De George set is satisfied in the Pepsodine case, Grey is obligated to avert the danger to life for the public. At the same time, De George's utilitarian approach would urge Grey to go about his objective by causing the least harm possible to his company. Given that the company has no past history of either corruption or failure to keep its word, Grey should accept the deal.

Recall that Baines conceptualizes the moral dilemma of the whistleblower as consisting of the conflict between his duty of care and his duty of loyalty. In the Omicron Pharmaceutical case, Grey can easily reconcile these conflicting duties by accepting the deal.

5. Better Late Than Never

In this scenario, the issue is whether the motivation of the whistleblower should be considered in accepting his report. De George's five-step procedure is explicitly addressed only to the would-be whistleblower who desires to make his disclosure for "moral reasons."[58] De George's guideposts hence provide no specific direction for the case at hand.

THE CASE STUDIES AND HALAKHAH

1. Fairway Electric

From the perspective of Halakhah, Bowen's disclosure finds two independent reasons for justification. One legitimate reason is Bowen's stated reason to *deter future fraud* by Fairway Electric. For all intents and purposes, Bowen's disclosure, as discussed earlier, will have no deterrent impact unless his documentation is sufficient to trigger the implementation of *new procedures* for companies in the business of selling construction designs for nuclear plants.

Another and independent reason for Bowen to make the disclosure is to *remedy* as much as possible the fraud of the past. To be sure, the public utility that used Fairway Electric's construction designs suffered no loss in the long run because it passed on the cost overruns to the ratepayers in the form of higher rates. The public, too, suffered inconsequential monetary harm, as the cost of the fraud was spread over a huge customer base. But these circumstances do not mean that remedy for the fraud is now entirely impossible and/or morally unnecessary. From the perspective of Halakhah, if the victims of a fraud cannot be identified, the perpetrator of the fraud is prescribed, as some measure of atonement, to perform public service.[59] This is done in the hope that the victims of the fraud will be included in the group that benefits from the service.[60]

Deterrence is hence not the only reason that legitimizes Bowen's disclosure. The disclosure should also be made to force Fairway Electric to make some form of amends to the victims of the fraud of 15 years ago. Donating money to a charity that serves the largest possible segment of its customer base makes amends of some sort to the original defrauded customer base or to their heirs.

There can be no doubt that the *steps* Bowen initially took when he stumbled across the 15-year-old report squarely met *Hafetz Hayyim's* criteria. By taking his concerns up the corporate hierarchy, Bowen's disclosure plan was to accomplish his objective with the least harm possible to the company.

What directs Bowen to agitate for disclosure is the *lo ta'amod* dictum. But consider that if Bowen is remiss, he violates a negative command of the Torah only in a passive manner. Accordingly, *lo ta'amod* does not direct

Bowen to risk losing his job to get his way. Bowen's struggle with management to force the disclosure must therefore be regarded as supererogatory conduct on his part.

The rebuff Bowen got from management drove him to go public with his disclosure. In deciding whether public disclosure was permissible for Bowen, recall *Hafetz Hayyim's* fifth condition—that *W's* objective should be to bring the matter at hand to *Bet Din* for adjudication. We take it as a given that a society governed by Halakhah would set up specialized courts in each industry. These courts would have both the legal and technical expertise to deal with disputes and issues of public policy pertaining to the industry under their jurisdiction. Let's assume for the moment that the Nuclear Regulatory Commission (NRC) is the *Bet Din* of the nuclear industry. Given the rebuff Bowen suffered at the hands of management, he would be entitled to hand over the evidence to the NRC for investigation. To ensure that Fairway would not suffer penalties disproportionate to its offense, which is *Hafetz Hayyim's* eighth condition, the investigation would have to be conducted discreetly, out of public view. This would ensure, as much as possible, that Fairway would not suffer reputation harm beyond what was warranted.

Bowen opted to break the story of the 15-year-old fraud to the newspapers. Because he was careless in the way he handed over the story, the journalist who wrote the story did not even read the document. In the exposé the journalist accused Fairway of deliberately withholding from its public utility customers that the design of the nuclear reactor was *unsafe*. Bowen's conduct hence grossly violated *Hafetz Hayyim's* fifth and tenth conditions.

Bowen's course of action of handing the document to a journalist for publication would have violated *Hafetz Hayyim's* criteria even if he would have taken all necessary precautions to ensure the accuracy of the article before publication. Recall condition ten that it is *W's* obligation to *minimize as much as possible* the degradation *S* will suffer as a result of the disclosure he makes. Since the wider the audience that receives the disclosure the greater will be the degradation the exposé brings to *S*, Bowen had no right to take the document to a journalist when the NRC route was available to him.

At this juncture, let's consider a variation of this case study: Bowen discovers that the nuclear plant his company designed is unsafe and threatens human life. Bowen brings his concerns to upper management, but his superiors downplay the risk to public safety and refuse to disclose Bowen's findings to the NRC. Bowen's superiors threaten to fire him if he does not lay the entire matter to rest. Is Bowen obligated to press on and lose his job over this matter? Yes. Recall *Hafetz Hayyim's* position that when danger to human life is what is at stake, anyone (R) in the position to avert this danger must take action to do so, even if it entails expending more than one-fifth of one's resources. As discussed earlier, not all decisors concur with this ruling of *Hafetz Hayyim*. But, let's not lose sight of the circumstance that this revised scenario entails a threat to the life of many people. In this instance, as will be recalled, R. Jehiel Yaakov Weinberg maintains that R is obligated, if necessary, to *risk his own life* in order to avert the threat to the lives of many people. If R must risk his own life here, he certainly, if necessary, must expend more than one-fifth of his resources to avert the danger from the public.

2. The Air Brake Scandal

From the perspective of Halakhah, the distinguishing feature of this case study is the circumstance that the whistleblower, Vandivier, was *party* to the fraud B. F. Goodrich committed against LTV and the Air Force. Recall that Vandivier wrote up the false report, in which he embellished Lawson's fabricated data with various false engineering curves and graphic displays. The fact that Vandivier inserted a sentence at the end of the report asserting that the A7D brake does not qualify is not a mitigating factor for him. Consider, Vandivier is the author of a technical document that *screams out* that the brake qualifies. At the time he wrote the report, Vandivier knew firsthand that upper management was fully committed to the report. Finally, Vandivier knew that his report would be reviewed before it would be sent out and the glaring mistake would, therefore, be found out and corrected. All this says that Vandivier's comment that negates the whole report is nothing more than a feeble and transparently insincere attempt to disassociate himself from the scandal that he, himself, was very much a part of.

Given that LTV relies on the report to go ahead to the next stage and test the brakes in an actual flight, any injury or death that results from the use of the faulty brakes is the responsibility of B. F. Goodrich. An analogous case discussed in the Talmud involves the liability of a professional money-changer for giving faulty advice that a coin shown him will circulate. If the moneychanger took a fee for his services, he is liable to make good on the client's loss.[61]

Let's examine the details of the moneychanger case and see why it relates to the case at hand. Some authorities understand the moneychanger case broadly as referring even to the circumstance where the advisee feels free to ignore the moneychanger's advice.[62] Others understand the case narrowly, as referring only to circumstances where the advisee, for all intents and purposes, feels compelled to accept the moneychanger's judgment.[63] This would be the case, for instance, when the advisee was a vendor who received cash payment for his merchandise and the moneychanger is called upon to resolve a dispute between the buyer and the seller as to whether the currency paid will circulate. Should the advisee be free to ignore the judgment of the moneychanger, the latter incurs no liability in the event that he made an erroneous judgment.

We take note that all disputants agree that communication on the part of the advisee that he relies on the judgment of the moneychanger makes the latter liable in the event of error.[64] Receiving payment for his opinion makes it as if the advisee enunciated to the moneychanger that he is relying on his opinion in the matter. Since the damage resulted directly from relying on the expert's advise, the latter's action is a form of *garmi* (indirect damage that should have been foreseen).[65]

There can be no doubt that the contract between LTV and B. F. Goodrich made it clear that LTV would be relying on B. F. Goodrich for the safety of the brake. Consider that LTV accepted B. F. Goodrich's unique, four-disk, lightweight design from among competitive bids. B. F. Goodrich hence knew that LTV would not be buying the same brake from other sources of supply and would be relying on them exclusively for its safety. More fundamentally, LTV required B. F. Goodrich to put the brakes through the qualification tests specified by the military. Any death or injury to test pilots resulting from the fraud should hence be the responsibility of those people at B. F. Goodrich who conspired to issue the false report.

Vandivier's clear-cut duty to take action to avert the danger does not, however, confer him a blanket license to drag the company down in the scandal. Rather, Vandivier is required to reconcile his *lo ta'amod* duty with the prohibition against talebearing. He achieves this reconciliation by pressing his goal to avert the danger while doing so in a manner that minimizes the harm to the company's reputation. Given that the defective brake presents no danger to human life *until* the test piloting stage, Vandivier must first direct his efforts up the corporate ladder at B. F. Goodrich. If these efforts fail, Vandivier is then required to go directly to the Air Force and alert them of the danger. Because breaking the story to the newspaper will probably maximize the harm to B. F. Goodrich's reputation, resorting to this medium should be only a last ditch effort to avert the danger.

The particulars of the air brake scandal point to another area of investigation. Let us add a fictional element to the moral dilemma. Suppose an employee of the firm that had no part in the fraud stumbles onto the fraud. What is the duty of that employee to stop the fraud? To illustrate, suppose Vandivier hands his original report to a management executive, Bertram Klintick. When Klintick notices that Vandivier inserted the phrase "does not meet the intent or the requirements of the applicable specification documents and therefore is not qualified" at the end of his report, Klintick blacks out this phrase with a magic marker and orders his administrative assistant, Abigail Richter, to retype the report and make a clean copy of it. Klintick assumes Abigail will never discover what was crossed out. Klintick is wrong! Abigail takes one look at the very technical report and realizes that she can't handle the graphical displays and hunts down the computer disk that has the original report. All that needs to be done, reasons Abigail, is to erase the last sentence from the report from the computer disk and make a new print-out. In taking this shortcut, Abigail stumbles on the last sentence of the original report that says that the air brake is unsafe. Consider that Abigail has no knowledge of the A7D project and her boss *ordered* her to retype the report. On the basis of what she discovered, Abigail has nothing more than a *suspicion* that something is wrong. Perhaps Abigail is entitled to conclude that she has, in fact, not discovered fraud and there is a perfectly legitimate explanation for what she found. But, suppose Abigail does pursue the matter further, discovers fraud and feels confident that her story will stick and have credibility. However, pursuing the matter internally will, in Abigail's own estimation, put her job in jeopardy. Is Abigail required to pursue this matter at the cost of losing her job? Consider that Abigail's duty to take action to avert the danger proceeds from the *lo ta'amod* interdict. If Abigail fails to take action, her transgression consists of her *inaction*. Because Abigail will lose her job if she takes action, perhaps the one-fifth rule should apply and

Abigail is exempt from getting involved. Recall, however, *Hafetz Hayyim*'s stricture that when loss of life is at stake the one-fifth rule does not apply. To be sure, R. Waldenberg applies the one-fifth rule even here. But, consider that what is at stake here is not just a single life. The faulty brake threatens the lives of all the aircraft and runway personnel and, perhaps, the safety of the general public as well. In this type of situation, according to R. Weinberg, an individual is obligated, if necessary, to put his or her own life at risk in order to avert the danger. Now, if one's life must be put at risk, if necessary, to avert the danger, consideration that taking action might or will result in job loss is certainly not an exempting factor.

Another issue for the last wrinkle in the air brake scandal is whether it is legitimate for Abigail to make use of bluffing. Without any intention to carry out her threat, perhaps Abigail can confront Klintick with the following ultimatum: "Unless you sign off right now on the original Vandivier document, I'll take what I know of the fraud directly to the company CEO." In actuality, Abigail does not have the fortitude to pursue the matter with the CEO. Accordingly, if Klintick does not cave in, Abigail will not pursue the matter further. Ordinarily, bluffing is prohibited conduct, as whatever one commits oneself to do, one should fully intend to carry out.[66] But, perhaps bluffing conduct is permissible here. Elsewhere in this volume, we have discussed the *mat'an* (lit., he deceives them) case. The model case involves a worker (*W*) who is engaged in a project that will cause the employer (*E*) material loss if *W* does not give the job his immediate attention. Suppose *W* wants to quit before the job is completed. Here, *E* has the right to cajole *W* to stay on the job by offering him a raise. If the tactic succeeds, *E* bears no responsibility to make good on his promise for a raise. Moreover, if *W* demands the extra fee up front, the differential pay is recoverable in a *Bet Din*.[67] The rationale behind the *mat'an* principle is apparently that *W*'s unethical conduct *forfeits* for him the entitlement to be treated with the *ordinary* rules of ethical conduct. Applying the *mat'an* rationale here results in giving Abigail license to neutralize the danger to life the A7D represents by the use of the bluff. The rationale behind the *mat'an* principle is, however, not forfeiture. Rather, *mat'an* finds its basis in the principle of *avid inish dina l'nafshai* (a man may take the law into his own hands for the protection of his interests, henceforth *avid inish*). Since the principle in defending one's entitlement is to take the course of action of least harm to the offender, *mat'an* becomes the first line of defense if all persuasion fails. *Mat'an* is the first line of defense because the defendant surely prefers that what is not his should be wrested away from him by means of deception, rather than by means of violence and/or injury.[68] Now, if *mat'an* is rooted in the minimum harm principle, it has no relevancy for the case at hand. Upon stumbling upon the fraud, Abigail is not confronted with a self-help setting, but rather with a duty to save the public from a danger. *Avid inish* hence does not apply to the situation at hand.

The legitimacy for Abigail to resort to bluffing as a first line tactic to prevent the fraud may, however, find legitimacy based on another principle. Consider that it is not Abigail's duty alone to shoulder the burden of extricating the Air Force from the danger of the unsafe brake, but rather this rescue duty theoretically devolves upon everyone. No quasi-contract between Abigail and society to guarantee her job can be identified, however. Since *mat'an* is acceptable in counteracting the unethical conduct of others, it should also be a permissible form of behavior to avoid the shouldering *alone* of a burden that everyone else is theoretically obligated to share. Nonetheless, if *mat'an* fails, Abigail must risk losing her job, if necessary, to save the public. This duty is based, as discussed previously, on the *lo ta'amod* principle.

3. The *Challenger* Launch

A critical feature in deciding Boisjoly's duty in this moral dilemma is the issue of who was on each of the two sides of the controversy as to whether the launch should be postponed. If other engineering experts from Morton Thiokol disputed Boisjoly's view that the launch should be postponed, the argument could be made that Boisjoly should defer to the judgment his firm reached regarding the safety of the launch in cold weather. If the weight of expert opinion was against Boisjoly, Boisjoly should certainly not have voluntarily testified before the Rogers commission, even if he was convinced that the experts were wrong and he was right. Under these circumstances, *Hafetz Hayyim*'s basic condition of *toelet* will not be fulfilled. Consider, however, that the controversy regarding whether the launch should be postponed was never between experts, but rather between management on the one side and the expert engineers on the other.

The controversy, as Professors Lisa Newton and David P. Schmidt put it, "was whether the focus should be on profits or risk."[69] Because there was no weight of expert opinion against him, Boisjoly had a duty to *volunteer* his testimony to the Rogers Commission. The *toelet* he sought was to force NASA to consider the engineering evidence regarding the potential fatal effects that cold weather has on the rubbery O-rings designed to seal the boosters' segments together.

Recall R. Nissim's contention that when the threat to life is not certain, but only probable, *lo ta'amod* requires the bystander's intervention. Accordingly, Boisjoly had a duty to get to the astronauts before the launch and warn them of his concerns.

4. A Whistleblower Makes A Deal

From the perspective of Halakhah, the duty of *W* is to fulfill his *lo ta'amod* duty while minimizing violation of the talebearing interdict. Recall *Hafetz Hayyim's* tenth condition that if *W's* legitimate objectives can be achieved by other means, *lashon ha-ra* should not be resorted to. The elements of the deal Omicron offers consists of forcing out the manager of the Pepsodine project and promising never to market the drug. This approach allows Grey to achieve the objective of averting the harm to the public without blowing the whistle on the company to the FDA. Because Omicron has no past record of committing these types of offences, Grey should not worry that Omicron will either renege on its word not to market the drug or repeat the offense.

5. Better Late Than Never

The distinctive feature of the last case study is *W's* motivation. Recall *Hafetz Hayyim's* ninth condition that *W's* reporting against a culprit should be entirely motivated by either a desire to secure what is rightfully his or to show zealousness for truth and justice. In a clarification of this point, *Hafetz Hayyim* writes that this condition should not be taken to mean that if *A* hates *B*, who is the target of his report, he should not make the disclosure. If *lo ta'amod* compels the disclosure, the report must, nevertheless, be made.[70]

In his work on *Hafetz Hayyim*, R. Binyamin Cohen (New York, contemp.) further clarifies the issue of whether *W* is permitted to make a disclosure against an evildoer (*E*) when he is driven to do so by the hatred he has for *E*. He posits that it depends on the type of benefit that *W* seeks to achieve from his report. If it consists only of a desire to *shame E* for the deterrence effect it would produce, *W's impure* motives *disqualify* him from making his report. This is so because *shaming E* is an aspect of the *mitzvah* of *tokhahah* (reproof), and having impure motives disqualifies an individual from administrating *tokhahah*. In sharp contrast, when the benefit *W* seeks is something tangible, as for example, the restoration of stolen property, *impure motive* is not per se a disqualifying factor. To illustrate, suppose *A* has testimony to offer on behalf of *B* in a monetary case. The testimony will force the defendant *C* to affirm his denial by means of an oath. Notwithstanding that *A* is biased against *C*, he should still offer his testimony, as the testimony will produce a tangible benefit for *B*.[71]

Let's apply R. Cohen's analysis to the case at hand. Consider that Holmes's revelation came about at a time when rumors were adrift that his job might be eliminated. Combine this with the circumstance that the evidence Holmes held against Pines was more than a year old. All this puts to question whether Holmes was truly motivated by zealousness for truth and justice. If Holmes would examine his motives, he would, perhaps, conclude that they are not pure. But, the evidence Holmes has against Pines will surely achieve tangible results. Accordingly, notwithstanding that this course of action will enhance his own job security, the *lo ta'amod* imperative tells Holmes to hand over the evidence.

LEGISLATION PROTECTING THE WHISTLEBLOWER

In this section we will review federal and state legislation designed to protect the whistleblower, and set that legislation against what Halakhah would regard as the proper public policy approach to this issue. On the federal level the most recent legislation is the Sarbanes-Oxley Act of 2002. Previous federal legislation that protected whistleblowers is the Federal False Claims Act of 1863 (amended in 1986) and the Whistleblower Protection Act of 1989. On the state level, more than 35 states have passed laws designed to protect whistleblowers.

Sarbanes-Oxley Act of 2002

Sarbanes-Oxley forbids any public company from discriminating against any employee who lawfully provides information or otherwise assists in an investigation of conduct that the employee "reasonably believes" constitutes a violation of the federal securities laws.

Relief under the statute includes compensation for damages, such as reinstatement with the same level of seniority and back pay with interest.

The statute requires that every public company establish mechanisms to allow their employees to provide information anonymously to the company's board of directors.

Sarbanes-Oxley affords protection only against retaliation based on securities fraud. Whistleblowing of other kinds of wrongdoing remain unprotected under the act. In these cases the whistleblower must rely on the state law, which gives preference to those allegations dealing with public safety.[72]

False Claims Act

Originally passed in 1863 to combat fraud committed against the Union government in the Civil War, a 1986 amendment to this statute is responsible for giving this act its present form. This act embraces the essential concept of a *qui tam* (lit., standing in the shoes of the King) suit. In a *qui tam* suit, an informer pursues a suit for the government as well as for himself. Under the False Claims Act (FCA), the party who is guilty of the false claim is subject to a stiff penalty and the informer is entitled to share in a percentage of the government's recovery.

The provisions of the FCA apply only when the defendant submitted his false claim *knowingly*. Innocent mistakes or mere negligence is a defense to the criminal charge or civil complaint. For the False Claims statute to apply the defendant must be guilty of either "deliberate ignorance" or "reckless disregard."

The penalty the law sets for violators is generally three times the amount of damages that the government sustains.

Finally, the FCA created a course of action for any employee who is "discharged, demoted, suspended, threatened, harassed, or in any other manner discriminated against in the terms and conditions of employment as a result of involvement in a *qui tam* suit."[73]

Whistleblower Protection Act (1989)

Expanding upon the Civil Service Reform Act of 1978, the Whistle-blower Protection Act (WPA) of 1989 protects federal employees against retaliation who engage in whistleblowing in matters relating to public heath and safety.

Under the 1978 act, the government set up an Office of Special Counsel (OSC) to hear complaints of reprisals against whistleblowers.

The WPA considerably advanced the protected speech of whistleblowers. Under the WPA, only content mattered. If the disclosure was reasonable and significant to public policy, then time, manner, place, form, motives, audience, and anything else were all irrelevant.

Under the WPA, an employee who prevails in exposing any prohibited personnel practice is entitled to all reasonable costs incurred in the process.

The WPA allows whistleblowers that prevail to petition for a transfer. This provision recognizes that it can be unrealistic to return to work under a vengeful supervisor after beating that official in litigation. The transfer provision is more an opportunity than a right. The agency's decision to grant the petition is discretionary. However, the employee has rights in respect to getting an explanation for rejection and appeal rights as well.

The heart of the WPA is the reduced burden of proof to win relief. There are three primary changes in the legal standard:

1. Decisions in personnel actions may not be based on whistleblowing disclosures, regardless of the presence or absence of animosity. This provision eliminates the common employer defense that there are "no hard feelings," but a supervisor no longer can work with a dissenter after what was said.

2. Corrective action must be ordered if the protected speech was a contributing factor in the personnel action.

3. The burden of proof is shifted to the employer. By a preponderance of evidence standard the employer must show that the personnel action would have occurred anyway in the absence of protected speech.

In 1994 Congress legislated amendments to the WPA. In these amendments the rights of legitimate whistleblowers were significantly increased. One provision calls for the manager who was responsible for the disciplinary action to be himself investigated when reprisal was a contributory factor in the personnel action.

Another amendment added a "catch-all" clause that effectively outlaws discrimination through "any other significant change in duties, responsibilities, or working conditions."

Another amendment states that employees can successfully prove the connection between whistleblowing and prohibited personnel practice through a time lag, as, for example, when an action is taken after protected speech but before a new performance appraisal.

Finally, it should be emphasized that the Whistleblower Protection Act of 1989 enhances protections for federal employees only.[74]

WHISTLEBLOWER PROTECTION IN STATE COMMON LAW AND LEGSLATION

In his survey of the law on whistleblower protection at the state level, Professor David Culp finds that the protection afforded is inconsistent from state to state. Some states provide no protection; others provide protection only to government employees; while others provide protection in varying degrees to private sector employees.

Michigan was the first jurisdiction to provide general statutory whistleblower protection when it enacted the Michigan Whistleblowers Protection Act in 1981. Covering public and private sector employees, the Michigan statute provides the whistleblower protection unless he knows that his "report is false."

Another salient feature of the Michigan act is that it does not require the whistleblower to report wrongdoing within the company before reporting the wrongdoing to a public body.

Legislation in other states does not follow the Michigan model in all respects. In Florida, for instance, the whistleblower does not receive protection unless she first informs her employer and allows the employer the opportunity to correct the problem. In addition, the whistleblower is protected only if she discloses or threatens to disclose the misconduct to the appropriate government agency. No protection is afforded the whistleblower if she discloses the misconduct to the public or to interested parties.

In contrast to Michigan law that protects the whistleblower under a subjective good faith standard, Florida and New Jersey law protect the whistleblower only if she acted reasonably (an objective standard).

The New Jersey statute is only concerned with illegal conduct that harms the public. Hence, it does not protect whistleblowing relating to fraudulent activity committed by management within the company itself.

Many states protect the whistleblower from retaliation only if the whistleblowing is in regard to the company having violated a law, rule, or regulation. The implication of such a rule, according to Culp, is that unless the whistleblower can pinpoint a statute that the company has violated, the law does not protect him or her from retaliation.

Another omission in the legislation and judicial decisions is protection for the whistleblower when he contacts the media or the public with his concerns.

In his critique of the current state of legal protection afforded the whistleblower, Professor David Culp makes a number of proposals and offers some new directions.

One of Culp's ideas is that the legal system should require employees, in all but the most exigent of circumstances, to raise their concerns initially through internal corporate channels before blowing the whistle externally to either a government agency or the public. This would give employers the initial opportunity to correct their own violations and put their house in order.

Internal whistleblowing, in Culp's opinion, carries little detriment for the firm. The firm will only benefit from a policy that encourages employees to come forward and discuss within the firm their concerns about the company's alleged mismanagement, negligence, or abusive practices. Such an open door policy may result in the company focusing clearly and thoroughly on a problem and averting potential losses. In sharp contrast, external whistleblowing carries with it the potential for considerable undeserved harm to a company's reputation if the accusations are either wrong or exaggerated. Recognition that wrongful accusation by the whistleblower carries with it much greater potential harm for the firm in the external case compared to the internal case leads Culp to propose that the external whistleblower should be subject to a greater burden before receiving protection under the law. For the internal whistleblower, Culp's standard for protection against retaliation is only that the report be made in "good faith." In sharp contrast, the external whistleblower should be protected only if he makes a good faith, reasonable investigation of the wrongdoing, and only when the company is actually guilty of the wrongdoing the whistleblower accuses it of.

Because the objective of whistleblower protection law is to avert harm to the public, the whistleblower should not be burdened to pinpoint a particular law that the company's practices or policies violate. To qualify for protection against retaliation, it should be sufficient for the whistleblower to demonstrate that the company's practices will generate harm to the public.

As far as coverage is concerned, whistleblower protection law, in Culp's view, should include private as well as public employees. Moreover, in the instance where there is a threat of substantial harm to the public or to individuals, the law should protect the whistleblower from retaliation regardless of the party to whom the employee reports the wrongdoing.

The *Challenger* space shuttle disaster of January 28, 1986, described earlier, provides a case in point. The *Challenger* tragedy demonstrates that when there is a clear-cut danger to life and both company and government officials turn a "deaf ear" to the danger, the whistleblower should have the right to go public as a means of averting the danger. Moreover, Culp argues that Boisjoly had the right, and indeed a moral responsibility, to go directly to the seven astronauts and voice his concerns to them. This would have shifted the decision to fly or not to fly to the astronauts themselves.

One of the lessons of the *Challenger* tragedy, according to Culp, is that there is a need to revise current statutes to expand protection for the whistleblower under certain conditions when he or she goes public. Ordinarily, the whistleblower should be expected to raise his or her concerns internally within the company before proceeding to the appropriate government agency. A government agency should be the recipient of a complaint only if the company's response is unsatisfactory. Nevertheless, in some situations, the employee should be permitted to blow the whistle directly to the public or to the people affected where the potential for harm is great and time is of the essence.[75]

WHISTLEBLOWER LEGISLATION AND HALAKHAH

In this section we will make the case for whistleblower legislation in the Torah society and extrapolate what the contours of this legislation would look like. We begin by recalling that the essence of the moral dilemma for the would-be whistleblower (*W*) is to properly reconcile his *lo ta'amod* duty with the prohibition against *lashon ha-ra*. If *W* observes *Hafetz Hayyim's* protocol, described earlier in this chapter, making the disclosure will either be *W's* absolute duty, or, at the very least, an act that is morally praiseworthy. But, often *W* will put his job at risk by making the disclosure. Under these circumstances, *W* will either be exempt from making the disclosure or find himself torn between his sense of duty on the one hand, and his self-interest on the other. Compounding *W's* dilemma is his facile ability to pretend he is not aware of the wrongdoing. In the absence of social pressure to urge *W* to do the right thing, *W* might very well be tilted in the direction of self-interest. Without a public policy that protects the legitimate *W*, the course of action *W* takes can often produce results that are unacceptable from a social standpoint. Society should not have to suffer the tragedy of severe injury or loss of life when *W* decides, rightfully or wrongfully, that silence is the appropriate course of action.

With the aim of encouraging the legitimate whistleblower to make his or her disclosure, society should protect him or her against reprisals of any shape and form. This protection amounts to nothing more than an encouragement to take the high moral ground and not to be penalized for doing so.

In Judaism, the guidepost for interpersonal conduct is the duty to emulate God's attribute of mercy. This behavioral norm is called *imitatio Dei* (imitation of God).[76] One aspect of God's mercy is the weakening of the power of the Evil inclination that He effects for those who strive for moral betterment.[77] Emulating this Divine Attribute translates into a duty for society to do its utmost to create a favorable moral climate that encourages people to do the morally right thing.[78] The aforementioned indicates that society should protect the legitimate whistleblower from reprisals. But, consider that disclosure by a whistleblower is legitimate only if the protocols of *Hafetz Hayyim* are followed before the disclosure is made. Protection against reprisals hence should be afforded to *W* only if he/she followed *Hafetz Hayyim's* protocols before making the disclosure. If *Hafetz Hayyim's* protocols shape the nature of the whistleblower protection act in the Torah society, many differences emerge between current legislation in the United States and the approach the Torah society would take. Let us examine these differences.

One fundamental difference is the ambit of protected speech. There can be no doubt that the ambit of protected speech is more expansive in the halakhic system than in secular law. Recall that the New Jersey statute does not protect whistleblowing relating to fraudulent activity committed by management within the company itself. From the perspective of Halakhah, the legitimate whistleblower should be afforded protection whether his/her report relates to misconduct within the firm or to the misconduct the firm committed against outsiders. In addition, within the halakhic system, both private and public employees should qualify for protection.

Another difference relates to procedure. Recall that federal law protects W when he reports misconduct of his firm to the government even if W did not first exhaust the internal hierarchy of the firm in making his disclosures. In the halakhic system, W should not be afforded protection unless he adheres to the following procedure. If A observes his co-worker or supervisor B engaged in wrongdoing, A's immediate obligation is to confront B with what he observed and urge him to make amends. To go over B's head and report B's misconduct to either someone within the firm or someone outside the firm is a *prima facie* violation of the prohibition against *lashon ha-ra*. Going over B's head becomes permissible only when either the confrontation produces no results or A assesses in advance that approaching B directly would be fruitless and/or result in retaliation against him. With the aim of achieving a remedy for the victim, but at the same time *minimizing B's* degradation, A must generally exhaust the internal hierarchy of command before disclosing the conduct to the government. Because disclosure of the misconduct to the media maximizes the humiliation of the one accused of the misdeed, taking this approach should be permitted only as a last resort, or when time is of the essence and going through channels will take too long.

Another difference relates to the degree of substantiation we expect from the whistleblower before we qualify his speech for protection. Consider that the prohibition against *lashon ha-ra* is suspended for W only because we expect a definite benefit (*toelet*) to proceed from his disclosure. No benefit is likely to proceed from W's disclosure when he cannot make *a case that will stick* against the defendant. If W has nothing going for him other than making his disclosure in "good faith," he has no business making the disclosure in the first place and hence should not qualify for protection.

One caveat should, however, be noted. In discussing the criteria for *toelet*, *Hafetz Hayyim* specifically includes the desire on the part of the whistleblower to vent his suspicions against someone as meeting the standard. *Hafetz Hayyim* bases this on the verse, "If there is concern in a man's heart *yashenna* and a good word will make it cheerful" (Proverbs 12:25). One opinion in the Talmud connects *yashenna* with the root *suh*, "to speak." The meaning of the verse is that *A* can mitigate the pain he feels when he has a worry or concern by sharing the disquietude with *B*. In *Hafetz Hayyim's* understanding, the disquietude spoken of in the verse includes the pain of being victimized. *A's* talk with *B* hence entails *lashon ha-ra*. However, by relating to *B* the evil that *C* inflicted on him, *A* can hope to mitigate his pain and even receive a comforting word from *B*. We will refer to the above dispensation to relate *lashon ha-ra* as the *venting out* caveat.[79]

The venting out caveat requires further elaboration. Relating *lashon ha-ra* is a moral pitfall regardless of what motivates it. If *A* does not preface his report by telling *B* that his intention is merely to use him as a sounding board, and he should not pass along anything he is about to say, *B* might accept the evil report and be guilty of accepting *lashon ha-ra*. Moreover, unless a relationship of trust exists between *A* and *B*, *A* can never be sure that his admonition for confidentiality will be heeded. These concerns lead to the proposition that *A* may not relate *lashon ha-ra* to *B* for the purpose of mitigating his disquietude *unless B* is a confidential person and A tells him that he desires only to use him/her as a sounding board and he/she should not pass on the information to anyone else.

Understanding *Hafetz Hayyim's* venting out caveat in this limited manner leads to the proposition that an ethics officer or ombudsman would serve a very useful purpose in reducing the occurrences of *lashon ha-ra* within the firm. The ombudsman would be the person to go to if anyone had concerns that the firm was committing wrongdoing. It would be the job of the ombudsman to evaluate the information provided and make the determination whether further action was warranted. The ombudsman must go about his investigation while maintaining *W's* anonymity. If *W* brings his concerns regarding company policy or the conduct of individuals within the firm to the ombudsman, his report, regardless of the evidence he presents to back it up, should be protected speech. The position of ombudsman hence fosters *healthy dissent* within the firm.

Once the ombudsman evaluates *W's* report and determines that the matter should be dropped, *W* may not engage in *lashon ha-ra* regarding the conduct or the policy. If *W* engages in *lashon ha-ra* after the ombudsman has determined that *W's* concerns are baseless, *W's* speech is no longer protected speech and the firm is within its rights to discipline *W* and even fire him. One caveat should, however, be noted. If *W* can make a case that will "stick" against the wrongdoer or can show that the firm's policy is dangerous to the public's welfare, *W's* speech should be treated as protected speech, notwithstanding the rebuff *W* receives from the ombudsman. In fact, *W's* ability to make the case against the wrongdoing should be taken as *prima facie* evidence that the ombudsman was not doing his job.

WHISTLEBLOWER LEGISLATION AND THE *MITZVOT* OF *HATZALAH* AND *HASHAVAT AVEIDAH*

The case for whistleblower legislation in the *Torah* society is considerably bolstered in consideration that *W* generates definite benefits for society. These benefits, although not necessarily measurable with precision, are at least identifiable. The whistleblower is very much akin to the one who rescues someone from peril (*matzil*) or restores lost property (*meshiv aveidah*) to its owner. The monetary protection Halakhah affords these benefactors provides an underpinning for whistleblower legislation in the *Torah* society.

One important principle, enunciated by R. Asher b. Jehiel (Germany, 1250–1327) and others, is that the would-be rescuer (*R*) is not required to expend resources saving someone (*V*) from mortal peril when *V* has the ability to save himself with his own money. *R* is hence entitled to full reimbursement of any expenses he incurred in effecting the rescue.[80]

Given that no advance arrangement was made between the parties, the legal principle behind *V's* reimbursement responsibility to *R* requires clarification. Perhaps the legal principle here is that an implicit or quasi-contract exists between *R* and *V*. *Two presumptions* stand behind this quasi-contract. One presumption is that *V* values his life more than his wealth.[81] Accordingly, if *V* finds his life in peril, he presumably *implicitly communicates* that he will pay, *if necessary*, any sum *R* demands to affect his rescue. At the same time, we may presume that *R* undertakes the rescue with the intention to be compensated for his efforts. Since *R* did not explicitly stipulate a price for undertaking the rescue, *R* is entitled to claim no more than what we may reasonably presume is his minimum demand to undertake the rescue. Now, if R would have been otherwise idle at the time, the expenses he incurred in effecting the rescue is the payment we should presume he would demand to undertake the task at hand. Increasing R's payment to include compensation for the toil and effort involved in the rescue operation itself is not done, however. This is so because in the face of V's life-threatening situation, R has a religious duty (*mitzvah*) to take on the work of rescue.[82] Taking compensation for the toil and effort one expends in doing a *mitzvah* is prohibited.[83] Although we may not reward R for the toil and effort he exerted on behalf of V, R is not required to incur any loss in rescuing V from mortal peril when V himself has the ability to pay. What loss does R incur when he interrupts his own job and takes on the rescue work? Given the assumption that R prefers leisure to work, compensating him with the sum he would demand if asked to abandon his work in favor of leisure makes R whole.

An extreme variant of the case where R abandons his work to save V from a life threatening danger occurs when R is told that he will be fired on the spot if he abandons his work. Because the cost of losing his job is both part of R's presumed minimum demand for getting involved in the rescue operation and is also, from the perspective of V, part of the minimum necessary cost to effect his rescue, this sum is included in the quasi-contract that exists between the parties.

Recall that whistleblowers usually fare very poorly at the hands of their company. Most are discriminated against, denied promotions, or fired because of the actions they have taken. Their reputations are forever sullied in their respective industries and they recognize that job loss and various forms of pernicious discrimination are almost inevitable. For this reason, protection for W against these expected debits becomes the necessary costs to bring forth W's disclosure. It is up to legislation to guarantee these protections.

Whistleblowers also expose fraud. The legal underpinning for legislation to protect W when the benefit he/she generates is only monetary in nature is the *meshiv aveidah* case. The Talmud discusses two variants of the *meshiv aveidah* case. In one variant the owner (O) is present as the *meshiv* (R) goes about the rescue operation; in the other, O is not present. Let's delineate both cases with the following example: Suppose a flood threatens to drown both R's and O's donkeys. O's donkey is worth \$200, while R's donkey is worth only \$100.

In the first variant, O is on the scene. With time to save only one donkey, R tells O that he will abandon his own \$100 donkey in order to save O's \$200 donkey. R stipulates that his compensation for saving O's donkey shall be \$100, which is the loss he suffers as a result of saving O's donkey. The stipulation is legally binding. If O is not on the scene, R can make this same stipulation to a group of three. This group can agree to a compensation for R up to and including the \$200 market value of the donkey R seeks to save.

If O is on the scene and R fails to stipulate his terms, R's reward for saving O's donkey consists of no more than the usual compensation taken for this type of work.[84] If O is not on the scene, then O's liability to R consists of the \$100 value of R's donkey. This value is the loss R sustains as a result of engaging in the rescue of O's \$200 donkey.[85]

Another variant of this case occurs when R interrupts his work to engage in the salvage operation. Here, if R stipulates with either O or, in his absence, with a group of three, that he undertakes the salvage operation only if he/she will be compensated for his/her entire foregone earnings, R's stipulation is valid.[86] If O was on the scene, but R failed to stipulate, O's liability to R consists of only the compensation that is usually taken for this type of work.[87]

One final case. Suppose neither O nor a group of three is on the scene and R interrupts his work in order to engage in the salvage operation. The compensation due R here is equal to the wages of a *po'el batei*l, (i.e., an idle worker).[88]

What this calculation entails is a matter of dispute. R. Asher b. Jehiel understands *po'el bateil* as the wages R would demand if he were asked to abandon his usual work in favor of the presumably lighter work of restoring lost property.[89] R. Jacob b. Asher (Spain, 1270–1343) calculates the sum to be equal to the amount R would demand if he were asked to abandon his usual work in favor of idleness.[90] Finally, Nahmanides (Spain, 1194–1270) understands the payment to be equal to the sum R would demand if he were asked to work at his usual job during the off season.[91] Underlying these calculations is the recognition that R's preoccupation with his own work at the moment he encountered the *mitzvah* of *hashavat aveidah* exempts him from getting involved in the *mitzvah*.[92] Because R need not involve himself/ herself in the *mitzvah*, he/she is fully entitled to some measure of compensation for his/her toil and effort for engaging in the task at hand. All these calculations represent different perspectives on how to calculate the *minimum compensation R* would demand for doing the work of *hashavat aveidah*.[93]

Once the nature of the relationship between *W* and the *meshiv aveidah* is recognized, it is but a small step to see that *meshiv aveidah* provides a basis for legislation to protect *W* when his/her disclosure exposes fraud. Let's use the following scenario to demonstrate this point:

> Nuclear Horizons, an engineering consulting firm, was hired by the Consolidated Energy Group of Eden Commons to blunt EPA demands that the power company should construct cooling towers to protect fish from excessively warm water that the company was discharging into the river. Nuclear Horizons submitted a report to the EPA contending that its research concluded that the long-term effects of the utility's effluent on fish were negligible. Morris Pillsberg, a scientist on the engineering consulting firm's team, knew that the report his company submitted was false. On the basis, of his own research, Pillsberg believed that the fish could be significantly harmed by the warm water discharge. For two years, Pillsberg tried to get his superiors at the engineering consulting firm to own up to the false report, but to no avail. The repeated rebuffs finally drove Pillsberg to send seventy documents supporting his allegations to the EPA. As soon as the firm got wind of the fact that Pillsberg had sent documents to the EPA, he was fired.[94]

In analyzing this case, there can be no doubt that Pillsberg is a legitimate whistleblower. Before blowing the whistle on Nuclear Horizons, he exhausted the internal mechanism of the firm to no avail. Given that Pillsberg was fired because he discovered that his company engaged in fraud, his discharge was unjust. Moreover, Pillsberg's disclosure will stop Nuclear Horizon's practice and generate a clear-cut benefit to society. At the very least, the benefit consists of markedly increasing the supply of healthy fish for the marketplace over the long run. Additionally, Pillsberg's action prevents future production of unhealthy fish, averting a heath hazard of unknown dimensions for the public. Clearly, a quasi-contract exists on an abstract level between Pillsberg and the public to make the disclosure and protect public interests in exchange for protecting him against retaliation of all sorts. But who will *enforce* this contract and encourage Pillsberg to do the right thing? No one. Because the marketplace breaks down here and fails to produce the desired result, the case for *legislating* protection for *W* is appropriate.

Relevant at this juncture is the view of R. Israel b. Gedaliah Lipschutz (Germany, 1782–1860) that the Talmudic sages enacted a special ordinance that the owner of a lost article must reward *R* for his efforts, even if *R* incurs no loss whatsoever in restoring the lost article. The Rabbis felt compelled to enact this legislation because they observed that people were generally lax in undertaking the *mitzvah* of *hashavat aveidah*, even when getting involved did not entail for the *meshiv* any loss whatsoever.[95] R. Lipschutz's expanded understanding of the monetary rights of the *meshiv* provides a halakhic underpinning for legislation to call for rewarding the one who uncovers fraud with a percentage of the recovered monies. To be sure, rewarding *W* for uncovering fraud is not in order unless he/she followed *Hafetz Hayyim's* protocols. Another important requirement for such a law is that it should be structured to maximally encourage *W* to exert his/her efforts to make the company own up to its wrongdoing, as opposed to going directly to the government with the information that he/she possesses.

PRECLUDING THE NECESSITY OF WHISTLEBLOWING

In this final section we will take up practices the firm can adopt to preclude the necessity for external whistleblowing.

In his treatment of this issue, Professor Michael Davis presents a number of ideas that relate to organizational structure and the incentive system of the firm. These ideas are designed to encourage employees to report wrongdoing through internal channels.

With respect to organizational structure, Davis recommends that the firm build invitations into its everyday routine to encourage employees to report bad news. One way to implement this idea is to include a space for "disadvantages" and "risks" in reporting forms employees routinely fill out. Along the same lines, the firm could schedule review meetings for the purpose of identifying problems.

Another idea relating to organizational structure is for the firm to create alternative channels for relating bad news so that no one in the firm is in a position to block its flow upward. This objective can be accomplished in many different ways. One way is for the firm to submit to a regular outside audit. Another is an "open door" policy that allows subordinates to go directly to a senior official. Still another method is to give employees routine access to more than one superior in the organization. Such arrangements give a manager reason to be thankful that he has heard the bad news from a subordinate rather than from a superior and to respond in a way likely to satisfy the subordinate. At the same time, the subordinate has saved the manager from being "blindsided." These arrangements would help correct the underlying problems, and at the same time would minimize the occurrence of whistleblowing.

Establishing the appropriate incentives for managers to accept bad news and to act upon it appropriately will also work to prevent external whistleblowing, and at the same time, work to make the members of the firm more committed morally. Toward this end, the firm should hold a manager responsible for what he or she does on the job, even if the consequences of the actions occur in a time frame beyond the manager's "watch." Assigning responsibility this way will give a manager the incentive to want subordinates to report the bad news about someone's work as soon as they learn of it.[96]

In theological terms, Davis's thesis recognizes the *moral weakness* of members of a firm, particularly subordinates, to question, to dissent, or to speak out against what appears to them as wrongdoing in the firm. Organizational structure and the proper incentive system can work, however, to make all members of the firm more committed to doing the right thing. On the basis of the principle of *imitatio Dei*, innovations that promise to fortify the *moral fiber* of the members of an organization should be implemented.

De George deals with the issue of precluding the need for whistleblowing as a means of correcting wrongdoing. One suggestion he makes is that a firm should establish the position of ombudsman. The purpose of the ombudsman would be to hear complaints or moral concerns of employees. The ombudsman would also participate in the formulation of company policy and it would be the function of the person occupying this position to recommend the appropriate course of action for the firm from a moral standpoint.[97]

De George's idea that the firm should hire an ombudsman to hear the complaints and moral concerns of employees is very much consonant with *Hafetz Hayyim's* notion, discussed earlier, that *A* does not violate the laws of *lashon ha-ra* if he vents out to *B* the anguish he feels as a victim. The implication to be drawn from *Hafetz Hayyim's* position is that the firm, as De George argues, should hire an ombudsman to hear out employee complaints and moral concerns. Complaints brought to the ombudsman would be treated in confidence and the employee would be protected against reprisal as long as the ombudsman does not tell him to drop the matter.

De George's proposal that the ombudsman should be given the task of presenting the ethical perspective in the firm's policy-making decisions is a *proactive* approach Halakhah would view very favorably. Let's consider the implications of De George's idea from the perspective of Halakhah. The most fundamental point is that if the firm is committed to moral conduct, it must educate its employees as to what the law says generally and how it pertains to the specific business in which the firm is engaged. Hillel's dictum is apt here: A boor cannot be fearful of sin; an unlearned person cannot be scrupulously pious (Avot 2:6). Educating a workforce to avoid illegal conduct and moral pitfalls requires the ombudsman not only to conduct seminars in the firm on commercial law, but also to demonstrate how the general principles apply to the specific business and practices of the firm.

Possessing precise knowledge as to what the law demands in respect to the situation at hand is only the first step in preventing wrongdoing. We must recognize that the marketplace is chock full of opportunities to engage in veiled misconduct. Unless an individual is truly God fearing, merely possessing the knowledge that the contemplated conduct is criminal or immoral will not be enough to deter him or her from committing the misdeed when he or she is convinced that the misconduct will go undetected. Elsewhere, we have demonstrated that the *Torah's* approach to overcoming veiled misconduct is through moral education. This program must begin at early youth and is the responsibility of parents and the educational enterprise. The program consists of training in truth telling, training against selfishness and envy, and the fostering of the attribute of gratitude.[98]

SUMMARY AND CONCLUSION

Our comparative study on how whistleblowing is treated in secular society and in Halakhah has uncovered significant differences in approaches. One significant difference is the protocol the would-be whistleblower faces. This point can be seen by setting De George's five-step procedure alongside

Hafetz Hayyim's criteria for reconciling the prohibition against *lashon ha-ra* with the duty of *lo ta'amod*.

De George proposes using his procedure only when the disclosure is done to avert a serious harm to the public, consisting of a threat to life or a health hazard. Moreover, De George intends his criteria to apply only to cases relating to nongovernmental, impersonal, external whistleblowing. In sharp contrast, the scope of *Hafetz Hayyim* procedures applies to any circumstance where a *toelet* will proceed from the disclosure.

De George's approach is a distinctly utilitarian approach. If whistleblowing is justified, it is only because the good it produces outweighs the harm it causes to those responsible for the harm. In contrast, *Hafetz Hayyim's* approach focuses entirely on the victim or potential victims. If the disclosure will produce a *toelet* in the form of restitution for a victim or deterrence against future harm, the disclosure should be made, provided, of course, that *Hafetz Hayyim's* other criteria are also met.

In De George's formulation, disclosure moves from the permissible to the mandatory level when one has documentation to make one's case and, in addition, is convinced that disclosure will result in the implementation of the necessary changes to avert serious harm. Satisfaction of these latter conditions is what is needed in *Hafetz Hayyim's* system to inspire confidence on the part of *W* that his disclosure will produce a *toelet*. But, once the *toelet* condition is in place, *W's* disclosure will be *mandatory*, provided, of course, that *Hafetz Hayyim's* other conditions are satisfied. Hence, the distinction between *permissible* and *mandatory* whistleblowing hardly exists within *Hafetz Hayyim's* system. This distinction comes into play only when the harm involved is merely financial in nature. Here, if *W* assesses that his disclosure will put his job in jeopardy, *W* need not make the disclosure. But, making the disclosure is permissible and regarded as supererogatory conduct. Another circumstance where whistleblowing is supererogatory, but not mandatory, is the instance where the disclosure puts *W's* life in peril. Nonetheless, if the disclosure averts a danger to the lives of many people, some authorities consider the disclosure here as mandatory.

De George's treatment of internal whistleblowing clashes severely with Halakhah. To be sure, the prohibition against *lashon ha-ra* is not absolute, but a wrongdoer does not forfeit protection against *lashon ha-ra*, as De George would have it, just because the wrong he commits is against an individual (e.g., an employer) rather than the public. Such an individual is no less entitled to *Hafetz Hayyim's* ten-step protection against *lashon ha-ra*. Likewise, the only consideration in deciding whether *lo ta'amod* is potentially operational is the determination that a *toelet* will be achieved. Consideration that the wrongdoing observed does not fall within the purview of the job description *W* was hired for does not relieve *W* of his or her *lo ta'amod* duty. Similarly, the concern that the disclosure might contribute to the fostering of an unhealthy corporate culture or the fostering of a police state mentality does not, other things equal, vitiate the anticipated *toelet for the victim*, and hence does not suspend *lo ta'amod*. *W's* concern that the disclosure might jeopardize his/her position in the firm is, however, a legitimate concern when the *toelet W* seeks is averting a financial loss for one or even many people.

Another point of difference between De George and *Hafetz Hayyim* is in respect to motivation. De George's five-step procedure explicitly addresses only the would-be whistleblower who desires to make his disclosure for "moral reasons." De George hence provides no guideposts for the whistleblower that makes his disclosure "not for moral reasons." In contrast, *Hafetz Hayyim* exhorts *W* not to make his disclosure either out of hatred for the wrongdoer or to acquire a benefit for himself. Rather, the disclosure should be made with the intention to accomplish a *toelet*. The implication to be drawn here is that in the absence of pure motives, the disclosure should not be made. Nonetheless, later authorities understand that if the *toelet* consists of making the victim whole, the absence of pure motivation on the part of *W* should not hold him/her back. If, on the other hand, the *toelet W* seeks is not tangible, but merely has the effect of deterring future harm, the disclosure should not be made unless it is rooted in pure motivation.

In Jewish society the guidepost for legislation is the *imitatio Dei* principle. As it pertains to whistleblower legislation, the *imitatio Dei* principle translates into a duty for society to do its utmost to create a favorable moral climate that encourages people to do what is morally correct. Given the severe reprisals the legitimate whistleblower has faced, there is a need for legislation that protects the legitimate whistleblower from discrimination. But, consider that disclosure by a whistleblower is legitimate only if the protocols of *Hafetz Hayyim* are followed before the disclosure is made. Protection against reprisals hence should be afforded *W* only if he followed *Hafetz*

Hayyim's protocols before making the disclosure. If *Hafetz Hayyim's* guidelines shape the nature of the whistleblower Protection Act in the Torah society, many differences emerge between current legislation in the United States and the approach the Torah society would take.

The monetary rights of one who restores lost property (*meshiv*) provide a legal underpinning for legislation that confers a reward for one who uncovers fraud. To be sure, rewarding *W* for uncovering fraud is not in order unless he followed *Hafetz Hayyim's* protocols. Another important requirement for such a law is that it should be structured to maximally encourage *W* to exert his efforts to make the company own up to its wrongdoing, as opposed to going directly to the government with the information that he has.

A fundamental moral challenge to the issue of whistleblowing is the setting up of both an organizational structure and a corporate culture that preclude this phenomenon in the first place.

In respect to organizational structure, our study presented the ideas of Professor Michael Davis. One of Davis's main ideas is that the firm should create alternative channels for bad news so that no one in the firm is in a position to block its flow upward.

Halakhah would fully endorse Davis's ideas. In theological terms, Davis's thesis recognizes the *moral weakness* of members of a firm, particularly subordinates, to question, to dissent, or to speak out against what appears to them as wrongdoing in the firm. Organizational structure and the proper incentive system can make all members of the firm more committed to doing the right thing. On the basis of the principle of *imitatio Dei*, innovations that serve to fortify the *moral fiber* of the members of an organization should be implemented.

In respect to the creation of a corporate culture that precludes the entire phenomenon of whistleblowing, we drew upon De George's idea that the firm should provide for the position of ombudsman. The purpose of the ombudsman would be to hear complaints or moral concerns of employees. The ombudsman would also participate in the formulation of company policy and would advise the firm with respect to the matter under consideration from a moral standpoint.

De George's idea that the firm should hire an ombudsman to hear the complaints and moral concerns of employees is very much consonant with

Hafetz Hayyim's notion that *A* does not violate the laws of *lashon ha-ra* if he vents to *B* the anguish he feels as a victim.

De George's proposal that the ombudsman should be given the task of presenting the ethical perspective in the firm's policy-making decisions is a *proactive* approach Halakhah would view very favorably. The firm must educate its employees about the boundaries of the laws pertinent to their particular business. Educating a work force about illegal conduct requires that the ombudsman conduct seminars in the firm on commercial law and its application.

Possessing precise knowledge of what the law demands in respect to the situation at hand is only the first step in avoiding wrongdoing. We must recognize that the marketplace provides many opportunities for veiled misconduct. A carefully developed program designed to properly educate people about ethical issues can help teach them ways to overcome the temptation of veiled misconduct. But, it must be recognized that moral education begins as the responsibility of parents and educators. Society would benefit tremendously by encouraging training in truth telling, stressing the deleterious effects of selfishness and envy, and emphasizing the importance of the attribute of gratitude.

NOTES

1. Manuel G. Velasquez, *Business Ethics Concepts and Cases*, 4th ed. (Upper Saddle River, NJ: Prentice Hall, 1998), pp. 454–455.
2. Leonard M. Baynes, "Just Pucker and Blow: An Analysis of Corporate Whistleblowers, the Duty of Care, the Duty of Loyalty, and the Sarbanes-Oxley Act," *St. John Law Review*, Fall 2002, Vol. 76, Issue 4, pp. 883–888.
3. Professor Richard T. De George, e-mail to the author, January 10, 2001.
4. Richard T. De George, *Business Ethics*, 5th ed., (Upper Saddle River, NJ: Prentice Hall, 1999), p. 250.
5. Ibid. p. 250, pp. 246–257.
6. Ibid. pp. 242–246, 257–259.
7. Maimonides (Egypt, 1135–1204), *Yad, Sekhirut* 13:7; R. Jacob b. Asher (Spain, 1270–1340), *Tur, Hoshen Mishpat* 337:20; R. Joseph Caro (Israel, 1488–1575), *Shulhan Arukh, Hoshen Mishpat* 337:20; R. Jehiel Michel Epstein (Belarus, 1829–1908), *Arukh ha-Shulhan, Hoshen Mishpat* 337:26.
8. *Kiddushin* 42b, *Bava Kamma* 79a; *Yad, Me'ilah* 7:2; R. Asher b. Jehiel (Germany, 1250–1327), *Bava Kamma* 7:9; *Tur*, op. cit., 350.
9. *Yevamot* 5b; *Mishna, Bava Metzia* 2:10; *Rif*, ad loc.; *Yad, Mamrim* 6:12; *Rosh, Bava Metzia* 2:27; *Tur, Yoreh De'ah* 240:15; *Sh. Ar., Yoreh De'ah* 240:15, 16; *Ar. ha-Sh., Yoreh De'ah* 240:34–35.

10. Leviticus 19:17; *Yad*, De'ot 6:7–13.

11. R. Mosheh Isserles (Poland, 1525 or 1530–1572), *Rema*, *Sh. Ar.*, *Orah Hayyim* 608:2. R. Isaac b. Jacob Alfasi advances a different opinion here. Following the position of R. Elazar b. R. Shimon and R. Abba at *Yevamot* 65b, R. Isaac holds that the *tokhahah* obligation is suspended when it is certain that the admonishment will not be heeded.

12. *Rema*, *Sh. Ar.*, *Orah Hayyim* 656:1. See also *Sedei Hemed*, vol. 9, pp. 7, 64.

13. R. Mosheh Sofer, Responsa *Hatam Sofer*, *Hoshen Mishpat* 177 and his gloss at *Sh. Ar.*, *Orah Hayyim* 656:1.

14. *Rema*, op. cit., 608:2.

15. R. Judah b. Samuel he-Hasid, *Sefer Hasidim* 413.

16. *Ar. ha-Sh.*, *Orah Hayyim* 608:7

17. The biblical source for the prohibition against slander is disputed at *Ketubbot* 46a. R. Elazar derives the warning from the verse: "You shall not go about as a talebearer among your people" (Leviticus 19:16). R. Natan derives the admonishment from the verse: "When you go out as a camp among your enemies, you must avoid everything evil" (Deuteronomy 23:10).

18. R. Israel Meir ha-Kohen Kagan (Radin, 1838–1933), *Hafetz Hayyim*, *Lavin* 1–17, *Essin* 1–14.

19. *Baraita*, *Sanhedrin* 73a; *Yad*, Rotze'ah 1:14; *Tur*, *Hoshen Mishpat* 426:1; *Sh. Ar.*, *Hoshen Mishpat* 426:1; *Ar. ha-Sh.*, *Hoshen Mishpat* 426:1.

20. This lesson is derived by R. Yishmael from the verse: "For he found her in the field; the betrothed *naarah* cried out but she had no rescuer" (Deuteronomy 22:27). The implication is that if there was someone who could have rescued her, he would have been required to rescue her in whatever way he could, including killing her pursuer (*Sanhedrin* 73a).

21. *Sanhedrin* 74a.

22. R. Nissim b. Reuben Gerondi, *Ran*, *Sanhedrin* 73a.

23. R. Meir ha-Kohen, *Haggahot Maimuniyyot*, quoted in R. Joseph Caro, *Kesef Mishneh*, *Yad*, *Rotzeah* 1:14.

24. R. David b. Solomon ibn Abi Zimra, *Radbaz*, *Lishonot ha-Rambam* 1582 (218).

25. Loc. cit., and Responsa *1052* (627).

26. R. Mosheh Schick, *Maharam Schick al Taryag Mitzvot*, mitzvah 238; R. Ovadiah Yosef, *Yehaveh Da'at* 84; R. Eliezer Yehudah Waldenberg, *Tzitz Eliezer* 9:45.

27. R. Jehiel Michel Epstein, *Ar. ha-Sh.*, op. cit., 426:4.

28. The one case where all disputants agree that if *R* would be at peril he should not undertake the mission regardless of the number of people who might be saved is the manslayer case described at *Mishnah Makkot* 2:7. The dispute between R. Meir Simha and R. Weinberg revolves around Maimonides' (Egypt, 1135–1204) presentation of this case:

> An exiled person may never leave his city of refuge, not even to perform a Scriptural commandment or give evidence in a civil or capital case. Or even to save a life with his evidence, or to save someone from invading troops or from a river in flood or from a fire or from a fallen ruin. Indeed, not even if all Israel needs his help, as it did that of Joab, the son of Zeruiah, may he leave the city until the High priest dies. If he does leave, he surrenders himself to death, as we have explained (*Yad*, *Rotzeah* 7:8).

R. Meir Simha notes that Maimonides' treatment of this law is not a verbatim codification of this law, as it appears at *Mishnah Makkot* 2:7. Specifically, Maimonides adds the phrase: "If he does leave, he surrenders himself to death . . ." What Maimonides wants to impart with this phrase, according to R. Meir Simha, is that the biblical duty of *lo ta'amod* does not apply when the rescue mission would put *R*'s own life at risk. When the rescue puts *R*'s life at risk, he is prohibited from undertaking the mission regardless of the numbers of people he seeks to save.

Disputing this interpretation of Maimonides' text, R. Jehiel Yaakov Weinberg contends that Maimonides never intended to espouse a general rule for the inoperativeness of *lo ta'amod* when undertaking the rescue operation would put *R*'s life at risk. To see that this was not Maimonides' intent, we merely need to take note that the *Mishnah* at *Makkot* 2:7 bases the prohibition for the manslayer to leave his city of refuge on the verse "The congregation shall protect the murderer from the blood avenger, and return him to his refuge city where he had fled *shamah* (there), and he must remain there until the death of the high priest who was anointed with the sacred oil (Numbers 35:25)." The *Mishnah* tells us that the word *shamah* (there) is superfluous, i.e., the city being discussed is obviously the one to which he fled. The word *shamah* therefore teaches us that there [in the city of refuge] shall be his dwelling place [and he may not leave for any purpose]. Ordinarily, other than in the manslayer case, *R* is, however, required to undertake the rescue operation when more than one person's life is threatened.

29. *Safra* at Leviticus 19:16 *ot* 41.
30. R. Israel Meir ha-Kohen Kagan, *Hafetz Hayyim, Be'er Mayim Hayyim, Hilkhot Issurei Rekhilut* 9:1.
31. *Talmud Jerusalem Pe'ah* 2a; commentary of R. Obadiah Bertinoro (Italy, c. 1445–1505) to T.B. *Mishnah Pe'ah* 1:1.
32. See *Sanhedrin* 73a.
33. Mishna, *Bava Metzia* 2:11; *Rif, Bava Metzia* 33a; *Yad*, Gezeilah ve-Avedah 12:1; *Rosh, Bava Metzia* 2:30; *Tur*, op. cit., 264:1; *Sh. Ar.*, op. cit., 264:1; *Ar. ha-Sh.*, op. cit., 264:1.
34. R. Goldberg notes two exceptions to this rule: (1) In connection with the *mitzvah* to honor one's parents, a son is not obligated to incur an expense in attending to the needs of his parents. Nonetheless, should attendance to the needs of parents entail an opportunity cost for the son in the form of foregone earnings, the son is required to incur this loss for the sake of his *mitzvah*; (2) A request by a *wealthy* Jew for an interest-free loan takes precedence over the opportunity to lend a non-Jew money with an obligation to pay interest.
35. R. Zalman Nehemiah Goldberg, *"Ba-Hiyyuvei Gemilut Hesed"* in *YadREM le-Zehker Eliezer Meir Lipschitz*, Jerusalem 1975, pp. 97–111.
36. R. Eliezer Yehudah Waldenberg, *Tzitz Eliezer* 19:1.
37. R. Meir Abulafia, *Yad*, Ramah, *Sanhedrin* 73a.
38. R. Mosheh Feinstein, *Iggerot Mosheh, Yoreh De'ah* 1:223.
39. R. Asher b. Jehiel, *Kitzur Piskei ha-Rosh, Bava Metzia* 5:6; R. Joseph b. Moses Babad (Poland, 1800–1872), *Minhat Hinnukh* 296:23; R. Meir b. Isaac Auerbach (Jerusalem, 1815–1878), *Imrei Binah, Orah Hayyim* 13:15; R. Eliyahu Eliezer Dessler (Israel, 1892–1953), *Mikhtav Me'Eliyahu* 4:353; R. Abraham Isaiah Karelitz (Israel,1878–1953), *Hazon Ish, Hoshen Mishpat, Likutim* 20.
40. R. Israel Meir ha-Kohen Kagan, *Ahavat Hesed* 20:2, note 2.
41. R. Hayyim Soloveitchik, *Hiddushei Rabbenu Hayyim ha-Levi al ha-Rambam, Yad, Yisodei ha-Torah* 5:1.

In his explanation of the dispute in the passive case, R. Soloveitchik preliminarily notes that the biblical source for the rule that the preservation of human life generally takes primacy over the performance of *mitzvot* is: "You shall observe My decrees and My judgments, which man shall carry out and live by them (*ve-hai ba-hem*)—I am Hashem" (Leviticus 18:5). Since Torah laws, as *Rashi* points out, were given "to live by them," it is generally preferable for someone to sin rather than to endanger his life. The above teaching is referred to in the rabbinical literature as the *ve-hai ba-hem* principle. Standing behind the dispute between R. Isaac and Maimonides is the issue of whether *mai hazit* negates the *ve-hai ba-hem* principle. In the opinion of R. Isaac, *mai hazit* does not entirely negate the *ve-hai ba-hem* principle. Accordingly, *A* is theoretically allowed to give his own life precedence over averting *B*'s death. What *mai hazit* prohibits *A* from doing is preserving his own life by taking the life of *B*. Agreeing to *C*'s demand to kill *B* as a means of averting his own death at the hands of *C* is a decision by *A* to engage in an act of murder. But, *A* has no right to decide that "his blood is redder than *B*'s." Since *mai hazit* does not negate the principle of *ve-hai ba-hem*, *A* may, however, allow *B* to hurl him on top of an infant as a means of saving his own life. Here, *A* is not guilty of taking *affirmative action* that decides that his life is more valuable than *B*'s life. Instead, *A* plays an entirely passive role. *A*'s *passivity* effectively turns the tables and says, "Who says that the blood of the infant is redder than my blood?"

Maimonides, on the other hand, applies *mai hazit* even in the *passive* case because *mai hazit* negates the *ve-hai ba-hem* principle. Accordingly, *A* has no right to save himself at the expense of *B*'s death. The circumstance that *A* will play only a *passive role* in *B*'s death is not a mitigating factor.

R. Isaac's position apparently finds support from the case referred to earlier in the text, involving two travelers in the desert: *A* has a jug of water and *B* has no water. *A*'s supply of water is sufficient only to allow one person to survive the desert trip. Recall R. Akiva's ruling, rooted in the *ve-hai ba-hem* principle, that *A* may keep the water for himself. Maimonides' position is entirely consistent with R. Akiva's ruling, however. In R. Akiva's case, *A* and *B* are separately and independently exposed to the same life-threatening force. *A* is capable of extricating himself from this threat to his life and *B* is incapable of helping himself from the danger. Here, R. Akiva rules that *A* has the right to give the *saving of his own life* priority. In contrast, if *C* threatens to kill *A*, *A* has no right to save himself from this threat by agreeing to cooperate in the murder of *B*. The prohibition should stand even if *C* demands only that *A* assume a passive role in the murder of *B*.

42. R. Solomon b. Isaac, *Rashi, Sanhedrin* 74a s.v. *sevarah.*
43. R. Mosheh Feinstein, *Iggerot Mosheh Yoreh De'ah* 1:145. In his analysis of the biblical prohibition against murder, "Thou shalt not murder" (Exodus 20:13), R. Zalman Nehemiah Goldberg (Israel, contempt.) demonstrates that *A* violates this injunction even if he causes *B*'s death by indirect action and even if *A* plays only a passive role in the murder of *B*, as would be the case if *A* allows himself to be thrown on an infant and thereby causes the child's death. Whether *A* must sacrifice his life in the *geramah* case to prevent *B*'s killing is, according to R. Goldberg, a matter of dispute between R. Isaac and Maimonides (*Moriah* 8, *Gilyan* 4–5, *Elul* 5736).
44. John R. Boatright, *Ethics and the Conduct of Business*, 2nd ed. (Upper Saddle River, NJ: Prentice Hall, 1997), p. 111; See also C. H. Farnsworth, "Survey of Whistleblowers

Finds Retaliation but Few Regrets," *New York Times*, February 21, 1988, p. 22.

45. *Hafetz Hayyim*, op. cit., *Hilkhot Issurei Lashon Ha-Ra* 10:1–2.

46. R. Binyamin Cohen, Sefer *Hafetz Hayyim im Perush Helkat Binyamin*, *Hafetz Hayyim*, p. 266 ot 11.

47. *Hafetz Hayyim*, op. cit., *Hilkhot Issurei Lashon Ha-Ra* 10:1–17; *Hilkhot Rekhilut* 9:1–15.

48. Sally Seymour, "The Case of the Willful Whistle-Blower," *Harvard Business Review*, vol. 66 (Jan/Feb 1988), pp. 103–110.

49. Kermit Vandivier, "The Aircraft Brake Scandal" in Thomas Donaldson and Patricia H. Werhane, eds., *Ethical Issues in Business*, 6th ed. (Upper Saddle River, NJ: Prentice Hall, 1999), pp. 285–296.

50. Russell P. Boisjoly, Ellen Foster Curtis, Eugene Mellican, "Roger Boisjoly and the *Challenger* Disaster: The Ethical Dimensions," *The Journal of Business Ethics*, April 1989, vol. 8, issue 4, p. 217.

51. Lisa Newton, David P. Schmidt, *Wake-Up Calls, Classic Cases in Business Ethics*, 2nd ed. (Mason , OH: Thomson South Western, 2004), p. 187.

52. Russell P. Boisjoly, Ellen Foster Curtis, Eugene Mellican, op. cit., p. 217.

53. John R. Boatright, op. cit., pp. 128–129. For this moral dilemma I have supplied the names of both the characters and the name of the drug.

54. loc. cit., pp. 129–130.

55. De George, op. cit., p. 251.

56. For an excellent exposition of utilitarian approach to business ethics issues, see Joseph R. Desjardins and John J. McCall, *Contemporary Issues in Business Ethics*, 4th ed. (Belmont, CA: Wadsworth, 2000), pp. 27–46.

57. Desjardins and McCall, op. cit., pp. 27–28.

58. De George, op. cit., p. 243–244.

59. See *Bava Kamma* 94b; *Rosh, Bava Kamma* 9:2; *Tur, Hoshen Mishpat* 366:2; *Sh. Ar.*, 366:2; *Ar. ha-Sh.*, 366:3.

60. R. Solomon b. Isaac, *Rashi, Bava Kamma* 94b s.v. Borot; *Ar. ha-Sh.*, loc. cit.

61. R. Jacob b. Asher, *Tur, Hoshen Mishpat* 306:6; R. Joseph Caro, *Sh. Ar.*, *Hoshen Mishpat* 306:6; R. Jehiel Michel Epstein, *Ar. ha-Sh.*, *Hoshen Mishpat* 306:13.

62. Rabbenu Yoel quoted by R. Israel of Krems, *Haggahot Asheri, Bava Kamma* 9:16; R. Jonathan Eybeschuetz (Prague, 1695–1764), *Tummim, Sh. Ar.*, op.cit., 146, n. 19; R. Mosheh Sofer, *Hatam Sofer, Bava Batra* 30b.

63. Rabbenu Efraim quoted in *Haggahot Asheri*, op. cit.

64. R. Shabbetai b. Meir ha-Kohen (Poland, 1621–1662), *Siftei Kohen, Sh. Ar.*, op.cit. 129, n. 7; *Ar. ha-Sh.*, op.cit. 306:13.

65. *Ar. ha-Sh.*, loc. cit.

66. For elaboration of this principle, please turn to pp. 152–154, 395–396 of this volume.

67. Please turn to pp. 77–80 of this volume.

68. Ibid.

69. *Wake-Up Calls Classic Cases in Business Ethics*, op. cit., p.187.

70. *Hafetz Hayyim, Hilkhot Issurei Rekhilut k'lal* 9, *Be'er Mayyim Hayyim ot* 3.

71. R. Binyamin Cohen, *Sefer Hafetz Hayyim im Perush Helkat Binyamin*, 266–267, 339, 352–353.

72. The brief summary of Sarbanes-Oxley is culled from Leonard M. Baynes, "Just Pucker and Blow? An Analysis of Corporate Whistleblowing, the Duty of Care, the Duty of

Loyalty, and the Sarbanes-Oxley Act," op. cit., pp. 888–896.

73. Marc S. Raspanti and David M. Laigaie, "Current Practice and Procedure Under the Whistleblower Provisions of the Federal False Claims Act," *Temple Law Review*, vol. 71, 1988, pp. 23–53.

74. "The Whistleblower Protection Act of 1989: Foundation For The Modern Law of Employment Dissent," *Administrative Law Review* 51:2, 1989, pp. 531–579.

75. David Culp, "Whistleblowers: Corporate Anarchists or Heroes? Toward a Judicial Perspective," *Hofstra Labor Law Journal*, vol. 13, 1995, pp. 116–138. For a more recent survey on whistleblower protection on the state level, see Julie Jones, "Comment: give a Little Whistle: The Need for a More Broad Interpretation of the Whistleblower Exception to the Employment-At-Will Doctrine," 34 *Texas Tech Law Review*, 1133. The author notes a trend of increasing number of state whistleblower statutes. Nonetheless, these statutes have proven to be very ineffective in encouraging whistleblowing or preventing retaliation.

76. *Sotah* 14a; *Sifrei* on Exodus 34:6–7; Maimonides, *Sefer ha-Mitzvot, Mitzvat Aseh*, no. 8, *Yad, De'ot* 1:6

77. *Resh Lakish, Kiddushin* 30b.

78. For an elaboration on this theme, see Aaron Levine, *Case Studies in Jewish Business Ethics* (Hoboken, NJ: Ktav Publishing Company, Yeshiva University Press, 2000), pp. 182–188.

79. *Hafetz Hayyim, Hilkhot Issurei Lashon ha-Ra*, k'lal 10:14.

80. R. Asher b. Jehiel, *Rosh, Sanhedrin* 8:2; R. Menahem b. Solomon Meiri (Perpignan, ca. 1249–1306), *Beit ha-Behirah, Sanhedrin* 73a; R. Jacob b. Asher, *Tur*, op. cit., 426:1; R. Jehiel Michel Epstein, *Ar. ha-Sh.*, op. cit., 426:1.

81. For the halakhic basis of this presumption see R. Joseph Engel (Poland, 1859–1920), *Gilyonei ha-Shas, Berakhot* 61b.

82. *Sanhedrin* 73a.

83. R. Asher b. Jehiel, *Rosh, Bava Metzia* 2:24. See, however, R. Solomon b. Isaac, *Rashi, Kiddushin* 58b and R. Mosheh Sofer, *Hiddushei Hatam Sofer, Bava Metzia* 69a.

84. *Bava Kamma* 115b; R. Asher b. Jehiel, *Rosh, Bava Metzia* 2:28; R. Jacob b. Asher, *Tur*, op. cit. 264:5; R. Jehiel Michel Epstein, *Ar. ha-Sh.*, op. cit. 264:3.

85. R. Mosheh Isserles, *Rema, Hoshen Mishpat* 264:3.

86. *Mishnah, Bava Metzia* 2:9; *Bava Metzia* 31b, 32a; *Tur*, op. cit., 265; *Sh. Ar.*, op. cit. 265; *Ar. ha-Sh.*, op. cit., 265.

87. *Rema*, op. cit., 265:1.

88. *Bava Metzia* 31b.

89. R. Asher b. Jehiel, *Rosh, Bava Metzia* 2:24.

90. R. Jacob b. Asher, *Tur*, op. cit., 265.

91. Nahmanides (Spain, 1194–1270), *Bava Metzia* 31b.

92. *Mishnah, Bava Metzia* 2:11.

93. For an analysis of the legal underpinnings of the three views regarding the monetary entitlement of the *meshiv*, see Aaron Levine, "*Be-Inyan Sekhar Betailah*," in Aaron Levine, Ed., *Kol Yaakov*, (New York: Rabbinical Alumni Rabbi Jacob Joseph, 1975), pp. 39–86.

94. Adapted from Andy Pasztor, "Speaking up Gets Biologist into Big Fight," *Wall Street Journal*, November 26, 1980, section 2, p. 25.

95. R. Israel Gedaliah Lipschutz, *Tiferet Yisrael, Mishnah Nedarim* 4:2, note 11.

96. Michael Davis, "Avoiding the Tragedy of Whistleblowing," *Business and Professional Ethics Journal*, vol. 8, no. 4, pp. 3–19.
97. Richard T. De George, *Business Ethics*, op. cit., pp. 259–261.
98. Aaron Levine, *Case Studies in Jewish Business Ethics*, op. cit., pp. 1–18.

VII. I'll Teach Them a Lesson

12

I'll Teach Them a Lesson

Our concern in this chapter is to identify the permissible bounds for protecting and defending one's property and other rights against infringement. Does this right extend even to causing possible harm, loss, and even death to potential infringers and intruders? By means of the case study method we will investigate this issue in the following settings: The right of a homeowner to protect his property against theft and the right and duty of a student to protect himself against cheaters. Finally, does the responsibility a teacher has to discipline his students extend even to the prerogative of confiscating the property of his students?

HOME SECURITY, PREVENTING CHEATING, AND CONFISCATING PUPIL PROPERTY

Returning late at night from a wedding celebration, Dror and Shulamit White were shocked to find that their home had been broken into and ransacked. In the three years they had lived in Eden Commons, a quiet, upscale neighborhood, the couple had never heard of any trouble, let alone a burglary. When the initial shock of the burglary settled down, Shulamit lashed into Dror and berated him for long ignoring her pleas to get a burglar alarm system installed in their home. No further delays could now be tolerated, she ranted. Resisting the notion of spending money to protect his home, Dror deflected his wife's strident plea for a home security system by saying:

> "Let us hold off on that for a while. First, let's figure out how the burglar made entry. My idea is to lay a trap for the burglar and teach him a lesson for life."

In short shrift Dror proved his mettle as a detective by discovering some telltale smudges on the exterior portion of a second story window. Once Dror discovered this clue, the mystery was solved:

> The thief, Dror exclaimed, "obviously stood up on the railing of the step at the back of the house and climbed from there on to the pole that supports the clothing line and from there angled to open the second story window. Shulamit, believe me, I don't mind spending the money on an alarm system, but I know that if we *don't* install an alarm, the thief will be back for another try. And I know how to catch him and teach him a bloody lesson he'll never forget. We'll just *loosen* the pole that supports the clothing line. We'll do it in a very inconspicuous manner. The thief will return and use the same *modus operandi*, and when he steps onto the pole he'll get the shock of his life. The pole will collapse under his weight and he'll come crashing down."

Dror's plan horrified Shulamit. In her mind the scheme amounted to an arrangement to trap and *injure* the thief. Shulamit's abhorrence toward the plan, however, quickly dissipated when she learned that neighbors adopted much more draconian measures to thwart would-be thieves. The Sheltons, for instance, had an attack dog in a hidden area on the sprawling grounds that surrounded their home. The attack dog, called Saddam, was trained to recognize the scent of the entire Shelton family. In the presence of the scent of any member of the Shelton family, Saddam was totally harmless. Pity, however, any intruder who came within the "scenting range" of Saddam. Similarly, the Drillmans dug a very deep trench in the border of their backyard and camouflaged the huge hole with a thin layer of shrubbery held up by poles. Invasion of the Drillman property would *automatically* result in injury for the trespasser.

Another neighborhood plan that arguably would be more punishing for an intruder was Rubie Indigo's scheme. Rubie's theory was that a thief would look for the *easiest* way to gain entry into a target home and use that route to enter. Taken to its logical conclusion, the easy entry should assume the form of a "lure." Toward this end, Rubie left the window that faced the back of his home slightly ajar. All that would be needed to gain entry was a small folding step ladder. To complete the lure Rubie would drive away at night for long periods of time. If the intruder managed entry an assortment of openly visible hazards would await him. Encountering a veritable minefield would surely convince any burglar on a cost-benefit basis to abandon the caper. Still better, let the burglar dare to navigate the minefield and get injured in the process. However, experience proved that the setup was an ineffective mechanism to trap burglars on the inside. A disappointed Rubie set out to introduce improvements in his system. The refinement consisted of substituting booby traps for the openly visible hazards. Serious injury for the infiltrator would now be a certainty.

Because Dror's plan was so much more civilized than the home security plans of her neighbors, Shulamit dropped her resistance to her husband's plan and allowed him to loosen the poles that supported the clothing line. Sure enough, as Dror predicted, the *modus operandi* of the first caper was repeated. This time the intruder's designs were thwarted. To boot, the perpetrator suffered serious injuries when the pole collapsed under his weight and he fell hard onto the pavement beneath. Never imagining that implementing Dror's plan would result in *actual* injury for a trespasser, Shulamit was overcome with guilt that she bore indirect responsibility for the severe injuries the intruder suffered. Within a short time, the police caught the perpetrator of the prior successful break-in and returned the stolen property to the Whites. The rude awakening that the two incidents were unrelated only exasperated Shulamit's sense of guilt as her husband's specific goal of laying a trap for the person who burglarized their home was hence not accomplished. Shulamit bemoaned to Dror:

"We could have thwarted the thief with the minimal expense of installing bars on the outside of the windows. We need to own up to the simple fact that the injuries the thief suffered are far disproportionate to the punishment he deserves for his crime." Dror snapped back, "The thief *brought on the injuries* to himself by attempting to break into our home."

With the aim of assuaging Shulamit's guilt and putting an end to her moping, Dror recounted two incidents of his youth. Both involved "teaching an evildoer a lesson." The first occurred in his college career:

> I was a student in Professor Regenstein's Intro Economics course. There were about 300 students in the class. We took the midterm examination in a large auditorium. We were told that the exam would be curved. The examination consisted of 50 multiple-choice questions. As I filled in the answers, I became aware that the fellow behind me, Boris Klugman, was copying my answers. Consider that the higher my relative score, the better off I would be. Boris's conduct was hence not only inherently dishonest, but also carried the prospect of lowering my *relative* score. I had to stop the cheating and protect my legitimate interests. What I did was to deliberately fill in wrong answers and give Boris a false impression that I was finished with the exam. The latter part was easy as Regenstein told us that we should be sure to fold the question sheets into our booklets before we handed in our exams. I folded the question sheets horizontally into the exam, exactly the way Regenstein liked it, and sat with my hands folded. Boris took these telltale signs to mean that I was finished with the exam and he therefore handed in his exam. After Boris was out of sight, I changed many of my answers. I must admit that I still relish the expression of horror and shock Boris had on his face when he got his exam back and his grade was 67.[1] Would you say that I did in Boris? Oh no! By freely choosing to cheat, Boris *brought his miserable grade on himself.*

Sensing that the Boris story did not change Shulamit's way of thinking, Dror had one more story up his sleeve about an evildoer that was taught a lesson. This time, Dror, himself, was the villain in the story:

> In the third grade, I occasionally became bored with the instructional material of my *rebbe* (teacher of Torah). In those moments of boredom, I turned to amusing myself with such challenging toys as Rubik's cube

and the long term project of constructing a merry-go-round from an assortment of small colored pads. Just as I would get into these "play things," the hand of my *rebbe*, Rabbi Sidney Kaplan, would suddenly appear and snatch away the toy. Rabbi Kaplan's confiscations were often of the permanent variety. Not infrequently, Rabbi Kaplan would accompany the confiscation with a harsh public reprimand. Let me tell you, I always felt the punishments Rabbi Kaplan meted out to me were disproportionate to my offenses and hence far too excessive. As I sobbed bitterly at the punishment, I remember Rabbi Kaplan's words: "*You brought this misery on to yourself.* I'm teaching you a lesson for life; it's for your own good."

Shulamit had heard the Rubrik's cube and paper merry-go-round story many times, but, in the past, the point of it was how creative and talented Dror was as a child. Dror's current application of the story appeared therefore to Shulamit somewhat strained and disingenous. But, Dror had the last word here: "You should be so proud of me. In loosening the pole, I just applied Rabbi Kaplan's lesson. You could say, *I finally got it.*"

Let's now turn to analyzing the ethics of the above three dilemmas from the perspective of Halakhah.

HOME SECURITY DEVICES IN EDEN COMMONS

Let us begin by examining the halakhic validity of the various home security devices the residents of Eden Commons adopted.

The common characteristic of all the alarms described in the opening vignette is that the homeowners designed their devices with the aim of attacking and/or injuring the burglar. Does the homeowner have any duty to control his or her actions and safeguard his premises so that a trespasser will not suffer injury?

Preliminarily, let's take note that the land occupier has a right to evict the trespasser from his premises.[2] If the trespasser refuses to leave, some authorities allow the householder, if necessary, to assault him as a means of advancing the ejection.[3] Moreover, if the land occupier's animal injures the trespasser, the land occupier bears no liability for the injuries.[4]

Does this mean that the land occupier has no duty whatsoever to the trespasser? No. R. Pappa, a fourth-century Talmudic Sage, punctuates this point:

> Rav Pappa said: This rule (that the homeowner is exempt from damaging the trespasser) was stated only regarding a case where [the land occupier] was unaware of [*lo hava yada beh*] the presence of [trespasser]— but in a case where [the land occupier] was aware of [*hava yada beh*] the presence of [the trespasser]—if the homeowner did damage to him he is liable.—What is the reason ? It is because [the trespasser] can tell [the land occupier]: It is granted that you have the right to evict me from your property, but *you do not have the right to damage* me.[5]

What R. Pappa intends to convey with his caveat is a matter of dispute. The dispute revolves around interpretation of the phrase *hava yada beh*. R. Solomon b. Isaac (*Rashi*, France, 1040–1105) understands R. Pappa to tell us that becoming aware of the presence of the trespasser requires the land occupier to exercise caution in his movements. Consequently, if the land occupier bodily harms the discovered trespasser, even if he inflicts the injury accidentally, the land occupier bears liability for the injury. But, if the discovered trespasser sustains injury by stumbling over the land occupier, the land occupier bears no liability for his injuries.[6]

Maimonides (Egypt, 1135–1204), however, understands the phrase *hava yada beh* to mean *willful intention*. What R. Pappa conveys here is that the land occupier has no license to *willfully* attack the trespasser.[7] Notwithstanding Maimonides's variant understanding of the phrase *hava yada beh*, some authorities interpret him, in the final analysis, to take on the same opinion as *Rashi*.[8] Other authorities, however, understand Maimonides to dispute *Rashi*. In this reading of Maimonides, the land occupier's duty to the discovered trespasser is no higher than it is to the undiscovered one.[9]

What remains to be clarified, as far as the duty of the land occupier to the trespasser, is whether the land occupier is permitted to set up his premises so that a trespasser will be automatically attacked. Relatedly, is it permissible for the land occupier to booby-trap his premises with the aim of trapping a trespasser and injuring him? In what follows we will introduce a number of different halakhic principles that bear on these issues.

1. *Shor ha-Itstadyon* (Arena Ox)

Providing a starting point for the issues at hand is a comparison of Maimonides's treatment of the case where the landholder's ox kills the trespasser with the case where the landholder's *shor ha-itstadyon* (arena ox) kills the trespasser. This comparison will shed light on Halakhah's attitude toward the use of certain home security devices.

Maimonides's presentation of the case where the landholder's ox gores the trespasser is as follows:

> [I]f, however, the plaintiff enters the premises of the defendant and the latter's animal causes him damage, the defendant is exempt from any claim, for he can say to the trespasser, "had you not entered my premises, no harm would have overtaken you." Moreover, Scripture says explicitly, "and lets his beast run loose, or allows it to feed in another man's field [of the best of his own field and the best of his own vineyard shall he make restitution], i.e., liability obtains only when the beast is let loose on someone else's field, (Exodus 22:4).[10]

Maimonides' formulation presents a difficulty. Once we are informed that the rationale for the exemption is that the trespasser brought the damage upon himself, what need is there for Maimonides to add: ". . . and lets his beast run loose. . . ." This apparent superfluous phrase leads R. Barukh Ber Leibowitz (Poland, 1866–1939) to read into Maimonides that the exemption is not just based on the notion that the landholder has no duty to guard his property to insure that his premises will be safe for the trespasser, but, it is rooted in the notion that in respect to an intruding trespasser, the landholder's animal is not regarded as a damager (*mazzik*) at all.[11]

Reinforcing the non-*mazzik* designation of the landholder's animal vis-à-vis a trespasser is the handling of the variant of this case when the animal was a habitual attacker (*mu'ad*). Ordinarily, if an animal attacks and kills a person, the animal is executed. In addition, if the animal had a record of three previous lethal attacks against people it is designated as a habitual attacker (*mu'ad*) and the owner of the *mu'ad* must pay an indemnity (*kofer*) to the family of the victim equal to the economic value of the victim.[12] These rules are modified when the victim was an intruder and was killed in the domain of the owner of the animal. Here, the animal is put to death, but no indemnity payment is imposed on the owner in the case of the *mu'ad*.[13]

In his treatment of the responsibility of the landholder for the injuries of the trespasser, R. Pesah mi-Kobrin (Poland, 1879–1939) concludes the same as R. Leibowitz that the landholder has no duty to safeguard his property to insure that a trespasser will not sustain injury and property damage.[14]

Once it is recognized that *mu'ad* is not a *mazzik* at all vis-à-vis a trespasser, the possibility of allowing a landholder to maintain an attack dog on his premises should be entertained. But, the analogy between a *mu'ad* and an attack dog does not hold. There is a basic difference between a destructive act that comes from an attack dog and one that comes from a *mu'ad*. The former is a programmed response whereas the latter is brought on by provocation.

Examination of the *mu'ad* scenarios described in the Talmud bear out the notion that the defining feature of *mu'ad* is an animal that attacks upon provocation: One scenario is the animal that gores upon hearing the sound of a *shofar* (Ram's horn). Upon the fourth such incident, the owner pays full damages.[15] Another scenario involves the animal that establishes a pattern of attacking only on the Sabbath. Here, on the fourth Sabbath attack the animal is a *mu'ad*. But, if the fourth incident occurs on a weekday, the animal is not treated as a *mu'ad*.[16] The importance of whether the fourth incident occurred on Sabbath or on the weekday is that we presume that there was something indigenous about the Sabbath that provokes the animal to attack. One explanation, advanced by *Rashi*, is that the animal is idle on the Sabbath and idleness breeds in the animal an arrogance that leads it to act upon its destructive urges.[17] *Tosafot* (Twelfth to Fourteenth century French commentators of the Talmud), quoting the Jerusalem Talmud, rationalize the provocation differently. On the Sabbath people are clad in their finery. The animal, unable to recognize the people in their Sabbath clothing, becomes agitated and attacks them.[18] One final point on the role provocation plays in the *mu'ad* scenario. If children tease a *mu'ad* and it does not attack, the animal loses its status as a *mu'ad*. Having withstood provocation, the animal is now regarded as having a clean record. Consequently, if the animal attacks again, the animal is treated as a *ta'am* (an innocuous animal), and the owner is liable to pay only for half of the damages.[19]

Recall Maimonides' reason why the landholder is not responsible for the injuries his animal inflicts on the trespasser: "Had you not entered my premises, no harm would have overtaken you." Now, this defense is understandable only if it takes provocation of some sort to make the landholder's animal attack. By entering without permission, the trespasser assumes the risk that there may be something about him, perhaps the manner of his gait, perhaps the color of his clothing, that will provoke the landholder's animal to attack him. If the landholder's animal does indeed attack him, the trespasser has brought the injury upon himself. But, if the landholder maintains an attack dog on the premises, the trespasser will be subject to an automatic programmed attack. It will be an unprovoked attack. Since a trespasser has a right not to be *deliberately* attacked, maintaining an attack animal on the premises should be prohibited.

It so happens that the modern attack dog has an ancient equivalent, discussed in the Talmud. This is the *shor ha-itstadyon* (lit. arena ox). The *shor ha-itstadyon* is an ox trained to attack other oxen or a man for the purpose of entertainment and sport.[20]

For the purpose of clarifying whether a householder is permitted to maintain an attack dog on his premises, let's take a brief look at the salient features of the *shor ha-itstadyon*. Ordinarily, an ox that kills a man is put to death.[21] In recognition that the *shor ha-itstadyon* does not attack out of provocation, but rather, is trained to do so, the *Mishna* exempts the *shor ha-itstadyon* from being put to death for killing a man:

> If an ox gores [a man or a woman and he dies, the ox shall surely be stoned].[22] –If an ox gores. This implies: – But not [an ox] that is trained to gore.[23]

Authorities dispute whether the exemption of *shor ha-itstadyon* extends to impunity for payment of damages caused. The mainstream view here is not to extend the exemption to impunity for damages caused.[24]

The qualitative difference between *shor mu'ad* and *shor ha-itstadyon* suggests that each category is governed by a different legal theory of liability. R. Yitzhak Ze'ev Soloveitchik (Israel, 1886–1960) explicitly proposes this thesis. He based his thesis on Maimonides' presentation of *shor ha-itstadyon*:

Oxen used for sport and trained to gore each other are not deemed fore-warned with respect to injury to each other. Even if they kill a person, they do not incur the death penalty, for Scripture says, "If an ox gore" (Exodus 21:28), not "has been incited to gore."[25]

Maimonides' presentation indicates that repeated instances of goring would not make the *shor ha-itztadyon* a *mu'ad*. R. Abraham b. David (*Rabad*, Posequeries, 1125–1198) avers, however, that repeated instances of goring renders the *shor ha-itstadyon* a *mu'ad*.[26]

The rationale behind Maimonides' view, avers R. Soloveitchik, is that "*But not* [an ox] that is *trained* to gore" takes *shor ha-itstadyon* out of the category of action by an animal that the Torah speaks of in the passage dealing with the goring ox (Exodus 21:28–32). Nonetheless, the owner bears responsibility for the damage of the *shor ha-itstadyon* because the owner *knows* that the ox will cause injury and he does nothing about it. The analogue here is the instance where *A* incites *B's* dog to bite *C*. Since the inciter *A* does not directly inflict the damage, but only indirectly causes it, *Bet Din* will not order him to make good on the damages. Liability for the *owner B* is, however, another matter. Since *B* knows that people incite *his* dog to inflict injury and he does nothing about it, *B* is at fault and to "fulfill his obligation to heaven" should pay the victim his damages.[27] Likewise, since the owner of a *shor ha-itstadyon* knows that his ox inflicts damage and he does nothing about it, the owner bears responsibility for the damages.[28]

R. Soloveitchik's understanding of Maimonides apparently turns the issue at hand into a mere theoretical one. Why? Irrespective of the duty of the householder, if any, to the trespasser, an attack dog is a menace to everyone who has a legitimate right to enter the premises. Accordingly, the householder may not maintain an attack dog on his premises, and his duty is to destroy the animal. The issue, however, remains. Consider that technology now and in the future makes it possible to automatically attack unwanted intruders with bullets, laser beams, and electric current. The presence of these intruders can be detected by means of various sensory devices, such as body heat and unique scent. Since the automatic attack mechanism does not become operative until the trespasser is detected, the householder cannot be said to be "maintaining a menace to society" on his premises. The issue therefore becomes entirely one of identifying the nature of the duty the householder owes the trespasser.

Recall *Rabad's* opinion that repeated instances of goring make a *shor ha-itstadyon* a *mu'ad*. In R. Abraham's view *shor ha-itstadyon* is not equated with the dog that bites when it is incited. The exegesis—*"But not* [an ox] that is *trained* to gore" –hence does not remove *shor ha-itstadyon* from the passage of the Torah that deals with a goring ox. It says only that the *shor ha-itstadyon* is not put to death. Given that, in Rabad's view, *shor ha-itstadyon* is essentially governed by the same legal theory of liability as the goring ox described in the Torah (Exodus 21:28–32), identification of the nature of the duty of the householder to the trespasser will determine whether the householder is permitted to maintain an attack dog to protect himself against trespassers. Likewise, identification of this duty will also determine if the householder is permitted to set up his household in a manner that would automatically attack the trespasser upon entry.

2. Liability of Man as a Damager

Resolution of this issue, we propose, turns on the following dispute regarding the parameters of the principle in tort law that says that an individual is fully liable for what he damages, even if the damage is inflicted through unavoidable mishap. This principal is referred to as *adam mu'ad le-olam* (lit. man [as far as being fully responsible for what he damages] is always [considered] forewarned.[29] How far this principle goes is a matter of dispute.

One school of thought, led by *Tosafot*, conceptualizes *adam mu'ad le-olam* narrowly. In this formulation, unavoidable mishap (*ones*) is categorized as either akin to theft (*geneivah*) or akin to becoming lost (*aveidah*). *Geneivah* is considered more of *ones* than *aveidah*. A person is responsible for damage only if the *ones* was of the order of *aveidah* or lower. But he is not liable if the *ones* was of the order of *geneivah* or higher.[30] We will refer to this view as the *ordinary ones* liability school. Maimonides and Nahmanides (*Ramban*, Spain, 1194–1270), however, formulate *adam mu'ad le-olam* more stringently. In their view, no distinction is drawn in regard to the category of *ones* that occurred.[31] Nonetheless, these authorities agree that if the victim (*V*) brought on the damage upon himself, the damager (*D*) bears no responsibility to him. Accordingly, suppose *D* is sleeping and *V* lies down next to *D* or places his utensils next to *V*. Subsequently, by turning or stretching in his sleep, *D* either inflicts harm to *V* or damages his utensils. *D* bears no responsibility here as *V* is regarded as having brought on the injury or damage upon himself.[32] We will refer to this opinion as the *ones gadol* liability school.

Let us apply the above dispute to the issue at hand. Now, if we adopt Maimonides' view, referred to earlier, that man is liable for damage his actions cause, even if the damage is the result of *ones gadol*, the householder's (*H's*) exemption from guarding his property so that it does no harm to a trespasser (*T*) must be rooted in the principal that *T* brought his injury on himself. Such a judgment makes sense only if what *T* encounters is a *visible* hazard or obstacle. Entering someone's property without permission puts the burden on *T* to exercise extreme caution in moving about not to get injured. But, if *H's* domain is laced with booby traps or, worse still, is designed to automatically attack *T* upon entry, no matter how circumspect *T* is, he cannot avoid injury. Since *T* is entitled not to be *deliberately* attacked without warning, we cannot tell *T* that he "brought the attack upon himself" by entering the householder's domain without permission.

To be sure, if *T* sustains injury from the automatic attacking device, the link between *H's* action and *T's* injury is only indirect. Engaging in an action that would cause someone injury only indirectly is called, in the terminology of the Talmud, *gerama* and is a prohibited action. Let us take note that *gerama* is actionable in Jewish law. This means that if a Jewish court (*Bet Din*) becomes aware that *A* has committed a *gerama* action, it will enjoin *A* to remove his potential harm immediately. Rather than deal with the *gerama* action only after it has inflicted damage or loss, *Bet Din* will take action to prevent the harm.

Illustrating the above principle is the restrictions the sages imposed on property owners not to use their own property in a manner that would potentially inflict a detriment to a neighbor. One such restriction is the prohibition for *A* to place his ladder within four cubits of *B's* dovecote. The concern here is that while *A* is placing his ladder against his own wall, a marten might jump onto the ladder and from the ladder spring into the dovecote.[33] Although there is usually no marten waiting to jump onto the ladder as one places it near a dovecote, it is nevertheless forbidden to place the ladder near the dovecote due to the possibility that such direct damage might occur.[34]

What emerges from the ladder-dovecote case is that a *gerama* potential action is enjoinable. Likewise, because of the *unlawful* harm an automatic attack burglar alarm system will inflict on a trespasser, *Bet Din* will order *H* to remove this type of alarm.

Proceeding from the *ones gadol* liability rule is the rejection of the Shelton plan, described in the opening vignette, of placing an attack dog in a hidden place on their grounds. Similarly objectionable is Drillman's plan of placing camouflage shrubbery on the border of his property with the aim of causing a trespasser to fall into the deep trench that is beneath it.

What about Rubie Indigo's plan of luring the would-be thief with an open window and having visible obstacles or booby traps placed inside the room? Should his plan be equated with the Shelton and Drillman plans? At this juncture our concern will only be with the aspect of Indigo's plan that entails the laying of the obstacles or booby traps. The ethics of *luring* an individual into committing a criminal act will be dealt with later. As far as the surprises that await the would-be thief when he gets his first glimpse of the room from the open window, booby traps and openly visible hazards should not be treated the same. Booby traps are objectionable because a circumspect thief cannot avoid them. Placing the booby traps in the room therefore amounts to a planned attack on him. Lacing the room with openly visible hazards is another matter. This method does not violate *H's* duty vis-à-vis *T*. Quite to the contrary, entering someone's property without permission places the burden on the intruder to be circumspect; therefore, if he stumbles on the hazards he encounters and injures himself he has brought the injury on himself.

Finally, let us turn to Dror's plan of thwarting the thief by loosening the poles that supported the clothing line. Perhaps, this method of thwarting the thief should be characterized as the *setting* of a booby trap for the intruder and therefore amount to a planned deliberate attack on the intruder? No. Consider that the ordinary and conventional use of a clothing line is to hang wet laundry to dry. Expecting the poles of the clothing line to support a weight beyond the usual laundry load is an unreasonable assessment. If a thief decides to jump on the poles with the expectation that the poles will support him, the thief is guilty of reckless conduct and has brought the injury on himself. Dror's plan of loosening the poles of the clothing line should therefore not constitute the laying of a booby trap to deliberately injure the intruder.

A different conclusion, can, however, be reached if we follow *Tosafot*'s approach to *adam mu'ad le-olam*. If man is not responsible for damage that is the result of *ones gadol*, then, the householder's exemption from guarding his property so that it does no harm to the trespasser is simply based on the principle that the householder does not have to *anticipate* that someone will enter his domain without his permission. Accordingly, setting up one's premises so that an intruder will automatically be attacked should not be viewed as a *gerama* potential action. Accordingly, the rights of a thief would not be a basis for *Bet Din* to enjoin the installation of a burglar alarm system whose salient characteristic is the automatic attack feature. To be sure, as we will discuss below, there may be other reasons to object to this type of alarm.

In his work *Mishpetei ha-Torah*, R. Tzvi Spitz (Israel, contemp.) addresses the legitimacy of thwarting the thief by using a camouflage shrubbery and loosening the poles of the clothing line. In his conclusion, R. Spitz finds no objection to the laying of hazards on one's property for the purpose of injuring the thief, provided that household members and invited guests are not at the same time put at risk by these burglar repellants.

R. Spitz finds support for his proposition from the following story recorded at *Derek Eretz Rabbah* 5:

> It once happened that a man came early in the morning [*hishkim etzlo*] to the home of R. Yehoshua. [R. Yehoshua] gave him to eat and drink and brought him up to the loft apartment to sleep and removed the ladder [that led from the loft to the ground floor]. What did that man do? He arose in the middle of the night, took the belongings [of R. Yehoshua] and wrapped them up in his garment. And when he tried to descend, he fell down and broke his neck. In the morning R. Yehoshua got up and found him and said: "Worthless man, is this the way people like you act"? "Master, I did not know that you had removed the ladder from under me." He spoke to him: "Worthless man, do not you know that [already] since last night [*emesh*] we are on guard against you"?

Note that the disastrous injury the thief suffered in attempting to escape did not make R. Yehoshua regret that he had pulled away the ladder. What can be drawn from this story, according to R. Spitz, is the permissibility to thwart a would-be thief by setting hazards in one's premises. In R. Spitz's mind the story provides support for the legitimacy for camouflage shrubbery and the loosening of the poles of the clothing line. R. Spitz has one caveat, however: These tactics enjoy legitimacy only if the safety of the members of one's household is not thereby compromised.[35]

The above conclusion is, however, unwarranted. What is crucial for the issue at hand is recognition that the removal of the ladder does not create a booby trap for the thief, but rather, only a hazard. Consider that R. Yehoshua led his "house guest" up the ladder to the second story loft. It should therefore have been plain to the thief that the ladder connecting the loft with the downstairs was *portable*. Only a reckless man would descend from the loft in pitch darkness without first checking to see that the portable ladder was still in place. The characterization of the thief as a reckless person can easily be read into R. Yehoshua's words of reprimand to him: "Worthless man, is this the way people like you act"?

It is in this vein that R. Shelomo Zalman Auerbach (Israel, 1910–1995) understands the above story. The lesson the story conveys, according to R. Auerbach, is not how expansive the license of the householder is to "do in" a thief, but rather is a sad commentary on how uncontrolled greed leads to reckless conduct and disastrous consequences.[36] R. Menasheh Klein (New York, contemp.) also understands the story in this manner.[37]

Supporting the notion that the whole point of the story is how uncontrollable greed leads to reckless conduct is an understanding of why the thief should have picked up that he was all along under suspicion. We can discover this detail by noting a slight discrepancy in the time line of the story. The narrative begins by telling us that a man arrived *early in the morning* (*hishkim etzlo*) to R. Yehoshua's home. But, in his dialogue with the thief upon seeing him injured, R. Yehoshua tells him: "Since *last night* [*emesh*] we were on guard against you." Now, if the man first arrived early in the morning, how could he have been under suspicion earlier from the previous night? The difficulty is easily resolved if we read into the words *hishkim etzlo* that the house guest banged on R. Yehoshua's door so early in the morning that he woke up R. Yehoshua and his family. Technically, the thief arrived in the very early hours of the morning, perhaps at the crack of dawn, but for R. Yehoshua and his family it was still night. Because it would be very reasonable for the thief to assume that R. Yehoshua's usual waking time for the morning prayer was anywhere between the crack of dawn and sunrise, the thief should have had a little patience and waited outside until R. Yehoshua exited his home. Barging in without showing a basic consideration not to wake up R. Yehoshua and his household created, we propose, an immediate tension in the air, and hence the thief should have picked up that he was from the beginning under suspicion.[38]

The upshot of the above analysis is that this story provides no basis for a householder to set a booby trap on his premises for the purpose of injuring an intruder. Relatedly, the story provides no basis for allowing a householder to set up his premises in a manner that will automatically subject an intruder to attack upon entry.

3. R. Natan's Dictum

The prohibition for a homeowner to *set up* his property in a manner that will *automatically attack a trespasser* can also be reached by analysis of the homeowner's duty to construct a roof fence (*ma'aka*): "When you build a new house, you shall make a fence for your roof, and you shall not place blood in your house, in case someone should fall from it" (Deuteronomy 22:8). Citing the *ma'aka* duty, R. Natan expounds:

> From where do we learn that a person should not raise a *kelev ra* (vicious dog) in his house – and should not place a rickety ladder in his house? – to teach this [the verse] states: "You shall not place blood in your house."[39]

Before we relate R. Natan's dictum to the home security scenarios, several preliminary remarks are in order. Authorities dispute whether the biblical *ma'aka* duty is rooted in a concern for a fatal accident,[40] or in a concern for injury.[41] In any case, R. Natan's dictum, as R. Avraham Duber Kahana Shapira (Poland, 1870–1943) points out, is rooted in the concern for even injury. Evidencing this is an incident, discussed in the Talmud, involving a cat that attacked and ate large chickens. The attack was regarded as an aberration and the owner was made liable for a half damage payment. But, based on R. Natan's dictum, *Bet Din* ordered the owner to destroy the cat. Finally, *Bet Din* warned the owner that if he failed to comply with the court order within the time the court gave him, the court would order a ban on him.[42] Given the controversy as to whether the *ma'aka* duty applies when the concern is only injury, R. Natan's dictum should be taken as rabbinical in nature, and a decree promulgated in the *spirit* of the biblical *ma'aka* duty.[43]

In his explication of R. Natan's dictum, R. Samuel Eliezer b. Judah ha-Levi Edels (Poland, 1555–1623) avers that R. Natan's concern is mainly not with the safety of members of one's own household. Because of their awareness of the hazard the rickety ladder presents, the members of one's household can guard themselves against this harm. Similarly, because the householder raises a vicious dog to protect his family at night against thieves, the family could avoid the danger of the vicious dog (e.g., the dog could be let loose outside the house only when everyone in the household was asleep). R. Natan's intention hence is to extend the duty of the householder to set up his premises in a manner that would not subject people outside his own household to hazards.[44]

What is the nature of the *kelev ra* R. Natan speaks of? Shedding light on this is the following ruling recorded in the *Mishna* along with a story the Talmud cites that demonstrates the practical wisdom and value of the ruling:

> A person may not raise *the* dog unless it is bound with a chain.[45] There was once a certain woman who entered a particular house to bake bread – and the owner's unchained dog barked at her. – Its owner said to her: "Do not be afraid of [the dog]. Its canines have been removed, and so it cannot harm you." [The woman] said to him in reply: "Your debt of gratitude is removed and cast onto thorns. For the fetus has already been dislodged from its place in the womb. Hence your reassurance is worthless."[46]

Noting that the *Mishna* makes use of the definite article (i.e., *the* [dog], in phrasing the prohibition of raising a dog without a chain, R. Yom Tov Lipmann b. Nathan ha-Levi Heller (Moravia, 1579–1654) avers that the type of dog the *Mishna* speaks of is the same type of dog R. Natan speaks of and the two dictums should be taken as complementing each other.[47] Once we accept the notion that the two dictums should be read together, we arrive at a definition of what exactly is meant by a *kelev ra*. What the above Talmudic story demonstrates is that *kelev ra* should be defined as a dog that barks, even if it does not bite. This type of dog presents a danger to a pregnant woman because without knowing in advance that the dog is harmless, a pregnant woman might become frightened upon hearing the dog's bark and may miscarry as a result. Once the dog is chained, no one will become frightened of the dog and its bark will present no danger, even to a pregnant woman.

Explicitly defining *kelev ra* as a dog that barks, even if it has been defanged and is therefore harmless, is R. Shelomo Kluger (Ukraine, 1785–1869). Specifically, he defines *kelev ra* as a dog that will bark at anyone it does not know. Such a dog, notwithstanding that it is incapable of biting, may not be kept unless it is chained.[48]

At this juncture let us take note of another halakhic objection of maintaing a *kelev ra* on one's premises. This is R. Shimon b. Lakish's dictum:

Whoever raises a *kelev ra* in his house prevents kindness from coming into his house.[49]

Expounding on R. Shimon b. Lakish's dictum, R. Solomon b. Isaac (*Rashi*, Troyes, 1040–1105) rationalizes it with the comment that "a *kelev ra* will not let the poor approach one's door."[50] Given the rationale behind R. Shimon b. Lakish's interdict, R. Kluger's definition of a vicious dog should apply here as well.

While R. Shimon b. Lakish speaks of the prohibition to raise a *kelev ra*, the underlying logic of the interdict should extend it to broadcasting a soundtrack of the howls and barks of a vicious dog. In both instances, the poor will be driven away and the householder's home will become a place that withholds kindness.

On the basis of R. Shimon b. Lakish's dictum, it should also be prohibited for a householder to affix a sign BEWARE OF DOG on his front door. This prohibition should hold irrespective of whether an actual dog lurks about inside or not. In both instances, the poor will be driven away and the householder's home will become a place that withholds kindness.

The upshot of this analysis is that R. Natan's dictum requires a householder to make his premises free of hazards. Relatedly, a householder must assure that his home will not become a place that withholds kindness. To be sure, these requirements don't stem from any duty the householder has to protect a potential trespasser. Instead, these requirements stem from the householder's duty to family members, invitees, implied invitees and poor strangers that have a right to approach him. Nonetheless, the householder's duty to an assortment of nontrespassers has the effect of constraining the type of burglar alarm system he sets up.

Clearly prohibited on the basis of both R. Natan's and R. Shimon b. Lakish's dictums is the Shelton home security plan of placing an attack dog in a hidden place on their grounds. Similarly prohibited is Rubie Indigo's plan of setting up a number of visible hazards in the second story room where he leaves the window open. Notwithstanding his intention to merely dissuade the would-be thief from navigating the room and convince him to withdraw from the enterprise, members of his household or invitees, especially children, might wander into the room and injure themselves on the hazards the householder places there. The same can be said of Drillman's scheme of placing camouflage shrubbery on the border of his property with the aim of causing a trespasser to fall into the deep trench that is beneath it. To be sure, no person with a legitimate purpose to enter the householder's premises would enter through the back via a neighbor's property. Nonetheless, camouflaged shrubbery presents a definite hazard for both the householder's family and other invitees in the long run. Setting up his property with a booby trap on a portion of it creates the specter that a person who legitimately is in the backyard, especially a child, will stumble into the abyss without being warned about the danger.

Let us now move to a consideration of whether Dror's plan of loosening the poles that supported the clothing line violates R. Natan's dictum. Perhaps the loosening of the poles should constitute the creation of a hazard? Addressing himself to this issue, R. Tzvi Spitz answers in the negative. In his view, an object should be categorized as a hazard only if its ordinary and conventional usage entails a danger for the user. Because the ordinary use of a knife or hammer entails no danger for the user, these ordinary household articles should not be categorized as hazardous objects. Likewise, the ordinary and conventional use of a clothing line is to hang wet laundry. Using the poles of the clothing line to support a person is definitely not a normal use of a clothing line. Loosening the poles so that they no longer can support a person standing on them does not hence constitute the creation of a hazard.

This analysis leads R. Spitz to find no halakhic objection for the scheme of loosening the poles of the clothing line as a means of thwarting would-be thieves in the future.[51] While loosening the poles may not violate R. Natan's dictum, the legitimacy of this particular method of thwarting would-be thieves can be questioned on other grounds, which will be discussed below.

One caveat should be noted. The prohibition against raising a *kelev ra* on one's premises is modified when the householder faces an imminent danger.[52]

4. Lifnei Iver

In assessing the halakhic validity of various burglar alarm systems, another issue to consider is the prohibition to *lure* someone into committing a transgression. Such conduct is an aspect of the interdict against facilitating a sin (*lifnei iver lo titen mikhshol*). The prototype case in the Talmud is the prohibition for L to lend money to B without the benefit of witnesses.[53] Such an arrangement effectively *tempts B* to repudiate his debt, as no one other than the lender can testify that the loan took place.[54]

Of the various alarm systems described in the opening vignette, Rubie Indigo's scheme of tempting the would-be burglar with an open window stands out as a violation of the *lifnei iver* interdict. Consider that checking that windows are not left open when one leaves one's premises is a protective precaution every homeowner understands as an absolute must. Not attending to this detail is gross negligence. Deliberately leaving a window open when one goes out of one's home therefore amounts to "luring" a would-be thief to break in and steal.

The notion that *deliberately* leaving one's premises with an open window amounts to luring a thief to break in finds support from a point in law in connection with the exemption of those who guard gardens and orchards from the mitzvah of *Sukkah*.[55] The Talmud is puzzled by this exemption. Why does the occupation of guard stand in conflict with the *mitzvah* of *Sukkah*? Could not the guard take up residence in a *Sukkah* in the orchard or garden he is watching and at the same time not compromise his duties as watchman? Addressing this issue, Abaye and Rava each provide a rationale for this exemption. Espousing the approach adopted in the codes,[56] Rava exempts those who guard gardens and orchards on the rationale that: *a breach* in the wall *invites the robber* to steal.[57] What Rava conveys here is that as soon as the guard sits in the *Sukkah* at night, the robber realizes that a portion of the garden is blocked from the guard's view and the robber seizes the moment to steal fruit from the orchard.[58]

In the thinking of the Talmud an obvious lack of security "invites" a robber to steal. By extension *deliberately* leaving one's premises with an open window amounts to "luring" a thief to attempt a break-in.

5. *Lo Ta'amod*

Another halakhic principle the setting up of home alarm systems must conform with is the prohibition of "Do not stand idly by the blood of your neighbor" (*lo ta'amod al dam rei'akha*, Leviticus 19:16). On the basis of this verse if *A*'s life is in danger and a bystander (*B*) is in position to extricate him from this danger, *B* must take timely action to do so.[59]

Does the duty of rescue apply even in the instance when the potential victim is poised to commit a transgression and the danger he faces threatens him only on account of the transgression he is bent on committing? Addressing this issue is R. Menasheh Klein (New York, Contemp.). The specific case he dealt with entailed the following elements:

M was a student in an American medical school. As far as his medical studies were concerned, *M* was an inept and poor student, but was an accomplished chemist. Because of his hapless performance in his medical studies, *M* was constantly ridiculed and mocked by his fellow students. One of the indignities *M* was subject to was that someone made a habit of stealing his lunch sandwich from his knapsack. Well, one day, after lunch, one student began to convulse and vomit violently. It was the thief who became violently sick from consuming the sandwich he stole. *M* got up and confessed publicly that he had laced his own sandwich with poison. The confession was followed by heroics by *M* to save the life of the sick student with an antidote. The incident transformed *M*'s image in the group and his prestige soared.

The ethics for *M* to ensnare the thief with a poisoned sandwich evoked heated debate in rabbinical circles.[60] The great majority of the rabbis, including R. Klein, felt it was terribly wrong for *M* to stop the thief in this fashion.[61] R. Klein's main objection to *M*'s conduct was that it amounted to a violation of *lo ta'amod* because the *lo ta'amod* interdict remains intact even if the potential victim faces the present danger only on account of the transgression he is actively committing. Accordingly, if *M* knows that the sandwich the thief stole contains poison, he is duty bound to inform the thief as fast as he can so that the thief will be saved from death or even from sickness. Now, if *M* must extricate the thief from the danger of the pilfered poisoned sandwich, he certainly should not poison the sandwich in the first place. *Lo ta'amod* requires this.[62]

R. Klein's assumption is that whenever there is a hypothetical duty to save someone from a particular danger, there must also be a prohibition to create that danger. How far does this principle go? Perhaps it holds only when it is more than just a remote possibility that the victim will be exposed to the danger. This is the salient feature of R. Klein's case. Consider that the sandwich was *unguarded*, and therefore easy prey for the thief. One might even argue that leaving the sandwich unprotected in the face of repeated incidents of theft, with absolutely no adjustment on the part of the victim, amounts to *luring* the thief to continue his conduct. Given the easy accessibility of the sandwich for the thief, the owner of the sandwich must take into account the likelihood that an attempted pilferage of his sandwich will be made. Poisoning the sandwich therefore violates *lo ta'amod*. But, if the likelihood that the victim will be exposed to the danger is, in any case, very remote, the action taken should not be regarded as creating a danger for anyone, with the consequence that *lo ta'amod* is not violated. To illustrate: *A* places poisoned candy in a locked safe that contains valuables. *A's* motive in doing this is the hope that in the event of a break-in, the thief would grab the candies along with the valuables and get his just desserts. *A's* intent in placing the poison candies in the safe is to harm or even kill the thief. *A's* intentions are clearly nefarious and shameful, but should not constitute a violation of *lo ta'amod*. Why? Given that the poisoned candy is absolutely secure against unauthorized entry and the authorized personnel are made fully aware of the danger, the danger the candies present to humankind is very remote. Placing the poisoned candies in the locked safe should therefore not be regarded as the "creation" of a danger for anyone.

Recall that R. Spitz found no objection for a householder to put hazards on his property for the purpose of injuring the thief, provided that household members and invited guests are not at the same time put at risk by these burglar repellants. In his analysis, the issue of *lo ta'amod* does not come up.

R. Spitz must therefore adopt a narrow conceptualization of the *lo ta'amod* interdict along the lines discussed previously.

Addressing the issue of placing poisoned candy in a safe, R. Yitzhak Zilberstein (Israel, contemp.) rules that such conduct is prohibited. If a break-in occurs and the thief consumes the candies and dies, the householder violates *lo ta'amod*. Given the hypothetical duty to save the thief from the danger of the candies, placing the candies in the safe violates *lo ta'amod*.[63] In R. Zilberstein's thinking the *hypothetical* duty of saving the thief from the poisoned candies alone creates a prohibition to place the candies in the safe, irrespective that nobody is placed in a peril.

If we adopt R. Zilberstein's broad conceptualization of the *lo ta'amod* interdict, none of the various burglar alarm systems described in the opening vignette will pass halakhic muster. Some of these devices may, however, survive under a much more narrow conceptualization of *lo ta'amod*. In what follows we will take the narrow conceptualization of *lo ta'amod* as our given.

The application of *lo ta'amod* to the various burglar alarm systems described in the opening vignette should turn on the dispute between the two schools of thought regarding *ones* liability.

If we adopt the *ones gadol* liability rule, the householder's exemption for the injuries of the trespasser is not rooted in the judgment that the householder need not take into account the possibility that someone might enter his premises without permission. Rather, the exemption is based on the principle that if someone enters another's premises without permission the burden is on the trespasser to be especially circumspect so as to avoid injury. If injury occurs, the trespasser is deemed to have brought the injury on himself. Accordingly, one may not set up one's premises in a manner that will automatically attack the intruder upon entry. Stationing a pitbull or installing camouflage shrubbery on one's premises therefore violates *lo ta'amod*. Moreover, setting up a trap for the thief designed to injure him, should also amount to a violation of *lo ta'amod*.

Within the *ones gadol* liability rule, does Dror's scheme of loosening the poles of the clothing line violate *lo ta'amod*? The issue turns on several considerations. The loosened poles represent a danger only to someone who both becomes a trespasser and also is willing to commit the reckless act of climbing on the poles. Because these combined circumstances are so remote, Dror cannot be said to be "creating" a danger for anyone when he loosens the poles. But, let us not lose sight of the fact that the poles of the clothing line proved to be "the breach that invited the thief." Accordingly, from the perspective of the original thief, climbing on the poles to gain entry is not a reckless act. Dror's motivation in loosening the pole is clearly to lure the thief into repeating his crime. Consider that Dror could just as easily have heeded the advice of his wife, Shulamit, and protected his home by installing bars on the inside of the vulnerable window. Instead, Dror opted to protect his home by loosening the poles only because he was convinced that the thief would repeat his *modus operandi*. Accordingly, Dror's action should be regarded as creating a danger, and hence is in violation of *lo ta'amod*.

Let us now analyze *lo ta'amod* as it pertains to home security devices within the framework of the ordinary *ones* rule of liability. If we adopt a lenient definition for *ones* liability, the householder's exemption for the injuries of the trespasser is simply rooted in the judgment that the householder need not take into account the possibility that someone might enter his premises without permission. Now, if the injury a trespasser sustains is regarded from the standpoint of the landholder as *ones*, then setting up one's property so that a trespasser will automatically be attacked upon entry should not be regarded as creating a danger for anyone. Note, however, that when the issue is danger to life rather than just the violation of a prohibition Halakhah takes a more protective stance.[64] The criteria for *ones* in respect to liability for damage should therefore not be equated with the level of risk that constitutes the creation of a life-threatening danger. Accordingly, the ordinary *ones* rule of liability school may very well be in agreement that setting up one's premises so that a trespasser will automatically be attacked without warning should be prohibited. In addition, this school of thought should be in agreement that any home protection device that lures the would-be thief into a dangerous predicament should constitute a violation of *lo ta'amod*.

6. Rodef

Another consideration in assessing the legitimacy of the various home security devices described in the opening vignette is the limitations Halakhah imposes on a householder in defending his property when engulfed in an *actual* confrontation with someone who invades his premises to rob him. Restraints that apply in the heat of battle with the thief should serve as a model for assessing the type of automatically triggered defenses one is permitted to set up in advance with the objective of intercepting and/or foiling a thief. The pertinent law here is the particulars governing *haba'a be-mahateret* (lit. one [who comes to rob someone's premises] by means of an underground passage). The biblical source of this law is: "If the thief will be found in an underground passage, and he is struck and dies, there is no blood for him" (Exodus 22:1). While the verse speaks of a thief who makes his entry by means of an underground passageway, the *Baraita* expands the case to include the thief who invades the property of a homeowner and is discovered on the roof, courtyard, or veranda.[65] The qualifying feature is that the thief invades the property under conditions when the homeowner can be expected to be on the premises.[66]

Breaking into someone's property brands the burglar a *rodef* (one who pursues another with the intent to kill him).[67] Although the burglar's original design is merely the theft of property, the presumption of resistance on the part of the proprietor forces the burglar to be prepared to eliminate his victim should he be discovered in the act.[68] Given the life-threatening danger the householder faces from the burglar, Halakhah confers him with a license to eliminate the burglar upon discovering him. Relatedly, Halakhah empowers a bystander with a license to extricate the proprietor from the life-threatening danger, even to the extent of eliminating the burglar, if necessary.[69]

Designating the thief as a *rodef* by no means denotes that the life of the thief becomes forfeit as soon as he enters the qualifying property without permission. The following caveats should be noted:

1) In the prototype *rodef* case, M pursues V with the intent of killing him. If the threat to V can be neutralized by means less drastic than killing M, the lesser means must be utilized.[70] If a rescuer (R) kills M, when it is evident that he could have accomplished the same end with less than lethal force, R is put to death on account of taking M's life.[71] This principle is called *yakhol le-hatziloh be-ahad ma-avorov* (lit. he could have saved him [the victim] with one of his [the pursuer's] limbs, henceforth *yakhol le-hatzilo*). Elsewhere in this volume we have discussed the parameters of this principle.[72] Several points are relevant for our case study. One point is that this

protocol, according to a number of authorities, applies not only for a bystander, but for the would-be victim as well. Another point is that the first line of defense against an intruder should be a warning to him to leave.

2) In his treatment of *haba'a be-mahateret*, *Rambam* designates the thief a *rodef* whether the perpetrator broke in at night or during the day.[73] Rabad, however, contends that the burglar should be treated as a *rodef* only if he breaks in at night. It is only in the evening hours, when the burglar must count on a strong likelihood that the householder will be home, that the psychology the sages ascribe to the thief is compelling. Because the burglar takes into account the strong probability that he will end up in a struggle with the householder, he makes up his mind in advance to murder the householder, if that happens. In contrast, in the daytime, the householder is probably away from home. Because the burglar does not expect to find the householder home in the daytime, it is much more likely that the burglar's plan in advance is to flee, rather than struggle with the householder, if he is discovered. Accordingly, the thief, in Rabad's thinking, should not be treated as a *rodef* if the burglary takes place in the daytime.[74]

3) One final caveat in regard to the thief's designation as *rodef*: The designation of *rodef* does not ordinarily apply if the householder discovers that the thief is his own son. Recall that the designation of *rodef* occurs because of the presumed resistance, to the point of a life-and-death struggle, the thief would encounter with the householder if the latter discovered him in the act. Because the thief realizes that upon discovery he is threatened with death, the thief makes up his mind to kill the householder as soon as he is discovered, before the householder kills him. This scenario makes no sense, however, when the thief turns out to be the householder's son. Because a father naturally loves his son, the thief has no right to presume that his father will resist his designs with a life-and-death struggle. Quite to the contrary, the son should feel confident that his father would surrender the booty, rather than struggle with him. Since the necessary scenario to make the son-turned-thief a

rodef does not occur, the householder (father) has no right to treat his son-turned-thief as a *rodef*. The same caveat applies when the thief is someone that the householder has a close bond with and would have compassion for if he discovered that person trying to steal from him.[75]

If Halakhah prescribes various constraints for the householder in defending his property in the heat of battle against a thief, these constraints should be operative, at least in some measure, in setting up an *automatic* response for a break-in.

Let us begin with the *yakhol lehatzilo* principle. Recall that issuing a warning to the thief to desist is ideally the first line of defense under the *yakhol le-hazilo* constraint. Now, if *yakhol le-hazilo* applies to the victim no less than it does to a bystander, a homeowner would be prohibited from setting up his premises so that *without warning* any intruder would be automatically attacked upon entry.

Recall that in the opinion of one school of thought the *yakhol le-hatzilo* rule applies only to a bystander, but is not a directive to the victim himself. If the *yakhol le-hatzilo* rule does not apply to the victim himself, the homeowner should apparently have no duty to sound a warning for the thief that if he does not leave the premises immediately he will be attacked. But this is not so. The rationale for dispensing with the *yakhol le-hatzilo* rule as far as the potential victim is concerned is only the recognition that the victim does not have the presence of mind to act with restraint. This consideration is inoperative when it comes to setting up a home security system. Here, the homeowner should be required to design his system in a manner that the first line of defense is to warn the intruder to leave on pain of possible serious injury or death. Moreover, the *yakhol le-hatzilo* principle would not validate attacking the intruder with a pitbull when technology such as stun guns could be employed instead.

Recall Rabad's view that if the break-in occurs in the daytime hours, the thief should not be regarded as a *rodef*. Recall also that if the intruder is the homeowner's son or someone else that the homeowner has a bond of affection for, the intruder is not regarded halakhically as a *rodef*. Consideration that the intruder might turn out to be someone that Halakhah would not designate as a *rodef*, should provide another solid basis for prohibiting a home security device that does not feature as the first line of defense a warning issued to the intruder.

Finally, recognition of the constraints Halakhah imposes on self-defense in the context of an actual encounter with an intruder should make it totally unacceptable for a homeowner to install a system that is designed specifically to ensnare and injure a thief, rather than just to repel him. Recall that Dror's plan of loosening the poles that supported the clothing line may very well be regarded as an ensnaring mechanism. If this characterization of Dror's plan is correct, his plan would also fall short of the model of self-defense the *haba'a be-mahateret* case presents.

7. Revenge

The driving force behind Dror's plan of loosening the poles of the clothing line was to get revenge against the thief. Elsewhere in this book we take up the biblical prohibitions against taking revenge, "You shall not take revenge *(lo tekom)*. . . ." (Leviticus 19:18) and against bearing a grudge: "[Y]ou shall not bear a grudge *(lo tittor)* against the members of your people" (Leviticus 19: 18).[76] Dror's conduct violates both injunctions. Consider that the Torah penalty for the thief is to make restitution to the victim along with the theoretical possibility that the thief will be ordered to make a double payment *(kefel)* to the victim. Dror's action of loosening the poles of the clothing line is designed to cause the thief severe injury or death. These measures go considerably beyond the penalties the Torah metes out to the thief. If Dror's plan succeeds because the original thief repeats his *modus operandi* and suffers severe injury or death, Dror violates the prohibition against revenge. Moreover, even if the loose poles never do any harm to the original thief, putting into motion a scheme to punish the thief beyond the penalties the Torah calls for violates for Dror *lo tittor*. Let us recall R. Ehrman's thesis in connection with *lo tittor*[77] and apply it to Dror's conduct. If Dror is overwhelmed with a passion for revenge when he initially becomes aware of the break-in, the Torah does not hold him accountable for this feeling. This emotion is spontaneous and involuntary, and the Torah does not legislate against human emotions that cannot be controlled. But, to avoid violation of *lo tittor*, Dror must take action to eradicate the initial passion for revenge that overwhelms him. Reporting the theft to the police and affixing bars on the window that the burglar used to enter the house, as Shulamit pleaded all along, constitute such actions. These actions by Dror are designed to recover no more than his entitlement and therefore violate for him neither *lo tekom* nor *lo tittor*.

DOING IN A CHEATER

Let us now move to a consideration of the ethics of doing in a cheater. Is it ethical for Dror to thwart Boris's designs to cheat off him by allowing him to copy his answers, only to change the answers once Boris hands in his exam?

Before we address the issue of the ethics of the specific tactic Dror adopted to deflect Boris's attempt to cheat off him, let us first identify the nature of the prohibitions the test taker violates for cheating on the exam and why another test taker may not allow anyone to copy answers off his or her paper.

In his treatment of the prohibition of cheating on secular education examinations, R. Menashe Klein (New York, contemp.) avers that this conduct entails a number of infractions. At once the cheater violates the prohibition against creating a false impression (*geneivat da'at*). To be sure, the cheater's immediate illicit gain is not a monetary gain, but only recognition in the form of a better grade than is deserved. But, the prohibition of *geneivat da'at* applies even when the gain achieved through the false impression is nonmonetary in nature.[78] Elsewhere in this book we have elaborated on many of the details of this prohibition.[79] The entire discussion on false good, in fact, illustrates R. Klein's point.[80]

In society today, many rewards are based on grades. These include eligibility for academic scholarships, the selection of new hires, and higher salaries. Individuals who secure these differential awards by means of dishonest grades are guilty of monetary fraud.[81]

Once it is recognized that the cheater violates *geneivat da'at law*, it becomes the duty of every exam taker not to assist anyone's cheating. Failure to thwart the designs of the cheater makes the assisting party guilty of facilitating a sin and hence violates for him or her the *lifnei iver* interdict.

The easy way for Dror to thwart Boris' cheating is to keep his answer key turned over when not filling in answers. While filling in the correct bubble for a particular question, Dror should make sure to cover with his hands the entire series of bubbles for that question. And, yes, Dror should check to make sure that his seat is not tilted in a manner that would give

Boris a glimpse of his paper. Making use of these methods thwarts Boris's designs and imparts no harm to Boris other than to frustrate his desire to cheat.

With the aim of teaching Boris a lesson, may Dror intentionally put down wrong answers on his paper and let Boris cheat off him? Let us consider three possible reasons why the ploy should be prohibited.

1) Dror's scheme is not acceptable because it *falls short* of *preventing Boris* from violating the prohibition against falsehood. Recall the dispute whether the *geneivat da'at* interdict is rooted in the prohibition against theft or is an aspect of the prohibition against falsehood.[82] The consideration that Boris' conduct, thanks to Dror's scheme, ends up *"fooling"* no one, perhaps, makes the case that the scheme *prevents* Boris from violating *genevat da'at*, even if this prohibition is rooted in falsehood. But, Dror's scheme does not entirely remove the falsehood element from Boris' conduct. Consider that up until the moment of truth when Professor Regenstein returns his exam, Boris imagines that his cheating succeeded in falsely inflating his grade. All along Boris is hence *"false to himself."* Recall that a misstatement that deceives no one is also a violation of the prohibition against falsehood.[83] Being *"false to oneself"* is certainly worse conduct than uttering a harmless lie to someone else.[84] Dror's scheme of filling in wrong answers hence does not *entirely prevent* Boris from violating the prohibition against falsehood. Accordingly, Dror's scheme *falls short* of his *lifnei iver* duty.

2) Another reason to object to Dror's scheme is that it does violence to the behavioral requirement expected of an individual when he becomes aware that his fellow is about to commit a transgression. Dror's awareness that Boris wants to cheat off him brings on the duty to remonstrate with Boris. The source of this duty is: "You shall not hate your brother in your heart; you shall reprove your fellow and you shall not bear a sin because of him" (Leviticus 19:17). In the explication of the sages, the end of the verse is connected with the beginning of the verse: "One might assume [this to be obligatory] even though his face blanched, therefore the text states: 'and you shall not bear a sin because of him.'"[85]

What the verse points to is that the remonstration should be delivered in a manner that will not make the remonstrator himself guilty of sin. Following this line, Maimomides presents the duty to remonstrate with the sinner as follows:

> If a man sees his friend sinning or following what is not a good path, it is his duty to restore him to what is better and make known to him that he is sinning against himself by his evil doings. As the verse states: "You shall reprove your fellow" (Leviticus 19:17). He who corrects his friend, whether the matter is between man and man, or between man and God, must do so between themselves; and he should speak calmly and in a gentle voice making known that he speaks for his friend's good and to bring him life in the "world to come." If the sinner accepts, it is good; but if not, he must be admonished twice, even thrice. It is always a duty to correct even until the sinner strikes one and says, "I will not listen." Anyone who has the power to prevent evil and does not do so will be overtaken by the evil that he could have prevented.[86]

There can be no doubt that thwarting Boris's designs by doing him in violates Maimonides' protocol to remonstrate with the sinner in "a quiet and soft manner." Proceeding in Maimonides' recommended fashion requires Dror to protect his examination in a manner that makes it impossible for Boris to cheat off him.

3) Another consideration here is the *yakhol le-hazilo* imperative discussed earlier. The relevancy of this principle is that Boris's design to cheat off Dror threatens to lower Dror's standing in the class. Recall that Professor Regenstein informed the class that the exam would be graded on a curve. If Boris is stronger than Dror in some of the tested material, Boris can decide to rely on his own judgments for certain questions. By selectively cheating off Dror, Boris can end up with a higher grade than Dror and thereby lower Dror's relative standing for the exam. Given that Dror's own interests are threatened by Boris's designs to cheat off him, Dror has a right to defend his interests. In fending off Boris's attack against his interests, the *yakhol le-hazilo* imperative should be operative. Preliminarily, let us note that this principle of restraint in self-defense

applies, according to R. Asher b. Jehiel, not only to a case where the victim faces a potentially lethal threat, but also to a simple assault case. In this regard, R. Asher rules that if *A* assaults *B*, *B* may respond only with the minimum force necessary to neutralize the threat he faces. If *B* responds with more force than is necessary, *B* becomes liable for his attack no less than *A* bears responsibity for initiating the attack on *B*. The principle that informs *B's* liability in the latter case, according to R. Asher, is the *yakhol le-hazilo* principle.[87] By extension, the *yakhol le-hazilo* principle should apply to the cheating case as well. Application of the *yakhol le-hazilo* principle should require Dror to exercise restraint in defending himself. Since Dror can easily defend his own interests by simply covering his examination paper, any defense that will bring Boris more anguish than this approach should be prohibited.

CONFISCATION FOR DISCIPLINARY PURPOSES

We now turn to Dror's third grade experience of having his *rebbe* confiscate, often on a permanent basis, the toys he caught Dror playing with. The ethics for a teacher to confiscate a pupil's item for disciplinary purposes has been dealt with in the rabbinic literature.

One problem with the confiscation is that despite the salutary intent of the teacher, the prohibition against theft should remain intact. As far as the prohibition against theft is concerned, the motivation of the thief does not matter. Thus, if the thief is not motivated by personal gain, but rather only to annoy (*lema'not*) the victim, the prohibition remains intact.[88] Moreover, even if the thief's plan all along is to get caught and get ordered by the court to pay the double (*kefel*) payment of the thief, the thief's salutary motive to enrich the victim does not legitimize the pilferage.[89]

Relevant to the issue at hand is the following criterion that R. Raphael Yom Tov Lipman Heilpern (Poland, 1816–1879) offers for the parameters of theft in connection with the *mitzvah* of *etrog* on the second day of *Yom Tov*. The case entailed the following: *A* makes it known that he gives no one permission to use his *etrog*. In full knowledge of *A's* prohibition, *B* snatches away the *etrog* from *A*. After fulfilling his *mitzvah*, *B* immediately gives the *etrog* back to *A*. Does *B* fulfill his *mitzvah* of *etrog*? Note that to fulfill the *mitzvah* of *etrog* on the second day of *Yom Tov* there is no requirement that the *etrog* must be the property of the person who performs the *mitzvah*. The issue at hand is therefore reduced to whether *B's mitzvah* should be disqualified on the basis that the *mitzvah* object is stolen property. R. Heilpern answers in the negative. In his view theft occurs when *B* snatches away *A's* item with the intent to either destroy or derive benefit from it. In the case at hand *B* takes the *etrog* with the intent to return it as soon as he fulfills his *mitzvah*. *B's* taking of the *etrog* should therefore certainly not be regarded as taking for the purpose of destroying the object of theft. Consider also that *B* takes the *etrog* with the sole intent to use it for a *mitzvah* (religious) purpose. The dictum here is that *mitzvot* (religious duties) were not given to us for the purpose of deriving benefit from them (*mitzot lav lehanot nitnu*). Since any benefit we derive from the performance of a *mitzvah* is entirely incidental to its purpose, the enjoyment we derive from the *mitzvah* is not reckoned as a benefit. Given that *B* has not violated the law of theft by snatching away the *etrog* and immediately returning it and there is no requirement on the second day of *lakham* (lit. your property) *B* fulfills his *mitzvah* with the snatched *etrog*.[90]

Referring to above ruling of R. Heilpern, R. Yaakov Yeshayahu Bloi finds a basis for a limited permissibility for a teacher to confiscate a pupil's item in a classroom setting. Consider that the teacher does the confiscation for disciplinary purposes and not for any personal gain. Confiscating a pupil's item on a temporary basis should therefore be in accord with the ruling of R. Heilpern.[91]

In his treatment of the confiscation case, R. Yehudah Herzl Henkin (Israel, contemp.) builds a case for limited permissibility around the opinion cited in *Shittah Mekubbetzet* that rules that theft with the intention to restore the item to the victim is not theft. R. Henkin interprets this opinion very narrowly. To be free of the prohibition of theft the expropriator must keep the misappropriated item only for a very brief period, and intend this from the beginning. This opinion builds into a case for permissibility for a teacher to temporarily confiscate a pupil's item when we consider that the teacher does this for disciplinary purposes.

R. Henkin's conclusion is that it is prohibited for a teacher to confiscate a pupil's property on a permanent basis. What the teacher may do is only deprive a child of an object temporarily. The teacher does this by placing the object on his own desk indicating to the pupil that he or she will get it back at the end of the day.[92]

In his critique of R. Henkin's work, R. Moshe Bleich (New York, contemp.) contends that there is no basis to read into the text of the permissive view the caveat that theft for anything longer than a "brief period" is prohibited. In R. Bleich's opinion, provided the intention of the thief is to eventually return the article he stole, the prohibition against theft is not violated. But, the permissive view quoted in *Shittah Mekubbetzet*, cautions R. Bleich, is definitely a minority view. Confiscating a student's property even on a temporary basis, accordingly, does not have a solid halakhic basis.

Another concern confiscation presents is the impact this practice might have on the moral development of pupils. Confiscation of property by a teacher "diminishes respect for the property rights of others and teaches that appropriating someone else's property is not always wrong." The practice may hence desensitize a child to the severity of the prohibition against theft.[93]

R. Tzvi Spitz expresses another opinion in the confiscation rights of teachers. Preliminarily, R. Spitz notes that for the purpose of achieving disciplinary objectives, a teacher of religious instruction (*rebbe*) has a right to administer corporal punishment. The latitude Halakhah grants a *rebbe* to administer corporal punishment is nowhere more evident than the ruling of the *Mishnah* that if a *rebbe* is engaged in chastising his pupil and inadvertently kills him, the *rebbe* is exempt from the punishment of exile.[94] Now, if the disciplinary authority of the *rebbe* extends even to corporal punishment, then, it certainly should include monetary penalties. This principle can be seen from a point in law in connection with *rodef*. Recall that the potential victim has a right to save himself by killing the *rodef*, if necessary. If killing the *rodef* is permitted, then the potential victim is certainly permitted to save himself by destroying the pursuer's vessels. Accordingly, no reimbursement is due for their destruction.[95] What proceeds from the logic employed by the Talmud is that corporal punishment is more severe than monetary punishment.[96]

Because confiscation is firmly rooted in the disciplinary authority of the *rebbe*, the issue of theft does not come up. To be sure, corporal punishment and confiscation of property are drastic disciplinary tools and should not be resorted to when less harsh methods will accomplish the disciplinary goals of the teacher. But, if the *rebbe* feels that confiscation is necessary, the property of a pupil may be taken away on even a permanent basis.[97]

Note that the lynchpin for R. Spitz's permissive ruling is that the right of the *rebbe* to confiscate flows naturally from his right to administer corporal punishment. Both R. Bleich[98] and R. Henkin[99] considered this argument and rejected it. Corporal punishment is within the disciplinary authority of the *rebbe* because hitting someone is prohibited only when it is conducted in the manner of an assault. In contrast, confiscation is inherently an act of misappropriation. The salutary motive of the *rebbe* in taking away the pupil's object should therefore not, as discussed earlier, remove the prohibition against theft.

CONFISCATION AS AN INSTRUMENT OF RESCUE

The controversy surrounding the issue of confiscating pupil property has, in the opinion of this writer, room for narrowing. Consider that Torah study stands on a higher level than any other *mitzvah*.[100] In the imagery of the sages, the enterprise of the *rebbe* is described as providing his pupils with the gateway to *hayyei olam* i.e. everlasting life.[101] Torah study is *qualitatively* superior to any other spiritual act. In this regard consider that the act of prayer rises only to the level of *hayyei sha'a* i.e. temporal life, compared to the *hayyei olam* status of Torah study.[102] The *hayyei olam* status of Torah study makes every *lost* moment of Torah study an irreplaceable loss. In the imagery of the sages, the Torah proclaims: "If you forsake me for one day, I will forsake you for two days."[103] The irreplaceable nature of time lost in Torah study makes the *rebbe* subject to immediate dismissal if he idles on the job.[104] The reason for this is that the idling causes a *peseida delo hadra*, i.e. an irretrievable loss for the pupils.[105] If a pupil can get away with playing with an item while the Torah lesson is going on, that pupil is destroying his own *hayyei olam* and the *hayyei olam* of his classmates. The disciplinary authority the school vests in the *rebbe* should therefore not be viewed as instruments of punishment, but rather as instruments of rescue. Disciplinary action saves the idling child from losing his or her *hayyei olam* and saves distracted classmates from the same fate.

Once it is recognized that Torah study in the classroom is a *hayyei olam* enterprise, any pupil who unlawfully disrupts the learning session or otherwise causes classmates to be distracted should be viewed as a *rodef*. If the distraction is done by means of a plaything, the plaything should be treated as a "bomb" that threatens the *hayyei olam* of the pupils. Given the *rodef* character of the disruption, the *rebbe* should have the theoretical right to smash or confiscate the plaything on a permanent basis. The guidepost here should be to remove the threat to *hayyei olam* with the *minimal* force necessary. If in the *rebbe*'s judgment smashing or confiscating the plaything is the only effective means of deterring this conduct in the future, the law of *rodef* should provide him with the license to take such action. Confiscation hence stands on solid halakhic grounds. But, the pupil that idles with a plaything does not become a *rodef* in the classical sense. The culprit's life does not become theoretically forfeit. Accordingly, the *rebbe* does not have *carte blanche* to do anything he feels necessary to stop the threat to *hayyei olam* now and deter this threat in the future. Does smashing the plaything or confiscating it *exceed* for the *rebbe* his disciplinary authority? No. A monetary penalty, as mentioned earlier, is never regarded as more severe than corporal punishment. If the *rebbe* has authority to administer corporal punishment, confiscating or smashing playthings should certainly fall within his discretion.

An objection to the above argument can, however, be raised. Consider that in many jurisdictions *dina de'malkhuta* (the law of the kingdom) prohibits the use of corporal punishment in the schools. Currently, twenty-two states permit some form of corporal punishment in school, while twenty-eight states ban this practice altogether. In the metropolitan area, New York, New Jersey and Connecticut all ban this practice.[106] In jurisdictions where corporal punishment is prohibited in the schools, the *rebbe* will have no authority to use this practice as a disciplinary tool. If the *rebbe* has no authority to make use of corporal punishment, his authority to confiscate playthings when a child idles with them on class time can be put to question.

The above objection can be dismissed. *Dina de'malkhuta* does no more than act as a *practical* restraint on the use of corporal punishment. The *theoretical validity* of its use from a halakhic standpoint remains intact.[107] If the *rebbe* is restrained from resorting to corporal punishment, he remains within authority to go down to the next level of harshness in his tool box, which is the use of confiscations in all its varieties.

PARENTAL ADVANCE CONSENT AND SCHOOL STUDENT PROPERTY CONFISCATION POLICY

While the *rodef* rationale gives the *rebbe* authority to confiscate pupil property for disciplinary reasons on a spontaneous basis without announcing the policy in advance, it is, nevertheless, desirable for the school to articulate this policy in advance and get parental consent for it as well.

Advanced articulation of the policy ensures that the school will not be guilty of creating a setting of veiled misconduct for its *rebbe* in respect to responsibility for the confiscated item in case it is lost, damaged, or destroyed. Consider the following scenario: Rabbi Kaplan catches Dror playing a video game on his palm pilot. Rabbi Kaplan confiscates Dror's palm pilot, but does not tell him for how long the confiscation will be in effect. Subsequently, Rabbi Kaplan puts the palm pilot in the unlocked drawer of his desk. The next day the item is gone. Is Rabbi Kaplan responsible for the loss? Dealing with a case of this type, R. Tzvi Spitz posits that if the *rebbe* makes up his mind to confiscate the item on a temporary basis, he becomes responsible to a certain degree to guard the item against theft or loss. Because the *rebbe* did not consciously undertake any responsibility to guard the item he confiscated, his responsibility to guard the item until he returns it cannot rise to anything more than the minimal level care. Hence, the level of care Halakhah imposes on the *rebbe* is no more than the level of care of one who accepts to be a guardian without pay (*shomer hinnum*). The *rebbe*'s responsibility extends therefore for negligence, but does not extend to responsibility for theft or loss. The fact that the *rebbe* receives compensation for his position as educator does not automatically impose on him the status of a paid trustee (*shomer sakhar*). This is so because the *rebbe*'s salary was never intended to cover the task of caring for confiscated objects.[108] What follows from R. Spitz's line, is that Rabbi Kaplan bears responsibility for Dror's palm pilot. Leaving Dror's palm pilot in an unlocked drawer in his desk overnight amounts to negligence on the part of Rabbi Kaplan. Notwithstanding that Rabbi Kaplan had only a duty of minimal care for the palm pilot while it was in his possession, the rabbi failed to meet even this minimum standard. But, Rabbi Kaplan can easily escape responsibility. What we have here is an opportunity for veiled misconduct. Recall that Rabbi Kaplan said nothing to Dror when he confiscated his palm pilot as to how long he intended to hold it. What is then to stop Rabbi Kaplan from getting out of responsibility for his negligence by claiming that his intention all along was to confiscate the palm pilot on a permanent basis and therefore bear no responsibility for the loss? Avoiding the unwitting creation of veiled misconduct scenarios, therefore, requires the *rebbe* and the school to clearly announce in advance the policy on confiscation.

One more concern. Notwithstanding the noble motive to prevent the disruption of "*hayyei olam*," confiscating the pupil's property runs the risk of teaching a false lesson that stealing "for any good reason" is not really stealing. Thus, the school's confiscation policy may inadvertently undermine in the eyes of all pupils the sanctity of private property. It becomes therefore desirable for the school to formulate its policy in such terms that it will be free of being characterized as "misappropriation for a good reason." Toward this end the policy would consist of getting parents to agree not to confer ownership to the child of the playthings they buy him or her. Instead, the parents would be asked to retain ownership of the toy and only let the child use the toy. The school would also request the parents to let the child know that they give both the child's teachers and the school administrators permission to "borrow" the toy anytime they felt a need to do so. The child would be made to understand that idling with the plaything on lesson time is the type of event that would trigger such a request. At the discretion of the teacher and other authorized personnel, the term of the "borrowing" could be temporary, indefinite or even permanent.

Helping along the objective of having the parents retain ownership of the playthings of their children is the ruling of R. Mosheh Isserles (*Rema*, Poland, 1525 or 1530–1572) in respect to the proprietary rights of gifts children receive from strangers. In *Rema's* opinion ownership of gifts strangers give to a minor who is supported by his father is retained by the father.[109] Given that children are legally regarded as not responsible, we assess that the donor desires to confer his gift in a manner that will allow the child to use the gift, but at the same time ensure that it will be guarded properly. This dual objective is achieved by reading into the mindset of the donor that his intention is to confer ownership of the item to the child's father and let the father make the item available to the child under his vigilance.[110] Once the proprietary right of the plaything resides with the father, teachers and administrators could use their discretion to "borrow" playthings from the pupils whenever disciplinary concerns called for such action without worrying that the policy violates someone's property rights. To insure that use of this disciplinary tool would not undermine in the eyes of the pupils the notion of the sanctity of private property, the teachers and administration should not refer or call this policy a "confiscation" policy. Instead, when the *rebbe* "takes away" the plaything he should tell the idling pupil: "As you know, your father has given me permission to borrow your toy. Don't worry. I'm not going to play with it! My enjoyment will, however, consist of the knowledge that you will no longer have a *distraction*, and instead, will concentrate your energies on your lessons." [A first or second grader might not understand every single word of this admonishment, but, will surely get the general gist of things, especially when he/she ends up *parting* with the "plaything."]

CONFISCATION OF STUDENT PROPERTY IN A SECULAR LEARNING SETTING

Recall that the lynchpin in the argument that gives the *rebbe* the authority to confiscate a pupil's plaything when he catches the child idling with it on lesson time is the *hayyei olam* nature of Torah study. Perhaps, a different conclusion is in order regarding the confiscation rights of a secular studies teacher. Notwithstanding that the secular studies learning session may very well take on the character of a *mitzvah* activity,[111] Torah study, and Torah study alone, is given the designation of *hayyei olam*. Because secular learning is not *hayyei olam*, its disruption, whether for the idling pupil himself or for his classmates, is qualitatively on a lower level of harm than the corresponding harm suffered when Torah study is disrupted. Since the harm of disruption is a lower level harm, perhaps, the disciplinary tool kit for the secular teacher does not include the confiscation of student property, which, as discussed earlier, is ordinarily treated as theft, even if done temporarily and for good purpose.

While the law of *rodef* will not serve as a basis for allowing the secular school teacher the right to use confiscation of student property as a disciplinary tool, R. Spitz's rationale, discussed above, should apply. This is so because Halakhah allows the secular teacher, as it does the *rebbe*, to use corporal punishment as a disciplinary tool.[112] Once corporal punishment is admissible, the use of monetary penalties applies, as discussed above, *a fortiori*.

Recall that other rabbinic scholars dispute R. Spitz. Accordingly, a much preferred approach is to get parental advance consent. The policy, as discussed above, should consist of getting parents to agree not to confer their child with ownership of the playthings they buy him or her, and, in addition, to tell their child that authorized school personnel have a right to "borrow" the toy upon request.

SUMMARY AND CONCLUSION

This chapter has investigated the limits Halakhah places on an individual in defending his property and rights against infringement.

The central issue we dealt with is to identify the parameters of the right of the homeowner to guard his property against theft and against trespassers.

One side of the issue is that the rights of the trespasser are very limited. In this regard, the land occupier has a right to evict the trespasser from his premises. If the trespasser refuses to leave, some authorities allow the householder, if necessary, to assault him as a means of advancing the ejection. Moreover, if the land occupier's animal injures the trespasser, the land occupier bears no liability for the injuries.

In the event the land occupier discovers the trespasser on his premises, the duty of the land occupier here is a matter of dispute. In the opinion of one school of thought becoming aware of the trespasser requires the land occupier to exercise caution in his movements. Consequently, if the land occupier bodily harms the discovered trespasser, even if he inflicts injury accidentally, the land occupier bears liability for the injury. But, if the discovered trespasser sustains injury by stumbling over the land occupier, the land occupier bears no liability for his injuries. Others authorities dispute this view. In the opinion of this school of thought the land occupier's duty to the discovered trespasser is no higher than it is to the undiscovered one.

In an affirmative sense, what measures may the landholder take to protect his property? In this regard we identified various restrictions in the use of home security systems.

Most objectionable are the home security devices that subject a trespasser to an immediate unwarned attack upon entry. If *adam mu'ad le-olam*

is broadly conceived to include even *ones gadol*, the homeowner must anticipate that someone might enter his premises even without his permission.
Setting up a home security system that is designed to automatically attack
the intruder with no warning amounts therefore to *gerama* conduct. Accordingly, *Bet Din* would enjoin the homeowner from protecting his home with
an attack first system. The case for a restraining order can be made even if
we conceptualize *adam mu'ad le-olam* as prescribing no more than a liability rule for *ordinary ones*. This is so because the *yakhol le-hatzilo* principle tells us that the trespasser, even if he takes on the status of a *rodef*, is
entitled to be warned first before being attacked. Moreover, even if the *rodef*
ignores the warning, the homeowner may not proceed to defend himself with
lethal force against the intruder when lesser force will neutralize the threat.
Accordingly, setting up the attack component of the home security system
to consist of a mechanism that aims to maul or possibly even kill the
intruder when the state of art technology allows for a system to neutralize
the harm with much less harm to the intruder, should be prohibited.

Another reason to object to the automatic attack system is the duty the
homeowner owes both to his own household and to invitees. By dint of Rav
Natan's interdict against raising a *kelev ra*, the homeowner must insure that
his premises are free of both openly visible hazards and certainly of booby
traps. The safety duty the householder owes to these innocents constrains
the type of security system he may set up to protect his home from intruders and thieves. The system of protection the householder opts for to keep
out those he has every right to keep out cannot be at the expense of com-
promising the safety of those he owes a safety duty to.

By dint of the *lifnei iver* interdict a householder is prohibited from
ensnaring someone into committing an act of theft. If the snare is designed
to insure that the thief will get injured in the act of committing the crime,
the householder is in violation of *lo ta'amod* as well.

If the homeowner sets up his security devices with the aim of foiling the
same thief from returning for a second ransacking, the particular design of
the system he sets up may be in violation of *lo tikom* and *lo tittor*.

Another area of investigation is the duty and rights of a student (S_1) who
becomes aware that another student (S_2) is trying to cheat off his or her exam
paper. Most fundamentally, the *lifnei iver* prohibition imposes a duty on S_1
to prevent the cheating. Frustrating the designs of the cheater by filling in

the wrong answers is, however, prohibited. Such conduct perverts S_1's *lifnei iver* duty, violates S_1's duty to remonstrate with S_2 in "a quite and soft manner." and, finally, fails the minimum harm defense protocol.

Finally, the limit set for the disciplinary discretion a teacher has in respect to confiscating the "playthings" of his or her pupils was investigated. When it comes to Torah study, the stock and trade of the *rebbe* is *hayyei olam*. The disciplinary authority the school vests in him should therefore not be viewed as instruments of punishment, but rather as instruments of rescue. Disciplinary action saves the idling child from losing his or her *hayyei olam* and saves distracted classmates from the same fate. With the aim of maximizing Torah study for the pupils, the pupil that idles away lesson time with a plaything should be regarded in a limited manner as a *rodef*. Because *hayyei olam* for the idler and the entire class is at stake, confiscation of the plaything, on either a temporary or permanent basis, should rightfully be part of the disciplinary discretion of the teacher. Nonetheless, the minimum harm defense principle should apply here.

While the *rodef* rationale gives the *rebbe* authority to confiscate pupil property for disciplinary reasons on a spontaneous basis without announcing the policy in advance, it is, nevertheless, desirable for the school to articulate the policy in advance. Articulation of the policy in advance avoids the inadvertent creation of settings for veiled misconduct for the *rebbe* in regard to claiming no responsibility for the confiscated item if it becomes lost or damaged. Moreover, to insure that the policy of confiscation should not diminish in the eyes of pupils respect for the property rights of others, the policy should be crafted in terms that make it free from being characterized as a "misappropriation for *good reason*." Toward this end the policy would consist of getting parents to agree not to confer ownership to the child of the playthings they buy him or her. Instead, the parents would be asked to retain ownership of the toy and only let the child use the toy. The school would also request the parents to let the child know that they give both the child's teachers and the school administrators permission to "borrow" the toy anytime they felt a need to do so. The child would be made to understand that idling with the plaything on lesson time is the type of event that would trigger such a request.

Another advantage of formulating the teacher's disciplinary right to appropriate pupil property in the above fashion is that the school can use this formula to vest the secular studies teacher with the same disciplinary authority as the *rebbe*. Without crafting the policy in terms of the right to "borrow" and getting parents in advance to agree to it, the halakhic authority of the secular studies teacher to appropriate pupil property for disciplinary purposes will stand on tenuous ground.

NOTES

1. Each of the multiple-choice questions was worth two points. Boris ended up with a 67 because Professor Regenstein gave a 15-point curve. Dror did a really good job of "doing in" Boris.

2. R. Pappa, *Bava Kamma* 48a; Maimonides (Egypt, 1135–1204), *Yad, Hovel u-Mazzik.* 1:16; R. Jacob b. Asher (Spain, 1270–1343), *Tur, Hoshen Mishpat* 421; R. Joseph Caro (Israel, 1488–1575), *Shulhan Arukh, Hoshen Mishpat* 421:6.

3. *Tur*, op. cit.; R. Solomon Luria (Poland, 1510–1573), *Yam Shel Shelomo, Bava Kamma*, 5:9. Maimonides, in the understanding of R. Judah Rosanes (Turkey, 1657–1727), disputes this view. Maimonodes, according to R. Rosanes, would not allow the landowner to assault the trespasser who refuses to leave, even if his continued presence on the premises represents a loss for the land occupier. In these circumstances, the land occupier will have to get the Jewish court (*Bet Din*) to force the trespasser off his property. *Bet Din*, can, of course, authorize the use of force, if necessary, to evict the trespasser. See *Mishneh le-Melekh, Yad, Avadim* 3:5.

4. *Yad*, Nizkei Mamon 1:7; *Sh. Ar.*, op. cit., 389:10.

5. *Bava Kamma* 48a.

6. R. Solomon b. Isaac, *Rashi, Bava Kamma* 48a.

7. *Yad, Hovel u-Mazzik* 1:16.

8. R. Solomon Luria, *Yam Shel Shelomo, Bava Kamma* 5:8–9.

9. R. Vidal Yom Tov, *Maggid Mishneh, Yad*, loc. cit.

10. *Yad, Nizkei Mamon* 1:7.

11. R. Barukh Ber Leibowitz, *Birkat Shmuel, Bava Kamma* 15.

12. For an explication of the *kofer* principle, please turn to pp. 539–540, 553–555 of this volume.

13. *Baraita, Bava Kamma* 23b; *Yad, Nizkei Mamon* 11:11.

14. For a detailed discussion and analysis of this case, see R. Pinhas Zevihi, *Ateret Paz*, part 1, *kerakh* 3, *siman* 8.

15. *Bava Kamma* 37b; *Yad*, op. cit. 6:11.

16. R. Yehudah, *Mishnah Bava Kamma* 4:2.

17. *Rashi, Bava Kamma* 37a.

18. *Tosafot, Bava Kamma* 37a.

19. R. Meir, *Mishna, Bava Kamma* 2:4; *Yad*, op. cit. 6:7.

20. R. Joseph Habiba (early fifteenth cent.), *Nimmukei Yosef* at *Rif, Bava Kamma* 39a. In R. Habiba's formulation the exemption of *shor ha-itstadyon* apparently applies only if it kills a combatant within the setting of an arranged contest. If, however, the *shor ha-itstadyon* attacks outside the contest setting, it is treated as an ordinary case of goring. R. Yisrael Zev Gustman (*Beit Aharon, Bava Kamma* 24b, 39a), however, proposes that the *shor ha-itstadyon* applies in both cases. In R. Gustman's conceptualization, the underlying legal theory for each of these exemptions is different (*Beit Aharon, Bava*

Kamma 24b, 39a).

21. See Exodus 21:28–29.
22. Exodus 21:28.
23. *Mishna, Bava Kamma* 4:4.
24. R. Abraham b. David (Posquières, 1125–1198), *Hiddushei ha-Rabad, Bava Kamma* 23b; R. Yom Tov Ishbili (Spain, 1270–1342), quoted by R. Joseph Habiba (early fifteenth cent.), *Nimmukei Yosef, Bava Kamma* 24b; R. David Tebele b. Moshe, *Nahalat David, Bava Kamma* 24b. R. Joseph Habiba, himself, takes the position that the exemption of *shor ha-itstadyon* is absolute and applies to the case of injuries as well.
25. *Yad*, op. cit., 2:5.
26. R. Abraham b. David, *Rabad, Yad*, ad loc.
27. *Bava Kamma* 24b; *Yad*, op. cit., 2:19.
28. R. Yitzhah Ze'ev Soloveitchik, *Hiddushei Maran Riz ha-Levi, Yad, Nizkei Mamon* 2:5.
29. *Bava Kamma* 3b.
30. *Tosafot, Bava Kamma* 27b; R. Asher b. Jehiel (Germany, 1250–1327), *Rosh, Bava Kamma* 3:1; R. Mosheh Isserles (Poland, 1525 or 1530–1572), *Rema, Shulhan Arukh, Hoshen Mishpat*, 378:1.
31. Maimonides, *Yad, Hovel u-Mazzik* 1:11; Nahmanides, *Ramban, Bava Kamma* 82b. Maimonides' formulation of *adam mu'ad le'olam* in terms of *ones gadol* is apparently inconsistent with his treatment of the case where *A* falls off a ladder and causes injury to *B*. The rule here, according to Maimonides, is as follows: If the rung was not strong and firmly fixed, *A* is liable. But, if it was strong and firmly fixed and yet it slipped, or if it was rotted, *A* is exempt, for this damage is "a blow from Heaven" (*Yad, Hovel u-Mazzik* 6:4). The exemption Maimonides confers on *A* when the rung *B* fell off of was firmly fit or rotted apparently places him in the ordinary *ones* school. R. Yosef Lev (Israel, contemp., *Birkat Yosef*, pp. 58–62) reconciles the two rulings. Preliminarily, he rationalizes the *ones gadol* school with the proposition that any action by man that causes damage, even if the action was done accidentally, is regarded by the Torah as if he caused the damage deliberately. But, if the action is not an action of man, but rather an *action by heaven*, man, even according to the *ones gadol* school, is exempt.
32. *Yad*, op. cit.; *Ramban*, op. cit.
33. *Bava Batra* 22b.
34. Nahmanides, *Ramban, Bava Batra* 22b.
35. R. Tzvi Spitz, *Mishpetei ha-Torah* 1:79.
36. R. Shelomo Zalman Auerbach, *Minhat Shelomo* 3:105.
37. R. Menasheh Klein, *"Hal'itehu la-Rasha ve-Yamut,"* in *Pa'amei Ya'akov be-Sedei ha-Halakhah, nisan*, 2000, pp. 114–115.
38. I thank my friend and colleague, Rabbi Dr. Hayyim Tawil, for helping me in the articulation of this idea.
39. *Bava Kamma* 15b.
40. Maimonides, *Yad, Rotzeah* 11:14; R. Menahem b. Solomon Meiri (Perpignan, 1294–1366), quoted in *Shittah Mekubbetzet, Bava Kamma* 51a.
41. R. Pinhas ha-Levi (Barcelona, 1235–1300), 447, 448.
42. *Bava Kamma* 15b.
43. R. Avraham Duber Kahana Shapira, *Devar Avraham* 2:37.
44. R. Samuel Eliezer b. Judah ha-Levi Edels, *Maharshah, Bava Kamma* 15b.

45. *Mishna, Bava Kamma* 7:7.
46. *Bava Kamma* 83a.
47. R. Yom Tov Lipmann b. Nathan ha-Levi, *Tosafot Yom Tov*, commentary at *Mishnah, Bava Kamma* 7:7.
48. R. Solomon b. Jehiel Luria, *Yam Shel Shelomo, Bava Kamma* 7:45.
49. *Shabbat* 63a.
50. R. Solomon b. Isaac, *Rashi, Shabbat* 63a.
51. R. Tzvi Spitz, *Mishpetei ha-Torah* 1:79.
52. For a detailed discussion and analysis of this case, see R. Pinhas Zevihi, *Ateret Paz*, part 1, *kerakh* 3, *siman* 8.
53. *Bava Metzia* 75b.
54. R. Solomon b. Isaac, *Rashi, Bava Metzia* 75b.
55. *Sukkah* 26a.
56. *Rif, Sukkah* 26a; *Yad, Sukkah* 6:4; *Rosh, Sukkah* 2:11; *Tur, Orah Hayyim,* 640; *Sh. Ar., Orah Hayyim* 640:10; *Arukh ha-Shulhan, Orah Hayyim* 640:21.
57. *Sukkah* 26a.
58. R. Solomon b. Isaac, *Rashi,* Sukkah 26a; *Yad,* loc. cit.; *Tur,* loc. cit.; *Sh. Ar.,* loc. cit.; *Ar. ha-Sh.,* loc. cit.
59. *Baraita, Sanhedrin* 73a; *Yad, Rotze'ah* 1:14; *Tur, Hoshen Mishpat* 426; *Sh. Ar., Hoshen Mishpat* 426:1; *Ar. ha-Sh., Hoshen Mishpat* 426:1.
60. The first authority to address the "poisoned sandwich" case was R. Yitzhak Zilberstein. R. Zilberstein voiced approval for the tactic the beleaguered medical student resorted to in poisoning his sandwich as a means of stopping the thief. From his treatment of the case in both his initial ruling (*Pa'amei Ya'akov, Kislev,* 2000) as well as in his later clarifications (*Pa'amei Ya'akov, Nisan,* 2000) it is clear that R. Zilberstein makes the assessment that the repeated instances of the pilfered "sandwich" was done by the same culprit. This assessment led him to conclude that the culprit was not your ordinary thief, motivated by greed, but rather was an incorrigible wicked person, deserving the designation of the "seed of *Amalek.*" Given this assessment of the character of the thief, it becomes legitimate, and even desirable, for the victim as well as bystanders to plot to "quicken" the death of the culprit. While taking action that would directly cause the death of the culprit is prohibited and amounts to murder, causing the culprit's death by means of indirect action is both permissible and desirable. Forming the lynchpin of R. Zilberstein's argument is his interpretation of the Talmudic dictum: "*stuff the wicked one* with the forbidden food *and let him die* (*hal'itehu la-rasha ve-yamut, Bava Kamma* 69a). In the medium of *Pa'amei Ya'akov,* many rabbis rebutted R. Zilberstein's ruling. In rejecting R. Zilberstein's thesis, the rabbis adduced various arguments, including variant interpretations on the Talmudic dictum of *hal'itehu la-rasha ve-yamut.* For an excellent article exploring the meaning and halakhic application of *hal'itehu la-rasha ve-yamut,* see also R. Yosef Ahitav, *"Hal'itehu la-Rasha ve-Yamut," Tehumin,* vol. 8, 1988, pp. 156–170.

It should be noted that the thrust of R. Zilberstein's clarifications was to limit *hal'itehu la-rasha ve-yamut* to a person who we are sure fits the description of a spiteful and irredeemable wicked person. In dealing with thieves that fall short of this description, R. Zilberstein is very strict in the defensive measures he would allow. Note, as discussed in the text, R. Zilberstein forbids a householder from stopping a thief by loosening the poles of the clothing line. Because this approach might cause the thief injury it violates *lo ta'amod*. Similarly, R. Zilberstein also prohibits a householder from placing poison candy in a safe. This action, in his opinion, also violates *lo ta'amod*.

61. *Pamei Ya'akov, Nisan*, 2000, pp. 107–129.
62. R. Menasheh Klein, *Pa'amei Ya'akov*, op. cit., pp. 115–116.
63. R. Yitzhak Zilberstein, *Pa'amei Ya'akov*, op. cit., p. 122.
64. *Hullin* 10a.
65. *Baraita, Sanhedrin* 72b.
66. *Yad, Geneivah* 9:12; R. Nissim b. Reuben Gerondi (Spain, ca. 1290-ca. 1375), *Hiddushei ha- Ran, Sanhedrin* 72b.
67. R. Mosheh Isserles, *Rema, Sh. Ar.*, op. cit., 425:1.
68. Rava, *Sanhedrin* 72a; *Yad, Geneivah* 9:9; *Ar. ha-Sh.*; op.cit., 425:10.
69. Exodus 22:1–2; *Yad*, op. cit., 9:7–89; *Ar. ha-Sh.*, op. cit., 425:10.
70. R. Yonatan b. Shaul, *Sanhedrin* 74a; *Yad, Rotzeah* 1:7; *Rosh, Sanhedrin* 8:1; *Sh. Ar.*, op. cit., 425:1; *Ar. ha-Sh.*, op. cit., 425:6.
71. R. Yonatan b. Shaul, loc. cit.; *Rosh*, op. cit., *Sh. Ar.*, op. cit., *Ar. ha-Sh.*, op. cit., Maimonides (*Yad*, op. cit. 1:13) understands the punishment to be "in the hands of Heaven," as opposed to being meted out by *Bet Din*. For an explanation of Maimonides' view, see *Ar. ha-Sh.*, loc. cit.
72. Please turn to pp. 245–247, 511–512 of this volume.
73. Maimonides, *Yad, Geneivah* 9:7.
74. R. Abraham b. David, *Rabad*, comments on *Yad*, loc. cit.
75. *Baraita, Sanhedrin* 72a; *Yad*, op. cit. 9:10.
76. Please turn to p. 252 of this volume.
77. Please turn to p. 252 of this volume.
78. R. Menasheh Klein, *Mishneh Halakhot* 7:275.
79. Please turn to pp. 8–17, 389–391 of this volume.
80. Please turn to pp. 1–42 of this volume.
81. *Mishneh Halakhot*, op. cit.
82. Please turn to pp. 8–9 of this volume.
83. Please turn to p. 392 of this volume.
84. In the ideology of the Hasidic sect called Kotzk, a major emphasis is placed on not being false to oneself. For an exposition of the ideology of Kotzk and many examples of the teaching that an individual should not be false to himself, see R. Ephraim Oratz, *And Nothing but the Truth* (New York: Judaica Press, 1990).
85. *Arakhin* 16b.
86. *Yad, De'ot* 6:7.
87. R. Asher b. Jehiel, *Bava Kamma* 3:13.
88. *Baraita, Bava Metzia* 61b; *Rosh, Bava Metzia* 5:3; *Tur*, op. cit., 348:1; *Sh. Ar.*, op. cit., 348:1; *Ar. ha-Sh.*, op. cit., 348:3.
89. Ibid.
90. R. Raphael Lippa Yom Tov Heilpern, *Oneg Yom Tov* 48.
91. R. Ya'akov Yeshayahu Bloi, *Pithe Hoshen, Hilkhot Geneivah ve-Ona'ah* 1:7, note 17.
92. R. Yehudah Herzl Henkin, "*Haharamat Hafetzim mi-Talmidim*," *Tehumim*, vol. 6, 1987, pp. 186–202.

93. R. Moshe A. Bleich, "Confiscation for Disciplinary Purposes," *Ten Da'at* 8:1, 1995, pp. 55–63.
94. *Mishnah, Makkot* 2:2.
95. *Bava Kamma* 117b.
96. This point is missing from the Hebrew source of R. Spitz's work referred to in the next endnote. R. Spitz, however, makes this point in the English version of his work *Mishpetei ha-Torah* (*Cases in Monetary Halachah* NewYork; Mesorah Publication, 2001, p. 73).
97. R. Tzevi Spitz, *Mishpetei ha-Torah* 1:77.
98. R. Moshe A. Bleich, op. cit. p.60. R. Bleich bases himself on R. Elhanan Wasserman (Poland, 1875–1941), *Kovets He'arot*, no. 70.
99. R. Yehudah Herzl Henkin, op. cit.
100. *Pe'ah* 1:1.
101. *Mishna, Bava Metzia* 2:11.
102. *Shabbat* 10a.
103. *Midrash Shumuel Rabbati Parshah* 1.
104. Rava, *Bava Metzia* 109a; Maimonides, *Yad, Sekhirut* 10:7; *Tur*, op. cit. 306; *Sh. Ar.*, op. cit. 306:8; *Ar. ha-Sh.*, op. cit., 306:8. R. Mosheh Isserles rules that deliberate idleness on the part of the *rebbe* for one or two days is sufficient grounds to dismiss him (*Rema, Sh. Ar.*, loc. cit.). See *Sema, Sh. Ar.*, op. cit. note 21.
105. *Tosafot, Bava Batra* 21b.
106. Dennis Randell,"Corporal Punishment in School," http://www.familyeducation.com/0,1120.1–3980,00.html.
107. For the interplay between Halakhah, American law and social morality on the issue of corporal punishment in the schools, see Rabbi Ronnie Warburg, "Corporal Punishment in School: a Study in the Interaction of Halakhah and American Law with Social Morality," *Tradition*, vol. 37, no. 3. Fall 2003, pp. 57–75.
108. R. Zvi Spitz, *Mishpetei ha-Torah*, op. cit.
109. R. Mosheh Isserles, *Rema, Hoshen Mishpat* 270:2.
110. R. Joshua b. Alexander ha-Kohen Falk (Poland, 1565–1614), *Sema, Hoshen Mishpat* 270 note 8.
111. *Kiddushin* 30b.
112. *Makkot* 8b; Maimonides, *Yad, De'ot* 6:10.

13

Premises Liability

Our purpose in this chapter will be to explore the duty a property owner has to ensure that his premises will not cause injury to someone who enters them. In addition, if the entrant sustains injury while on the property, to what extent is the owner of the property liable? We will explore this issue from the perspective of both American law and Jewish law (Halakhah).

PREMISES LIABILITY IN AMERICAN LAW

Premises liability law in the United States is in a state of flux. In most states, this issue is still governed by the old common law tradition. We will proceed to describe how common law treats premises liability and describe the modernization of this law as practiced in a growing number of states.

In common law, the status of the entrant determines what duty of care, if any, the property owner owes to the entrant. In this regard, an entrant is classified as either trespasser, licensee, or invitee.

A trespasser is defined as one who enters someone's property without permission and has no right to do so. The owner generally owes the trespasser no duty except to refrain from willful and wanton acts that might harm him.[1]

In the instance where the owner sets a trap for the trespasser, the owner is liable for the trespasser's injuries. A typical example is the setting of a spring or trap gun to stop or prevent depredations by animals or humans.[2]

Common law makes the trespasser assume the risk of injury from the condition of the premises.[3] Nonetheless, the owner becomes liable for the injuries of the trespasser if he sets up his premises with a dangerous condition hidden with sufficient cover to obscure it or render it unobservable to one who approaches it.[4]

The majority of courts today recognize a number of instances where the property owner owes a duty to the trespasser beyond the duty to refrain from willful and wanton acts against him. One circumstance, called the frequent trespasser case, entails the instance where the land occupier knows or should know that people constantly intrude upon a small area of his property. In these circumstances, if the land occupier maintains a highly dangerous and artificial condition on his premises, he must warn the trespasser of the danger he faces. The duty to warn the trespasser obtains, however, only if it is reasonable to assume that the trespasser will not discover the endangerment on his own.

Another exception to the no duty rule obtains when the land occupier knows or has reason to know of a trespasser's presence on the premises. Under these circumstances, some jurisdictions impose a duty on the land occupier to warn the discovered trespasser of dangerous conditions on the premises, which the intruder will not pick up on his own. Other courts, however, follow the general no duty rule on land occupiers, even if the trespasser's presence is known or reasonably discoverable, unless wanton conduct is found on the part of the land occupier.

Finally, the vast majority of jurisdictions, under certain conditions, impose upon land occupiers a duty to eliminate dangerous artificial conditions on their premises that are particularly attractive to children.[5]

The second category of entrant in common law is the licensee. The licensee is defined as one who enters someone's property with the owner's acquiescence or permission, but for purposes still not connected with the owner's interests. Persons labeled licensees usually include social guests, loiterers, and salespeople. The licensee is afforded more protection than a trespasser, but must accept the premises as the property owner maintains them. Although the owner is not required to make an inspection of the premises, he must warn a licensee of any concealed danger he knows about and that the licensee might reasonably be expected to encounter.

Finally, the third category is the invitee. The invitee is defined as one who enters someone's property at the owner's invitation and for a purpose beneficial to the owner. A property owner who encourages the invitee to come on the property must make a reasonable inspection of the property to discover defects and keep the property safe. The duty of the owner to the invitee is to exercise reasonable or ordinary care for his safety in a manner consistent with the invitation. In addition, the owner must warn the invitee of any latent or concealed perils present in the property. Common law does not, however, go so far as to make the owner the insurer of the invitee's safety. Accordingly, the invitee is liable for his own negligence.[6]

In 1968 the Supreme Court of California (*Rowland v. Christian*) took the state off the common law approach for premises liability. In its decision, the court ruled that the proper test for determining liability is whether the owner managed his property as a reasonable person would in view of the probability of injury to others. Although an entrant's status will have some bearing on what is reasonable care, the status of the entrant should not determine liability.[7]

In 1993 the Supreme Court of New Jersey adopted the Rowland standard. In its decision (*Hopkins v. Fox & Lazo Realtors*), the court held that a real estate broker owes a reasonable duty of care toward prospective buyers and visitors at an open house, including a duty to inspect the premises and warn of any known dangers. The court concluded, therefore, that an adequate inspection should include an examination of the house to ascertain latent defects affecting its salability, as well as those characteristics that a typical purchaser would examine. The majority eliminated from the broker's duty, however, are the obligation to warn against unknown dangers that are not revealed by his or her own inspection.[8]

In abrogating the tripartite common law classifications, the *Hopkins* Court noted that a majority of jurisdictions had either abolished the categories or at least eliminated the slight distinction between a licensee and an invitee.[9]

The trend in U.S. law is hence clearly in the direction of the "reasonable care against foreseeable harm" standard.

PREMISES LIABILITY AND HALAKHAH

In extrapolating Halakhah's view on the issue of premises liability, the classification of the entrant as trespasser, licensee, or invitee will prove a useful vehicle of analysis. We will show that the duty of the property owner toward the entrant will depend on which category the entrant falls in to.

Premises Liability and the Invitee

Of the three categories of entrants, the land possessor owes his strictest duty to an invitee.

One aspect of this duty is in respect to the land possessor's animals located on the premises. The land possessor must guard his animals to ensure that they don't injure the invitee. Failure to do so makes the land possessor liable for any injury his animal inflicts on the invitee while the invitee was visiting on the premises.[10] If the animal kills the invitee, the land possessor is obligated, under certain conditions, to pay *kofer*, (an indemnity equal to the economic value of the victim paid to the victim's heirs).[11] This would be the case when the animal had a previous record of fatal human gorings and the present goring was the fourth such episode.[12]

Another aspect of the land occupier's duty to an invitee is to ensure that his premises are free of hazards. This duty, based on R. Natan's dictum against raising a *kelev ra*, was discussed in the previous chapter. The issue we take up here is the matter of liability for the land occupier vis-à-vis the invitee in the event he did not make his premises hazard-free.

Suppose the hazard is in the form of an obstacle or pitfall. Does failure to meet R. Natan's standard result in liability for the householder if the invitee suffers injuries on his premises? One possible legal theory to impose liability is the consideration that creating or maintaining a hazard is prohibited and subjects the violator to liability under the rubric of the damager (*mazzik*) called *bor* (lit., pit): "When a man will open a pit, or when a man will dig a pit and he will not cover it, and an ox or a donkey fall into it. The owner of the pit shall make restitution; he shall return money to its owner, and the dead body shall be his" (Exodus 21:33–34). Talmudic understanding of *bor* expands the parameters of this damager (*mazzik*) to include any hazard, whatever form it takes.[13] Although the tortfeasor bears no monetary liability if the *bor* causes the death of a man,[14] the tortfeasor is liable for that person's injury.[15]

Bor does not, however, provide the legal underpinning we are looking for. R. Joshua b. Alexander ha-Kohen Falk's (*Sema*, Poland, 1555–1614) comment here is relevant. In his thinking, Exodus 21:33–34 is not a legal basis for premises liability and, for that matter, not even a basis for a prohibition against maintaining a hazard on one's own premises. In the Torah's formulation, the *mazzik* of *bor* ordinarily obtains when it is created in the public domain. Exodus 21:33–34 does not per se prohibit a householder from creating a *bor* in his private domain. The householder, argues R. Falk, should not be restricted in the free use of his property just because the *bor* would represent a hazard for someone who enters his domain. Nonetheless, if a *bor* exists in *A's* domain and *A* proceeds to disown his own domain except for the *bor*, he becomes liable for damages the *bor* causes.[16]

If *bor* is not the basis for premises liability in respect to the hazards located on one's property, perhaps R. Natan's dictum can provide the legal underpinning for this liability. Given the prohibition to maintain a hazard on one's premises, violation of this standard perhaps results in liability for the householder. Addressing this issue, R. Jehiel Michel Epstein (Belarus, 1829–1908) posits that violation of R. Natan's standard does not per se impose liability on the householder if the invitee sustains injury on his premises.

The issue of liability, according to R. Epstein, turns on a different principle. This is the issue of whether an invitation to enter the premises carries with it both an assurance that the premises are safe and an assumption of responsibility, in some measure, if the invitee sustains injury as a result of the unsafe premises. The analogue, according to R. Epstein, is the following dispute between Rebbi and the Rabanim: *P* gets permission to place his pots in *H's* courtyard. While the pots were there, *H's* ox breaks the pots. Rebbi frees the householder from any responsibility in the matter. The rationale behind Rebbi's ruling is that *H's* permission must be understood in the narrowest sense as granting *only* permission to place the pots in his premises with no undertaking to safeguard them from damage. Since the onus of guarding the pots against damage is entirely on *P*, *H* bears no responsibility for the loss. Rabanim, however, read into *H's* agreement to allow the pots to be deposited in his premises an implicit undertaking to guard the pots against loss as well.[17] Authorities are in dispute as to whether Rebbi's or the Rabanim's view should be regarded as normative. R. Isaac b. Jacob Alfasi (*Rif*, Algeria, 1012–1103),[18] Maimonides (*Rambam*, Egypt, 1135–1204)[19] and R. Joseph Caro (Israel, 1488–1575)[20] follow Rebbi's view, while R. Isaac b. Samuel of Dampierre (*Ri*, France, ca. 1120–ca. 1200),[21] R. Asher b. Jehiel (Germany, 1250–1327),[22] R. Jacob b. Asher (*Tur*, Spain, 1270–1343), and R. Mosheh Isserles (*Rema*, Poland, 1525 or 1530–1572)[23] adopt the view of the Rabanim as normative.

If we adopt Rebbi's view, the householder's invitation to enter does not carry any guarantee for the safety of the invitee. Quite to the contrary, the invitee enters at his own risk. If we, adopt the view of the Rabanim, however, an invitation to enter carries with it an assurance that the premises are safe. Since the invitee has a right to rely on this assurance, injuries he later sustains as a result of the unsafe premises are the responsibility of the householder.[24]

Premises liability in respect to an invitee is very limited. Consider that the authority for this liability is *Rabanim* in the pot-courtyard case just discussed. In his treatment of this case, *Rosh* explicitly limits the responsibility of the owner of the courtyard to the liability of an unpaid guardian (*shomer hinnum*).[25] The liability of the owner of the courtyard is hence limited only to being responsible for negligence and no more. By analogy, the householder's invitation does not make him an *insurer* of the safety of the invitee. Accordingly, the householder bears no responsibility for the negligence of the invitee. Moreover, suppose a hazard does exist on the premises. By dint of R. Natan's dictum, it would be unethical for the householder to extend an invitation to someone to come over and visit him without first *removing* the hazard. Leaving the hazard in place and only warning the invitee in very specific terms regarding the nature and location of the danger would not suffice. Nonetheless, from the standpoint of incurring liability for injuries of an invitee caused by a hazard located on his premises, the householder's advance warning to the invitee in specific terms regarding the nature and location of the hazard should be sufficient to absolve him from legal responsibility for the injuries.

Another limitation for premises liability is in the realm of liability to the invitee for the negligence of third parties. Ordinarily, failure to take reasonable steps to avoid foreseeable harm amounts to negligence on the part of the custodian. But, recognition that the duty for *H* to secure his premises for the invitee's sake does not derive from any duty imposed on him by the Torah, but is only voluntarily and implicitly assumed, makes *H* not responsible for the negligent action of third parties. The analogue here is the ruling of *Rosh* in the case of the pots deposited in a courtyard discussed above. Here, if *H* gives *P* permission to place his pots in his courtyard, *H* is responsible only for damage to the pots inflicted by his own animals. Damage to the pots caused by an animal that attacks from outside *H*'s premises is not *H*'s responsibility. The rationale here, as offered by *Rosh*, is that when *H* gave *P* permission to place the pots in his courtyard, *H* implicitly undertook to take reasonable precaution that his own animals, located in the courtyard, would do no damage to *P's* pots. But, *H's* intention was never to undertake custodial responsibility in respect to animals belonging to someone else.[26]

PREMISES LIABILITY AND THE LICENSEE

The prototype case of the duty a householder owes a licensee to safeguard his premises from harm is the case when the worker comes uninvited to the premises of his employer to put in a claim for his wages and gets killed on the premises by the employer's ox. Maimonides records this case as follows:

> No owner need pay *kofer* unless his animal kills outside his premises. But, if it kills on his premises, then although it is liable for stoning, the owner is exempt from paying *kofer*. Thus if one enters a privately owned courtyard without the owner's permission—even if he enters to collect wages or a debt from the owner—and the householder's ox gores him and he dies, the ox must be stoned, but the owner is exempt from paying *kofer* since the victim had no right to enter another's premises without the owner's consent.
>
> If one stands at the entrance and calls on the householder, and the householder answers, "Yes," and he then enters and is gored by the householder's ox and dies, the owner is exempt, for "Yes" means no more than "stay where you are until I speak to you."[27]

In the Talmudic discussion of the above case, a number of caveats emerge, but *Rambam* fails to record them.

One caveat is in respect to the whereabouts of the householder. The exemption of the householder from the *kofer* payment applies only if the householder is most frequently found in the city. But, if the householder is most frequently found at home, the worker has every right to enter his premises and put in a claim for the money owed him. In this case, if the householder's ox kills the worker, the householder must pay the *kofer* payment to the worker's heirs.[28]

Another caveat relates to the interpretation we give the householder's response of "Yes" to the call of the worker. In *Rambam's* formulation, the householder's response of "yes" is always taken to mean "stay where you are until I speak to you." But, the relevant Talmudic passage lends itself to limiting this interpretation to the circumstance where the householder is most frequently found in the city and possibly also to the circumstance where the employer is often but not commonly found in the city (*d'shakhiah ve-lo shakhiah*). But, if the employer is most frequently found at home, his response of "Yes" to the call of his worker certainly means "enter," with the consequence that if the worker is subsequently killed by the employer's ox on the premises, the employer bears responsibility for the *kofer* payment.[29]

Noting these omissions in Rambam's treatment of premises liability for the employer, R. Isser Zalman Meltzer (Russia, 1870–1953) avers that, in Rambam's thinking, liability for *kofer* obtains only when the victim had a *zekhut* (privilege to enter). This will obtain only if the employer gives the worker *explicit* permission to enter. Anything short of this gives the worker only a right or license to enter. Without *explicit* permission to enter, the worker enters the premises of his employer at his own risk. Consequently, if the employer's ox kills him, the employer is exempt from the *kofer* payment.[30]

Another lacuna in *Rambam's* treatment of premises liability for the employer is the issue of responsibility for injury caused by hazards located on the premises. Recall that a hazard located on one's own premises is not categorized as a *mazzik*. Liability for injuries caused by the hazard can therefore obtain only if the employer voluntarily assumes this responsibility. Recall also that Rambam follows the position of Rebbi that an invitation to enter does not convey an assurance that the premises are free of any hazard. Consequently, the employer bears no responsibility if the worker sustains injury caused by a hazard located on the premises. This will be the case even if the worker obtains explicit permission to enter.

Rosh espouses another view that places a much greater duty on the employer in respect to premises liability. In *Rosh's* formulation, the critical factor to consider is where the employer can be most frequently found. If the employer is most frequently found in the city, the worker has no right to come uninvited to the premises of the employer to put in a claim for his wages. If the worker does so, he does so at his own risk, with the consequence that if the employer's ox kills the worker, the employer is not liable for the accident and bears no financial responsibility in the matter. If, on the other hand, the employer is most frequently found at home, the worker has the right to come uninvited to the premises of the employer to put in a claim for his due. Consequently, in the event the employer's ox attacks the worker, the employer bears responsibility in the matter. In the instance where the employer is often but not commonly found in the city (*d'shakhiah ve-lo shakhiah*), the worker has no right to come uninvited to his employer's home, with the consequence that in the event the employer's ox attacks the worker, the employer bears no responsibility in the matter.[31]

Rosh posits that the above guideposts apply only in the time of the Talmud when employers made arrangements with moneychangers or storekeepers to pay their workers in currency or food. Within this system, a worker could effect the necessary arrangements with a meeting with his employer in the city. But, as soon as the payment method changed and employers began to directly pay their workers, nothing could be accomplished by a worker meeting with his employer in the city. Within the new system of payment, a worker typically went to the employer's home to get paid. Accordingly, even if the employer is most frequently found in the city, his worker has every right to approach him at home to put in a claim for his due. In recognition of the changed method of paying workers, the worker has every right to approach the employer at home, notwithstanding that the employer is most frequently found in the city. Given the worker's right to approach his employer at home, the employer will be responsible in the event his animal attacks the worker while the worker is on the premises.[32]

Noting *Rosh's* call for changing rules in response to changing socio-economic circumstances, R. Ya'akov Yeshayahu Bloi (Israel. contemp.) points out that it is not customary in contemporary times for an employer to have employees come to his home to be paid. Accordingly, the rules should change again to reflect the changed reality.[33]

Rosh does not deal with the instance where the worker is injured by a hazard located on the premises of the employer. Recall that *Rosh* follows the opinion that an invitation to enter carries with it an assurance that the premises are safe. Accordingly, if the invitee is given no specific advance warning regarding the hazard and sustains injuries while on the premises, the householder should be liable for the invitee's injuries. Does the householder's liability extend to the instance where the entrant was not an invitee, but rather only a licensee? One could argue in the negative. Consider that if the householder incurs liability, it is only because the householder implicitly accepted it upon himself. But, an implicit invitation to enter is not the same as a right to barge in. It is therefore not evident that the householder implicitly represents that the premises are safe when the licensee barges in on him.

The upshot of the above analysis is that animals and hazards are not treated the same. In respect to incurring liability for the damage or injury one's animal causes, liability proceeds from the biblical duty the owner has to prevent his animals from inflicting harm. This duty is absolute and does not depend on the particular category the entrant falls into. If there is a case of exemption from liability, it is based on the law of accident (*ones*).[34] In sharp contrast, a hazard located on one's premises is not categorized as a *mazzik*. If the householder has a duty to guard an entrant against this danger, it is based on a responsibility the householder undertakes voluntarily and must be dealt with on a case-by-case basis.

Tur espouses a third view on premises liability for the employer. It is almost identical with the view of *Rosh*, his father; however, one point of difference can be identified. In the *d'shakhiah ve-lo shakhiah* case, in opposition to *Rosh*, *Tur* holds the householder liable for the injuries his ox caused.[35]

PREMISES LIABILITY AND THE TRESPASSER

In the previous chapter, the issue of the land occupier's duty to a trespasser was dealt with.The reader is referred to the summary at the end of the previous chapter.

THE MERGING OF CATEGORIES—THE CASE OF THE CARPENTER'S SHOP

The Talmud deals with another case of premises liability, this one involving injury from flying pieces of wood that the carpenter's wood chopping produces. Moving away from the setting of the premises of a householder to a carpenter's shop has the dramatic effect of wiping out consideration of which category the entrant falls into as a criterion to decide liability for the carpenter. Maimonides' treatment of the carpenter shop case is as follows:

. . . If one enters a carpenter's shop, with or without permission, and a chip of wood flies up and strikes him in the face, the rule in each of these cases is that the one causing the injury is liable for *four effects* [actual damage, for pain, for medical expenses, and for loss of employment during the period of recuperation] but is exempt from paying compensation for humiliation.[36]

Most striking in Maimonides' treatment of the carpenter's shop case is the expansive rights he confers on the trespasser (*T*) who is hit by the flying chips of wood. Note that the carpenter's (*C*) liability is not just to pay for damages, but also to compensate *T* with four effects. Note also that Maimonides does not limit *C*'s liability to pay the four effects to the instance where *C* was aware that *T* entered his shop at the time he was doing the wood chopping. The implication is therefore that liability for *C* obtains liability even in the instance where he was not aware of the presence of *T* when the incident took place.

The key here is the constant flow of traffic of legitimate customers. The knowledge that implied invitees are constantly on the premises makes it reckless for *C* to conduct the wood-chopping activity on the premises. Given the obvious danger the wood chopping entails for implied invitees, any injury caused by flying chips should be regarded as being inflicted "almost deliberately." This harsh characterization of *C*'s action follows from Maimonides' ruling that *C* bears liability not just for actual damage (*nezek*) but also for *all* four effects. Now, if the injury from the wood-chopping activity makes *C* guilty of only not exercising proper caution, *C*'s liability would be limited to the payment of *nezek* under the *adam mu'ad l'olam* rule. But, *Rambam* says that *C* is assessed with payment for the four effects, which obtains only if the tortfeasor's conduct can be characterized as *shogeg karov le'mazid* (unintentional [act] bordering on deliberate [conduct designed to injure]).[37] To be sure, what designates the wood-chopping activity, as *shogeg karov l'mezid* conduct is the presence of a constant stream of customers in the shop while this dangerous activity is in progress. But, once the wood chopping activity gets its designation as gross negligence, this designation should pertain in relation to a trespasser as well. Consider that conducting the dangerous activity puts no particular person in peril, but rather is a threat to each and every person who is in the shop, including a trespasser.

Notwithstanding that a trespasser entered the shop without permission; he is entitled not to be attacked *deliberately*. Conducting a dangerous activity on one's premises that threatens entrants on a random basis amounts to a *deliberate* attack on a trespasser. The circumstance that the wood chopper was not specifically aware that the trespasser entered his premises when the injury occurred does not remove the *shogeg karov l'mazid* character of the wood-chopping activity vis-à-vis the trespasser. Given that people who are not customers come to the carpenter shop, the wood chopper *should have been aware* that a trespasser was in the shop when he was doing his wood chopping. In short, the wood-chopping should be treated as tantamount to a deliberate attack on the trespasser.

What emerges from this discussion is a sharp difference between how the wood-chopping incident is treated in the setting of the carpenter's shop and how the same incident is treated in the setting of the backyard of a wood chopper's home. Let's draw out this contrast. Suppose *T* suddenly enters *H's* backyard and gets injured from flying chips produced from *H's* wood chopping activity. Since *H's* premises are not open to the public and *H* is not expected to take into account the arrival of an intruder while he is engaged in the wood-chopping, the injury to *T* should in no way be characterized as the result of *H's* gross negligence. There can therefore be no question that *H* is not ordered to pay the four effects to *T*. But, perhaps payment for damages (*nezek*) is in order. Several factors, however, point to absolving *H* from liability even for *nezek*. One consideration is that the likelihood of *T* appearing on *H's* premises is remote. Accordingly, *H* need not refrain from wood-chopping on his own premises on account of the possibility that *T* might suddenly appear and sustain injury from flying chips. If this scenario does unfold, H will be regarded as faultless as far as *T's* injuries are concerned. Recall the discussion in the previous chapter regarding the theories of liability proceeding for a tortfessor from the principle of *adam mu'ad le'olam* (literally, man [as far as being *fully* responsible for what he damages] is always [considered] forewarned). If *adam mu'ad le'olam* applies even to *ones gadol* as Maimonides has it, *H* should still bear no responsilility for *nezek*, as *T* brought the injury upon himself. Suppose, however, that *H* became aware of the presence of *T* and, despite his awareness, continued with the wood-chopping and *T* sustained injury from the flying chips. Does *H's* continuation of the wood-chopping activity, despite his awareness that *T* is on the premises, constitute culpable conduct? Recall *Rashi's* view that once H becomes aware of the presence of *T*, the stricture of *adam mu'ad le'olam* is operative, with the consequence that if *H* bodily inflicts harm to *T* the circumstance that the assault was unintentional is not an exculpating factor. In the thinking of some authorities, as discussed in the previous chapter, Maimonides also subscribes to this view. Within this school of thought, conducting the wood-chopping operation in the yard despite the knowledge that *T* was present should also incur liability for *H* under the rule of *adam mu'ad le'olam*.

Recognition that the constant flow of invitee traffic makes for a much stricter premises liability rule leads to the possibility that this same stricter standard applies in respect to liability for hazards on the premises.

Recall R. Epstein's thesis that whether a householder's invitation to enter his home carries with it an assurance that the premises are safe from causing foreseeable harm is a matter of dispute between Rebbi and the Rabanim. Since the dispute revolves around identifying mutual expectations, the possibility opens up that under certain conditions all parties agree that an invitation to enter carries with it an assurance that the premises are safe from foreseeable harm. Pointing in this direction is the comment R. Isaac b. Moses (*Or Zaru'a*, Bohemia, b. late 12th century–d. mid.13th cent.) makes in connection with the potter case discussed above: If instead of giving *P* permission to deposit his pots in his courtyard, *H* gives *P* permission to deposit his pots in his home, Rebbi agrees that the invitation carries with it a custodial undertaking as well.[38] Changing the premises from a courtyard to a house apparently alters what the mutual expectations of the parties are regarding the custodial undertaking by *H*.

Taking our cue from *Or Zaru'a*, we propose that Rebbi agrees that when a store opens for business today, the owner's invitation to patronize his store carries with it an assurance that he has made the premises safe from causing foreseeable harm. If Rebbi rejects the notion of an implicit assurance to an invitee (*I*) that the premises are safe from causing foreseeable harm, it is because a compelling case cannot be made that the mutual understanding was that *I* should be relieved of the burden to be on guard for any hazards. Not relieving *I* of a duty to be on guard makes sense only when each person enters the householder's premises on an individual and controlled basis, and the entry of other people on the premises is separate and independent of his own entry. In the case of a store, the invitation to the public is to enter at any time. The owner must reasonably expect a diverse group of people over the entire continuum of business hours, including children, the elderly, and handicapped people. Although the burden on *I* to fend for himself in avoiding hazards might be reasonable for the average customer, it is not reasonable in respect to people who have below average capacity to fend for themselves in avoiding hazards. Because invitees have an invitation to enter at any time during business hours, the invitation of all invitees becomes integrated and intertwined. Accordingly, the implicit assurances regarding safety that the storeowner makes to his most vulnerable customers become the norm for everyone who enters the store during business hours. This assurance is that the premises are safe from causing foreseeable harm. Any one who enters a store during business hours has therefore a right to piggy-back on the implicit assurances the owner makes at that moment to the most vulnerable of his invitees.

PREMISES LIABILITY—AMERICAN AND JEWISH LAW COMPARED

In this section we will take up a few recent cases in American law involving the issue of premises liability and compare the ruling of these cases with the corresponding halakhic approach.

Lee v. Chicago Transit Authority

In this case, Jae Boon Lee brought a wrongful death action against the Chicago Transit Authority (CTA) to recover damages for the death of her husband, Sang Yeul, who was electrocuted while on land owned by the CTA.

Sang Yeul Lee was a 46-year-old Korean immigrant who was unable to read English. On the evening of October 21, 1977, Lee attended a party, where he became drunk. On his way home, Lee entered a CTA right-of-way, apparently in order to relieve himself. Lee was neither permitted nor invited to be on the property of the CTA at the time. The right-of-way was posted with signs placed on a utility shed and on sawhorses at each side of the tracks clearly warning "DANGER"—"KEEP OUT"—"ELECTRIC CURRENT." Lee made contact with the third rail and suffered fatal injuries.

Plaintiff's expert witness testified that the segment of track in question was the only one in the United States or Canada where an electrically charged grade-level third rail was unguarded, uncovered, or unfenced.

In the original proceeding the jury returned a verdict finding no willful and wanton conduct, but awarded $3 million on the negligence count, which was reduced by fifty percent based on Lee's negligence.

The Illinois Appellate Court reversed and entered judgment in favor of the CTA on the basis that the plaintiff was a trespasser. The Illinois Supreme Court, in a four-to-two opinion, reversed the Appellate Court and allowed the $1.5 million verdict to stand.[39]

Lee v. Chicago Transit Authority and Halakhah

Halakhic evaluation of the Lee case begins with a consideration of whether the CTA was guilty of a tort by maintaining the third rail in unprotected condition on its premises. Most fundamentally, we must identify the category of *mazzik* the third rail falls under.

In assessing the category of *mazzik* the third rail comes under, consider that the only human input as far as the creation of the dangerous condition of the third rail is concerned occurred when the power was turned on. But, this action, done long ago, has no connection to Lee's electrocution, even on the level of *gerama* (indirect causation), as it was Lee's action of coming into contact with the third rail that caused his death. The *mazzik* we are dealing with is hence certainly not *adam ha-mazzik* (the damager of man). Instead, we are dealing with damage caused by CTA's failure to properly *guard* its property from causing damage and injury.

R. Yaakov Yisrael Kanievsky (Israel, 1899–1985) discussion of the defining features of the *mazzik* of *esh* (fire) and the *mazzik* of *bor* raises the possibility that the third rail could be regarded as either *bor* or *esh*.

The third rail fits into the category of *bor* because the characteristic of *bor* is that the victim comes to the *mazzik*. But, consider that as far as *bor* is concerned, it is not its *inherent* property that injures the victim, but rather it is the impact of the victim's fall that does the harm. If we regard this latter feature as the defining characteristic of *bor*, the third rail will not fit into the category of *bor* as the third rail itself is inherently lethal and is responsible for the death of the victim.

Another possibility is that the third rail should be treated as the *mazzik* of *esh* (fire). It fits into the category of fire because, like fire, the third rail is inherently dangerous and can cause injury. But, the defining feature of *esh* is that with the aid of another force, (e.g., an ordinary wind), the fire moves from its original location and does damage in a new location.

Consider that the third rail remains stationary as it does its damage. Accordingly, if we take the defining characteristic of *esh* to be the feature that it moves with the aid of an outside force and does damage at a location different than its original source, the third rail would not fall under the category of *esh*.[40]

The consideration of which category of *mazzik* the third rail falls under is only a theoretical one. As a practical matter, the CTA was not guilty of being remiss in guarding its property from inflicting harm. This will be so whether we consider the third rail *bor* or *esh*. If the third rail fits into the category of *bor*, there should be no liability for injury, as the third rail is located on CTA's property. The CTA becomes liable for injuries the third rail causes only if subsequent to the setting up of the third rail on its own property, the company *disowns* to the public all their property that surrounds the third rail. Moreover, for the case at hand the entire discussion is academic, as *bor* never incurs liability when the harm consists of death to a human being.[41] If the third rail fits into the category of *esh*, the CTA also bears no liability on technical grounds. This is so because if *A* has a fire on his own property and the fire stays there, *A* incurs no liability for the damage it causes a trespasser. In this scenario, where *A* committed no wrong in making or having the fire, *A* incurs liability only if the fire moves out of his property and does damage outside his property. In this regard, consider that the CTA constructed the third rail on its own property and the third rail never moved outside the company's property. The *mazzik* of *esh* can therefore not be the basis for imposing liability on the CTA for Lee's death.

If the CTA is guilty in the matter of Lee it is only because it did not properly warn him of the exact location of the third rail and the life-threatening danger it posed to him. Two features of the case are particularly salient. One is that Lee was a trespasser; the other is that the CTA was aware that the occurrence of trespassing in the vicinity of the third rail was frequent.

We begin with the trespassing feature. Notwithstanding that Lee was a trespasser the CTA owed him a duty not to arrange its premises so that an intruder would be attacked. The primary purpose of the third rail is to provide power for the CTA's railroad trains. Given the business purpose of the third rail, it should in no way be viewed as a mechanism the company sets up to attack trespassers.

Ordinarily, a trespasser has no legitimate expectation to be warned of the presence of hazards on the premises he has entered without permission. But, if the householder is aware of the presence of a trespasser on his property and is also aware that the trespasser is in danger of being injured by a hazard on the premises, the householder must warn the trespasser of the danger. This duty proceeds from the biblical verse, "Do not stand idly by the blood of your neighbor" (*lo ta'amod al dam rei'akha*, Leviticus 19:16). On the basis of this verse if *A*'s life is in danger and a bystander (*B*) is in position to extricate him from this danger, *B* must take timely action to do so.[42] The *lo ta'amod* duty, according to R. Menasheh Klein (New York, contemp.), applies even in the instance when the potential victim is poised to commit a transgression and the danger he faces threatens him only on account of the transgression he is bent on committing.[43] Given the broad parameters of *lo ta'amod*, the prohibition certainly applies to warning an innocent trespasser of a life-threatening hazard on the premises. To be sure, no one was there from the CTA to warn Lee to stay away from the third rail on the night that he got electrocuted by coming into contact with it. But, it was an undisputed fact at the trial that the CTA was aware that occurrences of trespassing in the vicinity of the third rail were frequent. The issue then becomes whether the CTA properly discharged its *lo ta'amod* duty with the warning signs and barricades the company set up in the vicinity of the third rail.

The Adequacy of the CTA's Warning Against the Danger of the Third Rail and Halakhah

From the perspective of Halakhah, a relevant source in assessing the adequacy of the precautionary measures the CTA took is following Mishnaic teaching:

> If one places a pitcher in the public domain, and *another* person comes along and *stumbles over it and breaks it*, He [the pedestrian] *is not liable* to pay for it.[44]

The basis of the pedestrian's (*P*'s) exemption requires explanation. Why is *P* not held responsible to look out where he is going? Supplying the rationale for the exemption, R. Ulla tells us that P is not liable because "it is not the way of people to study the roads [on which they walk]."[45]

R. Ulla's dictum is apparently contradicted by the point in law that says that if a normal animal falls into a pit in daylight, the one who dug the pit is not liable because the animal should have watched where it was going.[46] If an animal is expected to avoid obstacles, we should have the same expectation for people. *Rishonim* offer several answers to this question. *Tosafot* answer that people walk upright and therefore do not automatically look down on the road. In contrast, animals that go on all fours look down and are therefore expected to avoid obstacles in their path.[47] R. Menahem b. Solomon Meiri (Perpignan, 1249–1316) resolves the issue with the proposition that people do not pay attention to the road because they are wrapped up in their thoughts and concerns.[48]

Providing further insight into the parameters of R. Ulla's principle is a variant of the above case: Suppose A placed his pitcher in the public domain in a spot where people usually place their pitchers, i.e., in the front area of an olive press. Here, P bears responsibility for the breakage because he is expected to anticipate that there will be pitchers lying about in that area and exercise the appropriate caution to avoid breaking them. But, if the incident occurred at night, P is exempt.[49]

Before we apply R. Ulla's principle to the Lee case, further clarification of his dictum is necessary. Exempting P for breaking the pitcher apparently clashes with the rule that man is responsible for damage he inflicts with his body, even if the damage was done inadvertently. The principle here, discussed in the previous chapter, is *adam mu'ad le'olam* (man is always considered forewarned). As a means of reconciling R. Ulla's dictum with *adam mu'ad le'olam*, several approaches are possible. One possibility is that "it is not the way of people to study the roads" describes an *almost inexorable human proclivity*. As such, if P breaks a pitcher that was in front of his path, the damage he causes falls into the category of accident (*ones*) that man bears no responsibility for. Another possibility is that although breaking the pitcher is not regarded as *ones*, nonetheless, P bears no responsibility for the breakage because the owner of the pitcher (O), to a certain degree, brought the damage on to himself because he placed it in the public domain.

Addressing the above issue, R. Menahem Mendel Schneersohn (Russia, 1789–1866) posits that "it is not the way of people to study the roads" puts

P's action into the category of *ones*. Accordingly, the exemption applies even when the circumstances were that *O* was right in front of *P* and put his pitcher down momentarily, with the aim of adjusting it to another position on his shoulder. Notwithstanding that *O* was fully within his rights to put his pitcher down momentarily for this purpose, P bears no responsibility for stepping on the pitcher and breaking it.[50]

R. Meir Brandsdorfer (Israel, contemp.) also understands R. Ulla's principle to be rooted in *ones*. The particulars of his case are as follows: *A* requests *B* to wake him at a certain hour. Unbeknownst to *B*, *A* places his eyeglasses at the foot of his bed. When *B* comes to wake up *A*, *B* inadvertently steps on *A's* eyeglasses and breaks them. Based on the principle of "it is not the way of people to study the roads [on which they walk]," R. Brandsdorfer absolved *B* of responsibility in the matter.[51]

Let us now apply R. Ulla's dictum to the Lee case. Preliminarily, we should not lose sight of the fact that Lee was trespassing on the property of the CTA. Accordingly, if Lee stepped on CTA property and damaged it, even inadvertently, while on the premises, R. Ulla's dictum cannot be invoked as a basis to free him of responsibility. This will hold even if the legal theory behind R. Ulla's dictum is *ones*. The guiding principle here is that any situation that begins with negligence, though it ends with an unavoidable mishap, incurs liability for the offender (*tehilato bi-peshi'ah ve-sofo be-ones hayyav*).[52] What is at issue here in the Lee case is not the parameters of liability for Lee if he damages CTA property. Rather, the issue is whether the CTA properly warned Lee of the danger he faced. Consider that because Lee had the status of a *frequent trespasser*, the CTA must be regarded as if it was aware of Lee's presence when he entered their premises. Accordingly, notwithstanding that Lee is a trespasser, he is entitled to an adequate warning of the presence of the third rail. Posting a sign on a shed that says "DANGER"—"KEEP OUT"—"ELECTRIC CURRENT" falls far short of this duty. Given that man is always wrapped up in his thoughts and concerns, the trespasser may not pick up in a timely way from a sign below his sight line the danger he faces. This will especially be so if the trespasser comes at night when the area is dimly lit.

At the legal proceeding against the CTA, the adequacy of the company's precautions against the danger the third rail represented was a point of contention. The CTA argued that the precautions it set up were adequate and therefore it was innocent of the charge of negligence in the matter. Plaintiff's expert witness, however, rebutted this claim. In his testimony, the expert witness testified that the segment of track in question was the only one in the United States or Canada where an electrically charged grade-level third rail was unguarded, uncovered, or unfenced.

In the Supreme Court review of the Lee case, the entire issue revolved around the adequacy of the CTA's warning of the danger of the presence of the third rail. Placing warning signs at the crossings demonstrated that the CTA felt that serious injury was foreseeable without warning. But, the precautions the CTA put into place were not adequate. Placing barriers and warning signs of a danger are not enough. Consider that the CTA trained its employees to recognize and work around the third rail. Recognition of the third rail and the danger it entails is therefore not something that we should take as obvious. Accordingly, the CTA's warning signs should have specifically identified the third rail and make it clear that electric current is transmitted via that rail. Another factor the court noted that made the CTA's warning inadequate was the close proximity of the grade-level rail to a pedestrian sidewalk.[53]

From the perspective of Halakhah the finding of the court that the CTA was remiss in making a proper warning to the frequent trespasser of the danger he or she faced is rooted in R. Ulla's principle that "it is not the way of people to study the roads [on which they walk]."

INDEMNITY TO LEE'S FAMILY AND JEWISH LAW

Before proceeding to assess the monetary award aspect of the case from a halakhic perspective, let us note that the authority of *Bet Din* to deal in criminal and tort law beginning from the middle of the fourth century, when the institution of *Semikhah*[54] discontinued, encounters a number of impediments.[55] Scholars have, however, found a solid basis for this authority. It applies for the State of Israel today and historically when the Jewish Communities enjoyed self-government in the Middle Ages.[56] Because one of the bases of the authority of the courts in these matters today is to deter wrongdoing, the courts have latitude to rule more strictly or more leniently than what Torah law calls for.[57] Notwithstanding this discretion, we take it as a given that the ruling of Jewish courts in these matters must fall roughly within the parameters of Torah law.

In the Lee case, the CTA is guilty of a failure to discharge it's *lo ta'amod* duty to the trespasser in respect to the danger of the third rail. Perhaps, the analogue for the appropriate penalty to impose on the CTA is the *kofer* payment. *Kofer* is an indemnity equal to the economic value of the victim paid to the victim's family. In ancient Israel, this payment was imposed on the owner of an animal when his beast gored a victim to death and this goring was the fourth such victim.[58]

Adoption of the *kofer* payment as the appropriate monetary award in the Lee case is, however, not a straightforward matter. Consider that in connection with the imposition of *kofer* on the owner of the killer animal the Torah says: "But an atonement payment shall be assessed against him, and he shall pay as redemption for his life whatever shall be assessed against him" (Exodus 21:30). The Talmud takes the concluding, apparently superfluous expression "against him" to convey that *kofer* is assessed only on the owner of the killer animal and not on man when, through his bodily actions, he is responsible for the death of a fellow.[59] Noting that the exclusion of the *kofer* payment for man when he himself is the tortfeasor is based on biblical exegesis, R. Aryeh Loeb b. Joseph ha-Kohen Heller (*Ketzot, Galacia,* 1745–1813?) posits that atonement for man when he is responsible for the death of a fellow can take on no form other than execution or exile, when applicable. The payment of *kofer* to the heirs of the victim is, however, not done even on the level of fulfilling one's obligation to heaven.[60] In his treatment of whether *kofer* can be imposed in wrongful death cases today, R. Yaakov Yeshayahu Bloi (Israel, 1929) posits that Maimonides takes this view as well.[61] *Rashi*, however, avers that the only reason *Bet Din* does not assess *kofer* on a murderer is the consideration that, from the standpoint of the murderer, execution is a more severe penalty than *kofer* and the rule is that when one is subject to two penalties *Bet Din* imposes only the more severe one. This holds even when the severe penalty is in actuality not imposed on account of some technicality in law.[62] *Rashi's* understanding of the *kofer* exclusion makes it a matter of fulfilling his duty to heaven for the murderer to pay *kofer* to the heirs of the victim.[63] R. Israel of Krems (fl. mid. 14th century) takes this view as well and posits that if the family of the victim seizes the murderer's assets for the *kofer* payment, *Bet Din* will not order the family to return these assets to the murderer.[64]

Consider that the above dispute regarding the applicability of *kofer* to a wrongful death case relates to a case where the defendant may be guilty of criminal homicide. But, the Lee case is not about criminal homicide. Instead, the CTA was guilty of not properly discharging its *lo ta'amod* duty. Accordingly, perhaps *kofer* is too harsh of a benchmark for the Lee case. Arguing in favor of the *kofer* benchmark, however, is that the issue at bar is not how to deal with an individual who, in an isolated incident, fell short of his *lo ta'amod* duty. Instead, the issue here is how to ensure that a large organization that provides services on a continuous basis to the public will run its operation in a manner that safeguards the public's safety. The objective here is not only to do justice for the family of the victim, but also to put in place a strong deterrence against negligent conduct by the CTA and other organizations serving the pubic.

CALCULATING THE *KOFER* INDEMNITY IN MODERN SOCIETY

In the previous section we argued that *kofer* is the proper benchmark to use as the indemnity payment to the Lee family. Consider, however, that *kofer* is equal to the economic value the victim would have fetched on the slave market. How can the *kofer* indemnity be calculated today? In western society, slave markets are a relic of the past. Nonetheless, an understanding of how the sages used the slave market to arrive at the *kofer* indemnity will show how this concept applies to wrongful death suits in modern society. Preliminarily, let us note that in ancient times the sages also referred to the slave market for the purpose of calculating part of the indemnity payment imposed on a tortfeasor in an assault and battery case. The reference to the slave market was made for the purpose of calculating the depreciation in earning capacity the victim sustained on account of his injury.[65] This payment is referred to as *nezek* (damages). We arrive at this figure by imagining that the victim could be sold as a non-Jewish slave on a permanent basis and calculate the difference in price he could fetch before and after his injury.[66] Conceptualizing *kofer* and *nezek* in these terms makes this payment the sum the victim could command for his labor services now and in the future. Calculating the victim's earnings now and in the future is hence vital for translating the ancient *kofer* concept into modern terms.

The aforementioned equips us to propose an award for the Lee case. We begin by noting that Lee's income at the time of his death was $8700. Since Lee was 37 at the time of his death, let us assume that if he was not killed his years' of gainful employment would have continued another twenty-eight years to the retirement age of 65. Next, we adopt the standard assumption in economic theory that Lee's earnings would, in all probability, increase each year over the remaining years of his working life by a factor equal to the extrapolated inflation rate and the labor productivity growth rate. An adjustment must be made for unemployment spells that Lee would most likely experience over the remaining years of his working career. In addition, another deduction for the taxes Lee would have been subject to over this period should be made. Finally, a deduction for work related expenses must be made. What remains is to shrink all the future income streams to the current time period. The method of doing this is the present value concept. We refer the reader to the appendix for the formula we use and the theory behind it. The figure we calculate is $229,164.

LEE'S NEGLIGENCE AND JEWISH LAW

In Lee's litigation against the CTA, the court cut the $3 million award in half in consideration that Lee was also guilty of negligence as he entered into the CTA property drunk. From the perspective of Halakhah, should Lee's trespassing and drunkenness reduce his award? The relevant principle here is Rava's dictum: Whenever one acts *irregularly* and someone else comes along and acts *irregularly against him*, [the second party] is not liable [to pay].[67] Examination of the seminal case will, however, show that this principle is not applicable here. Rava's case dealt with the instance where A was actively trying to incite B's dog to bite C and the dog, instead, turned on A and bit him. Here, Rava uses his rule to exempt B from any liability to A. Verily, B acted irregularly by being remiss and not guarding his dog against biting, but A is also guilty of acting irregularly by inciting B's dog. B bears no responsibility because A is regarded as if he brought the injury on himself.[68] Apparently, Rava's principle applies here too. The CTA acted irregularly by not properly warning Lee, but Lee also acted irregularly by becoming both a trespasser and entering into the CTA property in a drunken state.

Rava's dictum, however, has no relevancy here. The salient feature of the seminal case is that A's irregular act *provokes* B's dog to bite him. In contrast, where the irregular actions of the two parties are *independent* of each, the tortfeasor bears responsibility to his victim.[69] This is the case at hand: Lee's negligence did not bring on the CTA's negligence. Rather, each party was independently negligent and therefore the CTA bears responsibility. No reduction of the award is therefore in order on account of Lee's irregular action, consisting of committing an act of trespassing into the property of the CTA in a drunken state.

Another reason to object to the application of Rava's dictum to the Lee case proceeds from the assault and battery case dealt with by R. David b. Solomon ibn Abi Zimra (*Radvaz*, Egypt, 1479–1573): *A* initiated a soft blow to *B*, with the blow causing no injury to *B*. *B* responded to the blow by grabbing a stick and striking *A* in the eye and blinding him. Because *A* initiated the fight, *B* should perhaps bear no responsibility for maiming *A* by dint of Rava's dictum. *Radvaz* rejects this reasoning. Rava's dictum is an exculpating factor only when the issue at bar is whether man incurs liability for not properly guarding his property. Rava's dictum does not, however, provide an exculpating factor when the issue is whether man incurs responsibility by means of his own actions. Notwithstanding that *A* acted irregularly by initiating a blow to *B*, as a responsible person *B* is expected to exercise restraint and not issue a disproportionate blow to *A*.[70] *Radvaz's* ruling has much relevance to the Lee case. Consider that the third rail is on the property of the CTA and Lee is a trespasser. The basis for holding the CTA responsible for the death of Lee is therefore not that the third rail is a *mazzik* and the CTA was remiss in guarding their property against harming someone. Instead, the CTA is responsible for Lee's death because the railroad did not properly warn Lee. Notwithstanding that Lee was a trespasser, the railroad had a duty to warn him of the danger on the basis of the *lo ta'amod* imperative. Liability is based on the judgment that the CTA was remiss in discharging its *lo ta'amod* duty. No reduction in award is therefore in order on account of Lee's irregular action.

WRONGFUL DEATH SUITS—THE FORENSIC ECONOMIC APPROACH

In wrongful death suits today, the courts recognize that plaintiff is entitled to an award equal to the cost of replacing the economic value the victim had for his family.[71] This is a far different concept than estimating the loss in future earnings the victim suffered.

Let us use the Lee case as a means of illustrating the economic replacement approach. This approach begins by saying that the deprivation Lee's family suffered as a result of his death should not be reduced to merely a matter of lost earnings. Accordingly, the $229,164 figure for the present value of Lee's lost earnings is just the starting point for the calculation of the award. The next step is to subtract from this figure an estimate of Lee's self-maintenance costs over the period of his working life time. Next, we must note that had Lee not been killed he would have continued to provide his family with household production, companionship and advice. An economic valuation of these items is made. The economic loss Lee's family suffered as a result of his death is then upwardly adjusted to reflect these items. The above approach gives Lee's family an award of $503,899. The interested reader is referred to the appendix of this chapter for the mathematical formula we used to arrive at this figure.

THE "SOCIAL LOSS" TO SOCIETY AND HALAKHAH

At this juncture, let us take note that both the halakhic and the forensic economic approaches for calculating awards in wrongful death suits fall far short of the Lee court's $3,000,000 judgment. The $3,000,000 jury figure award reflected, as one commentator put it, a measure of the "loss of society."[72]

What "loss of society" means is elusive and certainly not amenable to quantification. Is it possible that the jury viewed the case as a battleground between a rich and powerful railroad that acted negligently and callously against a weak, downtrodden, and illiterate immigrant, and decided to use its judicial role to "cut the rich and powerful down to size?" If this was the intent of the jury, its actions violated the *spirit* of the biblical injunction "Do not bend justice [even] for your needy in his dispute" (Exodus 23:26). This verse prohibits the judge from perverting justice to favor the poor. Instead, the judge must seek out the truth and reach his decision irrespective of the economic status of the parties.[73] In the spirit of this prohibition, a jury may not use its judicial role to effect income redistribution between the very wealthy and the poor and downtrodden, or use its authority and power as jurors to make a statement on its opinion of what constitutes social justice.

THE FORENSIC ECONOMIC APPROACH AND HALAKHAH

The forensic economic approach we described above is significantly different from the concept of *kofer*. Yet, the forensic economic approach should have a place in the Torah society. Preliminarily, let us take note that the

Torah records the penalty for the taking of a fellow's limb in the stark terms of tit for tat: "A man who maims his neighbor just as he did so shall be done to him. A broken bone for a broken bone, the loss of an eye for the loss of an eye. . . ." (Leviticus 24:19–20). The sages, however, tell us that the biblical prescription for the penalty of maiming should not be understood literally, but instead what is meant is monetary compensation.[74] The question, though, remains. If monetary compensation is what is intended, why the use of tit for tat language in the Biblical verses? The answer, Biblical commentators offer, is that the Torah desires to impress upon us that we should not *reduce* the suffering of the injury to a mere matter of monetary compensation. No. For the incalculable suffering he caused, the tortfeasor deserves no less than tit for tat. But what the tortfeasor theoretically *deserves* is not done to him. Instead, he is assessed a monetary penalty.[75] Similarly, a human being cannot be reduced to an economic machine, with his or her value consisting of the current value of future income flows. The work of the forensic economist does much to drive home this lesson. Conceptualizing wrongful death in terms of the deprivation effects on the victim's family bespeaks of the humanity of the victim and the suffering the victim's family undergoes on account of the loss of this humanity. In his lifetime, the victim was to his family much more than just an economic engine. He provided his family with personal attention and services in the form of household production, companionship, and advice. By putting a monetary value on what we might call the humanity of the victim vis-à-vis his family, the deterrence effect of the indemnity award is enhanced.

Once it is recognized that the forensic economic approach expresses poignantly the humanity of the victim, this approach should be available to the court for cases where the transgression of the defendant is far more egregious than in the Lee case. A case of this sort, widely discussed in the secular business ethics literature,[76] is the Ford Pinto case. The particulars of the case are as follows:

To meet foreign competition for the small compact car market, The Ford Motor Company produced in 1971 a small, compact car, which it called the Pinto. Because of its accelerated production schedule, the Pinto was not tested for rear-end impact until after it was produced. The car was tested after production, and the test showed that a rear-end collision would rupture the Pinto's fuel system extremely easily. Though there were no Highway

Traffic Safety Administration rear-end impact standards at the time, the Pinto fell below the state of the art for cars of that size.[77]

Between 1976 and 1977 alone, Pintos suffered thirteen fiery rear-end collisions, which was more than double the number for comparable-size cars. Many civil suits were brought against Ford Motor Company.[78] In one suit alone, a California jury awarded damages of $127.8 million (reduced to $46.3 million on appeal) in a Pinto crash in which a youth was burned over 95 percent of his body.[79]

From the perspective of Halakhah, the issue against the Pinto is not that Ford had a responsibility to put on the road a safer car. No. There is always a trade-off between safety and cost. Rather, the complaint against Ford is that the company was egregiously remiss in its *lo ta'amod* duty. Consider that Ford did a study and determined that if a baffle, estimating at costing between $6.65 and $11, were placed between the bumper and the gas tank, the Pinto would be comparable to other cars with respect to the danger of fire from rear-end impact. But, on the basis of a cost benefit analysis, the company decided not to insert the baffle.[80] Not only did Ford opt not to install the baffle, but, in addition, it failed to give the consumer the right to choose the additional cost for added safety. Finally, the company lobbying efforts against the establishment of mandatory rear-impact standards delayed the adoption of these standards for eight years.[81] In comparing the Lee and Pinto cases, it is clear that Ford Motor Company's violation of its *lo ta'amod* duty is far more severe than the corresponding CTA violation of this duty.

What this points to is a need for the Torah society to have a range of deterrence penalties dealing with failure of the *lo ta'amod* duty, with the severest violations dealt with by means of the forensic economic approach.

SMITH V. WAL-MART STORES, INC.

In this case Mrs. Elizabeth Smith sued Wal-Mart Stores Inc. for injuries sustained when she slipped in a puddle of water that had accumulated in the small passageway between the outer door and entrance into the store. This area will be referred to as the vestibule of the store. The puddle resulted from Wal-Mart employees watering plants and shrubs in front of the store. The water ran across the parking lot, forcing customers to walk through the water and then track the water inside the store.

Wal-Mart argued that Smith had no case because the water she slipped on was an "open and obvious" condition.

The jury found Wal-Mart one hundred percent at fault and returned a verdict for Smith, awarding her three hundred thousand dollars.

Wal-Mart appealed the ruling to the Missouri Court of Appeals. The appeal failed. In upholding the verdict in favor of Smith, the court stated that an open and obvious condition does not automatically bar recovery and release a defendant from all liability. The court held that a defendant could be found liable if he should have anticipated that harm might occur to his invitees, despite the open and obvious condition. Wal-Mart should have anticipated harm to its customers because the store knew that the water from the parking lot was being tracked into the store's vestibule. Additionally, the store was aware that the floor was wet and could be dangerous because another customer had slipped and informed the store of the condition almost an hour before the Smith incident.[82]

SMITH V. WAL-MART STORES, INC., AND HALAKHAH

Let us now proceed to analyze the Smith case from the standpoint of Halakhah. Perhaps, the most fundamental point to be made is that from the perspective of Halakhah, the puddle of water in the vestibule does not take on the status of *bor*. This is so because the *mazzik* of *bor*, as discussed above, generally obtains only if *A* places a hazard in the public domain. If *A* places an obstacle in his own domain, the hazard takes on the status of *bor* only if subsequent to placing the obstacle down in his domain, *A* proceeds to disown his entire domain, except for the *bor*. Given that subsequent to the creation of the puddle in the vestibule of its store, Wal-Mart did not proceed to disown its entire premises, with the exception of the puddle and the ground beneath it, the *mazzik* of *bor* will not provide a theory of liability for Mrs. Smith.

While liability for Wal-Mart does not proceed under the rubric of the *mazzik* of *bor*, perhaps, R. Natan's dictum can be the basis for making a liability ruling against Wal-Mart. Before proceeding along this line we must take note of several extenuating factors in how the puddle was created. Perhaps, the weight of these factors leads to the conclusion that the puddle should not be categorized as hazard of the type R. Natan refers to. In assessing whether the puddle should fall under R. Natan's dictum we will assume that any stringency in the criterion for defining *bor* is equally applicable in defining an obstacle for the purpose of applying R. Natan's prohibition.

One extenuation in the Wal-Mart case is the consideration that the slippery puddle originated from the accumulation of water in the parking lot. If the accumulation of water in the parking lot is regarded as a hazard, Wal-Mart should be responsible for injuries resulting from its failure to remove the danger by cleaning up the puddle. This is so because Wal-Mart employees created this hazard by means of watering the plants and shrubbery. Under the assumption that the puddle in the parking lot is a hazard, is Wal-Mart responsible for the new hazard that was created in the vestibule of their store? In addressing this issue, let us use the *mazzik* of *bor* as the guidepost in this matter. Consider that it is the traffic of customers from the parking lot to the vestibule that effectively moved or "kicked" the hazard to a new location. As far as the *mazzik* of *bor* is concerned, A's placement of a *bor* in the public domain generates liability for him in the event someone sustains injury. This responsibility is not removed if pedestrian traffic "kicks" the obstacle to another location in the public domain and someone stumbles over the obstacle in the new location and gets hurt there.[83] Analogously, if Wal-Mart bears responsibility under R. Natan's dictum for the puddle in the parking lot, R. Natan prohibition remains intact when pedestrian traffic "kicks" this hazard elsewhere to a different location in their private domain.

At this juncture, let's change our assumption. Suppose the puddle in the parking lot is not considered a hazard because conditions in the parking lot are not slippery. In this scenario, it is pedestrian traffic that moves a harmless puddle to a new location, but in the process create a "slippery puddle." In this scenario, Wal-Mart has done nothing to create a hazard. Again, let's turn to the *mazzik* of *bor* as a guidepost. If the technicalities for responsibility are met, A's mere *knowledge* that a hazard is present in his domain requires him to remove it. The circumstance that A had nothing to do with placing the hazard in his own domain does not excuse him from a responsibility to remove it.[84] Likewise, the circumstance that pedestrian traffic created the hazard of the slippery puddle does not relieve Wal-Mart of the responsibility to clean up the puddle once management becomes aware of it.

Another point to consider is Wal-Mart's defense that it should not be held responsible for Mrs. Smith's injuries because the slippery puddle in the vestibule of their store was an "open and obvious" condition. Again, let's refer to the model of the *mazzik* of *bor*. Clearly, the "open and obvious condition" is not an acceptable defense in respect to the *mazzik* of *bor*. Recall the discussion on this point in the treatment of the Lee case.

What the above analysis has shown is that R. Natan's dictum serves well as a basis to require Wal-Mart to react quickly to remove the hazard of the slippery puddle in the vestibule, even though they were faultless in creating this hazard for their customers. Moreover, on a moral level, Wal-Mart is certainly responsible for Mrs. Smith's injury. The issue, however, is whether R. Natan's dictum can be a basis to impose liability on Wal-Mart for Mrs. Smith's injuries. Recall R. Jehiel Michel Epstein's point that violation of R. Natan's dictum cannot be a basis for imposing liability on the householder for the injuries of an invitee. Liability for Wal-Mart can proceed only if it is evident that Wal-Mart *implicitly* voluntarily undertook responsibility for the injuries of customers in the event it was negligent in preventing foreseeable harm.

Recall that the issue of whether a householder's invitation to enter his premises carries with it an undertaking that the premises will not cause foreseeable harm to the invitee is disputed between Rebbi and the Rabanim and that halakhic codifiers take opposing sides on this matter.

The model for the Smith case should, however, be the carpenter shop case, discussed earlier in this chapter. If Rebbi rejects the notion of an implicit assurance to an invitee (*I*) that the premises are safe from causing foreseeable harm, it is because a compelling case cannot be made that the mutual understanding was that *I* should be relieved of the burden to be on guard for any hazards. Not relieving *I* of a duty to be on guard makes sense only when each person enters the household's premises on an individual and controlled basis and the entry of other people on the premises is separate and independent of his own entry. In the case of a store, the invitation to the public is to enter at any time during store hours.

The upshot of the above analysis is that Halakhah agrees with the ruling against Wal-Mart. The amount of the award is, however, a different matter. Mrs. Smith was awarded $300,000. The Appeals court rejected Wal-Mart contention that the amount of the award was excessive. In defending the reasonableness of the award, the Court pointed to the various aspects of damage Mrs. Smith suffered. The itemization began with medical bills and lost wages. These two items amounted to $19,000. But, the list went out to include the adverse impact the injury and her continuing pain had on changing her daily routine, including reduced ability to take care of her children, do household tasks and enjoy a normal family life with her husband.

In assessing the "fairness" of the $300,000 award, one consideration is that the puddle in the vestibule technically speaking is not a *bor* and hence Wal-Mart's liability in this matter does not proceed from being remiss in guarding its property from causing foreseeable injury. Instead, liability proceeds from the presumption that Wal-Mart implicitly assures each customer and effectively each entrant that its premises would not cause foreseeable harm. If Wal-Mart is assessed liability for the injury a patron suffers on account of slipping on a puddle, it is because the customer had a right to rely on Wal-Mart's implicit assurance of safety. Because liability is based on what is reasonable to assume Wal-Mart implicitly volunteered to undertake, imposing liability on the company beyond payment for Mrs. Smith's injuries in the narrowest sense possible cannot be made. What follows from this line, in the opinion of this writer, is that Wal-Mart's liability to Mrs. Smith should be restricted to payment for her medical bills and for her losses in earnings while she was homebound recuperating from surgery. Imposing liability on Wal-Mart for the adverse impact Mrs. Smith's injuries and continuing pain had on changing her daily routine is a liability we have no presumption Wal-Mart implicitly undertook.

Arguing, however, for liability in more than just the most narrow sense is the circumstance that Wal-Mart did nothing to remove the danger even after an off duty employee had already slipped on the puddle and alerted management of the need to clean up the puddle. In not cleaning up the puddle, Wal-Mart was hence guilty of "gross negligence." With the aim of *deterring* such conduct in the future, it is perhaps in order for *Bet Din* to go beyond the narrowest conceptualization of liability. Recall, however, the proposition we made earlier in connection with the Lee case that if the goal is *deterrence*, then, perhaps, an assessment of the deprivation impact the injury has on the family of the victim is in order. Applying this notion to the Smith case should, perhaps, give some measure of validity to the Mrs. Smith's claims in respect to the impact the injury had on disrupting the quality of her interactions with her family. But, we should not lose sight of the fact that if any additional payment is due; it is only to promote the deterrence goal. Accordingly, a sliding scale of penalties beyond the minimum damage award should be available to the court. Depending on the severity of defendant's negligence, the various levels of penalties would kick in.

SUMMARY AND CONCLUSION

In extrapolating Halahkah's standard for premises liability, the common law categories and the doctrine of reasonable care against foreseeable harm both have their place. The category the entrant fits into will be very significant when people enter the premises on an individualized and controlled manner. This changes, however, when the general public is invited to enter. The constant flow of invitee traffic makes for a much stricter premises liability rule.

In the setting where people enter premises on an individualized and controlled basis, two schools of thought can be identified. One line of thought is R. Asher b. Jehiel and R. Jacob b. Asher and the other school of thought is Maimonides. In both schools of thought, the categories of trespasser, licensee, and invitee are useful in making a liability rule for the owner.

In the work of R. Asher b. Jehiel and R. Jacob b. Asher, all three common law categories can be identified:

1) As far as the trespasser is concerned, he is treated essentially the same way common law treats him.

2) In respect to the licensee, the household owes him a duty to maintain the premises in a manner that will prevent foreseeable harm. But, liability for the householder if he was remiss in this duty is limited. It obtains only if the householder's animal attacks the licensee. But, a case for liability cannot be made if the cause of the injury was a hazard located on the property.

3) The strongest duty is owed the invitee. Here, the householder not only owes a duty to the invitee to make sure that the premises are safe, but a case for liability can be made against the householder if he is remiss in this duty.

The second school of thought is Maimonides. In his formulation:

1) Anyone who falls short of getting explicit permission to enter the premises is treated the same way as common law treats a trespasser. Maimonides hence treats the trespasser and licensee the same way.

2) To anyone whom the householder gives explicit permission to enter, the householder has a duty to maintain his premises in safe condition. Making the householder liable for injuries an invitee sustains as a result of failing to meet the standard is, however, another matter. The case for liability holds up only if the invitee is attacked by the householder's animal, but does not hold up if the injury was caused by a hazard located on the premises.

In Halakhah, the common law categories lose, however, their determinative significance when the premises in question are open to the public. The salient feature here is that there is a constant flow of invitee traffic, consisting of a diverse group of people, including children, the elderly, and the handicapped. The store, hospital, park, and museum provide examples of this type of setting. If the land possessor is responsible for injury a hazard on his premises causes, it is only because it is reasonable to presume that the owner implicitly assures his invitees that his premises are safe from hazards. While the notion that the burden is on an invitee to fend for himself in avoiding hazards is reasonable for the average customer, it is not reasonable in respect to people who have below average capacity to fend for themselves in avoiding hazards. Because invitees have an invitation to enter at any time during visiting hours, the invitation of all invitees becomes integrated and intertwined. Accordingly, the implicit assurances regarding safety that the owner makes to his most vulnerable invitees becomes the norm for everyone who enters the premises during the hours the public may enter. This assurance is that the premises are safe from causing foreseeable harm. Any one who enters a place that is open to the public has therefore a right to piggyback on the implicit assurances the owner makes at that moment to the most vulnerable of his invitees.

Proceeding from the aforementioned discussion is a striking difference between American law and Halakhah in respect to the issue of premises liability. In American law, the historical common law categories are now giving way to a standard of reasonable care against foreseeable harm. In sharp contrast, as far as Halakhah is concerned, the common law categories and the standard of reasonable care against foreseeable harm have always been contemporaneous doctrines, with each applied to a different set of circumstances.

In the treatment of wrongful death suits, a difference in approach between Jewish and American law was uncovered. In American law, the approach is to calculate the economic value the victim had to his family and restore that value to his family. In Jewish law, the approach is to confer the heirs of the victim with the victim's lost, current and future earnings.

Once it is recognized that the forensic economic approach expresses poignantly the humanity of the victim, this approach should have a place in the Torah society in crafting an appropriate deterrence penalty for wrongful death and premises liability cases. In these cases, judges should have the option of drawing upon a range of penalties for violation of the *lo ta'amod* duty. The severest of these violations should be dealt with by means of the forensic economic approach.

NOTES

1. Kerrie Restieri-Heslin, "Negligence-Common Law Categories of Trespasser, Licensee, and Invitee that Govern a Landowner's Duty in a Premises Liability Action are Replaced by a Single Standard To Exercise Reasonable Care in a Premises Liability Action are Replaced by a Single Standard to Exercise Reasonable Care Against Foreseeable Harm— *Hopkins v. Fox & Lazo Realtors*, 132 N.J. 426, 625 a.2d 1110 (1993)," 24 *Seton Hall Law Review* 2227, 1994, note 2.
2. 45 C. J. 750, 751; *State v. Barr*, 11 Wash. 481 (39 P. 1080, 29 L R. A. 154, 48 Am. St. R. 890); *Scheuermann v. Scharfenberg*, 163 Ala. 337 (50 So. 335, 24 L.R. A. (N. S.) 369, 136 Am. St. R. 74, 19 Ann. Cas. 937).
3. Kerrie Restieri-Heslin, op. cit.
4. *Bohn v. Beasley*, 51 Ga. App. 341 (180 SE 656).
5. Mark J. Welter, "Premises Liability: A Proposal to Abrogate The Status Distinctions of 'Trespasser,' 'Licensee' and 'Invitee' as Determinative of a Land Occupier's Duty of Care Owed to an Entrant," *South Dakota Law Review*, 33, 1988, pp. 67–69.
6. Restieri-Heslin, op. cit.
7. *Rowland v. Christan*, 69, *Cal.* 2d 108, 70 Cal. Rptr., 443 P.2d 561, 565–68 (1968).
8. *Hopkins v. Fox & Lazo*, 132 N.J. 426; 625 A.2d 1110; 1993 N.J. Lexis 127.
9. Loc. cit. p. 437.
10. R. Asher b. Jehiel (Germany, 1250–1327), *Rosh, Bava Kamma* 3:12; R. Jacob b. Asher (Spain, 1270–1343), *Tur, Hoshen Mishpat* 389; R. Mosheh Isserles (Poland, 1525 or 1530–1572), *Rema, Shulhan Arukh, Hoshen Mishpat* 389:10; R. Ya'akov Yeshayahu Bloi (Israel, 1929–), Pithe Hoshen, *Hilkhot Nezikim* 5:13 n. 26.
11. Maimonides (Egypt, 1135–1204), *Yad*, Nizkei Mamon 11: 1.

12. R. Menahem b. Solomon Meiri (Perpignan, ca. 1249–1306), *Beit ha-Behirah, Bava Kamma* 33a. The fourth goring designates the ox a *mu'ad* (lit. forewarned). For the principle that only the owner of a *mu'ad* is assessed *kofer*, see *Mishna, Bava Kamma* 4:5. When the institution of *Sanhedrin* ceased to function, *kofer* was no longer assessed. CF. R. Jacob b. Asher, *Tur, Hoshen Mishpat* 389.

13. *Bava Kamma* 3a, b; *Yad*, Nizkei Mamon 13:2–3; *Tur*, op. cit. 411; R. Joseph Caro (Israel, 1488–1575), *Shulhan Arukh, Hoshen Mishpat* 411:1; R. Jehiel Michael Epstein (Belarus, 1829–1908), *Arukh ha-Shulhan, Hoshen Mishpat* 411:1.

14. *Bava Kamma* 28b; R. Isaac b. Jacob Alfasi (Algeria, 1012–1103), *Rif, Bava Kamma* 28b; *Yad*, op.cit., 13:1–3; *Tur*, op. cit., 410; *Sh. Ar.*, op. cit., 410:21; *Ar. ha-Sh.*, op. cit., 410:23.

15. Ibid.

16. R. Joshua b. Alexander ha-Kohen Falk (Poland, 1565–1614), *Sema, Sh. Ar.*, op. cit., 410 note 5.

17. *Mishna, Bava Kamma* 5:2–3.

18. R. Isaac b. Jacob Alfasi, *Rif, Bava Kamma* 48b.

19. *Yad*, op. cit., 7:5.

20. *Sh. Ar.*, op. cit.398:5.

21. *Tosafot, Bava Kamma* 48b.

22. R. Asher b. Jehiel, quoted in *Tur*, op. cit. 291.

23. R. Mosheh Isserles, *Rema, Sh. Ar.*, op. cit. 398:5.

24. R. Jehiel Michel Epstein, *Ar. ha-Sh.*, op. cit. 410:4.

25. *Rosh, Bava Kamma* 4:5.

26. *Rosh*, op. cit.

27. *Yad, Nizkei Mamon*, op. cit. 10:11–12. In light of the fact that since post Talmudic times *Bet Din* has no authority to assess *kofer* on the tortfeasor, it is striking why *Rambam* chose to formulate the case as involving the *killing* of the worker by the ox of the employer, rather than the instance when the worker sustained *injury* on the employer's premises by the goring of the employer's ox. To be sure, the *Baraita* (*Bava Kamma* 33a) records this case as involving the death of the worker, but *Rosh, Tur* and *Rema* all formulate the case as involving injury rather than death.

28. *Bava Kamma* 33a.

29. Ibid.

30. R. Isser Zalman Meltzer, *Even ha-Ezel, Yad, Nizkei Mamon*, 10:11–12.

31. R. Asher b. Jehiel, *Rosh, Bava Kamma* 3:12.

32. Ibid.

33. R. Yaakov Yeshayahu Bloi, *Pithe Hoshen, Hilkhot Nezikim* 5:12 note 22.

34. For a discussion of the two schools of *ones* liability please turn to pp. 495–500 of this volume.

35. R. Jacob b. Asher, *Tur*, op. cit. 389.

36. *Yad, Hovel u-Mazzik,* 1:17.

37. R. Solomon b. Isaac, *Rashi, Bava Kamma* 26a; *Yad, Hovel u-Mazzik*, op. cit. 1:12 (on interpretation of R. Meir Simha ha-Kohen (Dvinsk, 1843–1926), *Hiddushei R. Meir Simhah, Bava Kamma* 48a; *Rosh, Bava Kamma* 2:15; *Tur*, op. cit. 421; *Sh. Ar.*, 421:3; *Ar. ha-Sh.*, op. cit. 421:1.

38. R. Isaac b. Moses, *Or Zaru'a* quoted in R. Israel of Krems (Germany, d. 1375), *Haggahot Asheri, Bava Kamma* 5:3.

39. *Lee v. Chicago Transit Authority*, 152 Ill 2d 432, 605 NE 2d 493 (1992).
40. R. Kanievsky, *Kohelet Yaakov, Bava Kamma siman* 3.
41. *Bava Kamma* 28b; *Rif, Bava Kamma* 28b; *Yad*, op. cit. 13:1; *Tur*, op. cit. 410:21; *Sh. Ar* op. cit., 410:21; *Ar. ha-Sh.* op. cit. 410:23.
42. *Baraita, Sanhedrin* 73a; *Yad, Rotze'ah* 1:14; *Tur, Hoshen Mishpat* 426; *Sh. Ar., Hoshen Mishpat* 426:1; *Ar. ha-Sh., Hoshen Mishpat* 426:1.
43. R. Menasheh Klein, *"Hal'itehu la-Rasha ve-Yamut,"* in *Pa'amei Ya'akov be-Sedei ha-Halakhah, Nisan*, 2000, pp. 115–116.
44. *Mishna, Bava Metzia* 3:1; *Rif*, ad locum; *Yad, Nizkei Mamon* 13:5; *Rosh, Bava Metzia* 3:1; *Tur*, op. cit. 412; *Sh. Ar.*, op. cit. 412:1; *Ar. ha-Sh.*, op. cit. 412:1.
45. R. Ulla, *Bava Kamma* 27b.
46. *Bava Kamma* 52b.
47. *Tosafot, Bava Kamma* 27b.
48. R. Menahem b. Solomon Meiri, *Meiri, Bava Kamma* 27b.
49. *Yad*, op. cit. 13:6; *Tur*, op. cit. 412; *Sh. Ar.*, op. cit. 412:2; *Ar. ha-Sh.*, op. cit. 412:3.
50. R. Menahem Mendel Schneersohn, *Hiddushei Tzemeh Tzedek*, quoted by R. Yaakov Yeshayahu Bloi, *Pithe Hoshen, Nezikim* 8:10, p. 243.
51. R. Meir Brandsdorfer, Responsa *Keneh Bosem, Hoshen Mishpat* 154.
52. *Bava Kamma* 21b; *Rif*, ad loc.; *Yad, She'ela u-Pikkadon* 4:6; *Rosh, Bava Kamma* 3:22; *Tur*, 291; *Sh. Ar.*, 291:6; *Ar ha-Sh.*, 291:39.
53. 152 Ill.2d 432, 452,456; 605, N.E.2d 493, op. cit.
54. From biblical times, judges received their authority from their immediate predecessors by means of *Semikhah* (lit. laying of hands) in the manner that Moses laid his hands on Joshua (Numbers 27:23), thereby making him leader and supreme judge in succession of himself. The original practice of *Semikhah* ceased about the middle of the fourth cent. (See Haim H. Cohn, *"Bet Din,"* in Menachem Elon, ed., *Principles of Jewish Law* (Jerusalem: Encyclopedia Judaica, 1975), p. 563.
55. Since the practice of *Semikhah* ceased, Jewish courts exercise their judicial functions only as agents of, and by virtue of, an implied authority from the ancients (*Yad, Sanhedrin*, 5:8–9). See also *Rambam's* commentary on *Mishna Bava Kamma* 8:1.
56. C.F. Yehudah Kahana, Nathan Munk, Menachem Slae, "Estimating Bodily Damages According to Jewish Law: A Comparative Legal Study," in B. S. Jackson, Ed., *Jewish Law Association Studies* 11 (Atlanta, Scholars Press, 1986), pp. 125–141; Alan Mittleman, *"Mishpat Hamelukhah* and The Jewish Political Tradition in the Thought of R. Shimon Federbush," *Jewish Political Science Review*, 10:3–4 (Fall 1998), pp. 67–85.
57. Cf. R. Solomon b. Abraham Adret (Spain, ca. 1235- 1310), Responsa *Rashba* 7:311; R. Asher b. Jehiel, Responsa *Rosh* 101:1.
58. Exodus 21:28–32.
59. *Bava Kamma* 26a.
60. R. Aryeh Loeb b. Joseph ha-Kohen Heller, *Ketzot ha-Hoshen, Hoshen Mishpat* 410 note 4.
61. R. Yaakov Yeshayahu Bloi, *Pithe Hoshen, Nezikin*, p. 47 note 50.
62. R. Solomon b. Isaac, *Rashi, Bava Kamma* 53b. Another authority that adopts *Rashi's* position is R. Yitzhak b. Asher (*Riva*, Germany, c. 1130, *Tosafot, Bava Kamma* 4a).
63. *Ketzot ha-Hoshen*, op. cit.
64. R. Israel of Krems, *Haggahot Asheri*, comments on *Rosh, Bava Kamma* 4:4.

65. *Mishna, Bava Kamma* 8:1; *Rif*, ad loc.; *Yad, Hovel u-Mazzik* 1:2; R. Asher b. Jehiel, *Rosh, Bava Kamma* 8:1; R. Jacob b. Asher, *Tur*, op. cit. 420; R. Joseph Caro, op. cit. 420:15; R. Jehiel Michel Epstein, *Ar. ha-Sh.*; op. cit. 420:16.

66. R. Asher b. Jehiel, *Rosh*, op. cit., R. Yehonatan (Provence, c. 1150–c.1215), quoted in *Shittah Mekubbetzet, Bava Kamma* 83b; R. Moshe Isserles, op. cit. 420:15; *Sema, Sh. Ar.*, op. cit. 420:16.

67. Rava, *Bava Kamma* 24b.

68. Ibid.

69. R. Jehiel Michel Epstein, *Ar. ha-Sh.*, op. cit. 389:42; R. Abraham Isaiah Karelitz (Israel,1878–1953), *Hazon Ish, Bava Kamma* 24b.

70. R. David b. Solomon ibn Abi Zimra, *Radvaz*, 4: 1291 (220). See *Tosafot, Bava Kamma* 29a.

71. For a description of the methodology of modern forensic economics, see Elias Grivoyannis, *Forensic Evidence* (New York: Thomson-West Group, 2001).

72. "Significant Cases and Developments, Liability to Trespasser in Electrocution Case," *The Lawyer's Guide*, 1992, pp. 171–173.

73. *Midrash Agadah*, Exodus 23:6.

74. *Mishna, Bava Kamma* 8:1; *Rif*, ad locum; *Yad, Hovel u-Mazzik* 1:2; R. Asher b. Jehiel, *Rosh, Bava Kamma* 8:1; R. Jacob b. Asher, *Tur*, op. cit. 420; R. Joseph Caro, op. cit. 420:15; R. Jehiel Michel Epstein, *Ar. ha-Sh.*; op. cit. 420:16. For various reasons, the Rabbis felt that the penalty for mauling cannot be understood on a tit for tat basis, see *Bava Kamma* 84b.

75. Cf. R. Abraham Isaiah Karelitz (Isreal, 1878–1953), *Kovetz Iggerot Hazon Ish*, ot 82. R. Mosheh Shterbuch (Israel, contemp), *Ta'am va-Da'at*, vol. 1, p. 151.

76. Cf. Richard T. De George, "Ethical Responsibilities of Engineers in Large Organizations: The Pinto Case," *Business and Professional Ethics Journal*, 1, no. 1 (1981), pp. 1–14; Richard A. Epstein, "Is Pinto a Criminal,?" *Regulation*, March–April, 1980, pp. 16–17; Mark Dowie "Pinto Madness," *Mother Jones*, September/October 1977, pp. 24–28.

77. Richard T. De George, *Business Ethics*, Fifth Edition (Upper Saddle River, New Jersey: Prentice Hall, 1999), pp. 240–241.

78. Ibid.

79. *New York Times*, Feb. 8, 1978, p. 8.

80. Richard T. DeGeorge, op. cit., p. 241.

81. Mark Dowie, "Pinto Madness," *Mother Jones*, September–October, 1977, p. 30.

82. *Smith v. Wal-Mart Stores*, 967 S.W.2nd 198; (E. D. Mo. 1998).

83. *Bava Kamma* 6a; *Rosh, Bava Kamma* 1:1; *Tur*, op. cit. 411:6; *Sh. Ar.*, op. cit. 411:6 ; *Ar. ha-Sh.*, op. cit. 411:4.

84. R. Joshua b. Alexander ha-Kohen Falk, *Sema, Sh. Ar.*, op. cit. 410 note 5.

Appendix

The central idea in the calculation of the current valuation of a worker's future earnings is the concept called present value. An understanding of the present value concept begins with what is called the compound interest problem. This entails the question of how much a sum of money M_0 would be worth a year from now if it was invested in a riskless, secure investment. Let us call the rate of return or interest rate on this investment i. At the end of the first year, the value of the investment is $M_1 = M_0 + iM_0 = M_0 (1+i)$. Suppose M_0 is invested in a riskless investment that will first mature at the end of two years; we then have: $M_2 = M_1 + iM_1$, $M_2 = M_1 (1+i)$. Since $M_1 = M_0 (1+i)$ we can substitute $M_2 = M_0 (1+i)^2$. This leads to the generalization that if M_0 is invested in a riskless investment that will mature in year t, then the value of M_0 in year t will be found by: $M_t = M_0 (1+i)^t$.

The present value concept is the reverse of the compound interest problem. The question is what is the *current value*, M_0, of a sum of money M_t that will first be realized in year t. What we are looking for is a formula for the value of M_0: $M_0 = M_t/(1+i)^t$.

In the calculation for the present value of Lee's future earnings we need to adjust the numerator of the present value formula to account for the possibility of unemployment, for the payment of taxes, and for work related expenses. As a result, the relevant present value formula becomes:

$$PV = \sum_{t=1}^{28} \frac{[Y_t(1+(\Delta p + l)](1-u-tx-w)}{[1+(\Delta p + r)]^t}$$

where: PV_Y =   present value of net income = \$229,164

Y_t =   gross income at year t = starting income \$8,700 at year 1

p =   inflation rate (average CPI% change for past 28 years, 1949–1977) = 3.27%

l =   labor productivity (average output per hour 1949–1977) = 2.94%

u =   rate of unemployment (average 1949–1977) = 6.48%

tx =   effective tax rate = 15%

w =   work-related expenses as a percentage of gross income = 2%

i = $(p + r)$ = riskless investment return = U.S. Treasury Bill one year rate = 5.065% (average 1959–1977)

r =   real interest rate = $(i - p)$ = (5.065–3.27) = 1.795%

t =   number of years = 28 years

In the forensic economic approach, the estimate of the loss of Lee's earnings is just the beginning point for the calculation of the award. In this approach, the above formula expands to include the loss for Lee's family of his household production (HP), his companionship (C), and his advice (A). Because the focus in the forensic economic approach is on the deprivation Lee's death cause his family, it must be recognized that had Lee been alive, a portion of his salary would have, in any case, not be devoted to the welfare of his family. This component is the present value of Lee's self-maintenance or personal consumption costs (m). In calculating the loss for Lee's family, the estimate for Lee's self-maintenance must be subtracted from the above total to arrive at the sum the award comes out to. Incorporating the above variables into the present value formula gives us the following formula:

$$PV = \sum_{t=1}^{28} \frac{\{[Y_t(1 + (\Delta p + l)](1 - u - tx - w)(1 - m)\} + (HP_t + C_t + A_t)}{[1 + (\Delta p + r)]^t}$$

where m = 30% of net income = \$68,749; net present value of HP = \$108,259; net present value of C = \$218,963; and net present value of lost advice and guidance A = \$16,263. The award therefore amounts to \$503,899 (in 1977 dollars).[1]

NOTE

1. For the methodology employed in arriving at the specific sums for household production, see *Forensic Evidence* (New York: Thomson-West Group, 2001), pp. 186–188, 197–213. For the concept of advice and companionship, see Havrilesky, Thomas, "Estimating the Value of Companionship and Consortium" in Thomas R. Ireland and John O. Ward, eds., *The New Hedonics Primer for Economists and Attorneys* (Tucson, AZ: Lawyers & Judges Publishing Co., 1996), pp. 393–398.

Glossary of Economic, Legal, and Foreign Terms

AB INITIO. "From the beginning." Latin.

AGENT. A representative who acts on behalf of another person (the principal), or an organization.

ASKING PRICE. A seller's initial declared lowest price for the sale of an item.

ASSET. A physical property or intangible right that has economic value.

ASYMMETRIC ECONOMIC POWER. A business situation in which certain relevant information regarding a transaction is known to one of the parties involved in the deal, but not to the other.

BILATERAL MONOPOLY. A market situation with a monopoly on the selling side and a monopoly on the buying side. In other words, a situation where there is one buyer and one seller in a marketplace.

BOULWARISM. Named after Lemuel Boulware, former Vice-President of General Electric, Boulwarism is the attempt on the part of an employer to circumvent union negotiations by making a "take it or leave it" offer **directly** to the workers.

CARTE BLANCHE. Unrestricted power to act according to personal discretion, French.

CO-INSURANCE. A form of insurance under which the insured is required to pay a stipulated percentage of the total value of the loss.

COLLECTIVE BARGAINING. Method by which a union representing employees negotiates with an employer to determine the conditions of employment.

COMPETITION. A market situation in which multiple sellers of a standardized product compete with each other for customers and there is free entry and complete information available to all parties.

COMPETITIVE PRICE. The standard price of an object in a competitive market setting.

COMPETITIVE WAGE. The standard salary for a specific occupation in a competitive market setting.

CONSUMPTION. Spending by households on goods and services to satisfy their current desires/needs.

COST-BENEFIT ANALYSIS. An appraisal analysis method that places values on all the benefits arising from a project and then compares the total value of benefits with the total cost of the project.

DEDUCTIBLES. A stipulation in an insurance policy that the policyholder will pay a portion of the loss from his own assets before the insurance company pays the remainder of the obligation.

DEMAND. Desired quantity of a good or service by consumers in a market, usually dependent on price.

DIMINISHING RETURNS. The tendency of additional units of an input to have a smaller marginal effect on total output than the preceding inputs.

DISCRIMINATION. Treating individuals of a particular group of people less favorably than others due to their sex, race, color, nationality, ethnicity, or various other categorizations.

ECONOMIC EFFICENCY. Achieving maximum output value from a given set of inputs, or achieving the desired output with minimum cost of inputs.

ECONOMIC VALUE. The value of an asset based on its earnings potential.

EFFICIENCY WAGE. The hypothesis that over some range the relationship between wages and productivity is positive.

ELASTIC DEMAND. Market demand that is relatively responsive to changes in the price of the subject product. If the firm's total revenue changes in the opposite direction as its pricing changes, the demand it faces for its product is characterized as "elastic."

EMPLOYEE ASSISTANCE PROGRAMS (EAP). Programs run by large companies to assist workers to solve personal problems affecting their job performance.

EMPLOYEE-AT-WILL. An employee hired for an indefinite period of time without a formal contract.

EQUILIBRIUM PRICE. The market price that clears the market. At equilibrium, the number of units suppliers want to offer is equal to the number of units demanders want to buy. Given the stability of supply and demand influences other than the price of the subject product, market price will tend toward the equilibrium price.

FIRE WALL. A security device that can be installed on a computer to prevent unauthorized accessing of information and unauthorized transfer of documents.

FIRM SPECIFIC TRAINING. Narrowly concentrated training usually provided by an employer to employees that enhance an employee's ability to perform his job at the company.

FIXED COST. A cost that does not vary depending on production or sales levels.

FREE RIDER. Anyone who receives a benefit from a good or service without having to pay for it.

FREE ENTRY. The ability for companies to enter an industry with relative ease; a condition of a competitive marketplace.

FRINGE BENEFIT. Employee compensation other than salary, generally includes insurance and pension plans.

GENERAL TRAINING. Training that develops an employee's general abilities applicable to his performance of a wide range of occupations.

HUMAN CAPITAL. Capital in the form of various investments a worker has made (e.g., education, experience, skill development) that augment his productivity.

INELASTIC DEMAND. Market demand that is relatively unresponsive to changes in the price of the subject product. If the firm's total revenue changes in the same direction as its pricing change, the demand it faces for its product is characterized as "inelastic."

INFLATION. A rate of increase in the aggregate price levels of all goods and services.

INSIDER INFORMATION. Confidential relevant information about a company that has not yet been made public.

INTER ALIA. "Among other things," Latin.

INTEREST. The amount paid to a lender beyond the original sum borrowed.

INVENTORY CYCLE. The amount of time it takes for a company to generate earnings from the current stock of its product.

KALDOR-HICKS TEST. State A is to be preferred to state B if those who gain from the move to A can compensate those who lose and still be better off. Compensation here is hypothetical, and the Kaldor-Hicks criterion suggests that A is preferable to B even if compensation does not actually take place.

LABOR FORCE. People currently employed or available and looking for employment.

LABOR PRODUCTIVITY. Amount of output produced by a worker over a specified period of time.

LABOR SUPPLY. Amount of labor available from individuals in a market, dependent on price.

LACUNA. A gap in information, lacking, Latin.

LAISSEZ-FAIRE. Lit. "let things alone." Refers to an economic philosophy that embraces the notion that a market system operates most efficiently when government minimizes its activity in the economy. According to this philosophy, governments should provide national defense and police protection, specify property rights, and enforce contracts drawn up between economic agents—and little or nothing else, French.

LEMON. A poor investment, usually used to refer to a car with many defects.

LEVERAGE. A strategic advantage of one party in a business situation allowing the party to act effectively and gain an advantage. Alternatively, the use of borrowed funds to increase buying power and profitability.

LIQUIDITY. Relative measure of ease and speed in which an asset can be converted to cash for approximately its original cost plus its expected accrued interest.

LOAN. A sum of borrowed money from a lender.

LOSS LEADER. Retail goods priced at less than cost so as to attract customers who will then buy other, regularly priced merchandise.

MARGINAL COST. Additional cost involved in increasing production by one unit.

MARGINAL PRODUCT. Amount by which output increases with the addition of one unit of an input.

MARKETPLACE. A place where suppliers and consumers interact and products or services are bought and sold.

MIMIMUM WAGE. Lowest compensation rate permitted by federal law for employers to pay employees.

MONOPOLY. An industry in which there is only one supplier of a product for which there are no close substitutes.

MULTIPLIER EFFECT. The number of times by which the change in total income exceeds the size of the expenditure change that brought it about.

MUTUAL FUND. An open-end investment company that offers to sell an unlimited amount of its shares to obtain funds to invest in corporation stock, bonds, or money market instruments. The company redeems its shares on demand at a price that reflects the value of its asset holdings.

NATURAL MONOPOLY. A market situation in which one firm can satisfy the entire demand of the economy at a lower total cost than can a combination of multiple firms due to decreasing average long-run costs based on continued economies of scale.

NON-COMPETITION CLAUSE. A provision in a contract of an employee prohibiting certain competitive conduct with the employer during and for a specified time after employment.

OMBUDSMAN. A neutral individual who receives, investigates, and reports on employees workplace problems.

OPPORTUNITY COST. The value of the best alternative sacrificed when taking an action.

PARETO OPTIMALITY. A situation in which no reorganization or trade could raise the utility or satisfaction of one individual without lowering the utility or satisfaction of another individual.

POVERTY. A situation in which a person lacks the resources necessary to be able to consume a certain minimum basket of goods.

PREDATORY PRICE CUTTING. A business tactic of sustaining a short term loss by lowering prices below the marginal cost of production with the intention of driving competitive firms out of business and then subsequently raising prices once monopoly power is established.

PREMIUM. Amount paid for an asset in excess of fair or economic value.

PRESENT VALUE.   The value today of a future payment, or stream of payments, discounted at an appropriate interest rate.

PRIMA FACIE.   At first sight; before closer inspection, Latin.

PRINCIPAL.   A person who empowers another to act as his or her representative.

PROFIT MARGIN.   A measure of profitability calculated by subtracting cost of goods sold from income earned and dividing the result by net sales.

QUI TAM.   Lit. "standing in the shoes of the King." In a qui tam suit, an informer pursues a suit for the government as well as for himself, Latin.

RATIONAL.   Acting in an internally consistent manner and making optimal choices based on consideration of all available opportunities and information.

RESERVATION PRICE.   A seller's minimum acceptable price for a good or service.

SAVINGS.   The portion of an individual's income not used on consumption.

SCREENING.   Strategy of a less informed person in an asymmetric information game scenario to elicit information from the more informed player.

SELF-MAINTENANCE COST.   The amount of money a victim in a wrongful death litigation scenario would have spent on himself or herself had he or she not been killed. According to American Law, this cost is subtracted from the total value of lost earnings in the payment by the responsible party to the victim's heirs.

SHIRKING.   Avoiding work or responsibility.

STRIKE.   A group of employees' collective refusal to work in protest against unsatisfactory conditions.

SUPPLY.   Quantity of a good or service available from suppliers in a market, usually dependent on price.

TERM LIFE INSURANCE.   A type of life insurance contract that covers only a specific period of time. The policy does not build up a cash value over time and the premiums increase as the insured gets older. For the short term this policy gives the insured the cheapest death benefit per premium dollar spent.

TORT.   A private or civil wrong or injury, not involving a breach of contract.

TORTFEASOR.   One who commits or is guilty of tort.

TRANSACTION COSTS.   The time costs and other costs required to carry out a market exchange.

UNEMPLOYED. A jobless member of the labor force seeking employment.

UNION. An organization that represents employees on a collective basis and bargains with employers regarding employee contracts.

UTILITARIANISM. A philosophical/ethical doctrine that argues that all action should be directed toward achieving the greatest utility for the greatest number of people.

VALUE OF THE MARGINAL PRODUCT OF LABOR. The dollar change in total revenue that a firm will realize by employing one additional unit of labor under perfectly competitive market conditions. Algebraically, it is equivalent to the product of the marginal product of labor times the per unit price of the output.

VARIABLE COST. The component of cost proportional to the volume of output produced.

WAGE DIFFERENTIAL. Differences in average earned wages between employees of different sexes, races, colors, nationalities, ethnicities, or various other categorizations.

WHISTLEBLOWER. An employee who exposes illicit behavior practices of an organization to the public or to those in positions of authority.

WHOLE LIFE INSURANCE. A type of insurance contract that covers the entire life of the insured. The policy builds up cash value over time and the premium is guaranteed not to increase from what it is set when the policy is taken out.

Glossary of Halakhic and Theological Terms

ADAM HASHUV. A distinguished person combining in himself both halakhic expertise and recognized leadership in public affairs.

ADAM MU'AD LE-OLAM. Lit. "man [as far as being *fully* responsible for what he damages] is always [considered] forewarned."

AGAR NATAR. A premium for waiting. Such a charge is prohibited under the prohibition of interest.

AHAT BA-LEV VE-AHAT BA-PEH. Insincere speech. Concealing the true desires of one's heart in conversations with others.

AHAZUKEI INISH B'RESHIEI LO MAHAZIKINAN. Lit. "we do not presume people to be wicked." Refers to the principle that in the view of Halakhah there is not a priori assumption that a person is wicked.

AMORA, AMORAIM, AMORAIC. Designation of scholars who were active in the period from the completion of the *Mishnah* (ca. 200 C.E.) until the completion of the Babylonian and Jerusalem Talmuds (end of the 4th and 5th cent. respectively).

ANI HAMEHAPEKH BAHARARAH. Lit. "a poor man casting about [trying to take possession of a certain] cake." The nature of the "cake" the poor man seeks is a matter of dispute. If in this scenario another individual preempts the poor person and acquires the cake, the "interloper" is branded a wicked person.

ASMAKHTA. A conditional commitment made by a party who does not really expect to have to honor it.

583

AVAK LASHON HA-RA. Lit. "the dust of evil talk." Refers to speech that is not in and of itself evil talk but it provokes the listener to engage in evil talk. Such speech is prohibited by dint of rabbinical, as opposed to, pentateuchal law.

AVAK RIBBIT. Lit. "the dust of interest." Violations of Jewish law's prohibition against interest by virtue of rabbinical, as opposed to, pentateuchal, decree.

AVEIDAH. An object lost by its owner without his knowledge. One who finds such an object is required to return it to its owner.

AVID INISH DINA L'NAFSHAI. Resorting to self-help without taking the matter to a *Bet Din*.

BAKESH SHALOM. Active pursuit of peace. A proactive attitude toward generating positive feelings among others.

BARAITA. A teaching or a tradition of the *Tannaim* that was excluded from the *Mishnah* and incorporated in a later collection compiled by R. Hiyya and R. Oshaiah.

BET DIN. Jewish court of law.

BIKKUR HOLIM. A positive commandment to visit a sick person.

CANA'AN. The pentateuchal name for the modern state of Israel and the surrounding countries.

DARKHEI SHALOM. Lit. "the ways of peace." Refers to the duty to end discord. Toward this end, the use of untruths is, under certain conditions, permitted.

DAVAR HA-AVUD. Circumstance in which a worker would cause a loss to his employer if he would not give immediate attention to the job at hand.

DAVAR SHELO BA LA-OLAM. Something that has not yet come into existence, an inexistent object.

DINA D'MALKHUTA DINA. Lit. "the law of the Kingdom is law."

DINAR. A silver coin equivalent in value to a *zuz*.

DINEI SHAMAYYIM. Lit. "judgments of Heaven." Refers to the extralegal responsibilities incumbent on a person that are beyond the scope of Jewish courts to impose or legislate regarding.

DIVREI HA-RAV. Lit. "the words of the Master [God]" Refers to a concept in Halakhah that when there is a discrepancy between the responsibility an agent has to his principal and the responsibility he has to God, the agent should heed the commandment of God and neglect the command of the principal.

EFES KI LO YEHIYEH BEKHA EVYON. A biblical verse literally meaning, "except when there shall be no needy among you." The verse is interpreted to teach one that he should not engage in conduct that will impoverish himself.

EGLAH ARUFAH. Lit. "decapitated calf." Refers to a ritual the Torah prescribes for a situation in which a murdered victim is found and the identity of the murderer is unknown. The elders of the town closest to the location where the corpse was found bring a calf to an untilled valley and decapitate it. The elders then proceed to wash their hands over the dead calf and proclaim that they are not responsible for the murdered individual.

EIN ADAM RO'EH HOVA LE-ATZMO. Lit. "a person is not able to see culpability against himself." Refers to the idea that a person will be biased in his assessment of himself.

EIVAH. Lit. "resentment" or "enmity." Refers to a halakhic principle that takes into consideration the emotional impact our actions have on others and aims to prevent feelings of animosity.

EMET. Truth.

EPHAH. A dry standard unit of measurement.

ETROG. Citron. One of the four articles of plant life we are commanded to take and hold in our hands on the festival of *Sukkot*.

FOUR SPECIES. The four articles of plant life we are commanded to take and hold in our hands on the festival of *Sukkot*. These consist of: (a) willow branches; (b) citron; (c) myrtle branches; and (d) branch of the date palm tree.

GARMI. Indirect damage that should have been foreseeable.

GEMILUT HASADIM. Lit. "the bestowal of loving kindness." The duty that encompasses the whole range of the responsibilities of sympathetic consideration toward one's fellow man.

GEMIRAT DA'AT. A firm resolve to conclude an agreement at hand.

GENEIVAH. Stealing an asset of value without knowledge of the owner.

GENEIVAT DA'AT. Conduct designed to deceive or create a false impression.

GERAMA. An indirect cause, generally with regard to causing damage.

GEZEL. Robbery prohibited on a biblical level, generally robbery committed with physical force.

GEZEL MI-DIVREIHEM. Rabbinic robbery. The rabbinic definition of robbery expands beyond the scope of robbery according to biblical law, and includes unjust gains from practices such as gambling or charging interest on a loan.

GOREM DE-GOREM. Doubly indirect cause. An action that causes an action that, in turn, causes a consequence.

HABA'A BE-MAHATERET. Someone who breaks into a house. According to Halakhah, such a person can theoretically be killed with impunity on account of the assumption that he is prepared to kill the host.

HALAKHAH. Jewish law.

HALOT. Lit. "to take effect" or "to come into force." Used in reference to halakhic states or statutes.

HANUPPAH. Insincere praise of a fellow; or flattery of the wicked.

HASHAVAT AVEIDAH. A biblical commandment that a person who finds a lost article must return it to its rightful owner.

HASHAVAT GEZEILAH. A biblical commandment that a person must return a stolen object to its rightful owner.

HASSAGAT GEVUL. Lit. "removal of boundary." Trespass on economic, commercial and incorporeal rights.

HATARAT NEDARIM. Absolution from the obligation of a personal vow granted by a Torah sage.

HAYYEI NEFESH. Essential food.

HAYYEI SHA'A. Lit. "temporal life." A reference to life in this world.

HAYYEI OLAM. Lit. "life of eternity." A reference to the Afterlife or the World to Come.

HEFKER. Ownerless object.

HEKKESH. Comparison between two matters usually because of their juxtaposition in the Torah.

HETTER ISKA. Lit. "permissible business venture." Refers to an elaborate legal device creating a business partnership, on a strictly halakhic level, between a lender and a creditor that effectively amounts to a loan, but is carefully constructed in order to circumvent the biblical prohibition against usury.

HEVER IR. Congregation, group of people.

HEZEK RE'IYAH. Visual penetration of privacy.

HEZKAT KASHRUT. Presumption of righteousness.

HILLUL HA-SHEM. Lit. "disgrace of the [Divine] Name." Refers to an action that brings dishonor and disgrace to God.

HIN. A standard dry measure unit.

HIN TZEDEK. Lit. "a just *hin*." Refers to the duty to make commitments in good faith.

HULLIN. A secular or non-sacred object

IMITATIO DEI. "Imitation of God," Latin. Judaism's behavioral imperative consisting of man's duty to emulate God's attributes of mercy in his interpersonal conduct.

ISKA. Lit, "business venture." Refers to a form of business partnership consisting of an active partner and a financier who is a silent partner.

KABBELAN. A pieceworker hired to perform a specific task, with no provisions regarding fixed hours.

KAF ZEHUT. A positive mandate to judge others favorably and assume their actions are appropriate.

KALON. Dishonor, shame.

KARET. Lit. "excommunication" or "cut off." Refers to Divine punishment in the form of premature death.

KEFEL. A twofold remuneration penalty imposed upon a thief to pay the victim of his theft twice the value of his theft.

KELEV RA. Lit. "bad dog." Refers to a prohibition against having a dangerous dog or maintaining any potentially dangerous object in one's house.

KIDDUSH HA-SHEM. Lit. "sanctification of the [Divine] Name." Refers to an observable and noble action that brings glorification to God.

KINYAN. A symbolic action establishing an individual's legal ownership of an asset. Used to transfer ownership.

KINYAN HATZER. Objects placed in the private property of an individual are established as the possessions of the property owner. This means of establishing ownership takes effect even without the knowledge of the property owner.

KINYAN SHETAR. A legal form of acquisition of an object established via a legal document.

KINYAN SUDAR. A legal form of acquisition of objects or confirmation of agreements, executed by the handing of a scarf (or any other article) by one of the contracting parties (or one of the witnesses to the agreement) to the other contracting party as a symbol that the object itself has been transferred or the obligation assumed.

KOFER. A court imposed indemnity payment that the owner of a forewarned ox that kills a human must pay to the victim's heirs. The indemnity payment is equal to the economic value of the person killed.

KOFIN. Lit. "compel" or "force," refers to the Jewish court's ability under certain circumstances to compel individuals to act in a particular manner.

KONEM. Lit. "a consecrated animal," refers to a vow to refrain from benefiting from a certain object or person, just as one is forbidden to benefit from a consecrated animal.

KOR. A standard measure of capacity. In volume a kor is equivalent to 30 se'ah.

LASHON HA-RA. Talebearing wherein *A* delivers a damaging but truthful report regarding *B* to *C*, with *C* being neither the object of *B*'s mischief nor the intended target of his evil designs.

LE-SHEM SHAMAYYIM. Lit. "for the sake of Heaven." Refers to an action motivated by religious beliefs.

LIFNEI IVER. Lit. "in front of a blind person." Refers to (1) the prohibition not to cause those who are morally blind to stumble by giving them the means or preparing the way for them to sin; and (2) The prohibition against offering someone ill-suited advice.

LIFNIM ME-SHURAT HA-DIN. Beyond the letter of the law.

LO TA'AMOD. Biblical prohibition that a bystander not remain idle when another individual is in a life threatening situation.

LO TA'ASHOK. Biblical prohibition not to unjustly withhold that which is due to your neighbor. This prohibition is violated by using strong arm techniques to refuse to surrender upon request what belongs to someone else.

LO TAHMOD. Biblical prohibition not to lust. The prohibition is violated by pressuring another individual to sell you a certain asset of his against his will.

LO TEKOM. Biblical prohibition not to take revenge.

LO TESHAKKERU. Biblical prohibition not to speak falsely.

LO TIGNOVU. Biblical prohibition not to steal.

LO TIT'AVVEH. Biblical prohibition not to covet the assets of another individual. The prohibition is violated by devising plots of possible courses of actions to pressure the other individual to sell you an asset of his after he initially refuses to sell the asset.

LO TITTOR. Biblical prohibition not to bear a grudge.

MAI HAZIT. Lit. "what do you see," refers to a concept that an individual does not have a right to save his own life through taking the life of another individual. The expression "what do you see" is the opening clause of a longer statement, "what do you see to think that your blood is redder than the blood of your fellow, perhaps his blood is redder than yours." The intention of the statement is that one lacks the authority to assume that his life is of greater value than the life of another person such that saving his own life could warrant taking the life of another individual.

MATZAH. Unleavened bread. There is a commandment to eat unleavened bread the first night of Passover.

MATZIL. Saving, rescuing.

MAZZIK. A person or animal that causes damage or injury to another person.

MEHEZEI KERIBBIT. Lit. "having the appearance of a prohibited interest payment." Refers to practices that resemble usury and are prohibited on a rabbinic level although they do not violate the biblical prohibition of prohibited interest payments.

MEHUSREI EMUNAH. Lit. "lacking trustworthiness." Refers to someone who retracts on a verbal commitment.

MEKAH TA'UT. Mistaken transaction.

MESAYYE'A LIDEI OVEREI AVERAH. Lit. "abetting transgressors," refers to a rabbinic extension of the *lifnei iver* interdict that is violated by helping another individual transgress a prohibition.

MEUTEI DE-MEUTEI. Lit. "a minority of a minority," refers to a negligible and insignificant possibility that can be disregarded.

MIDDAT HASIDUT. Acting in a beneficent manner beyond what is required by the letter of the law.

MILLA BE-SELA MASHTUKA BI'TREIN. Lit. "a word is worth a sela, silence is worth two." Refers to the idea that at times silence is preferable to speaking.

MINHAG. Traditional custom or prevailing practice.

MI-SHE-PARA. Lit, "He who punished." Refers to a judicial imprecation imposed on a buyer or seller who retracts before a transaction is legally consummated, but after a deposit has been paid. The formula of the imprecation is: "He who punished the generation of the Flood and the generation of the Dispersion will exact payment from one who does not stand by his word."

MISHNAH. Compiled and codified by R. Judah ha-Nasi in 200 C.E. It contains the essence of the Oral law as it had been handed down from the time of the Bible.

MITKABBED BE-KELON HAVERO. Elevating oneself at the expense of another's degradation. A person who acts in such a manner is said to lose his share in the world to come.

MITZVAH. A religious act or duty.

MITZVAT ASEH. A positive biblical commandment to perform a particular action. There are a total of 248 positive biblical commandments.

MITZVAT LO TA'ASEH. A biblical prohibition not to perform a particular action. There are a total of 365 biblical prohibitions.

MI'UT HA-MAZUI. A small but nonetheless significant percentage. In a situation in which a small but significant minority exists, it is not permitted to rely on the rule of following the majority.

MOTZI SHEM RA. The utterance or spreading of a false statement harmful to another's character or reputation.

MU'AD. A forewarned animal, an animal that has demonstrated that it is habituated to attack people by attacking on three occasions. The owner of a forewarned animal that damages is liable for full compensation.

NASSAIT LO KE-HETTER. A concept that when one becomes accustomed to acting in a prohibited manner, he becomes desensitized to the depravity of his actions and will perceive his actions as being permitted conduct.

NAZIR. An individual who vows to abstain from eating or drinking all grape derivatives, cutting his hair, and coming into contact with the dead for a specified period of time.

NEVELAH. A carcass of an animal that was not slaughtered according to the procedure prescribed by Halakhah.

NEZEK. Damage.

NIDREI ZEIRIEZIN. A vow that a person makes solely in order to generate credibility for his bargaining position. Such a vow is not legally binding on a halakhic level.

ONA'AH. Price fraud involving selling above or below the competitive norm.

ONA'AT DEVARIM. Conduct causing others needless mental anguish.

ONES. Unavoidable circumstance.

PE'AH. Lit. "corner," referring to a biblical commandment that a farmer designate a corner of his field of crop for the impoverished to eat from.

PERUTAH. Smallest unit of currency in the times of the Talmud. Equal in value to one eighth of an *issur*.

PESEIDA D'LO HADRA. Irretrievable loss.

PIV VE-LEBO SHAVIM. Lit. "his mouth and heart are the same." Refers to a condition that a vow is not legally binding on a halakhic level unless the words uttered are in line with one's intentions.

PO'EL. Day-laborer hired for a specific period of time or required to work at fixed hours.

PO'EL BATEIL. Idle or unemployed worker.

RASHA. Wicked or evil person.

REKHILUT. Talebearing wherein *A* delivers a damaging but truthful report regarding *B* to *C*, and *C* is either the object of *B's* mischief or the intended target of his evil designs.

RIBBIT. Prohibition against interest.

RIBBIT KETZUTZAH. Stipulated and agreed upon interest payment in the context of a loan in violation of the biblical prohibition against charging interest. A

Jewish court has the authority in such a case to force a lender to pay back the interest payments to the borrower.

RISHON, RISHONIC, RISHONIM.   Designation of scholars who were active in the period from the eleventh to the middle of the fifteenth century.

RODEF.   Lit. "pursuer." According to Jewish law, if *A* pursues *B* with the manifest intent to kill him, everybody is under a duty to rescue *B*, even by means of killing *A*, if no lesser means are available to neutralize *A*. This general rule has been extended to cover the killing of a fetus endangering the life of the mother and the killing of a rapist caught before completion of his offense.

ROSH HA-SHANAH.   The holiday marking the New Year on the Jewish calendar.

SABBATICAL YEAR.   Every seventh year of a seven year cycle, there is a Sabbatical year during which it is biblically prohibited to work the land and all loans are canceled.

SANHEDRIN.   Assembly of ordained scholars that functioned both as Supreme Court and Legislature before 70 C.E.

SELA.   A silver coin equivalent in value to four *dinars*.

SEMIKHAH.   Lit. "leaning." Refers to the process of rabbinic ordination. Traditionally ordination was passed down through the generations by an individual with *Semikhah* putting his hands on the head of the appointee and conferring upon him the authority to judge.

SEMIKHAT DA'AT.   Mental reliance. Without the presumption of mental reliance on the part of the principals to an agreement the transaction lacks validity in Jewish law.

SEVEN NOAHIDE LAWS.   Seven duties that are incumbent upon non-Jews to observe. The seven duties are: 1) not to murder, 2) not to engage in incest; 3) not to rob, 4) not to eat flesh of animals taken from an animal while it was still alive; 5) not to worship idolatry, 6) not to blaspheme God, and 7) to set up courts.

SHADHAN.   Matchmaker.

SHEKEL.   A coin equivalent in value to two *dinars*.

SHEKER.   Falsehood.

SHEKHENIM.   Neighbors.

SHEKHIV ME'RA.   Lit. "lying dangerously ill." Refers to a seriously sick person who is confined to his bed and cannot get up and walk outside to the marketplace.

The rabbis conferred upon such a person a unique ability to affect a transfer of assets through mere words.

SHEMA TITTAREF DA'ATO. Lit. "lest his mind become muddled," refers to the idea that one should be extremely careful when speaking with a seriously sick individual and make sure not to aggravate him/her in any manner out of concern that aggravating the sick individual could cause his/her condition to deteriorate.

SHIKHHAH. Forgotten sheaves. This portion of the crop is the entitlement of the poor.

SHOFAR. Ram's horn sounded for memorial blowing on *Rosh Ha-Shanah* and other occasions.

SHOGEG KARUV LE-MAZID. Lit. "unintentional bordering on deliberate," refers to an action that is technically unintentional, though nonetheless to some extent borders on being a deliberate action.

SHOMER HINNUM. A watchman who watches the object of another individual at no charge. Such a watchman assumes no liability for the object provided that he does not act negligently.

SHOMER SAKHAR. A watchman who watches the object of another individual at a charge. Such a watchman assumes liability for the object in the event that the object was lost or stolen.

SHOR HA-ISTADYON. Lit. "arena ox," refers to an ox that is trained to attack other oxen or people for the purpose of sport.

SINAT HINNUM. Unwarranted hatred of other people.

SIRSUR. A commercial broker, or in general a middleman.

SODOMITIC. Exhibiting the character trait of a citizen of Sodom, i.e., denying a neighbor a benefit or privilege that involves no cost to oneself.

SUKKAH. A temporary dwelling that the Torah instructs Jews to dwell in for the seven days of the holiday of *Sukkot* ("Tabernacles" in English).

TALMID HAKHAM. Talmudic Scholar.

TALMUD. The record of the discussions of scholars on the laws and teachings of the *Mishnah*. The Babylonian Talmud was codified ca. 500 C.E., the Palestinian Talmud ca. 400 C.E.

TAM. An innocuous animal, one that has not demonstrated that it is habituated to attack people. The owner of an innocuous animal that damages is liable to pay for half the damages.

TANNA, TANNAIC, TANNAIM. Designation of scholars active in the period from the beginning of the common era up to 200 C.E. The period of the *Tannaim* spans six generations of scholars from Gamliel the Elder and his contemporaries to Judah ha-Nasi (the redactor of the *Mishnah*).

TELUHU VE-ZAVIN. Lit. "they suspended him and he agreed to sell." Refers to a case in which a buyer put undue pressure on a seller to sell his object. Such a sale is legally binding on a halakhic level.

TENAI KAFUL. Lit. "double condition." A technicality of Jewish contract law that makes a conditional clause unenforceable unless the stipulations expressly spell out the consequences of both fulfillment and nonfulfillment of the clause.

TOELET. Generating benefit; useful.

TOKHAHAH. Reproof.

TORAH SOCIETY. A community in which all of its members are committed to Halakhah.

TOSAFOT. Twelfth to fourteenth century French commentators of the Talmud.

TOSEFTA. A collection of *Mishnayot* under the redaction of R. Hiyya and R. Oshaiah.

TREIFA. A person, animal or bird that has a flaw in one of its organs that will cause its death within twelve months.

TZALEM ELOKIM. Lit. "in the image of God," refers to the idea that all people are created in the image of God in the sense that human beings have tremendous potential for righteousness.

TZEDEK. Righteousness and integrity.

UMDANA. Inferential fact finding.

VE-HAI BA-HAM. Lit. "and by which you shall live." Refers to a principle that one is to live through his adherence to the biblical commandments and prohibitions, and not die because of his adherence to them. Consequently, if a person is threatened with death unless he violates a prohibition, he should violate the prohibition and save his life. There are however three prohibitions that an individual should die rather than violate: murder, adultery, and idol worship.

YAD PO'EL KE-YAD BAAL HA-BAYIT. Lit. "the hand of the laborer is like the hand of the employer," refers to the concept that any work done by a laborer under contract is legally the property of the employer.

YAKHOL LE-HAZILOH BE-AHAD MA-AVOROV. Lit. "he could have saved him with one of his limbs." Refers to the scenario where *A* pursues *B* with the manifest intent to kill him. While *A* has the theoretical right to eliminate the threat to his life by even killing *A*, *B* has no right to kill *A* when he can neutralize the threat against him with less than lethal force. This dictum translates into a minimum necessary harm defense rule.

YEZER HA-RA. Evil inclination in a person.

YOM TOV. A generic term for a Jewish holiday; a day of festival on which certain activities are prohibited.

ZEHUT. Favorable judgment, acquittal.

Subject Index

Name Index

Aaron Levine is the Samson and Halina Bitensky Professor of Economics at Yeshiva University. A Phi Beta Kappa at Brooklyn College, he earned his Ph.D. at New York University. He was ordained in Jewish civil and ritual law at the Rabbi Jacob Joseph School and is the spiritual leader of Brooklyn's Young Israel of Avenue J.

A noted authority on Jewish commercial law, Professor Levine's research specialty is the interface between economics and Halakhah, especially as it relates to public policy and modern business practices. He has published widely on these issues, including four books and numerous monographs. His books include *Free Enterprise and Jewish Law* (1980); *Economics and Jewish Law* (1987); *Economic Public Policy and Jewish Law* (1993); and *Case Studies in Jewish Business Ethics* (2000).

An associate editor of *Tradition*, Rabbi Levine also serves on an ad hoc basis on the *Bet Din* (rabbinical court) of the Rabbinical Council of America for disputes in monetary matters.

Dr. Levine is a member of the World Jewish Academy of Science and the recipient of the Irving M. Bunim Prize for Jewish Scholarship. In 1982, he was respondent to Milton Friedman in the Liberty Fund symposium on the Morality of the Market.

Other Books in the JEWISH ETHICS SERIES

Israel Salanter: Religious-Ethical Thinker
by Menahem G. Glenn

Rabbi Israel Salanter was one of the most influential nineteenth-century Jewish thinkers who sought to innovate the yeshiva system as well as lay society from within, while simultaneously warding off the modernizing elements of less committed Orthodoxy. This book presents an academic biography full of interesting tidbits of information as well as an overview of Salanter's innovative ethical system.

The Pursuit of Justice and Jewish Law: Halakhic Perspective on the Legal Profession
(Revised and Expanded Edition)
by Michael J. Broyde

Michael Broyde, distinguished rabbi and professor of law, takes a fearless inside look at critical ethical and religious issues facing the Jewish lawyer. Rabbi Broyde provides a clear analysis of the ethical challenges facing lawyers, elucidating the issues with keen insight into American and Jewish law. He offers practical conclusions relevant to anyone involved in the legal system or interested in the unique place of the observant Jew in the modern world.

The Right and the Good: Halakhah and Human Relations (Revised Edition)
by Daniel Z. Feldman

Rabbi Daniel Z. Feldman explores the vital role that the masters of Jewish thought have ascribed to laws of interpersonal relations. The author explains—with style and grace—what Jewish law really has to say about ethics and human relationships. He answers the skeptics who dismiss *halakhah* as anachronistic "ritual" and gives new sense, meaning and relevance to traditional observance. Feldman gives a detailed, scholarly overview of the laws of ethics, citing a wide range of rabbinic opinions in a highly readable work accessible to all.

Visit www.YasharBooks.com